# REPORT

FROM

## SELECT COMMITTEE

ON THE

## EDUCATION

Of the Lower Orders in The METROPOLIS:

WITH

## THE MINUTES OF EVIDENCE

TAKEN BEFORE THE COMMITTEE.

---

*Ordered, by* The House of Commons, *to be Printed,*
7, 14, 19, & 20 *June* 1816.

---

498.
427. 469. 495. 497.

*British*
*Parliamentary Papers*

EDUCATION OF THE
LOWER ORDERS

[ 1816 (498) (427) (469) (495) (497) VOL IV ]

Education

Poorer Classes 1

IRISH UNIVERSITY PRESS SERIES

OF

# British
# Parliamentary Papers

## REPORTS FROM THE
## SELECT COMMITTEE ON
## THE EDUCATION OF THE
## LOWER ORDERS OF THE METROPOLIS
## WITH
## THE MINUTES OF EVIDENCE

*Education*

*Poorer Classes*

1

SHANNON · IRELAND

© *1968*

*Irish University Press  Shannon  Ireland*

*Microforms*

*Microfilm, microfiche and other forms of micro-publishing*
© *Irish University Microforms  Shannon  Ireland*

SBN 7165 0197 X

*Irish University Press  Shannon  Ireland*
DUBLIN CORK BELFAST LONDON NEW YORK
*Captain T M MacGlinchey  Publisher*

PRINTED IN IRELAND AT SHANNON
BY ROBERT HOGG PRINTER TO IRISH UNIVERSITY PRESS

# REPORT.

THE SELECT COMMITTEE appointed to inquire into the Education of the Lower Orders in The Metropolis, and to report their Observations thereupon; together with the MINUTES of the EVIDENCE taken before them, from time to time, to The House; and who were instructed to consider what may be fit to be done with respect to the Children of Paupers who shall be found begging in the Streets in and near the Metropolis, or who shall be carried about by Persons asking Charity, and whose Parents, or other Persons who they accompany, have not sent such Children to any of the Schools provided for the Education of poor Children;——HAVE, pursuant to the Order of The House, inquired into the Matters to them referred, and have agreed to the following REPORT:

YOUR Committee have examined a great body of Evidence, which has been reported and ordered to be printed, respecting the State of Education among the Lower Orders in The Metropolis; and they have found reason to conclude, that a very large number of poor Children are wholly without the means of Instruction, although their parents appear to be generally very desirous of obtaining that advantage for them.

Your Committee have also observed with much satisfaction, the highly beneficial effects produced upon all those parts of the Population which, assisted in whole or in part by various Charitable Institutions, have enjoyed the benefits of Education.

Your Committee have not had time this Session fully to report their Opinion upon the different branches of their Inquiry, but they feel persuaded that the greatest advantages would result to this Country from Parliament taking proper measures, in concurrence with the prevailing disposition in the Community, for supplying the deficiency of the means of Instruction which exists at present, and for extending this blessing to the Poor of all descriptions.

Although Your Committee have not been instructed to examine the state of Education beyond the Metropolis, they have, in addition to what has appeared in Evidence, received communications, which show the necessity of Parliament as speedily as possible instituting an inquiry into the management of Charitable Donations and other Funds for the Instruction of the Poor of this Country, and into the state of their Education generally, especially in the larger Towns: And Your Committee are of opinion, that the most effectual as well as least expensive mode of conducting such an Inquiry, would be by means of a Parliamentary Commission.

20 *June* 1816.

# FIRST REPORT.

## MINUTES OF EVIDENCE

Taken before The SELECT COMMITTEE appointed to inquire into the EDUCATION of the Lower Orders of The Metropolis.

Ordered, by The House of Commons, *to be Printed,*
7 *June* 1816.

# WITNESSES.

# FIRST REPORT.

## MINUTES OF EVIDENCE

TAKEN BEFORE THE

Select Committee on the Education of the

Lower Orders of The Metropolis.

*Mercurii, 22° die Maii,* 1816.

HENRY BROUGHAM, Esq. in The Chair.

Mr. *Thomas Augustine Finnegan,* called in, and Examined.

Mr.
T. A. Finnegan.

WHAT are you?—Master of the St. Giles's Irish Free Schools, in George-street.

In George-street, St. Giles's?—Yes.

How long have you been so employed?—Since June 1813.

Before that time were you employed in the education of children in that district?—In 1810 I was employed in Moorfields; I had a school consisting of about 120 children, boys and girls; I found a general disposition among the parents to have their children educated.

From your intercourse with the inhabitants of St. Giles's, in which you have resided since that time, can you speak to the state of the education and the situation of the lower orders generally?—I have taken a survey of the neighbourhood, and I have ascertained that there are upwards of 6,000 poor Irish in that neighbourhood, in the district of St. Giles, including the parts of Bloomsbury that are connected with it.

Do you mean 6.000 Irish families?—Six thousand poor Irish, exclusive of children; and they have all a general disposition to have their children educated, and not only send them, but many of the parents, who could not read or write themselves, attend to be taught; about 100 of them attend four nights in the week, to be instructed, some of them have been taught to read since January last, who exceeded forty-seven years of age.

Have you any means of informing the Committee how many children there are belonging to those parents?—Nearly 3,000.

In what state are those children generally as to education?—Entirely ignorant and destitute of any information whatever, unless those that are in schools at present.

In what state are they with respect to their morals?—Most depraved; they are exposed to every species of vice with which the streets abound; they generally associate with gangs of pickpockets: they are to be found in every quarter of the town, and particularly that quarter.

Do those children belong to labourers in very poor circumstances?—Generally.

Are the morals of the parents themselves very dissolute?—Very dissolute, generally; on Sundays particularly they take their children with them to public-houses, and the children witness the scenes of riot and sanguinary conflict that happen among the parents in the streets.

Is the whole Sunday spent in those public-houses?—Entirely so; while they have a farthing left of their week's wages, they spend it in those public-houses, and the children are left to the parish, for food, during the rest of the week.

You are yourself a native of Ireland?—I am.

How many schools of all sorts are now established within the district of St. Giles's and the neighbourhood?—I do not know of any other, but one, which I believe is

only

*Mr.*
*T. A. Finnegan.*

only for Roman Catholics. The St. Giles's Schools are called free; they are for Irish Protestants as well as Irish Catholics; we interfere not with their opinions.

You are now speaking merely of the schools where those children attend, whom you have been speaking of?—Yes.

Do the parents of those children belong to the Catholic persuasion?—Not generally; many of them are Irish Protestants.

When you mention that there are only those two schools within the district, do you mean there is no other charity school at all?—There are parochial schools.

Are the English inhabitants of that district materially different in their morals and education from the Irish, of whom you have been speaking?—They are; their morals generally are much better, and their strict observance of the Sabbath is exemplary, even of the lowest orders.

Your communication has principally been among the Irish?—Principally so; notwithstanding that, I have had much connexion with the English also.

How many are educated in the school of which you have had the charge?—There have been 774 received into the schools since 1813; out of that number, 520 have been so far instructed as to read the Scriptures.

How many on an average are in the school at any one time?—Two hundred on an average.

How many is the school capable of instructing at once?—Three hundred boys and girls.

What is the nature of the establishment?—To give the children of the poor Irish proper instruction, and useful information, in reading, writing, and arithmetic only, without interfering with the principles of their religion.

Are children of all religious denominations, provided they are of poor Irish parents, admitted?—They are; and are particularly directed to attend at such places of worship as their parents prefer.

By whom was the school founded?—The school was first founded by the Rev. Joseph Ivimey of Harpur-street, with my assistance.

By what fund is it supported?—By voluntary subscriptions; but now considerably in arrears.

What is the annual income of the establishment?—Not more than 200*l.*

Is it upon this 200*l.* you complain of arrears?—It is not; that is the average income; we have the expectation of donations.

To whom does the school-house belong?—I believe it belongs to Mr. Clarke of Bury-place.

Do you pay rent for it?—Yes; Mr. Clarke engaged the school-house on his own account, he pays a rent for it to Mr. Wallis of Long Acre.

Do the children pay any thing for their education?—Nothing: when the schools were first established, we endeavoured to assist the funds by requesting the parents to pay a penny a week, but we found the parents in many instances could not even pay that.

Was it from want of means, or inclination?—In many instances from want of means, particularly in the winter season; their supply from the parish was so very trifling, and they are so improvident in the summer, they have no savings for winter.

Are the children fed or clothed?—They are clothed, and in the inclement season we fed them, when their parents were out of employ; they would literally have perished had not a generous public subscribed towards their relief.

How long do they generally continue at school?—From nine in the morning till five in the afternoon, dinner hour excepted; in the evening many of the parents attend, as before described.

Are there any other schools than the one with which you are connected?—I have already remarked, there is another school, denominated "The St. Patrick's."

How many are taught in that school?—I do not know; they are all children of Roman Catholics, and instructed in the Roman Catholic principles.

Do you know any thing of the parochial schools in St. Giles's?—Very little; I know there is a parochial school.

You do not know how many are taught there?—No, I do not; they are boarded and educated there.

Have the poor Irish, of whom you have been speaking, any other means of education whatever, than the schools of which you have been speaking?—I believe not.

Has there been an arrear since the establishment of the school of which you have the charge?—There has been a considerable arrear.

Have

Mr.
T. A. Finnegan.

Have you any means of judging how many of the poor Irish, to whom you have referred, remove from the district in the course of a year?—I have no particular means of judging, but on a supposition I should say about 1,000; in the harvest season they generally go into the country.

By what means do you ascertain the number of which you have spoken?—I took a survey three years ago, and another six months ago; I went from house to house, and from room to room, and am particularly acquainted with the state of the families. I have stated before, that there were 3000 children; I mean children above the age of five years: when the children advance in years, they are generally sent to Ireland to their relatives, and that causes the number to appear so small.

At what age are they sent to Ireland?—As they grow up, the parents find it impossible to maintain them here, and they are sent to Ireland to their friends; particularly if there are any in circumstances capable of giving them some relief: many are also sent from the workhouse to Manchester, I am inclined to think, as apprentices.

At what age are they accustomed to send them as apprentices?—Between the ages of nine and twelve. The officers of the parish are so particular, when they apply for relief they take their children from them.

When you mentioned the district of St. Giles's, within what bounds are you speaking?—Only of the parish of St. Giles; I include Seven Dials, and as far as St Martin's Lane; it is an extensive parish: there are very few of the Irish in that part of Bloomsbury within the parish.

You have stated, that you had room for 300 children, and that only 200 attended; how do you account for your establishment not being full?—From the most unprecedented opposition, by the Roman Catholic Clergy, to the teaching the Holy Scriptures.

You have no want of funds, if parents would send their children to your school?—We are considerably in arrears now, and have been since the commencement of the schools: the schools are quite sufficient to contain 300 children, in their present state; our funds are certainly inadequate; notwithstanding, our Treasurer is willing to advance, in hopes of supplies from generous contributors.

You have said, you do not interfere with the religious principles of the children; what do you mean when you say you have met with unprecedented opposition from the Roman Catholics?—We make use, as a reading book in the school, of the approved version of the Holy Scriptures: the Roman Catholic clergymen are averse to that; they will not allow the children of Roman Catholics to read the Scriptures at all. What I mean by not interfering with religious opinions is, that we introduce or use no Creed, Catechism, or confession of faith, but leave the children to attend such places of worship as their parents prefer, and to be instructed in their peculiar modes of worship by their own clergy.

Their objection is to the children being taught to read the Scriptures?—The parents entirely approve of it, and wish their children to be taught to read them; but the Catholic priests oppose it, and threaten the parents to deprive them of their religious privileges if they suffer their children to read the Scriptures; and have done so in many instances.

Is this opposition of late?—It has been ever since the commencement; as soon as the plan and design of the schools were made known, their opposition immediately commenced; one of the Priests entered the school-room, and demanded permission to teach the Roman Catholic Catechism in the school; this was objected to: the Sunday following, he preached against the schools, addressing a Roman Catholic congregation, and the effect of the sermon was, the windows of the school-house were broken, my wife and I pelted with mud, and a few days after my child so beaten as to become a cripple, and is so to this day; the usual epithet whereby we are designated, is, "The Protestant Bible School," as a term of reproach.

How long ago is this?—Our Report particularly points out the time; Mr. Gandolphy preached the Sermon about two years ago.

Has your number fallen-off since that time?—At the time, the number decreased from 230 to 38 for one week; but the week following, the parents, satisfied with the mode of instruction, sent their children again; and in the course of six weeks our full number was completed, and it has continued at an average ever since. The violence of the priests is incessant, they go from room to room, endeavouring to persuade the parents not to send their children, and I endeavour to be as active as possible

Mr.
T. A. Finnegan.

in pointing out to the parents the advantages arising from a moral education, considering there can be no true religion that is not founded on the principles inculcated from the Bible.

Do you know whether those persons, when they attempted to prevent the parents sending the children to your school, attempted to persuade them to send them to the other school?—I cannot exactly say.

About how many are educated in the Catholic school?—About 200; their avowed hostility to our school is particularly expressed in their own declaration, which appears in one of their reports.

Of what principle are you?—I am myself of Protestant principle. There are a number of poor Irish in Saffron-hill; I made a survey there last week, and I found there were 3,420 Irish adults; the average of the children were three to each family, some five and some two, making about 5,000 of all ages.

What did you observe respecting the morals of those people?—Similar to that that I have observed in St. Giles's, but a disposition to give their children education, and to be taught to read themselves.

What means of instruction have those children?—They have none; I have solicited a few friends to endeavour to establish a school there, which they are now about doing.

Was there no free school for those children, before that?—I understood there was a free school, of the National establishment, in the neighbourhood; but the Irish have a disinclination to send their children to schools avowedly Protestant.

Do you know how many the National Free School educates?—No, I do not.

What wages do those poor Irish in St. Giles's earn a day?—Some of them have only two shillings a day; but very few exceed three.

What do they work at?—Generally they work at labouring work, as paviors' labourers, plasterers' and bricklayers' labourers; I know very few indeed have more than 3 s. a day.

What do the wives employ themselves in?—The greater part of them, in the morning, carry loads from Covent-garden and other markets for what they can get.

Do you know what wages they get?—There are no set wages; according to the discretion of the person who engages them. Since the schools were established, a very observable amendment has been seen in the conduct of the parents and the children connected with the schools; at the time they began in 1813, the language of the children was violent in the extreme; their general employment at present, when they have done school, is preparing their task for the next morning; they commit portions of Scripture to memory each day, and there are rewards distributed for the encouragement of reading the Scriptures at home: preceding the period of 1813, their sanguinary battles were frequent, particularly on Sundays, but since that period I have not witnessed above five, which I attribute to the influence their education has on their morals.

---

## Jovis, 23° die Maii, 1816.

### HENRY BROUGHAM, Esquire, in The Chair.

### Mr. John Kelly, called in, and Examined.

Mr.
John Kelly.

YOU are Treasurer of the Saint Patrick's School?—I am Secretary and Trustee.

How long have you been so?—Since its commencement in 1803.

By what funds is it supported?—By voluntary contributions.

What is the purpose of the charity?—For the instruction of the poor children in Saint Giles's and its vicinity; and if there is any superabundance of contributions, it is applied towards the maintenance of orphans.

Do you mean by children in Saint Giles's and its vicinity, the children of the poor generally, or only the Irish children?—The children of the poor generally, if they are Catholics; but we feel ourselves bound not to admit any persons into the school, but those who are of that religion.

How many children receive education?—I think there are at this moment about 400; I think it is rather beyond that number, of boys and girls.

Do

Do you think that 400 is the average number that are educated?—At present we have more than we usually have, more especially in the female school.

Is that increase of number temporary?—I believe it has been partly owing to a very excellent schoolmistress, who has undertaken that office from motives of humanity, without reward, and under her influence the female school has considerably increased.

What used the number to be, before that increase?—The school is divided into a boys school, situate in Dean-street, and the girls school in Denmark-street; till about two years ago, the number of girls used to be about sixty, and I believe at present there are about 200; the boys school has always averaged from 150 to 200.

Has the girls school had 200 in it permanently during the last two years?—It has been generally increasing, and the lady who has undertaken the management of it, says that if she had more space, she should be able to get more children.

Are the funds of the Society in a flourishing state?—They promised very well at the late annual meeting.

When was that?—On the 6th of May.

Do you mean to represent, you have as much funds as you have any occasion for in supplying the money requisite for educating the children?—If we abandon the intention of taking orphans, I presume the funds would enable us to take all the children our space would allow us to receive.

If you had a larger space, have you reason to believe that many more children would come for education?—The lady who conducts the female school has repeatedly urged that to the committee.

Are there as many boys and girls now educated in both those schools, as the schools will admit?—The boys school would admit 100 more, perhaps, than it has hitherto had.

To what cause do you take it to be owing that there are so few children in the boys school, compared to what it would admit?—I cannot rightly speak to that, except that there is another school existing in the neighbourhood.

Do you know how many children are educated in that other school?—I do not.

Do you mean the school under Mr. Finnegan?—I do.

Then do you apprehend that 330 children are the whole number of poor in your parish who require education?—I must answer that by saying I have never made it my business to go into Saint Giles's, to inquire as to what children stood in need of education.

Have you observed any indisposition on the parts of the Irish Catholics in that district, to educate their children in those schools?—By no means; but I believe it frequently happens that they have not clothes to send them in, and from other causes of poverty, they have almost abandoned all hopes of doing it; I believe the other school, and ours likewise, are endeavouring to furnish the children with the means of covering them, and I believe it is owing to that, that our school has become more numerous.

Do you know any thing of any other parish schools belonging to Saint Giles's?—I do not; there is another Catholic school, which has one of it establishments in Wild-street, and I believe they receive also some of the children from the Saint Patrick's Society.

What are the whole expenses of your establishment?—I think about 900*l.* is the whole expense of the establishment.

For which about 400 boys and girls are educated?—Yes, and I think about six or seven female orphans entirely provided for, and no boys; it was formerly both for boys and girls, but we made an agreement with the other Charity, that they should take the boys, and we the girls, for reasons which are obvious.

How much may the expense be of supporting those six or seven orphan girls?—We take it upon an average of 20*l.* each.

Then how is the other 760*l.* expended in the education of 400 children?—The two first items that strike me, are the rents of the two premises, which I think are about 170*l.* a year; from that I think 30*l.* a year is to be taken off, leaving 140*l.* the net rent we have stood at, including taxes.

What is the next expense?—The salary of the schoolmaster, I believe, last year was 60*l.*; that which would be the mistress's salary, she has to purchase rewards for the children, say 40*l.*; and there is occasionally printing.

What sort of printing?—Books and lessons, and some publications occasionally, to keep the thing alive.

When

Mr.
John Kelly.

When you reckon the whole expense at 900*l.* what is the whole income?—In speaking of the income this last year, ending Lady-day 1816, there was an excess of 150*l.*; we were indebted to the carpenter and builder, for sundry repairs in the school for two years and a half, and he brought in his bill this year, which I think was 220*l.* odd pounds. I have not mentioned yet, neither does it occur to me, what the sum was, but there is clothing provided for a great number of children at the anniversary dinner; but I do not call to mind what number of children were provided with clothes for the dinner of 1815.

You have mentioned 900*l.* as the expense of this last year; what is the average expense of the year 1814, or for any preceding year?—I think I may venture to say that the average has been from seven to nine hundred pounds; till this last year the orphan establishment has never been so low as seven; it used to be twenty.

From what you have stated, the average expense being small in former years, was the average income as much as 1,050*l.*?—We have always taken care to let our outgoings be something in proportion to our income.

Have you any salary for executing your office?—No.

Has any other person, except the schoolmaster?—None whatever.

What are the hours of instruction?—From nine to twelve in the morning, and from two to five in the afternoon, in summer; I believe there is a little difference in winter time.

The schoolmaster resides in the house, I suppose?—He does not at present; the matron resides in the orphan-house for the girls.

What are they taught?—Reading, writing, and arithmetic.

Are the girls taught any work?—Certainly; they are taught needle-work and household-work.

Upon what plan do you teach?—We attempted to teach, some time ago, upon Lancaster's principle, but not precisely upon his plan: we could not follow his plan precisely, but we followed his principle, so that the number of children, however great, does not become an inconvenience to the teacher.

Are the Scriptures taught?—The Catholic religion is taught, and every branch of the Scriptures are taught, as proposed by Catholics.

Are the children instructed from the Bible itself?—From the Bible, the Testament, and religious books; their lessons are pasted upon boards, according to Lancaster's plan, and those lessons are extracts from the Bible or Testament, and also lessons from their Catechism.

From what you know of the poor Irish, do you believe they have a great desire to give their children education?—I have no doubt of it whatever.

Do the children pay any thing for admission into the school?—Certainly not, in any way whatever; and if the master or other person about the school were to receive bribes, they would be discharged.

Has the schoolmaster any other profession or employment?—None at all.

What have you increased his salary to, lately?—It will be increased 20*l.* if not more.

Has he any perquisite of any kind?—None at all.

Does any part of the income which you have stated, arise from money in the funds?—I think there are 3,500*l.* in the 3-per cents.

Mr. *Thomas Leary*, called, in and Examined.

YOU undertook to survey the district in the neighbourhood of Saint Giles's?—I did.

As one of the gentlemen belonging to the West London Association?—Yes, one of the Committee.

When was that?—In 1813, I think.

Who accompanied you?—Mr. Doyle and Mr. Spratley.

What district was it you examined?—It was called the Covent-garden Division.

Can you tell us nearly what the bounds were?—The method in which the West London Association acted, was to divide their portion of the Metropolis into divisions that they intended to erect schools for, and then they subdivided those divisions into districts.

Which district was it you examined?—It was called the Covent-garden Division.

Can you tell us the streets?—From the corner of Catherine-street in the Strand,

to

Mr.
*Thomas Leary.*

to Exeter-court Strand, Exeter Change, Change-court, Burleigh-street, Marigold-court, New-street, Dennis-court Strand, Lumley-court Strand, Bullen-court Strand, Baylie's-court Strand, New Exchange-court Strand, and Bedford-street. I beg to observe here, that the remainder of the division was not visited, in consequence of the two gentlemen, who accompanied me, not being able to devote their time to it just at that period.

Did you yourself visit the whole of the district you have mentioned?—Not the whole of it.

How many houses did you visit?—Two hundred and fifteen.

Upon that number, what was the number of poor children educated and un-educated?—97 boys educated, and 145 uneducated.

How many girls?—75 educated, or with the means of education; and 112 un-educated, and without the means of education.

What age do you speak of?—Of an age fit to go to school, about four or five years of age; we sometimes did take an account of the children who would be likely to go to school when we erected one.

Were many of those people in a state of great misery?—Very great.

Were they chiefly composed of English, Irish, or Scotch?—I think they were chiefly composed of English and Scotch; but there was one Court (Dennis-court) which was entirely inhabited by Irish.

Did you perceive any difference in the different sets of English, Irish, and Scotch, which were worst educated?—Our association was founded upon a principle which excluded all party spirit.

In the survey you took of this district, do you think there was more want of education where the Irish were, or where the English and Scotch were?—The number of Irish was too small to enable me to make any observation upon that. In our district we took an account of all Irish families, and in the division I visited, we had only five Irish families that had children.

How many houses were there in the district?—Five hundred.

You did not visit any other district?—No, I did not.

Did all the persons, among whom you went in the course of your inspection, express a willingness to assist according to their ability in the plan of education?—Very much so, for there was hardly a person we went to, though they were some of the very poorest, that did not endeavour to contribute something, sixpence or a shilling, and they were very anxious that a school should take place.

How have those subscriptions been applied?—The undertaking was very extensive; the intention was to build schools in the West of London, bounded by Temple-bar and those districts which divide the West end of the town from the City, upon one side; the boundaries on the other side I do not now recollect. In order to accomplish that, a committee (which was appointed at a general meeting held for the purpose) separated the whole of the West of London into eleven divisions; those divisions they subdivided into districts, as they called them; in those districts they expected to get persons who would visit from house to house, and ascertain the number of children educated and uneducated, and to solicit subscriptions; there were a variety of causes afterwards which prevented the extensive object of the Association being carried into effect, and still remains unexecuted, but not given up. The great difficulty we found at that time was to get persons to visit the districts; it is very difficult to get men in trade to devote their time to that purpose, and those who undertook to visit that district got cool upon it.

How much was received from that division?—I received from those few streets 7*l.* 18*s.* 9*d.* and from the poorest classes 1*l.* 11*s.* 6*d.* in sums from twopence to one shilling.

How have those subscriptions been applied?—They have been applied in printing, in promoting the objects of the Association, in expenses of public meetings which were held in order to procure those subscriptions, in the rent of an office taken, and in a salary to an acting secretary.

Has any school been erected by the Association?—No school has been erected, but they have taken one which had been originally a Lancasterian school, in the Horse-ferry Road, in which they are teaching at present.

How many boys are taught in that school?—The number upon the books, I believe, is about three or four hundred, but of them I do not think more than 150 attend regularly.

From what parts do those children come?—From the neighbourhood of Tothill-street, Westminster, and thereabouts.

Who

Who is the master of that school?—Mr. Jameson.

In the course of your inspection, did you find great anxiety amongst the poorest classes whom you have described, to procure education for their children?—Very great, I think; in the short visit which I paid, I found the poorer classes particularly anxious upon the subject of education.

You know nothing of any parish school in the neighbourhood of that district?—No, I do not.

## Mr. *Francis Baisler*, called in, and Examined.

WAS it the parish of St. Giles's which you visited?—The left-hand side of Long Acre, along Drury-lane.

How many educated children did you find there?—417 educated.

How many uneducated?—497.

Did you find them in great distress?—Many of the families in very poor circumstances indeed.

Were those of the lowest orders, generally speaking, uneducated altogether?—The greater part of them, where there were three or four in a family; one or two of them perhaps could read a little, others not at all; and many had not the means of procuring education.

Did they seem anxious for it generally?—Extremely so; the general inquiry was, what time they might expect to get their children to school.

What nation were they chiefly, of the families you visited?—A good many Irish.

Did you find any difference in the Irish, as to their education?—Yes.

What was it?—There were generally more in their families uneducated than the others.

Did you find any difference in their anxiety to be educated?—Very little, they were generally as desirous of having their children educated as the others.

Were the families for the most part English, Irish, or Scotch?—A good many Irish, but some of all.

Do you know whether there were any schools established before your visit in the neighbourhood?—I do not think there was, in the district we visited.

When you speak of children, to what age do you refer?—From four to ten; after that time they generally send them out to do something, and do not keep them at home.

You saw a great deal of misery and filth?—Yes, very great.

## Mr. *Frederick Augustus Earle*, called in, and Examined.

HOW long have you been Clerk to the Vestry Clerk of the Parish of St. Giles?—About twelve years.

In the course of that time have you had occasion to attend at the Workhouse school?—Yes.

Is there any other parish school besides the workhouse school?—There is a charity school in Queen-street, Bloomsbury.

Who is at the head of that school?—There is at present no secretary to the school, but certain Trustees are appointed by the Subscribers, who manage the concerns of it; it is a school for 101 boys and 70 girls; there are but 60 girls at present in the school.

Is there any other school in the parish, besides Mr. Finnegan's and St. Patrick's schools?—There are several schools under the management of parish officers; I am speaking of the united parishes of St. Giles and St. George Bloomsbury; there is one established in Eagle-street, upon the Lancasterian plan, in which there are 100 boys educated, and fourteen pence a month is paid by the parents towards the schooling.

Is it supported by voluntary subscriptions?—I believe the remainder is paid by voluntary subscriptions.

Do you know of any other school?—There is one established in Store-street, Bedford-square, that purports to have thirty girls, but at present there is only twenty-two, and the parents pay a penny a week for each child, I understand.

Is that a Lancasterian school also?—That I am not aware of; there is another school likewise in Store-street, in which there are seventy children, who pay
two-pence

Mr.
F. A. Earle.

twopence a week each, that is on Dr. Bell's principle; there is another in Wild-street, in which there are 100 boys educated.

Do they pay any thing?—I believe not, I am not quite sure of it; there is likewise a free school in Wild-street or the neighbourhood, in which there are 40 boys and 45 girls; it is principally maintained by subscriptions from Queen-street chapel.

Are you aware that a number of children attending the schools you have mentioned, do not live in the neighbourhood?—A great number do not.

Are there any other schools that you can speak to?—There is one in West-street, in which there are 300 boys and 100 girls.

Do you mean actually educated?—I understand, from the master, there are 400 now.

Is that upon the National system, or the Lancasterian?—I do not think it is upon either; the master has the principal management of it, under the direction of the Rev. Mr. Gurney, and nine-pence a month is paid by each child.

Do you know how many masters there are in it?—There is a master and a mistress.

Are the funds of that school provided by charity?—I understand they are; there is another school in Gate-street, Lincoln's-Inn Fields, and I am informed there are about 300 boys and girls altogether there.

Supported by charity?—Yes.

Do they pay any thing?—I am not aware of that. There is a school now building, under a committee of parish officers, which is under the will of a Mr. Shelton, near the vestry-room of Saint Giles's, in which there are to be 50 children educated, 35 of the parish of Saint Giles, 10 of Saint Martin, and 5 of Covent Garden, agreeably to his will.

How much money did he leave for that purpose?—Having been called upon quite unexpectedly, I have not furnished myself with the particulars of that school: it is left by will to the management of the churchwardens and a committee of the vestry.

Are there no other foundations, of the same sort, in the parish?—I am not aware of any other but the workhouse school, which contains 63 children.

From whence do the funds come for that school?—From the poor rates; there are 30 girls and 33 boys.

Is it limited to that number?—No; it varies every day, in consequence of the admission of people to the workhouse, whose children are placed in the school.

Is that school merely for the children of persons admitted to the workhouse?—Yes.

What is the annual expense of that school?—We cannot ascertain that, it being blended with the workhouse, and being one branch of it.

What salary has the schoolmaster?—Twenty pounds a year, and his lodging and board.

What has the schoolmistress?—She has twenty-five pounds for two situations; she is housekeeper as well.

Is she the wife of the schoolmaster?—No.

Are the children boarded as well as lodged?—Generally.

How many years are they kept at school before they are apprenticed out?—They frequently go out of the school before they have been in long, being taken away by their parents; but about the age of ten years they have been apprenticed to manufacturers.

What are they taught?—Reading and writing, if they remain sufficiently long enough in the school, and accounts; a great many of them are taken away before they arrive to that. There is no other parish school under the Churchwardens and Overseers of the poor.

Do you know of any other charitable foundation within the parish, for the purposes of education, besides those you have mentioned?—No, I do not; there may be others.

Is there a grammar-school in the parish?—I am not aware of any. I beg to state, there may be some little variation as to the number of scholars I have mentioned, except as to the workhouse school; but I have spoken to them from the best information I could procure.

Have you sufficient knowledge of the state of the poor of the parish of Saint Giles, to inform the Committee respecting it?—Yes; I have been in the daily habit of seeing them, and visiting the district.

Are

Are there a number of children in the parish destitute of the means of education?—A great many.

How long have you known those schools of which you have spoken?—I cannot speak to that; the school in Store-street has been very recently established.

You have stated, that some of those schools are short of the number which they could accommodate; do you apprehend that the poorer classes require inducement to bring their children to school?—A great many do; and a great many are very anxious to get their children placed in schools.

What do you conceive to be the disposition of the poor Irish, with respect to their wishing their children to be educated?—The number that I see in the workhouse, generally speaking, are desirous their children should be educated; but they are deterred, in a great measure, from being in want of clothes, and from the mother not being able to attend to the children, from going out to market, and leaving them the whole day to themselves.

Are there any other obstructions which present themselves against the education of the poor Irish children of Saint Giles?—I am not aware of any so material as those I have mentioned.

Do you see any of the poor at their own habitations?—Very frequently.

What is the general state of the children in Saint Giles's, with respect to their morals and education?—In a very dreadful state, I am afraid.

Do you apprehend there are many children of very bad character in St. Giles's?—I do indeed.

Are there many thieves?—A great many.

Are girls early devoted to prostitution?—Very early. I had an opportunity of attending at the Public Office Marlborough-street but last week, where there were about 30 prostitutes that had been apprehended in the parish of Saint Giles, and several of them were very young, two or three of them not above thirteen or fourteen years of age.

Have you ever gone through the interior of Saint Giles's on a Sunday afternoon?—Many times.

In what state have you found the generality of the inhabitants?—The generality, I think, have been very peaceable and orderly; but I have frequently seen great affrays on a Sunday.

How do the children in Saint Giles's spend their Sundays?—A great many in playing about the streets.

Have you ever noticed any going towards the fields in great numbers, and in a riotous manner?—Very frequently.

Does it fall within your knowledge that a great number of children are gambling and behaving in a very riotous manner in the fields on a Sunday afternoon, in the neighbourhood of that parish?—I have, in that parish and St. Pancras, seen a great many.

How many?—Fifty or sixty.

In parties, or altogether?—In various parties about the fields; I do not mean to say together.

Do you apprehend there would be any improvement in those children, if more pains were taken with their education?—I have no doubt of it.

Have you any officers of your parish, constables, churchwardens, overseers, or any responsible person, to take cognizance of any of these irregularities?—The beadles are constantly employed in doing it; but immediately they go away, those children assemble again.

Are you aware, or have you not heard, that there is a system laid down by the parents of those children, to encourage them to go out thieving?—I have heard it, but do not know it personally.

Do you think that a want of clothing in the children prevents them from attending school, and likewise from attending divine worship?—I should apprehend that many parents will not send their children in the destitute condition in which they are; I do not speak generally, but we have them frequently come into the workhouse naked, or nearly so.

Have you known any instances in which children have been induced to come to school, and the parents afterwards have been very well satisfied with seeing their children informed?—Very many instances; some have been clothed by the churchwardens and overseers, and of my own knowledge they have got admission to the school of Mr. Finnegan.

Have you any establishment for the reception of prostitutes, after being before the

the Magistrates?—None but the workhouse, where they are sometimes kept for a short time; I am aware that there are many parents who will not send their children to school, because they send them out begging, that begging being the principal support of the parents.

Have you known of children, who were taught reading at the schools, going home and reading to their parents who had not the benefit of education?—I have; and have frequently seen children at the workhouse, who did not formerly go to school, and on speaking to them I have found they have made astonishing progress.

## Mr. *Edward Norris*, called in, and Examined.

YOU have heard the evidence given by the other Witnesses, respecting the state of the poor Irish in St. Giles's; does your information lead you to agree with it?—I partly coincide with the whole of it.

Do you know of any other schools in that neighbourhood, but those which you have heard spoken to?—There is one called " The Bedford," in Tottenham-court Road.

How many are educated at that school?—I really cannot say; I only know there is such an establishment.

Is the chapel you attend chiefly frequented by the lower Irish?—Chiefly by the lower Irish.

Is it a Catholic chapel?—It is.

From their appearance at chapel, should you conceive them to be in miserable circumstances?—They do make a very miserable appearance, frequently.

Do they bring their children with them?—They frequently do and frequently do not.

Are they very destitute of the means of education generally?—I should not exactly say that, because we have room in the school attached to the chapel for more than attend.

To what do you attribute there not being so many children there as the school could accommodate?—Partly neglect, and partly want of the inducement of clothing.

Is there a general anxiety prevalent among those classes to have their children educated?—They profess so.

From that, you do not appear to credit it?—While there are opportunities for them, I should not quite credit it.

In short they would rather spend their money in drink, than in giving clothing to their children?—Too many would.

Does any method strike you of reclaiming them from that perversion?—I do not know of any general remedy; we do as much as lies in our power.

Do you belong to the Benevolent Society of St. Patrick, or the United Society?—I belong to the Chapel of St. Patrick.

Is that a branch of the Society of St. Patrick?—It is neither one nor the other, it is quite a distinct thing.

## Mr. *John Honeyman*, called in, and Examined.

WHAT are you?—A silk manufacturer.

Are you acquainted with Spitalfields, and that neighbourhood?—Yes; I have resided there four and twenty years.

How are the poor children off, for education, there?—There are a great number of them uneducated.

Can you give us any idea of the number of children uneducated?—Not accurately I cannot.

Near about it?—I should suppose near 2,000.

In what population?—In a population of from 17 to 18,000.

Are those the children of the poorest classes?—Yes.

What means of education are provided in that district?—There is a parish-school which contains 110 children, and a parish Sunday school of 150; and there is a Protestant dissenting school of 100 children; there is a Methodist school, in Raven-row, of 500 children, that is a Sunday school.

Is that upon the Lancasterian plan?—I believe it is. There is a Sunday school,

in

Mr.
John Honeyman.

in Hope-street, of about 200; there is another Sunday school, belonging to Mr. Evans's Chapel, of 800, upon the Lancasterian plan partly, that is merely a Sunday school; there is Mrs. Buxton's school, of about 100 children, who pay about two-pence a week; all the rest are free. There is an adult school of 160; and a free school also, which is likewise held on a Sunday evening.

Are there any others, besides those you have mentioned?—I know of no others.

How are those different schools supported?—By subscriptions, except Mrs. Buxton's, which I believe is supported by herself.

Have you any parochial schools?—I have mentioned there is a parochial school of 110 children, and a parochial Sunday school of 150.

How are those supported?—By voluntary subscription; and part of the money is funded.

You do not know what the amount of the funds are?—No, I do not.

From all that you have stated, do you apprehend that there is a great want of the means of education in your district?—I think there is: there are as many uneducated as educated; there is a great deal of poverty and distress among those persons now; want of clothing is a very serious objection to their sending their children to school.

Are the schools worse attended in times of distress than at other times?—They are, certainly.

You reckon this a time of great distress?—I do; I think I could take the Members of this Committee, within ten minutes walk of my house, and show them 20,000 hands out of employ; there are about 7,000 looms unemployed, and each loom generally employs three hands.

Is there any indisposition on the part of the poor to send their children to those schools?—I never saw any whatever.

Have you observed any anxiety on the part of the parents to have their children educated?—A considerable anxiety; two years ago I was employed to take a survey of the poor, to know their distress for want of Bibles, and we went into almost every room, when we took an opportunity of recommending them to send their children to school; since that we have distributed upwards of 1500 Bibles and Testaments among them.

In the course of that survey, did you find great misery and ignorance prevailing among those orders?—Very great; there were very nearly 1000 adults who could not read, besides a great number of children, I presume about 2000 children.

Did they appear to regret the state of ignorance in which they were?—Many of them did very much. Of the schools which I have mentioned, six have been established within these twelve years.

In the Sunday schools, how many years attendance does it require to teach a child reading?—I really am not quite sure how long; if they attend constantly they will very soon acquire it; from the observation I have made, I am persuaded Sunday schools are by far the most efficient way of instructing children, their parents cannot spare them so well on other days, and their attendance is generally better on Sundays than on other days.

Could any of the schools which you have mentioned, accommodate a considerably greater number than attend them?—Yes, they could; the parish school, and the parish Sunday school, and the adult school, could all admit more.

How many more, do you think?—I am not quite sure; Mr. Evans's school, which educates 800, can only admit 400 at a time.

Is the school, which educates 500, full?—It is.

Are there any other schools full?—No.

Have you many Irish in your neighbourhood?—A very considerable number.

Can you form any idea of the number?—No, I cannot exactly; they are principally casual poor.

What are the Poor Rates in your neighbourhood?—Five shillings in the pound rack rent, and they are going to raise them next quarter another shilling; we are relieving now about 1200 poor every week, besides about 500 in the Workhouse.

*Veneris, 24° die Maii, 1816.*

HENRY BROUGHAM, Esquire, in The Chair.

---

### Mr. *William Hale,* called in, and Examined.

WHAT is the state of the lower orders in Spitalfields, in point of education?— Their education is much better attended to now than it was some years back.

Mr.
*William Hale.*

Are there many poor children without the means of education?—I should suppose about near one half.

How many may there be altogether uneducated?—I should think perhaps about 1500; that is a rough calculation.

Are there any establishments for education?—There is a parochial school, where there are about one hundred and ten children educated, and they attend regularly at the church; and there is a school, called the Protestant Dissenting School, where 100 children are educated: at both those schools they are educated principally upon the old plan, and are annually clothed.

How are the funds provided?—By annual subscriptions, legacies, and donations.

How long have they been established?—The parochial school has been established about 110 years; the Wood-street school 99 years.

What is the annual expense of the parochial school?—I am not aware of that.

Can you give a guess?—No, I cannot. There is some little funded property belonging to the Protestant Dissenting School.

You have read over the evidence given by Mr. Honeyman; do you agree with it?—In the general purport of it I agree; I see he has stated that about 2000 remain uneducated; I should think about 1500; by far the greater part of those who are now educated, are those who are educated in Sunday schools only.

Can you form any conjecture of the proportion between those children who are educated in day schools, and those educated in Sunday schools only?—Four-fifths at least, I should suppose, are educated in Sunday schools only; but in one or two of the Sunday schools they meet one evening in the week, for an hour or two.

Can you give the Committee the number of schools who have the custom of meeting one evening in the week?—One of the schools in Raven-row, in which there are about 500 children, and who attend at a place of worship under the denomination of Methodists, have a meeting once or twice a week.

The persons who frequent other places of worship, are they conformists with the Church of England?—Yes, there are about 150 that attend at the parish church. The great mass of those who are now educated, have been in schools which have been recently established, Sunday schools and other schools upon the Bell and Lancasterian system; and it has had a great effect in bettering the morals of the poor; it has been the practice of the managers of all the schools, the Methodist, the parochial, and all the schools, to make the children attend at their respective places of worship; by those means, a great number of poor children, who were formerly accustomed to spend their time idly in playing about the streets, are now under the necessity of attending at a place of worship; it has not only had an happy influence on their morals, but has been the means of inducing some of the parents of those poor children to go to a place of worship that never attended one before.

Is there sufficient room in the church of the parish to hold the poor?—I should think there is nearly; there are a great number of poor that attend at the parish church, and the Rector is constantly in the habit of visiting a number of the poor.

Is there sufficient room in the church to hold the poor, without the aid of other places of worship?—Not for the whole population; there are several chapels in the neighbourhood, not of the established church. I would just observe, but for the increase of those schools, I apprehend that the morals of the people, from one circumstance, would have been much more depraved than formerly, that is, the increase of liquor-shops in the neighbouring parishes all round, by which the poor have been more accustomed to take spirits than formerly; and I have invariably found that whenever they accustom themselves to take spirits, their morals are ruined.

### Mr. *Edward Meyrick,* called in, and Examined.

WHAT are you?—I am Treasurer of the parochial school of Christ Church Spitalfields, which office I have only held for a very few days.

Mr.
*Edward Meyrick.*

427.

What

What number of children are educated there?—One hundred and ten.

How is it supported?—By donations, annual subscriptions, charity sermons, and the interest of money in the funds.

That money in the funds arises from bequests?—Yes, and what has been saved out of the subscriptions.

What is the annual expense of the school?—As near as I can judge (I have only the treasurer's book for one year) it was 458*l.* 10*s.* for 56 boys and 54 girls.

Are they fed?—No; annually clothed.

Are they sufficiently clothed?—Yes.

Are you acquainted with any other schools in the parish?—Not intimately; we have 246 children educated and clothed in the parish altogether.

Do you know the whole number educated in the parish?—No, I do not exactly; but I should think about 2 or 3,000.

You heard the last Witness's account of the proportion between those educated in charity schools and those educated in other ways?—Yes.

Do you think he is correct in stating that 4-5ths received their education at Sunday schools?—I think he was very correct; but a great number of children in Spitalfields are educated in the neighbouring parishes; there are two or three schools upon the borders of the parish, where some of them attend.

Is any sum paid by the parents towards the education of those children?—No.

Do you know any thing of the number of children from your parish, who are educated in the neighbouring parishes?—No, I do not; there appears to be no want of the means of education in our parish, if the parents would send them.

What reason do you give why they do not send them?—Our Sunday schools are not full; and I ought to say, there appears to be a want of inclination on the part of the parents to send them.

By means of education, you mean the means of education in the neighbourhood?—There are means of education in the parish, which they do not take the opportunity of embracing.

What is the reason of their going to the neighbouring parishes?—There are two or three very large schools, upon the Lancasterian plan, upon the borders of the parish.

The Lancasterian method of instruction is not adopted in parish schools?—No, quite in the old way.

Is it adopted at any school within the parish?—No, I believe not.

What is the time that the children usually remain in your school?—Till the age of fourteen, unless they are taken out previously by their parents.

From what age?—From eight to fourteen; and if they conduct themselves well they have a little apprentice fee, something to pay for their indentures, and a Bible and Testament given them.

What becomes of the girls, in general?—In general they are put out to service.

The number of poor in your parish is very considerable?—Very considerable, no parish more so.

That extreme poverty must be one cause of the parents not sending their children to school?—I should hope that might be the reason of not sending them to Sunday schools; but I am sorry to say there seems to be very little inclination to exert themselves with respect to providing clothes for their children; we do not want any particular dress, if they are but clean.

Of what nation is the body of poor people of Spitalfields; Irish?—Not a large proportion of them; English generally.

Are there many French names remaining among them?—Yes, but that language is gone.

A great many of those are among the lowest?—Yes, and some among the most respectable.

The Reverend *William Gurney*, M.A. called in, and Examined.

YOU are Rector of Saint Clement Danes?—Yes.

And also Minister of the Free Chapel in West-street Seven-dials?—Yes, licensed Minister of the Free Episcopal Chapel.

How long have you been Rector of Saint Clement Danes?—About seven years.

And during what time have you been Minister of the Free Chapel?—Nearly fourteen years.

Are you acquainted with the state of education among the lower orders in those
parts

parts of the town?—I know a great deal about it in Saint Giles's, because there I have the greatest establishment for children.

Are there many of the poor children in the parish of Saint Clement's without education?—I should think there are a great many.

Have you any means of giving the Committee an estimate of how many there may be?—I do not know that I can mention the number, but a very strict examination has been made by the friends of the Sunday school, in order to ascertain the number of children without education, and to endeavour to bring them to the Sunday school; it was about three years back that the first attempt was made to establish a Sunday school, and the result has been, that we have collected together about 300 children, boys and girls.

What was the result of that examination, as to the state of the poor in point of education?—We found there were a great many who did not go to any school; the reason assigned in some measure for it was, their ragged condition, and their being unfit, from their great poverty, to appear decently at any school; and we found also, that a great many children went to Sunday schools belonging to Dissenters of various denominations, who had begun long before us to open schools; we found there was a very large Sunday school in Drury-lane, in which there were from 5 to 600 children; a very large number of our children, I believe, went there. But there are a great many mendicants in our parish, owing to the extreme lowness of some parts of the neighbourhood, and the more children they have, the more success they meet with in begging, and they keep them in that way; so that in the week-day we could not get them to a day-school without some different measures were adopted; neither are they fit to appear in them as they are; and on a Sunday they get more by begging than they do on any other day in the week, because more people are out and about; we tried the experiment in several instances, by giving clothes to some of the most ragged, in order to bring them decent to school; they appeared for one Sunday or two, and then disappeared, and the clothes disappeared also. We have two charity schools in the parish, besides the Sunday schools I have mentioned.

What foundations are they on?—Voluntary subscriptions: Sixty boys are clothed and educated, properly called the Parish Charity School; and we have an institution for the education and board of twenty females; that is by voluntary subscriptions; it is done by regular votes of the trustees; every subscriber of two guineas is a trustee, and can have a vote; they do not recommend, as in other charities, the cases are all put on a list, that fully explains the number of children in the family, and so on.

Have you any schools upon any regular foundation?—I am not prepared to say there is no school on a foundation; but I am very suspicious there has been some mismanagement; that there was once a school, which has disappeared.

Was it in consequence of any bequest by will?—That I am not quite certain about; I think it was called The Blue School, but the building was pulled down on the alterations about the church a great many years ago, and I never could get a clear understanding about it: I did make inquiries. Whether the fund arose from any thing that was perishable, and so has fallen down, I cannot tell; but I rather think not; I rather think it has been handed over in some way to the present school; I do not know that it is so, but I rather suspect it is.

Who are the managers of those sixty boys?—The trustees and subscribers of two guineas each; the treasurer is Mr. Johnstone.

What was the size of that Blue school?—Very small, I believe; yet it was something that, I think, might have been made the foundation for a good school, if we could by any means have raked it out of its ashes; but I rather think there was a building belonging to it, and that it decayed, or was pulled down; it is within the memory of many of the inhabitants. I believe a very considerable sum is spent upon those two schools annually.

Can you form an opinion how much?—Four or five hundred a-year, both of them; the girls are fed and completely clothed.

With the exception of those, you know of no other parish schools within your parish?—No others, that I know of.

Is there any large school in the neighbourhood, to which the poor of your parish go?—That one in Drury-lane, I rather think, is in my parish; there is no other, that I know of, to which any children go, unless they may be of different denominations of christians: there is one, not a parochial school, but within the parish, in New-court, Carey-street, connected with Dr. Winter's chapel there.

How

*The Rev. William Gurney.*

How many does it contain?—Two or three hundred, or more, I think.

What is the annual expense of your Sunday school?—Very trifling; I have one collection a-year at the church, at which we generally get about 40 *l.*; we do not go round to collect, it is a private thing done by the Teachers themselves: we have no master or mistress, or any expense of that kind; the Teachers are all gratuitous and voluntary; the whole expense consists in the books and rent of the rooms; in fact now I have by great exertion got part of the vestry for a Sunday, which saves us the expense of paying rent.

Then the whole expense of this school does not exceed sixty or seventy pounds?—Seventy or eighty pounds; we give a good many rewards, according to our funds; and we have a writing school in the week, for the children who behave the best.

What hours do the children attend on a Sunday?—From about half-past eight or nine till twenty minutes before the church service commences in the morning, and again at two till five in the afternoon; we have not proper accommodation at the church for them, that is one great grievance to me; and if we had, we could have four times the number attend the school; we cannot accommodate them at the church, and I am forced to send a detachment of them to another chapel; I wanted to have a gallery erected, and I would have done it without any expense to the parish; two or three charity sermons would have done it.

How long does a child take, at the Sunday school, in learning to read, having no other instruction?—Several have learnt to read in the course of about eighteen months; we would rather they would stay about two years, so as to be able to read a chapter in the Testament; but others, of course, will take much longer, in consequence of the difference of abilities and attention.

What should you take to be the average period in which a child may be taught to read well and easy, at a Sunday school?—I should prefer two years and a half, if I were to have my choice, and I think in that time they would do.

Has any plan been ever adopted in your school for visiting the children at home?—The teachers, I believe, of every class are expected to look after their children, and to know the reason why they are absent, and to inquire how they behave at home, and to present their account of every child at our monthly meeting.

Do they visit them in cases of sickness?—Yes, that they make a point of doing.

Do you think the plan of visiting the children at home is useful to their families?—No doubt of it.

Do you know what is the general moral character of the children in your school at St. Clement's?—We keep a regular account of their conduct with us, and can, by looking to our books, tell the character of every child that has been in the school from the beginning, as far as we have been able to judge.

When did you take an account of their character?—The teachers take an account, and keep an account regularly; and they bring an account of the conduct of every child at the meeting of the Teachers, which I make a point of attending.

Then you have the progressive improvement of your children entered in your books?—I apprehend so.

Do you know the moral character of the children in the West-street school?—I believe it is as good as that of the character of any other children in London; I am satisfied of it, because I made a strict inquiry myself.

Do you know of any Report made from Newgate, of the moral state of the children in charity schools in and about the Metropolis?—I did hear of it; and I had a communication made to me in consequence.

Did you ever see any part of that Report?—I did.

What is your opinion of it?—I formed my opinion in this way; in the first place, I considered the fountain from whence the Report came to be a very bad one, and therefore much to be suspected; in the next place, as the school with which I am connected was particularly marked as one, and knowing that the statements in that account were grossly false, I conceived that it was scarcely worthy my notice; and therefore I took no further steps than by simply stating, in reply to some questions that were asked me in writing by the Committee of investigation, that no such person was ever in the school as they referred to. I should state, there was a boy's name mentioned as having been in our school; the books were examined from the very commencement of the school; for we know every boy and girl that passes through the school, and we know the reason why they went away; and this boy, who stated himself to have been in the school, never was there.

As

As far as your knowledge goes, do you think there is any just foundation for the statements of that Report?—Certainly not, as far as regards my school in West-street: one great reason for my saying that, is this, that we never suffer any child to continue in the school that is detected in any immoral act.

*The Rev. William Gurney.*

Have you been able to form an opinion of the practicability of any general plan for the education of the poor?—I do not think there is any difficulty, myself.

You spoke of a bad fountain from whence the Report proceeded; to what did you allude?—I referred to the boys who gave that information in Newgate.

Were those boys confined in Newgate as criminals?—Yes, they were.

Did one or more of those boys give information respecting your school?—Yes; there was one boy particularly named, who stated that he had been in the school.

Was it true that that boy had been in the school?—No; I inquired of the master, and he examined the books, and he said that no such name had ever been in the school.

Do you believe that that boy ever was at your school?—Certainly not.

How many are taught at the free school at West-street?—Our number is four hundred.

When was it established?—It has been established ever since the chapel was opened, or within a year and a half of it; it has been established about twelve years.

Has it always educated as many?—No, at the beginning, of course it did not; it was not upon the same plan exactly then.

How is it supported?—By the parents of the children now; I began it by subscription.

What was the utmost expense it cost when it was upon subscription?—I can hardly tell that, because we clothed fifty children at first, that cost a guinea a head at that time.

What is the expense now?—Two hundred and ten pounds, including every thing; including a donation of ten pounds to the master and mistress, for their services during the year, in addition to their salary.

What is the salary of the master?—Fifty pounds, and his wife thirty pounds.

How much do the children pay?—Nine-pence per calendar month, which they pay beforehand, so that we never lose any thing.

Of what classes are those children?—They are children of industrious labouring mechanics.

Not of the lowest order?—Not of the very lowest order, not of the very raggedest.

Does it consist with your knowledge that in that district there are a great number of uneducated children of the lowest order, and have no means of education?—A great many; I see, I was going to say, hundreds about the streets, when my school is in operation, so that they cannot attend other schools.

At what age do the children come to your school, generally?—We take them as soon as ever the boys have got breeches; we do not consult their age, but their size; we keep them till they are fit to go out; they generally leave us before they are twelve years of age; they are generally five years of age before we take them. I think altogether we have had four thousand children pass through the school during the last eight years; there are about three hundred out of the four hundred attend regularly, that is a very good proportion; and we are open to all parishes, without distinction.

You confine yourselves to members of the Church?—No, we do not, we are quite free; we have several Roman Catholics, and they go with the rest of the children to church.

Do you teach catechism?—Yes, three times a week.

Does not that scare the Catholics?—Not the least.

Is the chapel at which they attend a free chapel?—Yes, the body of it is free for the accommodation of the poor, it is the only free chapel in London, that I know of.

Do you include, in the expense, the rent of the school?—Yes, fifty pounds rent.

With respect to the children going to church chiefly, in the Sunday school at St. Clement's, do you find great difficulty to procure accommodation for those children?—Yes, very great.

Has it a tendency to make those children leave the church, and go to no place of worship or else dissenting meeting-houses?—Yes, I think there is no doubt of it; those who have been some time in the Sunday school, having got into the habit of going to a place of worship, will not be satisfied when they leave school without going to one where they can be accommodated.

Does

Does any plan strike you, by which this defect could be remedied?—I have thought a great deal of it: I rather think the only way would be, if you can accomplish your object in procuring school-rooms in every parish, suitable in size to the population requiring instruction, to make every one of those schools a chapel for the poor, consecrated regularly as chapels for the poor, to be so used on the Sabbath-day, or any other time; and, where there are accommodations, for some of the children regularly to attend, as a sample of what is doing in the schools, to the congregation at large; the residue to attend in the chapel with their parents. They have got a school of that description, I think, at Whitechapel, of which the master is a clergyman; he is licensed as a preacher there, and the poor people are allowed to attend there, and there is a very large assembly; and it will always be a shelter for the children after they have quitted the school, as well as while they are in it. In my parish, where there are twelve thousand inhabitants, the church, if crowded, might contain nearly four thousand, but there are no accommodations in it for the poor, except about twelve benches in the middle aisle.

What are the expenses of West-street school?—The salary to the master was fifty pounds; to the mistress, thirty pounds; rent, fifty pounds; coals and candles, ten pounds; donation for additional services of the master and mistress, ten pounds; school expenses, sixty pounds. Those expenses, the Committee will observe, include white-washing and repairs, water rate, &c.

Are the children taught upon the National or Lancasterian plan?—They are taught upon a plan upon the principle of both, but in no connexion with either. Our catechetical examinations are rather important. I did make a calculation in my own mind of the expense of extending this school to twelve hundred children, if I had accommodation for them, by which it appears that this number might be educated in the same way for 380 *l.* a year.

Does this calculation include the increased expense for accommodation?—Yes. I was going to say, that in case schools were prepared in the way suggested, by being afterwards consecrated as places of worship for the poor, in large and populous neighbourhoods, that as there would be many children whose parents perhaps could not pay a penny or three halfpence a week, it might be, by any Bill that was brought in, provided that the overseers of the poor for the time being, who distribute the money to the poor to buy provisions, might reserve that penny, in order to pay for those parents who were unable to pay it themselves; that would be doing away any objection which might arise from this idea. You have got 400 children in the neighbourhood of St. Giles, whose parents can pay nine-pence per month; but perhaps there are 2000 in St. Giles's, whose parents cannot pay that; therefore, what are you to do about the funds; but the funds are so small, they are hardly worth mentioning, even if it was paid by the parish. I am satisfied that in St. Clement's parish, if the parish were obligated to find me a room of that description, that would hold 1000 children, and of course 1500 persons for worship, that that money that is now spent upon the eighty children would educate 1000.

In the parish of St. Clement's, what is the total number of children educated at all the schools, as far as you can estimate?—One thousand and thirty, of whom 950 are only at Sunday schools; and I dare say there are 1000 who are wholly uneducated; besides those who go to different day-schools, being children of more respectable parents.

### The Reverend *Charles M<sup>c</sup>Carthy* called in, and Examined.

YOU are Curate of St. Giles's?—Yes.

How long have you held that office?—Eleven years, next June.

Are there many children in the parish of St. Giles's, wholly destitute of the means of education?—I should conceive there must be an immense number, the population being so thick.

Can you form any estimate of the number in that parish without the means of education?—It has not been in my power to form any estimate at all, because my time is chiefly taken up by parochial duties, being the only curate in the parish.

Is there any parochial school, upon any foundation, within the parish of St. Giles?—Not that I know of.

Do you know of their having been one?—There is a school now building in the neighbourhood of the church, which may be called a foundation.

From your intercourse with the lower orders in that parish, do you perceive any disinclination to send their children to school?—Not generally; there are a variety

of

of applications made for admission into our charity school; I believe there are a great many on the books for admission in their turn now.

Are there many more applications than those schools could admit?—I should think there must be a great many more.

During the eleven years you have been curate, should you say the morals of the lower orders in your parish have improved?—I think the face of the general appearance of the parish has improved within that time; there is not so great an appearance of vice as there used to be.

Is there a greater or less appearance of distress and misery among the lower orders?—The appearance of misery is much the same; you find it in one part of the parish to a considerable degree, in the neighbourhood of Drury-lane, for instance; there are shocking places there.

When you say that the appearance of vice has diminished, to what vice do you refer?—I refer to going to gin-shops and public-houses, and fornications, and all those kind of things, which were very common in our parish.

Are the habits of the lower orders less filthy than they were formerly, or about the same?—I do not think we see quite so many as there were when I first came to the parish, but still there are a vast number of lamentable objects about the streets.

### Mr. *Thomas Cooke*, called in, and Examined.

WHAT is your occupation?—A tailor, in Bloomsbury.

Are you acquainted with the schools in the parish of Saint Giles?—Tolerably well.

Are there any charitable foundations for education there?—Not any others that I know of, except the parochial school.

Is there not a free school?—Not that I know of.

What is this parochial school?—It is for the clothing and education of 101 boys, and for the board, clothing and education of 60 girls; the original foundation was for 70 girls, but it was only, when it was first established, for educating and clothing them, but from time to time they have been taken in, and for a considerable time it remained at 35.

What are the funds?—The funds are considerable, and the expenditure, I think, as far as I can recollect, was 2,000 l. a year, if not upwards; I am one of the trustees; there was a committee for auditing the accounts and making a balance sheet, and I drew the balance sheet myself.

How is that fund raised?—By charity sermons, by annual subscriptions, and donations, which are very considerable; we have a fund of 10,000 l. Reduced, and 500 l. in the 4-per-Cents.

How was this fund raised?—By subscriptions from one to two guineas, and legacies.

Is there any will, directing any money to be applied in a particular way?—There are two legacies in reversion now coming due to the charity; we have had one fell in, which amounted to 150 l.

How long has this school been established?—Ever since the year 1706.

Has the fund been accumulating?—It has been very trifling till within these few years. When we took those five and twenty additional girls, it was found to be as many as the house could conveniently hold, and we had beds and every increased appendage to raise, and the consequence was, that several gentlemen in the parish took an active part; indeed we went round almost from house to house, to increase the subscriptions, by which means we raised a very considerable sum.

Is it confined to Saint Giles and Saint George Bloomsbury?—Yes. This class of children are rather above the lower orders; our rules may perhaps be considered strict in some respects, because we do not admit any children who receive parochial aid; things of that sort have crept in by some false statements of the parents, but it is our rule not to admit any who receive parochial aid.

Is the building your own property?—Yes, it is; we are on the Duke of Bedford's estate.

Where is the building?—In Bloomsbury church-yard, and extends into Queen-street Bloomsbury.

What is the salary paid to the schoolmaster?—80 l. a year, and 40 l. to his assistant.

The mistress?—I think she has 30 l.

Has

Has she any assistant?—No.

Are there any other persons employed, servants of any sort?—None but one household servant, who has 12 guineas a year; the children take the office of performing the duties of servants, housemaids for instance occasionally; they are all brought up in that way, and the rest of their time is devoted to needlework, unless the necessary time for taking air.

Has the schoolmistress board as well as lodging?—Yes.

Has the schoolmaster and his assistant?—No, he has coals and candles.

Is he lodged?—Yes.

Is his assistant lodged?—No.

Can you give the Committee any account of what the rest of the expenses amount to; for the Committee have only before them an account of 170 *l.*?—I think the expenses for board for the girls were 690 *l.* I would explain, that there are five quarters, we pair our accounts quarterly, and they all come into this year together, which make a considerable difference; the last year was less; we had not money in the hands of the treasurer to pay the last debts.

What do you think is the average annual expense?—1700 *l.* at least.

What does the other 930 *l.* go for?—There is the boys' clothing and the girls' clothing; then there are for books, stationary, and printing, I think that amounted to upwards of 100 *l.* In fact our object was, not only to take in those additional girls, but to increase our funds, if we could, and to take in the other ten girls; it was considered we were doing so much better for the girls than before; they had intercourse with their parents, and there was little or no progress, the bad corrupted those that were better.

How are the children elected into this school?—We consider it one of the best in London for the girls: they are elected once a quarter, and they must have been upon the books a given length of time, they must have remained in the parish ever since their first entering upon the book, and they must have been twelve months in the parish before their entry upon the books for examination; the girls are not admitted into the school under ten, some of them learn to read before they come: it was considered at that time the best calculated to take them from their dissolute parents, the girls particularly, and they are not kept in after fourteen, unless by a special leave.

Who elects them?—The Trustees; a list is taken of the children to be admitted, and there are in general four or five vacancies a quarter, then we take the eldest of them, or else they would be superannuated if they were taken in rotation.

Does any body recommend them?—The parents apply, and the name is put down, and it stands upon the book till the time of election comes.

Are there any fundamental rules which the trustees could not vary, in the management of this school?—I should think they could not vary them.

What prevents them from varying them?—I do not know of any endowment, it is true.

Have they ever varied from the year 1706?—I think but very little; I believe the first origin of the girls coming in was, that some gentleman or lady left a sum of money; it was an idea that suggested itself to them, that it would be much better to take the girls, and board them.

How many legacies altogether have been left to the school?—I should think there must be three hundred in number.

Any large sums?—Some 100 *l.* and sometimes 200 *l.* or 300 *l.*

Are those legacies left upon condition of lodging and boarding a certain number of girls, or any other condition?—I believe they have been left merely to the charity school of St. Giles and St. George Bloomsbury, except where, as I before stated, it was left upon condition of taking in one or two girls.

Does that apply to many?—No, very few indeed.

Has any discussion ever taken place among the trustees at any time, respecting the propriety of changing any of the rules?—Never; but I think it would be well received if it was.

What would be the objection to discussing any such proposed improvement?—I do not think there would be any objection to the discussion of it.

Suppose it was stated, that by boarding and clothing a smaller number of children, a fund would be left free for educating from 1000 to 1500 children at present wholly destitute of the means of education, what objection would there be on the part of the trustees to entertaining such a proposition?—The objection would be this;

this; that it has always been held out, that so far from diminishing the number we now board, we ought to increase it to the original number that the school was raised for.

Do you mean, then, that the objection would be, that the proposed change is a departure from the plan adopted in 1706?—I think it would entirely; a great deal of exertion was made to raise this money, and it would not have been raised if it had not been for the board of these twenty-five additional girls. The Bishop of Chichester gave us 100 *l.* for this express purpose, and he increased his subscription; Dr. Wallis the Rector did the same, he did not give us the same sum of money, he increased his subscription, and I think he doubled it; and there are many people in the parish who did the same.

What becomes of those girls, generally speaking, at the age of fourteen?—They are generally got into servitude by the attention of the ladies and trustees, who on seeing them, and knowing them to be well brought up, may suppose they would be an acquisition in any family; they are brought up as servants, and expected they will do their duty as such.

Have you and the rest of the trustees ever attended to what became of those girls when they left the school?—We have, sometimes; it has been a greater consideration so to attend to it within these few years, than it was formerly, when we had a day school in the house.

How many in the day school used you to have?—The number was always seventy, and of course the fewer there were boarders, the greater number of day-scholars. I think in the year 1795 there were but thirty children boarders, consequently we had forty day-scholars.

With respect to the one hundred and one boys, are they day-scholars?—Yes.

Clothed as well as educated?—Yes.

What is the expense of clothing those boys per annum?—I cannot speak to that exactly, I should think it was not so much as three hundred pounds; the cloth comes from Leeds, and is made up by a person in the neighbourhood, who does it very cheap indeed.

You having accommodations of every sort for a day school, supposing it were proposed, that instead of clothing a hundred boys, you were to educate eight hundred, which might be done at the same cost; what would be the objection?— I fancy it would be still the same, that it is not the purpose for which the money was first solicited; and I think the consequence would be, that a great many subscriptions would be withdrawn.

Do you think a great proportion of subscriptions would be withdrawn if such a use was made of it?—I think it would. I was going to observe, that Dr. Bell's plan was wished by some to be introduced; Sir John Nicholl was the first who proposed it, and Dr. Bell came; but we passed a rule, that so much of the plan should be introduced as was convenient; in fact it all might have been introduced; I was the principal one who supported it, but there were so few to support me, that it was not persisted in. The master was not sent to be regularly trained, nor any of the children; they did go once or twice; in my opinion it did not seem to meet the master's own ideas, and we could not compel them to do it; it was impossible for any one individual who was in business to go through with it.

You have said, that there are two masters; would not the Bell or Lancasterian system save one of those teachers?—I have always said so myself; I am convinced of it, from what I have seen.

Suppose it were proposed, that without any alteration respecting the girls, or any alteration respecting the one hundred and one boys at present taught and clothed, and retaining the master and his assistant, but only making them teach upon the new method, 1200 boys should be taught, that is to say 1100 taught only, and 101 as formerly taught and clothed; what objection would the trustees or subscribers be likely to make to this change?—I should think none, if we had accommodation.

How many is your school capable of accommodating now?—Very few more than it at present has.

Would any objection be made to paying for an additional school-room, or of employing a part of the fund now vested in Stocks, in enlarging the present premises?—I think there would.

Are the objections to which you have referred, to be apprehended from the trustees only, or from the subscribers also?—The trustees are the organs of the Institution, and they and the subscribers meet four times a year.

The

The restrictions on the introduction of Bell's plan was on the part of the trustees and the master, and not of the subscribers?—I cannot take upon myself to say that that was the case; the trustees meet once a fortnight for the conduct of the school generally.

How many are they?—They amount to a great many, but seldom from above ten to twelve attend.

Are they chosen by the subscribers?—The trustees are constituted by being two-guinea subscribers, or above that; but then there are eight elective trustees out of the body of subscribers, who are summoned to do the business by the other trustees.

How many subscribers are there altogether?—I am sure I cannot say; I think about five or six hundred at least; I may say more than that. The amount of our subscriptions collected in one year was eight or nine hundred pounds.

How many trustees may there be altogether?—I should think there must be about one-sixth or one-eighth of the number of subscribers.

Are there any salaries besides those to the schoolmaster, mistress, and assistants?—There is a singing-master for the children, and for charity sermons; and he provides the music and hymns; he has only ten guineas a year.

The treasurer has no salary?—None whatever.

Are children of all sects admitted indiscriminately?—No, only of the Church of England; I think not.

How do you know that; do you find out from the parents?—From the parents; before the child is admitted, whether boy or girl, there is a committee of trustees appointed to go and make the necessary inquiries.

Whether they are Dissenters or Methodists?—Whether they are of the Established Church; and there are several other little things to inquire into, whether they have received parochial aid, for instance.

Of what standing is that rule, of not receiving any child that has not received parochial aid; in your own time?—I cannot precisely say; there was an alteration took place in the Rules and Orders about three or four years ago, and that was one which was more strictly enforced. It was considered it was for a more respectable class, equally distressed, or perhaps more distressed than those who go to the parish for relief; that they struggled against the difficulties of the times, and were not willing to go to the parish for relief.

Do you know any thing of the Gower school, lately established by subscription?—No, I do not.,

The Bedford school?—No.

The workhouse school?—That I knew something of, when I was overseer.

Do you know of any other establishments for education in Bloomsbury or St. Giles's?—There is one Sunday school in Gate-street.

Do you know of any other Sunday school besides that?—No, I do not; there are not so many poor in our parish as in St. Giles's.

---

*Sabbati,* 25° *die Maii,* 1816.

HENRY BROUGHAM, Esquire, in The Chair.

---

Mr. *Daniel Beaumont,* called in, and Examined.

WHAT are you?—I am Treasurer of the Saint George's Bloomsbury school.

How long have you held that office?—About two years and a half.

From whence do the funds of that school arise?—From voluntary subscriptions and donations.

Including bequests?—Yes.

What are the annual expenses of the establishment, one year with another?—I should suppose near 1000*l.* a year.

Is

Is that a correct copy of the Audit of the Accounts of that school, ending the 13th of April 1815? [*handing a Paper to the Witness*]—It is.

Mr. *Daniel Beaumont.*

[It was read, as follows :]

Audit of the ANNUAL ACCOUNT of the Charity School of *Saint Giles in the Fields* and *Saint George Bloomsbury*, to 13th April 1815.

| Dr RECEIPTS: | £. | s. | d. | DISBURSEMENTS: Cr | £. | s. | d. |
|---|---|---|---|---|---|---|---|
| ANNUAL Bequest, Dr. Carter - - | 10 | — | — | Boys Clothing - - - - | 62 | 12 | — |
| Legacy of Daniel Herne, Esq. deducting £.2 Duty - - - - - | 18 | — | — | Girls Ditto - - - - - | 21 | 18 | 2 |
| Donations - - - - - | 144 | 4 | 10 | Shoes and Pattens - - - - | 70 | 12 | — |
| Girls Work - - - - - | 102 | 7 | 8¼ | Hosiery - - - - - | 52 | 16 | 6 |
| Collections at Charity Sermons - | 312 | 18 | —½ | Stationary, Books, and Printing - | 188 | 13 | 8 |
| Dividends on Bank Stock - - | 259 | 4 | — | Coals - - - - - | 64 | 9 | 1 |
| Subscriptions - - - - | 1,145 | 2 | 6 | Candles, Soap, &c. - - - | 43 | 19 | 3 |
| Rent, and Recovery of Dilapidations from School-house in King-street - - | 185 | 1 | 3 | Repairs - - - - - | 156 | 10 | 4½ |
| Sale of Exchequer Bill, and Interest - | 122 | 3 | 8 | Apprentice Fee - - - - | 2 | 2 | — |
| Balance in the Treasurer's hands upon Audit 1814 - - - - - | 208 | 13 | 10¾ | Water Tax - - - - - | 3 | 3 | — |
| | | | | Disbursements for Girls Board - | 634 | — | 1½ |
| | | | | Purchase of Stock - - - - | 263 | 10 | — |
| | | | | Ditto of three Exchequer Bills - | 308 | 15 | 10 |
| | | | | Master and Mistress's Disbursements - | 65 | 6 | 11 |
| | | | | Salaries, Poundage, &c. - - - | 228 | 4 | 10 |
| | | | | Linen and Haberdashery - - | 136 | 18 | 9½ |
| | | | | Incidental Expences - - - | 38 | 9 | 6 |
| | | | | Ground Rent, and Insurance - - | 21 | 4 | — |
| | | | | Law Expences in recovering Rent of House in King-street - - - - | 47 | 8 | — |
| | | | | Furniture - - - - - | 49 | 19 | — |
| | | | | | 2,460 | 13 | —½ |
| | | | | Balance in the Treasurer's hands - | 47 | 2 | 10 |
| £. | 2,507 | 15 | 10½ | £. | 2,507 | 15 | 10½ |

*Note.*
Tradesmen's Bills to the 1st April remain unpaid, amounting to - £.207 17 6
The Dividend due 5th April on £.10,000 Reduced Annuities, has not yet been received by the Treasurer - - - 150 — —
The return of the Property Tax for the year 1814, remains due to the Charity - - 28 16 —
Dr. Carter's Annual Bequest, due at Christmas last, has not yet been received - - 10 — —
Mrs. Thompson's Annual Bequest is now due - - 5 — —
Twenty-six Boys, and eighteen Girls have been admitted into the School during the last year; £.400 has been purchased into the Three per Cent. Reduced Annuities in the course of the last year; and two Exchequer Bills remain in the hands of the Treasurer.

FUND of the Charity Schools of *Saint Giles in the Fields* and *Saint George Bloomsbury*, as stated at the Annual General Meeting on Friday the 14th April 1815.

IN the Reduced Three per Cent. Annuities, standing in the names of Rev. Dr John Buckner Lord Bishop of Chichester, Rector of Saint Giles in the Fields; Rev. Dr. Thomas Willis, Rector of Saint George Bloomsbury; William Bray, Esq.; and Daniel Beaumont, Esq. of Great Russel-street Bloomsbury, Treasurer - - - - - - - £.10,000.
In the Navy £.5 per Cents, standing in the Names of Dº - - - - - 100.
Two Exchequer Bills (1,309 and 1,310) - - - - - - - 200.
Annual Rent of the School-house in King-street - - - - - - 45.
Dr. Carter's Annual Bequest of - - - - - - - - - 10.
Mrs. Thompson's Dº - - - - - - - - - - 5.

The following Legacies are left in Reversion:

By the Will of Mr. Thomas Edwards, on the death of John Evans, in the Four-per-Cents. - 150.
By Will of Mr. Richard Chappell, on the death of Mrs. Chappell, £.20 sterling - - 20.
By Will of Mr. Griffin Edwards, on the death of Mrs. Ann Read, (now Long) in the Three-per-Cents. - - - - - - - - - - - - - - 50.

This Account was audited on the 13th April 1815, by the Finance Committee.

JOHN LUSH, Secretary.

*Mr.*
*Daniel Beaumont.*

Is that the Balance of the Accounts for the year ending April 19, 1816? [*handing a Paper to the Witness*]—It was.

[It was read as follows :]

Audit of the ANNUAL ACCOUNT of the Charity School of *Saint Giles in the Fields* and *Saint George Bloomsbury*, to April 19, 1816.

| D<sup>r</sup>    RECEIPTS : | £. | s. | d. | DISBURSEMENTS :    C<sup>r</sup>. | £. | s. | d. |
|---|---|---|---|---|---|---|---|
| BALANCE in the Treasurer's hands } April 13, 1815 | 47 | 2 | 9¾ | Boys Clothing - - - - - | 126 | 16 | 11 |
| D° from the Master, on Disbursements } - - D° - - | — | 10 | 3 | Girls - D° - - - - - | 51 | — | — |
| Annual Bequest, Dr. Carter - - - | 9 | 19 | 6 | Shoes and Pattens - - - | 102 | 9 | — |
| D° - - - Mrs. Thompson - - | 5 | — | — | Hosiery - - - - - | 47 | 2 | 10 |
| Legacy of Mrs. Jane Thomas, deducting Duty | 90 | — | — | Stationary, Books, and Printing - - | 104 | 5 | 11 |
| D° - Mrs. Sarah Savage - D° - | 27 | — | — | Coals - - - - - - | 59 | 15 | 9 |
| Interest accruing on the Reversionary Legacy of Thomas Edwards - - - | 8 | 2 | — | Candles and Soap - - - - | 33 | 3 | 9 |
| Donations - - - - - - | 32 | 5 | 10 | Repairs - - - - - | 40 | 1 | 1 |
| Subscriptions - - - - - | 963 | 18 | — | Apprentice Fees - - - - | 8 | 8 | — |
| Charity Sermons - - - - - | 298 | 9 | 5 | Water Tax and Legacy Duty - - | 9 | 19 | 6 |
| Girls Work - - - - - - | 92 | 12 | 1¼ | Disbursements for Girls Board - | 692 | 19 | 4 |
| Dividends - - - - - - | 486 | 12 | — | Purchase of Stock - - - - | 325 | 6 | 3 |
| Rent of old School-house in King-street - | 20 | 16 | — | Master and Mistress's Disbursements - | 87 | 16 | 7 |
| Sale of Two hundred Pound Exchequer Bills, and Interest - - - - | 203 | 19 | 1 | Salaries, Poundage, &c. - - - | 218 | 17 | 8 |
| *Note.* | | | | Linen and Haberdashery - - - | 94 | 19 | 6 |
| The return of Property Tax for ½ year to April 1816, remain due to the Charity - - - - £. 16  4 — | | | | Incidental and House Expenses - - | 78 | 6 | 8 |
| Dr. Carter's Annual Bequest, due at Christmas 1815, has not yet been received - - - 10 — — | | | | Ground Rent, and Insurance - - | 32 | 18 | 3 |
| Mrs. Thompson's D°, to Lady-day 1816, is now due - - 5 — — | | | | Law Expenses - - - - | 27 | 10 | 9 |
| Half year's Rent of old School-house, to Christmas last - - 20 16 — | | | | Furniture - - - - - | 3 | 15 | — |
| 31 Boys and 15 Girls have been admitted into the School during the last year. | | | | Cash advanced to Master and Mistress for Disbursements - - - - | 10 | — | — |
| £. 450 has been purchased into the 4-per-Cent. Bank Annuities in the course of last year. | | | | £. | 2,155 | 12 | 9 |
| £. 150 4-per-Cent. Bank Annuities (being Mr. Thomas Edwards's Legacy, left in reversion in 1792) has been transferred into the names of the Trustees of the Charity Fund. | | | | Balance in hands of the Treasurer - | 130 | 14 | 3 |
| £. | 2,286 | 7 | — | £. | 2,286 | 7 | — |

FUND of the Charity Schools of *Saint Giles in the Fields* and *Saint George Bloomsbury*, as stated at the Annual General Meeting on Friday the 19th April 1816.

IN the Reduced £. 3 per Cent. Annuities, standing in the names of Rev. Dr. John Buckner Lord Bishop of Chichester, Rector of Saint Giles in the Fields; Rev. Dr. Thomas Willis, Rector of Saint George Bloomsbury; W. Bray, Esq.; and D. Beaumont, Esq. of Great Russel-street Bloomsbury, Treasurer - - - - - - - £. 10,000.

In the £. 4 per Cent. Bank Annuities standing in the names of D° - - - - - 600.

Annual Rent of the School House in King-street - - - - - - - - 45.

Dr. Carter's Annual Bequest of - - - - - - - - - - 10.

Mrs. Thompson's D° - - - - - - - - - - - 5.

The following Legacies are left in Reversion :

By the Will of Mr. Richard Chappell, on the death of Mrs. Chappell, £. 20 sterling - - 20.

By the Will of Mr. Griffin Edwards, on the death of Mrs. Ann Read (now Long) in the £. 3 per Cents. - - - - - - - - - - 50.

The Committee see here, in the Audit for 1815, salaries, poundage, &c. two hundred and twenty-eight pounds ; of what do those salaries consist ?—To the principal master, and to the usher.

Do you always attend the meetings of the trustees ?—Whenever I have leisure.

Mr.

### Mr. *Thomas Cooke*, again called in, and Examined.

WHAT is the salary of the master of this school?—80 *l.* and the usher 40 *l.*; mistress, 30 *l.* 5 *s.*; the singing master, for teaching the children, 10 *l.* 10 *s.*; the servant's wages twelve guineas; the rest arises in the poundage to the collector, he has ninepence in the pound; the poundage in the last audit amounts to about forty-three pounds.

The Committee see in these accounts, you purchased from 300 *l.* to 500 *l.* a year stock?—We have done so within these last two or three years, not so much previous; in 1816 it was 325 *l.* in 1815 it was 263 *l.* in 1814 it was 288 *l.*

According to this, you have a larger yearly income than covers your expenses?—Yes, certainly; we wish to take in the other ten girls, when we have an opportunity.

The incidental expenses amount to about 70 *l.*?—I will explain that; that has arisen by turnery, for brushes and brooms, and articles from the tinman's and the brazier's and ironmonger's; this year the incidental expenses amounted to a good deal, in consequence of two or three of the children being ill and going into the country, and I think two of them were buried there.

What compels the society to board and lodge, instead of merely educating?—I do not know.

Have you a copy of your Rules?—That is it [*handing in a paper*;] I inquired of Mr. Davies this morning, who is one of the oldest attendants at the meetings, and he said, he believed it arose merely from the idea of certain persons at that time of day, who thought it better to take the females out of the street, and that it would be a great advantage, both by relieving their parents and keeping the morals of the children better; that has been carried on from time to time as our funds would admit of it.

How many children of the lower order, altogether, are educated at those schools?—About eight hundred.

Are any of those Sunday schools?—The Gate-street school, I believe, is not solely a Sunday school, there are instructions given there every other day.

Do you know how many Gate-street school educates?—No, I do not. In the united parishes of St. George and St. Giles, I mentioned yesterday, with regard to the children of Roman Catholic parents, that we did not educate them; I have since found that we do.

Did you not state yesterday, you admitted none but those of the Established Church?—I think I did, that was the rule once, but we do not apprentice them to any other but those of the Established Church; they are not excluded because they are Roman Catholics or dissenters, but they are obliged to conform to the regulations of the school while they are in it.

Mr.<br>Thomas Cooke.

### Mr. *Richard Murphy*, called in, and Examined.

ARE you one of the trustees of this school?—I am.

What other office do you hold?—I occasionally officiate as secretary.

Wha do you apprehend obligates the trustees to continue the plan of boarding and lodging, instead of confining their school merely to education?—I am not aware of any reason.

Suppose that, instead of clothing the boys, a proposition was made to the trustees to educate a much larger number upon one of the new plans of education; what reception do you apprehend such a proposition would meet with?—I have no doubt it would be very fairly discussed.

Are you aware of any thing which renders it impossible to make any alteration, of this or any other description, in the plan of the school?—We are very confined for room.

Suppose that that difficulty was got over, are you aware of any thing in the fundamental rules of the society, or any condition under which the legacies have been bequeathed to it, which prevent the change in the management?—No, I am not.

Do you know of any legacies left upon the condition that a certain number of girls should be boarded and clothed?—No, I do not.

Do you know what is the amount of the largest legacy ever left to the school?—No, I cannot say.

Do you recollect any change ever having been made in the management of the school?—No.

Mr.<br>Richard Murphy.

427.

Do

Do you mean it has continued ever since the year 1705 as it is now?—It has, with the variation of the number of girls; the number of girls educated was at one period the same as our boys, an hundred and one.

What period was that?—Whether it was absolutely so, or not, I cannot say, but it appeared so by a paper I put my hand upon last night.

When did that change take place; when were they reduced from an hundred to thirty?—I cannot say that was the case; it appeared so upon the face of that paper.

The number has at different times been as low as twenty or thirty?—Yes, on the house establishment.

Did that variation take place from the state of the funds, or from a change in the system of the school?—I beg to observe, that I believe it was from our situation that we thought we could do more general good by taking the girls wholly away from their parents, than by having an extended number distributed about in the street after they quit the school.

At the time the number of girls were diminished, was the number of boys increased?—I believe they have always continued the same.

## Mr. *William Carmichael*, called in, and Examined.

HAVING heard the examination of Messrs. Cooke, Beaumont, and Murphy, have you any thing to add to the information given by them, upon the points to which they have been examined?—Not any thing.

Do you adopt any of the new plans of education?—No, not any.

Have you any assistant?—I have one.

How many could you, upon your present plan of teaching, instruct, in addition to the 101 now under your care?—I have got the girls as well to teach writing, they have a schoolmistress for reading.

Do you apprehend that in addition to those whom you now teach, you could instruct a greater number upon the plan you now teach upon?—No, I do not think I could, to do them justice.

At what age are the boys admitted under your care?—Not under eight, and the girls at ten.

How long do the boys remain under your care?—Till they attain the age of fourteen, unless they are taken out by their parents previously.

What are they taught?—Reading, writing, and arithmetic.

How many hours a-day are they at school?—From eight in the morning, in the summer, till twelve, and then from two to five in the afternoon; in winter, from nine to twelve, and from two to four in the afternoon.

What are their occupations at the time when they are not taught by you?—They go home to their parents.

Have you any other occupation yourself, besides schoolmaster?—Not any thing.

How soon does a boy, coming into the school at eight years old, and ignorant of reading, learn to read completely well?—Some boys will learn more in six months than others in six years.

Should you say two years was a fair time?—A very fair time for a boy of competent understanding.

What does such boy do during the remaining four years that he is under your tuition?—Learn writing and arithmetic.

Do you not think six years a long period for a boy to learn only reading, writing, and arithmetic?—It depends a great deal upon the capacity of the boy, it will not be sufficient time for some.

Suppose the case of a boy of good capacity perfecting himself in three or four years in those different branches, how does he occupy the remainder of his time?—We have not met with any instances of that kind, I have only been there two years.

Do you observe any improvement in the morals of the boys after they come to school?—Yes, we certainly see them improve in that respect; every attention is paid to them; we cannot see what they do at home, but at school we make them conform to our rules.

Do the boys at eight or nine years old, when they come to you, know any thing of reading?—Some do, and some do not.

Do some come who are wholly ignorant?—Yes, they do.

What

What are the number of boys that left the school last year, and have been apprenticed?—Four.

What became of the other boys?—They have other employments: some were taken out of the school.

## Mr. *Frederick Turner*, called in, and Examined.

HAVE you the custody of any of the papers belonging to Bloomsbury school?—Yes, I have.

From your knowledge of those papers, can you inform the Committee whether there is any considerable amount of legacies left, on the condition that a certain number of girls should be boarded, educated, and clothed?—I should think not, from frequent discussion having taken place as to the change in the mode of conducting the establishment.

Is there any play-ground for the children?—There is none.

Are you acquainted with the premises occupied by the girls' school?—I am.

Is there any play-ground there?—No, there is none; there is part of the church-yard in which I have occasionally seen some of the children playing, but there is no regular play-ground attached to the establishment. The boys are not in the house; they are only instructed.

Are the girls chiefly confined to the house?—The girls have been a great deal confined to the house; and there was a specific order made, that the mistress should take them out occasionally.

Has that been complied with?—It has; we thought they were confined too much in sedentary employments.

Are the rooms confined; do they want ventilation?—No, they do not; the house is very spacious, and well conducted in its various details.

Does the matron receive any benefit from the earnings of the children?—I apprehend not; I believe she brings forward the money to account: they are a great deal employed, I know.

Does any person regularly accompany the children, when they walk out after school hours?—Always; they never go out without an attendant; at least, I have never seen them out without.

Have you reason to believe that since the new regulation, the children have had regular exercise?—I believe they have; I have frequently seen them out myself.

## The Rev. *Tindall Thompson Walmsley*, called in, and Examined.

YOU are Secretary to the National Society?—I am; and have been so nearly from its commencement, except about a couple of months.

It is wholly supported by voluntary contributions and donations?—Wholly.

What is the amount of your funds; how much money have you altogether?—As to our funds, I am sorry to say we were obliged to tell the public that they were totally dilapidated; we made a fresh appeal, and I am happy to say with some success.

Can you tell the Committee how much money you have received, from your commencement?—From the establishment of the Society in 1811, to the beginning of June 1815, the whole sum was rather more than 24,000 *l.* the greater part of which had then been applied in the erection and enlargement of buildings for schools; since that time we have received an additional six thousand pounds, in consequence of a strong appeal made to the public on the exhausted state of our resources.

How much is your income in annual subscriptions?—I should suppose about 1,500 *l.* a year.

The regular subscriptions, or including casual donations?—No, annual subscriptions only.

How many schools have been erected since the beginning?—There is only the National School we have erected altogether.

Where is that?—Baldwin's-gardens, Gray's-Inn-lane.

How many schools have you contributed towards the erection or extension of?—Up to June 1815, a hundred and twenty-two schools have been erected or enlarged by the partial assistance of the National Society, in sums from 15 *l.* to 500 *l.*; considerable supplies of elementary books have been furnished; 336 masters, and 86 mistresses, have been trained in the principles and practice of the National

system,

system, and are now, with few exceptions, conducting important schools in town and country; whilst a succession of masters has also been kept in constant pay at the Central School, for the purpose of being sent out wherever their services were required for the formation of new or the regulation of old establishments; and, lastly, besides that great number of children who have already quitted the different National schools after having received a competent share of instruction, more than a hundred thousand children are actually returned to the Committee, as at this time under a course of education in 570 schools formally united to the National Society. Since that period, I should think about 140 schools have been united, in addition to that 570.

Do you include in the above calculation, the Sunday schools established in different parts of the country?—Yes.

Do you include the Sunday schools in different parts of the country, and which existed previous to the formation of the National Society?—That I can only speak to from some of those having previously existed separately; some of them are now united to us.

Can you give the Committee any estimate of the number of new schools established by the assistance of the National Society since 1811?—No, I cannot.

You cannot tell, then, how many, of the 122 schools you have helped, are new?—No, I cannot indeed.

What grants of money have been made to schools or societies in the year ending 1814?—With the permission of the Committee, I will deliver in a list, as contained in the Report of that year.

[It was read, as follows:]

GRANTS of MONEY made by the National Society to Diocesan and District Societies, and Schools in union with it, since the Annual General Meeting 2d June 1813, up to June 1814.

| £. | | £. | |
|---|---|---|---|
| 150 | to Bingley, Yorkshire. | 15 | to Old Windsor. |
| 100 | to Dalton, Yorkshire. | 100 | to St. Martin's-in-the-Fields. |
| 300 | to Sheffield, Yorkshire. | 100 | to Chesterfield, Derbyshire. |
| 30 | to Moulton, Northamptonshire. | 100 | to St. Martin's-in-the-Fields (additional.) |
| 25 | to Sidbury, Devonshire. | | |
| 80 | to Billinghurst, Sussex. | 100 | to Bromley, Kent. |
| 50 | to East Retford, Nottinghamshire. | 100 | to Nottingham. |
| 25 | to Cowfold, Sussex. | 30 | to Bangor. |
| 30 | to Mile-End Old Town. | 100 | to Feversham, Kent. |
| 50 | to Nayland, Suffolk. | 100 | to Southminster, Essex. |
| 80 | to Isleworth. | 31 10s. | to Aylsham, Norfolk. |
| 50 | to Witham, Essex. | 200 | to Macclesfield, Cheshire. |
| 50 | to Penshurst, Kent. | 100 | to Carlisle. |
| 16 | to Ilton, Somersetshire. | 30 | to Forncet, Norfolk. |
| 100 | to St. Saviour's, Borough. | 100 | to Acton Burnell, Shropshire. |
| 100 | to Eltham, Kent. | 300 | to Leicester. |
| 100 | to Deal, Kent. | 50 | to Guilford, Surrey. |
| 200 | to Leeds, Yorkshire. | 300 | to Halifax, Yorkshire. |
| 100 | to Wandsworth. | 20 | to Yarcomb, Devonshire. |
| 100 | to Winterborne, near Bristol. | 100 | to Ratcliff, in Stepney Parish. |
| 100 | to Hungerford, Berks. | | |

When the Society makes a grant of money to a school, or district society, what conditions does it impose?—That it should follow the National system in teaching, as to mechanism; and the children be instructed in the Liturgy and the Catechism of the Church of England; and that they constantly attend Divine Service in their parish church or other place of public worship under the Establishment, wherever the same is practicable, on the Lord's day, unless such reason for their non-attendance be assigned as shall be satisfactory to the persons having the direction of that school; and that no religious tracts be admitted into any school, but such as are or shall be contained in the catalogue of the Society for promoting Christian Knowledge.

Do you inquire from time to time into the progress of those schools?—Not regularly; but occasionally we require them to send annual reports of their proceedings, and of the state of the schools.

Besides

*The Rev.*
*T. T. Walmsley.*

Besides the school in Baldwin's-gardens, what other schools are there in the Metropolis connected with your Society?—The Westminster National free school, to which we gave 500 *l.*

How many children are educated there?—A thousand children it was built for.

How many are actually educated there?—That I cannot say.

Do you know how it is supported?—By voluntary subscriptions, I believe, or contributions.

What others are there?—The next is St. Martin's-in-the-Fields school, to that we have given 200 *l.*

How many are educated there?—It is intended for 500.

What others are there?—The next we assisted was the Whitechapel school; we gave them 500 *l.* towards building.

For how many children?—For a thousand children.

How many are educated?—Near that number, I believe. To the St. Saviour's Co-operating Society we gave 100 *l.* for enlarging and altering, and also for a new school.

For how many?—About 300, I believe.

How many are educated there?—I do not know, indeed.

What others?—There is Mile-End Old Town school, to which we gave 30 *l.* I believe.

Is that a new school?—It is for 400, of whom 360 are actually under instruction. The next is Limehouse school for 220 boys and 120 girls, and they have just began to build an additional room for the girls; we gave them, I think, 200 *l.*; that was one of the grants of last year, in addition to 100 *l.* we gave them before. These comprise all the grants made to schools in the Metropolis.

Besides those schools which you have assisted with money, what schools are there in connexion with you in the Metropolis?

[The Witness delivered in the following Paper.]

SCHÓOLS in LONDON, united to The NATIONAL SOCIETY:

| | Intended, and fitted for | Actually attended by |
|---|---|---|
| National school, Baldwin's Gardens - - - - | 1000 Children | 800. |
| Westminster Ditto - - - - - - - | 1000 - - | 670. |
| ***Three City of London Auxiliary Schools - - - | 900 - - | 711. |
| St. Saviour's, in the Borough - - - - - | 113 - - | 113. |
| *Bedford Girls School - - - - - - - | 100 - - | 100. |
| St. Martin's-in-the-Fields - - - - - - | 500 - - | 500. |
| *Mary-le-Bone - - - - - - - - | 540 - - | 540. |
| *St. Dunstan's, West, Sunday School - - - - | 100 - - | 100. |
| *Bishopsgate, Daily and Sunday - - - - - | 280 - - | 280. |
| *St. George the Martyr - - - - - - | (number not known.) | |
| *Offertory School, St. James's | | |
| *Whitechapel Parochial - - - - - - | 200 - - | 200. |
| Whitechapel (Society) - - - - - - | 1000 - - | 564. |
| *Gower's Walk - - - - - - - - | 260 - - | 260. |
| Mile-End Old Town - - - - - - - | 360 - - | 360. |
| Ratcliffe - - - - - - - | (number not known.) | 65. |
| Limehouse National - - - - - - - | 360 - - | 360. |
| Ditto - Charity - - - - - - - | 350 - - | 350. |
| ⎧ Charity School - - - - - | 350 - - | 350. |
| *Hackney - ⎨ School of Industry - - - - - | 58 - - | 58. |
| ⎩ Stamford Hill School - - - - - | 30 - - | 30. |
| St. John's Chapel Ditto - - - - | 90 - - | 90. |
| *Farringdon Ward within - - - - - | about 100 - - | 100. |
| *Aldgate Ward School - - - - - - | 130 - - | 130. |
| *Bishopsgate Charity School, which the Governors think of enlarging - - - - - - - - ⎰ | 100 - - | 100. |

Of this list, there are fifteen to which the Society has lent no pecuniary assistance; which are marked with an asterisk (*).

Is Mary-le-bone charity school a new school?—An old school, which has adopted our mode of teaching. The next are the three London Auxiliary National schools.

In what parts are they?—Shoe-lane, Fleet-street, another in Coleman-street Buildings, and another in Fish-street.

How many children are there in Shoe-lane school?—About 200.

**How**

*The Rev.*
*T T. Walmsley.*

How many in Coleman-street school?—I believe about 500; and in the third school, situate in old Fish-street, 200.

Do you mean that those several numbers actually attend?—The schools are formed for that, and I believe they do.

Are those three new or old schools?—The Fish-street school is an old charity school, the other two are both new.

What are the funds of that charity school?—Subscriptions.

No funded property?—To that in Fish-street I believe there is, because it is an old foundation.

What others are there, besides those four?—The last is the Farringdon Ward Within charity school.

For how many?—I think about 80 boys at present.

Is that an old charity?—An old Ward school reformed, and by adopting this system, they are enabled to take in a larger number.

How was the change effected, of introducing the National system into that school?—The school was originally established for 70 boys and 30 girls, all of whom were clothed; it occurred to the committee for the management of that school, that it would be extremely desirable to avail themselves of this new method of teaching, for the purpose of giving instruction to an increased number of children, without at all departing from the original institution, as you may say, of the school, merely clothing a given number; and I believe now the plan is to select from the general mass of the boys those who behave best, and to clothe them.

Has this increased the expense of the establishment?—The only increase has been by making some little alteration in the internal management of the school, and by this alteration a great deal of lumber was removed.

How is it supported?—By subscriptions; and I believe they have a little money in the Funds.

Was there any original foundation?—I do not believe there was.

How long has that been established?—Certainly above a century.

What are the two other schools?—The Ward of Aldgate is one.

For how many is that?—I may say a hundred at least.

When was the National system introduced into that school?—Within this twelve-month.

Is that supported in the same way?—Yes.

What is the third school?—The Ward of Bishopsgate.

For how many is that?—That is founded, I believe, for about 300; I do not know how many attend. There is one I omitted to mention, for 100 children, at Radcliffe, in the parish of Stepney. I have also omitted to mention the Bedford girls school, which is united with us, in which there are 70 girls; it is conducted entirely by ladies. There is also the Gower's Walk free school for 260 children, 130 boys and 130 girls: and in Whitechapel there is a parochial school for 100 boys and 100 girls. The former was originally established upon Dr. Bell's plan, prior to the institution of the National Society; the latter is an old parochial school, which has adopted that plan.

If the funds of those different schools which you have described, were larger, could they educate a greater number of children?—The present annual subscriptions would of themselves educate a greater number of children: there would be some additional expense in enlarging the buildings, of course.

What prevents them from educating more?—Want of space.

Is there any indisposition on the part of the parents to send their children?—I believe not: as far as my experience goes, there is a great desire to send them, even among the lowest orders. With the permission of the Committee, I would mention an anecdote: An old Irish barrow-woman, with a pipe in her mouth, came into the girls school one day, and said to the mistress, " Good madam, God Almighty has got a place for you in Heaven, for your kindness to my child."

This was a child that had been educated in that school?—Yes, and I believe was in the school at that time.

Do you perceive any difficulty on the part of the parents in sending their children to school, in consequence of the naked state of some of them?—No, we require nothing else but clean face and hands.

Is there any difficulty on the part of the parents sending them, for want of clothes?—I believe there is; they feel some reluctance to send them, which the gentlemen of the school endeavour to overrule.

If

*The Rev.*
*T. T. Walmsley.*

If the funds of the Society were increased, could they establish schools, or extend others already established?—I will undertake to say, give us funds, and in the course of three years there shall not be a child in the Metropolis to whom the benefits of education shall not be offered.

Are you not apprehensive that if any public grant of money were given, it would slacken the disposition of individuals to subscribe?—I am apprehensive it might, if given as an annual grant.

Suppose the grant of money were confined merely to the specific purpose of building houses?—In that case the subscription might be kept up for other purposes, as for the annual expenses, &c.

How many can one master superintend, according to your system?—I conceive I do not exaggerate when I say one thousand.

What would be the expense?—The room being given, the expenses are, salary to the master, and the expense of books, which, I hope I shall be able to prove to the satisfaction of the Committee, is a mere trifle; say 80 *l.* a year.

What would be the expense of such a room, to build it?—That must depend much upon the materials. The quantity of space we consider necessary for a child is six square feet; some people say seven, but we think six sufficient, allowing for absentees; so that a room 30 feet by 20 will hold 100 children.

Is there a disposition in different parts of the country to form auxiliary societies?—Very much so indeed.

Are all the schools you have now mentioned, free schools?—Yes, entirely.

---

*Lunæ, 27° die Maii,* 1816.

HENRY BROUGHAM, Esq. in the Chair.

---

The Rev. *Tindal Thomson Walmsley,* again called in, and Examined.

CAN you now inform the Committee respecting the disposition of grants by the National Society?—This paper contains an abstract of them.

[It was delivered in, and read as follows:]

1813:
26 Grants - - - of these, 16 towards building new schools.

1814:
40 Grants - - - 28 towards building new schools.

1815:
55 Grants - - - 42 towards building new schools.

1816:
46 Grants - - - 33 towards building new schools.

Total - 167 Grants - - - of these, 121 towards building new schools.

GRANTS of MONEY made by the National Society:

| | |
|---|---:|
| 1813 - - - - - | £.2,332 |
| 1814 - - - - - | 3,832 |
| 1815 - - - - - | 4,510 |
| 1816 - - - - - | 3,120 |
| | £.13,792 |

According to the plan of the National Society, what is the expense of books for fifty boys?—The total expense of books for fifty children is 1 *l.* 3 *s.* 11 *d.* amounting to less than sixpence for each child; but as under good management each of the tracts comprehended in this calculation will serve six children in succession, the real expense for books, for suitable instruction in reading and in the first rudiments of religion, cannot be calculated at more than one penny for each child.

What is the expense of slates and pencils for the same number?—Not more than twopence halfpenny a child.

Can

Can you give the Committee an estimate of the expense of teaching 500 children?—The room being given, I conceive four shillings and twopence a head abundantly sufficient.

And proportionably larger for a smaller number, and smaller for a larger number?—Yes, of course.

What is the longest time that you take a boy for education?—We admit them at seven years old, and they may remain till they are fourteen; I should conceive two years abundantly sufficient for any boy.

Does not one great advantage of this system consist in its keeping every one of the boys actively at work during the whole time?—Yes, and I may add that they have not an idle moment.

Have you any experience in Sunday schools?—No, I have not; I think most of the London schools are day-schools.

Can you give the Committee any estimate of the comparative time it would take for teaching a boy upon the National system at a Sunday school, instead of a day-school?—No, I cannot form any estimate.

Do you find the Dissenters are slack in sending their children to the National school?—I should say they are not slack; we have people of all denominations; we have even Jews in the school.

Do children of Dissenters go to their own places of worship?—I must beg leave to refer to the plan of union for an answer to that question, an extract from which I will read: " That the children of each school do constantly attend Divine Service in their parish church, or other place of public worship under the Establishment, wherever the same is practicable, on the Lord's day, unless such reason for their non-attendance be assigned, as shall be satisfactory to the persons having the direction of that school."

Do you find that in consequence of the children of Dissenters not being expressly permitted to attend at their places of worship, there is any reluctance on the part of their parents to send them?—I am not able to answer that question, for this reason, that the only question we ask when the child is admitted is, Are you seven years old?

What is the time it takes to educate a master?—If a man is clever and active, about six weeks or two months.

How many masters have you sent out during the last twelvemonth?—Masters sent out to arrange schools, 49; boys ditto, 18; mistresses, 33; girls, 16; masters received from the country for instruction, 50; mistresses, 41.

What do you mean by boys and girls sent out?—As teachers; a school is opened at Guilford, for instance, and they think a boy or girl sufficient, and of course we send them one.

Have the masters and mistresses given satisfaction, that you have sent?—Very much so.

Are those masters and mistresses you send out stationary?—We have ten masters constantly upon our pay at a guinea a week, ready to be sent out either for a temporary or a permanent purpose, to arrange schools all over the kingdom; and we have even sent masters to Guernsey and Jersey.

Have you a number of candidates for admission?—A great many.

Do parents ever take their children away after being admitted, and before their education is completed?—Sometimes they do, but in general they are very permanent, till their parents have found a situation for them.

Have you sent masters or mistresses to any of the old foundations in the Metropolis?—A great many to what they call the old Ward schools; and we have had thanks from them for the services they have rendered.

Have you had occasion to observe how far there is a repugnance on the part of parents not belonging to the Church, to send their children to the National schools?—I am not able to ascertain that there is any repugnance, for this reason, we only ask this question, namely, Are you seven years old?

Can you tell how many children belonging to sectarian parents attend the school?—I believe very few.

How many attend the Baldwin's-garden school altogether?—The total number of boys that attend constantly is very near 500; the girls about 200, or from that to 250.

In that number of 750, do you think there are 20 sectarian children?—I dare say there are more than that.

The

The Rev. *Robert Simpson*, called in, and Examined.

HAVE you the charge of the Whitechapel free school?—I have.

How many does it teach?—One thousand.

When was it founded?—In 1813, by the Whitechapel Society.

How is it supported?—By contributions, and the benevolence of the inhabitants.

It is entirely a new foundation?—Yes, entirely.

Is it in connexion with the National Society?—Yes.

And taught upon its plan?—Yes.

Did the National Society contribute towards its formation?—In some degree; I do not know to what extent.

How many years have you had the management of that school?—One year.

By whom was this Institution originated?—By a society denominated the Whitechapel Society.

How long has the Whitechapel Society existed?—The question was first agitated in 1812; it is not only a school, but divine service is performed there, I having a license for the purpose from the Bishop of London.

Was this establishment suggested or promoted by the National Society, or did it arise from local exertions?—From local exertions.

In what respect did the National Society promote the undertaking?—By the donation of a small sum of money. The expenditure will appear, by the Report, to be very great indeed.

Did they communicate any suggestions respecting the conduct or management of the school?—I am not aware of any.

Then in what does its union with the National Society consist, beyond the donation of 300*l.* which it has received from that Society?—From the circumstance of the instruction being conveyed in the same manner with the school in Baldwin's-gardens, and the same religious instruction being given.

Did you receive any master from the National Society?—There was one previous to my being there, and I had an extra assistant from the National Society; but the thing is so far established now as to go on without further assistance, except what I can give myself to the boys.

How did you learn the national system of teaching?—From Dr. Bell's instruction.

Where did you see it practised?—In Baldwin's-gardens school.

Did you ever attend regularly there, to receive instruction?—No, never.

Was there ever any master from the National Society at the Whitechapel school?—Yes.

Your predecessor?—Yes.

Do you mean that the instruction which you received was from Dr. Bell's book?—Yes.

What was the annual income of the establishment for the year 1815, altogether?—1,254*l.* 10*s.* 2*d.*

What was the expenditure for that year?—813*l.* 2*s.* 10*d.* besides a balance upon the former year, of 185*l.* 9*s.* 5*d*; 180*l.* 13*s.* 7*d.* for repayments of loans; and a further sum of 1,108*l.* 1*s.* 5½*d.* remains still due to different persons, for loans and expenses incurred since the establishment; and 75*l.* 4*s.* 4*d.* still due to the treasurer.

How many children can the establishment teach?—One thousand.

How many are actually there at present?—About seven hundred.

Have there ever been more?—Never more.

Have their numbers increased since you came?—Very much.

How many were there at first when you came?—Between three and four hundred.

Do they pay any thing at all?—Fourpence a month, which is given away again in rewards; but when the parents are so distressed as not to be able to pay, it is not exacted.

How does it happen that the number is not full?—We cannot persuade the lower orders of people at once to conform to our wishes, however good the object may be.

Are there a great number of the poor children in your neighbourhood uneducated?—That I cannot say, from the short time I have been there, but I think there are ample means to educate all there are; we have children from other parishes, as well some from Bethnal Green and Spitalfields.

What is the mistress's salary?—I believe 70*l.* a-year.

What is your salary?—157*l.* 10*s.*

Are

Are there many of the poor in your neighbourhood Catholics or Dissenters?—Yes, I should suppose there are a great many, but I cannot say exactly; we have some Jews also among the poorer orders.

Have you any children of Catholics, Dissenters, or Jews, at your school?—Yes, we have; but I cannot say to what extent; the question is not asked at the admission, respecting the sect to which they belong.

Do you mean to state that there is no exclusion of children who do not belong to the church?—So long as they conform to the system of education and religious instruction carried on there, there is not.

Can you give the Committee any conjecture as to the number of children not belonging to the Establishment, who are educated at your school?—No, I cannot.

Are there twenty, do you think?—I really cannot answer that.

Is the number very considerable, in proportion to the whole?—No, it is very inconsiderable, in proportion to the whole.

Are there many poor people uneducated in the neighbouring parishes to you?—There are a good many; but still there are the means, I think, of affording education to them, if they would embrace the opportunity.

What other schools are there besides yours, in that neighbourhood?—Gower's Walk school, and the Foundation school.

How many are educated in Gower's Walk school?—Between two hundred and three hundred.

Is it connected with the National Establishment?—Yes, just as much as we are, only it is under private sanction.

Who is it under?—The head of the school is Mr. Lovell.

Who supports it?—Mr. Davies entirely supports it; but now there is a printing press erected in the school, which supports itself, but I cannot tell to what extent it contributes towards the support of the school.

How many are educated at the Foundation school?—Two hundred.

Are the boys at your school lodged or clothed?—No, not at the Whitechapel Society's school.

Are the girls?—No; merely taught.

How long does a boy of ordinary abilities take to learn to read?—That is a question not very easily answered, because it depends upon his abilities; but I think a child constant in his attendance, would attain the object in two years.

### Mr. *Thomas Cooper*, called in, and Examined.

ARE you master of the Castle-street Leicester-fields school?—I am.

Is it in connexion with the National Society?—It is.

You have heard the evidence of the last Witness?—Yes.

Is your school any otherwise in union with the National Society than the Whitechapel school?—Nothing more; we had a donation from the National Society, as the Whitechapel school had.

How long has your school been established?—September 1814 was the first establishment of it.

By whom?—By the united parishes of Saint Martin in the Fields, and Saint Paul's Covent Garden, and supported by their mutual funds.

For how many children was the school established?—The rooms will contain about 500 children, not more.

How many attend?—Two hundred boys in round numbers, and 140 girls.

Do you know what the annual fund is?—I am speaking rather at random, but I think about 400*l.* independent of occasional parochial collections at the church; I should conceive the annual subscriptions amount to between 300*l.* and 400*l.* a year.

Is it much in debt?—I think not, as nearly out of debt as possible; we had a heavy debt, but I believe that is paid.

Is the school your own property?—It is held on lease.

What is the rent?—The rent I believe is somewhere about 100*l.* a year, the net rent.

Do you know what was paid for the lease?—I do not, nor do I know the length of it.

What is your salary?—For myself and my daughter who keeps the girls' school, our joint salary is 150*l.* a year.

Have you lodgings?—We have house rent, and coals and candles as well.

Are there many poor children uneducated in the parishes of Saint Martin's in the
Fields,

Fields, and Saint Paul's Covent Garden?—I am not prepared to answer that question; I should think they have, generally speaking, the opportunities of obtaining education.

What other schools are there in the parish?—The parochial school is the principal one, in Hemmings-row.

Do you know how many are educated there?—I think 80 boys and 40 girls.

Are they educated, lodged and clothed?—The girls are entirely kept, and the boys clothed.

Is there any other school in the parish?—I am not aware of any other; the Covent Garden is a parochial school on Doctor Bell's plan, which is not the case with Saint Martin's.

*Mr.*
*Thomas Cooper.*

## Mr. *James Wilmot*, called in, and Examined.

*Mr.*
*James Wilmot.*

YOU are the master of the Westminster National free-school?—Yes, at the back of Great George-street, near the Sessions-house.

When was it established?—In 1812, on Doctor Bell's plan: originally it was in Orchard-street, Westminster. I do not know how long the school had been established upon the old plan; it was established some years previous to my arrival there about four years ago, and conducted on the old plan.

In short, it was reformed four years ago?—Yes.

How many children is it capable of educating?—One thousand.

How many actually attend?—Three hundred and ten boys and 272 girls.

How is it supported?—By voluntary subscriptions.

You have heard the examinations of the last two Witnesses; is your school connected with the National Society in the same way with theirs?—It is.

What is the annual income of the school?—The income for the year ending April 1816, was 1,131 *l.* 8 *s.* 10 ½ *d.* including the balance of the last year's account; 183 *l.* 19 *s.* and 6 *l.* 19 *s.* 4 *d.* difference between Exchequer Bills sold and Exchequer Bills bought; 5 *l.* 12 *s.* 3 *d.* rent received for a quarter of the old school; the annual subscriptions were 648 *l.* 19 *s.*; collections by sermons, 238 *l.* 16 *s.* 3 *d.*; donations, 38 *l.* 6 *s.* 6 *d.*; deposits in the school boxes, 8 *l.* 16 *s.* 6 *d.* The whole expenses for the same period were 1,113 *l.* 8 *s.* 2 *d.*; including 539 *l.* 1 *s.* 10 *d.* to artificers, on account of the new building.

What is your salary?—One hundred pounds.

What is the schoolmistress's?—Seventy pounds.

The chaplain's salary?—Twenty-one pounds.

The needle-woman?—About sixteen pounds.

Are there many poor children uneducated in the neighbourhood?—I believe not; they may receive instruction, if their parents are desirous to put them to either of the schools established.

What other school is established in that part of the town, besides yours?—The school in the Horse-ferry Road.

Is there any other in the lower parts of Westminster?—Not on this plan: there are foundation schools; the first is the Green-coat school.

Do you know how many are educated there?—Not above nineteen.

What other school is there?—There is the Grey-coat school, situated near to the other.

For how many?—Sixty boys and 30 girls. The children on this foundation are clothed and boarded.

What other schools?—The Blue-coat school, situated in Saint John's parish.

For how many?—I believe 80 children; 50 boys and 30 girls.

Any others?—There is a school which they call Lady Dacre's Charity.

For how many?—I believe about twelve boys and ten girls, something of that description.

What do you take to be the reason why, your school being capable of educating 1000, there are not above 600 attend it?—I cannot give any reason for it.

What has been the decrease since last year?—About 45 boys.

And the girls?—Fifty-one during the year.

Are there a great number of Catholics or Dissenters in your neighbourhood?—I believe there are a great number of Catholics and Dissenters, but we seldom hear of them as being so.

Mr.

Mr. *Thomas Biggs*, called in, and Examined.

ARE you secretary to the West London Lancasterian Association?—Yes.
When was that established?—In July 1813.

Does it consist with your knowledge that a survey was undertaken of the Covent-garden Division, by the members of that Association?—Yes, it was commenced and partly executed in the latter end of 1813; the district which forms the object of the Association is divided into twelve divisions, bounded by the River, St. James's Park, extending as far as Vauxhall Bridge, and bounded by Grosvenor-place, Park-place, and the Edgeware Road; the New Road, North; and Gray's-inn-lane, that is the left boundary.

Have you got an abstract of the Returns made by the Committee who examined that part of this district?—I have.

[It was delivered in, and read as follows:]

### COVENT-GARDEN DIVISION:

| Section. | Houses. | Visited. | N° of Educated Children. | | | Uneducated Children. | | |
|---|---|---|---|---|---|---|---|---|
| | | | Boys. | Girls. | TOTAL. | Boys. | Girls. | TOTAL. |
| N° 1. | 240 | 230 | 87 | 63 | 150 | 313 | 366 | 679 |
| 2. | 200 | 180 | 124 | 78 | 202 | 174 | 182 | 356 |
| 3. | 260 | 260 | 213 | 211 | 424 | 228 | 269 | 497 |
| 4. | 210 | 210 | 74 | 58 | 132 | 129 | 146 | 275 |
| 5. | 260 | 240 | 197 | 163 | 360 | 68 | 68 | 136 |
| 6. | 220 | 200 | 115 | 106 | 221 | 106 | 91 | 197 |
| 7. | 320 | 315 | 175 | 226 | 401 | 226 | 195 | 421 |
| 8. | 500 | 215 | 97 | 55 | 152 | 75 | 112 | 187 |
| 9. | 380 | } Not examined. | — | — | — | — | — | — |
| 10. | 220 | | — | — | — | — | — | — |
| 11. | 190 | | — | — | — | — | — | — |
| — | 3,000 | 1,850 | 1,082 | 960 | 2,042 | 1,319 | 1,429 | 2,748 |

Supposing that sections Nos. 9. 10. and 11. should average with the former numbers, it would give for the whole of Covent-garden Division, containing about 3,000 houses,

Educated children 3,318 - and if multiplied by 12 - 39,816

Uneducated D° - 4,465 - - - - Ditto - - - 53,580

The division which was partly examined, is bounded by the River, Northumberland-street, St. Martin's-lane, St. Andrew's Seven Dials, Broad-street St. Giles's, Drury-lane, and Strand-lane.

Who examined the worst part of that division marked No. 1, in the above return?—Mr. Edward Wakefield and myself; I attended instead of Mr. Basil Montagu, who had undertaken it, and was prevented by professional engagements from performing that duty.

How did you proceed?—From house to house, and in many instances from room to room, for the purpose of ascertaining the number of those children that were educated, and those that were not; and we found a great number of the children in that place in extreme wretchedness, without instruction, or the means of procuring it; and the result of the investigation, which continued for several days from nine o'clock in the morning until dark in the evening, was, that we obtained this information, that there was a great proportion of children uneducated, as in the above Table. Wretchedness and filth were in the extreme; in many places, they had nothing to lie upon; and a great number of them subsisted by making clothes for the soldiers; many, who after they had been employed a whole day about a coat, got fivepence for it; their husbands were gone for soldiers, and that was the only employ they had to subsist themselves and family upon. They were all exceedingly anxious to have their children instructed, and seemed to be highly gratified in being informed that it was likely their wishes would be complied with.

Were

Mr.
Thomas Biggs.

Were they closely packed?—Exceedingly so; in every room of the house was a different tenant, from the ground-floor up to the garret.

To what streets or courts do you refer as the worst part of the district you surveyed?—Short's-gardens and the courts and alleys adjoining, and the courts united with Broad-street St. Giles's, particularly one filled with Irish, which were packed together in the most miserable state.

Were they in a state of great filth?—Extreme filth indeed; we were almost fearful of entering some of the apartments, but we received the greatest civility and kindness, and no doubt should have received subscriptions from them if they had been able, but they were totally unable to contribute any thing; the amount of subscriptions we received from the decent inhabitants was 6 *l.* 6 *s.*

Was it collected in small sums?—Generally 5 *s.*; I do not know that there was any body gave less than 5 *s.*; then they were considered members of the Association.

Were the children whom you saw in this miserable place, so deficient in clothing that they could not have attended any school, if there had been one?—They could not without being thoroughly cleaned, many nearly without covering, and mostly without shoes.

What has the West London Lancasterian Association done towards erecting schools, since its establishment?—It has not been able, by the smallness of its funds, to erect any schools; the only one which the Association has at present, is situated in the Horse-ferry Road, Westminster, calculated to hold 500 boys, and 300 attend.

Is it conducted upon the plan of the Lancasterian, or British and Foreign School Society?—It is conducted upon the plan of the parent institution, so as to admit children of all religious denominations, without exception.

And to instruct upon Lancaster's plan?—Yes, we use the same lessons as the British and Foreign School Society.

What is the annual expense of the school at the Horse-ferry Road?—I should conceive near 250 *l.* including the repairs, which it continually requires, and the master's salary, and incidental expenses.

What is the master's salary?—100 *l.* except half a year he had a gratuity, making it up to 125 *l.*

What is the reason that only 300 boys attend, when it is capable of accommodating 500?—I believe it has arisen from the parents sending their children to work; and in other instances, from their not having clothes to send them in; the children who attend, chiefly come from the lower parts of Westminster.

Can you inform the Committee whether in that part of the town there are a great number of uneducated children?—I should conceive there are a great many; we have not had it investigated. It should be observed that the school is not a free school, but the children pay a penny a week, and in many instances the parents are too poor to pay any thing; the penny a week from these children, in five quarters, amounted to 35 *l.* odd; but there are a great number who do not pay.

What has the income of the West London Lancasterian Association ever been in one year?—From May the 29th last year, up to the present period, it amounted to about 384 *l.* in subscriptions and donations, and it expended nearly that sum.

What are its funds in hand, besides the annual subscriptions?—1000 *l.* three per cent. To shew the readiness of some of the lower orders to assist the Society, I would mention, that between May 12th, 1814, and August the 21st, 1815, the journeymen tailors have subscribed a sum amounting to 69 *l.* 1 *s.* 3 *d.*

Have the West London Lancasterian Association any connexion with the British and Foreign School Society, further than similarity of plan?—None.

In what proportions have children belonging to different sects been admitted into the Horse-ferry Road school?—Of the Established Church, 195; Kirk of Scotland, 5; Methodists, 21; Catholics, 7; Jews, 2.

### Mr. *Maurice Edwards Marsault,* called in, and Examined.

Mr.
M. E. Marsault.

ARE you Master of the Blue-coat School, Westminster?—Yes.

When was it founded?—In the year 1668.

By what funds is it supported?—Voluntary subscriptions, chiefly.

Has the school any property?—Very little.

What are the yearly expenses?—About 350 *l.*

What is the yearly income?—Very uncertain; but we generally have from five to ten pounds over.

How

Mr.
M. E. Marsault.

How many boys are educated there ?—Fifty-two boys.

How many girls ?—Thirty-four.

Are they taught and clothed?—Annually clothed; shoes, stockings, and body-linen, twice a year.

At what age are they admitted ?—Seven.

How long do they remain?—Till fourteen, and then a premium given with them.

Who present the children to the school ?—The governors.

Are the governors chosen from among the subscribers?—They are the subscribers.

Are any children but those of persons belonging to the Established Church admitted ?—No.

Have the governors the power of altering the rules of the establishment ?—Not without calling a special meeting.

Do you mean a special meeting of the subscribers?—Of the governors.

How many are there ?—One hundred.

Does the building belong to the Society?—No, it belongs to the Dean and Chapter.

Do you pay a rent?—A ground-rent of 3 s. 6 d. a year.

Is it a long lease?—One and twenty years, renewable.

Is there a fine paid upon the renewal?—Yes.

What is the master's salary?—Sixty pounds a year.

The mistress's?—Five-and-twenty.

Are there any other salaries ?—No.

Can the governors alter the manner of conducting the charity, so as not to clothe, but only to educate ?—No, I do not think they can.

What prevents them?—The charter upon which the school was first founded.

By whom was the charter granted?—Thomas Green, originally the owner of the Stag brewhouse.

Did he endow it with money ?—A small sum; it was but a small school when he first established it; it was the first school of the sort established in England.

How much did he endow it with?—A very small sum, about 100 l. or 150 l.

Did he lay down rules?—No.

Have the rules ever been altered ?—No, very trifling indeed; there has been some little alteration for the better.

Have the numbers of the children always been the same ?—Yes, always the same.

Do they take seven years to learn to read, write, and account ?—Some do not, and some do.

Are they taught arithmetic?—Yes, the four first rules; that is the limit, we go no farther.

If there were a greater number of children attending, could you instruct them ?—Yes.

Do you teach upon the old or new method?—The old method.

What is the meaning of the charity called The Grand Khaibar?—I do not know; it consists of fifteen boys only.

Part of the fifty-two you have already mentioned?—No, in addition; I have an additional salary for that.

By whom was it founded?—It is not known; the particulars were burnt, years ago.

What is its income?—Voluntary subscriptions.

No others?—None at all.

What is your allowance for teaching those additional boys?—Twenty pounds a year; and I have to find them in all their books.

Are those children clothed, or only taught?—They are not clothed, they merely have their education.

How long have you been master?—Very near twelve months.

Were there ever fewer boys and girls?—Sometimes the numbers have not been complete, but very seldom.

Mr.
James Lancaster.

## Mr. *James Lancaster*, called in, and Examined.

WHAT are you?—Master of the Grey-coat school.

When was it founded?—In 1707, by Queen Anne.

Did she endow it?—I believe there was some benefit received from her, but I do not know any thing of the particulars.

Is

Is there a building belonging to it?—Yes, a very old building.

What funds have you?—We have some freehold property in and about Westminster, and some in the City.

What is the annual income from that property?—Suppose I say 1800 *l.* a year.

Is there any other fund besides that freehold property?—Some money in the Bank, and in South Sea Stock.

Do you include the income from your stock as well as from your freehold property?—Yes, I do; our freehold estate is about 1200 *l.* a year.

How many do you educate?—Sixty boys and thirty girls.

Do you board them?—Yes, and clothe and lodge, and every thing; we take them off their parents' hands entirely, both boys and girls.

At what age do you admit them?—Between seven and ten they are taken in, and dismissed at fourteen.

Is there any income arising from voluntary contributions?—Very small; so uncertain, that I cannot speak to it.

A hundred pounds a year, do you think?—No, by no means.

What are they taught?—We profess to give them mathematical education; and those who are inclined to go to sea, are taught the principles of navigation.

Do you teach reading, writing, and arithmetic?—Yes.

What are your salaries?—My salary as master is 50 *l.*; my wife, as matron, 20 *l.*

Have you lodgings?—Yes.

Board?—Yes.

Coals and candles?—Yes, every requisite.

Are there any other salaries?—A mathematical master.

How much has he?—45 *l.*; but he does not live in the house, he only attends three afternoons in the week; I have an assistant at 30 *l.* board and lodging; likewise the matron, an assistant at 10 guineas, with board and lodging also; and five women servants.

What do their wages amount to, altogether?—About 220 *l.* including board wages.

Are there any other salaries?—No.

Who present the children to that school?—The governors.

Who are they?—They principally live in Westminster.

What constitutes a governor?—After a nomination at a quarterly meeting.

By whom?—The chairman and treasurer, and confirmed at the quarterly meeting.

Do you mean quarterly meetings of the governors?—Yes.

How many governors are there?—Fifty-two.

Are there any rules laid down by the charter?—Yes.

Is the hospital obliged to abide by the number of boys and girls you have mentioned?—No.

Were there ever fewer?—Yes; and there have been more.

Could the governors alter the rules, if they pleased?—They can make bye-laws.

Could they give up the boarding a certain number of children if they chose, and expend the funds in educating a greater number?—No, I do not think they could do that.

What prevents them?—The charter, I presume.

Have you ever seen it?—Yes.

Does the charter specify the number who might be educated?—No, it does not specify the number of children; the number of governors is regulated by the charter.

Does it specify what use is to be made of the funds?—I believe not any, otherwise than for the provision, maintenance, and education of children.

How do the governors present children?—In rotation.

Have they ever altered the plan of the establishment from the beginning?—I presume they have, for, sometime after the establishment, the children were employed in spinning and combing wool; that has been done away a long time; now they attend to their education only.

What are the whole annual expenses, as nearly as you can estimate?—That is uncertain; I have known them exceed our income materially.

Do they materially fall short of the income?—Very little.

427.

*Martis, 28° die Maii*, 1816.

HENRY BROUGHAM, Esq. in The Chair.

_____

*Edward Wakefield*, Esq. called in, and Examined.

*Edward Wakefield,*
*Esq.*

DID you survey, with Mr. Biggs, part of the Covent-garden district mentioned in yesterday's evidence?—I went through two sections.

Did you make a report to the West London Lancasterian Society?—I made a report on the 16th of September 1813.

Have you that Report here?—I have.

[It was delivered in, and read, as follows :]

" To the Chairman of the General Committee of the West London Lancasterian Association.

" Sir,

" Mr. Basil Montague having declined to act as a district visitor, I determined no longer to delay an examination of the section which I undertook to visit, and accompanied with your messenger, Mr. Biggs, I began at the corner of New Betton-street, in Short's-gardens, nearly the whole of which we found occupied by poor room-keepers, generally with families, living in apparent wretchedness, unhealthy, filthy in their persons, their rooms, and their bedding ; the staircases of the houses of course common to the numerous families which occupied them, and being common to all, appeared to be cleaned by none ; the rooms in want of ventilation and white-washing, two objects which would conduce more to the comfort of the occupiers of these mansions of misery than any other which I can point out, objects attainable by those who let out the houses in rooms. It frequently happened, that more than one house, sometimes as many as four, had been hired of their owner by an individual, who let the house out in rooms, in some cases with furniture, but in all with the rent paid weekly. It must not be calculated upon, that the room-keepers are permanent inhabitants of the places they occupy ; their change of abode is frequent, and whenever your schools are built, it will be found that many of the children, now returned in your book as uneducated, will be gone ; but it may be reasonably expected that their places will be occupied by others similarly circumstanced. We were received with great civilty ; our enquiries readily answered. The men were generally absent, being labourers, and many of the women (particularly widows) occupied in making soldiers clothing, for which they stated being paid five-pence for a pair of trowsers, they finding the thread. The very great majority of the children were ignorant, and without the means of education ; but it would be doing the parents great injustice, were I to omit stating, that they seemed anxiously desirous that their children should receive this blessing. I cannot pass by the filthy state of the street, and the alleys and yards in Short's-gardens, which is of a fair width, and requires nothing but the attendance of the scavenger, to be as clean as any other part of the town ; on the 10th of September at the ends towards Drury-lane there was a quantity of human ordure floating down the kennel, apparently the emptyings of many privies, and causing a stench sufficient to breed a pestilence. Crown-court, as marked in the Map, is not in existence. From Short's-gardens we proceeded up Drury-lane, which is chiefly occupied by shopkeepers, many of whom already subscribe to parish or sectarian schools ; but although we were unsuccessful in procuring money of any consequence, still we experienced so much civility, that it may be expected that persons known in the neighbourhood will eventually procure subscriptions in Drury-lane ; for which purpose I should recommend application being made to Mr. Woodhead, Distiller, Mr. Vaughan, Butcher, and Mr. Ewing, Cutler. Ragged-staff-court has only four houses in it, inhabited by much cleaner people than those in Short's-gardens. The houses in Broad-street St. Giles's are occupied by shopkeepers, having very few lodgers ; and the same remark will attach to them as has already been made upon those in Drury-lane ; persons known to the inhabitants will in time procure many subscribers. Mr. Turtle, Butcher, in Middle-row,

are persons who should be applied to. There are three courts in this part of St. Giles's, viz. Lascelles-court, Salutation-court, and another, occupied almost entirely by Irish ; and it would be difficult to exceed the truth in describing the peculiar wretched situation of these people. The narrowness of these alleys will partly account for the increased state of dirt over those in Short's-gardens. These persons flocked around in great numbers, all anxious to avail themselves of the

proffered

proffered boon. But it is necessary to remark, that some plan must be thought of by *Edward Wakefield, Esq.* which these miserable children can be cleaned, previous to their admission into schools. Lascelles-place consists of fourteen private-houses, let out in floors to the clerks of brewhouses, timber-yards, &c. We generally saw the female of the families, who expressed so much good-will towards the Association, that I can hardly doubt but that if one efficient *local collector*, living in the place, could be found, that most of the families would be subscribers; and if the schools formed should be pay, rather than charity schools, many of the children from this place will be sent to them. In King-street are many respectable shopkeepers, who will subscribe if such schools are formed as they may esteem adapted to the instruction of their own children. Upon this subject I had much conversation with numbers, and I perceived a very general anxiety to avail themselves of schools which should afford education at a cheap rate. And, aware of that most active of all principles in the conduct of man, viz. self-interest, I cannot but strongly recommend to the attention of the Association to adopt the principle of cheap pay schools, rather than charity schools; the former will at once instruct, and render the people respectable in their own eyes; the latter, although they may inform, will degrade the children to the class of charity children, and exclude thousands of subscribers willing to contribute towards the teaching of their own offspring at a cheap rate, but who possess an honest pride above gratuitously educating them, and yet unless they feel an interest will not subscribe. If this plan be adopted, no reliance must be placed upon the column of "educated children," for the majority of those so returned will become your scholars. The object of your Association I conceive to be no less than that of bringing home instruction to every man's door at the cheapest possible rate; and I am sanguine in the hope that the period is not very distant, when knowledge will flow like water from the public conduits. But you must bear in mind, that the houses in this great Metropolis are not supplied with *water* GRATIS. The public companies have found out the easiest method of furnishing that necessary commodity; and if you succeed in creating schools for all, I am convinced your success will arise from the support which will be derived from those who can afford to pay for instructing their children, rather than from the gifts of the rich to bestow it upon those who are unable to pay any thing. Consider the difference in effect between a people independently educated through their own means, rather than a nation of charity children. I dwell upon this subject, because I conceive it to be a very important one for every district visitor to bear in mind. It is to this point that he must direct his conversation with all persons of property; it is by convincing them that your schools, when built, will be the means of enabling them to bring their children up at a cheaper rate and in a better manner, that you will receive their support; and if any doubt be entertained, reference may be made to the High School at Edinburgh, where the very highest classical education is received for 10s. 6d. per quarter. The side of Andrew-street which is included in my section is almost entirely occupied by a respectable class of room-keepers, most of whom were aware of the Association. Some will subscribe, and the majority send their children, some of whom are now brought up in the Rev. Mr. Gurney's school, at the cost of 9d. per month, and books; others are in day-schools, paying from 4d. to 8d. per week. From Andrew-street we proceeded into the remainder of Short's-gardens, New Bolton-street, Bowl-yard, and Vinegar-yard; the whole of which is inhabited by room-keepers, unable to subscribe, but abounding with uneducated children. The object of your Association is that of instructing the children of the Western part of the Metropolis; but the individual exertions of the gentlemen who have associated is no doubt for a much higher purpose, it is certainly with the hope that he is assisting in ameliorating the condition of his countrymen; and perhaps I should not say too much were I to add, his species. A district visitor will therefore attend to the state of the section which he agrees to superintend. An ancient philosopher has said, That a people are formed by laws, manners, and philosophy; and narrow would be your pursuit, were you only endeavouring to form a herd of reading and writing machines: it is through that instrument, by the study of useful books, that you will form moral habits; and a moral and instructed population will take care to be governed by laws that will suit their habits; and such a people will no doubt learn to exercise the reasoning faculties by which they will be enabled to judge of cause and effect, which is the philosophy of which Aristotle has spoken. In the course of my visits, I witnessed great misery; wretchedness which appeared to me to be very permanent, since though I met but with one person in a fever, but one child in the small pox, but one woman lying in, one child blind, and one deaf and dumb; yet the unhealthy appearance of the majority of the children was too apparent. It would seem that they came into the world to exist during a few years in a state of torture, since by no other name can I call sickness, and dirt, and ignorance.

"It appears to me that every district visitor should consider the section, as placed permanently under his care; that his business must not end with the first examination; that he must pursue his enquiries until he find a *sufficient number of persons, to act as local collectors,* as will keep every family in his view; that thus,

when

*Edward Wakefield,*
*Esq.*

when the schools are formed, every child will be accounted for, and the parents readily made acquainted with their duties, the chief of which will no doubt be that of attending to the personal cleanliness of their children. If the schools be pay-schools, the very payment will form the great stimulus for attendance, since a parent considers the money thrown away if the child neglects to go to school.

" In this section I have found,

| | |
|---|---|
| 224 Houses. | 4 Schools, containing 110 Children. |
| 472 Families. | 6 Manufactories. |
| 150 Educated Children. | 9 Publick-houses. |
| 679 Uneducated Children. | |

And I have collected contributions to the amount of £. 4. 11. 6.

" Although I have not been successful in collecting money, I have been eminently so in finding uneducated children, the exposure of which fact will probably ultimately be the means of procuring the necessary funds for the erection of schools. It also must be recollected, that the section which I have visited is inhabited by persons very unable to contribute in money; and that of those who are placed in happier circumstances, more will be obtained when they are convinced of the utility of your Association, and feel confident in the success of your exertions.

" *Edward Wakefield.*"

Have you another Report?—I have.

[The same was delivered in, and read, as follows :]

" To the Chairman of the General Committee of the West London Lancasterian Association.

" Sir,

" WE received on the 5th November the district book, No. 4, of the Covent-garden division, marked in your Map, C. No. 2 ; and soon after proceeded, agreeably to the written directions, to visit the householders in James-street Covent-garden. In this street we called upon the Rev. Mr. Embry, the Rector of St. Paul's Covent-garden, who was unable to see us ; but we had, at two visits, some conversation with a young lady, his niece, who was pleased to convey your Address to this gentleman, and who was commissioned by him to state, that he declined contributing to your Association. We then requested that he would either preach a sermon, or lend his church for that purpose, in order that contributions might be collected in your favour; but we were assured that a resolution of the Vestry prevented any sermon from being preached in this parish church, except for the local purpose of the parish ; and that there was no institution, however benevolent, to which the parish of Saint Paul Covent-garden could render assistance. James-street is inhabited by respectable housekeepers, who seldom take in lodgers. The same remark may apply to the whole of Long Acre: on the south side of Long Acre are several courts and alleys, viz. Leg-alley, Banbury-court, Conduit-court, Lazenby-court, Angel-court, and Rose-street. The houses in these courts are occupied by room-keepers, generally in a state of poverty. In Leg-alley we visited a hair-dresser, Wm. Radcliff, who had lately had three children, one of whom was dead, and a second dying, to whose case no medical assistance was called in, the father alleging that it was useless, and complaining alone of their funeral expenses, without appearing to consider their death as any affliction. In this alley we found a Mrs. Russel, a Jewess, who appeared delighted to hear that her children would be admitted into your schools, as she had formed an idea that their religion would have precluded them ; she promised to become a subscriber to the Association. The people residing in Angel-court and Rose-street are living in a peculiarly wretched manner; the former is chiefly inhabited by Irish, and in the latter the cellars are filled with human beings, existing in a state of peculiar wretchedness. We must particularly observe, that the outside of those houses do not by any means exhibit signs of that wretchedness which we found to pervade their interior; a passing stranger might imagine them to be respectably tenanted, but if the rooms are visited, it will be found that few parts of the Metropolis can exhibit individuals in a much greater state of poverty. From Long Acre we proceeded down St. Martin's-lane, and through New-street to Rose-street, and afterwards visited the inhabitants of the north side of King-street, and Queen's-court in King-street, also Rose-street and Hart-street. In King-street, the upper stories are generally let to lodgers. Rose-street and Hart-street have many poor inhabitants, and some manufactories. On the whole we have been received with great civility, particularly by that class of persons likely to be benefited by your Association. In no instance did we hold out the expectation of forming charity schools ; to all we stated, that the Association wished to afford instruction at the cheapest possible rate, and that the principle, if acted upon, would not reduce them to a state of obligation to any one. We cannot name the individual who dissented from this system; and we are convinced that the majority

of

of those whose children are intended to receive a common education, will subscribe *Edward Wakefield, Esq.* to your Association, and avail themselves of the opportunity of independently instructing their children. Mr. Jones, of Long-acre, secretary to the Sunday school Union, is willing to become a member of your committee ; Mr. Minchet, of St. Martin's-lane, is ready to assist; and we believe that Mr. Applegarth, of James-street, may also be rendered useful.

" We visited 209 Houses,
316 Families, having

> 74 Boys educated.
> 128 Girls ditto.
> 58 Boys uneducated.
> 146 Girls ditto.

> 406 Children; 13 of whom are Irish.

" We found two schools, that of Mr. Turner, in Hart-street, and Mr. Lee's, in King-street, who, although favourable to your exertions, complained of the injury done to their profession.
" In this section are 5 gin-shops, 9 public-houses, 2 hotels, 7 brothels, 5 manu-factories. And we collected 6 l. 14 s.
" We are your obedient humble Servants,
*Edward Wakefield. Thomas Graham. Abraham Clarke."*

Besides the observations contained in these two Reports, did any other informa-tion present itself to you in that examination ?—I found amongst the persons who I thought might become contributors to general schooling, which was the great object of the Association, an objection made to that object, in consequence of their subscribing to sectarian schools of their own religious belief.

Do you mean by " general schooling," schools for all sects ?—The formation of the West London Lancasterian Association arose with the Earl of Darnley, who, I believe, is a trustee to the St. Patrick's Society ; and the St. Patrick's Society does or did possess a large fund for the purpose of educating Irish children ; in the con-versation which I had with Lord Darnley, it struck us both that the fund might be most beneficially applied in the erection of a school in the neighbourhood of Saint Giles's, where so many Irish are known to live ; in consequence of this conversation, Lord Darnley met some gentlemen at the house of the late Mr. Fox, of Argyle-street, when it was determined to enlarge the idea that had been thrown out, and, if general schools could be formed, to take in the children of the whole district; and it was considered as probable that the Saint Patrick's Society would pay pro rata for the children of such Irish parents as might be educated in the schools ; as the meet-ings of those gentlemen increased, the plan was greatly enlarged, and an Associa-tion was formed to take in the whole Western District of the Metropolis, with the hope that the funds might be found to create schools for the general schooling of children of every sect and every description.

Would it be desirable to unite all sects of religion in supporting day schools, leaving such to adopt their own methods of conveying religious instruction in Sun-day schools?—My opinion decidedly is in favour of mixing the children of the different sects, and whose parents come from different countries, and the bringing them up in terms of intimacy and affection, under the roof of a common school-room.

What were the difficulties to which you alluded in a former answer ?—Several housekeepers gave us as a reason for not subscribing to the West London Lancasterian Association, that they subscribed to a school of their own religious sect, which they thought sufficient ; many of the common people, who were Irish Catholics, said their children went to the school of the Irish religion; there is also a Methodist school there, and some of the housekeepers stated that they already subscribed to that.

Suppose there is a small district only in which it is proposed to plant a school, would it be inconvenient for that purpose that one school should be planted, from which all sectaries were excluded, in order to take the chance of another school being established to which all persons indiscriminately might be admitted ?—If there were not sufficient funds, there must be a great number uneducated.

Suppose the case of a large district, in which there are large numbers both of the church and sectaries, would there be any material inconvenience in having a school upon the exclusive principle, and another for all?—As far as my opinion goes, I should much rather prefer a common school; I think children as they are

trained

Edward Wakefield, Esq.

trained up afterwards divide into parties as it were, and if the church is to have one school, and all out of the pale of the church another, I think it may eventually be attended with bad consequences.

But the question supposed, that the school for all should comprehend churchmen as well as sectaries; are you apprehensive that in such case the children of churchmen would not be sent to such school?—I am inclined to think that would be the case; and although there may be children who in a common view of the thing might be called children going to the National Church, are children of those parents who are of no religious sect whatever.

Then is it your opinion that the principal objection to the exclusive system, where there is no want of funds, and in a large district, is this, a tendency to perpetuate distinctions and religious parties?—That is my opinion.

From your intercourse with the inhabitants of this City, and your experience in the West London Lancasterian Association, do you apprehend that there is a facility of considerably increasing the amount of the present yearly sum raised for the purpose of educating the poor?—I think by no means; for the West London Lancasterian Society for education has fallen to the ground for want of funds, and every pains has been taken to raise them.

Do you apprehend that the disposition to subscribe has diminished of late?—I think it has; I have no doubt that money was more easily got when the thing was novel, than it is now.

Suppose Government were to assist the different societies with money, do you apprehend that the effect would be to slacken the subscription?—I think that might depend upon how the money was applied; it strikes me, that all that could be expected from Government, would be the providing the school-rooms, and that afterwards the schools might be maintained by being cheap pay schools.

Do you mean, that as much as possible of the current expenses should be defrayed by small sums received from the scholars?—I believe that by the Lancasterian or Madras system, a school-room filled with scholars is fully capable of defraying the expenses of that school, at the payment of a penny per week per child; and I think that a people educated independently from their own funds, must be very superior to a nation of charity children.

Upon what number of charity children do you found your calculation of a penny per week being sufficient?—I am not speaking from any calculation of my own, but from the information which I have received in conversation with the different committees to which I belong, for schools under the Lancasterian system.

Then you do not apprehend that if Government were merely to assist in the first outlay of the money, and then wholly to withdraw their supplies, that part of the yearly funds which arises from subscription would be materially affected?—I think that if Government were to provide the school-rooms, it would be so great an encouragement to the system, that subscriptions would increase, and not diminish by any means; and the general zeal for superintendence would also greatly increase, which I consider very important.

Mr. *James Lancaster*, again called in, and Examined.

[The Witness delivered in the following Paper, which was read.]

Mr. James Lancaster.

" The Charter of the Governors of the Grey Coat Hospital, in Tothill Fields, of the Royal Foundation of Queen Anne.

Preamble.

" Anne, by the Grace of God, Queen of England, Scotland, France and Ireland, Defender of the Faith, &c. To all Christian people to whom these Presents shall come, greeting : Whereas in or about the month of January in the year of our Lord 1698, a Charity School was erected in the parish of St. Margaret Westminster, (by the name of the Grey Coat School) for the education of poor children in the principles of the Christian religion, teaching to read, and instructing them in the Church Catechism and discipline of the Church of England, as by law established, and for teaching to write and cast accounts, and (when fit) binding them apprentices to honest trades and employments; which said school was supported by the voluntary subscription and benevolence of charitable persons: And whereas the persons who have acted as trustees of the said school, having found encouragement in the said undertaking, and designing to enlarge the said charity, did, in the year 1701, take into their care several other poor boys and girls of the said parish, and provide them, together with the other poor children of the said school, with cloathing, meat, drink, washing, lodging and other necessaries, in a large house, known at present by the name of the Grey Coat Hospital, in or near Tothill Fields,

Fields, appointed to them of the vestry of the said parish, rent free, for that purpose; in which said hospital all the said children are not only taught and instructed as above mentioned, but such of them as are capable are also kept to work, as spinning, knitting, sewing, and other employments, to inure them to honest labour and industry; towards the maintenance of which last mentioned children the parish gives the usual allowance of six shillings per calendar month for each child, and thirty shillings a piece towards binding them apprentices; and the whole charge of the said undertaking, being upwards of eight hundred pounds per annum, is made up by the voluntary subscriptions and benevolence of charitable persons: And whereas We are credibly informed that several persons are willing to bestow gifts and legacies, and to settle messuages, lands, tenements, rents, and hereditaments, for making a more solid foundation for the support and maintenance of the said hospital; but in regard the trustees, who have the care and management thereof, are not incorporated, they are not persons capable in law to receive such settlements, nor are well empowered to sue for, receive or recover any gifts or legacies which may be hereafter from time to time bequeathed by charitable persons to the said hospital; whereby the said hospital is in danger of losing such gifts, legacies, and charitable benevolences: And whereas We have been well assured that if We should be graciously pleased to incorporate the trustees of the said hospital now and for the time being, it would greatly encourage and promote the said undertaking;

1. Know ye therefore, That We of Our special grace certain knowledge and mere motion, have ordained, willed, constituted, and appointed, and by these presents, for Us, Our heirs and successors, Do will, ordain, constitute, declare and grant, That the right reverend father in God John lord bishop of Ely, the reverend Nicholas Ouley, Robert South, and George Smallridge, doctors in divinity, Our trusty and well beloved James Vernon, esquire, of Our privy council, William Lowndes, Thomas Frederick, Hugh Squier, Charles Twitty, Thomas Cross, James Vernon, junior, Thomas Addison, Thomas Railton, Tanner Arnold, John Chamberlayne, William Clayton, Lionell Herne, Lancelot Burton, Samuel Edwards, Thomas Baker, Samuel Edwin, esquires, Charles Rampaine, William Green, John Dive, Peter Walter, Henry Ballow, John Thurston, Henry Lloyd, Thomas Green, gentlemen, John Clayton, Robert Cross, John England, Leonard Martin, Samuel Paul, and John Bedwell, brewers, captain Thomas Morgan, Mr. Jonathan Freeman, Mr. Emery Arguis, Mr. Robert Cousins, Mr. Arthur Swift, Mr. Edward Boulte, Mr. James Eales, Mr. Thomas Yeomans, Mr. John Holmes, Mr. Thomas Wisdom, Mr. Simon Boulte, Mr. Mark Hall, Mr. John Wilkins, Mr. Richard Files, Mr. Francis Mackreth, Mr. Henry Priest, and Mr. Samuel Michell, the present subscribers and benefactors to the said hospital, and their successors, to be elected in manner as hereafter is directed, be, and shall for ever hereafter be, by virtue of these presents, one body politic and corporate, in deed and in name, by the name of The governors of the Grey-coat hospital, in Tothill-fields, of the royal foundation of Queen Anne; and them and their successors by the said name, We do by these presents, for Us, Our heirs and successors, constitute and declare to be one body politic and corporate, in deed and in law, and by the same name they and their successors shall and may have perpetual succession.

*Names of the Governors.*

*Name of the Corporation.*

*To have a perpetual succession.*

2. And that they and their successors, by that name, shall and may for ever hereafter be persons able and capable in law to purchase, have, take, receive and enjoy, to them and their successors, manors, messuages, lands, tenements, rents, annuities, and hereditaments, of whatsoever nature or kind, in fee and perpetuity, not exceeding the yearly value of two thousand pounds beyond reprizes; and also estates for lives and for years, and all manner of goods, chattels and things, whatsoever, of what nature or value soever; for the better support and maintenance of such poor children of the said parish of Saint Margaret Westminster, taught and instructed in manner and form as aforementioned; and to give, grant, let and demise, the manors, messuages, lands, tenements and hereditaments, whereof or wherein they shall have any estate or inheritance, or for life, lives or years, as aforesaid, or any of them, by lease or leases, for term of years, in possession at the time of granting thereof, and not in reversion, nor exceeding the term of one and forty years from the time of granting thereof, on which, in case no fine be taken, shall be reserved the full value, and in case a fine be taken, shall be reserved at least a moiety of the full value that the same shall be reasonably and bonâ fide worth at the time of such demise.

*May purchase Lands, &c. in perpetuity, not exceeding £.2,000 per annum ultra reprizes.*

*And Estates for Lives, Goods, Chattels, &c. of any value.*

*May grant and let Leases not exceeding 41 years, of Land, &c. in possession.*

*In case no Fine be taken, the full value to be reserved; and a Moiety at least, if a Fine be taken.*

3. And that by the name aforesaid, they shall and may be able to sue and to be sued, plead and be impleaded, answer and be answered unto, defend and be defended, in all courts and places whatsoever, of Us, Our heirs and successors, in all actions, plaints, matters and demands whatsoever; and to act and do in all matters and things relating to the said corporation, in as ample manner and form as any other Our liege subjects, being persons able and capable in law, or any other body politic or corporate in this Our realm of England, lawfully may or can act or do.

*May sue and be sued, &c.*

4. And

May have a Common Seal, which they may alter at pleasure.

On the 6th of January yearly, unless it be Sunday, and then on the Monday following, may choose a President, Treasurer, Auditors, and Secretary, &c.

If any of those so chosen, happen to die, the Treasurer, Secretary, or any three Members, may at any time summon the Society to meet, to choose persons in the room of any of those so dying.

On the first Tuesday after Lady Day, Midsummer, Michaelmas, and Christmas, yearly, may choose Members of the said Corporation.

And on the Tuesday aforesaid may execute Leases and make Bye Laws;

and displace Officers and Servants at their pleasure.

If any Officer misbehaves himself, any Five Members may give Notice for a General Meeting, where they may dismiss him, if they see cause, and choose others in his place.

No act valid at a Quarterly Meeting, unless seven Members present, and major part consenting

May depute persons to take Subscriptions and collect Monies.

Time of meeting to transact the Business relating to Receipts and Payments.

4. And that the said society for ever hereafter shall and may have a common seal for the causes and businesses of them and their successors; and that it shall and may be lawful for them and their successors to change, break, alter and make new the said seal from time to time, as they shall think best.

5. And for the better execution of the purposes aforesaid, We do give and grant that they and the said society, and their successors for ever, shall and may, upon the sixth day of January in every year, unless the same happen to be on a Sunday, and then on the Monday following, meet at the said hospital, where they or the major part of them then present shall choose a president, one or more treasurers, two or more auditors, one secretary, and such other officers and servants as shall be thought convenient to serve in the said offices respectively for one year then next ensuing, and till others shall be chosen in their places respectively, and to allow them such salaries or other allowances as the said society or major part of them present at such annual meeting shall think reasonable.

6. And if it shall happen that any of the said persons so chosen shall die at any time between the yearly days of election aforesaid, that then it shall and may be lawful to and for the treasurer and secretary for the time being, or any three or more of the members of the said corporation, to issue summonses to the several members of the said society to meet at the said hospital, who, or the major part of them present, have hereby power to choose others, in the room or place of such person or persons so dead, to serve in such office respectively until the day of the next annual meeting hereby appointed for making new election of officers as aforesaid; at which annual meeting the officer or officers so put in to serve per interim, as aforesaid, may be continued or not continued, according to the direction of those who are to make the annual election as aforesaid.

7. And that the members of the said corporation and their successors shall and may, on the first Tuesday after Lady-day, Midsummer, Michaelmas, and Christmas yearly, for ever, elect such persons to be members of the said corporation as they or the major part of them then present shall think beneficial to the charitable design of the said corporation; which members so elected shall be members of the said corporation by virtue of these presents as fully as if their names respectively were inserted to be members thereof in and by this Our charter.

8. And Our further will and pleasure is, That at the said meetings on the said first Tuesday after Lady-day, Midsummer, Michaelmas, and Christmas, yearly, and at no other meetings of the said society, the said society or the major part of the members thereof then present shall and may execute leases for years as aforesaid, and shall or may ordain and make laws orders and constitutions for the well government of the said society, which laws and constitutions, not being repugnant to the laws and statutes of this realm, shall and may be effectually observed and kept; and the members to be present at such quarterly meetings, or the major part of them then present, are hereby empowered from time to time to remove and displace any of the officers before mentioned, or any other officers and servants belonging to the said hospital, at their will and pleasure, and to put others into their places from time to time, according to the best of their judgment and discretion.

9. Provided always, that any five or more of the members of the said society for the time being, upon information that any officer or servant of the said hospital has misbehaved himself, shall have power forthwith to give notice for a general meeting of all the members, at which such misbehaviour shall be examined, and the major part of the members then present having thereby power, if they see cause, to dismiss such officer or officers, servant or servants, from his or their office or offices, place or places in the said hospital, and to place others in his or their places, although it is not a quarterly meeting of the said members.

10. Provided always, that no act done in any of the said quarterly meetings shall be effectal and valid, unless seven or more members of the said corporation be present, and the major part of those present be consenting thereunto.

11. And We do likewise grant unto the said society and their successors, that they and their successors and the major part of them, as shall be present at any quarterly meeting of the said society, shall have power from time to time to depute such person or persons as they shall think fit to take subscriptions and to gather and collect such monies within the said parish as shall by any person or persons be contributed for the purposes aforesaid.

12. And Our will and pleasure is, and We do hereby further grant unto the said society and their successors, That they and their successors shall and may on Tuesday in every week forever hereafter, or oftener if occasion requires, meet at the said hospital, and they or the major part of them then present shall and may then or there transact any business of the said society, relating to the receipts, payments and accounts of their monies, and the expenditure thereof, for the

charitable

charitable purposes aforesaid; and make such orders as shall be reasonable, and not repugnant to the bye-laws or orders to be made at any such yearly or quarterly meetings.

13. And Our further will and pleasure is, That the said society shall cause fair and just accounts in writing to be kept, of all receipts, payments, and doings by them, their officers and agents repectively, in relation to the premises; which shall be liable to the view and inspection of any subscriber or benefactor upon occasion; which said accounts shall on the sixth day of January in every year, or within fourteen days after, be examined, audited and adjusted, and subscribed by the members present at such meeting, or the major part of them.

14. And lastly, Our pleasure is, That these Our letters patent, or the inrolment of them, shall be good, firm, valid and effectual in law according to Our royal intentions hereinbefore declared, without any fine to be paid in Our Hanaper. In witness whereof We have caused these Our letters to be made patents. Witness Ourselves at Westminster the nineteenth day of April in the fifth year of Our reign.

(By Writ of Privy Seal)   Cocks.

It appears by the Charter that has just been read, that a charity school, called the Grey Coat School, was erected in 1698, for the education of poor children in the discipline of the Church of England; and that Queen Anne granted a charter for the same the 19th of April 1706?—It was opened the 27th of May 1706.

The charter incorporates certain persons by the name of the Governors of the Grey Coat Hospital, enables them to purchase lands and tenements not exceeding 2,000 l. yearly value, and to chuse their successors, and make bye-laws for their government, seven being a quorum?—It does.

Is there any restriction, either as to the number of children, or the manner in which they shall be educated?—No, there is not; at present there are 90 children; in 1812 there were 120.

What is the income of the establishment?—1,300 l. a year ground-rents; dividends upon stock, 467 l. 16 s.; grants from the Exchequer, 20 l.; annual subscriptions, 147 l.; making in all 1,934 l. 16 s. per annum.

What was the total receipt for 1814?—2,269 l.; besides 980 l. by the sale of Bank stock, and a legacy of 270 l.

What do the yearly expenses usually amount to?—They amount to between 1,900 l. and 2,000 l.; of which, 219 l. go for salaries and wages.

Have any great alterations been made in the regulations of the establishment?—In June 1813, a great alteration was made, beginning with the following Resolution: " That whereas the several standing orders, resolutions, and bye-laws, for the government of the said hospital, heretofore agreed upon, and now entered upon the books thereof, are in a great measure become obsolete and inexpedient, the same be rescinded and annulled, except as to such parts thereof as shall be expressly confirmed by the regulations and bye-laws which shall now or hereafter be enacted and agreed upon; and for the better regulation and government of the said hospital, the following bye-laws and standing orders were resolved and agreed upon by the said governors at their quarterly meeting aforesaid."

## Mr. *Robert Blemell Pollard*, called in, and Examined.

ARE you master of the Green Coat School, Westminster?—I am the master of Saint Margaret's Hospital, called the Green Coat School, of the royal foundation of Charles the First.

What is the income of the establishment?—I am not competent to state exactly; as our property lies, some in the funds and some in estates, it is very fluctuating; but I should think about 700 l. a year.

What are, as nearly as you can tell us, your yearly expenses?—The expenses are to the full amount of the income; our buildings are very extensive, and much money is expended perpetually in repairs.

Are the buildings your own property?—Yes.

Does any part of the income arise from subscriptions?—None; entirely from estates, and money in the funds; we have no subscriptions and no charity sermons.

How many boys?—24; originally 20; there are 20 governors, and each governor has a boy upon the foundation, of his presenting; but the funds were more prosperous at the commencement of the French Revolution than they are now; the governors from year to year increased the number from 20 to 24, and we have found the bad effects of it since.

  In

In what manner?—In the increase of all the necessaries of life; they are fed, lodged and clothed, and taught commercial education.

Are there any girls?—None.

Are boys apprenticed out?—There is a fund arising from the will of Sir John Cutler, granting to each boy 5 *l.* as an apprentice fee.

Are there no other allowances, upon leaving the school?—None.

What is the master's salary?—30 *l.* with 20 *l.* for board.

Coals and candles found?—Yes.

Has the master any other perquisite?—The indulgence of taking some boarders, and some day scholars, and a house.

What other salaries are there on the establishment?—I am allowed for two servants.

Is there any other master employed beside yourself?—None.

Any other teacher?—At my own expense; therefore the hospital has nothing to do with it.

How many does the school consist of altogether, at present?—24 upon the foundation, and the others are fluctuating; but they may at present be 40; I cannot state exactly, I think that is about the number.

Is there a matron in your school, and what salary has she?—There is: the salary is 20 *l.*; board, &c. 18 *l.*

Is there nothing in the fundamental laws of the hospital which obliges them to board and lodge, as well as to educate the children?—It is expressed according to the charter.

Does the charter oblige the managers to support the children in that way?—Yes, to board, clothe, lodge, and educate them.

Does it oblige the managers to support a certain number of children in that way?—No, the number is indefinite.

Is there any thing to prevent the managers from boarding and lodging a smaller number than they now do, and to apply the surplus to a more general plan of education?—They are confined to board, to lodge, and educate as many boys within the hospital as the funds will admit them.

That is by the charter?—Yes.

Who are the governors?—There are twenty in all.

How are they chosen?—By ballot.

Who ballots for them?—The governors, at a board called for the purpose.

They chuse, then, their own successors?—Yes, according to the terms of the charter.

Do they present the boys in rotation?—Yes, they do.

Are the boys obliged to be taken from a particular class?—The class of people that they are taken from is poor and decayed housekeepers, and others having a legal settlement in the parishes.

Are they bound by the charter to chuse from parochial residents?—Yes, they are.

Copy CHARTER of Saint Margaret's Hospital, commonly called The GREEN COAT SCHOOL.

" CHARLES by the grace of God of England, Scotland, France, and Ireland, King, Defender of the Faith, &c. To all to whom these present letters must come, greeting. Whereas divers of Our loving subjects, dwelling within Our city of Westminster, have resolved to settle a certain house in which poor boys and girls of tender years may not only carefully be maintained with meat, drink, and apparel, but also instructed in manual arts in a certain part of a farm of the Dean and Chapter of the Church of St. Peter's Westminster, and have humbly supplicated Us, so much as in Us is, to found and erect that house into an hospital, and that We wou'd vouchsafe to appoint perpetual governors of the same to be a body corporate and politic, to whom the government of that hospital, and of the lands, tenements, goods, and chattels of the same may be committed: Know ye, That We, being willing to further their pious intentions, of Our special grace and certain knowledge and meer motion, Do for Us, Our heirs and successors, will and ordain that that house hereafter be an hospital, and that the same hereafter be called by the name of The Hospital of St. Margaret's in the city of Westminster, in the county of Middlesex, of the foundation of king Charles; and We do erect and found the same house for an hospital, by the name aforesaid, for ever to endure by these presents. We will also, and by these presents do ordain, for Us, Our heirs and successors, That for ever hereafter there be twenty honest and discreet men within the city and parish aforesaid, dwelling, who shall stand governors of the hospital aforesaid for perpetual time to come and under-written, that is to say, sir Robert Pye, knt.; sir Edward

Wardowre,

Wardowre, knt.; John Packer, Thomas Packer, William Man, Henry Lide, Peter Heywood, Henry Wetlefield, Thomas Morris, William Ireland, esq. John Elstone, gent. Bartholomew Parker, William Bell, John Bridgham, Richard Procter, Thomas Gabriel, James Parcal, James Chapman, Richard Bridges, and Robert Towley, dwelling within the city and parish aforesaid, We create and ordain into one body corporate and politic, in deed and in name, by the name of The Governors of the hospital of Saint Margaret's in the city of Westminster, in the county of Middlesex, of the foundation of King Charles. And We will, by the name aforesaid, they be called by these presents; and that they and others dwelling within the city and parish aforesaid, for the time being, in form following, to be governors of the hospital aforesaid, to be chosen and admitted, and their successors by the same name, may hereafter have perpetual succession; and that they and their successors be, and shall be for perpetual time to come, persons able and capable in the law to have, perceive, possess, and retain the lands tenements and hereditaments in fee, and perpetuity for term of life and years, and the goods and chattels, and rights and debts what kind soever; and also to give, assign, demise, and dispose of their lands and tenements and hereditaments, goods, chattels, debts, rights and credits; and also by the name aforesaid, that they may implead and be impleaded, defend and be defended, in whatsoever courts and places, before whatsoever judges and justices, or other Our officers and ministers, or of Our heirs and successors, in all manner of actions, pleas, plaints and damages, in manner and form as any of Our liege people able and capable in the law, or any other body corporate or politic whatsoever, may or can; and that they may have a common seal to serve for their causes and business, and of their successors, whatsoever is to be done, and that it may be lawful for them and their successors that seal to break and change, and to make a new from time to time, as to them shall seem expedient. Moreover We will, and by these presents for Us, Our heirs and successors, Do grant to the aforesaid governors, that it shall be lawful for them and their successors, or the greater part of them, for the good government, supportation and bettering of the hospital aforesaid, to make, ordain and establish statutes laws and ordinances whatsoever concerning the aforesaid hospital, boys, girls, and others living within the same hospital for the time being, and there to be put into due execution, so as notwithstanding that the same statutes laws and ordinances and decrees be not contrary to the statutes and laws of this Our realm of England; and that the governors aforesaid, and their successors hereafter for ever, may have the government and oversight as well of boys and girls as of others living in the said hospital, and the disposing of the lands tenements and hereditaments belonging to the said hospital, or being now or hereafter parcel of the possession thereof. We also will, and by these presents for Us, Our heirs and successors, Do grant to the said governors and to their successors, that it may be lawful for them or the greatest part of them in the hospital aforesaid from time to time themselves to meet together; and after the deaths of any of the governors aforesaid, or when any of them shall go to dwell in any other place, or from his place shall be lawfully removed, one other honest discreet man dwelling within the parish and city of Westminster aforesaid, in the place of him so departing or going away or removing, to nominate him thus for one of the governors of the aforesaid hospital, to supply the number aforesaid, which person so nominated and chosen shall be one of the governors of the aforesaid hospital, and him one of the governors of the hospital aforesaid for Us, Our heirs and successors, We do make, create and ordain by these presents, for Us, Our heirs and successors, We do make, create and ordain by these presents so often as the cause shall require. And further know ye, That We of Our special grace and out of Our certain knowledge and meer motion, Do grant to the aforesaid governors and their successors, that it may be lawful for them and their successors from time to time to purchase and hold in fee, or for term of life or years, land and tenements which are not holden of Us, Our heirs or successors, or of any other by knight service, or any of Us by service of soccage in capite, to the yearly value of five hundred pounds. We do likewise give, license and grant by these presents, That it shall be lawful for the same governors and their successors to aliene and grant for term of life, all the said lands and tenements of the yearly rent aforesaid (the Statute de Terris, &c. notwithstanding.) We will also, and by these presents do grant to the aforesaid governors, That they may and shall have these Our letters patents under Our great seal of England, in due manner made and sealed without fine or fee great or small, to Us in Our hanaper or elsewhere to Our use therefore by any ways to be yielded paid or made, so that there be express mention of the true yearly value or certainty of the premises, or of any of them, or of other gifts or grants, by Us or by any of Our progenitors or predecessors to the aforesaid governors or any of them, before these times made, and in these presents not granted, or any statute, act, ordinance, provision, proclamations or restraint to the contrary thereof theretofore had, made, set forth, ordained or provided, or any other thing, cause or matter whatsoever, in anywise notwithstanding. In witness whereof We have caused these Our letters to be made patents. Witness Ourself at Westminster the fifteenth day of November in the year of Our reign the ninth.

(By Writ of Privy Seal.)

427.

## Mr. *James Wiggins*, called in, and Examined.

ARE you master of the foundation school in Whitechapel-Road?—Yes, I am, and have been so for 31 years.

This is not Simpkin's school, to which you allude?—No, the old school.

When was it founded?—In the year 1680.

By charter?—By the Rev. Ralph Davenant.

Did he endow it?—Yes.

By will?—Yes.

For what did he found it?—For 60 boys and 40 girls; but it has been increased since that time from 100 to 200 children.

How many boys and girls are there now?—One hundred of each.

Does that number attend at the school now?—Yes, punctually; they never fail to attend.

How is it supported?—By funded property, and by subscriptions.

It appears that there is, by this paper you have handed me, 410*l*. odd paid for rent?—Yes.

There is 122*l*. odd, dividends; and above 330 *l*. subscriptions, and collections from charity sermons?—Yes.

Are the children taught only, or boarded and lodged?—Only taught.

Are they clothed?—Yes, they are.

What is the master's salary?—One hundred pounds a year.

Is there a matron; and what is her salary?—Thirty-eight pounds.

What is the expense for books?—Fifty pounds.

For clothes?—Three hundred and ten pounds, making a yearly expense of about 690*l*. in the whole.

Is there any thing to compel the plan of clothing the children?—No, I do not know that there is.

Who are the managers of the charity?—The rector, the treasurer, and others, making 15 in all; and these are collected out of the elders of the parishes, who, as they die, chuse the successors in perpetuity.

How long has the number of 200 been educated there?—When we began the Madras system about seven years ago, it was then increased from 100 to 200 children.

Do you mean that your funds were then increased?—They added subscriptions to it; previously, only the collections from charity sermons were taken.

Could the school now educate a greater number upon the new system than it does?—No.

Why?—It could not without re-building, which it was the intention to do, in proportion as the funds increased.

Were the 100 children, taken seven years ago, clothed as well as educated?—Yes, all clothed as well as educated.

Are there many poor children uneducated in your neighbourhood?—There were, some time ago; but, since we have had the large school, there are not so many.

Of what school do you speak?—I speak of Mr. Simpkins's, which joins us.

## Mr. *James George Wilson*, called in, and Examined.

ARE you master of the parish school in Hemmings-row?—Yes, I am

In what parish is it?—In the parish of St. Martin's-in-the-Fields.

How long has it been established?—Ever since the year 1699.

By charter?—No.

How then?—It was established by the minister, then Vicar, at the instigation of the principal inhabitants.

By what funds is it supported?—By annual subscriptions, benefactions, collections from charity sermons, and we have some funded property.

What is the total yearly income?—The last year it was little more than 1200*l*.

How much of that was casual subscription?—Nearly 500*l*. were annual subscriptions.

Was the remaining 700*l*. income from the funds?—No; the funded property produces between 70*l*. and 80*l*. a-year.

Then how is the rest of the money raised?—From collections of charity sermons, and occasional donations.

How many children do you educate?—80 boys and 40 girls.

Do you clothe them as well as educate them?—Yes, both; the girls are entirely
maintained

maintained in the house, boarded, lodged, and educated; the boys are clothed and educated only.

What are they taught?—Reading, writing, and arithmetic; the girls are taught plain-work, so as to fit them out for service.

What is the general yearly expense?—The expenses nearly amount to our receipts; there was a balance in our hands, by the last year's account, of only 12 *l*.

What is the master's salary?—One hundred guineas, finding himself board and lodging. I should wish to mention, with regard to the salary, 10 *l*. was allowed for teaching them to sing psalms.

Are there any other salaries?—The matron has 30 guineas; and there is one servant, to whom wages are paid.

Who are the governors?—They are chosen from the annual subscribers and benefactors to the charity.

From whom are the children taken?—The boys are the children of distressed people in the parish; and the girls are the daughters of those who have kept houses in the parish, that is, those who either are or have been housekeepers, who have paid the parish rates.

Are they obliged to conform to the discipline of the church?—Yes; the school is connected with the Established Church.

Who presents them?—They are recommended by subscribers, and admitted by the board of governors.

Are there any fundamental regulations for the establishment?—None particularly to which I can speak.

Is there any thing to oblige the governors to clothe and board the girls?—I should suppose not, from the way in which the school was first established.

Was there any charter?—There was no charter.

Were there any rules laid down at the time of the establishment?—None that I know of; I cannot speak to that.

Were there ever fewer girls boarded in the school than there are at present?— There might be at the foundation, I think there were then.

Did the governors change the rules from time to time, under which the school was carried on?—Yes; but they did it very seldom, and altered none of any importance.

How long have you been in that school?—I have been master for three years, and I was assistant a few years before that.

What is the salary of the assistant now?—There is no assistant now.

Do you practise the new, or the old mode of teaching?—Chiefly the old mode; we have a school on the new system already in the parish.

Until what age do you keep the children in your school?—We keep the boys from the age of eight till 14, and the girls from 8 to 15; the boys are sent out to apprentice, and the girls to household service.

### *Joseph Fletcher*, Esq. called in, and Examined.

HOW long have you lived in Shadwell?—Twenty years.

Are you well acquainted with that district?—Yes, I am.

Have you turned your attention to the education of the poor in your neighbourhood lately?—I have.

Are you engaged in the foundation of a society for that purpose?—In the formation of a school for that purpose, called The British Union School.

To what parishes does the plan extend?—To the six parishes of Wapping, St. George's Middlesex, Limehouse, Shadwell, and the hamlet of Ratcliffe.

What is the population of these parishes?—I should suppose at least 100,000

In that population, how many poor children do you estimate that there are without education?—There are only 18,000 educated; what proportion they bear to the population I do not know.

How are they educated?—In the parochial class, connected with the Church of England, there are 360: 180 boys, and 180 girls, clothed, educated, and regularly attend divine service at the Established Church of their several parishes. There are two National schools in the district, one of Ratcliff, originally the parochial charity school. It was enlarged about two years ago, by contributions from the friends forming the National school; and the rest of the building was paid for by voluntary subscriptions: there are now in it 145 boys and 65 girls; 210 children in all, part of whom are clothed or educated. In Limehouse there is a National school, which has been recently built, and contains 264 boys and 135 girls; making in the two

National

*Joseph Fletcher,*
*Esq.*

National schools 609 children. Of the Dissenters, there are six charity schools in the district: there are 250 boys, and 187 girls, making 437 children, the greater part of whom are clothed; I may certainly say the whole of them. In the Roman Catholic school there are 72 boys, and 36 girls, making 108 children, of which 84 are clothed. There are general schools in the district, one of which is The East London Orphan Asylum, having 5 boys and 21 girls, boarded, clothed, and educated.

What is the expense of that establishment?—I cannot say, although I have been upon the committee. It has been very recently established; not more than two years ago. There are altogether 1,540 children educated in the six parishes. The children of the Middlesex and Tower Hamlet school occasionally attend the Established Church; but in the above calculation they are reckoned among the Dissenters, because they frequent the Dissenting chapels more than the church. There are likewise a great number of Sunday schools, in which 2,549 children are educated, in the six parishes of the district.

Are there any Irish, among the lower orders in the six parishes?—A very great number indeed. I am told, by the Roman Catholic clergyman, that there are 1400 persons belonging to his chapel, and the district of his chapel is nearly the same as that of our school.

Are these persons in low circumstances?—Almost the whole of them; they are the labourers of colliers and ballastmen, &c.

Are their children badly off, in respect of education?—Extremely so.

Can you form any estimate of how many of their children are educated?—Only the 108 which I have already expressed. It is possible there may be some educated in the National and Dissenting schools, but there cannot be many, if any.

Is there any indisposition on the part of these poor Irish to have their children educated, if they had the means?—Under certain restrictions they would have no objection; but they would not allow them to go into any of the schools at present established.

Why?—On account of the peculiar tenets of their religion.

Do any of them attend the Sunday schools?—I cannot answer that question; I do not attend, as teacher, any of the Sunday schools, and therefore I do not know.

Are your schools full?—The school I am speaking of is not open.

But of the schools which you have spoken of, are they full?—They are not filled; the number of children in them are given.

How many more are they capable of accommodating?—Nearly as many more, or more than as many more.

How do you account that they are not full?—For want of funds, I should presume.

There is no indisposition on the part of the poor to send their children?—On the contrary, the Shadwell Walk charity school has 50 in the school, and 71 in the the nomination list, waiting for admission.

Then they have other advantages besides education, in that school?—In that school they are clothed.

How long has it been established?—Since the year 1712.

How is it supported?—By voluntary contributions. It has 1,000*l.* 5 per cent. stock, which has been gradually accumulating by the legacies of persons who have died.

Do the managers consider themselves bound to clothe, as well as educate the children?—Yes, certainly. At the annual dinner yesterday, a sum of money was subscribed for clothing 20 more, thereby increasing it to 70.

Is the old, or the new method of teaching, used in the different charity schools mentioned?—With the exception of the National schools in Ratcliff and in Limehouse, the old method is used in them all.

Are the habits of the lower people very dissolute in these parishes?—Very much so indeed; the children are in a very depraved state.

Suppose free schools to be established, would there be any difficulty, from the want of proper clothing, in getting the parents to send their children?—I think there would; the clothing the children is a great relief to the poverty of the parents, and it is in itself an inducement for sending their children to the schools; in too many instances this is the case, but I hope not in all.

Have you observed that the morals of the lower orders have grown better or worse within the last 20 years?—I think the population having increased, the

morality

morality of the lower classes is more observable; there are a greater number of children round us than we used to have.

*Joseph Fletcher, Esq.*

Are the poorest classes generally married?—I am sure I do not know; there are a great number unmarried.

For instance the Irish?—I believe they are generally married, so far as I know.

But whether married or not, have they generally families?—Yes, they have; the Irish, particularly, in some of the rooms, have two or three families: it is impossible to describe their poverty, or the situation in which they live.

Are their wages considerable?—While at work they earn a great deal of money, but their employment is casual, depending upon the arrival of ships.

Do they save for a bad day?—They are not provident.

Have you any Savings Bank in your district?—There is one about to be established, from which we expect great benefit. I am of opinion that it will tend more to the improvement of the morals of the people, when coupled with education, than any other establishment whatever.

What are the highest wages that the poor Irish in your neighbourhood get?—The whole of the Irish work by the task; they deliver by the ships, by the score, and can make any sum they please by exertion.

What will a good workman make in a day?—From ten to twenty shillings a-day, when they work hard; the average may be taken from eight to ten shillings; this is only for one or two days in the week.

The rest of the week they are idle, then?—Unless the colliers are in; it depends entirely upon the arrival of the coal ships.

When they are not occupied, what do they do then?—They walk about and drink. Sometimes they spend their time in a public-house, but not generally so.

Do they not find it necessary to drink a great quantity of beer, when they are working so hard?—A very great deal; the quantity they drink is very great.

How much have you known a man to drink in a day, when at work?—I cannot tell; the quantity of beer they drink is proverbial; indeed they find it necessary to drink while they are at work.

Have you known a man drink four or five shillings worth of beer a-day?—I cannot answer that question; they drink a very great deal; they drink almost all they earn.

Do their wives work?—Only in the family; a few of them however go out to washing, and some sell fruit; the lower classes of the Irish are very industrious.

Do they employ their children in begging?—I believe not, generally.

If schools were established for them, would there be any risk of their taking the children from the schools, in order to beg?—I should think not; in our district we have few if any begging; now and then one or two blind children are seen to beg, but none else.

How many children is your new establishment intended to accommodate?—About 1000 children.

Is there any foundation school in the six parishes in question?—There is Ranies's Hospital.

When was that established?—About 60 years.

Is it endowed?—Yes.

What is the income?—I cannot say; a part of it consists in landed leasehold property, the leases of which have run out; its funds are in a very low state; they clothe and educate, and give a marriage portion of 100*l.*

It has 30 girls?—There are 30 in it at present; it is a very excellent institution.

From what class are they taken?—From the parishioners.

Without distinction of sect?—It belongs to the Church of England, and the discipline of the church is used there; I put it in the number of my former estimate.

## Mr. Henry Althens, called in, and Examined.

ARE you secretary to the East London Auxiliary Sunday school Union Society?—I am one of the secretaries.

*Mr. Henry Althens.*

How long has it been established?—Rather more than two years.

How many Sunday schools has it established?—About ten since its first commencement.

How many children are taught at these ten schools?—1,296 children.

What district does the care of this Society extend to?—The Union is confined to Sunday schools within the following limits; the River Thames, Gracechurch-street,

Bishops-

Bishopsgate-street, through Shoreditch and Kingsland to Stamford-hill, allowing any Sunday school in the county of Essex to unite that may find it convenient; that is the line of demarkation, and we take all on the east of that line.

What assistance do you give to schools, as established in your parish?—We assist them by giving them money for the purpose of fitting up their schools, or providing books for the commencement of them, and any other assistance that they may apply to the committee for, which are found necessary.

How are your funds raised?—Partly by subscriptions of the existing Sunday schools, and partly by voluntary contributions.

What is your yearly expenditure?—During the two years it has been 50*l* and 60*l.* each year.

What are the receipts?—They are about the same.

Is the teaching in these Sunday schools performed gratuitously?—Entirely so.

How many hours on the Sunday do the children generally attend?—I think, upon an average, we may say about five hours, besides attending a place of worship.

Are children admitted without any distinction of sect?—Entirely.

Are they obliged, in any of these schools, to attend the National Church?—I do not know that there is any compulsion.

Is there any reluctance on the part of the Dissenters to send their children to them?—They are quite willing.

On the part of Catholics there is a reluctance?—Yes; we have had in our Sunday schools instances of the children of Roman Catholics attending them with the consent of their parents, but after having attended a few Sabbaths, the children tell us that they are not to come any more; we presume on account of the interference of the parent.

So that in point of fact few or no Catholics do attend these schools?—Certainly.

What are the children taught in these Sunday schools?—First, they are taught to read, and our main object is to teach them to read the Bible, and we exhort them to attend to all the moral duties of life. Our chief object is to convey religious instruction to the children, believing that to be the foundation of all moral good.

Do you teach any particular catechism in these schools?—No particular catechism, unless in schools connected with the Established Church. The chief catechism we use is that of Dr. Watts.

Are many of the ten schools mentioned, so connected with the Established Church, as that a Dissenter could not, consistently with his tenets, send his children to them?—I believe there is not one of them connected with the Established Church; when I spoke of the schools so connected, I meant the schools formerly in existence, independent of the ten new ones.

How many schools then are connected with your Union altogether?—Fifty-nine.

How many children are taught in those 59 schools?—There are 913 teachers, and 9,291 children.

In what way are these connected with your Union?—By sending subscriptions and representatives to the committee of our Union.

Do they receive any assistance from your Society?—They are at liberty to apply for whatever assistance they may require, and if it is found necessary, and the committee think proper, such assistance will be granted.

At what age are the children generally admitted into these Sunday schools?—I believe not under six years of age.

How long do they continue in them?—Usually until they are fourteen years of age; but upon an average, we think that our children do not continue with us above two years.

Are they children of the poorest classes?—We consider them the chief object of Sunday schools.

Do any children of a somewhat higher class attend?—There are several respectable persons children who attend, on account of the religious instruction given.

Do you receive any pay?—None whatever. In some schools, the children and monitors subscribe; but it is an act entirely of their own, without being asked for it.

From what you know of Sunday schools, how long do you think a child takes learning to read?—I have known a boy of 14 years old come into a Sunday school, who was scarcely able to read a letter, and by the time he had been in a twelvemonth he was able to read correctly in the Testament, and had no other instruction whatever, excepting that he received at the Sunday school. But in a
general

general way, we think, upon an average, the children learn to read in about three years.

Do you teach writing?—On the week evenings, which is always gratuitous.

Is that taught to all, or only meant as a reward?—It is a reward for proficiency and good behaviour.

Have you any adults in these schools?—We have adults to the number of 580, taught within the limits of our Union; and there are other adult schools connected with the City of London Adult Society, that has been recently formed; but we take no notice of them in our own.

How long does an adult take to learn to read at an adult school?—About five months; they are taught on Sunday, and one or two evenings in the week.

When you say that a boy at a Sunday school will learn to read in three years, do you mean a boy of ordinary abilities?—I do.

Having no other instruction in the week day?—None; but then we recommend the children to be taught by their parents, and brothers and sisters, at home, to acquire all the assistance they can by that means.

Have you had the means of comparing the progress made by children of the same description at a Sunday school and a day school?—We have had many instances occur, where children who go to day schools have been taken from them by their parents, and sent to our Sunday schools, on account of their education being so much neglected.

Have you had any means of comparing the progress made, where there was no neglect of the day schools?—I have not.

In these Sunday schools, is the new method of teaching adopted?—Only partially.

Is there any deficiency of teachers?—We consider that we have teachers sufficient to instruct the children we have at present in the schools, but that if we could have more commodious school-rooms, we might have a greater number of teachers, and more children might be instructed.

How many teachers, in general, are there, in proportion to 100 children?—About ten, in some of these schools; the ten teachers attend each Sunday. To 100 children, in other schools, there are a greater number of teachers, and they take it in rotation.

How many of these others attend each Sunday?—Where they have few children and a great number of teachers, the teachers attend once a fortnight or three weeks.

How many children can the teacher teach at once?—Ten or fifteen children; but the numbers of children vary according to the particular circumstances in the school.

Is there any instance of one teacher in a Sunday school taking charge of 90 or 100 children?—I believe not; they cannot take the whole charge.

Do you mean to represent the teacher to teach, upon an average, 10 or 15 children at once?—Yes, about that.

Have you any further information to give to the Committee?—I undertook to raise a Sunday school in that deplorable part of London called St. Catherine's, there being a great number of children in that neighbourhood who are totally uninstructed. About eighteen months ago a school was formed there, which now contains nearly 200 children; and many of these children who are now in the school, when first they came were unable to read, but now they are able to read well in the Bible. Finding that neighbourhood to be one in which there was a great deal of iniquity practised, I endeavoured, through the means of children whom we employed as monitors, to ascertain the ways in which children were led into such iniquitous practices; and by this means I found out that there are four Jews, who live in St. Catherine's-lane generally, but they have other places of abode, and these four Jews have got a gang of 21 boys, whom they are bringing up as reputed thieves. One or two of these boys, and perhaps more of them, have been in our Sunday schools. One, upon being talked to upon the subject, seemed very much affected. He said he did not know what to do about it; he wished to leave that mode of life, and he sometimes never went near his companions for a week or two together; but they would decoy him out to go and play with them, and by that means they got him along with them again, and he could not resist the temptation held out to him. Through this boy I learnt that this gang of boys emulate each other to do the most daring actions. One of them said, " I got a gold watch out of a gentleman's pocket, in the Borough, and you never did such a thing as that yet." By this emulation they go on from one thing to another, until they perpetrate the most wicked deeds, and until they come to the gallows at last. And we have also likewise children attending our Sunday schools, who are either the servants or children of

prostitutes

prostitutes living in the neighbourhood; and it appears that they have children bred to the same mode of life, who would be very glad to leave it, if any other means were presented by which they might earn their livelihood.

### John Nunn, Esquire, called in, and Examined.

YOU are District Secretary to the East London Sunday school Union Society?—Yes, I am.

You have heard the evidence of the last Witness; as far as your information goes, does it coincide with what he has stated?—I believe it to be quite correct.

Of what districts are you secretary?—Of Bow, Bromley, Old Ford, Stratford, West Ham, East Ham, and Plaistow.

What are the schools within that district?—

[The Witness handed in the following paper:]

| | | Children actually Educated. | Of these are Clothed. |
|---|---|---|---|
| | **BOW and OLD FORD.** | | |
| C. | Mr. Cobourn's charity, as many as can be obtained - | 80. | |
| C. | Drapers' Company's School - - - - - | 40. | |
| D. | Sunday school - - - - - - - - | 235. | |
| D. | Female Charity School - - - - - - | 20 | 20. |
| | **BROMLEY.** | | |
| C. | Parish School - - - - - - - | 114 | 114. |
| | **STRATFORD and WEST HAM.** | | |
| C. | Supported by a Lady - - - - - - | 60 | 60. |
| C. | Parish Boys - - - - - - - - | 120 | 40. |
| C. | Dº - Girls - - - - - - - - | 60 | 20. |
| D. | Female Charity School - - - - - - | 20 | 20. |
| D. | Sunday School - - - - - - - | 40. | |
| D. | Dº - - - - - - - - - | 39. | |
| | **EAST HAM.** | | |
| C. | Supported by three Gentlemen - - - - | 60. | |
| D. | Sunday School - - - - - - - | 46. | |
| | **PLAISTOW.** | | |
| D. | Female Charity School - - - - - - | 10 | 10. |
| D. | Sunday School - - - - - - - | 42. | |
| D. | Dº - - - - - - - - - | 30. | |

**C.** Denotes schools where the children are obliged to attend the Established Church.
**D.** Where no such regulation exists.

---

### Mercurii, 29º die Maii, 1816.

### HENRY BROUGHAM, Esq. in The Chair.

---

### Mr. Frederick Turner, again called in, and Examined.

HAVE you looked into the particulars referred to upon a former occasion?—I have.

Can you inform the Committee whether there is any thing to prevent the trustees of your school from altering the mode of conducting the charity?—It appears to have been originally formed by some private gentlemen, who met together for the purpose of instituting it; and it was established for the purpose of educating 101 boys and 101 girls.

Did they tie down their successors to that particular form of proceeding?—I do not find that they are actually tied down; but the description which is used in all the deeds I will just read, it is called "A Society or Charitable Institution, or Foundation, supported by voluntary subscriptions, contributions, devises and
bequests,

bequests, and the donations of well disposed persons, for the purpose of clothing and educating 101 poor boys and 101 poor girls, and at a competent age placing out to trades and businesses the said poor boys and poor girls, of or belonging to the several parishes of Saint Giles in the Fields and Saint George Bloomsbury, in the county of Middlesex." There appears to have been a great many bequests and donations, and they are generally given to the trustees of the charity, without any specific direction as to the mode of application; but there are some exceptions to that rule. I have a publication here, which contains a list of the donations and legacies.

Which of the legacies are accompanied with conditions?—We have not copies of all the wills; but I find, among those I have, the will of Mrs. Sarah Power, which is dated the first of October 1792, which was a bequest for the girls; there is another, the will of Mrs. Elizabeth Seawell, dated the 5th of January 1813, which is also a bequest for the girls; there is also the Reverend Benjamin Carter's deed of settlement, dated the 12th of March 1727, which is a bequest of 10 *l.* a year for the use and benefit of the girls.

Are there any other legacies with that condition?—There is another from a lady unknown, in 1803, on condition of taking an additional girl into the house, a donation of 100 *l.*; and there was an additional girl taken into the house in consequence of that donation.

Can you take upon you to say there is not 50 *l.* a year left under those conditions?—No, I cannot.

What sum should you think altogether is restricted by conditions of this sort?—Not much more or less; we circulate a copy of a will, in which a trust is described, " Upon trust that they or one of them do pay the same to the treasurer or treasurers for the time being of the charity school of Saint Giles in the Fields and Saint George Bloomsbury, in the county of Middlesex."

Do you apprehend there is any thing in the constitution of the charity to prevent the trustees from diminishing the number of boys clothed, or the number of girls boarded?—Certainly not, unless the word " clothing," used in the deed above referred to, might be considered as contradictory; this form of deed being used in all the transactions of the charity, may be supposed to have made it known to the public that it was an institution for clothing as well as educating.

Is there any mention of boarding, in that form?—None whatever.

Have the trustees ever made any material alterations in those particulars?—They have made alterations from time to time in the number of girls; some time ago there were very few girls in the house, not above five; but they have since been considerably increased.

## The Reverend *Anthony Hamilton*, called in, and Examined.

YOU hold the office, in the church of St. Martin's, of Clerk in Orders, and Master of the Librarian School?—I do.

What endowment has it?—It is an endowment of Archbishop Tenison, in the year 1697.

By will?—By donation in his lifetime.

Of freehold property?—Of certain sums of money, and leasehold property.

What is the amount of it?—The amount at present is 91 *l.* odd shillings.

Including the leasehold property?—Yes.

To what purposes was it given?—Originally there was an appointment of librarian, master, usher, and writing master, all out of that sum.

Was there a library left?—There is a library also, consisting of between four and five thousand books.

Has there been any subsequent addition to the endowment?—There has been a considerable addition to the library, by Dr. Courayer, of a considerable number of books.

Was he librarian?—I do not think he was.

Any subsequent donation of money?—None at all.

In whose gift is the place?—It is in the election of the trustees, the vicar, the churchwardens of the parish, and certain other persons.

Who are those other persons?—I cannot say.

How are they chosen?—Elected by one another.

Upon what conditions was the gift made?—It was given for salaries to the master, usher, writing master, and librarian.

To

To what purpose was the library given?—It is expressed for general purposes, but particularly for the clergy of the parish (which then included St. George, St. James, and St. Anne Soho,) and the King's Chaplain in Ordinary during the time of waiting.

Have you a copy of the deed of gift?—Yes, I have.

### Here follow EXTRACTS from the Same.

" AND whereas the said Lord Archbishop, out of his pious and charitable inclination for promoting such a publick benefitt, is willing to make some further provision for the master of the said schoole, who likewise is intented to be the keeper of the said library, and for the usher of the said schoole; and that such schoolmaster for the time being shall be in priests orders, and read or cause to be read morning and evening prayers duly in the said church, according to the Will of the said Dr. Willis."

" The books in the said library to be for publick use, but especially for the use of the vicar and lecturer of the said parish, and of the said schoolmaster and usher for the time being, and the parsons of the parish churches of St. James and St. Anne's Westminster, and the King's chaplains in ordinary for the time being; to which library they shall have free access at all seasonable time, to read or peruse any the said books without fee or reward."

" The said schoolmaster for the time being shall teach and instruct ten boyes, and the usher twenty boyes, of the said parish of St. Martin, from time to time and at all times, gratis, without sallary or other reward, such boyes to be chosen by the vicar and churchwardens of the said parish for the time being and the within mentioned trustees, to continue to be taught untill they be respectively putt forth to trades or attain the age of twelve years, and then others to be taken in their place, as any of them goe out to trades or attain the age aforesaid; and so from time to time as the same shall happen: But if any of the said boyes shall have an extraordinary genius for learning, to be approved of by the vicar of the said church, and the greater number of the trustees of the two messuages within menĉoned and of the lands and tenemᵗˢ within directed to be purchased, that then such boy or boyes to continue to be taught untill fitt to be sent to one of the universities."

" That all such boys as are now of the said schoole, and there taught gratis, shall be examined by Dr. Lancaster and the major part of the other trustees; and such as are the sons of wealthy parents, or are above twelve years old, to be discharged, unless their parents or relations shall agree and satisfy the said master for teaching of them; and the rest of the said boyes to be taught gratis untill they shall be putt out to trades, or attaine the said age of twelve years; and after their number shall decrease and be less then tenn, to be taught by the master, and twenty by the usher, then the constituĉon above, for ten to be taught by the master and twenty by the usher, gratis, to take place, and not before."

" The method now used in the said schoole to continue untill altered by the Archbishop of Canterbury, and vicar of the parish church of St. Martins, and the said trustees for the time being, or by Symon now Bishop of Ely, who shall have power to make such orders or constitutions concerning the same, as they from time to time shall think fitt."

How long have you held the office?—Since 1803.

Is it an open library?—It is accessible to the public, if I am there.

Is there a regular attendance given in the library?—I am in town for five months in the year, and during that time I live there.

Can a person have access to the library during those months at any time?—During certain hours.

What hours?—In the course of the day, from breakfast to dinner. It is very little frequented; one reason is, that there are no books of a later date than the date of the foundation; and Dr. Courayer's books are nearly of the same date. When I say there have been no donations since, there may have been a few donations of books, which are entered in a separate catalogue, but a very trifling number.

Is the office held by you for life?—I should consider not, because in former years there was an annual election, but it has always been the same person re-elected; they cannot be removed without the consent of the Archbishop, who is visitor.

Is he appointed visitor by the deed?—Yes.

Has any person a right to take away books for reading?—Many persons have borrowed books for reading, entering their name in a catalogue.

Is there a school?—There is.

How many boys are educated there?—Thirty boys; that was the original number fixed by the founder.

Are they lodged?—No.

Clothed?—No.

Mr.

Mr. *Dignum* was here Examined with Mr. *Hamilton*.

WHAT are they taught?—Reading, writing, and arithmetic; and a few of the head boys, navigation and mensuration.

At what age are they admitted?—They should be admitted at nine years of age.

Are any admitted younger or older than nine?—Yes, they have been admitted at all ages.

How long do they remain?—Till they are fifteen.

How are they chosen?—I am totally ignorant of that; but the vicar of the parish and the senior churchwardens send a written order, and I receive them.

What is your salary?—Thirty pounds a year, for which I teach thirty children, with the privilege of taking pay scholars.

How many of those do you take?—They are limited; at present I have ten or twenty.

Is there any other master?—None; I employ gentlemen sometimes to teach them Latin and French.

Is your salary paid out of the 90 *l.* a year given by the founder?—Part of it is.

*(To Mr. Hamilton.)* How is the master's salary paid?—Out of the funds.

How much of it out of the funds?—The salary of the master and the librarian is 30 *l.* a year, for which the master was to teach ten boys; originally it was ten pounds more, making 40 *l.*; out of that 40 *l.* I allow 10 *l.* to the under master; one 5 *l.* is paid by the funds and the other 5 *l.* by the churchwardens, according to the order in the year 1774.

Then to what does the rest of the 90 *l.* go?—For the support of the building and the payment of taxes, which eats up the whole of it, and more. The funds are considerably in arrear at present. The original constitution of the school required the master, who was to be a master of arts, and in priest's orders, to teach ten boys, and the usher twenty; and in the year 1724 there was a librarian and schoolmaster in the same person. There was an usher and a writing master in 1732. The appointment of the writing master was relinquished on account of the deficiency in the funds; in 1742 the appointment of usher was relinquished also, probably for the same reason, but no minute appears of that. In the year 1766, Mr. Wright was appointed librarian and schoolmaster, with a salary of 40 *l.* In the year 1774, Mr. Applegarth was appointed to teach thirty boys, with a salary of 5 *l.* from the trustees, 10 *l.* from the schoolmaster, and 15 *l.* from the churchwardens. There is no minute respecting the reasons of this alteration, but it probably arose from there being no boys applying for instruction to the upper master, he was restricted to ten; it was a grammar school, and probably there were no boys coming under his direction, and therefore it was changed into a reading and writing school, which it was not originally.

*James Palmer*, esq. (Treasurer of Christ's Hospital, and who stated that he had been so for eighteen years;) and

*Richard Corp*, esq. (chief clerk to the hospital, who stated that he had been so twenty-six years, and had been in the department forty-one years;)

Examined, as follows:

WHEN was the hospital founded?—In 1552, another part in 1673.

It is incorporated by two royal charters, is it not?—Yes, one from King Edward the Sixth, and the other from King Charles the Second.

Are there any other charters relating to the corporation?—Not that I recollect.

Have you got copies of those charters here?—No.

They are printed, are they not?—I believe not.

What was the endowment of the charity?—We are really not in possession of any knowledge what was the precise endowment of the institution; we certainly know that part of the premises we occupy, commonly called Grey Friars, and the Cloisters, with a part of the building, were given us by King Edward, the founder; but further than that it does not occur to us we can give the Committee any information upon that point. We are come here prepared to give the Committee every possible information in our power, and not to withhold a single circumstance.

You

You understand then that King Edward the Sixth endowed the charity with lands and tenements?—If you embrace the buildings and the site upon which they stand, it would certainly be lands and tenements. The mathematical school was either built or given by King Charles the Second.

Did King Edward endow it in no other way than by giving the house and site?—I really cannot answer that question; we have little or no income under the charter; I apprehend the estates were first given to the City of London, and afterwards apportioned to the royal hospitals as they thought fit. We can trace all our other estates.

From whence does the other property of the corporation come?—From legacies and donations at different periods.

Can you give the Committee the amount of those legacies altogether?—No; we can give the Committee an account of our present expenses.

Have the legacies been numerous at different times?—Very.

Have any of them been to a great amount?—Yes.

Can you give us about the largest?—Lady Ramsey's is the largest; the rental of it is near 4000 *l.* per annum.

Where does the estate lie chiefly?—In Essex and Surrey, and one house in London.

About what time was the legacy left?—1592 or 1593; it is charged with payments of 240 *l.*; the rent then might have been 400 *l.* or upwards.

Do you remember any other great legacy to the charity?—There is a very capital estate in Lincolnshire, a legacy from Mr. Henry Stone, left in the year 1693.

About what income is derived from that now?—About 3,200 *l.* a year; but perhaps it might be more proper to state, that in order to get that rent, the hospital has been at the expense, of drainage, inclosures, new buildings, and other improvements, of upwards of 40,000 *l.*

Have you had, generally speaking, a great defalcation of rent within the last two years?—Very little, but expect defalcations, for we have already found great difficulty in getting payment of rents; but have made only one deduction, and that a small one. We have arrears, heretofore unusual.

Did King Charles the Second give any thing to the charity?—An annuity of 370 *l.* 10 *s.* payable at the Exchequer.

Was that all that King Charles gave?—It is all that we now receive under the charter, and we receive that for the special purpose of placing out yearly ten boys in the sea service; those are the boys that used yearly to be presented to the King. King Charles gave 1000 *l.* a year, for seven years, besides the above annuity, to establish a mathematical school of 40 boys. From that endowment the hospital is certainly minus.

Do you recollect any other considerable legacy?—Mr. Garway, of Sussex, left five farms, the present rent of which is 1810 *l.* a year.

Do you know the date of that donation?—I think just before the Mortmain Act, about 1702.

Any other considerable one?—There are several; Mr. Barnes gave us some very good estates in London; Mr. Barnham, Sir Martin Bowes, and Mr. Blundell, are also considerable benefactors, with many others.

Were those, or any one of them, legacies left upon conditions?—There are many that are left upon conditions; such as payment of the outgoings charged upon the property, the admission of children, some also for scholarships at the university; Lady Ramsey particularly left some charged with payments to old soldiers and widows, Mr. Barnes to pensioners, &c.

What was the whole gross income of the charity, for the last year to which your accounts have been made up?—In the year 1814, the income was 44,625 *l.* arising from all sources; that was the receipt, rather more than the stationary income perhaps.

Does that include any balance in the treasurer's hands?—Certainly not.

Could you tell the Committee what was the income for the year 1815?—43,386 *l.*

What were the expenses for the year 1814?—41,061 *l.*

For 1815?—40,420 *l.*

What is the average balance in the treasurer's hands?—Cannot say precisely, but think it may be about 2000 *l.*; the balance is at particular periods much larger, at other

other times very small. The nurses are paid weekly; the masters and officers, and provision bills, quarterly; and the workmen and tradesmen's bills half-yearly. The cash-book is balanced every week, signed by the treasurer, and laid before the committee every time they meet; the general account of receipts and payments is made up at the end of every year, and reported to the court in March.

*James Palmer, Esq.*
*and*
*Richard Corp, Esq.*

How many children have you upon the establishment?—Our accommodation is for 1156, including 80 girls; there are now in the house 1062, including about 65 or 70 girls. There are now outstanding about 120 presentations, which are daily coming in for admission.

Does this include the establishment at Hertford?—Yes.

Is that a preparatory school for Christ's Hospital?—It may be so esteemed, but it is not altogether so.

Do any boys continue there the whole time?—Only those whose friends particularly request it; perhaps never more than two at a time.

Do you reckon 1156 your full number?—Our beds and other accommodations are for 1156.

Are you limited, by any clause in your charter to that number?—No; but we maintain as many as we can accommodate, and our funds will support.

What ages are the boys admitted at?—From seven to ten; that is the rule established in 1809; they may have been admitted older than ten, but none under seven; before 1809 there was no strict rule as to that point.

How long are they allowed to remain?—Till 15; with the exception of those who go to college, and those who go to the sea service.

Are they taught, lodged, and clothed?—Yes, without a shilling expense to their parents; and are also provided at our expense with all the books which they have occasion for; and with such as are bound out, an apprentice-fee of 5*l.* is paid, several of the benefactors having left that sum for this purpose.

Translation of the CHARTER of King EDWARD the Sixth of Foundation of the Hospitals of CHRIST, BRIDEWELL, and ST. THOMAS the APOSTLE.

EDWARD the Sixth by the grace of God of England France and Ireland King, Defender of the Faith, and in Earth of the Church of England and of Ireland Supreme Head. To all to whom the present Letters shall come, greeting. Whereas We, pitying the miserable estate of the poor fatherless decrepit aged sick infirm and impotent persons languishing under various kinds of diseases; and also of our special grace thoroughly considering the honest pious endeavours of our most humble and obedient subjects the Mayor and Commonalty and Citizens of our city of London, who by all ways and methods diligently study for the good provision of the poor and of every sort of them, and that by such reason and care neither children yet being in their infancy shall lack good education and instruction, nor when they shall obtain riper years shall be destitute of honest callings and occupations whereby they may honestly exercise themselves in some good faculty and science for the advantage and utility of the commonwealth; nor that the sick or diseased, when they shall be recovered and restored to health, may remain idle and lazy vagabonds of the state, but that they in like manner may be placed and compelled to labour and honest and wholesome employments: Know ye, that We, as well for the considerations aforesaid as of our special grace and of our certain knowledge and meer motion, desiring not only the progress amplification and increase of so honest and noble a work, but also condescending in our name and by our royal authority to take upon ourself the patronage of this most excellent and most holy foundation, now lately established, have given and granted, and by these presents do give and grant, to the Mayor and Commonalty and Citizens of our city of London, All that our manor capital messuage and tenement and our mansion-house called Bridewell other Bridewell Place, with all and singular its rights members and appurtenances, situate lying and being in the parish of Saint Brigid in Fleet-street London, and all and singular houses edifices lands tenements rents reversions and services chambers curtilages gardens void grounds places spaces ways easements profits and commodities whatsoever to the said house called Bridewell Place in any wise howsoever belonging or appertaining, or as being parts members or parcels of the same heretofore had known used or demised; and all those our messuages tenements cellars sollars houses edifices and hereditaments whatsoever, situate lying and being in the parish of Saint Sepulcre without Newgate, London, to the late royal hospital called the Savoy, in the parish of Saint Clement Danes without the bars of the New Temple London, now dissolved, formerly belonging and appertaining, and being parcel of the possessions thereof; and also all the messuages tenements cottages cellars sollars houses edifices and our hereditaments whatsoever, situate lying and being in the parish of Saint Michael at Corn, London, to the said late hospital formerly belonging and appertaining, and being parcel of the possessions thereof; and also all that messuage and tenement, and all our houses edifices shops cellars sollars and hereditaments whatsoever, with their appurtenances, situate lying

and

*James Palmer, Esq.*
*and*
*Richard Corp, Esq.*

and being in the Old Change, in the parish of Saint Augustine, London, to the said late hospital formerly belonging and appertaining, and being parcel of the possessions thereof; and also all those our five messuages and tenements, with the appurtenances, in the parish of All Saints Honey-lane next Cheap, London, to the said late hospital formerly belonging and appertaining, and being parcel of the possessions thereof; and also all those our messuages and tenements, with the appurtenances, lying in the parish of Saint Anthony, called Saint Anklyn's parish, in Budge-row, London, to the said late hospital formerly belonging and appertaining, and late being parcel of the possessions thereof; and also our messuage and tenement, with the appurtenances, lying in Pankerith-street in the parish of Saint Bennets Sherehog, London, and to the said late hospital formerly belonging and appertaining, and late being parcel of the possessions thereof; and also all those our messuages and tenements, with the appurtenances, in the parish of Saint Bennett, London, to the said hospital formerly belonging and appertaining, and being parcel of the possessions thereof; and also all those our messuages and tenements, with the appurtenances, in the parish of Saint Andrew Undershaft, London, to the said hospital formerly belonging and appertaining, and late being parcel of the possessions thereof; and also all other our messuages cottages tofts tenements shops cellars sollars rents reversions services and hereditaments whatsoever, with their appurtenances, situate lying and being in the parish of Saint Sepulchre without Newgate, London, to the said late hospital formerly belonging and appertaining; and all the messuages lands tenements rents reversions services and other hereditaments whatsoever, with their appurtenances, in the city of London and the suburbs of the same, which were parcel of the possessions and revenues of the said late hospital; and all our lordship and manor called Shoreditch Place otherwise Ingibrow-hold, with all its rights members and appurtenances, in Hackney and elsewhere in our county of Middlesex, to the said late hospital formerly belonging and appertaining, and late being parcel of the possessions thereof; and also all those our lands meadows pastures and hereditaments whatsoever, called Robbyes, in our said county of Middlesex, now or late in the tenure or occupation of Edmund Lyecz, to the said late hospital formerly belonging and appertaining, and being parcel of the possessions thereof; and also all those our lands meadows feedings pastures and hereditaments whatsoever, called Goldbetters, with the appurtenances, lying and being in Enfield in our said county of Middlesex, now or late in the tenure or occupation of Catherine Alychell, and to the said late hospital formerly belonging and appertaining, and late being parcel of the possessions thereof; and also all our lordship and manor called Oxenford in Colkerington in our said county of Middlesex, with all its rights members liberties and appurtenances, to the said late hospital formerly belonging and appertaining, and being parcel of the possessions thereof; and also all those our lordships and manors of Denge Hillions Albethley and Gerons, with their rights members liberties and appurtenances, in our county of Essex; and also our messuage and tenement called the Newhouse; and all our lands meadows feedings pastures commons rents reversions services and hereditaments whatsoever, with the appurtenances, called or known by the name or names of Tarlfees and Stewards; and all other our lands tenements meadows feedings pastures rents reversions services and hereditaments whatsoever, in Great Perington otherwise Parndon in our said county of Essex, to the said late hospital formerly belonging and appertaining, and late being parcel of the possessions thereof; and also all that our lordship and manor of Lynsters otherwise called Langleys, with all its rights members and appurtenances, in our county of Hertford, to the said hospital formerly belonging and appertaining, and late being parcel of the possessions thereof; and also all those our lordships and manors of Denham Duredent and Maskworth, with all their rights members and appurtenances, in our county of Buckingham, and to the said late hospital formerly belonging and appertaining, and late being parcel of the possession thereof; and also all that our manor and our tenements of Topcliff in Melryth, and of Melbourn Royston Feversham and Great Eversden, with the appurtenances, in our county of Cambridge, with all their rights members liberties and appurtenances, to the said late hospital formerly belonging and appertaining, and late being parcel of the possessions thereof; and also all that our lordship and manor of Netherhall in Hinton, with all its rights members liberties and appurtenances, in our said county of Cambridge, and to the said late hospital formerly belonging and appertaining, and being parcel of the possessions thereof; and all that our lordship and manor of Burdlyns in Comberton in our said county of Cambridge, with all its rights members and appurtenances, now or late in the tenure or occupation of John Ranger, and to the said late hospital formerly belonging and appertaining, and being parcel of the possessions thereof; and also all that our lordship and manor of Allens, and all our lands meadows feedings pastures and hereditaments whatsoever, called Maners, with their rights members and appurtenances, in Feversham and elsewhere in our said county of Cambridge, now or late in the tenure or occupation of William Wise, and to the said late hospital formerly belonging and appertaining, and being parcel of the possessions thereof; and also all those our messuages lands tenements meadows feedings pastures commons and hereditaments whatsoever, with the appurtenances, now or late in the tenure or occupation of the said William Wise, situate lying and being in Fulborne in our said county of Cambridge, to the said late hospital formerly belonging and appertaining, and being parcel of the possessions thereof; and also all that our lordship and manor of Astinleigh otherwise Hastingleigh and Aldeloss, with all its rights members liberties and appurtenances, and all our messuages lands tenements meadows feedings pastures and hereditaments whatsoever, with the appurtenances, in Hastingleigh and Aldeloss aforesaid in our county

of

of Kent, now or late in the tenure or occupation of Edward Grey, to the said late hospital
formerly belonging and appertaining, and being parcel of the possessions thereof; and also
all that our lordship and manor of Crofton, with all its rights members and appurtenances,
in our said county of Kent, to the said late hospital formerly belonging and appertaining,
and being parcel of the possessions thereof; and also all that our lordships and manors of
Combe Grove and Fienscombe, with all their rights members and appurtenances, in our
said county of Kent, to the said late hospital formerly belonging and appertaining, and
being parcel of the possessions thereof; and also all that our lordship and manor of
Tibshelf, with all its rights members liberties and appurtenances, in our county of Derby,
and to the said late hospital formerly belonging and appertaining, and being parcel of the
possessions thereof; and all those coalpits in Tybshelf aforesaid, to the said late hospital
formerly belonging and appertaining; and all that our lordship and manor of Bewyke,
with all its rights members and appurtenances, in our county of York, to the said hospital
formerly belonging and appertaining, and being parcel of the possessions thereof; and
also all and singular messuages mills tofts cottages houses edifices barns stables dovehouses
yards orchards gardens lands tenements meadows feedings pastures commons furze heaths
marshes woods underwoods waters fisheries fishings rents reversions and services and rents
reserved upon any demises and grants whatsoever; and also courts leet, view of frankpledge, chattels, waived estrays, free warrens, chattels of felons and fugitives, and felons of
themselves, and persons put in exigent and deodands; and also knights fees wards mar-
riages escheats reliefs heriots fines amerciaments, and all other our rights profits commodities emoluments revenues and hereditaments whatsoever, with the appurtenances, in
Hackney Rabbys Enfield and Oxenford in our said county of Middlesex, and in Denge
Hillions Albethley Tailfees Stewards Great Perington and Gerons in our said county of
Essex, and in Linsters otherwise Langley in our said county of Hertford, and in Denham
Duridont and Maskworth in our said county of Buckingham, and in Topcliff Mebryth
Melborne Royston Great Everdens Burdlins Comberton Netherhall Hinton Allens Manors
Feversham Fulborne in our said county of Cambridge, and in Hastingley Aldcloss Crofton
Combegrove and Femescombe in our said county of Kent, and in Tibshelf in our said
county of Derby, and in Bewyke in our said county of York, and elsewhere wheresoever
in the said counties to the said lordships manors and tenements, or to either of them, in
any wise howsoever belonging or appertaining, or as being members parts or parcels of
the same lordships manors and tenements, or either of them, heretofore had acknowledged
accepted used or reputed; and also all other our manors lordships lands tenements and hereditaments formerly belonging or appertaining, and late being parcel of the possessions thereof;
and also all and all manner of advowsons donations nominations presentations and rights of
patronage of the rectories vicarages and churches, to the said late hospital formerly belonging
or appertaining, and late being part of the possessions thereof; and also all and all manner of
rectories tithes oblations obventions pensions portions and other tithes whatsoever or of what
kind nature or sort soever they be or have been, or by what name soever they are called deemed
or known, to the said late hospital formerly belonging or appertaining, and late being parcel
of the possessions and revenues thereof (Except and always to us and our heirs reserved
the capital messuage to the said late hospital called the Savoy House, with the site and
church thereof, and all the houses edifices and tenements to the same capital messuage
and site adjoining, called the Savoy Rents.) Also We have given and granted to the aforesaid Mayor Commonalty and Citizens of the city of London and their successors, for the
further sustentation of the same poor who shall be and shall be supported in our aforesaid
manor of Bridewell, and all manner of the implements and utensils belonging or appertaining
as well to our aforesaid house of Bridewell, as all and all manner of bedding utensils and necessaries which formerly belonged to the said late hospital of the Savoy, by what name soever they
may be known; except nevertheless, and to us reserved, one great bell and one small bell now
remaining and being in the chapel of the said late hospital, and one chalice for the administration of the communion, and other the necessary implements and things to be had and
used in the said chapel for divine service and administration of the sacraments there. Also
We have given and granted to the aforesaid Mayor and Commonalty and Citizens of the
City aforesaid, and their successors, all and all manner of our woods underwoods and trees
whatsoever of in and upon the premises growing and being, and all the land soil and
ground of the same woods underwoods and trees, and the reversion and reversions whatsoever of all and singular the same premises and of every part thereof, and also the rents
and yearly profits whatsoever reserved upon any demises and grants whatsoever of the
premises or of any part thereof in any wise howsoever, made as fully freely and entirely and
in as ample manner and form, and with all and singular the like liberties franchises jurisdictions and commodities, as any master or governor of the said late hospital, or any other
or others heretofore having possessing or being seised of the premises or any part thereof,
are had held and enjoyed the same or any part thereof, or ought to have had held or enjoyed
the same or any part thereof, and as fully freely and entirely and in as ample manner and
form as all and singular the same premises came or ought to have come to our hands by
reason or pretext of the dissolution of the said late hospital, or by reason of the gift grant
or surrender thereof to us made, or by any other manner right or title whatsoever, and as
the same now are or ought to be or to have been in our hands; and which manors lands
tenements and all and singular other the premises with their appurtenances (except before
excepted) are now extended to the clear yearly value of four hundred and fifty pounds and
no more; To have hold and enjoy the aforesaid manor capital messuage and tenement
called Bridewell Place, and all and singular the aforesaid manors messuages lands tenements

*James Palmer, Esq.*
*and*
*Richard Corp, Esq.*

hereditaments,

*James Palmer, Esq.*
*and*
*Richard Corp, Esq.*

hereditaments, and all and singular other the premises, with all their appurtenances (except before excepted) to the aforesaid Mayor and Commonalty and Citizens of the City aforesaid and their successors, to the proper use and behoof of the same Mayor and Commonalty and Citizens of the City aforesaid and their successors for ever; to hold of us our heirs and successors as of our manor of Greenwich in our county of Kent, in free socage (to wit) by fealty only and not in chief, for all services and demands whatsoever for the same to us our heirs or successors in any wise howsoever to be rendered paid or done. And further, of our more abundant grace and of our certain knowledge and meer motion, We have given and granted, and do for us our heirs and successors by these presents give and grant, to the aforesaid Mayor and Commonalty and Citizens of the City aforesaid and their successors may have hold and in full right enjoy and use all and all manner of the like, the same, so many, and such sorts of courts leet, views of frankpledge and all things which to view of frankpledge belong or appertain or which may or ought to appertain, assize and assay of bread wine and beer, estrays, goods and chattels waived, and goods and chattels of felons and fugitives, parks free warren and all things which to free warren do or may belong, and other the rights liberties privileges jurisdictions profits commodities and emoluments in the aforesaid manors lands tenements and other the premises, with their appurtenances, and in every part thereof, as and which we now hold and have held, and in as ample manner and form as we now have hold and enjoy, or as our progenitors at any time heretofore have had held and enjoyed our aforesaid manor and house of Bridewell and every part and parcel thereof, and which now are or heretofore have been had held or acknowledged to be parcel or member of or in any wise howsoever belonging or appertaining to the manor aforesaid, and also as and which the last master of the said late hospital or any other or others of his predecessors in right of the same late hospital at any time have or hath had held or enjoyed or ought to have held or enjoyed in the aforesaid manors lands tenements and other the premises with their appurtenances or in any part thereof, by reason of any letters patent of us or of any of our progenitors, or by reason of any charter of gift grant prescription use or custom, or in any other manner howsoever. And further, We give and by these presents grant to the aforesaid Mayor and Commonalty and Citizens of the City aforesaid, all and all manner of issues rents revenues and profits of the aforesaid manors lands tenements and other the premises, with all and singular their appurtenances, from the twelfth day of June last past in the seventh year of our reign, hitherto issuing arising or growing, To have and receive all the aforesaid issues rents revenues and profits to the same Mayor and Commonalty and Citizens of the City aforesaid, as well by their own proper hands as by the hands of the receivers bailiffs farmers tenants and occupiers of the said manors lands tenements and other the premises with their appurtenances, without account or any other thing for the premises or any of them to us our heirs or successors to be rendered paid or made. And further, We will and by our royal authority, which we exercise of our special grace, and of our certain knowledge and meer motion, have given and granted, and by these presents for us our heirs and successors do give and grant to the aforesaid Mayor and Commonalty and Citizens of our said city of London, and their successors, license faculty and full power to have hold possess and enjoy all and singular the rectories vicarages and churches of the said late hospital of the Savoy, with the right of patronage of the same, and all and singular the messuages houses edifices lands glebes annuities portions pensions fruits tithes oblations and other the rights profits commodities and emoluments whatsoever to the same rectories vicarages and churches, or to either of them, assigned appointed belonging or appertaining or hereafter happening to be assigned appointed or to belong or appertain, and that they may and shall have power to convert and retain the same to their own proper use without the impeachment or impediment of us our heirs or successors, or of any of the archbishops archdeacons sheriffs escheators justices commissioners or other the officers or ministers of us our heirs or successors, and without account first fruits or tenths or any other thing to us our heirs or successors in any wise howsoever to be rendered paid or done for the same, and without the nomination presentation institution or collation of any rector in either of the churches or rectories aforesaid, the statute of not putting lands and tenements to mortmain, or the statute of granting the first fruits and tenths of spiritual and ecclesiastical benefices dignities and promotions, to us our heirs and successors lately made and provided, or any other statute act ordinance provision prohibition restriction or law ecclesiastical or temporal, to the contrary thereof heretofore had made passed ordained or provided, or any other thing cause or matter whatsoever in any wise notwithstanding, and without any writ of " ad quod dampnum" or any other writ mandate or precept of our heirs or successors in this behalf in any wise howsoever to be prosecuted sued forth or made, and without any inquisition thereof to be made or taken. Moreover know ye, that We of our more abundant grace, and of our certain knowledge and mere motion, will and have given licence, and by these presents for us our heirs and successor do give and grant licence to any of our subjects and liege men whomsoever, that they either or any of them may and may have power to give grant sell alien or devise to the aforesaid Mayor and Commonalty and Citizens of the said city of London and their successors, for ever, any manors rectories lands tenements tithes rents reversions services or other possessions revenues or hereditaments whatsoever, to the yearly value of four thousand marks, in our city of London or elsewhere within our kingdom of England or in Wales, or elsewhere wheresoever within our dominions or power, besides the aforesaid manors rectories lands tenements and other the premises above by these presents given and granted as aforesaid, although they be held of us in chief or otherwise. And to the same Mayor and Commonalty and Citizens and their successors We do likewise by these

presents

presents give and grant special licence, that they may and may have power to have receive and purchase of any of our subjects and liege men such manors rectories lands tenements tithes rents reversions services possessions revenues and hereditaments, to the yearly value aforesaid, besides the aforesaid manors rectories lands tenements and other the premises by these presents above given and granted as aforesaid, the statute of not putting lands and tenements to mortmain, or any other statute act ordinance or provision to the contrary thereof heretofore had made ordained or provided, or any other thing cause or matter whatsoever in any wise notwithstanding.  AND that our aforesaid intention may take better effect, and that the lands tenements rents revenues and other things to be granted assigned and appointed to the sustentation of the said hospitals or houses of the poor aforesaid may be the better governed; for the continuation of the same, We will and have ordained that the Hospitals aforesaid, when they shall be so founded erected and established, shall be named and called The Hospitals of Edward the Sixth, king of England, of Christ, Bridewell, and Saint Thomas the Apostle; and that the aforesaid Mayor and Commonalty and Citizens of the city of London aforesaid, and their successors, shall be named and called governors of the said hospitals and of the possessions revenues and goods of the said hospitals commonly called and to be called the Hospitals of Edward the Sixth, king of England, of Christ, Bridewell, and Saint Thomas the Apostle; and that the same governors be and shall be hereafter in deed fact and name one body corporate and politic of themselves for ever by the name of the governors of the possessions revenues and goods of the hospitals of Edward the Sixth, king of England, of Christ, Bridewell, and Saint Thomas the Apostle, incorporated and erected, and them the governors of the possessions revenues and goods of the hospitals aforesaid We do by these presents incorporate, and a body corporate and politic by the same name to continue for ever really and fully do create erect ordain make and constitute by these presents; and We will that the same governors of the possessions revenues and goods of the said hospitals of Edward the Sixth, king of England, of Christ, Bridewell, and Saint Thomas the Apostle, may have perpetual succession, and that by the same name they may be and shall be persons able and capable in the law to have and receive as well of us as of any other person or persons whomsoever, any lands tenements rents reversions hereditaments and goods and chattels whatsoever, To hold to them and their successors for ever.  And further We will, and for us our heirs and successors by these presents grant to the aforesaid governors and their successors, that hereafter for ever they may have a common seal, to serve only for their businesses touching and concerning the premises and other the things in these our letters patent expressed and specified, or any part thereof; and that the same governors by the name of the governors of the possessions revenues and goods of the hospitals of Edward the Sixth, king of England, of Christ, Bridewell, and Saint Thomas the Apostle, may plead and be impleaded, defend and be defended, answer and be answered, in any courts and places whatsoever, and before any judges whomsoever, in any causes actions suits plaints pleas and demands whatsoever, of what nature or kind soever they shall be, touching or concerning the premises and other the things underwritten, or any part thereof, or for any offences trespasses things causes or matters by any persons or person done or perpetrated in or upon the premises or any part thereof, or in or upon any thing in these presents specified.  And further, of our more abundant grace and of our royal authority certain knowledge and meer motion, We have given and granted for us our heirs and successors as much as in us lies, and by these presents do give and grant to the aforesaid Mayor and Commonalty and Citizens of London aforesaid, and their successors for ever, and the major part of them, that it shall or may be fully and entirely lawful to the same Mayor and Commonalty and Citizens for the time being, at all times and always hereafter, when and as often as to them it shall seem expedient or necessity shall so require, to ordain constitute and make all such fit wholesome and honest ordinances statutes and rules for the right government of the poor in the same manor or house called Bridewell Place, or in the same other houses called Christ Hospital and Saint Thomas's Hospital in Southwark aforesaid, or either of them, to be supported, as to them shall seem good; and also that they may have full power and authority to examine all and singular idle persons wandering about within the city aforesaid and the liberties thereof, and to compel them to employ and exercise themselves with all their might in some honest labour and work.  Also We give and by these presents for us our heirs and successors grant to the aforesaid Mayor and Commonalty and Citizens of London aforesaid, and their successors, full power and authority from time to time to nominate appoint make create and ordain such and so many officers ministers or governors under them, in the aforesaid hospitals or houses or in either of them, who may from time to time provide for the poor therein, that they may be well and justly ordered and taken care of, and also for the order and government of the same poor, as to them shall likewise seem good and convenient, without the impeachment of us our heirs or successors, or of the justices escheators sheriffs ministers servants or other of the subjects whomsoever of us our heirs or successors, any statute act law or ordinance heretofore made or hereafter to be made to the contrary notwithstanding, so that the same ordinances laws and statutes be not contrary or repugnant to the laws and statutes of our kingdom of England or to our royal prerogative. And further, We give and grant, for us our heirs and successors, to the aforesaid Mayor and Commonalty and Citizens of our city of London aforesaid and their successors, for ever, that it may and shall be lawful as well to the aforesaid Mayor and Commonalty and Citizens for the time being, as to the same and such officers ministers or governors as to the aforesaid Mayor and Commonalty and Citizens as aforesaid shall from time to time appoint or ordain to be officers ministers or governors under them of the same manor or house called Bridewell

*James Palmer, Esq.*
*and*
*Richard Corp, Esq.*

Place,

*James Palmer, Esq.*
*and*
*Richard Corp, Esq.*

Place, or the other houses or hospitals assigned for the aforesaid poor as aforesaid, and of two or three of them, at all times hereafter from time to time, as well within the city of London aforesaid and the suburbs of the same, as within our said county of Middlesex, diligently to inquire and examine by all ways and methods by which they may better know according to their prudence and discretion of all and all manner of suspicious houses inns taverns gaming-houses playhouses dancing-houses and other places whatsoever, and the liberty or liberties and places exempt whatsoever within the said City and the suburbs thereof and of our said county of Middlesex, by what names or titles soever the same or either of them are or shall be called or known, and also to examine investigate and inquire of all and singular houses or places whatsoever in anywise suspected for idle lazy ruffians haunters of stews vagabonds and sturdy beggars or other suspected persons whomsoever, and men and women whomsoever of ill name and fame, and the same ruffians haunters of stews vagabonds and beggars not only to apprehend within the same suspected houses or places liberty or liberties and places exempt, being within the said county of Middlesex, but also the tenants masters owners or keepers of such houses or places where any such shall be found, to the house of labour of Bridewell to commit, or in any other manner all and singular the same persons to punish as to them it shall then seem good and lawful, unless the tenants masters owners or keepers of such houses and places can honestly and justly excuse and discharge themselves before the aforesaid Mayor and the Aldermen of the same city for the time being, or before the officers ministers or governors under them of the aforesaid houses, why they have so cherished and entertained such idle ruffians and suspected persons and vagabonds, or permitted them to lie converse and frequent in their houses, and also unless such men so suspected, and vagabonds being so taken, may sufficiently and fully declare for their honest and good conversation, and render a just reason by what manner they may get their living, and why they do so wander about and daily frequent such sort of suspicious and secret and prohibited houses or places, and shall also find sufficient surety that they and every of them shall afterwards behave themselves and himself honestly. And moreover We will, that it shall be lawful to the Mayor and Aldermen of the city aforesaid for the time being, or for other the officers or governors of the poor under them in the hospitals aforesaid for the time being, to use such correction and order in the premises as to them shall seem most convenient or profitable, without the impeachment of us our heirs or successsors, or of the justices escheators sheriffs or other the ministers servants or subjects whomsoever of us our heirs or successors, any statute act ordinance restriction law or custom to the contrary thereof in any wise notwithstanding. Also We will, and by these presents grant to the aforesaid Mayor and Commonalty and Citizens of our city of London, that may have and shall have these our letters patent under our great seal of England, in due manner made and sealed, without fine or fee great or small to us in our Hanaper or elsewhere to our use for the same in anywise howsoever to be rendered paid or made, although express mention of the true yearly value or of the certainty of the premises or either of them, or of other gifts or grants by us or by any of our progenitors heretofore made to the same Mayor and Commonalty and Citizens of our city of London, is not made in these presents, or any other statute act ordinance provision or restriction to the contrary thereof made passed ordained or provided, or any other thing cause or matter whatsoever in anywise notwithstanding. In testimony whereof, We have caused these our letters to be made patent. Witness ourself at Westminster the twenty-sixth day of June in the seventh year of our reign.

*Cotton.*

(Great Seal.)    By Writ of Privy Seal and of the date aforesaid,
by authority of Parliament.

Inrolled before John Hornyoke, Auditor.
Inrolled before John Purevey, Auditor.
Inrolled in the office of Bryan Taillor, Auditor.

[In addition to the former Witnesses, *Dr. Trollope*, the Head Master of the School, here joined in the Evidence.]

*Dr. Trollope.*

WHAT are they taught?—They are taught to the utmost extent that they are taught in any other great school; reading, spelling, writing, arithmetic, all classical learning, and Hebrew, part in mathematics, part in drawing.

How many scholarships have you at the university?—Seven at Cambridge, and one at Oxford.

What are those scholarships in value?—Exhibitions we call them; I think they are 60l. a year at Cambridge, and at Pembroke they have an additional exhibition from the college, making about 90l. for four years, and 50l. for the last three years; to which we should add the expenses of bachelors' and masters' degrees, that are paid.

What are the Oxford exhibitions?—10l. more, or 70l. We pay all fees of entrance, 20l. toward furnishing their rooms, 10l. for their books, and 10l. for their clothes, which is at least 50l. for the outfit altogether.

When you represent the classical education as consisting of the particulars above mentioned, you do not mean that all or even the bulk of the boys are so taught?—Not to the extent.

What

*Dr. Trollope,*
*James Palmer, Esq.*
*and*
*Richard Corp, Esq.*

What proportion now may be taught Greek and Latin?—According to a recent regulation of the governors, the whole of the boys proceed as far in the classics, as their talent or age will allow them. They all leave us at fifteen, except those who go to the university, or go to sea.

About how many boys on an average, do you think, are taught in the classics?—In the upper grammar school I have 60, which is my department; the second master has, I think, about 150; but upwards of 500 will be instructed in Latin, &c. *and as far as we can say, I do not think that they can go further, and even with some of them it is quite the utmost.*

How many boys should you say, in general, went through a classical course completely?—About eight or ten, to fill up the university exhibitions as they become vacant.

How many at the Hertford seminary are taught in the classics?—About 200, there being there 416, when full; and they are drafted in general at the age of twelve to London.

How many boys generally attain the last stage of what may be called the ordinary classical education?—Those who reach the upper school; viz. about 60.

How are the scholars chosen for exhibition?—They are selected by the head master, according to their talent and behaviour.

In making this selection, does any person interfere with the choice of the head master?—No person.

Is any recommendation used with him in behalf of any scholar?—Frequently by their parents and friends.

Has he the absolute disposition of the exhibitions?—I have always found it so, since I have been head master.

Do you chuse directly, or only recommend to the governors?—I make the choice; I do not consult at the time; I chuse them when they would otherwise be discharged, or about the age of fifteen.

In the event of more boys than one being equally qualified, how would such choice be made?—If they were equally qualified in point of talent, it would be given to the boy of the best behaviour; or if the talent and behaviour were both equal, it would be regulated by age; it is a case which must happen constantly, from the number of applications, and but one exhibition.

How many exhibitions go every year?—One to Cambridge, and one every seventh year to Oxford, forming eight in seven years altogether; there have been no instances of vacancies by death in those exhibitions, except one, during the last forty years, which happened in the year 1789.

In the competitions for those exhibitions, is any interest used by any person or from any quarter whatever?—Applications are frequently made by the relations of the boys; but certainly the decision is always by me.

Do the governors interfere at all?—Never; since I have been there, the choice has been altogether with myself.

How many teachers are there altogether?—In London, four classical masters, two writing masters, and two ushers; a mathematical, drawing, and singing master. At Hertford, a classical master, writing master, two ushers, and two mistresses to the girls school.

Is there a matron?—At each place, and a steward at each place; six beadles in London, and two at Hertford; thirteen nurses in London, and nine at Hertford; and a cook at each place; besides physician and surgeon, attached to the establishment; a resident apothecary in London; the apothecary at Hertford is not resident.

Is that the whole establishment?—No: there are four clerks; a surveyor and architect; land surveyor, and solicitor. We also elect and pay three street keepers, who act under the orders of the Lord Mayor, as constables, to clear the streets, and keep the peace.

What is the salary of the head master?—As head master, 240*l.* 16*s.* 8*d.* A Sunday evening lecture was established by the governors in 1804, for the more effectual instruction of the children in the fundamental points of the Christian religion, which is delivered by the upper grammar master in the great hall, during eight months of the year, for which he has 50 guineas; it is only eight months in the year, because the children for three months have public suppers, and prayers, when it would be inconvenient to attend the lecture; and the other month is the month of vacation; we have a month vacation in August, a fortnight at Christmas, and eleven days at Easter, with the Bank and City holidays.

427.                                                                              Has

Has the master any other emoluments?—A house rent and tax free, no coal, candle, nor any further perquisite; all the officers have houses, and the rent and taxes paid.

Have any of them any perquisites?—No, not besides their salary, except medical attendance and medicines; one or two of the beadles have a chaldron of coals. A library has been established within the hospital, for the use of the children; and no book is permitted to be used by the children, till it has been inspected and approved by the head master.

What are the school hours?—From the first of March to the last day of October, they begin school at seven and continue till eight; then they have an hour's play; then from nine to twelve; then they have two hours for their dinner; and from two to five; seven hours in the whole. In the winter, from the first of November to the last day of February, they begin school at eight or nine; then they have their hour's play; and from ten to twelve; in the afternoon, from two to four, excepting the whole of Saturday afternoons and Thursdays after three, throughout the year.

What is the salary of the second master?—205 l.; the third master, 180 l.

What is the salary of the master at Hertford?—The same as the salary of the second master in London, 205 l.

Has he a house too?—Yes. It happens that the fourth master in town has not a house, but he has an allowance till one can be provided for him.

What is the salary of the treasurer?—Not any, but he has a house, and medical attendance if he wants it; the hospital pay the taxes for the house.

Has the treasurer the use of the balances that happen to be in his hand?—Certainly.

What is the amount annually of the whole salaries?—5,244 l. in London, which includes the wages to all the servants; the Hertford establishment, 1,746 l. being in the whole for salaries 6,990 l. There are pensions to retired officers and widows, in this year, to the amount of 1,054 l. which is included in the 6,990 l.

What is the average of the house expenses in the year?—The expense of clothing, salaries, and other charges of each child, was 32 l. 11 s.; if we include building and every thing, it will amount to 37 l. 8 s. 8 d.

Is the expense of managing the estates included in the former estimate?—Yes, completely; the only officer we have in the country is a steward in Lincolnshire, at a salary of 70 l.

What were the house expenses of last year?—The expenses for provisions, apparel, medicine, nurses wages, and stationary, for the year 1815, came to 21 l. 8 s. 3 d. per child, being in the whole 22,547 l.

Does this include Hertford?—It does; this account includes salaries to the apothecaries, wages and board wages of the nurses and servants; it includes every thing relating to the children, except the salaries of the masters and officers.

Is the new mode of education adopted in any part of the seminary?—Doctor Bell's plan is pursued with the younger boys at Hertford.

How many boys are admitted yearly into the establishment?—One hundred and thirty have been voted for admission to be presented this year on governors' presentations, besides six girls, who are admitted by lots being drawn for them; independent of presentations from gifts.

What do you mean by presentations from gifts?—We are obligated, out of estates given, to receive many children; of this description are four every year from Guy's Hospital; the others are chiefly from parishes and companies, entitled to present by virtue of old wills or other donations.

What is the annual number of those not admitted by governors presentations?—We generally discharge about 170 or 180 boys in a year, including all the ways of dismissal; we have known 200 discharged, at the time when there were more children than at present.

To supply those vacancies, the governors present?—Yes; 130 boys and six girls were agreed to be presented each of the last two years; the number is regulated by the finances, after the report has been made, on the examination of the accounts: The remaining vacancies are filled up by gifts. There are 90 children constantly maintained from different gifts in the hospital; the vacancies in that number are supplied as they arise, without waiting for the annual period. When a boy of this description is discharged or dies, notice is given, and his place is filled up.

Are those thus entitled, restricted to the boys whom they are to present?—The wills are various; many leave it to the governors to present in the usual way; some
particular

particular benefactors state that they shall be of particular ages; but there are very few exceptions to the general regulations of the house; whatever limitations are put in the will of the benefactor, we see performed in the selection of that object. There are a certain number of children that are presented every year, sons of lieutenants in the navy, under the will of Mr. Travers, not included in the 130 above specified; there are fifty of these lieutenants sons always maintained.

*Dr. Trollope.*
*James Palmer, Esq.*
*and*
*Richard Corp, Esq.*

Who are the governors of the hospital?—The Mayor and Commonalty and Citizens of the City of London, as represented by the lord mayor, aldermen, and twelve of the common councilmen chosen by the rest of the common council out of their own body.

By what law or custom is the Corporation of the City of London so represented for the purposes of this Charity?—The Act of Parliament in the year 1782, the 22d of the King, settled the disputes between the City of London and the Hospital; it is intituled, " An Act to render valid and effectual certain Articles of Agreement between the Mayor and Commonalty and Citizens of the City of London, governors of the possessions revenues and goods of the Hospitals of Edward King of England the Sixth, of Christ, Bridewell, and Saint Thomas the Apostle, and of the Hospitals of Henry the Eighth King of England, called the House of the Poor, in West Smithfield near London, and of the House and Hospital called Bethlem, and the Presidents, Treasurers, and acting Governors of the said several Hospitals." Since the passing of this Act, the share of the government of this hospital belonging to the corporation of the city of London, has become vested in the mayor, aldermen, and twelve common councilmen chosen by the whole common council.

Who are the governors, beside the Corporation of the City of London?—Noblemen and gentlemen of all ranks, who become benefactors to a certain amount.

What entitles a benefactor to be a governor?—Four hundred pounds, after passing a ballot as to character, in this manner; viz. The treasurer, upon receiving a benefaction of 400 *l.* informs the committee, who recommend to the court, that from its specialty the gentleman should be made a governor, if qualified; the court then refer it back to the committee to consider his qualifications, and to report, which is done by ballot

After they are so recommended to the court of governors, they vote them a staff?—Yes. No benefaction governor has ever been rejected by the court of governors, or the committee of almoners, for the last forty-one years.

How many governors are there now upon the list by benefactions?—There have been made of benefaction governors, within the last ten years, one hundred and five, who have given 39,330 *l.*

Are all those governors made by virtue of having given 400 *l.* each?—No; twenty governors are to be named in two years, by the governors in rotation : if there are twenty governors made from benefactions, there are no nominations, except in the case of a new alderman being made in the two years.

Then are the Committee to understand that the Mayor, each alderman, and each of the twelve common council chosen by the rest of the body, have all the privileges of individual governors?—Yes, they have; each of them is a governor; the aldermen have exclusive rights, which will afterwards appear.

Have the common council such privileges?—No exclusive privileges; the Act settles that they are to act in common with all the other governors, have the same privileges and powers, and no more; and if they quit the common council they are no longer governors; the same is to be observed with regard to the aldermen : they can make permanent governors during the time they are governors.

Besides the corporation of the city, and the governors by benefactions, and the ten governors a year chosen in rotation by the other governors, are there any other governors?—Every alderman, at the first biennial nomination after he comes into his office of alderman, is allowed to name a governor, which governor is to be a benefactor of 200 *l.*, although the number should be full of twenty nominated by the other governors or benefactions : thus, suppose there are seventeen benefaction governors in two years, the governors in rotation, beginning where the last nomination left off, fill up those three, unless an alderman is come into office since the last nomination, in which case he makes one, and the governors name the other two ; but if there are twenty benefaction governors, and a new alderman has come into office, he names the twenty-first governor, and there is no rotation governor named at all, We do not limit the number of benefaction governors; every governor, nominated in what way soever, must become a benefactor to the amount of 200 *l.*

Does

*Dr. Trollope.*
*James Palmer, Esq.*
*and*
*Richard Corp, Esq.*

Does every alderman, upon becoming a governor, become a benefactor also?—Not necessarily; some do.

How often do the governors hold a court?—There are five appointed courts; and as many other courts as the business requires.

Do all the governors attend there?—They are all summoned, and may attend.

Has each a vote?—Yes; fifteen is a quorum.

Who is at the head of the charity?—A president, elected by the body of the governors; and no instance has been known of its being otherwise than an alderman of London.

Is he elected for life?—Yes, as long as he continues an alderman; in ceasing to be an alderman he ceases to be a governor, and of course to be a president, unless he happens to be a governor by benefaction or otherwise before he was an alderman.

How do the governors present to the charity?—The Lord Mayor presents two, one being extra, as Lord Mayor; the president, as president, two, and one as alderman; the other twenty-four aldermen each one annually, provided any children are admitted. In the year 1767 or 1768 was the last time when there was no presentations for that year, except that they complimented the Lord Mayor with his extra presentation.

Suppose the Lord Mayor was president?—He would have two as Lord Mayor, and two as president.

How do the other governors present?—The treasurer, who is also a governor, is complimented with two presentations, and one in his turn as governor: the ordinary governors fill up the remaining number in rotation, beginning each year where the last presentation ceased.

Suppose a person has presented as a privileged governor, by which is meant president, mayor, alderman, and so forth; does he present in his rotation as an ordinary governor?—The treasurer is the only person to whom that applies.

From what class of children must the presentations be made?—This appears by the regulations established at different periods, but last especially revised and settled at the court held the 28th of April 1809, a copy of which I will deliver in.

[It was delivered in, and read, as follows:]

" REGULATIONS for the Admission of Children into Christ's Hospital, London\* :—Specially revised and settled at a Court, 28th April 1809.

1. That every governor may present the child of a parent not free of the city of London, nor a clergyman of the Church of England, either on his first, second, or third presentation, as he shall think proper, and so on, one every three presentations.

2. That no children be admitted but such as shall be between the age of seven and ten years; which is to be proved by such certificates, affidavits and vouchers, as are now or shall be hereafter required by the order of the general court.

3. That a child whose parent or parents has or have two other children under fourteen years of age to maintain, may be admitted by a presentation, although such child has one brother or sister, and no more, already on the charge of this hospital.

4. That no child shall be admitted, who is a foundling, or maintained at the parish charge.

5. That no children of livery servants, except freemen of the city of London, or *children who have any adequate means of being educated or* MAINTAINED, or who are lame, crooked or deformed, so as not to be able to take care of themselves, or have any infectious distemper, as leprosy, scaldhead, itch, scab, evil, or rupture, or distemper which shall be judged incurable, shall be taken into this hospital, on any account or by any presentation whatever; and if any such shall happen to be admitted, and afterwards found disqualified in some or one of these instances, they shall be immediately sent home to their parents, or to the parishes from whence they came.

6. That none be admitted without a due certificate from the minister, church-warden, and three of the principal inhabitants of the parish from whence such children come, certifying the age of the said children, and that they have no adequate means of being educated and maintained; the said minister, churchwardens and inhabitants engaging to discharge the hospital of them before or after the age of fifteen years, if the governors shall so require.—If the father is minister of the parish, the certificate to be signed by the officiating minister of a neighbouring parish.

7. To

---

\* See Orders of Court, of the 28th of March 1765, the 4th of July 1765, and the 7th of March 1777.

Dr. Trollope.
James Palmer, Esq.
and
Richard Corp, Esq.

7. To prevent children being admitted contrary to the above rules, they shall be presented to a general court, who will examine into the truth of the certificates, vouchers and testimonials required, touching their age, birth, orphanage or other qualifications, or refer the same to the committee of almoners, strictly to examine whether the allegations contained in each separate petition and presentation are true, and conformable to the right of the presentee and the above regulations; and all such as shall be found otherwise, shall be rejected."

Have those regulations been strictly adhered to ever since the 28th of April 1809?— There has been only one exception, and that relates to the age which arose upon the doubtful construction of a will, under which the boy was presented, it being a parish presentation.

What was the name?—Carpenter.

In what year was it?—About the year 1814.

Previous to April 1809, were any children admitted, whose parents were able to educate and maintain them?—They all produce a certificate of their inability so to do.

When was this the old rule of the establishment?—The old form of the presentation before 1809, was always upon the certificate of the inability of the parents to maintain and educate them.

By whom was that certificate signed?—The minister, churchwardens, and three housekeepers of the parish where the party resided.

Was any examination, before 1809, made into the truth of the certificates?— No other examination than what is pursued now; previously, not perhaps quite so strict; in fact, the examination did not go so strictly into the capability of the parents to maintain them, great dependence being placed upon the honour of the governor, that he would conform himself to the rules respecting the qualifications.

Have the examinations since 1809 been rigorous into the question of the capability of the parents?—They have been very particular; we have no means of ascertaining except by the credit of the statement; in fact, the officers always inquire of the parent, when the presentation is filled up, what is the income, &c.; and the governor knowing what class of child he is to present, of course is a good deal depended upon that he will select a proper object. There have been presentations which the court and committee have refused; we look at an income not exceeding 300 *l.* a year as the largest, unless there happens to be a very large family. No general rule is adopted, but every case is examined upon its own merits.

Are there many instances of children being admitted, whose parents are totally destitute?—Very many.

Is that the case with the majority of children admitted?—No. It appears, " that on the 17th of February 1809, when there were upon the charge of the hospital, children 1065, sixty-five of whom were girls;

" That of the 1000 boys,

   161 were admitted on gifts from companies, parishes, &c.
   498 sons of freemen.
   239 sons of nonfreemen.
   102 sons of clergymen, who had, exclusive of the boys in the hospital, other children - - - - - - -} 578.

" That the parents of 871 boys, had, exclusive of those in the hospital, other children - - - - - - -} 3606.

" And that 27 boys had neither brother nor sister.

" That out of the 973 boys, there were as under;

| | | |
|---|---|---|
| Orphans - - - - - - - - | 57 | |
| Sons of widows - - - - - - - | 210 | 360. |
| Motherless boys - - - - - - - | 93 | |

" Of the above number, 400 were at Hertford."

Did it appear that in those cases the parents of the children above enumerated were in distressed circumstances?—It appeared so at the time of their admission, because they produced certificates that they could not otherwise procure education.

427.

What

*Dr. Trollope.*
*James Palmer, Esq.*
*and*
*Richard Corp, Esq.*

What sort of examination, beyond merely looking at the certificate, was gone into?—There was no means of ascertaining the income of the party, but from their own declaration.

Who are present at the examination?—The presentation is filled up by a clerk, and it is always reported to the court or committee; and the statement read.

Are the committee present when the parent is examined?—In the first instance it is done at the public office; they are afterwards admitted at the committee, and the parent or friend of the child is called in before the committee, and such questions put as the committee may think necessary, upon reading the prayer of the petition and the statement of their circumstances.

Are the Committee to understand, that before a child is admitted upon a presentation, the parents are examined and questioned as to their circumstances, by a committee of governors?—No; the parent or friend is ordered to attend and do attend in consequence, to answer any questions that the committee may think necessary; if there is nothing particular in the presentation, no question is asked; but the statement of income is made in the presentation, with their number of children, particulars, and ages of the rest of their family, and read in their presence.

Have you frequently seen an actual examination by questions, at the committee?—Very often; particularly so by the treasurer, and many other governors, sitting at the board.

Has this been more strict since 1809 than it was before?—Certainly, infinitely more.

Do you know of any one instance since that, of a child being admitted, whose parents were able to maintain and educate it?—No, I think not, as far as the statement in the presentation went; it is taken on the credit of the party. There are many instances of children being removed by their parents of their own act, when they found themselves equal to support their family.

That was the understanding of the hospital committee, you mean, at the time of the admission; but has it often happened that, notwithstanding the certificates, children were admitted, whose parents could otherwise have maintained and educated them?—It has never come to our knowledge; we know no instances of our having been deceived; but we cannot take upon us to say that the parents may in all cases have been in the circumstances represented; but at the time there was no reason to believe they were otherwise than represented.

How often does the hospital committee meet?—The second Wednesday in every month, for the admission of children, and oftener if required.

### Mr. *Thomas Huggins*, called in, and Examined.

*Mr.*
*Thomas Huggins.*

ARE you steward of Christ's hospital?—I am.
You have heard the examination of the last Witnesses?—I have.
As far as your knowledge goes, do you agree with them?—I do.
Have you any thing to add to the evidence they have given?—Nothing.

[The witness was directed to withdraw]

*Jovis, 30° die Maii,* 1816.

HENRY BROUGHAM, Esquire, in The Chair.

---

THE Chairman laid before the Committee a Statement transmitted by
Mr. Althans in compliance with their request; which was read, as follows:

" I HAVE endeavoured to ascertain the number of Untaught Children within
the general district of our East Union; and I herewith transmit the following Calculation:

" In the district bounded by the River Thames, Gracechurch-street, Bishopsgate-street, through Kingsland-road to Stamford-hill, the population east of this
boundary amounts to about - - - 250,000 persons.

| | | |
|---|---|---:|
| One half of this number are above 20 years of age - | - | 125,000 |
| One quarter under 6 years, and from 16 to 20 | - - | 67,500 |

One quarter, from 6 to 16 years of age:
- Number of those whose parents can pay for their education, - - - about 12,000
- Number of those who are taught in Charity, Parochial, and National Schools, about 5,000
- Number of those who are taught in Sunday Schools, by gratuitous teachers, - about 10,000
- Untaught, - - - - - about 30,500

Total - - - 250,000

" I submit the above, believing it will, upon investigation, be found nearly
correct: if so, a similar calculation, to include the other three parts of London
and its vicinity, will leave 122,000 children, between the ages of six and sixteen,
destitute of instruction in the Metropolis.

" As a Sunday school teacher, I have been in the habit of visiting the houses
of the poor; and in the neighbourhood of St. Catherine's, East Smithfield, and
the Hermitage to the Wall of Wapping Dock, I have made frequent visits to
upwards of 500 houses, which are numerously inhabited; and the result of my
enquiries in these parts fully convince me of the great want of education among
the children of the poor, between the ages of six and sixteen years; and great
numbers of the parents are also unable to read."

Dr. *Thomas Waters*, called in, and Examined.

YOU are master of Emmanuel Hospital?—I am.
How long have you been so?—Twelve years.
On what foundation is it?—Lady Dacre's.
Of what date?—The 20th of December 1594. The following is a copy of that
branch of the Will which relates to this foundation:—

" AND whereas my Lord, in his lifetime, and myself, were purposed to erect an
hospital in Westminster, or in some other place near adjoining thereunto, and to
give one hundred and ten pounds in monies towards the building and edifying
thereof, and forty pounds a year in lands, for ever, towards reliefe of aged people,
and bringing up of children in vertue and good and lawdable arts in the said
hospital, whereby they might the better live in time to come by their honest
labour; and for y⁰ pfecting of our said purpose were minded to become humble
suitors to the Queen's most excellent Maᵗʸ, for her princely incorporation of the
same hospitall for ever : To the end therefore that the same may be done accordingly with a further augmentation I will and devise that mine executors, if
I shall not live to perform this myselfe in my lifetime, shall, of the issues sales
and profits of my mannors lands and tenements to them hereafter in and by
this my said last will devised lymitted and appointed for and towards y⁰ payment of my debts and legacies, and the performance of my last will and testament,
cause to be erected and built a meet and convenient house, with roomes of
habitation for twenty poor folkes, and twenty other poor children, imploying and
bestowing thereupon three hundred pounds; and that also my said executors
shall in like sort as my Lord and I had purposed (if we had lived) become
humble suitors to y⁰ Queen's Majesty, and prosecute the same with their best
good meanes and endeavour for incorporating of the same hospital; and after
such incorporation procured, my will and mind is, that my said execut**
or y⁰ survivor of them, shall assure the mannor of Brainsburton in the county
of

*Dr.*
*Thomas Waters.*

of Yorke, with y^e appurtenances, and all other my lands tenem^{ts} and hereditaments in Brainsburton aforesaid or elsewhere in the county of Yorke that I have any way to me and mine heyres, not being parcell of y^e mannor of Woodhall Elwarbie and Thorclebye, and not lying or extending in Elwarbie Woodhall or Thorclebye, to the said Incorporation and their successors for ever, for which purpose I have hereafter devised lymitted and appointed the said mannors and lands by this my will to my said executors and their heirs; Nevertheless, my will and meaning is, if I demise not nor lease not the same hereafter in my lifetime, that then my said executors or y^e survivors or survivor of them, or y^e heires of the survivor, before such assurance to be made to y^e said Incorporation as aforesaid, shall lease demise and grant for the terme of one hundred yeares, or for some lesser terme at their discretion, the said mannor of Brainsburton and y^e said lands and tenements limitted and appointed to be insured to the said Incorporation, with their appurtenances, to such pson or psons as to them or to y^e survivor or survivors of them, or y^e heirs of y^e survivor, shall seem good; upon which lease to be made, there shall be reserved and yearly payable during the said terme for which y^e said lease shall be made, the yearly rent of one hundred pounds yearly to be paid at two feasts in y^e year by even and equal portions; and the same lease so to be made as aforesaid, I will and devise shall be good and effectual in law against me, my heires executors and assigns, and their heires and assignes; after which lease so to be made, I will the reverĉon of the said mannor of Brainsburton, and of y^e said lands tenements and hereditam^{ts}, with their appurtenances, together with y^e said rent of one hundred pounds yearly to be reserved upon y^e said lease, shall by my said executors, or the survivor or survivors of them, or the heires of the survivor, be conveyed and assured to the said Incorporation, and their successors, for ever; and y^e same conveyance and assurance so to be made, shall stand and be good against me and mine heires, and against my said executors, and their heires and assignes as aforesaid, other than y^e lease or leases aforesaid: And whereas I have had speech and communication with Edw^d More, Esq. for the purchase of certaine ground of his, conteyning about four acres, situate lying and being in or near Tuthill Fields in y^e county of Middlesex, for erecting and placing the said Hospitall thereupon, or some part thereof, I will that the same shall be purchased of him by my executors, at such price as he hath offered y^e same unto Mr. Goddard, who hath dealt with him therein; and that afterwards my executors shall build thereupon one Hospital or messuage as aforesaid, with convenient roomes of habitation for the said Incorporation; and after the same so bought, and y^e housing so edified, then I will the same be assured to the said Incorporation and their successors for ever accordingly; and my desire is y^t y^e said Hospital shall be called Emanuel Hospital in Westminster, or such like good name as shall please my Lord Treasurer to name, or in his default as my said executors, or y^e most part of them, or the survivors of them, or y^e heirs of the survivor, shall name or appoint; and whatsoever my said executors shall do in the premises, or for y^e making or executing of the said lease and assurance of y^e said mannor, and other y^e premises to the said Hospital meant or intended to be limitted or assured, I the said Lady Dacre do will that the same shall stand and be of full force and effect in law against me and mine heires, and against mine executors and assignes, and against their and every of their heires and assignes, saving y^t the said lease for term of one hundred years to be made of the premes in forme aforesaid, rendring y^e yearly rent of one hundred pounds aforesaid, shall be good and effectual for and during the said terme, to such person or persons, and their assignes, to whom the said lease or demise shall be made."

After this will, was there a charter of incorporation?—There was; dated 17th December in the 43d of Elizabeth, according to the tenor of the foregoing will, and appointing the Lord Mayor and Aldermen of London, after the decease of Lady Dacre's executors, the governors of the hospital.

How many poor children are now maintained in the said hospital?—Twenty-two; we have two more girls than are named in the will.

Are they boarded, lodged, and clothed?—Yes; and taught.

Are there twenty aged people maintained also?—There are.

Has the number always been full?—Ever since I have been there.

Do you know the yearly income of the hospital?—I believe at the last letting it was let for 2,900*l.* together with 90*l.* for garden-ground in Westminster, that is subject to a deduction of 940*l.* for the Rector of Brandsburton; his predecessor had 200*l.* only; within three or four years back, he, being a mathematical man, measured the land, and increased it to 940*l.*

Does the rector's income arise from land?—I know nothing of the Brandsburton business, merely that there is such a man, and that he receives so much.

In whose gift is the living?—St. John's Cambridge; the rector is a fellow of that college, of course.

In

In whose gift is the mastership of the hospital in Westminster?—In the Lord Mayor and court of Aldermen.

Has the hospital any other establishments besides those you have mentioned?—None that I know of.

Any funded property?—That I do not know; but I imagine not much; there must arise an annual surplus from the income, but that we require, the premises being very large, for repairs; it is like an old castle; and it is necessary to make preparation for those repairs, which occur almost every seven years.

As nearly as you can estimate, what is the annual expense of the establishment? 1300*l.* or 1400*l.* I suppose.

What is your salary?—130 *l.* including that of the mistress, who is my wife.

Have you a house?—Yes, and a garden.

Any other emoluments or perquisites?—Coal and candle, and those kind of things, which are common to the situation.

Have you board besides?—No, no table.

Have you any allowance for servants?—Not a farthing.

Are there any other salaries belonging to the establishment?—I believe not.

Are there no porters or servants kept?—No; one of the old men is called warden, and gets 10*l.* a year upon the binding of apprentices, and taking care of the gates, but nothing from the charity.

Is it understood to be incumbent upon the hospital to clothe and feed the children, as well as to educate them?—I have always understood so; by the statutes and ordinances made by the governors, the diet of the children and all other particulars are regulated.

Are those ordinances strictly observed?—Very strictly, excepting that they have been modernized.

Was the number of children ever greater than 22?—It has been, but not here; they tried the scheme of sending eight children to Yorkshire, but the distance was so great, and the inconveniencies so numerous, that they withdrew from it; but they have ten out-pensioners, which I believe are not at all named, who have 10*l.* a year till they are elected into the house, and out of those we take the others, if their character be good.

How are they chosen?—They are appointed by the Lord Mayor and Court of Aldermen; they are the same description of people, of course.

When were those out-pensioners first taken?—That I do not know; before my time; but I rather suppose when the last regulation took place.

Do you mean in 1802?—Yes.

Are the children chosen, as well as the pensioners, by the Mayor and Aldermen?—They are appointed by them; there is a notice sent to the parishes, and it is published in the church, and all persons who are eligible make their applications; it is necessary for the parents of the children to have been housekeepers, never to have received alms either as paupers or beggars, and to be Protestants, and members of the Church of England.

Is it necessary for them to produce a certificate of not being able to maintain or educate their children?—I believe not; I never heard of such a thing.

Then how do they state or prove that their children come within the description of poor children?—They state it in the body of the petition, and that is authenticated by the minister and churchwardens of the parish.

Are they obliged to state that their circumstances are such as to render them incapable of educating and supporting their children?—Yes, they must produce certificates to all those things from the clergymen and churchwardens of their parishes.

From your knowledge of the children now in the Establishment, can you take upon you to say that the whole 22 are poor children belonging to parents who have no other means of supporting and educating them?—Every one of them, I believe, I can say very conscientiously.

In what rank of life are their parents?—They are in general of the lowest orders of people, journeymen brewers and carpenters, and that description of people; there is not one who has been got in by favour or affection.

Mr. *William Freeman Lloyd*, called in, and Examined.

WHAT is your business, and where do you reside?—I am a Blackwell-hall factor, carrying on business at Mason's-hall, Basinghall-street.

Are

Mr.
W. F. Lloyd.

Are you acquainted with the state of the children of the poor in the Metropolis?—Yes; chiefly from my acquaintance with Sunday schools, and with those who conduct them, and from having visited the poor at their own habitations.

Are there in your opinion many who have no instruction?—Certainly a great many.

In what parts of the town chiefly?—In St. Giles's, Saffron-hill, Tothillfields, St. Catherine's, and Wapping, where there are many Irish children.

Do you think that Irish children are the most neglected?—Certainly.

From what cause?—From the priests discouraging their attendance at schools where the Bible is used; the Catholic children sometimes come into a school, but they seldom stay long.

Do you belong to a society called the Sunday School Union?—Yes, I am one of the secretaries.

What is the nature of that society?—It is a voluntary association of gratuitous Sunday school teachers, and others feeling an interest in the instruction of the young, for the purpose of extending Sunday schools as much as possible.

By a voluntary association, do you mean an association of teachers of various sects of religion?—Yes, certainly.

What are its objects?—Its objects are to promote the extension of Sunday schools, to lead to the formation of new, and the revival of old schools, and to the establishment of similar institutions throughout the kingdom.

Does it extend to the kingdom at large, as well as to the Metropolis?—Primarily to the Metropolis, and more remotely to the kingdom at large.

Are you able to form an opinion of the number of children educated in Sunday schools in the Metropolis?—I have drawn out a statement as nearly as I can, which I will deliver in.

[It was read, as follows:]

| SUNDAY SCHOOLS: | | | | | | Scholars. |
|---|---|---|---|---|---|---|
| East London District | - | - | - | - | - | 9,291 |
| D° - - - - - Adults | - | - | - | - | | 580 |
| West D° - - D° | - | - | - | - | - | 8,708 |
| Southwark - - D° | - | - | - | - | - | 7,361 |
| North and Central D° | - | - | - | - | - | 9,520 |
| | | | | | | 35,460 |

I think there are several Sunday schools, either not known or not reported in the above; I think the number of Sunday scholars in the Metropolis is about 40,000.

How many teachers are employed in those schools?—About 4000.

Are all the teachers gratuitous?—All of them.

And the secretaries and other officers of the society?—Entirely gratuitous.

What particular advantages do you think arise from this association?—It tends to promote general zeal and union in advancing the cause of Sunday schools.

Has it been the means of producing an increased desire in the poor for the education of their children?—Certainly.

Do you imagine there is any difference in the progress which children make in Sunday schools and day schools?—They seem to pay more attention on Sundays, but it depends upon the system on which the schools are conducted; in some Sunday schools, the teachers not only instruct on a Sunday, but in addition to this, the most advanced scholars are taught writing and arithmetic during the week; the scholars also attend regularly public worship, and are taught to reverence the Sabbath.

How many children does one teacher generally instruct?—From ten to fifteen is the general average; some teachers attend only part of the day.

What difference is there between a Sunday school and a day school?—Sunday schools instruct those poor children whose time is fully employed in labour during the week days, and to them this is the only opportunity of gaining instruction; the children also learn their lessons during the week, to repeat to their teachers on Sunday; and the teachers visit their children at their own habitations, and procure the co-operation of their parents, and watch over their conduct as much as they can.

What in your opinion could be done to extend the benefit of education throughout the Metropolis?—I conceive it would be desirable to investigate the situation of the poor.

What

Mr.
W. F. Lloyd.

What is the advantage of gratuitous teachers over paid teachers, in Sunday schools?—It is the great excellence of the Sunday school system, that it employs gratuitous teachers, who are incalculably preferable to paid teachers, because they perform their duty better; many of them are persons in respectable situations of life, and the children perceive the disinterested attention of their teachers, and therefore feel a greater regard for them, and pay more attention to their instructions. If the 4000 teachers in the Metropolis were paid at the rate of 2s. each Sunday, it would cost upwards of 20,000 l. per annum.

Do you imagine that the generality of poor children in the various parishes of London are educated in the parochial schools?—No, comparatively very few.

Do you know of any plan which could be adopted to increase that number in the day schools?—I think it would be desirable for the inhabitants of the several parishes where they are formed, to investigate the state of the schools, and to superintend them as much as lies in their power.

What do you calculate the expense, per annum, of teaching a child in a Sunday school?—Exclusive of the expense of rent (of which it is impossible to form a general calculation) sixpence per head is as much as it costs.

Does that include books?—Books, fire, candles, and all other expenses, except rent.

Are there candles used in a Sunday-school?—Yes.

Do they teach them in an evening?—Many of them, where the children attend public worship in the afternoon.

If children were not clothed in parochial schools, but that expense saved, might not a much greater number of children be educated than are now, in the respective parishes of London?—Certainly the expense of clothing one child would educate several; a great many more might have instruction; I suppose nearly the whole uneducated poor of the Metropolis.

Do you think it is better to give education to a great number, than instruction and clothing only to a few?—Certainly, much better.

Are there not many poor children in want of clothes to appear decent in schools? —There are some few; but they are chiefly of the lowest description of poor; I think most of the parents are in general very well able to clothe their children.

Would not occasional clothing, by way of reward, have a better effect than regular clothing at certain periods?—I conceive so, because it would be unexpected and conditional

Might not a smaller number in parochial schools be regularly clothed, and children taken, either in rotation or according to their behaviour, into that number?— Certainly, I think it would be preferable to giving clothes indiscriminately to the good and the bad.

Have occasional rewards a good effect in stimulating children to exertion?—A very good effect.

Have you ever witnessed any of those effects, in the schools to which you belong? —Yes; I have known of children excited to uncommon exertion and assiduity.

Do not the poor frequently claim regular allowances as a right, rather than receive them as a boon?—Very frequently so.

Are they not more grateful for occasional gifts than regular bounty?—Certainly.

Have you ever observed that children in Sunday schools improved in their dress and appearance, within a short time after their admission?—Yes, exceedingly so; their habits of decency and order vastly improve; they become clean in their persons and respectful in their behaviour, and, from being dirty, ill-behaved children, become decent and creditable.

What is the cause of this?—When they see other children better clothed than themselves, they apply to their parents for clothes, and generally succeed and get better clothes.

Do you imagine this induces parents to be more industrious and frugal?—Certainly; they are very desirous for the creditable appearance of their children, and they often deny themselves many gratifications to procure clothing for them.

If this occurs with the parents of Sunday-school children, might not the parents of children in day-schools be induced to adopt the same frugality and industry and care of their children?—I can see no difference, except that the parents of Sunday-school children are generally more necessitous than those of charity-school children, because they want their labour in the week.

Is it the practice in charity schools, where they do not give regular clothing, for benevolent individuals frequently to make presents of clothing to the children?— Yes, it is very frequently the case when any children are observed by benevolent

persons

persons to be in a very destitute situation, to give clothing to the most ragged, which excites their gratitude to their superiors.

Is it not desirable to excite a more general disposition to instruct the children of the poor throughout the parishes in the Metropolis?—Certainly; I conceive all parish schools would be more useful, if the housekeepers and inhabitants properly looked after them, and felt an interest in their prosperity; it would be desirable if masters, when they wanted servants, would see that they were well educated, and this would induce parents to pay more attention to the education of their children.

If an annual examination of the children in parochial schools were to take place, might not this excite an additional interest in the parish?—Certainly so, if it were properly conducted; but I think girls on those occasions should not be brought too forward, as modesty is the ornament of the female character.

Do you think the object of parochial schools might be promoted by an annual meeting?—It would excite the benevolent regard of the inhabitants, and increase the interest felt for the prosperity of the school.

Would this annual examination stimulate the master to prepare the children?—Very much so, and would induce the children to strive to get forward.

Would the school rooms be large enough to admit the parents, the subscribers, and the children?—I think not in general; commodious school rooms are wanted very much, all over the Metropolis.

Then how could they be accommodated?—I should think the parish church would be a very suitable place in general.

What has been your plan of annual examination?—The children are generally informed on what subjects they will be examined, and the teachers prepare them accordingly.

In what way are they examined?—They are generally called up, and they repeat chapters or psalms from the Scriptures, and hymns and poetry, which they have committed to memory; and sometimes are asked plain questions from the Scriptures.

Do the moral sentiments conveyed by the pieces committed to memory, in your opinion, produce right principles in the minds of children?—Yes, they very frequently recur to their minds, and when they are exposed to temptation, guard them against the evil.

Are children fond of poetic pieces?—Very much so indeed; and they are very useful, because they so soon come to their minds; we also aim to imbue their minds with the Scriptures as much as we possibly can.

If any general plan of education for the poor throughout London could be adopted in the respective parishes, do you imagine it would produce a change for the better in the character of the poor?—Very much so indeed.

Have you observed this in the schools to which you belong?—Yes, I have frequently observed the children very much improved in their moral character as well as in their condition.

Have you had much intercourse with their parents?—I very frequently visit the parents of the Sunday-school children at their own habitations; they are very grateful for the instruction their children receive, and for the visits of the teachers, from which they often likewise derive many benefits.

Do you think parish officers might more strongly recommend the education of poor children to their parents who apply for relief?—Yes, if they did it without any partiality or preference of religious sect or party, leaving it to the parents to choose which they thought preferable.

Would not poor children be greatly benefited by being kept out of the streets, and sent to day-schools?—Exceedingly so; the morals of children derive a vast deal of harm from their playing with idle and depraved children in the streets, and especially upon a Sunday, when children very often herd together, and initiate each other into the commission of crimes, it being a day of leisure.

Do you think the employment of children in schools produces habits of industry?—Very much so.

Has it the effect of fitting them for useful employments?—I have known many cases of great improvement in that respect. I happened to meet two or three children, coming here this morning; one was the first child admitted into the Sunday school with which I am connected; she made a courtesy: I have learned she lives in a creditable situation, as housemaid in a respectable family in the City: and I met one or two others, who are likewise filling creditable situations with their fathers.

Would children be more likely to meet with employment, in your opinion, if they were better educated?—It is one of the first inquiries we make, when we want
                                                                                    servants,

servants in trade, how they have been educated ; and they are very frequently incapacitated from filling many situations, because they have not been taught when young.

Do you know whether shopkeepers and wholesale houses, in the City, prefer youths from the country, to those born and educated in London?—Very frequently so.

Do they prefer youths in the various capacities of porters, warehousemen, and clerks, and in short, in all the departments of trade?—In most cases they certainly do prefer lads from the country.

Are they also preferred as domestic servants?—In general, so far as my experience extends.

For what reason are they preferred?—Because their character is better known, their morals more frequently uncontaminated ; and I think the education of those who are sent off to Town has been much better attended to than those persons born in London.

Have you any idea how many young men come up to London annually to seek for situations, both domestic and in trade?—It is impossible to speak with any accuracy ; but I have heard many intelligent men, who have had long experience on the subject, calculate that nearly 10,000 come up annually.

Including footmen, porters, and clerks?—All descriptions of servants.

Are you acquainted with any of the principals of the trading and commercial houses of the City of London?—Yes, many of them.

Do you know whether they originally came from the country, or were born in London?—I should think the majority came from the country.

Is it not a remarkable fact, and well known, that the large proportion of the housekeepers in the City of London came from the country?—Yes, I conceive so.

And generally without property?—Most of them, I think.

They have generally risen by their own merit?—Yes, from clerks, or even many of them from inferior situations ; they have risen from their attention to business, and good education. Several of our Lord Mayors have risen from clerks situations.

Have they chiefly risen by their own merit, and having had the advantages of a useful education?—Yes, I conceive so, and a steadiness and perseverance in their conduct.

If parochial schools in London were better attended to, might not masters and mistresses be more disposed to receive servants from among the children brought up in those schools?—Yes, if the procuring of suitable situations for the children when they left the school were made an object of importance by the governors of the school. I fear it is too often neglected : the children are left entirely to themselves when they leave parochial schools. In Sunday schools we often obtain situations for the children, either in our own businesses or among our acquaintance.

Do the teachers generally feel an interest for the welfare of the children under their care?—When we see a steady attentive boy, we generally recommend him to some situation where he is likely to be well attended to and prosper. Many of them have succeeded remarkably well, and have become teachers themselves; and many of them, from the lowest state of society, have become respectable characters, and fill useful situations, if not very high ones.

Do you think it of importance to convey moral instruction while communicating knowledge to the children?—Yes, it is of the highest importance ; for knowledge, unaccompanied by virtue, very frequently only capacitates for increasing mischief in society.

Is there much difference between the moral character of the Scotch and Irish?—No one, who has been accustomed to visit them at their own habitations, can have failed to observe a marked and decided distinction.

Whence does this distinction arise?—The Scotch are constantly taught, when young, to read their Bibles, and accustomed to moral and religious instruction.

From your knowledge of the trading world, and of the children of the poor, do you think a more extensive plan of education would be a public benefit?—I think it would be one of the greatest public benefits.

Would it, in your opinion, lessen public crimes?—I have no doubt of it ; for the most guilty criminal characters are commonly the most ignorant; in fact we cannot get them to stay in our schools; we have sometimes gathered them from the highways, and brought them into our schools, but we could never keep them long together.

From

Mr.
W. F. Lloyd.

From your knowledge of the benefits of education, is it your opinion that a more extended plan would greatly promote the public benefit?—I think it would exceedingly so; in Wales, owing to the general establishment of Sunday schools there, in one or two of the counties the prison-doors have been thrown open, and I attribute it to education, because nearly every individual throughout those counties attended the schools.

Are you acquainted whether maid-servants in London generally come from the country?—I know it is often the case that they are preferred from the country, unless their character can be well ascertained by a respectable and well-known person with whom they have lived before.

Are they not, in a general way, preferred to London servants?—They are in general very much preferred; they have not such connexions, and are in general more steady.

Are they not in general of a better moral character?—Decidedly so.

Does not this partly arise from having a better education?—I think so.

### Mr. *Thomas Davis*, called in, and Examined.

Mr.
Thomas Davis.

WHAT are you?—A distiller, in Old-street, Saint Luke's.

Are you acquainted with the state of the poor in that neighbourhood?—More so at the parochial school.

How long has that school been established?—In 1698.

Was there another founded in 1761, in addition to the former?—There was.

Upon what foundation is it?—Partly supported from funded property and annual subscriptions.

How was it founded?—I cannot trace the foundation of it; it began upon a small principle; and by the savings of the annual income, the charity has now 6,300 *l.* in the three per cent. consols.

What is the annual income of the society?—The yearly income, on the average of the last three years, is 752 *l.* per annum.

What have been the yearly expenses, for the same period?—As near 700 *l.* as possible.

How many children are educated there?—100 boys and 85 girls now; within these four years, there have been 65 children added to the number.

How many masters have you?—Only one.

Do you teach upon the old or new plan?—Upon the old, generally.

Are the children clothed?—Yes.

Are they boarded?—No.

Nor lodged?—No.

What is the schoolmaster's salary?—100 guineas a-year, and some perquisites.

A house?--Yes; and two chaldron and a half of coals. The girls, 85 in number, one guinea per annum for the instruction of each child.

To whom is that paid?—To the mistress.

Has the mistress any other perquisite?—She has; the mistress has been many years in the employ of the institution, and she has the privilege of letting children work for the persons who want needlework and such kind of things done; the present conductors of the charity very much object to that part of her emolument, but, being so old a servant of the institution, they find it difficult to get over it.

What is the yearly expense of clothing?—As near as possible 3 *l.* 18 *s.* per child, both boys and girls.

Is there any thing in the institution which renders it necessary to clothe as well as educate?—I should think so.

Upon what is that opinion founded?—My opinion is, that the parents of children seek as much for the clothing as they do for education.

Have any of the legacies which have been left to the establishment had any condition annexed to them, of clothing the children?—I should think so; I cannot answer positively.

Who are the trustees of the charity?—They are chosen by the general body of subscribers.

Do you apprehend that any proposition made to them for increasing the number of children educated, and diminishing the number clothed, so as to teach a larger number, and clothe a few by way of reward to those who conducted themselves well, would be favourably received by the trustees?—I should think not.

What objection are they likely to make to that proposition?—Strictly adhering to the old principles of the establishment.

Is

Is there any thing in those principles which is compulsory on the trustees?—That is a question I cannot answer correctly.

Have the trustees ever made any alteration in the management of the charity?—Within these four years there have been alterations made.

What are they?—Visiting committees, who take it in turn to inspect the schools weekly.

Have any alterations been made in the number of children educated?—Within these four years, we have regularly added fifteen each year to the former number.

Then there is no particular number which you are bound to educate?—No.

And consequently, nothing to prevent you extending the education, and diminishing the number clothed?—We clothe all.

When you added fifteen each year to the number, was there any thing to prevent you from adding a greater number to be educated, and not clothed?—The school would not admit a larger number.

But you have added altogether sixty-five?—Yes.

Might you not, the first year, have taken those whole sixty-five in?—We could not, because our funds would not admit of us maintaining them.

But suppose you had not clothed, but only educated sixty-five, might you not have done so for a smaller sum than the fifteen were clothed and educated for?—Certainly, without clothing them, we might have extended the education a considerable deal further.

Does it not then appear that you might the first year have taken in the whole sixty-five to educate, at a less cost than you took in fifteen, who were both clothed and educated?—We certainly might have admitted sixty-five, had we not clothed them.

Of what classes are the children, generally?—The children of labouring manufacturers, recommended by subscribers, generally very poor.

Have you accommodation for any more children than you now teach?—Not among the boys.

Among the girls?—With some little alterations that are now going on, it is the intention of the committee of the managers to add fifteen more to their number, after their next anniversary, so as to make up the number of 200 children, 100 of each sex.

Do the premises belong to yourselves?—They do, the ground given, and the place built upon it.

Have you ground upon which to build another school?—We have not; we threw out a wing to the boy's school, so as to admit of our taking in the forty-five which we have added to their number; and we are about making the same improvement in the girls department.

Must the children be of the Church of England?—They must go to church; we do not object to a child coming from a parent who is not of the church, but the child must go to church.

Have you seen a Report by the Schoolmaster of Newgate, respecting your school?—I have.

Have you any thing to say touching that statement?—On receiving that Report, I considered it my duty as treasurer, to go to Newgate, and to make the best inquiry I was able, as to the materials upon which the Report was founded. The keeper of Newgate called the master, Mr. Godinge; and I had a conversation with him, how he came to suffer such a report to go abroad, that in the parochial school of St. Luke's we had five hundred thieves; he informed me, that the only foundation he had for so framing the Report, was from the information he had obtained from a boy, or young man there, of the name of Filby White, who was three or four years prior to that educated in the parochial school. I endeavoured to obtain from him, whether he could furnish me with any further specific cases; he informed me, no; and the only reason that he had for making such an assertion, was from the information furnished by this Filby White, sentenced for seven years transportation. I went to Newgate a second time; I could gain no further information from Godinge than I obtained the first time. His Report appeared to be exceedingly unfounded, for he could not, on examining the reports of the convicted persons, find one other person who had been educated in the school, but this Filby White. I was fearful that such report might have injured the interest of the charity very much, for in St. Luke's parish, independent of the parochial school, a vast number of children are educated by charitable persons, to the amount of 1227 children, at different schools and charities. We have a gift called Worrel's

Charity,

*Mr.*
*Thomas Davis.*

Charity, which is an endowment of forty children; Fisher's Charity, to clothe and educate twenty; I am treasurer of that also; and there are children educated in the workhouse to the number, I believe, of about forty; there is another charity called Finsbury school, which is the lordship part of the parish, educating about fifty-two boys and girls; the Lancasterian school in the City Road, for five hundred boys; Wallbrook school, for fifty boys and thirty girls; the Orphan working school, ninety children; the Catholic school, 160 boys and sixty girls; making a total of 1227 children. I have no doubt but what there are a great many bad disposed children out of so great a number; but at the same time I found myself hurt, as treasurer, that all the odium of so many children should be placed to the discredit of 185 poor children; the master, who is of fifteen years standing, never knew but one child being discarded the school for theft; in these last four years, we have only discarded eight children for non-compliance with the rules and orders; and on the first day of February 1816 we discharged a boy, of the name of John Payne, for theft; those are the only instances that ever I knew, since I have had the conducting of the school, or been at the head of the charity. In Worrel's charity, the children are obligated to go to church; the children of Saint Luke's parochial school are obliged to go to church, likewise; the workhouse children go to church; Finsbury school children go to church; the Lancasterian children, of course go where their parents wish to take them; the Wallbrook school children go to church; the Orphan school are Protestant Dissenters; and the Catholic school go to their own places of worship.

In addition to the sources of income formerly specified, namely, money in the funds, and annual subscriptions, what other means have you to make up the income above stated by you?—Three charity sermons, from which we generally average about 100*l.* per annum; the next source of income is not always to be depended upon, because it a vast deal depends upon the exertions of the steward on the day of the anniversary dinner; but we have these last three years raised 150*l.* from that resource: the various subscriptions amount to above 313*l.*; gifts and subscriptions amounting in the whole to about 715*l.* per annum.

The Rev. *William Johnson*, called in, and Examined.

*Rev.*
*William Johnson.*

YOU are master, chaplain, and accountant, of the Central National school, situated in Baldwin's-gardens?—I am.

How long have you been so?—Four years last March.

How many children are educated there?—About 860 boys and girls.

How many boys and how many girls?—Five hundred and sixty boys and three hundred girls.

For what number have you accommodation?—Not much more than 900; it was intended, in the first instance, to contain 1000. The boys school is complete in number; the girls school might contain 100 more, but the defect of the girls is made up partly by a class of masters and mistresses, who attend for training, exclusive of the others; the average number in attendance at one and the same time may be between 25 and 30, and in the course of a year we have 150 or 200 of them; they do not stay longer with us than a month or six weeks, or two months.

In what way are children admitted into the school?—Once a month, which is the first Friday in every month, we have a day of admission, when the parents attend with their children, and they are then received into the school, provided there be vacancies to receive them.

On priority of application?—Yes; or in some particular cases, where they are very distressed and urgent, they are preferred, the poorest and the most abject.

Do you receive the children of persons not members of the Church of England?—Yes, we do; there is no question ever put to any parent, respecting their religion.

What sort of religious instruction do you give the children?—The course of religious instruction is, we begin with the Lord's prayer, a short grace before and after meat, the two first collects at morning and evening service, taken from the Liturgy of the Church of England; a prayer on taking their place in church, and on leaving it; the Church catechism, and then the same broken into short questions; and the highest class of children, or classes, use Crossman's Introduction to the Christian Religion.

Do you take those children to church?—The school-room is licensed, not having any accommodation in the church; the majority of them attend divine service there,

according

according to the form of the Church of England; but on an average, 100 go to the parish church.

Rev. William Johnson.

Have you in fact, according to the best of your knowledge, many children of Dissenters in that establishment?—Many are Dissenters, and Dissenters of every description.

As nearly as you can estimate, how many may there be?—I cannot tell that exactly.

Are there twenty?—More than that; I might say one third, if not one half, are Dissenters; and at this time we have seven Jews.

Do you include in your class of Dissenters, the children of people called Methodists?—Certainly; and also those whose parents go to Spafields chapel.

You neither clothe nor feed?—No, not generally; we give clothing to some deserving teachers of classes; fifteen or twenty suits may be given in the course of a year, but to none of the children; we give it for exemplary conduct in the teachers.

Is this establishment conducted upon the principle of Dr. Bell's plan?—Exclusively.

Have you any regulation in this establishment for preserving personal cleanliness among the children?—We have, and a copy of the regulations is given to each parent on the admission of their children.

Have there been, to your knowledge, any objections stated by the parents of children sent to this institution, on account of your teaching the Catechism according to the Church of England?—Not one, excepting in one case, and that was complied with; it was one Jew boy, whom we have at this moment, and since that he complies with all the regulations of the school.

Do you consider yourself authorized to attend to the feelings or prejudices of individuals upon that subject, by not permitting them to attend to that part of your instruction?—No, I do not; all are expected and all do comply with the rules of the school.

What are the funds of this institution, and from whence do they originate?—From benefactions and voluntary subscriptions.

Can you give any account of the amount of those benefactions and subscriptions?—No, I cannot.

Have you a treasurer to that institution?—Yes.

Who is he?—Mr. Joshua Watson.

What is the yearly expense of Baldwin's-garden school?—The yearly expense nearly 180 *l*. a year. I act both as accountant and chaplain, and in the capacity of under secretary to the National schools generally, as well as schoolmaster.

What is your salary altogether?—One hundred and fifty pounds a year.

How much of that as schoolmaster?—I should think about 80 *l*. or 100 *l*.; but it is not kept separate.

What is the yearly expense of slates, books, &c. as nearly as you can tell?—The books, as far as I can judge, about 20 *l*. a year; slates and pencils, 10 *l*. or 12 *l*. This calculation I take to be considerably over the mark; for a complete set of our elementary books cost only sixpence, and the same set of books, on an average, will serve three children in succession, before the books are worn out. Each slate costs three-halfpence; the pencils, two-pence; pens and ink, two-pence halfpenny; making eight-pence for each child. We do not use paper more than once a week, at present.

How long has this institution been established?—Four years in June, since it was opened.

You have stated, that you had Jews under your care, and many Dissenters; have you found any indisposition among the parents of children to send them to this school, in consequence of their religious persuasion?—Not one instance, but rather the reverse.

Are there, to your knowledge, many schools, on the Lancasterian or other plan, in that neighbourhood?—There were two on the Lancasterian plan, one in Holborn, which is broken up, on some account, and another in Eagle-street.

Does that school still continue?—I believe it does.

Are you at all acquainted with the number of children there?—No, I am not; but I believe about one hundred.

What number of young persons qualified as teachers have been sent annually, since the commencement of this institution, into the country, or other parts of London?—On the average, about fifty male and thirty female, making eighty in the whole. In addition to that, we have received from the country to a still larger amount.

Explain

Explain the different descriptions of persons whom you receive?—The Society have on the list always ten, who receive from the institution an allowance, while they are training, of one guinea per week, in order that they may be ready, when application is made for such from the country, to act either as permanent or temporary masters. There may be, in addition to that ten, as many candidates for the situations, and they are appointed to this pay-list, as we call it, according to exemplary conduct or seniority, as candidates. The other description of masters and mistresses have been previously appointed by the local committees in the country, and sent up merely to receive instruction.

Have you any copy of the instructions given to those masters and mistresses sent from your institution, for the regulation of their conduct with regard to education?—Not any; that generally is regulated by their own committees to which they belong; but with regard to the mode of instruction they are to pursue, they have a copy of Dr. Bell's instructions for conducting schools, but purchased at their own expense.

Are those male and female teachers uniformly members of the Church of England?—I believe so; we have had some exceptions.

Do you, in any instance, send teachers to any body of Dissenters?—No, I believe not.

But they are exclusively sent to members of the Established Church?—Yes, I believe so.

Who is the President of this Institution?—His Grace the Archbishop of Canterbury.

At the commencement of the school, is any part of Divine Service performed by you?—By one of the boys.

What is read?—The two Collects of the morning service, the Lord's Prayer, and the Grace of our Lord.

Any thing at the breaking up of the school?—The Collects of the evening service only, and in addition to that, one verse from the Evening Hymn is sung, or the Doxology.

Mr. *John Clement*, a Trustee of Raines's School, and Mr. *John Verrall*, Master of the said School, called in, and Examined.

WHEN and by whom was that school founded?—By Mr. Raines, in the year 1719, for educating 50 boys and 50 girls in the principles and duties of the Christian religion as were taught by the Church of England.

Did he endow it?—He did.

How did he endow it?—With freehold and leasehold estates, and monies in the public funds.

What is the yearly income of the charity?—The average income is something above 1000 *l.* a year, and the expenses between 900 *l.* and 1000 *l.*

What proportion of the income arises from subscription and charity sermons?—About 190 *l.* a year, and about 62 *l.* from the needlework; the remainder is fixed income.

How many children are educated?—The establishment is for 50 boys and 50 girls.

Is it full?—There are now that number.

Are they clothed?—Yes.

Are they fed?—No. In 1776, an hospital was added by Mr. Raines to the two schools, for 40 of the most deserving girls selected from the old school.

Are they maintained at this hospital?—Entirely.

What do they do in that hospital?—Learn needlework, and fitted out for service.

How long are they to remain there?—The maidens educated in the hospital remain there four years, and then are put out to service; and on attaining the age of twenty-two, continuing members of the church of England, and producing testimonials of their good behaviour, six of them are entitled to draw lots for a marriage portion of 100 *l.*

What proportion of the expenditure belongs to the hospital, and what to the schools?—Under 500 *l.* a year for the hospital, and the rest for the schools.

What is the schoolmaster's salary?—Fifty pounds, a house, and coals.

Any

Any other perquisite?—A number of boys, in addition, what we call day boys, whom he is allowed to take.

What is the matron's salary?—Thirty pounds a year.

Is there any assistant master?—Yes, but the master pays him; there is a master to the hospital also.

How are the trustees chosen?—The number of trustees is 47, filled in, when they are reduced to 25, by themselves, under Mr. Raines's will and the Act of Parliament incorporating the charity.

How many years are the boys at school?—They are taken in between eight and nine, and between nine and ten, and continue till they are fourteen, and then put out apprentice, with 3 *l.* premium.

What are they taught?—Reading, writing and arithmetic.

Are the trustees bound to clothe as well as to educate?—They are by Mr. Raines's will and the Act of Parliament. The funds being inadequate, the trustees have been obliged to reduce nearly one half of the number of children in the hospital; the original number was 40.

Do you admit children of any religious principle, or those of the Established Church only?—Only those of the Established Church.

Is that by his will?—It is.

Are there any other salaries in the establishment, besides those you have mentioned?—I know of none.

## Mr. *Edward Wentworth*, called in, and Examined.

ARE you master of a Sunday school?—I superintend one gratuitously, with 60 teachers, who also give their labours gratuitously.

How many children do you educate?—From 850 to 1000.

Of all religious persuasions?—Yes.

How long have you been so occupied?—Nearly fourteen years.

How long does a child of ordinary capacity take to learn to read?—About three years.

Do you observe any improvement in the children after they come to the school, in their manners or their morals?—Particularly so; I do not know of any institution better calculated to improve their morals.

Do you adopt the new method of instruction?—It is not adapted for Sunday school instruction.

How so?—As it precludes a number of respectable persons from being teachers, which is a great obstruction to the improvement of the children. Sunday school instruction is very much wanted in the parish of Bethnal-green; our school is not sufficient to hold half the number of children that would apply. The Lancasterian institution is not half filled, because the children in that parish are employed at a very early age in the silk manufacturing business, as early as the age of five or six years, and the funds of that institution are inadequate to its support.

## Mr. *David Goff*, called in, and Examined.

HAVE you been engaged in the conduct of the school to which the last Witness has spoken?—I have.

How long?—About eight years.

Do you agree with the last Witness?—I do.

In all respects?—Yes.

## The Reverend *Charles Champnes*, called in, and Examined.

WHAT are you?—A clergyman, and master of the Coburne school, situated in the parish of Saint Mary Stratford-le-Bow Middlesex.

How long have you been so employed?—Two years last March, at which time the school was opened; it was not a school until then.

From what do the funds arise?—A bequest of Prisca Coburne, who died in the year 1701.

427.

Who

Who are the trustees?—The trustees are in number nine, five clergymen and four officers of the parish.

How are the vacancies filled up?—By the appointment of the clergy to the livings.

How many boys and girls?—At present 100 boys and 50 girls.

Are they clothed and fed?—No; 25 boys and as many girls have shoes and stockings twice a-year.

What is the nature of their instruction?—They are instructed precisely on the plan of Dr. Bell; and I believe exactly similar to the system used and pursued at Baldwin's-gardens.

Do you take in children of all religious persuasions?—Certainly.

There is no exclusion by the will of Mrs. Coburne?—No, there is not, except that the children, I believe, are obliged to attend church; we do not enquire what are the religious tenets they profess, but they must attend the church while in the school.

The religious instruction you give is conformable to the tenets of the Church of England?—Yes; and we learn them the Catechism; in fact, precisely as they do at Baldwin's-gardens.

What is the annual income of the charity?—It is now about 300 *l.* per annum.

From what does that arise?—From land situated chiefly in the parish of Bow, and some in Essex, from freehold and copyhold property.

What is the salary of the master?—One hundred pounds per annum.

The mistress?—Sixty pounds.

Any assistants?—At present the funds are inadequate to employ the assistants who ought to be employed; but as the leases fall in, the rent will be advanced; and it is the intention of the trustees, when their funds will admit, to allow the master and mistress an assistant each.

What is the mode of receiving children into this charity?—It is in the will specifically stated, that there shall be five-and-twenty children, of either sex, educated, inhabitants of Bow parish; but we have enlarged, in consequence of an application to Parliament, the number of children.

Are they selected by the trustees, or by any one of them; or how otherwise?— An application is made for admission, and if the trustees have not been particular, I have admitted all resident within the parish of Bow.

At what age do you admit them?—Seven is the age we lay down, but I sometimes admit them earlier.

How long do they continue there?—Till either their education is completed, or their parents chuse to withdraw them from the school.

There is no precise period fixed by the founder?—No, none; generally at fourteen they are supposed to leave, because we apprentice them; we apprentice a particular fifty, which we designate the upper scholars; we give a small fee with them.

Was the number to be educated limited by will?—Yes, limited to 50.

Have you since got an Act of Parliament to increase that number?—Yes, we have.

What other expenses are there?—The expense of 100 pair of shoes and stockings, those are given at the option of the trustees; nothing is mentioned in the will but the apprenticing the children, and the fee.

Is there any other article of expense, besides those you have named?—Mops and brooms, and things of that sort, and six pounds per annum for a person to take care of the boys to and from church, and whilst at church.

Is the management of the estate in the hands of the trustees alone?—Yes, namely, five clergy and four parish officers.

How are the children admitted?—They apply to me.

Then in point of fact does not the power of receiving the children remain with yourself?—I have power to receive; and since I have been master I believe I have never refused one; the will states, that we shall receive Bow children, but as our school will contain considerably more than we have, I have never or seldom objected to take the children from another parish.

Have

Have any children, to your knowledge, been admitted by the authority of any other person besides yourself?—The trustees.

They have directed you to receive children in some cases?—They have; I remember a case where I was desired to admit a child of another parish.

Who are the trustees?—The rector of Whitechapel, the rector of Bow, the rector of Stepney, the rector of Bromley, and the rector of Poplar, the two churchwardens and two overseers of Bow parish, for the time being.

From whom do you receive your salary?—I receive my salary by means of a check drawn upon a banker, which must be signed by either the rector of Whitechapel or the rector of Stepney, and there is also, in addition to that, the signature of one of the officers.

Does it consist with your knowledge, that there are children of all religious persuasions in the school?—Yes.

Can you state correctly the number of those who profess a different religion to that of the Established Church?—I should think about a quarter of the children are Dissenters, those who are not members of the Church of England.

Have you any Roman Catholics?—I am not aware of it, or Jews either.

Have you found any difficulty in taking those children to church; any reluctance?—Not the least, in no case; and even those parents that I knew were Dissenters, were very willing that their children should go to church, because upon admission, I tell them, and they afterwards receive a paper to the same effect, that they must attend school at particular hours, come clean, and that they must attend church twice on a Sunday.

The Committee are to understand, then, that it is an indispensable part of your plan that the children cannot be admitted unless they consent to go to church?—We tell them they are to go to church if they come to school, and I know of no instance in which they have not complied with that direction; neither am I aware that any child has been withheld from school in consequence of the necessity of their attending church.

But it is a regulation of this charity, that all the children should be taken to church twice on a sabbath-day?—Yes, it is, where a gallery has been built for their reception.

*Veneris, 31° die Maii*, 1816.

HENRY BROUGHAM, Esq. in The Chair.

---

The Reverend *George Gaskin*, D.D. called in, and Examined.

*The Rev.
George Gaskin,
D.D.*

ARE you Secretary to the Society in Bartlett's-buildings for promoting Christian Knowledge?—Yes; and the Society has always had for one of its leading objects the assistance of parochial schools in connexion with the Church of England, and that from the year 1698, which is the date of our foundation.

In what way do you render assistance to parochial schools?—By assisting them with books at about half the prime cost, that is one of the modes; all the books that are used in the parochial schools of London, and not only in London, but all over England, where they apply for them, they have them on the terms of the society, which is about half prime cost.

In order to render assistance to any school, do you require they should comply with any other terms than being merely connected with the Church of England?—No.

Whence do your funds arise?—Partly from voluntary contributions, and partly from funded property.

What is the amount of your annual income?—Our annual income is to be considered in different points of view, it arises partly from the produce of the funded property, partly from the annual subscriptions of the members, partly from casual donations, and partly from the payments that are made for books.

What should you say, one year with another, was about your expenditure?—Last year our expenditure was little less than 40,000 *l.* and our income was not so much; our expenditure exceeded our income. I have not a very accurate statement of it present, but upon consideration I rather think the income was about 40,000 *l.* and the expenditure was nearer 50,000 *l.*

Are the parochial schools in London supplied by you?—They are, on the terms of the society, and throughout England likewise.

Will you be pleased to furnish the Committee with a list of the schools within the Metropolis supplied by you, and naming, if you can, the master and the treasurer of each?—I am apprehensive there may be schools furnished by us in the Metropolis, a precise detail of which we cannot give, but all the established schools we annually print a little account of.

---

The Reverend *James Stewart*, called in, and Examined.

*The Rev.
James Stewart.*

YOU have heard the examination of the last Witness?—I have.

Have you any thing to add to those particulars he has stated?—He is secretary, and of course much better acquainted with the society than I am; I am only a member, attending sometimes their meetings, and have nothing to add to what Dr. Gaskin has stated.

Are you acquainted with the establishment at Percy Chapel?—I am both the proprietor of it, and the minister of it.

When was that established?—In November 1812, or the beginning of 1813.

Upon what plan?—It is in some measure a plan of my own. When I came to Percy Chapel, which is a chapel in the parish of St. Pancras, and is connected with the parish church, and is private property; when I bought that chapel, I found that there was no place in the parish, in the Established Church, where the poor could attend for divine worship, or where the children were much attended to; the only society for educating the poor was a female parochial school, which had at that time forty children; and I went round to some of the poor people in the neighbourhood, and told them it was my wish to have a Sunday school for teaching children, and that it would begin on the next Sunday, and there were 120 children applied for admission; in consequence of this, I then drew up a plan for their regular instruction; they are taught by ladies and gentlemen, who come to the chapel, and are divided into small classes of from nine to fourteen each: each lady and gentleman instructs them gratuitously.

How

The Rev.
James Stewart.

How many are taught altogether?—There are 220.

Every Sunday?—Yes. And then there is besides that, a school which was set on foot almost immediately after by some ladies, a day-school of industry, where there are seventy girls taught.

What are the funds of the first of these establishments?—It is supported by voluntary contributions.

What is the yearly amount?—The expense is very small, something about 80 *l.* a year; the expenses are, that of books, and the remuneration to the persons who keep the children in order during divine service; but there is no expense for teachers, they are all taught by ladies and gentlemen, and the school is held in the aisles of the chapel, and part in the gallery, which was built for their accommodation.

Is there any other day for instruction?—Not in the first mentioned school.

Are they taught any thing but reading?—No.

How long have you found that a Sunday school takes to instruct a child of ordinary capacity in reading?—It varies; there are some of them have been taught in three months; but our object is not so much to teach them to read, as it is to give them religious instruction; they are taught to read, and some of the classes are taught upon Dr. Bell's plan; we do not wish so much to have those children who cannot read, because there are more applications, or at least fully as many, for religious instruction, as there is room for, of those who can read.

What are the ages?—From seven to fourteen.

How long may the average be, of those who cannot read, before they are taught to read?—I think in six months, generally; they do not read in the Bible in general; there is a regular course in which the classes go forward, and it would be two years before they got into the Bible class, but that arises from other circumstances.

You have no doubt that instances have occurred, in which you have taken in children who could not read at all?—Yes.

Can you give any idea of what the average time is before a child can read tolerably well?—I can scarcely say, because there are other circumstances which prevent their being in the Bible class; they are not moved into that class till they have learned the Church Catechism, and so many of Dr. Watts's hymns, and so many chapters in the Bible.

Independent of the Bible class, how long does it take, generally speaking, before a child, knowing nothing of his letters, can learn to read easily?—I should think they would learn in nine months; we have had several of them who have not been in the Bible class.

Without any intermediate instruction between Sunday and Sunday?—Only what they give themselves.

But suppose a child has no intermediate instruction between Sunday and Sunday, in what time do you think he would be able to read; in nine months?—No, I do not think he would.

In short, you have no means of forming an accurate estimate upon the subject?—No; our object is to bring them on as fast as we can, and we give them small books to take home to read in the course of the week.

Are you not of opinion that it requires eighteen months or two years to teach a child to read, who has only instruction afforded him on a Sunday?—A child, if he will read during the week any book, and take the opportunities that may be afforded him, with the instruction that may be given on a Sunday, will learn to read in a much shorter time. I have no means of ascertaining how long it would take, supposing a child was only to have a book just on a Sunday, and then to have the book shut and not opened again till the following Sunday morning.

Are you not of opinion that it would require eighteen months or two years to teach a child to read a chapter in the Bible?—I think it might.

From what you know of the day-school, how long do the children there take to learn to read?—There are other circumstances in the day-school which prevent them being put into the Bible class.

How long does a child in the day-school, of ordinary capacity, take to learn to read?—About eight months; we have had some instances of their learning much quicker, but I should think that that was the average time.

*Richard*

*Richard Corp,*
*Esq.*

*Richard Corp,* Esq. again called in, and further Examined.

HAVE you brought the account of the admission of children into the Hospital ?—The account of certain children, to which the Committee alluded to, I have ; here are seven accounts of the admission of the children who have been complained of as improper objects of charity.   [They were delivered in.]

[The following was read :]

9.                                                                    " 23d March 1792.

" To the Right Honourable, Right Worshipful, and Worshipful the
Governors of Christ's Hospital, London.

" The humble Petition of Thomas Penn, of the parish of Saint Nicholas,
in Rochester, Kent, Ironmonger,

" Humbly Sheweth,

Exam^d Reg. C.

" That the Petitioner has a wife and five children to provide for, and he finds it difficult to maintain and educate so large a family without assistance ; therefore he humbly beseeches your Worships, in your usual pity and charity to distressed men, poor widows, and fatherless children, to grant the admission of one of his said children into Christ's Hospital, named Thomas Ford Penn, of the age of nine years and upwards, there to be educated and brought up among other poor children.
    Born 18 April,⎱ 1783."
    Bapt^d 18 May,⎰

" We, the minister, churchwardens, and others of the parish of Saint Nicholas, in Rochester, Kent, whose names are hereunto subbscribed, Do certify, that Thomas Penn, father of the said Thomas Ford Penn, is a freeman of the City of London and company of patten-makers, and that the said child is at present of the age of nine years and upwards, having been born in the month of April 1783, and is no foundling, nor maintained at the parish charge ; and that we know of no probable means for the education of the said child, unless the said Governors of Christ's Hospital should admit him into the said hospital, which if they shall be pleased to do, we, together with the father of the said child, do fully consent and agree to leave the said child to the disposal of the Governors of the said hospital, to bind him an apprentice to such trade or calling, whether for land or sea employments, as they shall judge the said child most fit and proper for ; and we, together with the father of the said child, do promise and oblige ourselves not only to ratify and confirm the same (in case the Governors of the said hospital shall please to dispose of the said child) but also we, the minister and churchwardens aforesaid, for ourselves and our successors, promise and oblige ourselves to discharge the said hospital of the said child at the age of fifteen years, or at any time before or after the said age, whensoever the said hospital shall require the same of us.   Witness our hands, this              day of March one 'housand seven hundred and ninety-three.

Reg. fo. 189.

| | |
|---|---|
| " Adm. Comm.  13⎱ March 1793.<br>     Clothed  14⎰ | *Charles Allen,* - Minister.<br>*Cha^t Bond,*  ⎱<br>*James Jeater,*  ⎰ Churchwardens.<br>*E. Dyne,*  ⎱<br>*Walter Prentis,*  ⎰ Three housekeepers.<br>*Matt^w Heath,*<br>*Thomas Penn,* - The Petitioner." |
| " Rochester, Kent. | |

Exam^d M. C.

" I present Thomas Ford Penn, Free ; the child mentioned in the certificate on the other side, and believe the same to be a true certificate, the christian name and sire-name of the said child being by me inserted at full length, according to Order of Court the 20th of June 1759.   Witness my hand this 12th day of March 1793.

                                                                    *Nath^l Newnham.*"

" 13 March 1793,
            *Tho^s Ford Penn.*
" Exam^d     *W^m Long.*
            J. Roberts.

" These are to certify, That Thomas Ford Penn, son of Thomas Penn and Anne his wife, was born the eighteenth day of April, * and was baptized the eighteenth day of May, one thousand seven hundred and eighty three, as appears by the register-book of christenings belonging to the parish of St. Nicholas, Rochester, in the county of Kent, and extracted from the said register this eighth day of March 1793.
                    " Witness my hand, *Charles Allen,*⎰ Vicar, and
                                                    ⎱ Register Keeper."

" * If the time of the child's birth does not appear in the register, this line may be obliterated."

" Kent.   Rochester, Saint Nicholas.

" 1782.

" Page 32.

" N° 128.

" Thomas Penn, of this parish, a batchelor, and Ann Pluckwell, of the same parish, spinster, were married in this church by banns, this seventeenth day of June in the year one thousand seven hundred and eighty-two, by me,

*Charles Allen,* Vicar.

" This marriage was solemnized⎱ *Thomas Penn,*
        between us  - - - - -⎰ *Ann Pluckwell.*"

" In the presence of ⎰*Will. Saltonstall.*
                      ⎱*Jemima Arne.*"

" The above-written is an extract from the marriage register belonging to this parish.  Witness my hand, this eighth day of March 1793.

" *Charles Allen,* Vicar."

[The following Petitions were read :]

Of Thomas Penn, of the parish of St. Nicholas Rochester, in the county of Kent, ironmonger, dated 4th April 1794 ; Shewing, that he has a wife and six children, one of whom is under their Worships' care in the hospital, and the remaining five are under fourteen years of age, and dependent upon him for maintenance and education.  With the date of the admission of his child ; viz. 17th Sept. 1794.

Of George Young, of the parish of Edmonton in the county of Middlesex, jeweller, dated 7th April 1797 ; Shewing, that he has a wife and five children to provide for, the charge of whose maintenance and education he finds difficult to support.  With the date of the admission of his child ; viz. 10th January 1798.

Of George Young, of the parish of Edmonton in the county of Middlesex, jeweller, dated 21st March 1800 ; Shewing, that he has a wife and six children, the eldest of whom is now under their Worships' protection, and he finds the profits of his business unequal to the maintenance of so numerous a family.  With the date of the admission of his child ; viz. 11th June 1800.

Of Thomas Penn, of the parish of Saint Nicholas in Rochester, in the county of Kent, ironmonger, dated          1801 ; Shewing, that his wife died in July 1799, leaving him with a family of six children, four of whom were under fourteen years of age, and dependent upon him for support.  With the date of the admission of his child ; viz. 9th Sept. 1801.

Of John Bridges, of the parish of All Saints in Malden, in the county of Essex, merchant, dated 2d April 1802 ; Shewing, that he has a wife and eight children, six of whom are under fourteen years of age, and dependent upon him for maintenance and education.  With the date of the admission of his child ; viz. 14th July 1802.

Of the Reverend Dawson Warren, vicar of the parish of Edmonton in the county of Middlesex, dated the 20th of March 1807 ; Shewing, that he has a wife and seven children, to whom he is desirous of affording a good education, which his preferment in the church does not enable him to do without assistance.  With the date of the admission of his child ; viz. 8th July 1807.

Of the Reverend Baptist John Proby, of the parish of Saint Mary in Litchfield, clerk, in orders, dated 15th March 1808 ; Shewing, that he has a wife and four young children to provide for, and his church preferment does not exceed three hundred pounds per annum, against which there are large deductions and considerable outgoings, so that he is in circumstances of difficulty and distress. With the date of the admission of his child ; viz. 26th April 1808.

Are those papers which you have delivered in, some of those which were before the Court of Chancery, in a proceeding instituted there in 1811 ?—They are.

By whom was the proceeding in Chancery instituted respecting these cases ?— By a petition of individuals, who were understood to be a certain number of the select committee appointed by the court of common council, "To inquire and report whether the Corporation of the City of London have any and what means of obtaining inquiry into, and reforming, the presentations and admissions of children into the Hospital ; and who, in presenting such Petition, acted under the Resolution of the Court of Common Council, whereby it was referred to the same Committee to take such measures in the business as they should be advised."

Do you remember the names of any of the individuals who promoted that proceeding, and that signed that petition ?—I remember some names who signed the petition ; Mr. Waithman and Alderman Goodbehere, were two ; there were 14 persons signed.

Upon

Upon what ground did the application to the Chancellor proceed?—By stating that the governors had admitted children improper objects of a charitable institution, or to that effect.

Did it set forth the above as instances of such improper admissions?—It did.

Was it from any thing that appeared upon the face of the presentations themselves?—I believe not, because I do not think they had seen them.

What objections had been stated, in the proceedings, to those admissions?—Generally, that the parents were in better circumstances than they ought to be, to have a child maintained in a public charity.

Did those objections apply to the truth of the statements upon the face of the certificate?—I believe it was only from opinion formed and statements made of individuals, that those boys were not fit objects of that charity.

Do you mean that that opinion and those statements went to deny the statements in the certificates?—I believe, if the Committee refer to it, it will virtually deny it.

Do you recollect, for instance, any objections that were made to Thomas Ford Penn's admission?—There was no objection ever stated to his admission.

In the course of those proceedings in Chancery, were there any stated?—The objections were, like all the others, that they were generally in circumstances unfit for a charitable institution.

Were any particulars gone into with respect to Penn, in the proceedings in Chancery?—There was an affidavit in Chancery, of Charles Turner, Esquire, of Mount-hill House, near Rochester, stating that the man was in opulent circumstances, and able to maintain and educate his children without the assistance of the hospital, and giving the particulars of his income and property.

Was there any evidence given in answer to Mr. Turner's affidavit, and in support of Penn's statement in his certificate?—The boys were discharged.

Were they discharged upon this proceeding being instituted in Chancery?—They had left the school before that time.

Was there any answer made to Mr. Turner's affidavit, or any other evidence given to show that Penn was in distressed circumstances?—I believe a reference was made to the affidavit; we had only those presentations in opposition to that affidavit. I was sent down to Rochester to acquire what information I could, but could not find any person able to state in what circumstances he died.

Did you speak to the clergyman of the parish?—I inquired of many housekeepers in the street where he lived, but not of the clergyman.

Did you inquire of the housekeepers who lived next door to him?—I believe I inquired of the person who succeeded to his trade in the very house; and all that I could collect was, that he was a very penurious man, and close as to the situation of his property.

But you did not inquire of the two people who lived next door to him?—I think I did; also of a gentleman who had many years resided there, a tenant of the Hospital's, in the hope of his being able to give me information, but he could not.

How long after Mr. Penn's death did you go to Rochester?—When the bill was filed in 1811.

When did he die?—In 1808.

Did the governors put in an answer to the before-mentioned affidavit?—I believe they did.

Are you aware of what answer they made to this complaint respecting Penn?—I have not a copy of the bill and answer.

Are you aware of what evidence was produced to rebut the accusation contained in the affidavit which has been read?—There was no other opportunity that we had, but producing the presentations themselves.

What were the objections made to Young's two children?—They had left the hospital before the proceeding took place, but the affidavits in Chancery went to show that Young, the father, died worth somewhere about 5000l. subject to debts; he was known to have been a shopkeeper in no flourishing circumstances: there was an affidavit, also, of Mr. Young's brother, stating that Young's income did not in his lifetime amount to more than 300l. or thereabouts, and that his circumstances were in no degree better, but rather worse at the time of the child's admission; and that he verily believes that what he left, after paying his debts, would not afford an income of more than 200l. a year; he also states the freehold estate at 1335l. instead of 1521l. which the other affidavit made it; and that during his lifetime, he was much afflicted with the stone, which rendered him incapable of any active employment.

Was

Was there any evidence as to Bridges?—There was an affidavit of John Wyatt Lee, Esq. of Munden-hall, near Malden, stating generally that he was informed and and believed that Bridges was in opulent circumstances, without stating any particulars.

What were the objections stated to Mr. Warren's case?—Mr. Warren, I think, attended at the hearing in the Court of Chancery to answer any questions, but I believe he declined making an affidavit; there was an affidavit of John Merrington, who had been churchwarden and overseer of the poor in his parish, and had resided twenty-five years in it, stating Mr. Warren's income, from his own knowledge of the particulars of it, as amounting in the whole to 1200 l. a year.

Relate what took place, to the best of your recollection, with the assistance of the minutes, at the admission of Warren?—At his admission eleven members of the committee were present, and some conversation of considerable extent arose, because a member considered Mr. Warren had too large an income to ask for the admission of his son; it was put to the vote whether he was a fit object or not, and his admission was ordered by a small majority; then afterwards the question came before the committee of Almoners, upon the eighteenth day of March 1809, when a long letter was read from the Rev. Dawson Warren, the father, upon his case; he states at the bottom of his letter thus : " When I attended the committee, on the admission of my boy, I considered that my income, on the average of my whole residence at Edmonton, had been 710 l. per annum; on the average of the three years then expired, 850 l. If I now consider it up to last Christmas, I should call it 860 l."

That is the close of a long statement he made respecting his circumstances?—It is ; the committee thereupon resolved, that the president should be requested to submit that letter to the consideration of the general court, and to order that notice thereof should be given in the summons.

Did the general court take it up in pursuance of that notice?—They did; they met the 4th of March, pursuant to the notice in the summons, to consider the case of the boy Dawson Warren.

What proceeding then took place?—I will read the minute of the court, which is as follows : " After some debate, it was moved and seconded, that the said child should be sent home to his father; upon which an amendment was proposed, but after some further debate withdrawn; the question was then put upon the original motion, which the president considered to be carried in the affirmative; whereupon a division was demanded, and in such division, the numbers appeared to be, for the question 41, against it 45; the court was then moved to resolve, that the governors now assembled in court are of opinion that Dawson Warren, admitted on the foundation, is not a child that comes within the rules and regulations established for the admission of children to the benefits of this charity, but this court, in pronouncing this opinion, would feel themselves much concerned to act with that rigour which would prejudice or injure the child, they therefore suffer him to be continued; which motion, having been seconded, was, upon the question being put, carried in the negative." There was nothing further done at that meeting.

What further was done?—On the 28th of March 1809, I entered on the register his discharge in these words, " Dawson Warren, discharged, with consent of the president, by his father, the Minister of Edmonton, in consequence of the regret he felt upon learning that the question respecting the continuance of his son upon this foundation has produced a disunion of sentiment among the governors, likely to be prejudicial to the interests of the establishment."

How long had the boy been upon the establishment altogether?—He was clothed upon the 9th of July 1807.

When was the first notice taken of his case?—In March 1809, in consequence of a motion made in the Common Council.

Were there any further proceedings with respect to Mr. Warren?—Nothing further.

What were the proceedings with respect to Mr. Proby's case?—There were affidavits produced, and one from himself, showing the state of his circumstances, by which it appeared that he had two livings, amounting to about 400 l. a year, out of which he had to pay a curate; that he had received 3500 l. from his father, and had an expectancy, on his mother's decease, of 3000 l. more, besides being entitled to about 80 l. a year in right of his wife, together with 1000 l. of marriage portion, but that his father had left him 5 l. only by his will, and that he was himself in debt.

What other proceedings were held with respect to Mr. Proby's case, by the Hospital?—At a meeting of the committee, upon the 11th of January 1809, at which

which fourteen members were present, the Rev. Baptist John Proby, father of the boy John Carysfort Proby, admitted in April 1808, attended the committee, to answer the assertion in a pamphlet recently published, signed by Robert Waithman, respecting his income ; and it was ordered, that the committee should be summoned to consider specially of this case. The committee accordingly met the first of February 1809, seventeen governors present; it is recorded thus: "The committee having been summoned to consider the case of the boy, John Carysfort Proby, as by order of the last committee, in consequence of the public charge, that the said boy is not, from the circumstances of his father, the Rev. B. J. Proby, a proper object of admission into this hospital ; it was resolved, after very mature deliberation and investigation, that the said child is a fit and proper object for maintenance and education in this hospital."

How long did the boy remain altogether ?—He was admitted in April 1808, and discharged in July 1810, the father then writing a letter, in which he stated he found his circumstances sufficiently improved to enable him to educate his child himself.

Besides those cases brought forward in the proceeding in Chancery, have you any others, of persons who improperly or doubtfully availed themselves of the charity, which have come to your knowledge ?—I know of none, of my own knowledge.

If any complaints respecting such had been made to the governors, must they not have come to your knowledge, from your official situation ?—They must ; I received a notice from the City, mentioning other cases as being improper objects, preparatory to the above-mentioned suit ; Mr. Newman, the City solicitor, inclosed me the particulars, as under, in which the following cases, besides those already mentioned, were specified ; the two sons of Egerton Stafford, the son of Mason Wright, the son of Jonathan Hammond, the son of the Reverend M. Wild, the two sons of Dr. Markham, the son of ———— Ives of Chertsey, and the son of Thatcher.

Upon receiving this notification, what did you do ?—I laid it before the general court the day after, who ordered, after some debate, That such letter, and its inclosure, should lie upon the table ; and the clerk was directed to inform the City solicitor of this resolution ; and nothing further was done.

Did you find the papers respecting those persons last mentioned ?—I did not search for them.

Are you aware of the objections made to their admission, by the parties who served you with the above notice ?—It was a general objection, that they were improper objects, from the situation of their families.

Did the particulars upon which those objections were founded, ever come to your knowledge ?—Never.

Was any notice taken of these cases, in the proceedings in Chancery ?—I believe they were all abandoned ; but I cannot speak to it with certainty.

Do you know any thing of Mr. Egerton Stafford, whose two sons were admitted ?—No.

Were there any such boys as the sons of Dr. Markham, ever admitted into the hospital ?—Certainly not.

Were not you directed by the governors of the hospital to allow any governor to inspect and take copies of all petitions and certificates of boys that had been admitted into the hospital, which they might think proper ?—I was.

Since receiving those directions, have you ever refused any governor ?—Certainly not.

Have you found any of the names of the cases now last referred to ?—I have found four cases, of the names of Hammond, Wild, Ives, and Thatcher.

In the proceedings in Chancery, what took place after the affidavits already referred to were filed ?—After the petition was presented, the governors were obliged to appear upon it ; and in consequence of the necessity so imposed, of appearing, such proceedings as it was imperative upon them to take, were taken under the general authority vested in the committee of the hospital for the time being, to guard the interests of the house, after the subject-matter, on which the petition was grounded, had been considered at four general courts ; and they were taken by and under the direction and advice of Chancery barristers of the first eminence ; the petition came on before the Lord Chancellor, and the arguments upon it occupied the 12th, 13th, and 15th days of July 1811 ; the Lord Chancellor reserved his decision, and has not yet pronounced judgment.

Were all the proceedings on both sides finished as long ago as July 1811 ?—I have not heard from the solicitor that any thing further has transpired ; but that is not in my department.

Has

Has the Chancellor ever taken any steps since that, in the case of this charity, the parties having then severally closed their cases?—The solicitor has not informed me that any further notice has been taken of it.

Have you any doubt that nothing further has been done by the Chancellor?—I have no doubt in my mind that it rests where it did.

Richard Corp, Esq.

## Mr. *Francis Jowers*, called in, and Examined.

Mr.<br>Francis Jowers.

WHAT are you?—By trade a builder.

Do you know any thing of Mrs. Coburne's charity?—Yes, I do.

When was it founded?—One hundred and two or one hundred and three years back.

For what description of children?—For the education of 25 boys and 25 girls.

For their board as well as education?—No.

Clothing?—Education only, except shoes and stockings, which I believe is not mentioned in the will.

How is it endowed?—Through a widow of the name of Coburne, who left certain property in lands and houses, producing an income of about 303 *l.* per annum.

In what property?—In freehold land and other property, in Mile-End Road, consisting of one house and between six and seven acres of land; some freehold houses or copyhold, in the parish of Bow; a farm at Bocking; and a piece of copyhold land in Old Ford, which is in the parish of Bow also.

What are the salaries of this establishment?—The master has 100 *l.* per annum; the mistress 60 *l.*

There are 100 boys and 50 girls?—I think not.

How may are there?—To the best of my observation there may be from 80 to 90 boys, and from 30 to 40 girls.

Now?—Yes.

Then how does it happen that Mr. Champnes, the master, states the boys at 100, and the girls at 50?—That I am not prepared to answer, for I have not seen Mr. Champnes.

Are there more names on the book than actually attend?—No doubt there are; there are frequently children taken in, and frequently children leaving.

Do you mean, when you say how many children there are, to refer to the present time?—I do mean at this time; nor do I think that the master himself could ascertain the number of children that he had in reality.

Why could not he ascertain?—As many leave without giving notice.

Are you acquainted with the property from whence the revenue of this school arises?—I am.

Will you repeat its annual amount?—I do not know that I can distinctly repeat every individual one; the gross amount is 303 *l.* 10 *s.*

Are you acquainted with the value of this property at the period of the decease of Mrs. Coburne?—At the period of the decease of Mrs. Coburne the property was certainly materially less, but what the amount was I do not know.

Are you acquainted with the value of this property twenty or twenty-five years ago?—I think that the value of it was nearly where it is now, for at that time it was let upon leases; but some of those leases have since expired.

Have you any expectation of an improvement of this property at the expiration of the present leases?—We have.

To what extent?—My idea is about 300 *l.* in addition to the present revenue; it has been stated at 500 *l.*

State to the Committee, to the best of your knowledge, the mode in which the present revenue of the charity is applied?—One hundred pounds to the master, 60 *l.* to the mistress; coals may be about 25 *l.*; we have now fixed it to seven chaldron and a half; and we have given 100 pair of shoes and stockings per annum.

How much in value?—I cannot say; I should think the shoes and stockings stand us in from 25 *l.* to 30 *l.*

Are there any other expenses?—There are; there are expenses for the school books, for the use of the children, which is defrayed out of the income.

To what amount are those expenses?—I cannot say what the amount is.

Can you form any estimate?—About 20 *l.*

Any thing else?—Six pounds we pay a man to attend the children to church; 5 *l.* we allow for expenses of brooms and brushes, and various other incidental expenses.

Independent of the sundry expenses?—Yes.

427.

Any

Any thing else?—There are four sermons in the year ; each sermon there is 5 *l.* paid to the rector by the will, and 1 *l.* to the clerk; there are also 5 *l.* given to the poor four times a year, and that on certain days, on the days that the sermons are preached.

In conformity to the will?—Yes.

Any thing further?—That is the principal of our expenditure.

Has there not been, for a great many years back, an accumulation from the profits and interests of those estates ?—There has.

To what amount ?—The accumulation is between 900 *l.* and 1000 *l.*

Up to what period?—The year 1812 or 1813.

In what way was that accumulation disposed of?—Prior to our present situation we had no regular school ; it was a school-house, an old building that stood in the parish, left by Sir John Jolis ; the charity availed themselves of it, and made use of this place, it being rent-free. In consequence of the accumulation of our property, an application was made to the Chancellor, for permission to build a school upon a part of the estate left by the deceased : a grant was given, and the school was built, with school-house for the master and mistress : that school-house far exceeded in expenses what was calculated upon at the time.

To what extent ?—Fourteen hundred pounds was our calculation, and 1900 *l.* was our expense, which left us minus a considerable sum.

Do you consider that the estate is liable to that debt ?—We, as trustees, borrowed money upon our own responsibility. We applied to the Master for permission to sell part of the estate holden by Lord Henniker ; he has an estate situate at Stratford ; a very small portion of our land, not more than three quarters of an acre, is inter-mixed with his lordship's property, which he holds on lease. His lordship applied to the trustees, for the purchase of this estate. The Master, considering the bargain which we had made with Lord Henniker, subject to his approbation, a provident and good one, confirmed it, subject to the Bill now passing through Parliament : that Bill, I believe, has nearly passed the House ; it is a Bill allowing the trustees of the Coburne estate to sell certain property situated at Stratford, in the county of Essex, to Lord Henniker. The sum Lord Henniker was to pay for this land was 1900 *l.* Our intentions were, with the Master's permission, to pay off the debt which we had accumulated, and to lay out the surplus money in such freehold or other property as the Master should approve. The sum which we now receive from Lord Henniker, or did prior to this bargain, was 50 guineas per annum. My calcu-lation is this, that we shall be able to reimburse that 50 guineas per annum out of the surplus money that will be left after we have paid our debt, so as not to diminish our present income at all ; we shall still have the same income as before. I calculate further, that at the end of twelve years, a valuable plot of ground, situated upon the Bow Road, the lease of which will expire shortly, and which ground forms part of our Bill before Parliament, we shall be able to let on building leases ; the rent of which now produces us fifty pounds a year, and which I calculate will then produce from three to four hundred pounds.

In what way and by what authority are children received into the school?—We have not sufficient applicants according to the room of our school ; perhaps there has not been that strictness which there should have been ; it was arranged that they should be received or admitted by a committee, but in consequence of the frequent leaving of the children, and the committee not meeting often enough, the master has been permitted to admit the children.

Do you know at present how many children there are who attend that school ?—I have noticed the children as they have passed along, and I have noticed them in the church, and I should think from 80 to 90 boys, and from 30 to 40 girls; in stating this, I do not say there are not a greater number of names down, for the children are so frequently changing, and this may be done without the master wishing to make the number appear more than they really are. Our schools are capable of holding a much greater number, our calculation being, at the time we built them, for room enough to contain 150 of each sex in the two distinct schools. And there is one thing I would state in relation to the funds, it does appear that at about the end of three years we shall be able to educate and clothe 300 children ; but my opinion is, not more than those.

What is the reason why a greater number of children do not apply for educa-tion?—I have inquired of several of the parents, who pleaded their poverty as the cause ; as soon as their children get to be six or seven years of age, if any kind of employment, such as silk mills, chalk-cutting, or any thing else can be found, they are under the necessity of taking them from their school to assist in earning their maintenance.

In

In your opinion, does the present schoolmaster and the present schoolmistress perform respectively their duties?—I think more might be done.

### The Rev. *Daniel Mathias,* called in, and Examined.

YOU are rector of Whitechapel, and one of the trustees of Mrs. Coburne's school?—Yes, I am.

Are you in the habit of frequenting that school, and observing what passes?—I have been an active member of the committee since my residence in the parish, which is about seven or eight years; the rector of Stepney I considered as the head of the trustees.

The head rector was a very active person in this trust?—Certainly.

Are not the schoolmaster and schoolmistress paid by your draft, or by yourself in some way?—I sign the draft, after it has been previously settled and approved of by the trustees upon the spot, and then it is brought to one of the clergymen trustees, generally to me, and I sign it; and it is paid at the bankers.

Do you consider yourself, as a trustee, authorized to apply the funds of this charity to the clothing and maintenance of children, as well as to their learning?—By the powers of our new Bill it is part of our Act of Parliament so to empower us.

Has that Bill passed the Lower House?—I think it is now in the Lower House.

Are you acquainted with the number of charity schools?—There are three charity schools; there is the original foundation of a former rector, the Rev. Ralph Davenant, which was founded, I believe, somewhere about the Revolution, or ten years before.

What are the revenues of that school?—I do not know the exact particulars, but I should think the endowment is about 300*l.* a year, the subscriptions perhaps as much, and some funded property likewise.

Part of your property is leasehold and freehold estates?—It is all freehold, consisting of two estates left by the original founder.

How many children are educated in that school?—The original foundation was for forty, it was increased then to 100; at what time the increase took place, I cannot tell, but it continued at 100 till 1807, when, by the savings and further exertions in the parish, the numbers were increased to 200, where they now are.

Do you feed and clothe those children?—Clothe and educate them.

Do you confine the scholars of this school to children whose parents are members of the Church of England?—By the founder's will they must be born in the parish, and baptized in the parish, and bring a certificate of their baptism from the parish-register: the parishioners are preferred; those that have a settlement are preferred; but when there is not enough of them, then the non-parishioners.

Can you state any particulars of any other school?—The Gower's-walk school is the concern of a private individual, carried on at his own individual expense, and now nearly supporting itself by the work conducted in that school, which is printing; and with very little aid, I believe, it nearly supports itself. Mr. William Davis is the founder and conductor of it.

For how many children?—I believe 250.

For education alone?—Education, and rewards of merit, which are distributed and kept in a peculiar way; and when a good child leaves the school, he will have to receive rewards to the amount of five, six or eight pounds, perhaps.

Do they clothe at this school?—Occasionally give clothes to part of the children.

Any other school?—The great school, which was built for 1000 children; I was the first planner and promoter of it; the National school, for education alone.

Are you in the habit, in that school, of admitting any children but those of the Church of England?—Of every description, without any distinction whatever; and the rule we laid down, which was prepared by myself and submitted to the Bishop of London, who approved of it very much, was, that children of every denomination, without any inquiry whatever, should be admitted into the school.

Have you then in fact, in that school, Dissenters of various descriptions?—Dissenters of all descriptions, and even some Jews; if a Dissenter sends his child, and makes any objection to the child being taught the Catechism, he is not obliged to learn it or submit to be taught; if a Dissenter objects to his child being brought to church on the Lord's day, he is not to be obliged, but assurances are to be given to the master that the child is taken to some place of divine worship.

427.

*Sabbati*, 1° *die Junii*, 1816.

HENRY BROUGHAM, Esquire, in The Chair.

THE Chairman delivered in the following Letter; which was read:

" SIR,

" I TRANSMIT to you a Paper containing an Account of the Receipts and Payments of the Society for promoting Christian Knowledge, for one year, ending at the annual audit in April last. From that paper it will appear, that besides the sums actually paid, there still remains a very considerable sum due to the booksellers, the difference between 32,357 *l*. 7 *s*. 8 *d*. and 20,214 *l*. 5 *s*. 7 *d*. I also transmit a " General Account of the Society," printed in the year 1813, the last that was printed; and the annual Report for the year 1814, that for 1815 not being yet ready for delivery. In the former of these you will find, page 275, an account of the Charity Schools of the Metropolis; but they are only such as compose the annual assemblage in St. Paul's Cathedral. To these schools, and to all other charity schools in connexion with the church, that apply for them through the medium of Members of the Society, books are furnished on the customary terms, the Society being at about one-half of the expense. I shall be happy to furnish any other information in my power; and remain,

Sir, very respectfully Yours,

" Bartlett's Buildings, May 31, 1816.          *Geo. Gaskin.*"

" P.S.—The names of the treasurers and schoolmasters I do not know."

" Henry Brougham, Esq. M. P."

SOCIETY FOR PROMOTING CHRISTIAN KNOWLEDGE.

The RECEIPTS and PAYMENTS of the Society, between the Audit, April 20, 1815, and the Audit, April 18, 1816.

| RECEIPTS. | £. | s. | d. |
|---|---|---|---|
| Received Benefactions and Legacies to the general designs of the Society | 4,729 | 3 | 10 |
| Received Subscriptions from the Members of the Society | 8,655 | 12 | 3 |
| Received of the Members on account of packets of Books on the terms of the Society | 16,505 | 16 | 2 |
| Received Dividends of funds for the general designs | 1,846 | 5 | 10 |
| Received D° - at the Accountant General's Office | 3,003 | 7 | 6 |
| Received D° - on account of the Manks impression | 37 | 16 | 0 |
| Received D° - of £.100. in trust for a Sacrament on holydays at Bow church | 2 | 14 | 0 |
| Received D° - towards the support of a Mission and Schools in the Scilly Islands | 49 | 15 | 2 |
| Received D° - and Rent for Mr. Belke's charity | 63 | 12 | 4 |
| Received D° - in trust for Mrs. Negus's charity for the distribution of Bibles, &c. in Rotherhithe | 72 | 18 | 0 |
| Received D° - in trust for Mrs. Negus's Welsh charity | 27 | 0 | 0 |
| Return of Propert Tax on Dividends | 391 | 16 | 4 |
| Received of the Members on account of Welsh Bibles | 6 | 0 | 0 |
| Received Dividends on account of the East-India Mission | 313 | 3 | 4 |
| Received Benefactions to the East-India Mission | 579 | 5 | 0 |
| Received from the Lords of the Admiralty, through the hands of the Chaplain General | 86 | 11 | 2 |
| D° - - for balance of a former account, and for Bibles, &c. since the last Audit | 278 | 1 | 6 |
| Received Benefactions on account of the Family Bible | 15 | 0 | 0 |
| Received on account of the sale of ditto, and in advance from Members | 10,400 | 0 | 0 |
| Received by sale of £. 5,000. 3 p' cent. Cons. | 3,050 | 0 | 0 |
| Received a Special Donation from Mrs. Ann Jenkins, Wells, Somerset | 105 | 0 | 0 |
| Balance in favour of the Treasurer | 7 | 11 | 8 |
| | £.50,220 | 10 | 1 |

| PAYMENTS. | £. | s. | d. |
|---|---|---|---|
| Paid Messrs. Rivington the Balance of Account last Audit | 7,531 | 12 | 9 |
| Paid D° - in part of £. 32,357. 7 s. 8 d. for Books and packets, delivered to Members on the terms of the Society, since the last Audit * | 20,214 | 5 | 7 |
| Paid D° - on account of Bibles and other books gratuitously distributed since last audit | 1,178 | 7 | 9 |
| Paid D° - on account of Bibles, &c. distributed to the Navy, &c. since last Audit | 277 | 6 | 9 |
| Paid for Paper and Printing for the Anniversary Sermon, with the Annual Account of the Society, and for sundry Tracts and Papers gratuitously distributed | 1,645 | 14 | 6 |
| Paid toward the Expenses of the Anniversary Meeting of the Charity Children, June 16, 1815 | 50 | 0 | 0 |
| Paid for Salaries and Gratuities to the Missionaries in the East Indies | 1,097 | 10 | 1 |
| Paid for Expenses on account of the Scilly Mission | 395 | 15 | 3 |
| Paid for Packing-boxes, Postage, Stationary wares, House repairs, dispersing the Anniversary Sermon and Report, Stamps for receipts, insurance, and other Incidental Expenses | 812 | 19 | 8 |
| Paid Salaries to the Officers of the Society and their Assistants, to Lady day 1816, and parliamentary and parish Taxes | 1,115 | 19 | 0 |
| Paid on account of Mr. Belke's charity for books | 27 | 16 | 11 |
| Paid an Annuity to the Rev. Mr. Triebner, late Missionary at Ebenezer, in Georgia | 70 | 0 | 0 |
| Paid on account of an Annuity to the Rev. Mr. Davis, late Missionary at Tresco, Scilly | 37 | 0 | 0 |
| Paid on account of Mrs. Negus's Rotherhithe Charity | 50 | 2 | 10 |
| Paid on account of the Family Bible | 14,926 | 13 | 0 |
| Paid for the purchase of £. 867. 13 s. 7 d. 3 per cent. Cons. for the East-India Mission | 500 | 0 | 0 |
| Paid Rent and House Expenses | 190 | 6 | 0 |
| Paid for the purchase of £. 175. 3 per Cent. Red. Ann. Mrs. Ann Jenkins of Wells | 105 | 0 | 0 |
| | £.50,220 | 10 | 1 |

* The Amount of Books and Packets delivered to Members on the terms of the Society, between the Audits of 1815 and 1816, is £. 32,357. 7 s. 8 d.; of which £. 19,774. 13 s. 6 d. is the Members' part, and £. 12,582. 14 s. 2 d. the Society's part.

Account

Account of Bibles, Common Prayer Books, Tracts, &c. dispersed by The Society, between the Audit, April 20, 1815, and the Audit, April 18, 1816.

The Society have sent 3,453 packets of Books to their Members on the Terms of the Society, between the Audits of 1815 and 1816; consisting of

| | |
|---|---|
| Bibles | 24,471 |
| New Testaments and Psalters | 38,406 |
| Common Prayers | 66,048 |
| Other bound Books | 55,554 |
| Small Tracts, half-bound, &c. | 788,387 |

Packets of Books issued gratuitously, and charged to the account of Stores;

| | |
|---|---|
| Bibles | 147 |
| New Testaments and Psalters | 380 |
| Common Prayers | 209 |
| Bound Books | 117 |
| Small Tracts, half-bound, &c. | 6,590 |

Special Account for the Royal Navy;

| | |
|---|---|
| Bibles | 60 |
| New Testaments and Psalters | 1,200 |
| Common Prayers | 800 |
| Bound Books | 180 |
| Small Tracts | 660 |

Books and Papers distributed gratuitously by the Society;

| | |
|---|---|
| Tracts distributed with the annual Packet | 16,000 |
| Directions for a devout and decent Behaviour in the public Worship of God, in 8vo. | 5,581 |
| Ditto, in 12mo. | 60,671 |
| Summary Account of the Society, on a folio sheet | 5,000 |
| Ditto, in 8vo. with a List of the Books | 5,000 |
| Stonhouse's Admonitions, on a broad sheet | 10,000 |
| Papers on Sunday Schools | 15,000 |
| - - - Jesus Christ a Pattern of Religious Virtue | 12,500 |
| - - - On praying to God | 15,000 |
| - - - On singing Psalms | 15,000 |
| - - - On the Sacrament | 15,000 |
| - - - On the Church Catechism | 15,000 |
| - - - Invitations to Church | 15,000 |
| - - - On Confirmation | 15,000 |

The whole Number distributed, on the Terms of the Society, and gratuitously, is,

| | |
|---|---|
| Bibles (exclusive of the Society's Family Bible*) | 24,678 |
| New Testaments and Psalters | 39,986 |
| Common Prayers | 67,057 |
| Other bound Books | 55,851 |
| Small Tracts, &c. half-bound, &c. | 795,637 |
| Books and Papers, issued gratuitously | 219,752 |
| Total | 1,202,961 |

* Of the Society's Family Bible with Notes explanatory and practical, three Impressions have been printed, and about 15,000 copies have been sold.

May 27, 1816.                 GEO. GASKIN, D.D. Secretary.

---

The STATE of the CHARITY SCHOOLS in The Metropolis, according to the latest Accounts which have been received.

C. Signifies Clothed.          B. Children who wear Badges on their Clothes.
M. Maintained.                 W. Set to Work.

| Charity Schools in the Parishes of | Nº of Schools. | BOYS. | GIRLS. | Boys put out since setting up of the School, to Apprentice-ships. | Services, or taken out by Friends. | Sea. | Girls put out since setting up of the School, to Apprentice-ships. | Services, or taken out by Friends. | Nº of Children Educated in the Schools, including those now in them. |
|---|---|---|---|---|---|---|---|---|---|
| St. Andrew, Holborn,* erected 1696, C. B. | 2 | 80 | 80 | 1,538 | 853 | 125 | 488 | 1,344 | 4,508 |
| St. Ann, Aldersgate, 1709, C. B.: Boys—Apprentices, Servants, and Sea - - 685 Girls—Apprentices and Services - - 480 } 1,165 | 2 | 60 | 30 | - | - | - | - | - | 1,255 |
| St. Ann, Limehouse, 1779, C. B. | 2 | 50 | 50 | - | 286 | 13 | - | 343 | — |
| St. Ann, Soho,† 1699, C. B. Boys, 1699 - - Girls, 1704 | 2 | 50 | 40 | 500 | 526 | 26 | 182 | 604 | 2,828 |
| St. Alphage, Boys, 1751 - - Girls 1753, C. B. | 2 | 18 | 7 | — | — | — | — | — | — |
| Aldgate Ward, 1717, C. | 2 | 70 | 30 | 198 | 417 | 32 | 18 | 64 | 829 |
| Aldersgate Ward, 1702, C. B. | 2 | 33 | 33 | 72 | 941 | 2 | 1 | 542 | 1,624 |
| St. Botolph, Aldgate, Boys, 1688 - - Girls, 1700, C. B. | 2 | 60 | 40 | 524 | 478 | 31 | 21 | 543 | 1,697 |
| St. Bartholomew the Great, Boys, 1717 - - Girls, 1727, part C. | 2 | 20 | 16 | — | — | — | — | — | — |
| St. Bride's, 1711, C. B. | 2 | 40 | 30 | 30 | 978 | — | — | — | — |
| St. Botolph, Bishopsgate, 1702, C. B. | 2 | 40 | 40 | — | — | — | — | — | — |
| Billingsgate Ward, Boys, 1714 - - Girls, 1803, C. B. | 2 | 30 | 10 | 267 | 707 | 59 | 2 | 16 | 1,091 |
| Bridge, Candlewick, and Dowgate Wards, Boys, 1710 - - Girls, 1717, C. B. | 2 | 55 | 35 | — | — | — | — | — | — |

* Twelve Girls wholly maintained in the house.                    (continued.)
† Ten Girls taken into the school house, wholly maintained, and when qualified, put out to service.

State of the Charity Schools in The Metropolis—*continued.*

| Charity Schools in the Parishes of | Nº of Schools. | BOYS. | GIRLS. | Boys put out since setting up of the School, to | | | Girls put out since setting up of the School, to | | Nº of Children Educated in the Schools, including those now in them. |
|---|---|---|---|---|---|---|---|---|---|
| | | | | Apprenticeships. | Services, or taken out by Friends. | Sea. | Apprenticeships. | Services, or taken out by Friends. | |
| Broad-street Ward, Boys, 1709 - - Girls, 1714, C. B. | 2 | 50 | 30 | 489 | 682 | 32 | 130 | 605 | 2,018 |
| St. Clement Danes, 1702, C. B.* | 2 | 60 | 40 | 616 | 716 | 78 | 320 | 272 | 21 |
| Cripplegate Ward Within, Boys, 1712 - - Girls, 1714, C. B. | 2 | 50 | 25 | 152 | 315 | 10 | - | 523 | 1,075 |
| Christ Church, Spital-fields, 1703, C. B. | 2 | 50 | 50 | 264 | 570 | 23 | - | 409 | 1,305 |
| Coleman-street Ward, Boys, 1712 - - Girls, 1758, C. B. | 2 | 40 | 25 | 285 | 463 | 35 | 147 | 178 | 1,173 |
| Cordwainer and Bread-street Wards, Boys, 1701 - - Girls, 1714, C. B. | 2 | 50 | 30 | 390 | 894 | 31 | 105 | 524 | 2,024 |
| Cornhill and Lime-street Wards, 1710, C. B. | 2 | 40 | 40 | 306 | — | | | — | |
| Castle Baynard Ward, Boys, 1710 - - Girls, 1720, C. B. | 2 | 30 | 20 | - - | - | 2 | | — | — |
| St. Dunstan in the West, Boys, 1708 - - Girls, 1710, C. B. | 2 | 40 | 30 | 424 | - - | 63 | 375 | - - | 932 |
| St. Ethelburga, Boys, 1719 - - Girls, 1774, C. B. | 2 | 36 | 20 | 294 | 520 | 17 | - | 153 | 1,040 |
| Farringdon Ward Within, Boys, 1705 - - Girls, 1720, C. B.† | 2 | 60 | 40 | 289 | 270 | 60 | 199 | 234 | 1,152 |
| Finsbury, Boys 1792 - - Girls 1795, C. B. | 2 | 31 | 21 | 52 | 66 | 27 | 12 | 59 | 268 |
| St. Giles in the Fields, and St. George Bloomsbury, 1705, C. B. | 2 | 101 | 60 | 981 | 867 | - | 480 | 165 | 2,854 |
| St. George Hanover-square, day schools of Instruction and Industry, 1804, C. | 2 | 65 | 45 | — | — | | — | — | — |
| St. George the Martyr, Queen-square, Boys, 1708 - - Girls, 1709 | 2 | 40 | 30 | 476 | | | 271 | | 817 |
| St. George the Martyr, Southwark | 2 | 60 | 40 | — | — | | — | — | — |
| St. Giles Cripplegate Ward Without, Boys, 1698 - - Girls, 1709, C. B. | 2 | 102 | 100 | 866 | 1,934 | 108 | - | 1,625 | 4,735 |
| St. John, Horsleydown, 1735, C.‡ | 1 | - | 36 | — | — | | —— | — | — |
| St. James, Clerkenwell, 1697, C. B. | 2 | 60 | 40 | 573 | 332 | 21 | - | 372 | 1,398 |
| St. John, Wapping, Boys, 1704 - - Girls, 1708, C. B. | 2 | 50 | 40 | 545 | - - | 356 | 5 | 548 | 1,544 |
| Joyes, founded by Peter Joyes, esq. 29th June 1705, C. | 2 | 30 | 20 | — | — | | — | — | — |
| St. Katharine by the Tower, 1707, C. | 2 | 35 | 15 | — | — | | — | — | — |
| St. Luke, Middlesex, Boys, 1698 - - Girls, 1761, C. B. | 2 | 100 | 55 | 707 | - - | - | - | - - | 862 |
| St. Leonard, Shoreditch, Boys, 1705 - - Girls, 1709, C. B. | 2 | 100 | 50 | 500 | 700 | 20 | 97 | 820 | 2,287 |
| Langbourn Ward, Boys, 1702 - - Girls, 1800, C. B. | 2 | 30 | 20 | 421 | - - | 28 | | 32 | 531 |
| St. Mary, Lambeth, 1661, C. B. | 1 | 70 | | — | — | | — | — | — |
| St. Mary Magdalen, Bermondsey, Boys, 1712 - - Girls, 1722, C. B. | 2 | 30 | 50 | — | — | | — | — | — |
| St. Mary, Whitechapel, 1705, C. B. | 2 | 100 | 100 | 14 | - - | - | 11 | — | — |
| St. Mary, Islington, 1710, C. B. | 2 | 46 | 34 | — | — | | — | — | — |
| St. Mary le-Strand, 1708, C. B. | 1 | 30 | — | — | | | — | — | — |
| St. Mary-le-Bonne, 1750, C. B.§ | 2 | 50 | 50 | 540 | 401 | - | 192 | 418 | 1,651 |
| —— School of Industry, 1791 ‖ | 2 | 60 | 60 | 30 | 500 | 20 | - | 309 | 979 |
| St. Matthew, Bethnal Green, Boys, 1765 - - Girls, 1762, C. B. | 2 | 30 | 30 | — | — | | — | — | — |
| Mile-End Old Town | 2 | 30 | 30 | — | — | | — | — | — |
| St. Paul, Covent-Garden, Boys, 1701 - - Girls, 1712, C.¶ | 2 | 13 | 15 | 265 | | 10 | 138 | - - | 441 |
| St. Paul, Shadwell, Boys, 1669 - - Girls, 1712, C. B. | 2 | 45 | 35 | 372 | 887 | 104 | 40 | 654 | 2,137 |
| St. Pancras | 1 | - | 30 | — | — | | — | — | — |
| Poplar and Blackwall, 1711, C. B. | 1 | 50 | - | 709 | 516 | 66 | - | - | 1,341 |
| Pentonville, 1788, C. | 2 | 15 | 15 | — | — | | — | — | — |

\* Eight Girls are lodged and boarded in the house.
† Twenty of the Girls wholly maintained in the house.
‡ The Trustees have taken fourteen into the house wholly to be maintained.
§ They are boarded, lodged in the house, and every necessary found.
‖ One hundred and fourteen are clothed from their own industry.
¶ Fourteen boys and fourteen girls are maintained in the house.

(*continued.*)

State of the Charity Schools in The Metropolis—*continued*.

| Charity Schools in the Parishes of | N° of Schools. | BOYS. | GIRLS. | Boys put out since setting up of the School, to | | | Girls put out since setting up of the School, to | | N° of Children Educated in the Schools, including those now in them. |
|---|---|---|---|---|---|---|---|---|---|
| | | | | Apprenticeships. | Services, or taken out by Friends. | Sea. | Apprenticeships. | Services, or taken out by Friends. | |
| Paddington, 1802, C. - - - - | 2 | 20 | 20 | — | — | — | — | — | — |
| Queenhythe Ward, 1717, C. B. - - | 2 | 20 | 20 | - | 338 | | - | 330 | 708 |
| Raine's Hospital, St. George's in the East, 1719, C. B. ☞ - - - - | 2 | 50 | 90 | 339 | - - | - | - | 321 | 800 |
| - - - Asylum, 1736, C. B. ☞ - - | 1 | - | 40 | — | — | — | — | — | — |
| St. Sepulchre, Ladies school, 1702, C. B. * | 1 | - | 51 | — | --- | — | — | — | — |
| St. Sepulchre, London, 1702, C. B. - - | 1 | 51 | - | 1,095 | 216 | 26 | - | - - | 1,388 |
| St. Sepulchre, Middlesex, Boys, 1702, C. - | 1 | 30 | — | — | — | — | — | — | — |
| St. Sepulchre, Middlesex, Girls, 1702, C. - | 1 | - | 26 | — | — | — | — | — | — |
| St. Stephen, Walbrook, Boys, 1698 - - Girls, 1778, C. B. - | 2 | 50 | 30 | — | — | — | — | — | — |
| St. Thomas, Southwark, 1703, C. B. - | 1 | 30 | — | — | — | — | — | — | — |
| Tower Ward, Boys, 1709 - - Girls, 1707, C. B. - | 2 | 60 | 60 | 78 | 1,242 | 137 | 186 | 1,339 | 3,102 |
| Vintry Ward, 1710, C. B. - - - | 2 | 48 | 17 | 266 | 963 | 10 | - | - - | 1,304 |

☞ RAINE'S Asylum, set up in the same Parish of St. George in the East, 1736, for 40 Girls. These Girls, being transplanted from the Parish School into the said Hospital, are entirely maintained and trained up for services.—After the age of 22, six of them, producing certificates of their good behaviour during their servitude, draw lots, twice in the year, for a marriage portion of £ 100. to settle them in the world with an honest industrious mechanic;—80 have received it, and 527 have been educated since its institution.

\* Forty-three wholly maintained in the house.

### Mr. *Charles Francis Jameson*, called in, and Examined.

Mr. *C. F. Jameson*.

YOU are master of the school in Horseferry Road?—I am.

How long have you been so?—Ever since the school was opened.

When was that?—16th of January 1815.

How many are educated there?—We have about 250 on the books at present.

How many actually attend?—The attendance is very irregular, sometimes 205, sometimes 170 or 180.

Two hundred on an average?—No, about 180; but although these boys do not attend, the principal part of them are in the school in the course of the week, though they are not present at the same time. The number admitted since the 16th of January 1815, is 413; 359 of the Church of England, 3 Jews, 5 of the Kirk of Scotland, 7 Baptists, and 36 other Dissenters. We take in all religions; we only ask the question in order to know what religions we have; they may attend what place of worship they please. At the present moment, we have 195 of the Church of England, 3 Jews, 5 of the Kirk of Scotland, 1 Baptist, 4 Catholics, and 35 Dissenters.

Could the school hold more?—It was built for 400, and will hold 500.

Would the funds allow of more boys being educated at the school?—I am not able to say any thing about the funds.

Do you know any thing of the expense of the school?—Yes.

What is your salary?—100*l.* a year.

Without perquisite?—I have no perquisite at all.

What is the annual expenditure of the school?—50 *l.* a year.

How long do you find the boys have taken to learn to read?—That depends upon the abilities of the child; they read two hours a day, and write and cipher the same.

How long does a child of ordinary capacity take to learn to read?—I cannot tell how to answer that; some boys much longer than others; I think in about a year and a half, a boy would learn to read very well, provided he knew his alphabet before he went into the school; I could produce some boys that have learnt very well in that time.

Do you know any thing about Sunday schools?—We have one on the same premises.

Are they taught on the same principles?—They do not allow any writing or ciphering; it is a Church school, that is held on the same premises; the Rev. Mr. Saunders carries it on.

Do

Do you know how long the children are learning to read, then?—No, I am not able to state how long they take.

How many attend there?—I believe about 415 boys and girls. There is a division in the school by green curtains between the boys and girls, and although it is in one school-room, yet there are separate places for boys and girls.

Do you know what is the mode of teaching?—No, I do not; the committee I serve have nothing to do with the Sunday school; they pay 15 l. a year rent for it.

When you say that a boy will take a year and a half to learn to read at a day-school, what proficiency do you allude to?—I mean, that he shall be able to spell any word that shall be put to him out of book: I class my boys by spelling: and if I find a boy can read well in the Testament, and cannot spell a word of two syllables, I put him down in the fifth class.

In what time will a boy get into that fifth class, from the time of his admission into the school?—In five months; we allow a month to a class.

Do many of your children leave you before you wish them?—I never wish them to leave till they are thirteen years old.

Do many leave before that period?—In a year and a half 170 have left, out of 413.

Most of them under thirteen?—Yes.

Do many leave you before they attain the fifth class?—Very few indeed, unless they go away to other schools: there are other charities in Westminster, where the parents find it more their interest to get them in; the Blue-coat school, the Grey-coat school, and the Green-coat school, for instance.

Do many leave you before they attain that proficiency in spelling which you before mentioned?—That depends on circumstances: some go away, and spend their time in the streets, without any education; they leave the school, and refuse to give any reason why: I have repeatedly seen boys that have been admitted, running the streets, and I believe they are not sent to any school at all; very many, I could say to the amount of fifty or sixty, out of the 170 that have left.

Is this your own doing, or is it with the consent of their parents?—I never turn any boy away, unless I inform the committee that I am going so to do; and only two boys have at any time been sent out of the school for misbehaviour.

Do those boys that you represent as having left the school, and running about the streets, act in this manner with the consent of their parents, or not?—Of course the parent must consent, because they know they are playing about, and not at the school; and I repeatedly, day by day, send after those boys, in a very different method from any school in London; I mean those boys who remain on the books, but who are not crossed out.

Have you any rules respecting the expelling of a boy after a certain degree of non-attendance?—If he does not attend in six weeks, unless he is ill, his name is crossed out; if his name is crossed out, and he applies again for admission, he is re-admitted by another number, and then he is classed afresh. I compel each boy to wear a number on his head, which number they keep constantly, in order to distinguish them apart; and if a boy who has number 2 or 3 on his head is present in the morning, he hangs his ticket on a nail drove in the desk for that purpose; if he is absent in the afternoon, his ticket remains hanging on the nail, there is no owner for it, consequently those numbers are brought up at five o'clock in the afternoon, at the time I dismiss them. In order to ascertain who are absent, I hang this number up behind where I sit on the platform, and every morning and afternoon I send after the absentees; I send after them by calling out, Who knows where No. 2. lives? the boy that knows will hold up his hand, and then I place his number exactly opposite to the boy's that I send after him, and then that boy cannot go to his seat, because he has not got his ticket, it is hanging behind me. The boy that I send after him brings me an account where he is; and the boy, by receiving his ticket, also gives me an account where he has been, so that if the accounts agree, I know whether the boy has played truant or not.

Are boys who, after having been dismissed for non-attendance, and have been re-admitted, allowed to be non-attendants for six weeks, before they are again expelled?—After they have been once crossed out of the books, I generally ascertain from their parents where they have been, and the reason of their leaving the school; and I make a memorandum, under my observation, of the answer which I receive from the parents; and when they are re-admitted, I generally have better and more regular attendance from them.

Are

Are any applicants to be admitted into this school refused admission, who are of a proper age?—None at all.

Has the school increased or decreased in its numbers, of late?—Decreased, but not many.

Within what time?—During this last winter; we consider it to be owing to the want of employment.

Do you consider the want of such numbers in the school is to be considered to proceed from any thing peculiar in the school, or from a general disinclination in the poor in the neighbourhood to receive instruction?—The general objection appears to be on the part of parents sending them to a charity school.

You mean where they have education gratis?—Yes, I have heard the observation repeatedly made.

They do not pay any thing in your school?—A penny a week each boy: it was introduced by some member of the committee, in order to do away the objection that many had, under the idea of its being a charity school; but there are very few that pay, among the boys; I never enforce it, nor ever turn away any child on account of it.

You have formed a regulation, then, of taking a penny a week from those who choose to send their children to the school?—It is what our committee, at present, will not give up: I have repeatedly written to them on the subject; for I have found parents, where they have four or five in a family, who have not paid perhaps for three or four weeks; and, for want of money, the parents have taken the children away altogether. But to remedy that evil, I generally call on the parents, and take them for nothing; that is the case with the three Jew boys I have, and five Catholics of one family, in the school at this present time.

The Committee are to understand, then, that some parents do not like to send, except they may pay, and others do not like it, except they can have it gratis?— They cannot afford it: and I believe I have children in the school, who are in decimals and fractions, whose parents are perhaps worth several thousand pounds.

And who pay regularly?—Yes; I know it is the case with three or four.

You mentioned the disinclination of some to send their children to a school at which they were not to pay something, and a regulation of the committee to receive a penny a week in order to meet the objection of such parents; did you find that such regulation to receive a penny a week so far did away prejudices as to increase the number in your school?—Certainly; I opened the school on the 16th of January 1815, with 37 boys only, which have now increased to 250. It had been a school before, but it was shut up for a twelvemonth, in consequence, as I understood, of some disagreement of the committee that had belonged to it; and the whole of the boys principally left, for the National and other schools.

Can you state any other circumstances which, in your opinion, prevent the school from being filled?—No, not particularly; I am unable to state exactly what is the reason why the parents of the children will not allow them to come to school; but there certainly is that which does prevent them, and which I think nothing but some compulsion will make them accede to.

Has it come to your knowledge that any of the regulations of the school are complained of in the neighbourhood?—No, I have never heard of any, except it is the punishment that is used in the school.

What punishment is used in the school?—No particular punishment, except it is for playing the truant, or stealing.

What is that punishment?—I always flog them when they play truant, and for nothing else, except it is stealing, and then I set one boy to flog another, because I think it disgraces the boy more.

Do you adopt the general system of the Lancasterian schools in all other respects, except that?—I do not follow the Lancasterian system altogether; I differ a great deal.

Were you taught at the school in the Borough Road?—Yes, I was; but the Earl of Stanhope, who is a member of the committee, has taken a great deal of interest in the school lately, and has given full permission that any improvement to render the system more easy may be adopted, which has been sanctioned also by the other members of the committee.

All the alteration, then, the Committee are to understand, that has been made, is sanctioned by the committee?—Yes, what are for improvements; if any gentleman comes into the school and suggests that any thing is an improvement, in order to make the system more easy, I immediately adopt it.

*Mr.*
*C. F. Jameson.*

Do you conceive any of those improvements have been distasteful to the poor?—Certainly not; the groundwork is the same as all other Lancasterian schools in London.

Do you conceive that the alterations that have been made has been the cause that has prevented parents from sending their children?—Certainly not.

Has any complaint been made by the parents of the children, respecting the books which are read?—None with respect to the parents; there has been some objection among some members of the committee, which has made the thing rather unpleasant for me; very much so.

Has any complaint been made with respect to your excluding certain books?—We never use any thing but the Bible and Testament, and that is without any comment at all; the Scripture is not at all interpreted, in any way.

Have the parents complained of the Scriptures not being interpreted?—I never heard of it.

Have they complained of your not using any catechism?—I never heard of it.

Do you conceive the want of clothing is an objection to the poor sending their children to school?—That has been an objection at times; but I have endeavoured to remedy that evil; for Mr. Sanders will, on application, if it is particularly wished, give a pair of shoes to a boy, if he attends the Sunday-school and day-school as well.

Do you believe, from your knowledge of the district, that poor persons would send their children if they were able to clothe them properly?—I do not think it would. If a boy has no shoes, I take him in: I have had boys come to me without shoes, and we have never refused to admit them into the school.

Do you then imagine your school would be at all benefited, if the discipline you mentioned were altered; by which is meant the discipline with respect to truants?—No, I do not apprehend it would at all.

Has the circumstance of the corporal punishment being in use, subjected it to any hard name in the neighbourhood?—O, dear, no; it is scarcely ever inflicted on any boys, except upon those boys whose parents can do nothing with them at home.

Have you any rewards for good behaviour in your school?—Every boy that gets out of any one class to a higher class, receives a penny; and the monitor that teaches that class, he also receives a penny for every boy; that is the only reward.

Have you no rewards for punctual attendance?—None at all.

What are the hours of attendance?—From nine to twelve, and from two to five.

*Mr.*
*James Miller.*

### Mr. *James Miller*, called in, and Examined.

WHAT are you?—Assistant secretary to the British and Foreign School Society.

What is the paper you have in your hand?—An Account of Schools in the parish of Shoreditch, which is one district of the North-east division of London. And we shall be able to bring in three or four more in the course of Monday and Tuesday; and likewise some account of the want of education. We have a number of hands employed, who are visiting the houses of the poor, to discover who have education, and who want it. [It was delivered in, and read, as follows:]

#### NORTH-EAST LONDON SCHOOLS FOR THE POOR.

| Instituted. | Where situated. | Description. | Day School. Boys. | Girls. | Sunday School. Boys. | Girls. | If boarded or clothed. | Treasurer or Secretary. | Master or Mistress. | Annual Expense. | Remarks. |
|---|---|---|---|---|---|---|---|---|---|---|---|
| | SHOREDITCH : | | | | | | | | | £. s. d. | |
| 1705 | Kingsland Road - | Church - | 100 | - | - | - | Clothed - | Chas Lush, Charles-square | Clifford Elisha | 380. 0. 0. | |
| 1705 | - - Do - - - | Do - - | - | 60 | - | - | Do - | - Do - - - - - - | Mary Tucker | 150. 0. 0. | |
| 1803 | Shoreditch, &c. - | Do - - | - | - | 327 | 282 | - | Revd R. Crosby - - - | Sundry - paid | 233. 19. 7. | |
| | Hill Court - - - | Dissenters | - | - | 60 | 60 | - | John Ludlow, Primrose-street - - - - - - | Do - gratuitous | 25. 0. 0. | |
| | Hoxton Chapel - | Do - | - | - | 320 | 270 | - | Thomas Hardy, Hoxton - | Do - - Do - | 75. 0. 0. | |
| | Land of Promise | Methodist | - | - | 150 | 150 | - | Willm Marriott, York-place | Do - - Do - | } 53. 0. 0. | |
| | Haggerston - - | Do - - | - | - | 50 | 50 | - | - - - Do - - - - - - | Do - - Do - | | |
| | Union-Street - - | Do - - | - | - | 75 | 75 | - | — Dowset, Steward, &c. | Do - - Do - | 30. 0. 0. | |
| | Holywell-street - | Dissenters | - | - | 50 | 50 | - | Revd W. F. Platt - - - | Do - - Do - | 20. 0. 0. | £. 10. 10. extra paid for teaching to |
| | Cumberland-street | Do - - | - | - | 50 | 50 | - | Revd — Frere - - - - | Do - - Do - | — | write 2 Evenings per week. |
| | Total - - - | | 100 | 60 | 1,082 | 987 | | | | | |

Mr. *Henry Woodthorpe*, Jun. called in, and Examined.

Mr.
*Henry Woodthorpe.*

WHAT is the paper you have in your hand?—An account of the Receipts and Expenses of Emanuel Hospital, for 1814 and 1815.

[It was delivered in, and read, as follows:]

A Statement of the RECEIPT and EXPENDITURE of the Fund for the Support of Emanuel Hospital Westminster, for the Years 1814 and 15.

| RECEIPT. | For the year 1814. | | | For the year 1815. | | |
|---|---|---|---|---|---|---|
| | £. | s. | d. | £. | s. | d. |
| To Amount of the Rents of the Estate at Brandsburton, from Lady-day to Lady-day - - - - - - - | 2,989 | 15 | — | 3,078 | 17 | 9½ |
| To Rent of Premises at Westminster, per Annum - - - | 110 | — | — | 110 | — | — |
| To Interest on £.5,400 Consolidated £.3 per Cent. Annuities - - | 162 | — | — | | — | |
| To - Dº - on £.7,900 of the said Stock - - - - - | - | - | - | 199 | 10 | — |
| *Note.*—£.2,500 of the said Stock was purchased on the 10th May 1815, per Order Court of Aldermen. | | | | | | |
| To Property Duty returned, for the years 1811 and 1812 - - | 197 | 2 | — | 193 | 7 | — |
| £. | 3,458 | 17 | — | 3,581 | 14 | 9½ |
| Average of Income - - - £.3,520. 5. 10. | | | | | | |

| EXPENDITURE. | For the year 1814. | | | For the year 1815. | | |
|---|---|---|---|---|---|---|
| | £. | s. | d. | £. | s. | d. |
| By Tithes to the Rector of Brandsburton (after deducting the Property Tax - - - - - - - - - | 819 | 18 | — | 819 | 18 | — |
| By Property Duty on Rents - - - - - - - | 283 | 5 | — | 284 | 7 | 1½ |
| By Agent's Allowance, and sundry Repairs - - - - | 460 | 2 | 2 | 781 | 1 | 9 |
| | 1,563 | 5 | 2 | 1,885 | 6 | 10½ |
| By the Allowance to Ten poor Men and Ten poor Women, residing in the Hospital - - - - - - - - - - | 403 | 8 | — | 403 | 8 | 6 |
| By Allowance to Out-Pensioners - - - - - - | 90 | 2 | 8 | 100 | 3 | — |
| By expenses of Bread, Meat, Medicines, and various other necessaries for the maintenance of Ten Boys and Ten Girls, residing in ditto - | 461 | 14 | 10 | 434 | 13 | 6 |
| By Allowance to the Master, for educating the said Children, doing the duty of Chaplain, and superintending the whole of the Concern within the Hospital - - - - - - - - - | 80 | — | — | 80 | — | — |
| By Allowance to the Mistress, including £.20. for Laundry - - | 70 | — | — | 70 | — | — |
| By Clothing, Linen, and Shoes, for the Children - - - | 149 | 17 | 7½ | 121 | 17 | 11 |
| By Coals - - - - - - - - - - - | 109 | 10 | 6 | 90 | 8 | — |
| By Premiums (£.10.) on apprenticing Children - - - | 20 | — | — | 35 | — | — |
| By Rent and Taxes for the Hospital, &c. - - - - | 57 | 18 | 4 | 69 | 5 | 10 |
| By Repairs of the Hospital - - - - - - - | 177 | 5 | 9½ | 163 | 1 | 3 |
| | 3,183 | 2 | 11 | 3,453 | 4 | 10½ |
| Average of Expenditure - - - £.3,318. 3. 11. | | | | | | |

Chamberlain's Office,⎫
June 1st, 1816. ⎭

B. W. SCOTT.

What is the meaning of this item, of " tithes to the rector of Brandsburton?"—It is a composition in lieu of tithes on the estate of Brandsburton.

How long has this been paid?—I hardly recollect how long; I believe for about six or seven years.

# SECOND REPORT:

pp. 111——164.

## MINUTES OF EVIDENCE

Taken before The SELECT COMMITTEE appointed to inquire into the EDUCATION of the Lower Orders of The Metropolis.

*Ordered,* by The House of Commons, *to be Printed,*
13 *June* 1816.

# WITNESSES.

# SECOND REPORT.

## MINUTES OF EVIDENCE

Taken before the SELECT COMMITTEE on the EDUCATION of the Lower Orders of The Metropolis.

*Lunæ, 3° die Junii,* 1816.

HENRY BROUGHAM, Esquire, in The Chair.

Mr. *George Griffiths,* called in, and Examined.

WHERE do you live ?—Saint Katharine's, near the Tower.

Are you a schoolmaster in the neighbourhood ?—Yes.

Of what school?—Saint Katharine's charity school.

Upon what foundation is that school ?—It is supported by voluntary contributions.

Have you any other funds?—There is a fund established by the contributions, which is placed in the Bank.

To what does it amount ?—The last purchase that was made has made it up to 1550 *l.*

What is the amount of annual subscriptions ?—It has varied very much within the last seven or eight years; it formerly used not to amount to more than sixty or seventy pounds, it has in the last six or seven years amounted to upwards of 100 *l.* by subscriptions and donations.

What is the whole amount of the yearly income ?—I am not prepared to state that, exactly.

Is it 200 *l.*?—Yes, it must be that, because our expenses amount to that.

How many children are educated there?—Fifty.

Boys and girls ?—Yes.

What are they taught?—Reading, writing, and arithmetic, and clothed.

What is the master's salary?—The master and mistress, 60 *l.* a year between them.

Are there any other salaries than the master's and mistress's ?—Nothing more than a trifling salary, for teaching psalmody, of four guineas a year.

Have the master and mistress any perquisite ?—None.

A house ?—A house to live in, and coal, but no candle.

Are there ever fewer children than fifty ?—No.

How long have you been master ?—About eight years.

How many were there when you came ?—Fifty.

Have there never been fewer, at any one time of the year, since the time you have been there?—There may have been so for a month or six weeks; the committee meet the first Tuesday in every month, and if there is a vacancy they admit whatever child is next in rotation to come in.

How long has the school been established ?—Since the year 1707.

Had it never any more property, besides the money in the funds?—The chapter of St. Katharine's has made it a present, at several times, of the leases of three houses towards its support.

Have they that leasehold property at present ?—They have.

At what are the houses underlet ?—Sixty pounds a year, the three.

Then the school has this 60 *l.* a year in addition to the interest of 1550 *l.* in the funds, and 100 *l.* a year subscriptions?—The increase of stock has doubled since I have been schoolmaster, owing to a lady who died and left us 500 *l.*

In what stock is it ?—Navy 5-per-cents.

Then instead of nearly 200 *l.* it appears the income of the school is above 230 *l.* a year ?—I was not aware of any question of the kind being asked, or I would have been prepared to answer it.

Is

*Mr.*
*George Griffiths.*

Is there any other property whatever belonging to the establishment?—None.

Any other salary paid, besides the master and mistress's?—None.

How are the children clothed?—They are completely clothed at Midsummer, and extra shoes, stockings, and linen, at Christmas.

Do the premises belong to the Institution?—During the lease; the schoolhouse is a gift of the chapter of St. Katharine's, during their pleasure, for which no rent is paid; there is a ground-rent paid for the other property.

Are there any occasional contributions and donations, besides the annual subscriptions?—I include those in the annual subscriptions.

Any charity sermons?—Yes, we have about one a year.

Is that included in the former account of 100*l.*?—No, that is not, so that the produce of this is to be added to the former sum.

What are the hours of teaching?—From nine to twelve, and from two to five; six hours a day.

Have you any other occupation than schoolmaster?—I am parish clerk.

Any other occupation?—As parish clerk, I do a little business in the undertaking line, which I employ other people to do.

Any other?—I do make a trifle as a musician; I am chorus singer to His Majesty's ancient concert of music in Hanover-square.

Have you any other employment?—No.

Do you teach any other scholars besides those in the school?—I am allowed to take a few, as they offer, such as sixpenny scholars per week; and very often I give several children their education, without charging them any thing.

Do the fifty children upon the foundation pay any thing?—Nothing.

Are they in general children of very poor people?—In general very poor.

Are there many poor children, in the neighbourhood in which you reside, destitute of instruction?—The generality of the children are poor people's children; the neighbourhood is a very poor neighbourhood.

Have those children the means of instruction?—Not till they are placed on our establishment, or other establishments in the neighbourhood.

Are there sufficient establishments in the neighbourhood for educating all those children?—I think there are.

Name them?—Aldgate charity school.

How many are educated there?—There are 120 or 140, I am not quite sure which.

What other schools are there in that neighbourhood?—The Middlesex charity school.

How many are educated there?—I do not know exactly, upwards of one hundred, I believe.

What other schools are there in that neighbourhood?—The Tower Hamlet school.

How many are educated there?—I do not know.

Is there any indisposition among the lower orders to send their children to those schools?—None; the parents are very anxious to get their children on the establishment.

In all those schools do they clothe?—In all the schools I have mentioned.

They do not board them?—No.

---

Account of RECEIPTS and DISBURSEMENTS, for the Clothing and Educating Fifty poor Children in St. Katharine's Charity School, for the year ending at Michaelmas 1815.

| 1814. RECEIPTS: | £. | s. | d. | 1814. DISBURSEMENTS: | £. | s. | d |
|---|---|---|---|---|---|---|---|
| To voluntary Subscriptions from the Inhabitants, &c. of the Precinct of St. Katharine's | 121 | 3 | — | By Clothing - - - - | 98 | 18 | — |
| | | | | By Stationary, Books, &c. - | 16 | 2 | 10 |
| To Interest of Money in the Funds | 74 | 17 | 6 | By Coals and Candles - | 15 | 17 | — |
| To Rents - - - - | 26 | — | — | By Schoolmaster's and Mistress's Salary - - - - | 64 | 4 | — |
| To Collection at Charity Sermon | 33 | 13 | 4 | By Repairs of School-house - | 5 | 15 | 6 |
| | | | | By sundry petty Expenses - | 9 | 10 | 2 |
| £. | 255 | 13 | 10 | £. | 210 | 7 | 6 |

Rents due to the Charity at Michaelmas last, £. 34.

*Geo. Griffiths,*
Schoolmaster.

### Mr. *John Crompton Bishop*, called in, and Examined.

WHERE do you reside?—St. Katharine's.

Are you treasurer to the school there?—Yes.

What is the yearly income of that establishment?—I am not in possession of sufficient information to answer that question, I am merely the treasurer; the committee are present at the different meetings, and I can give every information by applying for it to them.

What is the yearly income generally, without entering into particulars?—The only stable income we have is the interest of 1550 *l.* 5-per-cents.; the rest is subscriptions.

What do the subscriptions generally run at?—I cannot correctly answer that question.

One hundred pounds a-year?—From seventy to one hundred.

What is the value of the leasehold premises given you by the chapter?—It consists of the school-house, and three dwelling-houses underlet; the dwelling-houses are let, and the school house is occupied by the master and mistress.

What do those three houses let for?—Something more than 30 *l.* a-year; but I am not correct, probably.

### Mr. *Oliver Hatch*, called in, and Examined.

ARE you connected with the National Establishment?—I am treasurer of the National Society.

How many schools have you in your immediate connexion?—Five.

Where are they situate?—The first school is in Coleman-street Buildings.

How many does it educate?—I think there are about 360 boys and 180 girls.

Is it a day school?—Yes.

Is it a free school?—No, it is supported by voluntary subscriptions.

Do the children pay?—No.

You educate them?—Yes.

How much does it cost a year?—We have only been established about two years; the cost of the education is very small indeed.

What salary has the master?—Eighty pounds, and the mistress thirty pounds and a house.

Any perquisite?—No.

No coals?—No.

Do you know what the annual expense of the books may be?—Since our establishment it is so definite a sum we can hardly tell; the whole expense has been between sixty and seventy pounds in books.

Are the expenses of the other schools nearly the same?—Exactly; we do not pay the masters so much by 10 *l.* a year as we do in this school.

Do you find any want of education among the lower orders of the people?—We have scarcely a child but whose parents are unable to pay for their education. At the present time we are obliged to turn away about twenty children a week, who apply for admission, and we are unable to take in any more.

Did you understand that those poor children, whom you turned away, were wholly destitute of the means of education?—I believe wholly so, and from their appearance I know they must be so.

Is there any indisposition in the parents in that neighbourhood to send their children to school?—Not the least, but quite the reverse; I have not a doubt but if our school was large enough to take 1000 children, we should have it full in a very short time.

Are the children in the school you have described, prevented from coming, for want of clothing?—Not in that neighbourhood, we have not found any hardly; we have given them shoes now and then; they are very poor, chiefly the children of brewers and draymen, but in general we have not found that an obstacle, they come, many of them, without shoes.

Is the Catechism taught in the school?—Exactly the same as the National schools.

Are there many Dissenters?—A great many.

How many may there be?—It is impossible to tell; we ask no questions, they are all told that we send them to church; we do not ask them, when they come, whether they belong to the Church or not, but they know that all who attend the school must learn the Catechism, and go to church.

What do you do with the Dissenters, on Sundays?—They all go to church; we have never met with any objection.

Do

Do the Committee understand rightly, that the Dissenters go to church?—A great many.

Of all descriptions?—Yes, as far as I know.

Do the Catholics go to church?—There are no Catholics living in that neighbourhood; in our second school there are a great many Catholics.

Do the Catholics in that school go to church?—Yes.

How many children are there altogether?—225 actually under education in that school, which is situated in Shoe-lane.

Do you know of your own knowledge that twenty of those are Catholics?—I cannot answer as to numbers; I believe there are many.

What reason have you to believe there are many among those children who are Catholics?—Because many of their parents have said they were.

How long have you known a boy, who was undoubtedly a Catholic, go to church regular and learn the Catechism?—I cannot answer that question.

Have you ever known any one boy, who was undoubtedly a Catholic, go to church and learn Catechism three months?—I should think a much longer time; when we first commenced, we found there were many Catholic boys who were admitted into the school, but the priests came and took them out. The parents have always been told, when they brought their children, that they were to go to church, and they made no objection.

Is it the same with respect to Dissenters from the Church of England?—There are very few others who have stated what they were; they have stated that they went to chapel, but we have never asked any further question, for fear it should be an objection to them; on their admission into the school, they have a card given them, containing the rules. We have a third school, which consists of 154 children, in Fish-street, Doctors Commons.

Are there many children uneducated in that neighbourhood?—I believe very few poor live in that neighbourhood.

What time, in your opinion, is the average period in which a boy will learn to read?—If a boy is attentive, in two years he will learn to read.

To read perfectly?—Yes.

To read a word of any length, and of any number of syllables?—Yes.

A boy would learn to read tolerably in a less time than that?—Yes, in less than a twelvemonth.

Have you any instances of adults learning to read?—We have one, and only one. Our children we take in at seven years of age and upwards.

Have you ever known instances of children, when they return home, teaching their parents to read?—I have known it; we had an instance of a Black, that Mr. Beeston Long sent to us about six months ago, that did not know the sound of a letter, or the shape of a letter; he was taught by a very little boy in the school, who did not exceed nine years of age; he left us after he had been about nine weeks in the school, and was then perfectly competent to read a chapter in the Bible.

Are there many charity schools in the district?—There are a great many more than there are children to fill in that particular district.

The admission of children into these charity schools being according to the sect of the parents?—Yes; they are different to the National schools.

Some of the charity schools take in all children?—There are several that have joined with our school, that form a part of our National school.

Do they add their funds to yours?—They have no funds; they are supported chiefly by voluntary contributions, and we do not touch their funds at all; they continue to clothe their children as they did before, but their annual subscriptions we take.

Have you seen any improvement in the behaviour and morals of the children in that district, since the establishment of that school in Coleman-street?—Very great indeed.

What assistance have you received from the general society?—None at all; our subscriptions are confined entirely to the City of London.

### Mr. *William Allen*, called in, and Examined.

YOU are treasurer to the British and Foreign School Society?—Yes.

How long have you been so?—About two years; but I have been virtually treasurer almost from the beginning of the society in 1808.

How long has your attention been turned to the education of the poor?—From the middle of the year 1808.

With whom did you co-operate at that time?—With the late Joseph Fox; Sir John Jackson, M. P.; Joseph Foster, of Bromley, Middlesex; William Corston;

and

and Thomas Sturge; who had formed themselves into a committee, for the purpose of assisting and promoting Joseph Lancaster's plan of education.

What were your first operations?—About the middle of the year 1808, I became first acquainted with the benevolent exertions of my late friend Joseph Fox; previous to that period, I had merely paid my annual subscription to the Borough Road school, conducted by Joseph Lancaster, but had never attended particularly to the subject; when informed of the interest taken in the concern by Joseph Fox, I inquired more minutely into the nature of the establishment, and visited it myself. I saw that it was an institution pregnant with the greatest benefits, not only to this country, but to the whole world; I saw a system in action capable of affording instruction to poor children, at the expense of from five to fifteen shillings per head per annum, according to the magnitude of the school, ranging from a thousand to a hundred boys; indeed a school of a thousand might be conducted at the expense of only four shillings and sixpence per head per annum. It appeared that as far back as the year 1798, Joseph Lancaster taught a few poor children in the Borough Road; himself and parents were in low circumstances, but he seemed to be actuated by a benevolent disposition, and to possess great talents for the education of youth; he was countenanced and supported by a few benevolent individuals, and as the subscriptions were limited to a very small sum, he was obliged to devise the most economical plans. By a series of improvements, he at length demonstrated the possibility of instructing even a thousand children (if so many could be collected together in one room) by a single master; he divided his school into eight classes, each of which was managed by a monitor, whose duties were exactly prescribed to him, and who was made responsible for the good order of his class; over these, a monitor-general was placed, who regulated the business of the whole school, under the immediate direction of the master. Upon Lancaster's plan, a single book was found sufficient for a whole school, the different sheets being put upon pasteboard, and hung upon the walls of the school. He avoided the expense of pens and paper in the first stages of education, by substituting slates; he also introduced the plan of teaching the younger children to form the letters in sand, which plan was borrowed, I believe, from Dr. Bell, who had imported it from India; he contrived to teach writing and spelling at the same time, and he made a single spelling-book serve for a whole school, however large. He taught arithmetic from lessons which he had constructed for the purpose, whereby the monitor might correctly teach the principles of it, even if he were not fully acquainted with them himself; in this case also, one book of arithmetic served for the whole school. So that the expense of teaching on this plan, consists in the salary of the master or mistress, the rent of the school-room, and from ten to twenty pounds per annum, according to the size of the school, for the necessary apparatus. I was particularly struck with the liberality upon which the system was conducted, for, while the reading lessons consisted of extracts from the scriptures, in the very words of the authorized version, no peculiar catechism or creed was forced upon the children thus promiscuously collected together, and who must obviously consist of those belonging to persons of different religious persuasions; and I could not but perceive at the same time, the immense advantages which would arise to the community by thus educating children of different religious persuasions together, inasmuch as it would tend to lessen those prejudices and animosities which often have been found so mischievous to society. The children might naturally be expected to acquire an attachment for each other, which they would in many instances carry with them through life. We all recollect that when a person whom we have not seen for twenty or thirty years past, is introduced to us as a schoolfellow, the recollection of the circumstance brings with it generally claims of attachment and regard. At this period, Joseph Lancaster was involved in great pecuniary difficulties; his debts amounted to between six and seven thousand pounds, while his effects were estimated only at about 3,500 *l.*; and if they had been sold, they would not probably have realized much more than a third part of that sum. Upon examination into the accounts, it appeared that Joseph Lancaster, in his ardour to propagate the system, had entered into pecuniary engagements which it was impossible for him to fulfil with the subscriptions he then had. Some time previously to this period, our venerable Sovereign had condescended to give him a personal interview, and was so much impressed with the value of this simple and economical plan, and the probable benefits which the country and the world might derive from it, that He became an annual subscriber of 100 *l.* per annum, and recommended the Queen and other branches of the Royal Family also to become subscribers to a considerable amount. The prejudices which had been

*Mr.*
*William Allen.*

469.                                                                    operating

operating against the founder, had so far diminished the subscriptions in the beginning of the year 1808, that they amounted then to little more than those of the King and Royal Family. Joseph Fox saw that, unless a vigorous exertion was immediately made, the whole plan was in danger of being utterly lost. At this period but few schools upon the system existed in the country, the public were not aware of the value of the plan, and nothing but a bold and decisive measure could possibly save it. Joseph Lancaster's creditors were at that moment harassing him with legal proceedings; and it was under these circumstances that Joseph Fox advanced nearly 2000*l.* of his own property, and made himself responsible for as much more, by bills drawn by him and accepted by William Corston, as were necessary to settle in full with all the creditors. This measure was arranged before I became acquainted with the circumstance. It was obvious, that though the plan was thus saved, it would be quite impossible to carry it on without a great increase in the annual subscriptions. The expenditure at that time, for the training of masters for the purpose of establishing this economical plan in different parts of the kingdom, involved an expense of from two to three thousand pounds per annum. I then determined to render all the assistance in my power, and to procure the co-operation of as many of my friends as possible, provided Joseph Lancaster would agree that the whole business should be managed by a committee of a few gentlemen, to be chosen by himself, that regular accounts should be kept of all receipts and expenses, as well as fair minute books of all transactions. To this he at length agreed, and appointed the following members of the committee; Sir John Jackson, M. P. Joseph Fox, Wm. Corston, Wm. Allen, Joseph Forster, Thomas Sturge; and from that period down to the present day, the account books and minute books have been regularly kept. In addition to the patronage bestowed upon this institution, almost from its very beginning, by the Duke of Bedford and Lord Somerville, the Royal Dukes of Kent and Sussex, about the year 1811, having minutely inquired into the nature of the plan, gave it their decided and warm support; and through all the difficulties that have attended its progress at different periods, these illustrious personages have rendered most important assistance, and have uniformly shown the most lively interest in its final success. In the year 1811, several distinguished persons also came forward to its support, and, by their kind assistance and countenance, the committee were encouraged to bear up under all their difficulties. In the years 1808 and 1809, the sum of 4000*l.* was raised, mostly in shares of 100*l.* each, from several benevolent individuals, which loans were to bear interest at five per cent.; and the annual subscriptions were increased, so as more nearly to meet the expenditure. But with all these exertions, the sum necessary to be employed in capital for the stock of lessons, slates, and apparatus, for the supply of country schools, rendered it necessary for the committee to advance sums of money, which at the end of 1811 amounted to 5,400*l.* About this period, the committee had much opposition to encounter, from those who were advocates for an exclusive plan of education, and who wished to insist on the Church catechism being taught in all schools for the general education of the poor. The subscriptions were, however, still very considerable; and though they did not equal the annual expenditure, the trustees made the necessary advances from their own private property. Joseph Lancaster, being set at liberty from his pecuniary embarrassment, travelled throughout the country, explaining his plan in public lectures; and by this means the public became so much interested in the business, that a great number of schools were established in different parts of the kingdom, which occasioned an extensive claim upon the parent institution for masters and mistresses. At this period, the advocates for an exclusive system established schools, which they called National, and insisted that children introduced into them should learn the Church Catechism and go to Church. Down to the year 1812, the system had been progressively making its way throughout the country; and the demands upon the parent institution, for masters and mistresses, whose training had incurred a considerable expense, became more and more urgent. A great number of accounts were now opened with new schools, for lessons, slates, &c. In 1813, Joseph Lancaster, without the knowledge, and contrary to the advice of the committee, engaged in an establishment at Tooting, on the plan of a boarding-school for the children of the middle ranks of society, from which he expected to derive emolument; he then proposed to the committee, that if they would exonerate him from all claims for their advances, amounting to between 5 and 6,000*l.* he would make over the premises and all the stock at the Borough Road, and commit the whole business to their management; promising, that if this request was acceded to, he would still render every assistance in his power. The

committee,

committee, upon deliberate consideration, agreed to his proposal; and the necessary deeds were drawn up and signed. The committee was now enlarged, by the addition of several highly respectable persons. From the great extension of the plans, not only in this country, but to all the quarters of the world, this measure had become absolutely necessary. And it is a gratifying reflection, that all these important benefits to mankind have been procured at an expense which must be deemed comparatively trifling. The total amount of subscriptions and donations received since the year 1808, when the committee first took charge of the concern, down to the end of the year 1815, amount only to 16,127 *l.* 7 *s.*: and it is further to be remarked, that the committee, from its very commencement, have had to struggle under a very heavy debt, which the increasing demands upon the establishment would never permit them to liquidate. They resolved, however, about two years ago, to make an attempt to raise 10,000 *l.* which they calculated would discharge the whole of the debt, and place the institution on a permanent basis. Upwards of 7,000 *l.* are already subscribed; and the committee are confident, that if the nature and value of the plan were but sufficiently known, the remaining 3,000 *l.* would be immediately supplied.

What is the annual income at present?—It varies in different years; for the last year it was only 1,600 *l.*

Does that include donations as well as subscriptions?—Yes.

What was it the year before?—The year before it was nearly 2,700 *l.*

How do you account for the difference?—Some of the persons who have subscribed, one in particular, who gave a donation of 500 *l.* would have given it to the general subscription, had it not been that the invested subscriptions were afloat, and it was invested there.

Have you ever received any considerable sums from persons who have refused their names to be mentioned?—Yes; and I regret that I am prohibited mentioning one in particular, without whose large pecuniary aid, advanced at different times through the course of several years, it would have been almost impossible to have supported the institution.

How much has he given altogether?—About 3,000 *l.*; but he insisted that his name should be strictly concealed, stating, that if it were made known, he would discontinue his aid.

How much are the trustees in advance?—We are altogether in advance between 6 and 7,000 *l.*; in which advance there is an increase, since last year, of several hundred pounds.

What are the average yearly expenses?—Between 2 and 3,000 *l.*

In what are those sums expended?—In the board, lodging, and clothing, of persons learning the plan, and qualifying for teachers either in this kingdom or foreign parts; in the maintenance of schools for about 700 children, boys and girls, in the Borough-road; in the support of some schools whose funds were inadequate; and in promoting the plan in foreign parts.

What is the annual expense of the Borough-road establishment?—It was stated in 1814 at 380 *l.* 7 *s.* 10 *d.* which includes merely the boys and girls school.

What other schools in London were established by the British and Foreign School Society?—There is some difficulty in replying to that question, because the existence of many schools is only known by applications for slates, lessons, &c.; as few of those schools are regularly connected with the parent institution, we must probably remain ignorant of one half of those which are actually established. In and near the Metropolis there are at least seventeen schools for boys, upon the plan of the British and Foreign School Society, which are perfectly known to us, and which educate nearly 4,000 boys; and we know of at least eight schools for girls, in which above 900 are receiving education. Several of the schools called National are also conducted upon this plan.

Does the Society actually assist the above number of schools?—It has rendered many of them material assistance, by supplying them with masters and mistresses, which is one great object of the parent institution, and a great source of its expense.

How many schools, besides the one in the Borough-road, are wholly maintained by the Society?—I do not now recollect that any schools are at present wholly maintained, except the school at Chelsea, it being an object with the committee to make the schools stand upon their own foundations as soon as possible, otherwise no funds that we could expect to raise would be sufficient for the purpose

Is there any school, besides the one in the Borough-road, of which the Society pays the master's salary?—I think not at present; we have paid the masters' salaries and

*Mr.*
*William Allen.*

469.                                    the

the other expenses for several schools, to set them going, or when they got into difficulties; we did so for the Chelsea school at one time; and to support the Horse-ferry-road school, several hundred pounds were expended.

What schools, in connexion with the Society, have been established in different parts of the country?—The number of boys schools, in the list I now produce, amounts to about 200; but I am perfectly aware of the existence of a great number more, from the applications made to our committee for school apparatus: And here is another list, of seventy-four girls schools, established in like manner.

[They were delivered in, and read, as follows:]

### SCHOOLS for BOYS, on the BRITISH SYSTEM, have been organized at the following Places in Great Britain:

| | | |
|---|---|---|
| Aldborough. | Eagle-street. | Margate. |
| Alnwick. | East Bourne. | Montrose. |
| Abergavenny. | Exeter. | Minchin Hampton. |
| Arundel. | Ebbu Vale. | Martin's St. (Shropshire.) |
| Borough Road. | East Looe. | Mary-le-bone. |
| Bath. | Fenny Stratford. | Neath. |
| Bermondsey. | Falmouth. | Newcastle-upon-Tyne. |
| Birmingham. | Felton (Shropshire.) | Newbury. |
| Bocking and Braintree. | Fincham. | Newport Pagnell. |
| Brecon. | Folkstone. | Newport (Isle of Wight.) |
| Bristol. | Falkland. | Nottingham. |
| Brompton Park. | Glasgow. | Norwich. |
| Belfast. | Gloucester. | Needham Market. |
| Brighton. | Godalmin. | Northampton. |
| Bury St. Edmunds. | Guernsey. | Newport (Monmouth.) |
| Blandford. | Handly Potteries. | Oswestry. |
| Bilston. | Hitchin. | Oxford-street. |
| Bridgnorth. | Hertford. | Oxford. |
| Bradford. | Halsted. | Pettenhall (near Wolver- |
| Boston. | Hampstead. |   hampton.) |
| Blackheath. | Horseferry Road. | Plymouth. |
| Chatham. | Horsell. | Plymouth Dock. |
| Chichester. | Hailsham. | Poole. |
| Clewer. | Harlow. | Portsea. |
| Carlisle. | Huddersfield. | Portsmouth. |
| Coggeshall. | Horncastle. | Peebles (N. B.) |
| Colchester. | Hastings. | Peckham. |
| Crickhowell. | Hockliffe. | Pill. |
| Chelmsford. | Halesworth. | Peterhead. |
| City Road. | Hunmanby. | Reading. |
| Croydon. | Homerton. | Ross (Herefordshire.) |
| Cirencester. | Halifax. | Rochford (Essex.) |
| Camberwell. | Ipswich. | Ryde (Isle of Wight.) |
| Caermarthen. | Kidderminster. | Ramsey (Isle of Man.) |
| Chipping Norton. | Kingsland. | Seaford. |
| Chester. | Luton. | Sheffield. |
| Cork. | Leeds. | Southampton. |
| Cambridge. | Leicester. | Southgate. |
| Coventry. | Lynn. | Swansea. |
| Chalvey. | Launton. | Shefford. |
| Cardiff. | Lamb's Buildings. | Stirling. |
| Charlbury. | Lavenham. | Swaffham. |
| Chudleigh. | Leighton Buzzard. | Saltash. |
| Clouance (Cornwall.) | Lostwithiel. | Shrewsbury. |
| Deptford. | Lewes. | Spitalfields. |
| Derby. | Liverpool. | Scarborough. |
| Dundee. | Loddon. | Sherbourne. |
| Darlington. | Lanark. | Staines. |
| Downham. | Llantrissaint. | Sunderland. |
| Doncaster. | Lakefield. | Shields, North. |
| Dorrington Castle. | Low Moor Iron Works. | St. Ives. |
| Docking. | Llandilo. | St. Giles. |
| Douglas. | Llanfihangel. | Seven Dials. |
| Debenham. | Llansilin (Shropshire.) | Selattyn (Shropshire.) |
| Ditchling. | Llanyblodwell. | Tullamore. |
| Dover. | Lancaster. | Tavistock. |
| Dublin. | Maidstone. | Tyne Iron Works. |
| Dewsbury. | Manchester. | Tewkesbury. |
| Edinburgh. | Machan. | Tottenham. |
| Etruria Potteries. | Middleton. | Talgarth. |

Tynemouth.

| | | | |
|---|---|---|---|
| Tynemouth. | Wakefield. | Wooburn (Bucks.) | *Mr.* |
| Uxbridge. | Wisbech. | Wadebridge. | *William Allen.* |
| Usk. | Weymouth. | Warrington. | |
| West-street. | Woodbridge. | Whittington. | |
| Waterford. | Worthing. | Woburn (Bedfordshire.) | |
| Wellington. | Woodborough. | Worcester. | |
| Whitby. | Winslow. | Youghall. | |
| Wycomb. | Walberton. | Yarmouth. | |

SCHOOLS for GIRLS, on the BRITISH SYSTEM, have been organized at the following Places in Great Britain:

| | | |
|---|---|---|
| Aberdeen. | Edinburgh. | Norwich. |
| Abergavenny. | Exeter. | Newbury. |
| Borough Road. | Farnham. | Portsea. |
| Bristol. | Godalmin. | Peckham. |
| Birmingham. | Guilford. | Rennishaw. |
| Bath. | Hitchin. | Rotherham. |
| Boston. | Horsell. | Rochford. |
| Brecon. | Harlow. | Ross (Herefordshire.) |
| Belfast. | Halifax. | Swansea. |
| Blandford. | Horncastle. | Shrewsbury. |
| Chichester. | Ipswich. | Sheffield. |
| Clewer. | Kingsland. | Seaford. |
| Chertsey. | Knutsford. | St. Giles's. |
| Chelsea. | Lewes. | Spitalfields. |
| Chesterfield. | Lynn. | Tottenham. |
| Camberwell. | Lanark. | Tewkesbury |
| Coventry. | Llandilo. | Tavistock. |
| Charlbury. | Lamb's Buildings. | Uxbridge. |
| Chatham. | Leighton Buzzard. | Woodborough. |
| Colchester. | Maidstone. | Wycombe, High. |
| Coggeshall. | Middleton. | Whittington. |
| Chudleigh. | Margate. | Whitby. |
| Dudley. | Mary-le-bone. | Wadebridge. |
| Ditchling. | Manchester. | York. |
| Douglas (Isle of Man.) | Newcastle-upon-Tyne. | |

Can you form any estimate of the number of children educated at those schools?—I think the average could not be taken much lower than from 150 to 200 in each school; there are some of 500, and others of 200: our plan cannot operate with advantage in a very small school.

Do you correspond with all those schools?—But few of them have any regular connexion with us at present, they are supported by local funds, but some of them at their first establishment were connected with the institution.

Have you any auxiliary societies connected with the central establishment?—The city of Bristol in the year 1815 established an auxiliary society, principally intended in aid of the funds of the parent institution; and it has actually since that period sent us near 300 *l.* besides providing large schools under its immediate superintendence. An auxiliary society has been very recently established in Southwark, which will be a most important step in our proceedings, inasmuch as it proceeds upon a plan calculated to provide for the education of every poor child in that district of the Metropolis, and to contribute also to the clothing of a large proportion of them. The Auxiliary Society collects subscriptions principally from the middle and upper ranks of society, for the purpose of providing school-rooms in all the subdivisions of its districts, and engages, after it has provided for the education of all the poor in its district, to remit the surplus funds to the parent institution, in aid of its operations at home and abroad. The committee of the Auxiliary Society in the first place, having agreed upon the number of subdivisions which may be requisite, is to form in each a school association, with a committee of its own, in order to diminish the labour. The association committee forms itself into numerous sub-committees, each of which takes a street or two, and is prepared with books ruled for the purpose, and containing certain heads of inquiry, calculated to ascertain the want of education in the district, and also the number of the poor and others who would be willing to become members of the association by subscribing one penny per week; their information, when obtained, is to be sent up to the auxiliary committee, from all the school associations under it, who, thus being acquainted with the state of their district, will finally determine upon the

number

Mr.
William Allen.

number of schools to be established, and will apply to the parent institution for teachers, school apparatus, &c. The school associations will establish collectors, who will apply not only to the poor, but from house to house, for those moderate sub-scriptions of one penny per week, all of which are to be wholly expended in the subdivisions where they are established. There is to be a general meeting of all the subscribers every half year in each subdivision, when the accounts of the school are to be made up, and the salary of the master and mistress, and other expenses attending the school, are to be paid; and the surplus is to be appropriated, under the direction of the committee, to the purchase of useful articles of clothing, which are to be distributed among those children who shall have distinguished themselves by their good conduct. All the children, on coming into these schools, are to be classed according to the religious profession of their parents, and provision made for securing their attendance, on the day called Sunday, at such place of worship as their parents may prefer.

What are the principles approved by the Society, and recommended for the for-mation of auxiliary societies?—I beg leave to offer a paper, which gives a full explanation of the subject; and if we were aware of any alterations that would tend to make it more generally useful, we should be happy to adopt them, indeed we should be happy to have them suggested to us.

[It was delivered in, and read, as follows:]

" HINTS for the Formation of AUXILIARY SOCIETIES in Aid of The BRITISH and FOREIGN SCHOOL SOCIETY.

RULES and REGULATIONS:

1. THAT this Meeting cordially approve of the object and constitution of the British and Foreign School Society.

2. That a Society be now formed, to be called *The Auxiliary School Society,* *for                          and its vicinity,* for the purpose of establishing schools within these districts, and of co-operating with the British and Foreign School Society in promoting the great cause of *Universal Education,* to embrace the same districts with the                          Auxiliary Bible Society.

3. That conformably to the fundamental principles of the Parent Institution, the schools to be established by this society shall be open to the children of persons of every religious denomination. No catechism peculiar to any religious sect shall be taught in the schools, and the general reading lessons shall consist of extracts from the authorized version of the Holy Scriptures.

4. That the parents or relations of every child admitted into the schools of this society shall engage that their children shall attend every Sunday at such place of religious worship as they may prefer, under the superintendence of such persons as may be appointed by the committee.

5. That all persons subscribing one guinea per annum, or ten guineas or upwards at one time, and all executors paying bequests of fifty pounds or upwards, shall be members of this society.

6. That the business of this society shall be conducted by a president, vice pre-sident, treasurer, three secretaries, and a committee consisting of forty-eight other members; and that five members constitute a quorum.

7. That every clergyman and dissenting minister who is a member of this society, shall be entitled to attend and vote at the meetings of the committee.

8. That the committee shall meet once every month or oftener, on some day to be fixed by themselves.

9. That the committee shall divide the district embraced by this society into sub-divisions, and appoint two or more of their members for each, for the purpose of soliciting subscriptions and donations from the inhabitants.

10. That in consequence of the Parent Institution furnishing schoolmasters and mistresses, properly qualified and trained in the British system, and also providing slates, lessons, &c. to be paid for by the Auxiliary Society at the usual charge, until it shall remit part of its surplus funds, the Auxiliary Society shall be entitled to receive them without any charge, provided the amount does not exceed one half the sum remitted.

11. That for the purpose of giving full effect to the benevolent design of the British and Foreign School Society in their universal extension of the blessings of education, the committee shall make it their business to inquire, by means of district committees, what number of children and of adults are unable to read, and report the same monthly to the general committee.

12. That for the purpose of still further promoting the great cause of education amongst the labouring classes of society, *through their own agency,* it is highly
expedient

expedient to encourage the formation of school associations throughout these districts, of which every person subscribing one penny a week or over, shall be a member; the funds of such societies to be exclusively applicable to the maintenance of the respective schools of the districts in which they are established.

13. That a general meeting of the subscribers be held on such a day as the committee shall appoint annually, when the accounts, as audited, shall be presented; the proceedings of the past year stated; a new committee appointed; and a report agreed on, to be printed under the direction of the committee, and circulated among the members; and that copies of all the district reports of the proceedings of the school associations, be sent as soon as convenient to the committee of the Parent Institution.

14. That on the formation of a new committee, the treasurer, secretaries, and such three fourths of the other members as shall have most frequently attended the committee, shall be re-eligible for the ensuing year.

15. That subscriptions and donations be now entered into; and that they be also received by the treasurer, secretaries, and members of the committee."

---

## "SCHOOL ASSOCIATIONS.

### Rules and Regulations.

THAT in consequence of the 12th Resolution of the Auxiliary Society, the whole district shall be formed into divisions of such size that each may be presumed capable of supporting schools for 3 or 400 children of each sex.

That a short paper, stating the advantages of education, the privileges of members, &c. shall be printed and circulated amongst the poor.

That after the divisions are agreed upon, means be taken to procure a large and respectable committee in each; and that these committees shall subdivide their department into streets, &c.; and a sub-committee shall be appointed for each of these smaller divisions, which shall be furnished with books ruled in columns, with heads of inquiry, as to names, residence, occupation, religious denomination, number of children above six years of age, how many educated and where, how many without education, whether willing to subscribe and how much, &c.; and that the printed papers, descriptive of the plan, shall be distributed to every house a few days before the inquiry is begun. That these committees meet as frequently as they conveniently can, in order to receive the report of their sub-committees.

That the information thus obtained of the state of the districts, be transmitted to the committee of the Auxiliary Society, which shall thereupon take measures to provide school-rooms for the accommodation of the children, and shall give notice to the Parent Society to provide suitable teachers, lessons, slates, &c.

That by extended subscriptions of small sums weekly, from all who are willing to contribute in the division, a fund shall be raised, not only sufficient to defray the current expenses of the school, but also to provide articles of clothing for the most deserving of the scholars.

Every subscriber of one penny per week or upwards to be a member of the association, and have the privilege of recommending one child to the school for every penny per week subscribed. Persons in all ranks of society to be also invited to subscribe.

That by an arrangement of sub-committees chosen from among the subscribers, application shall be made at every house in the division, and the subscriptions be collected weekly: these collectors to pay the money to the treasurer, and report regularly to every committee, with a list of the contributors.

That all the subscriptions raised by the association in any division, be expended upon the children in that division.

That the general committee of the division shall appoint a chairman and secretary, and meet at least once a month, to consider the reports of the visitors of the school, the collectors, &c.; the secretary having power to summon a meeting at any intermediate time, on a written application signed by three members.

That the accounts of the school be balanced every half year, or oftener if the committee shall see fit, and a report of the state and progress of the school made in writing to a half-yearly general meeting of the subscribers; and the surplus, after defraying the current expenses of the school, shall be invested by the committee in the purchase of useful articles of clothing for the children, or in any other way which the committee may judge most for their benefit.

That the providing the clothing be entrusted to a committee of females, who shall make their report to the general committee.

That the girls school shall be under the management of a female committee, who shall conduct it according to the general rules, and shall report regularly to the general committee of the division.

That

*Mr.*
*William Allen.*

That all the children, on their entering the schools, shall be registered under the religious denomination to which their parents belong; and that they be required to assemble at the school-house at an early hour, say nine o'clock, on every Sunday morning, where they are to be met by certain persons from the different religious denominations, who shall attend the children of their own sect to a place of worship; and that these persons be furnished with tickets, one of which they shall deliver to each child after the worship is over, as his certificate to the master of the school, on Monday morning.

That the regular attendance of the children at some place of divine worship be essential to the receiving of prizes.

That the distribution of prizes shall be made publicly in the school-room, at each general meeting, and at the same there shall be a public exhibition of the school.

That a printed report of the state of the school, with the names of those who have received prizes, &c. shall be published immediately after every general meeting; but the cost of each report not to exceed one halfpenny; and those to be regularly distributed by the collectors throughout the division.

That the distribution of prizes shall be as general as possible.

That the committee shall establish a gradation in the value of prizes, founded upon the number of tickets each scholar may acquire.

That the school be regularly visited by two members of the committee of the association, in rotation, who shall enter into a book, to be provided for that purpose, the date of their attendance, the number of children present, and the state of the school at the time; this book to be kept in a box or drawer in the school-room, under lock and key, accessible only to the committee.

That the committee keep a list of those children who, having distinguished themselves for good conduct, shall have nearly completed their education, and endeavour to find suitable places for those who may need it; and that children so placed out be occasionally inquired after and visited; and that also the auxiliary committee be solicited to appropriate a part of its funds in bestowing rewards upon those who shall have supported a good character for one, two, or more years.

That every half year a conference be held in the district, consisting of deputies from the committees of all the divisions in the district; and to this meeting every Association shall send its report, stating the number of scholars, their progress in learning, general conduct, distribution of prizes, &c. and an Abstract shall be prepared from these reports for the auxiliary committee of the district.

That a report from the Auxiliary Society be sent every half year to the Parent Institution.

That a library be attached to every school; the books to be lent out to the scholars under regulations to be fixed by the committee.

That no books shall be admitted into the library, but such as are approved by the Parent Society, or by the Auxiliary Society of the district.

That no religious opinions, peculiar to any sect or party, be taught in any of the school-rooms."

Are you acquainted with the establishment of the school in Spitalfields?—I was concerned in the first foundation of it. In the course of the proceedings of the soup committees established to assist the poor during seasons of scarcity, it occurred that the same class of individuals who superintended that charity, would extend their benevolent exertions to procure the means of education for the objects of their care; this being suggested to them, a special meeting of the committee was called, which proceeded immediately to form a school society on the British system, and to erect a school-house, which cost about 1,700*l.* This school has already educated 2,000 children.

What year was it established in?—In the beginning of 1812.

How many can it educate?—If the children could be procured, it would contain full 800.

How many actually attend?—On an average 320.

What should you take to be the cause of the deficiency?—One cause in that district, is the employment of the children in the manufactures; but I have no doubt that if the school associations were made to operate, that the school would not only be filled, but a necessity would appear for another being established.

From what you know of the state of education in different parts of the Metropolis, do you consider there are a great number of poor children without the means of education?—From what I have seen, which is principally founded upon the investigation, which took place a few years ago, into the circumstance of fifteen hundred poor families in and about Spitalfields, who received assistance from the soup institution, it appeared that a great proportion of the parents were totally unable to read; and I beg to state, that in some cases there was clear evidence of

persons

persons dying through scanty and insufficient food, which brought on incurable maladies. The following is the general result of the investigation above alluded to. [It was read.]

| — | N° of Families | N° of Adults | Cannot read | N° of Children | How many can read | Weavers, &c. | Church | Dissenters | No religious Profession | Catholics | Without Bibles | Much distressed from want of Work | More distressed | Still more distressed | In extreme Distress |
|---|---|---|---|---|---|---|---|---|---|---|---|---|---|---|---|
| North-West | 611 | 1,083 | 457 | 1,837 | 331 | 290 | 225 | 217 | 118 | 16 | 336 | 193 | 278 | 129 | 20 |
| South-West | 297 | 513 | 195 | 800 | 227 | 85 | 146 | 79 | 45 | 16 | 145 | 28 | 165 | 29 | 3 |
| North-East | 481 | 878 | 347 | 1,547 | 406 | 324 | 197 | 165 | 92 | 1 | 183 | 127 | 169 | 56 | 8 |
| South-East | 115 | 208 | 70 | 340 | 121 | 24 | 55 | 31 | 24 | 1 | 29 | 3 | 28 | 2 | — |
| Totals - | 1,504 | 2,682 | 1,069 | 4,524 | 1,085 | 723 | 623 | 492 | 279 | 34 | 693 | 351 | 640 | 216 | 31 |

Can you form any estimate of the number of poor children in this Metropolis, who are without the means of education?—It is almost impossible to answer this question, until the inquiries now on foot shall be further advanced ; but I have every reason to believe considerably more than 100,000. I beg this to be considered merely as a vague estimate, arising only from the opportunities that I have had of witnessing the want of education. I am confident that one half and upwards of the children of the poor are destitute of the means of education, and that a large proportion of them, through the neglect of society, are actually training in vice.

Mr *James Millar*, again called in, delivered in the following Papers; which were read.

### NORTH-EAST LONDON SCHOOLS FOR THE POOR.

| Instituted | Where situated | Description | Day School Boys | Day School Girls | Sunday School Boys | Sunday School Girls | If Clothed | Treasurer or Secretary | Master or Mistress | Annual Expense | |
|---|---|---|---|---|---|---|---|---|---|---|---|
| | BETHNAL GREEN : | | | | | | | | | £. s. d. | |
| | Church-street - - | Church - | 35 | 35 | - - | - - | Clothed - | Joseph Merceron - - | - - - - - | - - - | Mr. Merceron declines giving further information, in consequence of having attended the Committee himself. |
| 1720 | Parmeter's School, St. John-street - | D° - - | 60 | - | - - | - - | D° - - | Peter Renvoin - - - | John Wybird | 215. 10. 0. | |
| | Friars Mount - - | Methodist | - | - | 486 | 482 | - - | William Marriott - - | Sundry gratuitous | — | |
| | Virginia Row - - | Dissenters | - | - | 35 | 55 | - - | - - - - - - - | D° - - D° - | — | |
| | Globe Fields - - | D° - - | - | - | 89 | 60 | - - | Mr. Piggott - - - - | D° - - D° - | 20. 0. 0. | |
| | D° - - - - | D° - - | - | - | 40 | 41 | - - | Revᵈ G. Evans - - - | D° - - D° - | 6. 0. 0. | |
| | Darling Place - - | D° - - | - | - | 101 | 95 | - - | Revᵈ Mr. Shenston - - | D° - - D° - | — | |
| | Bethnal Green - | D° - - | - | - | - - | 70 | - - | Revᵈ Mr. Kello - - - | D° - - D° - | — | |
| | D° - - - - | D° - - | - | - | 60 | 51 | - - | Mr. Mandino - - - | D° - - D° - | — | |
| | Church-street - - | D° - - | - | - | - - | 70 | - - | — Fox - - - - - | — | — | |
| | Gibraltar Chapel - | D° - - | - | - | 150 | 100 | - - | Revᵈ Mr. Acutt - - - | D° - - D° - | 30. 0. 0. | |
| | Wilmot Square - | D° - - | - | - | 126 | 103 | - - | - - - - - - - | D° - - D° - | — | |
| | Middlesex Chapel | Methodist | - | - | 110 | 90 | - - | William Marriott - - | D° - - D° - | — | |
| | | | 95 | 35 | 1,188 | 1,217 | | | | | |
| | TOTAL - - - | | | | 2,535 | | | | | | |

(continued)

SCHOOLS FOR THE POOR—*continued.*

| Instituted. | Where situated. | Description. | Day School. Boys. | Day School. Girls. | Sunday School. Boys. | Sunday School. Girls. | If Clothed. | Treasurer or Secretary. | Master or Mistress. | Annual Expense. | |
|---|---|---|---|---|---|---|---|---|---|---|---|
| | HACKNEY : | | | | | | | | | £. | |
| 1715 | Paradise Field - | Church - | 181 | 90 | - | - | 100 boys all the girls | D. Duval, Esq. - - | Rich$^d$ & Chas. Hirgill | 500. | Number unlimited, National. |
| 1789 | Thomas-square - | Independent | - | 20 | 55 | 55 | 20 Girls - | Mr. Wafford, Mrs. Lewin | Sundry - - - - | - - | Voluntary Contributions. |
| 1800 | Dalston-lane - - | Church - | - | 30 | - | - | Clothed - | T. F. Foster, Esq. - - | Ann Adaman - - - - | - - | Supported by Industry. |
| 1810 | Grove-street - - | D° - | 57 | 26 | - | - | 26 Girls - | Rev. H. Norris - - - | Mr. & Mrs. Williams | - - | By Mr. Norris, National. |
| 1810 | Morning-lane - - | Unitarian | 28 | 28 | - | - | Clothed - | Rev. G. Smallfield - - | Mr. Newman, Mrs. Best | - - | Voluntary Contributions. |
| 1803 | Bohemia-place - | Independent | - | 31 | - | - | D° - - | Mr. Mather - - - - | Mrs. Punchard - - | 163. | - - D°. |
| 1806 | Wells-street - - | D° - - | 60 | - | - | - | - - | Mr. W. Loddign - - | Mr. Barrett - - - | 200. | - - D°. |
| 1812 | - - D° - - - | D° - - | - | - | 56 | 42 | 42 Girls - | Mr. White - - - - | Sundry, gratuitous - | - - | - - D°. |
| 1804 | Man-street - - | Baptist - | - | - | 30 | 30 | Partly - | Mr. W. Fox - - - - | - - D° - - - | 35. | - - D°. |
| 1813 | Shore-place - - | Methodist | - | - | 46 | 92 | D° - - | T. Page - - - - - | - - D° - - - | 30. | - - D°. |
| 1813 | CLAPTON - - | Independent | - | 14 | - | - | D° - - | - - - - - - - - | Mrs. Nash - - - - | | - - D°. |
| 1804 | HOMERTON - | Church - | 25 | 25 | - | - | Clothed - | Mr. Gaviller - - - - | Mr. Whitehead, Mrs. Coram | - | - - D°. |
| 1814 | - D° - - - - | Independent | - | - | 19 | 30 | Partly - | Mr. Holden - - - - | Sundry, gratuitous - | - - | - - D°. |
| 1816 | CLAPTON - - | Church - | 14 | 18 | - | - | D° - - | Rev. Dr. Watson - - | Mrs. Lee - - - - - | - | Supported by Dr. Watson. |
| | | | 365 | 282 | 206 | 249 | | | | | |
| | TOTAL - - - | | | 1,102 | | | | | | | |

" THE Kingsland and Newington schools owe their origin to a few individuals who commenced a Sunday school in the neighbourhood of Kingsland, and afterwards in Stoke Newington, which were held at each place in a small room at a private house. This was for many years the only means of instruction for the children of the poor, in these increasingly populous neighbourhoods. In 1808, by great exertions a small school-house was erected, and opened as a day-school for 25 boys and 25 girls, besides the school held on the Sunday. In two or three years the poor became more desirous of obtaining education for their children, and application for admission was increased, so as to render it necessary to augment the number of children in the schools, and after that to a still greater number. At length a difficulty was experienced in procuring suitable persons as master and mistress, to instruct upon the old plan of education. This led to an acquaintance with the system of Mr. Lancaster, now the British and Foreign. In 1811, application was made to the Institution in the Borough Road, and a master was supplied for the boys' school, which was immediately filled with boys, as far as was prudent for the health of the children. The girls' school was still continued on the old plan. In this way both schools were continued till the beginning of the last year 1815, at which time the applications for admission were more numerous than there were even children in the schools; but no more could be received, for want of room. The committee therefore determined to make an effort in order to raise money sufficient to build a more commodious room for a boys' school, and to convert the two day-school rooms into a school for girls. This was effected in the summer of last year, and cost but little more than 400*l.* The schools were opened on the 9th of last October; a mistress was then provided from the Borough Institution for the girls' school; so that now both schools are conducted on the British system, and are open for the children of the poor of all denominations, in Kingsland, Stoke Newington, and the adjacent villages. The boys' school is capable of containing from 200 to 300 boys, and there are 150 in daily attendance; the girls' school contains from 80 to 100, and is quite full. The committee are anxious to effect an enlargement of the girls' school, it being far too small and incommodious, but cannot at present, for want of the means. In the above school-rooms the Sunday school is continued, and more than 200 children are regularly assembled on the Sunday, and are instructed on the same plan as on week days. The annual expenditure on the present scale, including the Sunday as well as the day-schools, is 153*l.* The children are not clothed in these schools, except some of the girls, and those only in part, and which is done by a private subscription among the ladies and their friends, but quite independent of the fund of the schools. The advantages arising from this

institution

institution are already abundantly apparent in this neighbourhood. The facility with which instruction is communicated on the improved system astonishes all who will take the trouble to inspect the schools, and to notice its operations. Its good effects on the children are particularly observable, by its inuring them to habits of good order and subordination. It is also worthy of remark, that a considerable alteration for the better has taken place among the parents, their general character and conduct being undoubtedly much improved by the orderly habits and good conduct of the children : numbers of the poor are now seen attending their different places of public worship on the Sabbath, when they used to be either in the alehouse or engaged in other vicious practices. It has been remarked by old inhabitants of Kingsland (and by persons who feel not sufficient interest in the welfare of the poor as to induce them to assist in the removal of that which is in a great measure the cause of their wretchedness) that Kingsland and its vicinity is certainly much improved, as it respects the moral character and condition of the poorer classes of the inhabitants. Another advantage that has resulted from the instruction of the children is, that a desire has been created in the parents to obtain education for themselves. This being made known, an adult school was commenced in the beginning of the last winter, and was held in the boys' school-room, and continued during the four winter months, four evenings in a week, from seven till nine o'clock; in which time 106 men received instruction. They were taught upon the same plan as the boys, and were much more rapid in their progress, both in reading, writing, and arithmetic. Numbers of them, when they first attended, did not know the alphabet; but in the short space of four months could read easy lessons selected from the Scriptures, and could write legibly words of five or six letters. Several instances occurred, of men upwards of 60 years of age attending, and making surprising improvement. Other instances might be mentioned (to show how desirous they were of obtaining instruction) of men, after finishing their day's work, walking from two to three miles to attend the adult school, and from which no weather, however severe, prevented them. The writer has often witnessed them coming into the school during heavy rain and snow, when nothing but an eager desire to gain instruction could possibly have induced them to leave their dwellings. The British system of education is particularly applicable to the teaching of adult persons, as has been experienced in this neighbourhood. Had it not been for this invaluable plan, 106 poor ignorant men could not possibly have been attended to by the superintendence of only two persons. The average number attending each night was from 50 to 70; consequently it would have taken more persons as teachers than could have been procured, had it been on any other system. The whole expense attending their instruction did not exceed 10*l.* which was defrayed by a private subscription.

Kingsland, 30th May 1816. (Signed) *T. Tayler*, Secretary."

"This Report may be submitted to the Honourable the Committee of the House of Commons, as a specimen of well-conducted schools, and of economy.

The building of the boys school, which is capable of
receiving 250 boys, cost not quite  -  -  -  - £.400.

The education of 200 boys ⎱
 -  -  -  -  - 100 girls ⎰ cost  -  -  -  - £.153.
Which sum includes the salaries of master and mistress.

The education of 106 adults cost not more than -  - £.10.

*George Green*, Esquire, called in, and Examined.

WHERE do you reside?—At Blackwall.

Are you acquainted with any school established there?—I am treasurer of the Blackwall free school; and I am likewise treasurer of the Stepney Meeting Dissenting school; and I was lately treasurer of the parish school.

Are there many poor in that neighbourhood without the means of education?—A great many indeed.

Can you give the Committee any estimate of the number?—We ascertained, as well as we could, before we established the Poplar and Blackwall free school, that there were 700 children destitute of education in that immediate vicinity, and a very large proportion of them are Catholics; the parish school not being calculated to receive them, because they were all compelled to learn the Church Catechism, and go to Poplar Chapel.

How many are educated at the free school?—It is calculated to receive 500; at present we have about 360.

Upon what plan is it?—The plan is principally upon Dr. Bell's, and partly upon Lancaster's; but we allow them to go to any place of worship they think proper,

receiving

*George Green,*
*Esq.*

receiving certificates that they have been to some place of worship ; and the Cate-chism is taught to Church boys on a Sunday morning; the Dissenters are learnt at the Sunday school, we do not interfere with them.

Do Dissenters learn any Catechism at your school?—No, we only teach one Catechism.

Are a great proportion of your children Catholics or other Dissenters?—Our place abounds with Dissenters : we have got four Dissenting meeting-houses, which are nearly all filled, and only one chapel of the Established Church of England ; therefore they were very much alarmed at our school, fearing we should make Dissenters ; on the contrary, we are reducing the number of Dissenters, and increasing the number of Church people: we find persons leaving Dissenting schools and coming to our schools. There is not above one in six that call themselves Dissenters, the rest all go to Poplar Chapel ; so that out of 360, we have now at the school nearly 300 of them that go to Poplar Chapel.

That last number is rather more than one half you found uneducated in the dis-trict?—They were principally Catholics that we found uneducated in the district : they were so much alarmed at us, lest we should interfere with their religion, that they are now establishing a school of their own, but which must soon fall to the ground, for the want of finances, and we have no doubt they will very soon all come to our school ; at present we have only five of them.

Do you propose extending the limits of the school in proportion?—We have pledged ourselves to give education to the whole of the poor in the district.

When you have educated the whole of the children at present in the school, do you apprehend the children who are at present beyond the limits to which you have hitherto confined yourselves, will be admitted?—We take them of any age beyond seven years. The Minister of Poplar Chapel at first was alarmed, lest we were giving too much encouragement to the Dissenters ; he is now completely with us, and recommends an old parish school to be given up, and that the free school should be the only school in the parish.

What are your receipts?—Our building was paid for by donations, and we are supported by the annual subscriptions of about 600 persons, which produce upwards of 800 *l.* a year at present. We have been very extravagant in our hamlet, by having four different schools, besides Sunday schools ; we have got two masters and two mistresses ; besides a Catholic school and a Dissenting Sunday school. When the church people are satisfied that the Church of England boys are taken care of by their learning the church Catechism, and not being induced to go to any other place of worship, we are in hopes this will be the only school in the hamlet, by which a great saving will be made.

What is the reason of only 360 children attending, when you have accommodation for 500?—We wish to give an opportunity to the children of Catholics coming in ; at present they have not come forward ; we turn away generally twenty or thirty applicants ; every day we are receiving children.

How many days in the week do you receive children?—About once a fortnight.

Where do those children resort for education, whom you turn away?—They remain uneducated.

What is the reason of turning children away ; is it from want of funds?—A great many children have come, from their parents being very much distressed from the times, whom we have not received, but in preference we should rather receive the children of Catholics ; we had an opportunity of doing it by our rules, in which we say, every subscriber of a guinea a year shall have the liberty of nominating a child, and until they find out a subscriber of a guinea a year we do not take them in ; but we keep a good many of our subscribers in the back ground, in order to intro-duce the children of Catholics.

Is it a rule in your school, that the master and mistress should be members of the Church of England?—It is ; and that is the only rule which has given offence to some of the Catholics and Dissenters ; but we could not satisfy the church people without it, and now all the liberal church people are satisfied.

Do you conceive that in your district there is occasion for more schools?—I think our school is not large enough to supply the demand.

Suppose assistance were given by the public for building a school, would the subscriptions by which you have been supported be slackened on that account?—Not at all, it would be rather an encouragement to many of the church people who are now wavering.

*Martis,* 4° *die Junii,* 1816.

HENRY BROUGHAM, Esquire, in The Chair.

---

The Reverend *Philip Fisher,* D. D. Master of the Charter-house ;
*Thomas Ryder,* Esquire, Registrar and Solicitor; and Mr. *Robert Barbor,* Receiver;
Called in, and Examined.

WHEN was the Charter-house established ?—In the year 1611.

Was it by charter ?—By charter of King James the First, confirmed by Act of Parliament in 3 Charles I.

Have you more than one charter ?—No, only one.

Is there any other Act of Parliament relating to the Charter-house ?—The founder, Thomas Sutton, intended to have had this hospital at Hallingbury in Essex, which is about three or four and twenty miles from London; and he obtained an Act of Parliament for that purpose. Afterwards, Lord Suffolk was about to sell his house, now the Charter-house, and he treated with him for the purchase of it. It was an old Carthusian Monastery, but had ceased to be so at the reformation of the religious houses in Harry the Eighth's time. The Duke of Norfolk and Earl of Suffolk then made it their principal residence. Upon this purchase being made, the founder, having formerly obtained an Act for Hallingbury, he had changed his intention as to the place; and consequently the objects were not locally confined to the Metropolis, but for a general hospital, and it is still so considered and acted upon, without any regard to the Metropolis.

What are the funds generally, without entering into particulars ?—*Mr. Ryder.* I do not conceive, so far as I am to answer, that it is fit for me to make any reply to that question.

> [*The Witnesses were directed to furnish the Committee with an attested copy of their Charter and Acts of Parliament in an hour and a half ; and that the Receiver do attend then.*]

Mr. *Carew Thomas Ellers,* called in, and Examined.

DOES the book in your hand contain an attested copy of the charter of the Charter-house?—It does.

Does it contain the Act of Parliament also?—Yes ; it contains an exemplification of the Act of Parliament of Charles the First, and of that of George the First.

[They were read, as follow :]

### THE EXEMPLIFICATION

Of the Charter graunted by his Maiesties Letters Patents under the Great Seale of England, unto Thomas Sutton, Esquire, for the erecting founding and establishinge of an Hospitall and Free Grammar Schoole in the Charter-house in the County of Middlesex.

JAMES by the Grace of God Kynge of England Scotland France and Ireland, Defender of the Faith, &c. To all to whom these Presents shall come greetinge: Whereas at the last Session of Parliament last past one Act was made and passed, intituled, An Act to confirme and enable the erection and establishment of an Hospitall a Free Grammar Schoole and sundrye other godlie and charitable actes and uses done and intended to be done and performed by Thomas Sutton Esquire (as by the same Act of Parliament more at large yt doth and may appeare:) And whereas sythence the said Act the said Thomas Sutton hath purchased to hym and his heires of our righte trustie and righte well beloved cousin and councellor Thomas Earle of Suffolke, lord chamberlaine of our househoulde, a greate and large mansion-house, commonlye called the late dissolved Charter-house besides Smithfeilde, together with divers houses buildinges courts yardes gardens orchards closes and other hereditaments to or with the same mansion-house used or enjoyed or reputed as part parcel member or belonging thereunto, within our countie of Middlesex; which mansion-house and other the premisses the said Thomas Sutton doth conceive to be a more fitt and commodious house and place to place erect and found the said hospital and free schoole and other the godlie and charitable uses afore sayed, then in Hallingbury alias Hallingbury Bouchers in the saied Act mentioned ; and to that end the saied Thomas Sutton hath been an humble sutor unto Us, that we would be graciouslie pleased to give license power and authoritie unto hym the saied Thomas Sutton to founde erect and establish an hospitall and free

*[side note: The Rev. Ph. Fisher, D.D. Tho. Ryder, Esq and Mr. R. Barbor.]*

*[side note: Mr. C. T. Ellers.]*

*[side note: Charter-house purchased by Mr. Sutton, of the Right honourable Thomas Earl of Suffe.]*

*[side note: Charter-house conceyved to be a fitter place for an hospital than Hallingburye.]*

free schoole and other the godlie and charitable uses by hym intended in the said house called the late dissolved Charter-house besides Smithfield, and the saied premisses in our saied countie of Middlesex, and to incorporate the governors of the same hereafter named to be a bodie corporate and politique, and to have perpetuall succession for ever in fact deed and name, and by suche name of incorporation as is hereafter mentioned to have full authoritie and lawful capacitie and abilitie to purchase take houlde receive and have to them and theire successors for ever mannors landes tenements tythes rents reversions annuities pensions hereditaments goodes and chattels whatsoever, as well of us our heires and successors as of any other person and persons whatsoever, for the better maintenance of the saied hospitall, free schoole, and other the godlie and charitable uses aforesaid : KNOWE ye therefore, that we graciouslye affecting so good and charitable a worke, of our princelye disposition and care for the furtherance thereof, and of our especiall grace certaine knowledge and mere motion have given granted and confirmed, and by these presents do give grante and confirme for us our heires and successors, unto the said Thomas Sutton his heires executors administrators and assignes and to every of them, full power licence and lawfull authoritie at all tymes hereafter at his and their will and pleasure to place erect found and establish at or in the saied house called the late dissolved Charter-house besides Smithfield, and other the premises within our saied countie of Middlesex, one hospital house or place of abiding for the finding sustentation and reliefe of poore aged maimed needy or impotent people ; as also that the saied Thomas Sutton during his life, and after his death the governors hereafter named and their successors and the survivors and survivor of them and his and their successors for ever, and the governors thereof for the tyme beying and their successors, shall have full power licence and lawful authority at his and their wills and pleasures respectivelye from tyme to tyme and at all tymes hereafter to place therein such master or head of the saied hospitall and numbers of poor people, men and children, and such other members and officers of the saied hospitall, as to him the saied Thomas Sutton during his life, and after his death, to the said governors and their successors and to the survivors and survivor of them and to his and their successors, and to the governors thereof for the tyme beying and their successors and the survivors and survivor of them and to his and their successors, and to the governors thereof for the time being and their successors, shall seem convenient. And further, we of our saied especiall grace certaine knowledge and meere motion have given granted and confirmed, and by these presents do give grant and confirme for us our heires and successors, unto the saied Thomas Sutton his heires executors administrators and assignes and to every of them, at his and their wills and pleasures, full power licence and lawful authority at all times hereafter to place erect found and establish at or in the saied house called the late dissolved Charter-house besides Smithfield, and other the premises in our saied countie of Middlesex, one free schoole for the instructing teaching maintenance and education of poor children or schollars, and that the said Thomas Sutton during his life, and after his decease the governors hereafter named and their successors and the survivors and survivor of them and his and their successors for ever, and the governors of the saied hospitall for the time beying and their successors, shall have full power licence and lawful authoritie, at his and their willes and pleasures, from tyme to tyme and at all tymes hereafter to place therein such numbers of poore children or schollars as to him the said Thomas Sutton duringe his life, and after his death to the said governors and their successors and to the survivors and survivor of them and his and their successors, and to the governors of the said hospital for the time being and their successors, shall seem convenient, and likewise one learned able and sufficient person to be schooll-master of the said schooll, and one other learned able and sufficient person to be usher thereof, to teache and instructe the saide children in grammar, and also one learned and godlie preacher to preach and teach the word of God to all the said persons, poor people and children, members and officers, at or in the said house. And further, we of our said especiall grace certaine knowledge and meere motion have ordained constituted assigned limited and appointed, and by these presents for us our heirs and successors do ordain constitute assign limit and appoint, that the said house and other the premises shall from henceforth for ever hereafter be remain and continue and be converted employed and used for an hospital and house and place for the abideing dwelling sustentation and reliefe of such numbers of poor people men and children as the said Thomas Sutton during his life, and after his death the governors hereafter named and their successors and the survivors and survivor of them and his and their successors, and all and every the governors of the said hospitall for the time being and their successors, shall name assigne limit or appoint to be lodged harbored abide and to be maintained and relieved there, and for the abiding dwelling sustentation and relief of such numbers of poor children as the said Thomas Sutton during his life, and after his death the governors hereafter named and their successors and the survivors and survivor of them and his and their successors, and the governors of the said hospitall for the tyme beying and their successors, shall from tyme to tyme name assigne limit or appoint to be lodged harbored abide and to be maintained and relieved there, and for the abiding dwelling sustentation and finding of one schoolmaster one usher and one preacher as is aforesaid and of one head or master of the said house and hospitall ; and that it shall and may be lawful to and for the saied maister preacher school-maister usher poor people children members and officers of the saied hospitall or therein to be placed for the tyme beying to assemble be remain abide and cohabite together in the saied hospitall ; and that the saied hospitall shall for ever hereafter be incorporated named and called, The Hospital of Kynge James founded in Charter-house in the countie of **Middlesex**

Governors enabled to purchase take and receyve as well from his Maiestie as any other person manors landes ten'ts, &c. for the maintenance of an hospital and free schoole in Charter-house.

Power and authoritie given to Thomas Sutton esquire to erect and found an hospital in Charter-house.

Power and authority given to Thomas Sutton, esquire, to erect and establish a free grammar schoole in Charter-house.

The Charter-house for ever hereafter to contynue an hospital.

The foundation of the hospital.

Middlesex at the humble petition and only costs and charges of Thomas Sutton esquire; and the same hospitall and free schoole by the name of The Hospitall of Kynge James founded in Charter-house within the countie of Middlesex at the humble petition and only costs and charges of Thomas Sutton esquire, we do firmly by these presents, for us our heires and successors, erect found establish and confirme to have continuance for ever. And for the better maintenance and continuance of the said hospitall and free schoole and the said godlie and charitable uses intents and purposes, and that the same may have and take the better effect, and that all and every the maanors landes tenements rents reversions services and hereditaments goodes and chattels to be given granted conveyed assigned devised willed limitted or appointed for the maintenance sustentation and reliefe of the persons aforesaid in the same hospitall may be the better governed used employed and bestowed for the maintenance of the persons in the saied hospitall for the time beying, to have continuance for ever; We will and ordain and do appoint assigne limit and name, and for us our heires and successors do grant and ordain by these presents, that there shall be for ever hereafter sixteen persons which shall be called governors of the landes possessions revenues and goods of the hospital of Kynge James founded in Charter-house within the countie of Middlesex at the humble petition and only costs and charges of Thomas Sutton esquire; and for that purpose we have elected nominated ordained assigned constituted limited and appointed, and by these presents do for us our heires and successors elect nominate ordain assign constitute limit and appoint, the right reverend father in God George now archbishop of Canterbury, our right trusty and well-beloved councellor Thomas lord Ellesmere lord chancellor of England, our right trustie and right well-beloved cousin and councellor Robert earl of Salisbury lord high treasurer of England, John the elect bishop of London, Launcelot now bishop of Ely, sir Edward Coke knight chief justice of the common pleas, sir Thomas Foster knight one of our justices of our court of common pleas, sir Henry Hobart knight and baronett our attorney general, John Overall now dean of the cathedral church of Saint Paul in London,             Mountaine deane of the collegiate church of Westminster, Henry Thuresbye esquire one of the maisters of our court of chancerye, Jeffery Nightingale esquire, Richard Sutton esquire, John Law gent. Thomas Browne gent. and the maister of the hospitall of Kynge James founded in Charter-house within the countie of Middlesex at the humble petition and only costs and charges of Thomas Sutton esquire, and such person and persons as shall from tyme to tyme be maister or maisters of the saied hospitall, for and during such time as they shall be maister or maisters thereof, to be the first and present governors of the landes possessions revenues and goodes of the hospitall of Kynge James founded in Charter-house within the countie of Middlesex at the humble petition and only costs and charges of Thomas Sutton esquire; and that they and the survivors of them and suche as the survivors and survivor of them from tyme to tyme shall elect and choose to make up the number of sixteen, when and as often as any of them or any of their successors shall happen to decease or be removed from being governors or governor thereof, shall be incorporated and have a perpetuall succession for ever in deed fact and name, and shall be one body corporate and politique, and that the said persons and their successors and the survivors and survivor of them and his and their successors, and such as shall be elected and chosen to succeed them as aforesaid, shall be incorporated named and called by the name of the Governors of the landes possessions revenues and goodes of the hospital of kynge James founded in Charter-house within the countie of Middlesex at the humble petition and onlye costs and charges of Thomas Sutton esquire, and them by the name of the governors of the landes possessions revenues and goodes of the hospital of Kynge James founded in Charter-house within the county of Middlesex at the humble petition and only costs and charges of Thomas Sutton esquire, one body corporate and politique by that name to have perpetuall succession for ever to endure, We do by these presents for us our heires and successors really and fully incorporate make erect ordaine name constitute and establish; and that by the same name of the governors of the lands possessions revenues and goodes of the hospital of Kynge James founded in Charter-house within the countie of Middlesex at the humble petition and only costs and charges of Thomas Sutton esquire, they and their successors and the survivors and survivor of them and his and their successors, and the persons to be elected and chosen as aforesaid, shall for ever hereafter be incorporated named and called, and shall by the same name have perpetual succession for ever; and that they by the same name be and shall be and continue persons able and capable in the law from time to time and shall by that name of incorporation have full power authoritye and lawful capacitie and abilitye to purchase take hold receive enjoy and have to them and to their successors for ever, as well goodes and chattels as mannors landes tenements rents reversions annuities and hereditaments whatsoever, as well of us our heirs and successors as of the said Thomas Sutton his heires executors and assignes, or of any other person or persons whatsoever: And also that the said governors for the tyme beying and their successors shall have full power and lawful authoritie by the aforesaid name of governors of the landes possessions revenues and goodes of the hospital of Kynge James founded in Charter-house within the countie of Middlesex at the humble petition and only costs and charges of Thomas Sutton esquire, to sue and to be sued, implead and to be impleaded, answer and to be answered unto, in all manner of courts and places that now are or hereafter shall be within this our realm or elsewhere, as well temporall as spirituall, in all manner of suits whatsoever and of what nature and kinde soever such suits or actions be or shall be, in the same and as ample manner and forme to all intents constructions and purposes as any other person or persons bodies politique or corporate of this our realme

*Sixteen persons appointed for governors.*

*The names of the first and present governors of the hospital of Kynge James founded in Charter-house, &c.*

*The maister of the hospital to be one of the governors.*

*Governors incorporated by his Majesties letters patents.*

*Governors to sue and to be sued, ymplead and to be ympleaded by the name and title of their incorporation.*

469.                               of

Governors to have a common seale.

of England being able persons in law may doe. And furthermore we will and grant by theise presents for us our heires and successors, unto the said governors for the time beying and theire successors, that they and their successors shall have and enjoy for ever a common seale, wherein shall be ingraven the name and armes of the said Thomas Sutton, whereby the same corporation shall or may seale any manner of instrument touching the same corporation and the mannors landes tenements rents reversions annuities and hereditaments goodes chattels and other things thereunto belonging, or in any wise touching or concerning the same: Nevertheless it is our true intent and

Governors not to do any acte whereby any the mannors landes &c. may be transferred to any use contrarye to the true meaninge of these presents.

meaning, that the saied governors for the tyme beying and their successors, nor any of them, shall do or suffer to be done at any time hereafter any acte or thinge whereby or by means whereof any of the mannors landes tenements rents reversions annuities or hereditaments of the said incorporation, or any estate interest possession or propertie of or in the same or any of them, shall be conveyed vested or transferred in or to any other whatsoever contrarie to the true meaning hereof, other than by such leases as are hereafter mentioned, and that in suche manner and form as is hereafter expressed and not otherwise;

Construction to be made for the benefit of the poor.

and that such construction shall be made upon this foundation and incorporation as shall be most beneficial and available for the maintenance of the poor; and for the repressing and avoiding of all acts and devices to be invented or put in ure contrarye to the true meaninge of these presents, and therefore our will and pleasure is, and so for us our heires and successors we do ordaine, that the said governors for the tyme beying or their successors, or any of them, shall not make any lease grant conveyance or estate of any the saied mannors landes tenements or hereditaments which shall exceed the number of one and twenty years, and that either in possession or not above two years before the end and expiration or determination of the estate or estates in possession, and whereupon the accustomable yearly rent or more by the greater part of five years next before the making of any such lease reserved due or payable shall not be reserved and yearly payable during

Governors dyeing or beying removed, the residue surviving to remain incorporated.

the continuance of every such lease. And also we do ordain grant and appoint by these presents for us our heires and successors, that so often and whensoever any one or more of the said governors for the tyme beying, or any other governor or governors that shall be chosen hereafter, shall fortune to depart this life, or to be removed from his or their place of governor or governors, that then and so often the residue of the said governor and governors and their successors shall be continue and remain incorporate by the same name of the governors of the landes possessions revenues and goodes of the hospitall of Kynge James founded in Charter-house within the county of Middlesex at the humble petition and only cost and charges of Thomas Sutton esquire, to all intents constructions and purposes, accordinge to the true meaning of these presents, as if all the said governor and governors had continued; and that then and so often it shall be lawfull for the rest of the governors, or the greater number of them, to elect nominate choose and appoint one or more meete person or persons, according to the true intent and meaning of these presents, into the room and place or rooms and places of every such governor or governors which shall so depart this life or be removed, which person and persons so nominated elected chosen and agreed upon by the said governors, or by the greater number of them, shall be and shall be reputed and taken from the time of his or their election to be from thenceforth, together with the other governors of the saied hospitall; and after this manner to proceed

Electione of governors to be made within two monthes after any shall decease or be removed.

whensoever and as often as need shall require, and the same election to be made within two monthes that any of the saied governor or governors shall depart this life or be removed; and that the saied Thomas Sutton during his life, and after his decease the saied governors for the tyme beying, or the more part of them, shall have full power and authority to nominate assigne and appoint, and shall and may name assigne and appoint when and as often as he and they shall think goode, such number and numbers of person and persons as he and they shall think convenient to be poor men children and schollars master preacher schole maister usher members officer and officers of or for the said hospitall, as the said Thomas Sutton during his life, and after his decease the governors for the tyme beying and their successors, or the more part of them, shall

The number of poor people and children to increase and be maintained according to the ncrease of the revenues.

think meete and convenient: Nevertheless if the rents revenues or profits of all or any of the mannors lands tenements and hereditaments goodes or chattells at any time to be granted and conveyed to the saied governors of the saied hospitall and their successors, for the maintenance of the people in the said hospital, shall happen to increase or be raised or augmented to a better or greater yearly value than formerly the same was, or that the rents revenues and possessions of the saied hospitall shall be further increased bye the detirmination of any former estates in any of the saied possessions of the saied hospitall, or otherwise, that all and every such increase shall be employed to the maintenance of more and other poor people to be placed in the said hospitall, or to the further augmentation of the allowances of those persons that for the tyme beying shall be in the saied hospitall, accordinge to the true intent and meaning of these presents, and shall not be converted or employed

New election of officers poor people or scholars to be made by Mr. Sutton duringe his life, and after by the governors when any place shall become voyde.

to any private use. And also we do bye these presents, for us our heires and successors, will grant and ordaine, that whensoever and as often as any of the said places or roomes of any of the saied maister preacher scholemaster or usher, poor men or children, schollars members or officers, or any of them, shall happen to become voide by deathe resignation deprivation or otherwise, that then and so often it shall and may be lawfull for the said Thomas Sutton during his life, and after his death for the saied governors for the tyme beying and their successors, or the most part of them, within one month after such avoydence, by wrighting under the seale of the saied Thomas Sutton during his life, and after his death by the saied governors for the tyme beying and their successors, under their common seale,

to

to nominate and appoint other meet person and persons in the rooms place and places of them and every of them so deceasing resigning or otherwise becoming void; and if in case the said governors and their successors for the tyme beying, or the most part of them, shall not within two months after suche avoydence nominate assigne and appoint as is aforesaid, that then and so often and in every such case, from and after the death of the saied Thomas Sutton, it shall be lawful for Us, our heires and successors, by letters patents under the greate seale of England or privy seale, to nominate and appoint meete person and persons to all and every such office rooms place and places as shall remain voyde for the tyme aforesaied by the default of the saied governors and their successors as is aforesaid. And we do further, of our especiall grace certaine knowledge and mere motion, for us, our heires and successors, give and grant that the saied maister preacher schollmaister usher poor men children schollars members and officers of the saied hospitall, and every of them, shall be allowed ordered directed visited placed or displaced by the saied Thomas Sutton during his life, and after his death by the saied governors for the tyme beying and their successors, or the more part of them, according to such allowances rules statutes and ordinances as shall be appointed set forth made devised or established by the said Thomas Sutton during his life, in wrighting under his hand and seale, and after his death by the governors for the tyme beying and their successors, or the more part of them, under the said common seale. And further we have given and granted, and by these presents do give and grant to the said Thomas Sutton duringe his life, by wrighting under his hand and seale, and to the saied governors and their successors for the tyme beying, or the more part of them, after his decease, under the saied common seale, to make set down and appoint such rules statutes and ordinances for the rule government and well ordering of the saied hospitall, and of the saied maister preacher schollmaister usher poor people children schollars members and officers for the tyme beying, and for their and every of their wages stipends and allowances for and towards their or any of their mayntenance and relief, as to the saied Thomas Sutton duringe his life, and after his decease to the saied governors and their successors for the tyme beying, or the more part of them, shall seem meete and convenient; and that the same orders rules statutes and ordinances, so by him them or any of them to be made set downe and prescribed as aforesaid, shall be and stand in full force and strength in law to all constructions intents and purposes, the same beying not repugnant to our prerogative royal, nor contraire to the laws and statutes of this our realm of England, nor to any ecclesiastical canons or constitutions of the church of England which then shall be in force. And that for the better government of the saied hospitall, the same Thomas Sutton during his life, and after his decease the saied governors for the tyme beying or the most part of them, or such and so many of them as the saied Thomas Sutton shall by his wrighting under his hand and seale thereunto assigne appoint and nominate, shall and may after the decease of the saied Thomas Sutton have full power and lawfull authority to visit order and punish or displace the maister preacher schoolmaister usher poor people schollars members and officers of the saied hospitall and every of them, and to order reform and redress all and every the disorders misdemeanors offences and abuses in the persons aforesaid and every of them, or in the saied hospital or free-school, or in or touching the government order and disposing of the same, and to censure suspend deprive and displace the saied maister preacher schoolmaister usher poor people schollars members and officers, and all every or any of them, as to him the saied Thomas Sutton duringe his life, and after his death to the saied governors for the tyme beying and their successors, or the more part of them, or to such and so many of them as the said Thomas Sutton by any his writing under his hand and seale shall thereunto assigne nominate and appoint, shall to him or them respectively seem fit just and convenient; so allwaies that no visitation acte or thing in or touching the same be had made or done by any person or persons during the life of the saied Thomas Sutton, other than by the said Thomas Sutton, and after his death by the said governors for the tyme beying and their successors or the more part of them, or by such or so many of them as the saide Thomas Sutton by his writing under his hand and seale shall nominate and appoint thereunto. And we of our further especiale grace certain knowledge and mere motion, and by our supreme power and authority, for us our heirs and successors, do will ordain and grant that that the saied hospital and the maister preacher schoolmaister usher members officers, and all other the persons to be placed in the saied hospitall, shall be for ever hereafter exempted and freed of and from all visitation punishment and correction to be had used or exercised in or upon them or any of them by the ordinary of the diocess for the time beying, or by any other person or persons whatsoever, other than by the saide Thomas Sutton during his life, and after his death by the saied governors for the time beying and their successors. And further know ye, that we, for the considerations aforesaid, of our especiale grace certain knowledge and mere motion, have given and granted, and by these presents for us our heires and successors do give and grant, to the said governors of the landes possessions revenues and goods of the hospital of Kynge James founded in Charter-house within the county of Middlesex at the humble petition and only costs and charges of Thomas Sutton esquire, and to their successors for ever, our especial licence and free and lawful libertye power and authoritye to get purchase receive and take to them and their successors for ever, for the maintenance sustentation and relief of all and every the person and persons to be placed in the said hospitall, of and from the said Thomas Sutton his heires and assignes, the said great and large mansion-house commonly called Charter-house besides Smithfield, together with the houses buildings courts yards gardens orchards closes and other hereditaments lately purchased by the said Thomas Sutton of the said Thomas earl of Suffolk, and all those his manors and lordships of South-

minster

minster Norton Little Hallingbury alias Hallingbury Bouchers and Much Stambridge in the countie of Essex, with all their and every of their rights members and appurtenances whatsoever; and also all those his manors and lordships of Bustingthorpe alias Buslingthorpe and Dunsbye in the county of Lincoln, with their and every of their rights members and appurtenances whatsoever; and also all those his mannors of Salthorpe alias Salthorp alias Halthorpe Chilton and Blackgrove in the countye of Wilts, with their and every of their rights members and appurtenances; and also all those his landes and pasture grounds called Blackgrove, containing by estimation two hundred acres of pasture, with the appurtenances, in Blackgrove and Wroughton in the saied countye of Wilts; and also all that his manor of Missenden otherwise called the manor of Misunden in the parishes of Wroughton Lydeyerd and Tregoce, in the said county of Wilts, with all his rightes members and appurtenances, and all that his manor of Elcombe and Parke, called Elcombe Park, with the appurtenances, in the said countye of Wilts; and also all that his manor of Watlescote alias Wiglescote alias Wigelscote, with the appurtenances, in the saied county of Wilts; and also all that his manor of Wescote alias Wescete, with the appurts: in the said county of Wilts; and also all those his landes and pastures, containing by estimation one hundred acres of land and threescore acres of pasture, with the appurtenances, in Wiglescote and Wroughton, in the saied county of Wilts, and all that his manor of Uffcote, with the appurtenances, in the saied countye of Wilts; and also all those his two messuages and one thousand acres of land two thousand acres of pasture three hundred acres of meadow and three hundred acres of wood, with the appurtenances, in Broadhinton, in the saied countye of Wilts; and also all those the manors and lordshipes of Campes alias Campes Castle otherwise called Castle-campes, with the appurtenances, situate lying beying and extending in the counties of Cambridge and Essex or in either of them, or elsewhere within the realm of England; and also all that his manor of Balsham in the countye of Cambridge, with all and singular the rights members and appurtenances thereof whatsoever; and also all those his messuages and landes situate lying and beying in the parishes of Hackney and Tottenham in the county of Middlesex, or in either of them, with their and either of their rights members and appurtenances whatsoever, which said messuage was lately purchased of Sir William Boyer knight, and the saied landes in Tottenham now are or late were in the tenure or occupation of William Benning yeoman; and also all and singular the mannors lordshipps messuages landes tenements reversions services meadows pastures woodes advowsons patronages of churches and hereditaments, of the said Thomas Sutton whatsoever, situate lying or beying within the said counties of Essex Lincoln Wilts Cambridge and Midlesex, or in any of them, with all and every their rights members and appurtenances whatsoever, or such and so many and such part of the saied mannors advowsons landes tenements and hereditaments, or of any part thereof, as the said Thomas Sutton shall think meet; and also all letters patents indentures deeds evidences bonds and writings concerning the premises, or any of them, which shall be so given and granted by the said Thomas Sutton to the said governors and their successors, and all such conditions warranties vouchers actions suits entrys benefits and demands as shall or may be had by any person or persons upon or by reason of them or any of them (except all his mannors or lordshipps of Littlebury and Hadstocke, with the appurtenances, in the saide countye of Essex aforesaid) or in either of them, though the premises or any of them be holden of Us immediately in chief or by knights service or otherwise howsoever, and without any licence or pardon for alienation of them or any of them, the statute of Mortmayne or any other acte statute ordinance or provision to the contrarie in any wise notwithstanding. And also we do give and grant like licence power and authority to the saied Thomas Sutton his heirs and assigns, to give grant and assure unto the saied governors and their successors, for the uses intents and purposes aforesaid, all and every the said great and large mansion house commonly called Charter-house besides Smithfield, together with the houses buildings courtes yardes gardens orchards closes and other hereditaments lately purchased by the said Thomas Sutton of the said Thomas earle of Suffolk; and all those his manors and lordships of Southminster Norton Little Hallingbury alias Hallingbury Bouchers and Much Stambridge, in the saied countye of Essex, with all their and every of their rights members and appurtenances whatsoever; and also all those his mannors and lordshipps of Bustingthorpe alias Buslingthorpe and Dunsbye, in the county of Lincoln, with their and every of their rights members and appurtenances whatsoever; and also all those his mannors of Salthorpe alias Saltrope alias Stalthrop alias Staltrop Chilton and Blackgrove, in the county of Wilts, with their and every of their rights members and appurtenances; and also all those his landes and pasture grounds called Blackgrove, containing by estimation two hundred acres of pasture, with their appurtenances, in Blackgrove and Wroughton in the saied countye of Wilts; and also all that his mannor of Missenden otherwise called the mannor of Missunden in the parishes of Wroughton Lydeyard and Tregoce, in the saied county of Wilts, with all his rights members and appurtenances; and all that his mannor of Elcome and Parke called Elcombe Parke, with the appurts: in the said county of Wilts; and also all that his mannor of Watlescote alias Wiglescote alias Wigelscote, with the appurtenances, in the said county of Wilts; and also all that his mannor of Wescote alias Wescete, with the appurtenances, in the said county of Wilts; and also all those his landes and pastures, containing by estimation one hundred acres of lande and threescore acres of pasture, with the appurtenances, in Wiglescote and Wroughton, in the said county of Wilts; and all that his mannor of Uffcote, with the appurtenances, in the said county of Wilts; and all those his two messuages and one thousand acres of land two thousand acres of pasture three hundred acres of meadow and three

three

three hundred acres of wood, with the appurts: in Broadhinton, in the saied county of Wilts; and all those his mannors and lordshipps of Campes alias Campes Castle otherwise called Castle Campes, with the appurtenances, situate lying beying and extending in the counties of Cambridge and Essex or in either of them, or elsewhere within the realme of England; and also all that his mannor of Balsham in the countye of Cambridge, with all and singular the rights members and appurtenances thereof whatsoever; and all those his messuages and landes situate lying and beying in the parishes of Hackney and Tottenham in the county of Middlesex or in either of them, with their and every of their rights members and appurtenances whatsoever, which said messuage was lately purchased of sir William Bower knighte, and the saied landes in Tottenham now are or late were in the tenure or occupation of William Benning yeoman; and also all and singular the mannors lordshipps messuages landes tenements reversions services meadows pastures woods advowsons patronages of churches and hereditaments of the said Thomas Sutton whatsoever, situate lying or beying within the saied counties of Essex Lincoln Wilts Cambridge and Midlesex, or in any of them, with all and every their rights members and appurtenances whatsoever, or any suche and so many and suche parts of the saied mannors advowsons landes tenements and hereditaments, or of any part thereof, as the said Thomas Sutton shall think meete; and also all letters patents indentures deeds evidences bonds and wrightings concerning the premisses, or any of them, which shall be so given and granted by the saied Thomas Sutton to the saied governors and their successors, and all such conditions warranties vouchers actions suits entries benefits and demands as shall or may be had by any person or persons upon or by reason of them or any of them (except all his mannors or lordshipps of Littlebury and Hadstocke, with the appurtenances, in the saide countye of Essex aforesaid) or in either of them, though the premises or any of them be holden of Us imediately in chief or by knights service or otherwise howsoever, and without any licence or pardon for alienation of them or any of them, the statute of Mortmayne or any other act statute ordonance or provision whatsoever to the contrarie in any wise notwithstanding. And oure further will and pleasure ys, and we do by these presents, for us our heires and successors, ordaine and straigtly charge and command, that whensoever and as often as any of the churches parsonages uicarages chapells or other spirituall livings (the advowsons patronages or donations whereof are hereby meant or mentioned to be licenced to be given by the said Thomas Sutton to the said governours and their successors, for and towards the maintenance of the said godly and charitable uses) shall happen to be voyde or become presentative or presentable, or to be given or collated unto by reason of the death resignation or deprivation of any incumbent or incumbents of them or of any of them, or by any other means howsoever, that then and so often the said governors for the tyme beying, and their successors or the greater part of them for the time beying, shall present preferr and collate thereunto such meete and sufficient persons as they shall think fit: Nevertheless our full meaning and direction in this behalf is, and so we do by these presents, for us our heirs and successors, ordain and declare, that such and so many of the schollars as shall from tyme to tyme be brought up and taught in the saied hospitall, and every of them as shall after be fully qualified and become meete to take upon them or any of them the charge of the said churches rectories parsonages vicarages chapells or other spiritual livings aforesaied, shall as near as may be from tyme to tyme be by the saied governors and their successors presented preferred and collated thereunto, before any other person or persons whatsoever, avoiding as much as may be the giving of more benefices than one to any one incumbent. And to the end that all suspicion of indirect dealing, which might hereafter be used or put in practice by the aforesaid governors or their successors, or any of them, contrary to the true intent and meaning of these presents, may be prevented and taken away, Oure will and pleasure is, and we do by these presents, for us our heirs and successors, ordain and streightly charge and command, that the mannors landes tenements and hereditaments and other things, which at any time hereafter shall be given granted or conveyed for the maintenance of the said godly and charitable uses before in theise presents mentioned, nor any part or parcell of them or of any of them, shall at any time hereafter be by the saied governors or their successors, or any of them, leased demised granted or conveyed to them the saied governors or their successors or to any of them, or to any other person or persons whatsoever, for or to the use benefitt or behoof of the saied governors or of their successors or any of them, although express mention of the true yearly value or certainty of the premises or any of them, or of any other gifts or grants by us or any of our progenitors or predecessors, to the foresaied Thomas Sutton heretofore made in these presents, is not made, or any statute acte ordinance provision proclamation or restraint to the contrary hereof, had made ordained or provided, or any other thing cause or matter whatsoever, in any wise notwithstanding. IN witness whereof We have caused these our Letters to be made Patents: Witness Ourself at Westminster the two and twentieth daye of June in the nynthe year of our raigne of England France and Ireland, and of Scotland the fower and fortie.

Per Breue de Privato Siggillo, &c.

*Lukyn.*

This agrees with the Original, and
    is examined therewith by me,
        *Thoᶜ Melmoth, Regᵗ.*

The EXEMPLIFICATION

Under the great Seale of England of the Acte of Parliament for confirmation of the foundation of the Hospitall of King James, founded in Charter-house in the countie of Middlesex, at the humble petition and only costes and charges of Thomas Sutton, esquire, and of the Possessions thereof.

CAROLUS Dei gratia Anglie Scotie Francie et Hibernie Rex, fidei defensor, &c. Omnibus ad quos præsentes litere pervenerint salutem. Inspeximus quoddam breve nostrum de cerciorand e Curia Cancellarie nostre nuper emanan' una cum quodam retorn' indorso ejusdem brevis fact' in filaciis dicte Cancellarie nostre de recordo residen' in hæc verba: Carolus Dei gratia Anglie Scotie Francie et Hibernie Rex, fidei defensor, &c. dilecto nobis Henrico Elsyinge, Armigero Clerico Parliamentor' nostror' salutem : Volentes certis de causis certiorari super tenore cujusdam Actus Parliamenti nostri apud civitatem nostram Westm. Decimo septimo die Martii ultimo præterito inchoat' & ibidem usque vicesimum sextum diem instan' mensis Junii tent' ac deinde usque ad             vicesimum diem Octobris, proxime sequen' prorogat' intitulat' " An Acte for the establishing and confirming of the foundation of the Hospitall of King James founded in Charter-house in the countie of Middlesex at the humble petition and only costs and charges of Thomas Sutton, esquire, and of the Possessions thereof." Tibi precipimus quod tenorem actus predicti cum omnibus ill' tangen' nobis in cancellariam nostram sub sigillo tuo distincte & aperte sine dilatione mittas & hoc brevi T. me ipso apud Westm. XXVIII° die Junii anno Regni nostri quarto. Cæsar Ra : Execucio istius brevis patet in Scedula huic annexat' H. Elsyinge Cler. Parl. Inspeximus etiam predicta Scedulam eidem bri annexat' in Filaciis dicte Cancellarie nostre de Recordo similiter residen' in hæc verba, In Parliamento inchoato & tent' apud Westm' Decimo septimo die Marcii anno Regni serenissimi & excellentissimi Domini nostri Caroli Dei gratia Anglie Scotie Francie & Hibernie Regis, fidei defensor', &c. tertio & ibidem continuat' usque in vicesimum sextum diem mensis Junii, tunc proxime sequen' communi omnium Dominorum tam spiritualium quam temporalium & communium consensu & Regie Majestatis assensu (inter alia) Sancitum inactitatum & stabilitum fuit hoc sequens statutum, " An Acte for the establishing and confirming of the foundation of the Hospitall of King James founded in Charter-house in the county of Middx at the humble petition and only costs and charges of Thomas Sutton, esquire, and of the Possessions thereof ;" Cujus quidem statuti tenor sequitur in hæc verba, videlicet ;

Whereas our late sovereign lord king James of blessed memory, at the humble suit of Thomas Sutton, late of Balsham in the countye of Cambridge, esquire, deceased, by his highness letters patents under the great seale of Englande, bearing date the two-and-twentieth day of June in the ninth year of his Majesty's reign of England, did give and grant unto the said Thomas Sutton full power licence and lawful authoritie to erect and establish, at or in the late dissolved Charter-house besides Smithfield in the countie of Middlesex, an hospitall and free schooll in such sort as in and by the said letters patents is expressed; and did further by the same letters patents nominate ordain assign constitute limit and appoint certain persons, in the same letters patents named, to be governors of the landes possessions revenues and goods of the said hospital ; and did by the same letters patents incorporate the said governors and their successors to be a body politique and corporate, to have continuance for ever by the name of " The governors of the landes possessions revenues and goods of the hospitall of king James founded in Charter-house within the countie of Middlesex at the humble petition and only costs and charges of Thomas Sutton esquire ;" and did further by the same letters patents give licence to the said Thomas Sutton, to give grant and assure to the said governors the mansion-house commonly called Charter-house besides Smithfield in the said countie of Middlesex, and divers and sundry other manors messuages landes tenements and hereditaments mentioned in the said letters patents, as in and by the said letters patents more at large appeareth : And whereas the said Thomas Sutton, minding the performance of the said charitable work, by his indenture of bargain and sale, bearing date the first day of November in the ninth yeare aforesaid, and inrolled in his said late Majesties high court of chancery, did, according to the said licence to him in that behalf given, for the consideration in the same indenture mentioned, give bargain sell grant confirm and convey to the said governors of the landes possessions revenues and goods of the hospitall of king James founded in Charter-house within the countie of Middlesex at the humble petition and only costs and charges of Thomas Sutton esquire, and to their successors for ever, the said mansion-house commonly called Charter-house besides Smithfield in the said countie of Middlesex, and divers and sundry other mannors messuages landes tenements and hereditaments in the same indenture mentioned and expressed, upon especiall trust and confidence that all and singular the rents issues revenues commodities and profits of all and singular the said manors houses landes tenements and hereditaments should be for ever truly faithfully and wholly distributed converted and employed to and for the maintenance and continuance of the said hospitall and free school and other the charitable uses in the said deed indented mentioned, as by the said deed indented more at large appeareth : And whereas since the death of the said Thomas Sutton one Symon Baxter, the heire of the said Thomas Sutton, hath attempted and endeavored to impeach and overthrow the incorporation and foundation of the said hospital and the endowment thereof, and so to obtain and get to himself the mannors lands tenements and hereditaments that were the said Thomas Sutton's, and by him conveyed to the governors of the said hospitall for maintenance of the poor there ; howbeit the said heire drawing the same in question in his said Majesties courts of king's bench and chancery

---

The writ of Cerciorari.

The retorne thereof.
The time of the beginning and the contynuance of the Parliament.

The title of the Acte.

THE ACTE.
Recital of the letters patents.

Recital of the founder's deed of bargain and sale.

Recitall of the heires suits in law against the foundation.

chancery, and the case beying adjourned by the then justices of the king's bench into the exchequer chamber, after solemn argument and deliberate advice of all the then justices of both benches and barons of the exchequer, it was clearly resolved that the said foundation incorporation and endowment of the said hospitall was sufficient good and effectual in the law; and judgment was thereupon given accordingly in the said court of king's bench, and also a decree agreeing with the said judgment was had in the said court of chancery: Upon consideration whereof, and for that the said foundation and endowment doth daily maintain fourscore poore men, some maimed in the wars, some undone by shipwreck and misfortune on the seas, and fortie poore schollars, with a master preacher teachers and attendants and other officers, in very ample manner with good and sufficient allowance in all things; It is most humbly desired in the behalf of the governors and poor people of the said hospital, that it may be enacted by the King's most excellent Majestie, the Lords Spirituall and Temporall, and Commons, in this present Parliament assembled, and by the authority of the same, AND be it enacted by the authority aforesaid, That the said house *The body of the Acte.* called the late dissolved Charter-house besides Smithfield, and all the said houses edifices *The place of the hos-* buildings orchards gardens landes tenements and hereditaments within the scite circuit and *pitall.* precinct of the same, was is and shall be for ever hereafter an hospital in deed and in name, and is and shall be called by the name of The Hospitall of King James founded in Charter- *The name of the hos-* house within the county of Middlesex at the humble petition and only costs and charges of *pital.* Thomas Sutton esquire; and that such of the said governors named or mentioned in the *The governors incor-* said letters patents as are yet living, together with such others now living as have sithence *porated, and by what* been named or elected or mentioned to be elected into the room or place of such of them *name.* as are since dead or are removed, or have relinquished their places and are now esteemed governors, now are, and they and their successors for ever hereafter shall be and continue and shall be adjudged deemed and taken to be, a body corporate and politique by the name of the governors of the landes possessions revenues and goodes of the hospital of king James founded in Charter-house within the countie of Middlesex at the humble petition and only costs and charges of Thomas Sutton esquire, and by that name shall have and may have and enjoy all and *The governors ca-* singular such and the like capacitie power and abilitie to all intents constructions and purposes *pacitie.* as any other corporation lawfully incorporated may or ought to have. And be it further enacted by the authority aforesaid, That the said governors and their successors for the tyme beying *Power given to govern-* or the most part of them, from tyme to tyme and at all tymes hereafter, as to them or most *ors to make lawes and* part of them shall seem fit and convenient, shall and may have full power and authority by *orders under their* writing under their common seale to make ordain set down and prescribe as occasion shall *common seale.* require such rules statutes and ordinances as they shall from time to time and at all tymes think fit, as well for and concerning the naming and electing of such person and persons as shall succeed into the place and room of any the said governors, when and as often as any of them shall die or be removed from such place or places of governor or governors, or volun-luntarily shall relinquish their places, as also for and concerning the election order rule and government of the master preacher schoolmaster usher poor men poor children and all other members officers or servants of the said hospitall, in their several places offices and rooms, and for their and every of their stipends or allowances; and that the same rules orders statutes and ordinances so from time to time to be made set downe and prescribed as aforesaid shall be and stand in full force and strength in law, and be executed in all things according to the true intent and meaning thereof, under the several pains forfeitures and penalties as shall be expressed and contained in the same ordinances statutes and rules respectively: Provided always, that the said rules ordinances and statutes or any of them be not repugnant or con-trary to the laws or statutes of this realm of England, nor against the purport or true intent of the recited letters patents. And be it enacted and established by the authority aforesaid, *The governors hence-* That every person that shall from henceforth be elected a governor of the said hospitall shall, *forth to take the oaths* before he exercise the place of a governor, take the several oaths of supremacy and allegi- *of supremacy and* ance, which any two others of the said governors for the time being shall have power and *allegiance.* authoritie by this Acte to administer unto them; and that the master from henceforth to be *The master to take the* elected shall, before he exercise or take any benefit of the said place, take the said several *same oaths henceforth.* oaths of supremacy and allegiance, and shall also take an oath, that neither he nor any *The master's oath.* other for him with his privitie allowance or consent, hath given or shall give directly or indirectly any money or other gratuity or reward for or in respect of the having or enjoying of the said place; all which said oaths to be taken by such master, any two of the said governors for the tyme beying shall have power and authority by this Acte to administer; and that the preacher minister schooll-master usher officers poor men and *The oaths of the* every of them from henceforth to be elected and admitted shall, before he exercise *preacher schoollmaster* or take benefit of any such place, take the said severall oaths of supremacy and *usher officers and poor* allegiance, and shall also take an oath, that neither he nor any other for him with *men.* his privity allowance or consent, hath given or shall give directly or indirectly any money or other gratuity or reward for or in respect of the having or enjoying of the said place; all which said oaths by the said preacher minister schoollmaster usher officers and poor men to be taken, any one of the said governors and the said master for the time being shall have power and authoritie by virtue of this Acte to administer. And be it further enacted and established by the authoritie aforesaid, That the said governors *The governors to hold* and their successors shall and may for ever hereafter have hold and enjoy, according to the *for ever the hospitall* purport true intent and meaning of the said indenture of bargain and sale, the said hospital *and the possessions* house and all buildings gardens courts orchards and backsides thereto belonging, and all *thereof against the* and singular the mannors messuages lands tenements liberties franchises and hereditaments *King and others.* by the aforesaid letters patents or by the said indenture of bargain and sale given granted

conveyed

conveyed and assured, or meant mentioned or intended in or by the said letters patents or indenture to be given granted conveyed or assured to the said governors, against oure sovereign lord the King's Majesty his heires and successors, and against all other person and persons of whom the said hospital house mannors landes tenements and hereditaments or any of them were holden at the tyme of the said indenture made, and against theire heirs and issues, notwithstanding any title accrewed for or by any alienation in Mortmain, and also against all and every other person and persons of whom the said Thomas Sutton did purchase the said hospitall house mannors lands tenements and hereditaments or any of them respectively, and against theire heirs issues and assigns, and also against all and every other person and persons claiming or that shall claim any estate right title or interest of in out or unto the said hospitall house mannors landes tenements and hereditaments or any of them, by from or under any person or persons of whom the said Thomas Sutton did purchase the same; unless such other person or persons do pursue their title claim or interest by way of action or lawful entry within ten years after the end of this present **Exceptions and savings.** session of parliament: Saving to the King's Majesty his heirs and successors all such estate right title and interest as his Majesty had or might have had into any the said mannors lands tenements or hereditaments before the said indenture made, other than for or by reason of any alienation in Mortmayn; and saving to all and every other person or persons bodies politique and corporate and their heirs and successors (other than the heires of the said Thomas Sutton, and other than suche person and persons from whom the said Thomas Sutton purchased the said hospitall house mannors landes tenements and hereditaments or any of them, their heires issues and assigns, and persons claiming by from or under them respectively, and other than such person or persons as shall claim the title of alienation in Mortmayn of any the said mannors landes tenements and hereditaments) all such estate right title claim custom interest and demand whatsoever as they or any of them have or shall have, in as large and ample manner and form to all intents and purposes as if this **The governors disabled to convey the hospitall house or landes to the Kinge.** Acte had never been had nor made. And be it further enacted and established by the authority aforesaid, That the said governors and their successors shall be from and after the end of this present session of parliament for ever wholly and utterly disabled in law to make do levy or suffer any act or acts thing or things whereby or by means whereof the said hospitall house mannors lands tenements or hereditaments, or any part of them or any of them, shall or may be aliened assured given granted demised charged or in any sort con- **All conveyances to the Kinge of any the hospitall landes to be voyde.** veyed or come to the possession of our said sovereign lord the King, his heires or suc- cessors; and that all alienations assurances gifts grants leases charges and conveyances whatsoever from and after the end of this present session of parliament, to be done suffered or made to our said sovereign lord the King, his heires or successors, by the said governors or their successors, of or out of the said hospitall house mannors landes tenements or here- ditaments, or of or out of any part or parcel of them or any of them, shall be from and after the end of this present session of parliament utterly voyd and of none effect to all intents constructions and purposes, any former law statute act ordinance or other matter or thing to **The governors disabled to make any estates but for 21 years or under, or for one two or three lives, or for any yeares determinable upon one two or three lives, by indenture in possession and not in reversion, at the usual rent or more than the true yearly value thereof.** the contrary notwithstanding. And be it further enacted and established by the authority aforesaid, That the said governors and their successors and every of them be also from henceforth for ever wholly and utterly disabled in law to make do levy or suffer any act or acts thing or things whereby or by means whereof the said hospitall house mannors lands tenements or hereditaments, or any of them or any part of them or any of them, shall or may be aliened assured given granted demised charged or in any sort conveyed to any person or persons bodies politique or corporate, other than leases and demises by indenture of the said mannors lands tenements and hereditamen s, and every or any of them (other than of the said hospital house orchards gardens backsides or any of them or any part of them, or any of them now used for the habitation or use of or for the master preacher schoolmaster usher poor schollars and poor people of the said hospitall or any of them) for the term of one and twenty years or under, in possession and not in reversion, or for one two or three lives, or for any number of years determinable upon one two or three lives, in pos- session and not in reversion, and whereupon such usual yearly rent or more shall be reserved to the governors of the said hospitall and their successors, during the continuance of every such lease, as is now reserved upon any demise thereof, or otherwise the true yearly value thereof, **An exception for grants by copy of court roll. Reservation of power for the governors to graunte annuities rents or fees to officers for life or at will, soe as the present number be not encreased.** and other than grants by copy of court roll according to the customes of the severall mannors respectively: Provided nevertheless, that it shall and may be lawful to and for the said governors and their successors to grant reasonable and convenient annuities rents or fees to such person or persons as shall be officers ministers or needful attendants con- cerning the affaires of the said hospital, only for life or at will, so as the number of the officers ministers or needful attendants be not increased above the number which now is, as fully and amply as they should or might have done if this Act had never been had or **A proviso for the Lord North.** made. Provided always, and be it enacted, That this Act or any thing hereinbefore con- tained shall no way extend to give any title to the said hospitall in or unto the mansion house now in the possession of the right honourable Dudley lord North or of his assigns, at or near the East end of the said hospitall, nor unto any of the buildings edifices courts gardens orchards or grounds thereunto belonging or therewith used or enjoyed, nor unto any other the messuages tenements or hereditaments of the said lord North, being within or near the scite or precincte of the said hospitall; but that it shall and may be lawful to and for the said lord North his heires tenants and assigns, for ever hereafter to hold and enjoy against the governors master and other the owners or possessors of the said hospitall or Charter-house, now and for the tyme being, the said mansion house and premises and all ways and passages by cart or otherwise, easements waters watercourses channels pipes

conduits

conduits cocks liberties profits and hereditaments to the same or any of them belonging, or therewith or with any of them now used or enjoyed, or the which by the true meaning of any grant covenant clause or agreement contained in one deed of feoffment made by Edward late lord North unto sir William Peter knight and others, bearing date the sixth day of November in the fifth year of the reign of the late Queen Elizabeth, and in one other deed made by Roger late lord North and others, to the right noble prince Thomas late duke of Norfolk, bearing date the last day of May in the seventh year of the reign of the said late Queen Elizabeth, were meant and intended to belong unto or to be enjoyed with the said mansion house or any other the said messuages tenements or hereditaments of the said now lord North, according to the true meaning of the said several deeds; and that it shall and may be lawfull at all times hereafter to and for the said Dudley lord North his heirs tenants and assigns, and all others inhabiting and possessing the said mansion house or any other the said messuages tenements or hereditaments of the said lord North, for themselves their servants and workmen, to have free ingress and regress into and from the orchards gardens or other places of the said hospitall, where it shall be needful to survey repair cleanse amend and new make the said pipes conduits cocks channels and water-courses, and all other pipes conduits cocks channels and watercourses that hereafter shall be erected or placed within the precinct of the said hospitall for the conveying of water unto the said mansion house or other the messuages tenements or heredita-ments of the said now lord North or any of them, and to that purpose to subvert and digge up the soyle of the said orchards gardens or other places of the said hospitall where it shall be needful. Provided also and be it enacted by the authority aforesaid, That this Act or any thing therein contained shall not in anywise extend unto the mansion house of the right honourable Elizabeth viscountess of Maidstone, scituate and being in Charter-house churchyard near unto the said hospital, nor to any the buildings outhouses gardens or grounds therewith used or thereto pertaining, nor to any mansion houses buildings or grounds therewith used of any other person or persons within or near the precinct of the said churchyard or hospital, and not conveyed or mentioned to be conveyed by the said Thomas Sutton to the said governors by the said indenture of bargain and sale; but that it shall and may be lawfull to and for the said viscountess of Maidstone, and all and every other person and persons whatsoever, to hold and enjoy the said several mansion houses and pre-mises therewith used or thereto pertaining, together with all ways and passages by carts or otherwise, and all liberties profits easements water and watercourses pipes cocks and pas-sages for water, and liberty to digg cleanse amend and new make such pipes cocks and watercourses, as fully and as amply as if this Act had never been had nor made. Ego Henricus Elsyinge Armiger Clericus Parliamentorum virtute brevis dicti Domini nostri regis de Certiorando mihi direct' & hiis annexat certifico superius hoc scriptum verum esse tenorem Actus Parliamenti supradicti in eo brevi mencionat. In cujus rei testimonium sigillum nomenque meum apposui atque subscripsi. Dat' secundo die Julii anno regni dicti Domini nostri Regis Caroli quarto. H. Elsyinge Cler. Parl. Nos autem superales tenores brevis & schedulæ predict' ad requisition' Gubernatorum terrarum possessionum revercionum & bono-rum Hospitalis predict' duximus Exemplificand' per presentes. In cujus rei testimonium has literas nostras fieri fecimus Patentes Teste meipso apud Westmonasterium decimo octavo die Julii anno regni nostri quarto.

A proviso for the Viscountess of Maidstone.

Endorsed. In Rotul' Patent' Cur' Cancellar' Domini Regis Caroli infra script' de anno regni ejusdem Regis Angliæ &c quarto.

Examinat' per nos $\left\{ \begin{array}{c} \textit{Rob. Riche} \\ \& \\ \textit{Edw}^d \textit{ Clarke,} \end{array} \right\}$ Clericos.

This agrees with the Original, and is examined by me,

*Tho. Melmoth,* Reg.

## ANNO REGNI OCTAVO GEORGII REGIS.

An Act for preventing delays in the execution of the trust reposed in the Governors of the Hospital of King James, founded in Charter-house at the charges of Thomas Sutton Esquire, for the benefit of the said Hospital.

WHEREAS the governors of the Hospital of King James founded in Charter-house within the county of Middlesex at the humble petition and only costs and charges of Thomas Sutton esquire, are a body corporate and politique by the name of The Governors of the lands possessions revenues and goods of the Hospital of King James founded in Charter-house within the county of Middlesex at the humble petition and only costs and charges of Thomas Sutton esquire: And whereas the number of the said governors is six-teen; and consequently whilst the said number is full by law there must be nine of the said sixteen present to make any corporate assembly or do any corporate act: And whereas by reason of the great quality and stations of several of the governors, and the distance of their respective habitations and places of abode, it is by experience found difficult to get an assembly of nine so often as the affairs of the said corporation do require; and inasmuch as by law the consent of five is sufficient to do a corporate act, supposing nine be present; May it therefore please your Majesty that it may be enacted, and be it enacted by the King's most excellent Majesty, by and with the advice and consent of the Lords Spiritual and

Temporal,

Temporal, and Commons, in this present Parliament assembled, and by the authority of the same, That if any number of the said governors under nine and not less than five shall meet and assemble together at the Charter-house for the affairs of the said corporation, notice of four days at least of the time and place of such meeting having been first given or left at the usual places of abode of the governors within the City of London or bills of mortality, and five of the said governors so met shall by their joint consent act or do any matters or things relating to the said corporation, such acts or deeds shall to all intents and purposes be and be deemed and taken to be the acts and deeds of the said corporation, and shall be of the same force validity and effect as if done at a corporate meeting by all the governors; any law to the contrary notwithstanding.

Mr.
Robert Barbor.

## Mr. *Robert Barbor*, called in, and Examined.

WHAT are the number of poor men at present in the Charter-house?—It is at present limited to eighty; they fluctuate according to the vacancies, from 77 to 80.

Those are fed, clothed and lodged?—They are fed and lodged, and they have a cloak, but merely a cloak, towards their clothing; and an allowance of 20*l.* a year for pocket money, having been lately increased from 14*l.*

How many scholars are there upon the foundation?—The number at present is limited to 42.

Is this limitation of the number in consequence of the state of the funds?—I presume so; but it is altogether in the discretion of the governors, and of course they will keep the expenditure nearly to correspond with the income of the hospital.

Besides the scholars on the foundation, are there not a number of young men educated at the school, independent of the foundation?—Yes.

About how many is that number?—It does not fall within my province to know; but from the information of the schoolmaster, the number at present is about 160 or 170; that is a larger number than there has been for some time past; I believe the school is fuller now than it has been for many years.

Do those boys not upon the foundation pay for their education?—Entirely, precisely upon the same footing as they are in the other public schools.

And receive no advantage whatever from the foundation?—None whatever; none but the 42; they live in boarding houses, for which they pay exactly as they do at other public schools.

With respect to those on the foundation, are they supported entirely by the house?—Entirely by the house, during their stay there.

How many years is that?—That depends upon the progress they make in their education, I believe there is no limited time; whatever part of the school the boy comes into, he stays there till he has completed his education; the longest time that a boy can stay in the school, if he goes through class by class, is nine years; there are nine classes, allowing a year to each class; they do not admit them on the foundation under ten, by which time a lad is supposed to have acquired the rudiments of education; they admit them between ten and fourteen.

Besides their lodging and board, have the children on the foundation any clothing given them?—They have an uniform precisely like the Westminster boys, a cap and gown, jacket and breeches, shirt, stockings and shoes.

How are the boys presented?—They are appointed, I believe, in rotation, by the governors. A good deal of this information is out of my peculiar province as receiver; but I happen to have been educated myself upon the foundation.

Is there any regulation by the bye-laws of the house, with respect to the children who shall be presented?—The only regulation that I am aware of upon that subject is, that they shall be natives of Great Britain, I believe; and I believe that they must be protestants of the church of England; but I speak with uncertainty upon that point.

Is there any rule established by the bye-laws with respect to the circumstances of the parents whose children shall be presented?—I apprehend that that rests entirely in the breast of the governor who makes the nomination.

Then is it your understanding, that no rules have ever been established interfering with the absolute option of the individual governor in presenting?—That is a question which I cannot answer with any degree of certainty whatever; I am entirely ignorant upon that point.

But you do not know of any such interference having ever taking place by the bye-law?—I am not aware of any such interference.

When

When a governor presents, is it upon a vacancy always?—I believe the rule to be, that after the rota has been made for the governors, which rota is made, I understand, according to the rank of the governor individually, that governor, I understand, after that rota has been made, which takes place when they have got to the bottom of the old list, is to be entitled to fill up his warrant for the admission of the scholar immediately, such warrant to be effectual when the vacancy occurs.

*Mr.*
*Robert Barbor.*

Who are the present governors?—The two Archbishops, the Lord Chancellor, the Duke of Marlborough, Marquis Camden, Earl of Liverpool, Earl Spencer, Earl of Chatham, Earl Grey, Earl of Harrowby, Viscount Sidmouth, Earl Moira, Lord Grenville, Lord Ellenborough, Lord Erskine, Dr. Fisher the master, ex-officio.

How many vacancies on an average happen in the course of a year in the school?—I suppose upon an average, from four to six, they fluctuate; I speak now of a time of war, when many of the boys used to go off to the army and navy.

Have you known of any instances of any control being exercised by the governors, upon the presentation of an individual governor?—None whatever; it would not fall within my knowledge; I might hear of it accidentally, but as an officer of the house I should not know it.

Is it, generally speaking, understood to be the absolute privilege of every individual governor to fill up his warrant as he pleases?—I believe so.

Do the number of children on the foundation vary?—Of course the number varies in a very slight degree, by reason of the lapse of time between a vacancy being created and a vacancy being filled up, but not more than that.

Since you have known the house, has there ever been fewer than 42?—Certainly; the number when I was a boy at the school, and till within these two years, was 40; the governors have lately added two to the number.

Has that addition been in consequence of the increasing state of the funds?—I presume so.

Have you ever known more than 42?—Never.

Have the numbers of poor men varied?—They have never exceeded fourscore.

Have they ever been fewer?—They have, for the same reason which I alleged before, that the governors do not fill up their warrants immediately; but they must necessarily be under fourscore occasionally, because if a pensioner dies between Christmas and Lady-day, his successor is not admitted into the house till after Lady-day.

Do you never remember them being considerably under fourscore?—I never remember them, I believe, being under 75, generally about 78.

From what classes in society are the poor men generally taken?—That depends also upon the discretion of the governor giving his nomination; but by a modern regulation of the governors, the pensioner, I believe, is required to have been a housekeeper for a certain period prior to his election; what that period is I do not know.

In point of fact what are the classes of society generally from which the pensioners are taken?—I really cannot answer that question.

Are they persons of decayed fortunes?—They must be of decayed fortunes, because they declare their poverty upon coming in.

Do they declare under a particular sum?—They do; I think it is under 20 *l.* a year, or under a given sum in the whole; but the amount of that sum I do not know.

Is there any oath or limitation imposed upon the admission of the scholars?—I am not aware that there is any.

Is there any certificate signed at the presentation of the scholars?—I do not know what are the requisites for a scholar's admission, except that there is a certificate of his age.

Does the parent certify any thing?—I really do not know; the warrant is issued by the governor presenting, to the master and registrar, and does not fall within my knowledge.

Can you tell the Committee what in point of fact is the general description of the boys who are upon the foundation?—I am not competent to do that from my own knowledge; of a few of them I can speak, knowing them.

As

As to those whom you personally know?—There is a son of Mr. Chester, deputy master of the ceremonies; there is a young man of the name of Fuller, whom I know.

Who is he?—His father is a surgeon in the country.

Do you know of any others?—There is a boy of the name of Proby, the son of a clergyman.

Is he a kinsman of Lord Carysfort?—I rather think he is; there is also a young man of the name of Ramsden, the grandson of the late master of the hospital, whom Dr. Fisher has succeeded; there is also a boy of the name of Fisher, a nephew of the master; but there are no others that I know of.

Should you say, generally speaking, the boys are gentlemen's children?—Generally speaking I should suppose the boys upon the foundation of the Charter-house were the children of gentlemen of moderate fortunes, with large families, to whom academical education is a great object.

What are the boys taught at this school?—They are taught the classics, precisely in the same way as they are at the other great schools; they have also a writing master, who teaches them writing and accounts.

Are they taught mathematics at all?—That I do not know.

What are the exhibitions?—The exhibitioners are allowed 80 l. a year for the first four years; and if they have graduated regularly, they are allowed 100 l. a year for the next four years, upon producing certificates of residence and good behaviour to the master of the hospital.

How many exhibitions are there belonging to the house?—I believe the number is limited to 29; but it has never reached that number in my time, and I have been in office twenty-seven years.

Is it to Oxford and Cambridge?—To either of the universities, at the option of the exhibitioner; it is attached to the person of the exhibitioner, and goes to either university and any college, and does not interfere with any promotion he may get afterwards; the number was very small during the war, but it is now increasing.

How are the exhibitions given?—The exhibitioners are elected to the university by the board of governors, after undergoing a public examination.

Are they elected by merit?—I presume they are elected by merit, because they undergo a public examination, and the exhibitioner, I believe, is certified by the examiners, who are generally the Archbishops' chaplains, to be competent.

Are they chosen from boys upon the foundation?—They are confined to boys upon the foundation.

Are they obliged to undergo any course of education at the university?—I apprehend not, and they are not obliged to go into the church.

Do you know any of the present exhibitioners?—I think I do; the master of the hospital has two sons upon the foundation, who are exhibitioners; those are the only two whom I know personally.

Do you know any others, who they are?—No; I of course have their names in my books, because I take their receipts for payments made to them; I could tell you some others by name; there are two young men of the name of Clerke, there is another of the name of Young; Barnard is another.

Have any funds been left to the house besides the original endowment by Mr. Sutton the founder?—Not to the hospital; there has been a donation to the exhibitioners, by dame Elizabeth Holford, of money, directed to be laid out in the purchase of estates for the exhibitioners upon the Charter-house foundation to four colleges, of Christ Church, Worcester College, Pembroke, and Hertford which is now transferred to University College.

Were those estates considerable?—The management of those estates is with the members of the colleges, they are not under the control of the Charter-house at all, except as to University College, the money directed to be laid out in the purchase of estates remains vested in the funds in the 3 l. per cents. reduced, and the interest upon that fund enables the governors to pay two exhibitioners at University College 20 l. a piece annually, with an allowance of 25 l. to the head of the college, to furnish them with chambers.

How does it happen that the money was not laid out in lands?—That is not in my power to know.

How long is it since Lady Holford died?—That I do not know, but it is an old will; Lady Holford founded ten exhibitions for Charter-house boys at the university

of

of Oxford; the colleges elect eight out of the Charter-house boys, the governors of the house only choosing the two who go to Univertity College.

Since the founder's time, have there been any other gifts made to the Charter-house?—None that I am aware of, except a very small bequest by Bishop Benson, of about 50 l. which is now an accumulating fund.

Is there any other limitation by Lady Holford, except that they shall belong to the foundation?—I am not aware of any; the only qualification I apprehend is, that they shall be upon the foundation of the Charter-house school, and I am not aware of any instances where others than those upon the Charter-house foundation have been elected.

Are there many livings belonging to the Charter-house?—I think there are about eleven.

Are they valuable livings?—They are of all sorts; there are some very good ones, and some very indifferent.

What do you take to be about the best?—I should apprehend the best is worth from 1000 l. to 1200 l.

Who are promoted to those livings?—It is matter of election by the governors.

Are the governors bound to give them to Charter-house scholars?—I think the Committee will find that mentioned in the Statute.

You cannot speak to that of your own knowledge?—I cannot; it is a limitation in the charter.

With what estates did the founder chiefly endow the house?—Chiefly freehold property, in various parts of the country, to which considerable additions were made by the executors upon winding up the accounts, they being directed to bestow the residue in additional purchases.

Do you recollect what the income was at first?—Certainly not; I have no other means of knowing, except from Mr. Herne's account, who makes it somewhat above 5,000 l. a year at that time.

What is the rental for the last year to which your accounts are made up?—The rental consists of farm rents, quit rents, manorial profits, timber and underwood; and I think the aggregate of the year ending at Michaelmas last was rather more than 22,000 l.

Do you mean the net rents, after paying the expense of collecting?—There is no expense of collecting, because the rents are all brought to me.

Do you mean after deducting the expenses of repairs?—Certainly not; the repairs of the farms have generally been done by the governors; the tenant pays his rent, and if any repairs are necessary, the governors make an order for that purpose. In like manner, the expenses of valuing and cutting the wood is to be deducted. The above is the gross rent.

Do you consider the farms to be moderately let, or high?—That is a question I cannot answer.

Are the governors generally supposed to be good landlords?—Within the last two or three years some leases have been renewed, and in those cases the tenants have applied for an abatement of their rent.

Have any abatements been given?—The matter is postponed till the next meeting of the governors.

Have you had any considerable defalcation in your receipts, in consequence of the distress of the times?—The arrears for the last year were much greater at the usual time of making up my accounts at Christmas, than they were at any former year that I have been in office.

What is the yearly expense of the house?—I cannot tell without my books; but I think it was somewhere about 17,000 l. or 18,000 l. including all outgoings.

Do you consider the estates as well circumstanced in point of management?—I do not think there is a better managed estate in England, whether regarding the condition of the premises, the responsibility of the tenants, or the mode of cultivation.

What is the general expenditure of the hospital, including diet, maintenance, clothing, pocket money, repairs upon the premises, salaries to the officers, and wages to the servants?—About 15,000 l. a year.

What is the master's salary?—800 l. a-year.

Has he a house?—He has.

Has

Has he coal and candle, and perquisites of any sort?—No other perquisites than candles and a small triennial allowance for linen, and he has the use of the garden for vegetables.

Has he fees or emoluments of any other description?—None whatever, I believe.

How many children has he?—Six.

Does he hold any of the Charter-house livings?—No.

Could he, without giving up his mastership?—That I do not know; I conceive he could not.

Does he combine any other office with that of master, within the Charter-house?—None, it would be quite incompatible; he is not only an officer, but he is a governor.

Has he any other employment?—None other beyond his clerical duties, that I know of.

What preferment has he, independent of the Charter-house?—I can only speak from report, I have no knowledge of it; he has, I believe, a living at Elton in Huntingdonshire, which is, I believe, a college living.

Do you know of any other preferment that he has?—He has a stall at Norwich.

Do you know of any other?—I believe he has a living also in Lincolnshire.

Did you ever know an instance of any exhibitions being given to any person not upon the foundation of the Charter-house?—Certainly not.

What is the salary of the master of the school?—Between 280 l. and 300 l. a year.

Has he a house?—Yes.

Any perquisites?—I do not know that he has, except a triennial allowance of linen, and the perquisites arising from the town boys, that we know nothing about.

Has he any church preferment?—I do not know but that he has a small living in Wiltshire.

What is the salary of the usher?—I think it is under 160 l. a year, and a house capable of containing a large number of boarders, which is an addition to his income.

What other salaries are there?—There is the registrar's salary.

How much is that?—I think his salary is 290 l. a year, with a house; there is a preacher, 250 l. and a house; the reader has 120 l. and an apartment.

Are there any other salaries?—The receiver has 250 l. and a house.

What are the wages?—Upon the aggregate, little more than 400 l. a year; physician, 100 l. and a house; surgeon, 100 l.; organist, a house and about 80 l.

How many servants are there?—I really do not know.

Can you give any idea of the amount of the repairs for the Charter-house itself?—From 1,000 l. to 2,000 l. a year.

What may be the expense of the repairs of the master's house?—The master's house was put into repair upon his coming into office, and it has not cost much since.

How long ago is that?—He came into office in the year 1804.

You do not recollect what the cost of those repairs was at the time?—No, I do not; it is a very large house, and the repairs were heavy.

Is he allowed to take any boarders?—No such thing was ever thought of.

Do you know what the repairs of the house of the master of the school cost?—No, I do not; it is a large house.

Are the estates at rack rent, or let upon fines?—All at rack rent, and none upon fines, and generally upon twelve years leases; the estates have increased more than double within the last twenty-seven years.

## Mr. *Joseph Booker*, called in, and Examined.

WHAT are you?—Secretary to the Association of Catholic Charities.

How long has this association existed?—Since the year 1811; it was not entirely carried into effect till 1812, but we date it 1811, because we partly acted upon it.

What is the nature of the Association?—It consists of what was formerly three societies, one for education, one for apprenticing, and one to provide for destitute orphans.

What are the funds by which it is supported?—We have some funded property, but it all consists of subscriptions and donations which we get in the course of the year.

What is the income of the Association, one year with another?—For the last three years, about 2,000 l. a year; with the permission of the Committee, I will deliver in an account of the receipts and expenses for the last year.

[It was read, as follows:]

ABSTRACT

ABSTRACT of the ACCOUNTS from the 1st April 1815 to the 31st March 1816.

| RECEIPTS. | £. | s. | d. | DISBURSEMENTS. | £. | s. | d. |
|---|---|---|---|---|---|---|---|
| Balance in hand - - - - - | 22 | 13 | 3 | Mr. Ireland, on account of his remaining Bills - - - - - - | 185 | 7 | — |
| Ditto - not therein inserted - - - | 10 | 8 | 4 | Mr. Richardson's Account due for Coals - | 48 | 7 | — |
| Collected at the Sermons at the five Chapels, in 1815 - - - - - - | 424 | 14 | 3 | Expenses of the Asylum - - - - | 594 | 15 | 10 |
| Subscriptions and Donations received at the Dinner, 20th April 1815 - - - | 334 | 2 | — | Clothing Department - - - - | 162 | 3 | 8 |
| By the hands of Rev. W. B. Fryer, the net produce of £. 1,000 Stock 3-per-cents. - | 564 | 13 | — | Educating Department; i. e. Rents of the five Schools, Salaries of the Masters and Mistresses, and other Expenses - - | 644 | 15 | 4 |
| By the Dividends due Michaelmas 1815 - | 152 | 19 | 5 | Apprenticing Department - - - | 59 | 10 | — |
| Donation from R. P. Lahy, Esq. - - | 50 | — | — | Miscellaneous Expenses - - - | 238 | 10 | 4 |
| Return of the Property Tax on the Dividends received in 1815 - - - | 33 | 19 | 10 | Annuity for £. 1,000. sunk with the Society at simple Interest - - - - | 50 | — | — |
| By Rent for 1815, and Arrears of 1814 - | 24 | 2 | 6 | Purchase of Stocks - - - - | 198 | 3 | 1 |
| Donation of Mrs. E. Stock, by Rev. Josh Hunt - - - - - - | 40 | — | — | Insurance on the Buildings of the Asylum and East School - - - - - | 7 | 10 | — |
| Subscriptions and Donations collected during the year, including previous Arrears | 553 | 10 | — | Balance in hand - - - | 22 | — | 4 |
| £. | 2,211 | 2 | 7 | £. | 2,211 | 2 | 7 |

How many children are educated at this establishment?—The general average is between 600 and 700.

Are they all in one school?—No, in five schools; three for boys and two for girls, in different parts of the town.

Are they clothed and fed as well as educated?—Part of them are clothed, just to enable them to attend divine service on Sundays and other days; and we maintain and keep twenty orphans also.

From what parts of the town are the objects of this charity principally taken?—They are not confined to any part of the town.

Are they the poorest Catholics?—Entirely.

Are they girls as well as boys?—Yes; two girls' schools.

When was this charity first instituted?—In 1811.

Have the number of children increased since that period?—Yes.

You are a Catholic yourself?—I am.

What were the numbers in 1811?—I should suppose then they did not exceed above 300 or 400.

Have they gradually increased?—Yes.

Has that been in consequence of the increase of subscriptions?—I am rather inclined to think it has been in consequence of greater exertions among the parents to send their children.

Have you room for more children now?—Yes.

Do you take in all the children that offer?—We do; except they are of bad character, we refuse none.

By bad character, you mean dishonest?—Yes.

Have you any particular age when you begin to admit them?—Six years old.

How long do you keep them?—We have never come to a decision on that point.

How long do you keep them practically?—Till fourteen.

Do most of them stay till they are fourteen?—No; I should hardly conceive more than a quarter.

What should you think is the average continuance of the children with you?—I should think rather longer than two years.

Three years?—Thereabouts.

Have you adopted any new mode of teaching?—We teach upon the Lancasterian mode.

Is it a day school?—Yes.

Do you enforce attendance pretty strictly?—We do all we can, but we find the greatest difficulty we have to encounter is on that head.

Out of the 700 you have upon your list, what number, upon the average, should you think attended at the different schools?—I think I may safely say 500 out of the 700.

In pursuing the Lancasterian mode, do you explain to the children what they are reading?—Our orders are such; but I have not sufficiently attended the schools myself to be able to answer that question distinctly; I have however little doubt that it is done. It may be necessary perhaps to observe, that it is our intention in the course of the summer to appoint a select committee, to inquire into the state of the whole of the schools, whether they have become more perfect or gone backwards, in the course of which examination all these circumstances will of course be attended to; we have every reason to think they have materially advanced.

469.                                                                          How

How long have you been connected with the schools?—From the beginning, with these associated charities.

You are not the master?—No.

You have probably been at the school occasionally?—Every month.

You know probably whether the masters do explain to the scholars while they go on, or ask the scholars questions about the sense?—I can answer to the arithmetic part that they do, but I cannot immediately bring to my recollection whether in the reading classes they do.

Do you make use of rewards in your school?—We did at one time, but from the multiplicity of business that part is not attended to so much as we had originally intended; the clothing, for instance, is only distributed to those whom we consider to deserve it by their assiduity and attention.

You have said in a former answer, that clothing was given to some children, to enable them attend a place of public worship; do you mean that it is given to all those children who could not attend public worship without that assistance?—Generally, except where there is indifferent behaviour, which we consider as not to entitle them to it.

Are you obliged frequently to dismiss children from the school?—Yes, but not so often as we were formerly.

You dismiss for bad attendance or bad behaviour?—Just so.

And do you attribute the less frequency of dismission to the good effects produced by the schools on the children?—Certainly; I should beg leave to add to that, that I conceive the greater extent of the school, the high rank of the persons who attend to it at this time, and the clothing, have had that effect upon the parents, because it is often owing to them that they have not attended, at least to their want of zeal to attend to it as they should do.

Do you imagine the dismissions have been one-half in any given number of children, in any period of time, from the causes you have mentioned?—I cannot answer that question distinctly, from the great disparity of numbers.

Per 100 per annum, for instance?—I should conceive it has in the proportion of half.

You spoke of the exertions you used to persuade the children to come to you, or the parents to send them; to what exertions do you allude?—To there now being places for their reception to any extent, and the Roman Catholic clergy and others who had any influence, having been better able to insist on the parents sending their children.

To what extent would your schools now hold children?—I suppose we could accommodate one thousand easily.

Have you altered your mode of teaching in any way since the association took place?—No; we began this association with the Lancasterian system, and have not since altered.

Do you find the number of scholars continually increasing, or have they been stationary for any length of time?—Increasing continually.

Have you the satisfaction of hearing good accounts of those you have put out apprentices?—Mostly, I should say latterly; for we have been more successful latterly than we were formerly.

To what extent do you carry the system of education?—No further than the Lancasterian system, plain reading, plain writing, and the first rules of arithmetic; in some instances we go further, in the instance of our orphans.

In what districts are the schools?—A boys school and girls school in Lambs Buildings, Moorfields, in which there are from 80 to 100 girls, and I conceive about 150 or 160 boys; and what we call the central school, which is a boys school, contains about 200, which is situated at the back of Little Wild-street, near Lincoln's-Inn Fields.

What is the next school?—The two next schools are in Paddington-street, Baker-street.

How many children are there there?—From eighty to a hundred boys, and about seventy or eighty girls.

In some of those places at least there are a good many Catholic children who still remain not in the school, whom you wish to bring there, are there not?—I have no doubt there are many.

In all the places, or only in some?—I may say all the places.

Are there any other charities for the education of Catholic children, in the neighbourhood of your schools?—Yes.

Are they large or small?—Very small.

Can you speak of the aggregate number of children they may contain?—No, I am not competent to do that.

Can

Can you speak of their probable number?—At a rough guess I should conceive they could not contain more than between 100 and 200 children at the very utmost, altogether.

Do you imagine your charities and those charities take in half of the Catholic children who stand in need of education in the district in which your schools are?—I should conceive at present they do.

More than half?—Yes, considerably, two-thirds full.

Have you seen Mr. Montagu Burgoyne's calculation of the poor in a certain distance?—I have only had a glance of it.

Do you consider them as pretty accurate?—Yes, they are, as far as they go.

Does the number of children that are ready to come to your schools approach to the number that might be expected from those calculations, and from your conversations with Mr. Burgoyne?—No; I only saw his first calculations, before he had gone minutely into the subject.

Do you conceive that there are a good many of the lower Catholics who would be induced to send their children if more were done in the way of reward?—We have been exceedingly careful with respect to the extending rewards, lest it should be thought that we were desirous of making converts.

Do you see a reasonable prospect, from the increase that has taken place in your schools, of their containing the great mass of lower Catholics that want education, in some reasonable time, say three, four, or five years?—Yes, I do.

Do you apprentice out all the boys who stay till the age of fourteen, if they wish it?—No.

In what proportion?—The proportion is very small, from the difficulty of getting masters.

Do you provide in any way for the girls who leave you?—At present not; no application in fact has ever been made by them; but we have an intention to endeavour to put them into services.

Do you take care that all the children in the schools shall attend divine worship on the Sunday?—Yes, we are very particular on that head; but we cannot succeed to the extent of our wishes.

Do the parents begin to feel the benefits which result from the education their children receive?—Much more so than they used to do.

Do you contemplate any schools in new situations?—Not at present.

Are there parts of the Metropolis where new schools for Catholics would be advantageous?—I should conceive there are.

What Catholic schools are you acquainted with, besides the five you have mentioned of the Associated Charities?—The first is the St. Patrick charity school, in Dean-street Soho, the treasurer is Mr. Longnan, the secretary Mr. Kelly, 45, Fleet-street; there is a school in St. George's-fields, the president the Rev. Mr. Bramston, London Road St. George's-fields; there is another school attached to the Virginia-street Catholic chapel, the president the Rev. Mr. Dobson.

Where does he live?—In the house contiguous to the chapel. There is a school at Somers Town, under the care of the Rev. Mr. Nerincks, who lives in Clarendon-square, Somers Town; and there is one at Rotherhithe, under the care of the Rev. Dr. O'Brien, East-lane. Those are all that I recollect.

Have you seen, of late years, an increasing attention to the charity schools for the poor, among your own connexion?—Yes.

And a disposition to find any funds that may be necessary for that object?—Certainly.

Are the funds of the Associated Catholic Society amply sufficient for their object?—Not entirely

Have you a prospect of their increase?—Yes, we hope for an increase.

In what other quarters do you conceive Catholic schools would be advantageous, besides those in which your schools are, and the other schools you have mentioned?—Not knowing exactly the extent of the other schools, I cannot answer that question.

Do the committee of governors often visit the schools?—Individuals of them, frequently.

And show an interest in them?—Yes.

What salaries are allowed to the masters and mistresses?—Eighty pounds a year to the masters, forty pounds a year to mistresses, with apartments.

Is the Lancasterian mode liked in those schools?—Yes.

Is it found to answer the purpose better than the system that was pursued before it was adopted?—Most certainly; particularly for a large number.

What

Mr.
Joseph Booker.

What are the hours of attendance?—From nine to twelve, and from two to five: In the winter they leave off at four, or soon after.

Do they attend also on a Sunday?—Yes.

What hours?—From half past nine to one, on the Sunday morning, and from half past two to half past four in the afternoon.

### *Thomas Babington*, Esquire, a Member of the Committee, Examined.

Thomas Babington,
Esq.

HAVE you been engaged in the superintendence of Sunday schools?—I have attended for more than 30 years at a Sunday school in my own parish in the country, at Rothley in Leicestershire, whenever I have been in that quarter. I have found that to induce the children to come and to continue in the school, and to attend to their business with advantage, it was absolutely necessary to interest their minds, and that this was best done by communicating to them knowledge by suitable explanations of the Scriptures. Till lately, I never had a master who was qualified for attending to this subject, and in consequence I always found the attendance in the school slack, and a considerable disposition in the boys to leave the school, in my absence during the sitting of Parliament; since I have obtained a better master, I find these evils have much diminished. My experience has shown me, that an endeavour to open the minds of the children, and to make them enter into what they read, that is, enter both into its sense and its object, secures their attention, and produces a willingness to continue much longer at the school as scholars, than was the case before this was done to the same extent as at present. It is unnecessary to say how much this method of exciting an interest, and so obtaining good attention from the children, coincides with the great and leading object of their education, namely, to inform and regulate the mind and impress the heart. I think I can say from my experience, that where the sort of explanation of which I have been speaking is practised, with due attention to the state of information, intellect, and feeling, in the children, that it will tend to produce a great effect on their manners and habits; they will contract deference and respect for those who instruct them, and a desire of information; and on leaving the school their gratitude will be very apparent, for years, towards those who have taken such pains with them, and their characters will appear to have undergone a very important change. My object has been to lead, and enable the children to read, not mechanically, but with their understanding, and to interest them in the subject-matter of what they were reading, so that after leaving the school they might not only be improved in their general character and in their knowledge, but might be qualified and disposed to take up the Bible in after-life with satisfaction and profit. Those who have not had experience in schools for the poor, would scarcely conceive in how great a degree young children read without understanding, or making any effort to understand, what they read. This habit, very early contracted, is apt to continue with most in a very high degree during the whole of their school education; and they leave the school very able indeed to read, but little disposed to do so, because the reading is not interesting to their minds; and therefore the benefits of education are attained very imperfectly. The explanations have been given to the children in a series of easy and familiar *viva voce* questions, and with comparatively little in the way of address, which has been chiefly employed when it was desired to impress the importance of truths, and to make some, though always a moderate impression on their feelings. Great care has been taken to accommodate such questions and little addresses as much as possible to their state of intellect, and knowledge, and feeling, and to give them that complexion which might be agreeable and interesting to their minds. When once, by the pursuit of this system, the child is brought to understand in a small degree what he reads, and to take some interest in it, the progress is astonishingly great. A course of this kind, pursued for only three quarters of an hour each Sunday, brought the children forward in their understandings, at a period when no assistance whatever was derived at any time from the regular master of the school, to such a degree as to enable the children who had been a year under it, to answer questions in general with ease and pleasure. Care is taken never to make ignorance any fault, except when accompanied with inattention or perverseness, but to proceed with kindness and good humour, and to support the child with encouragements, until the matter is understood. When this mode was first adopted, the common habit of taking places for good answers was practised; but it was soon found that this led to self-conceit and pride in some of the ablest of the boys, and to depression of spirits and a consequent listlessness in a greater number of those whose faculties were inferior; this practice was in consequence discontinued.

*Mercurii, 5° die Junii,* 1816.
HENRY BROUGHAM, Esq. in The Chair.

---

*Thomas Babington,* Esq. a Member of the Committee,
again Examined.

TWO striking instances of the ill effects produced in two of the most able boys, contributed, probably, to draw my attention more immediately to this point. Since the change, I have found the progress in learning greater than before in the school at large, though less, probably, in a few of the more able boys; and I find no difficulty in keeping the attention alive, and in exciting a sufficient interest in the bosoms of the scholars. We have proceeded without any of those bad effects which before we experienced, and we have now had the new plan, of not taking places, ten or twelve years in operation. With respect to rewards and punishments, we are not profuse in the former, and very sparing of the latter; our punishments, if I may be allowed the expression, consist chiefly in the withholding rewards; corporal punishment is almost altogether avoided, and in strong cases resort is had to expulsion from the school. I have always found that the best mode of noticing faults is to talk in a friendly and rational way to the culprit, in the presence of his school-fellows, and that there are few minds on which a due impression may not be made in this manner; and a far better and more durable impression is produced upon the school at large, than by any of the common modes of punishment which were in use when I first knew the school. I have not been desirous to carry on the children fast in mere reading and writing, wishing always to have them for several years in the school, and finding that the parents, estimating their progress by their advancement in those mechanical parts of instruction, (the parts on which their own attention is generally most fixed,) were not desirous of continuing them in it after their children had, to their apprehension, acquired sufficient attainments of that kind. I have wished to keep the children as long as I could in the school for the sake of communicating to them a tolerably competent knowledge of religion, and of impressing on them a regard for the Scriptures, and a respect, to say the least, for their doctrines; advantages which were scarcely to be attained, except they continued there for a considerable time. I have also thought it of high importance that the habits acquired in the school should be well confirmed, esteeming them a very valuable part of school education, namely, regularity of attendance on divine worship, cleanliness, deference to authority, civility, punctuality, method, and abstinence from disturbing others, and from talking when they ought to be silent. These, with other good habits, in my opinion, can scarcely become established parts of the character, except the continuance at school be considerably prolonged. The affection also of the children for those who teach them, if they are well taught, is a very important instrument to secure their good behaviour in future life; it greatly softens their minds, and is a strong barrier against conduct which they know will be highly displeasing to their former teachers; this affection will seldom become a settled habit of mind, except their schooling be continued during several years. I have also been averse to a very swift progress in those mechanical branches of learning, which the poor can best understand and therefore will most highly esteem, having found in some instances that it tended to intoxicate the minds both of the parent and the scholar: and conceiving the most important fruits of education to be those which regard the principles, the dispositions, and the habits, I have been very careful to avoid any system, for accelerating the learning of the scholars, which might be adverse to such fruits. I have thought it desirable to make the attendance at school on Sunday as little burthensome as might be, and therefore the children have been kept to their business only about one hour before church in the morning, one hour before church in the afternoon, and an hour or an hour and a half later in the evening. I have found no difficulty with respect to the children of Dissenters, though the children in this school learn the Catechism, and regularly go to church in a body: such children have cheerfully acquiesced in the general course pursued. I should not have objected to any of them going to the meeting with their parents, but have insisted on their going to church, on the ground of their probably spending their time in play instead of going to the meeting, if they did not go to the church. With respect to the Catechism, I do not believe any difficulty

*Thomas Babington, Esq.*

whatever

*Thomas Babington, Esq.*

whatever has at any time occurred. In the explanations of Scripture given to the children, which are found to interest their minds more than any thing, controversial points are carefully avoided, and nothing is said which could be offensive to Dissenting parents, if repeated by the children on going to their homes. The Dissenters among the children are not numerous, perhaps a fifth of the whole, perhaps fewer. The children have an opportunity of learning to write gratis on the evening of one of the week days; and the very small ones, who are engaged in the manufactures at their homes, are permitted to go to a day-school, when their parents find it most convenient to send them, which may be perhaps three days in a week upon the average, and they receive this education gratis till they can read a verse in the Testament without much difficulty. The whole expense of the school, which consists of between eighty and ninety, including every thing, may be about 10s. per head. Some articles of dress are given or furnished at a cheap rate to the girls, but not to the boys. The general result of this mode of education, with respect to both, has been, I think, very favourable; they very generally leave the school with mild and modest dispositions, and such habits as suit their station in society.

Do you insist upon the children attending your own church, that is, the Established Church?—I have hitherto insisted upon the children of Dissenters going with the other children to church, because the meeting-house of the Dissenters is so situated that their actually going thither could not well be secured, and I feared that many who professed that they would go, would in fact play truant.

Then all you require is, that they should go to some church?—That is all I required in my own mind, though I never held it out to the school; but my language to the Dissenters, and respecting the Dissenters, has always been very conciliatory, and such as would prevent them from considering themselves objects of contempt or ill will.

Do you find any repugnance on the part of parents to allow their children to attend your church?—I never had an application from any parent to have his child released from going to church, nor from any of the children, except on one occasion, when two of the boys, slipping away from the school as it was passing to church, excused themselves on the alleged ground of their having gone to the meeting, and they expressed a wish to be permitted in future to go there. The man who was the parent of one of the children, and the master of the other (his apprentice) was a Dissenter. I do not exactly remember what I said to the boys, but more or less to the following effect; that I feared if I granted their request, they would be very slack in their attendance on the meeting; that my wish was that they should punctually go to a place of worship on the Sunday, and I did not know how to secure this but by carrying them to church with the other boys, and that this was my only reason for doing so. They have since attended the school and gone to church, apparently quite cheerfully, and I have had no remonstrance from the family to which they belong.

Do you conceive, from what you have observed of schools generally, that there would be any difficulty, with respect to Dissenters, in an arrangement of this sort; suppose a school in which the children were taught upon the plan of the National establishment, but such as belonged to sectarian parents were not compelled to attend divine service in church, but only required to satisfy the directors of the school that they shall attend some place of worship regularly?—I think not, provided no offensive language whatever was used to them by the masters or directors of the school on the ground of their being Dissenters, or permitted to be used towards them by their school-fellows. If this course were not strictly followed, I should conceive that the greatest obstacles to the success of such a plan would arise.

With respect to the Catechism, do you from your experience apprehend that a mode might be fallen upon, of teaching all the poor children of the school that large proportion of doctrine in which the church and the sects are all agreed, and confining the instruction with respect to the remaining part of the doctrine, upon which they differ, to the children belonging to the Establishment, leaving the Dissenters to instruct their own children in their own peculiar tenets?—If a difficulty were made by dissenting parents, as to teaching the Catechism, I question whether any such plan as that mentioned would answer, for it is called the Church Catechism, and the name would set such Dissenters against any part of it being taught, even though they might have no objection to the religious truths contained in the parts proposed to be taught, if those religious truths were offered to their children under another title and in another form.

Do

Do you apprehend that if Dissenters sent their children to a school upon the *Thomas Babington,* National plan, and such modifications of that plan were made, with respect to *Esq.* teaching the Catechism and church attendance, as to render this practicable, that the children would by degrees be allowed to attend the church, and would gradually fall into the Establishment?—I should be of opinion that a considerable portion of them would ; what proportion I really cannot say. All the children of the school of which I have been speaking, receive a Prayer-book and Bible, as well as Watts's Hymns for Children, on leaving the school, and none of them object to the Prayer-book ; nor do they object to the getting of a Collect by heart every Sunday, which is one of our practices, during the latter years of their attendance at the school, when they become old enough to do this. I believe they leave the school with a respect for the church and churchmen, even though they may return to the habit of frequenting the meeting-house with their parents ; so that their prejudices as Dissenters appear to be so far softened as to pave the way for their entire removal. The success of such a system for conciliating Dissenters, must materially depend on the spirit in which it is carried on.

### The very Reverend Dr. *Ireland,* Dean of *Westminster,* called in, and Examined.

ARE you acquainted with the National Establishment as far as regards the *Dr. Ireland.* Westminster school?—Very little ; I have but just entered upon my situation as Dean, to which I succeeded upon the death of Dr. Vincent, nor have I yet had time to inquire into the particulars.

The committee presume you are not acquainted particularly with the state of education among the lower orders in the district to which you now belong?—Not yet ; but I am with respect to Croydon, from which I have removed.

Will you be pleased to state to the Committee, in what way you have had an opportunity of seeing the education that is there practised?—By inviting the parents to send their children, and by attending the school two or three times in the week.

Was it a free school?—It was.

In connexion with the National Society?—Yes.

Did you find any repugnance amongst Dissenters to sending their children to that school?—There was an inclination on the part of the Dissenters to join their efforts with mine, for the purpose of a combined school ; but the business went off in consequence of a want of agreement as to the mode ; the Dissenters claimed a portion of the management of the joint school, and demanded that one-half of the managers should be Dissenters, though the proportion of Dissenters, in comparison with the number of Church people, was not more than one-tenth or one-twelfth part : the project was accordingly dropped, and the parties formed separate schools of their own.

Has this difference tended to prevent the Dissenters from sending their children to the National school?—Yes ; they send to their own school.

Do any children of Churchmen attend the dissenting schools?—Yes.

Do you think any considerable number?—Not many ; but they are much invited so to do by the Dissenters.

Suppose no difference, as you have referred to, had taken place, was it a plan to have accommodated the National system, so as to make it possible for Dissenters to send their children to the school?—There was no plan to cut down the National system in order to meet the demands of Dissenters, but it was completely understood that the school should be open to all who would take the run of it.

Do you apprehend that any material difficulty would have occurred from recommending the children to attend the church?—Some difficulty, certainly ; but more with respect to the teaching of the Church Catechism within the walls of the school.

Might it not have been so accommodated, as to have allowed the Dissenters children to go to their own place of worship, upon satisfactory security being obtained that they had attended regularly upon divine service, and by teaching only such parts of the catechism as both church and sect were agreed upon?—The Dissenters always claimed a part of the management of the school, together with any such intended arrangement ; of course that separate question was not persisted in ; I found that they demanded a part of the management, and in a way which I could not possibly accede to, and the matter was not fully discussed.

469.                                                                          Do

Dr. Ireland.

Do you, from your observation, think that there is any insuperable obstacle in the way of such accommodation as has just been alluded to?—Considering both the parties together, I think there is an insuperable objection; I mean, considering the principles and prejudices of both.

In what way do you take that objection to consist?—In the unwillingness of Churchmen to part with the general teaching of their catechism within the walls of the school, and the unwillingness of Dissenters, generally speaking, to partake in the education of such schools without such accommodation.

Croydon being sufficiently large to support two schools, one upon the National plan, and another upon the British and Foreign plan; do you apprehend that any such inconvenience would result in the education of the lower orders, from one of those schools being such as Dissenters could not attend?—None, except from the indulgence of the passions of one or both parties in drawing scholars to their respective school.

Have you ever witnessed a thing of that kind at Croydon?—I have indeed; I was not aware of the obstacles until the plan was started for an union, when we came to discuss them, and to perceive how they operated.

Do you conceive that the efforts of the Dissenters to obtain the attendance of the children of Churchmen at their school, has been accompanied with the conversion of those children to their peculiar tenets?—The children are at such a tender age that it is impossible to pronounce upon that; but if such a mode of education will have that tendency, I am very well persuaded that for that purpose the respective parties should attend merely to their own children; this however has not been attended to, and invitations have been profusely given to some parents belonging to the church, to send their children to the dissenting school, while every forbearance on the other side was practised on the part of the National school.

Did you perceive any disinclination amongst the lower orders to send their children generally to school?—They were desirous to send them, generally.

Have you had any experience in Sunday schools?—Previous to the establishment of the National schools at Croydon.

What progress have you found the children make at such establishments?—The progress was desirable, where better instruction could not be had; but, on the whole, it was but moderate.

Have the goodness to inform the Committee what is the foundation of the Westminster school?—The school was founded by Queen Elizabeth.

Do you recollect how it was endowed?—It is endowed with various lands and possessions, not the school's separately; but the Dean and Chapter are invested with all the possessions belonging to the foundation, they being bound to maintain forty scholars there.

Is the management of the school under the Dean and Chapter?—Yes, conjointly and in some respects with the Dean of Christ Church and the Master of Trinity College Cambridge, who have shares in the election of scholars to their respective colleges; but the general management is local. We have, besides that, twelve poor pensioners, for whom we are bound to provide; there are also donations of beef, meat, and so forth, to other people, through the year.

Do you think that a good result might be expected, if no endeavour was used to form an union with Dissenters in any school plan, but if the clergyman were to establish a school, in which he should profess, that upon receiving due security that the children of Dissenters should be taken by their friends to the meeting, he would permit them to go there, instead of going with the rest of the scholars to church; and also, that if the Dissenters objected to their children learning the Church Catechism, they should be employed in some other way at those times when their class-fellows were learning it; do you think that in this case the poor orders of Dissenters would gradually slide in considerable numbers into such a school, supposing it to be well conducted?—I believe that the poorer orders would be very glad to have their children so instructed; but from the experience I have had, they have been prevented by their leaders from allowing their children to attend such schools, without a demand of participation in the management.

### The Rev. *John Basset Campbell*, called in, and Examined.

YOU are one of the ushers of the Westminster school?—Yes.

Are there forty boys upon the foundation?—Yes.

Is the number always full?—Yes, generally full, except during the few days interval in filling up any vacancy.

The Rev.
J. B. Campbell.

Are

*The Rev.*
*J. B. Campbell.*

Are they boarded and lodged as well as taught at the school?—Some of the boys of the school are boarders, others come to the school as home-boarders. I understand that the statutes allow 120 boys, viz. 40 King's scholars, and 80 town boys; but I do not know that that is the case; the masters take more town boys, about 260 instead of the 80; hence it is necessary to have ushers; they are not members of the school.

Are the 40 King's boys the boys upon the foundation?—Yes.

Are those 40 boys boarded and lodged, as well as taught at the school?—Yes; they also half board occasionally, but not necessarily, at the boarding-houses; having been town boys, they remain half-boarders; they sleep in the dormitory of the college, and they have dinner and supper in the hall, and breakfast of beer, with bread and butter, if they please.

Then they are not understood to be wholly at the expense of the foundation?—No; at least not by the usage.

Do they wear a particular dress?—Yes; a gown, a cap, and college waistcoat.

Do the other boys wear any particular dress?—No, we call them town boys; there is a gown furnished once in a year to the King's scholars, but they get also others, for these are rather coarser than they wish to wear.

Then has a foundation boy any other advantages, besides those you have mentioned, over the town boys?—No other advantage, while at school.

Do they pay, like the other boys, for their education?—Yes.

The same sum?—Yes.

What does a boy pay?—It is different in different years, it depends upon the year; it is 13 guineas the first year, which is the same for a town boy or a King's scholar, 10 guineas the next two years, and 8 guineas the last year.

How do they go off to college?—They are generally at the end of the fourth year elected for Christ Church Oxford, or Trinity College Cambridge; the Dean of Christ Church perhaps takes four or five, as may be, according to his vacancies; and the master of Trinity, the remainder of the eight candidates, or fourth-year King's scholars.

How many scholarships may there be altogether, at Oxford and Cambridge, belonging to Westminster?—I believe there is no limited number; the Dean of Christ Church will take three, four or five, as he chooses; they must take the eight between them, viz. Oxford and Cambridge; eight go off every year; they have studentships at Christ Church, and scholarships at Trinity; the scholarships are not very much worth their having.

What are the studentships at Christ Church worth?—I do not know exactly; these are the same as the other studentships, they are indeed made rather better; as I understand, they are now worth about 50 or 60 *l.* a year, having lately fallen.

Are those studentships given entirely to foundation boys?—Yes, these; but our town boys also get studentships in common with all other young men, but these three, four or five, are confined to the King's scholars; the scholarships at Trinity are worth very little indeed.

How are boys put upon the foundation?—About 30 town boys annually propose themselves as candidates from the fourth, fifth, and shell forms; they contend with each other in Latin and Greek, particularly in grammatical questions, speaking only Latin; two boys will challenge for five hours together in grammar questions. At the end of eight weeks of constant challenge, the eight head of the number are chosen into college to fill the vacancies caused by the eight elected to the universities; the other of those who presented themselves, but ended below those eight, are chosen according as any vacancies may occur in the year. The head master sits as umpire during these eight weeks of contest.

Then the forty foundation boys are chosen, in the way you have just now described, out of the town boys?—Yes.

Can no boy be put upon the foundation without such election as you have described?—No, it is not possible, as I believe.

Is there no instance of any such thing?—No, it is not possible.

How are the foundation boys chosen for scholarships or studentships?—At the end of their four years in college, the Dean of Christ Church, and the Master of Trinity College Cambridge, elect these fourth-year boys at their pleasure, and take the eight between them.

And without any trial?—There is an examination, but it is rather a matter of form.

Are there any boys presented, or otherwise put upon the foundation at Westminster, than by examination?—No, it could not be.

What

What are the Bishop's boys?—There are four boys appointed by the Dean; they, as I hear, are called Bishop's boys, because the Dean had also been a bishop; they get their education free, and have a purple gown given them annually.

Are they boarded and lodged as well as educated?—No, they usually live in the neighbourhood, and board at home.

Do they get any other advantage besides their education and gown?—If a Bishop's boy has gone through the school, he gets an exhibition at St. John's college Cambridge, but I do not know the amount; I fancy 20 l. a year, but I do not know exactly.

Is the situation of King's scholars much sought after among the boys?—Yes, in consequence of its being obtained by an examination, and creditable, boys of distinction and all ranks are anxious for it.

Has the mode of choosing King's scholars been always the same?—I believe always; it has certainly for 80 or more years back, if not a greater length of time.

## Mr. *John Henry Gell*, called in, and Examined.

WHAT are you?—Receiver of the Dean and Chapter of Westminster.

What revenue belongs to the Westminster school?—There is no particular part of our revenue applicable to the school or the charities mentioned by the Dean; but out of the gross revenue the expenses of these three must be paid; there are twelve poor almsmen mentioned, about 12 l. each, and forty women, who receive weekly donations of bread, beef, and money, and then the forty boys on the foundation.

What is the expense of the school of forty boys?—It varies according to the price of articles; but I should think between 1,000 l. and 1,200 l. a year, including all expenses incident to those boys.

Then do you understand that the King's scholars pay for their own education?—Not to my knowledge.

Do you pay the salary to the master?—Yes, besides what they have privately from the town boys, with which we have no concern.

What is the salary of the master?—39 l. 6 s. 8 d.; and he has no perquisites, to my knowledge.

Has he a house?—Yes. The second master has 15 l. and a house.

The ushers?—We know nothing of them; we pay nothing to them.

Are those all the salaries you pay on account of the school?—Yes; when I mentioned from one thousand to twelve hundred pounds, that includes every expense, as I stated before.

Does it include the whole expense which the Westminster school is of to the Dean and Chapter?—They have the repairs of the two masters houses, as they happen to become necessary.

## Mr. *William Hargrave*, called in, and Examined.

WHERE do you live?—No. 1, Bishopsgate-street.

Are you acquainted with the state of the children of the poor in any part of the Metropolis, and what part?—In the North-east district, including Spitalfields, Shoreditch, and that neighbourhood.

What led you to this knowledge of the state of the poor?—I am a member of a society which is entitled the Juvenile Benevolent Society, for clothing and promoting the education of destitute poor children, and improving the condition of the poor.

Are there many poor children uneducated in those parts of the town?—A great number.

Are they desirous of instruction?—They are very desirous.

State the limits of the North-east district?—I think, as near as I can recollect, Hackney is the extent of it, bounded on one side by Bishopsgate-street, and on the other by Whitechapel; the same district as the Auxiliary Bible Society. It does not extend so far as Houndsditch; there is a small street which divides it.

If the children of the poor are desirous of education, what is the reason they are prevented receiving the benefit of it?—They are prevented, from two reasons: I have visited a great number of families to ascertain the cause of that prevention, and have discovered, when the parents are ignorant, and do not know how to appreciate the value of education, they appear very indifferent whether their offspring are educated or no. There is another reason, which appears to operate very much against

against children being sent to schools, particularly Sunday schools; that is, a sufficient portion of clothing to render them tolerably decent, to place them upon a par with other children who are generally placed in those schools. The general objection to their being sent to school, which is urged by their parents, upon our committee applying to them upon the subject, is this; they appeal to us in this way, "You see our children, is it possible we can send them to school in this state?" This observation applies to a very large portion of the poor in that vicinity.

Are they poor mechanics, that make objections of this sort?—They are generally Irish, who are labourers. The object of this society, on whose account I visit the poor, is to obviate that difficulty; and they have procured a cheap kind of clothing, with which they clothe those poor children, a boy for the expense of 8 s. and a girl for 10 s. and place them in a Sunday school.

What articles are you now describing for a boy?—For a boy, a leather cap costing 1 s. 1 d.; a pinafore, made of a brown kind of sheeting which is very strong, extending from the neck down to the feet, and covering the arms, and which costs 3 s.; and shoes, good ones, for 3 s.; that constitutes the whole of the boy's dress: The girl's dress consists of a bonnet and ribbon, costing 2 s.; a pinafore, made of gingham instead of sheeting, 3 s.; a pair of shoes, 3 s.; which renders these children, when clean, very respectable. This question appears to involve a point which I suppose I may allude to, that is, the benefit of Sunday schools over that of other schools: we have found, generally, that once a week, which is on the Sabbath day, the child will learn as much in that time as he would if placed in a National school, or in a school on the British system of education, in a week.

How do you account for this?—The number that is admitted to those schools is so great, that we are apprehensive that every child does not receive the same attention as that child does in a Sunday school; on the other hand, in a Sunday school the children are taught to read by young men and young women, who volunteer their services on those occasions.

Are there a sufficient number of schools for the poor in the district with which you are acquainted?—I do not think there is.

Do you know the number of schools?—I do not know the exact number; I know some, but I do not know the precise number.

Why do the parents object to their children going to Sunday schools, on account of their dress, more than day schools?—They do not object more to one school than the other, but many children are engaged on the week day.

Have you observed any improvement in the moral condition of the poor, when the children have been educated in the free schools in or near your neighbourhood?—In the particular families under my care, I have noticed a considerable improvement; and as reports are brought up from every district in London every month to the committee of the Juvenile Benevolent Society, which I attend, and from the many facts and observations recorded in those reports, it evidently is the case throughout London, where our committee have extended their care.

Do you know any particular reason which occasions the great distress among the poor?—I am of opinion, from the observations I have made amongst the poor, that it arises from the parents in the first place not being educated; when they become enlightened, we find they become economical, and acquire more stable habits.

Are they more industrious?—Yes.

More frugal?—Much more so.

Have you any adult schools in your neighbourhood?—We have.

Do many of the poor attend those schools?—Not a great many; we find it is better to send children to school than adults; they are in general more attentive, continuing a greater length of time at school.

Do you know the number of children that are in the free schools in your own district?—I do not.

Are you able to speak to the length of time a child takes to learn to read the Bible at a Sunday school?—I am not a teacher in any Sunday school, but my observations proceed entirely from what I have ascertained and inquired among the poor; but I should think they would learn in twelve months.

Can you give a general opinion upon the best means of improving the children of the poor in your district?—The only plan that I could suggest would be, by the establishment of more schools, and an additional number of masters among the poor, which operates as a stimulus: we have found when children are desirous of coming to school, the parents were unwilling they should come; and we have found, that by visiting the parents two or three times, and talking to them upon the subject, that such remonstrance has been effectual, and they have generally in consequence

suffered

suffered their children to come to the Sunday school; we can get them to a Sunday school when we cannot get them to a day school.

Are the children employed on a week day, which prevents them attending a day school?—A great number of them are; the Juvenile Benevolent Society summon, in their different districts, all the children under their care once a week, to a room appointed for the purpose, to ascertain what progress those children have made in their learning. Nine children out of ten that we visit, who have not been placed under the care of this institution that I allude to, are unable to read.

Have you visited some of the very lowest classes of society?—That is the description of poor that we take particularly under our cognizance.

What number have you clothed?—About 200 within the last 18 months. A family who are natives of Scotland, the man a weaver, but not able to work, from having broken his leg, and the woman having charge of four children, consequently unable to assist her husband in procuring a livelihood; their distress was so great, that this family, which consisted of six persons, laid and slept in one bed; two of the children were about 13 years of age at that time; they have been taken under the notice of this institution from its formation, and assisted with pecuniary aid, and their children sent to Sunday schools. Since that was done for them, they have been progressively improving. I visit them weekly, and they appear altogether much more comfortable; two of their children have got employment; the other two continue to attend the Sunday school, and at what is termed a weekly conference with some of the committee of the Juvenile Benevolent Society, which is merely an examination, they receive a little advice how to conduct themselves when they are at school. The boy sometime ago was absent from home; his mother told me she believed he was connected with some of the juvenile depredators, who procure a subsistence by stealing; but I have now the satisfaction to say that this boy is restored to his parents, has got work, and conducts himself with propriety; his only sister has also got a comfortable situation. The two eldest children, in consequence of being employed, have left the school, but they can read, which they have principally learnt to do at the Sunday schools; the other two children, who are attending Sunday schools, are making progress in their learning; and the family, although very poor, are much improved in their condition and comfort.

It has been stated to the Committee, that where clothing has been furnished to children, it sometimes has happened that after it has been worn for a few times, that they and the clothing have disappeared together; has your society suffered in that way?—Our society has suffered very little in proportion to the number of children it has clothed, owing to the precautions which is used by the committee; they supply them in the first place with clothing of little value, the clothing is stamped with permanent ink in the inside, " J. B. S. Charity," which prevents pawnbrokers receiving the same; this clothing is not given to the children, it is merely lent them, they take it out from the depôt on Saturday, and return it on the following Monday; in case they omit to do so, where such omission has taken place, the parties are visited by a member of the committee who has the particular charge of them; and we have found that that plan answers the purpose better than any other. But we are not confined entirely to that plan; when a child who has been under the care of the institution some time, and demean themselves in such a manner as to merit a peculiar mark of distinction, that child receives a gift of clothing, and is placed in a day-school, which is done publicly before the rest of the children, that it may stimulate them to act equally consistent.

Do you know in point of fact whether all the children so supplied with clothes go to Sunday schools, or if not, what proportion?—We have regular information from the Sunday schools, by tin tickets, stamped J. B. S. that are given to each child, which child is well known by its peculiar dress; in the Sunday schools it is given to each child that has attended school; and as all the children under our care are summoned together once a week, we have an opportunity of ascertaining correctly what children have attended, and who have not attended; if any deficiency appears in that respect, the committee man, who has particular charge of the delinquent, is obliged, according to the rules of the institution, to visit that child in the course of the same week.

When you recommended children to any Sunday school, do you send them to schools of any particular religious sect, or to all indiscriminately?—We send them to all indiscriminately, it is quite optional on the part of the parents.

Do you recommend them to that school nearest their residence?—We do, if that school meets with the approbation of their parents.

Are you of the society of people called Quakers?—I am a member of that society.

Mr.

Mr. *William Nettlefold*, Junior, called in, and Examined.

ARE you Secretary to the Hoxton Academy Sunday school?—Yes, I am.

Are you acquainted with the state of the children of the poor in your neighbourhood?—I visited a considerable part of the neighbourhood when our school was first opened, to obtain children to fill it; but we have now in the school about 560; and in going round the neighbourhood, I discovered that one-fourth, I should suppose, of the parents that I called upon, had children that were uninstructed.

Were they desirous to be instructed?—They were desirous of having their children instructed. On one Sabbath morning I collected 73 children who had never been in any Sunday school, and out of the 73 there were but two that could read, and that not sufficient to read in the Testament.

Are there now a sufficient number of schools in your neighbourhood to instruct all the children?—I consider not; I am convinced that if our school could instruct more children, that is, if we had more room, we could readily get 100 more.

Do you conceive very large schools are the best for Sunday schools, or to increase the number of small ones?—I should consider there was no particular choice in that respect; as Sunday schools are divided into classes, the children being regularly under the attention of one individual, one may consider each class as a distinct school, only, being congregated, they have all the advantage of one general exhortation or admonition.

How long have you taken an active part in this school?—Three years.

Have you observed any particular improvement in the children?—Considerable.

In what respect?—As it respects the improvement in the children, their attention to the reverence of the Sabbath is to be discovered, and their increasing delight in attending the school, to what they had when they first came; and the parents, upon visiting them, one may perceive a very considerable improvement in their domestic circumstances. When first called upon, the parents appeared to consider that they were obliging us, by sending their children; after the children had been at the school, probably a month or two, we have had the thanks of the parents for instructing them; they have considerably more parental obedience to what they were accustomed to receive from the children; and if the parents are poor, greater willingness on the part of the children to assist in the support of the family, if they require their assistance. Previous to the children attending the school, one might understand, from the acknowledgment of the parents, that they (the parents) would occupy the Sabbath at work; washing, for instance, on the part of the mother, and the occupation of the father continued likewise; but from the books which the children have carried home from the school, and the information that they have given their parents from the instruction and exhortations they have heard, have been, in a number of cases that I could mention, induced to regard the Sabbath themselves by attending a place of worship.

Have you reason to believe that moral principles are fixed in the minds of the children, by the instruction they receive at the school?—Yes; we never discovered in our school one of the children that had been there ever committing any act of delinquency. The number of children in our school is 560.

Do you limit the time which children shall remain in the school?—No.

Are there any advantages which the children receive by continuing in the school, beyond those of merely learning to read?—No particular advantages, except presents at times for their good behaviour.

Do they improve in behaviour?—Yes, they do.

You conceive an increased number of Sunday schools throughout the Metropolis would benefit the lower classes of society?—Materially so, because a number of the children of the very poor are occupied in the week by obtaining a portion of their livelihood, which will preclude their attendance at National schools. In one case I know a blind man, and the wife who is so infirm from affliction, that they are both dependent upon three small children for their support, the eldest of which is not twelve years of age.

How do they obtain it?—They obtain it by selling various articles in the street.

Do those children come to your school?—They do.

How long does it require to teach a child to read in a Sunday school?—A great deal depends upon the abilities of the child to receive instruction.

What is about the average?—We have had children leave the school at the end of nine months, who, when they entered, did not more than know the alphabet, and, when they left, could read in the Bible.

You

You would not state that as the average length of time?—I should consider twelve months sufficient.

With the education he would receive at the Sunday school alone; or do you include the additional instruction he would receive at home?—Those cases I have mentioned have not been in the habit of receiving any instruction at home.

The children are only taught to read in the Sunday school?—Yes.

Do the children not learn to write?—They do.

On a Sunday?—No.

When do they learn to write?—On Monday evening.

Any other evening?—No other.

Do you teach them arithmetic?—Yes, on the Monday evening.

Do you find the parents of poor children very desirous that their children should be instructed?—Where the parents could read themselves, but not otherwise, unless they conceive they shall be receiving some pecuniary aid by allowing their children to come.

Are you aware of any particular impediments which prevent poor children from receiving instruction?—Where the parents are poor, the impediment arises from the want of suitable clothing to attend it.

After children have been in your school for any length of time, have you found that their dress has been improved, and their general appearance?—Yes, because the conduct of the parents have been improved in proportion to the conduct of their children.

Is your school in connexion with the National Society?—No, it is not.

Do you know the average annual expense?—Seventy pounds.

Does that include rent?—We have no rent to pay.

What are the expenses?—The expense is for books, fire, candle, and door-keepers.

Do you give any rewards to the children for good behaviour?—Yes, and for attending in time.

What rewards do you give?—We give them small tickets, a certain number of which purchase books, according to their wishes; they have an opportunity of making a selection; but we always place into their hands, for their first reward, a Testament.

What is the nominal value of the tickets?—Twelve tickets are valued at three halfpence.

Have you any circulating library attached to your school?—We have.

What entitles a child to the benefit of the circulating library?—A recommendation, from a teacher, for good behaviour.

Do they take those books home with them?—They do.

Have you any reason to believe they read the books from the circulating library on an evening to their parents?—We have known in each case, from recent examination, that they do.

Are the parents pleased to hear their children read to them of an evening?—Particularly.

Have you any reason to believe that the children, reading the library books, prevent the father spending the evening at a public-house?—I know one family, where a girl took home a tract that has been written by the Reverend Leigh Richmond, called "The Dairyman's Daughter;" the father, who was in the practice of spending the whole of his Sunday at a public-house, overheard the girl reading this tract to her mother, and said that he thought he would go to the chapel; an opportunity occurred for him to carry the younger child to meet his daughter coming from school, and through the little girl's entreaty he attended the chapel; and since that time he has been in the habit of attending a place of worship instead of the public-house.

Have you reason to believe his moral habits are much improved?—Yes; he is a weaver by trade, but the want of employ has reduced the family to great distress; but the distress is not more, not for the mother and the children, than they were in the habit of enduring from his improper conduct when in work.

Do the children consider it as a great reward to be admitted to the benefits of the circulating library?—Those children who have an opportunity of reading; but most of the children having to work on the other days, have little time for reading, except on the Sunday.

Do you find, in general, the children are fond of books?—Yes, when they have learnt to read with readiness.

Do children in your schools commit portions of Scripture to memory?—They do, and are rewarded for it.

Is

Is that the practice of the school?—It is.

Is there any annual examination of the children?—Yes, the first Sabbath in April.

And the improvement noted down?—Yes; each teacher is in the habit of putting down every Sabbath what the child learns, to prevent the child repeating the lesson a second time, and being able at any period to discover what that child has learnt while in the school.

Have you made any calculation of the annual expense of each child?—I have not.

But the whole of your expenses do not exceed 70 *l.* per annum?—They do not, for 500 children. We receive 500 nearly, in the course of the year : upon the average, we have admitted twelve children every Sabbath for the last three months. As a proof of the willingness of the poor to learn, we have no trouble now to go round to get children into the school; they come with their parents.

Do you make a point of examining the children with respect to cleanliness?—We do; and consider it the duty of the teacher to impress upon the minds of their parents, when visiting, that we require them to come in a cleanly condition ; that is the only provision we make; we regard not their dress, if they are cleanly.

How many teachers have you in the school?—About twenty, male and female.

Do they attend twice a day?—Three times each teacher.

How many children are attached to one teacher?—In the Bible and Testament classes about eighteen to each teacher, sometimes twenty; in the lower classes, thirty or forty; they are taught, by lessons hung against the wall, in distinct classes.

Have you any monitors to assist the teachers?—Only in the lower classes.

The monitors are selected from the senior children?—Yes, and those who are most sedate in their conduct.

Are you of opinion that the extension of Sunday-schools throughout the Metropolis would greatly benefit the lower classes of society?—Yes, judging from the manifest improvement in the vicinity of our schools, among the families of the very poorest who attend.

*Mr.
W. Nettlefold, jun.*

Mr. *Robert Barbor*, again called in, and Examined.

WHAT change has taken place within your knowledge in the salaries of the Charter-house?—I am afraid I cannot give the Committee any exact account of that; they have been increased lately.

When was the last increase?—About two years ago.

Do you recollect generally the amount of the increase?—No, I do not; the masters' salary has been increased considerably; at the time of Dr. Fisher coming into office it was only 200 *l.* a year; it was afterwards increased to 450 *l.* but he had then other perquisites and small allowances, which are now included in the aggregate allowance of 800 *l.* a year.

When he came into the office what might the whole, including the perquisites, amount to?—I should suppose that they were then 300 *l.* a year; I speak now of money allowances.

You speak of that part of his income which answers to the present 800 *l.*?—Yes.

Are the other salaries increased in the same proportion?—Certainly not; but the salaries as they are now increased include all the former small allowances, except the triennial allowance for linen.

Can you tell the Committee how many of the other salaries are increased?—My own was 80 *l.* a year when I came into office 27 years ago; it was afterwards increased by 50 *l.* but I was then supposed to have made some advantage, or to have had the opportunity, I would rather say, of making some advantage, by the balances remaining from time to time in my hands, which however I never availed myself of, certainly not to more than 20 *l.* in the course of the 27 years; since that, the allowance which I now have is supposed to be in lieu of any such advantage which I might so make. The registrer's salary has also been increased nearly in a similar proportion; and all the salaries indeed have increased, but I cannot speak with certainty to the amount of that increase.

Has the pocket-money of the pensioners been increased?—The pocket-money of the pensioners has been increased within my time, from 14 *l.* to 20 *l.* a year; the wages of the servants have also increased.

By whom is the increase in the salaries made?—By orders in assembly of the governors. I might probably here say that no monies are issued except by special

*Mr.
Robert Barbor.*

orders

*Mr.*
*Robert Barbor.*

orders of assembly, or by warrants signed by the master, in the ordinary expenditure of the establishment.

What is the duty of the registrar?—The registrar acts as secretary to the governors; issues summonses for meetings, draws up the orders of assembly, prepares the leases, and all applications to the governors for renewals of leases, or for any other matters that are brought before them, and the petition necessarily passes through his hands; and he is also the solicitor for the conduct of any law proceedings.

Does he charge separately for his labour or attendance in any of those duties?—He has a fee of a guinea for every petition, and the tenants pay for their leases.

Does he bring in his bill separately for any law proceedings, besides money out of pocket?—I believe he makes out a regular bill of costs, as in ordinary cases.

Has he any other fee besides a guinea upon a petition?—An allowance of 40 l. a year for the expenses of coach hire, sending messengers to the governors, postage of the letters of correspondents; and I suppose 40 l. a year does not pay him.

Has there been any increase in the exhibitions, of late years?—When I was an exhibitioner, in the year 1808, at Christ Church, the exhibition was limited to 40 l.; it was afterwards increased on behalf of the bachelors of arts to 60 l.; and the subsequent increase made the 60 l. 85 l.; and the 40 l. for the under graduate was increased to 65 l.

In what year did that take place?—1812; in the year 1813 the bachelor's exhibition was increased to 100 l. and the under graduate's to 80 l. and that is their present standard.

Should you say that, generally speaking, the boys upon the foundation are in the present day of superior or inferior rank to that of the boys formerly?—I should not suppose that much alteration has taken place either way, since I was a boy on the foundation.

Do you know that Mr. Russel has introduced the new plan of education under Dr. Bell, and adopted it in the instruction of the classics?—I understand he has introduced it into the school; whether it extends into the higher departments of the school I do not know; I do not happen to know that he has applied it to the teaching the Greek grammar, it may be so, but I am not aware of the particulars.

Are the boys upon the foundation of a different description with the town boys?—I apprehend they are nearly of the same description.

Have you got a statement of the revenue and expenditure of the house?—I have.

[It was delivered in, and read, as follows:]

**CHARTER-HOUSE.**—State of the REVENUE for One Year to Michaelmas 1815; and of the Arrears thereof, which remained due on 5th January 1816.

| Charter-house Square and Lane : | Annual Rents. | Arrears due 5th January 1816. | Carthusian Street : | Annual Rents. | Arrears due 5th January 1816. |
|---|---|---|---|---|---|
| | £.  s.  d. | £.  s.  d. | | £.  s.  d. | £.  s.  d. |
| William Mountague - - | 46 16 6 | — | William Haines - - | 20 4 — | — |
| John Robinson - - | 46 16 6 | — | Felix Calvert - - | 16 12 — | — |
| Marg‍t Jarman - - | 52 3 6 | — | Rep‍s of C. Smith - | 63 6 — | 94 19 — |
| Rev. D. Shackleford - | 46 16 6 | 23 8 3 | | 100 2 — | 94 19 — |
| Dr. Fane - - - | 46 16 6 | — | Sutton Place : | | |
| Cha‍s Spurden - - | 41 16 6 | — | | | |
| John Rowlatt - - | 92 15 — | — | James Sorrell - - | 13 6 8 | 13 6 8 |
| Sol‍n Hougham - - | 78 15 — | — | James Collins - - | 66 13 4 | — |
| James Priest - - | 20 9 — | — | | 80 — — | 13 6 8 |
| J. W. Long - - | 18 9 — | — | Southminster : | | |
| Tho‍s Slowers - - | 22 4 — | — | Sam‍l Bawtree - - | 1,012 — — | 506 — — |
| Messrs. Purdas & Co. - | 7 3 — | — | James Clarke - - | 803 7 6 | 401 13 9 |
| Rev. Jn‍o Russel - | 48 10 — | — | John Bawtree - - | 400 — — | — |
| Small acknowledgements for | | | Joseph Kitcher - - | 310 — — | 155 — — |
| liberties in the Square - | 6 13 2 | — | Impropriate Tithes - | 1,489 16 — | 331 16 — |
| | 576 4 2 | 23 8 3 | John Wade - - | 48 15 — | — |
| Clerkenwell : | | | Quit Rents - - | 39 — 3¼ | 78 — 6½ |
| John Herbert - - | 25 — — | 25 — — | Profits of Courts - | 276 — — | — |
| Amb‍e Ashby - - | 25 — — | — | | 4,378 18 9¼ | 1,472 10 3½ |
| Jn‍o Hewett - - | 25 — — | — | | | |
| Sam‍l Boulton - - | 28 — — | 56 — — | Cold Norton : | | |
| Will‍m Wilson - - | 30 — — | 60 — — | Rich‍d Clarke - - | 578 — — | 1,156 — — |
| Cha‍s Warne - - | 25 — — | — | Quit Rents - - | 16 15 2 | 33 10 4 |
| Sam‍l Pullen - - | 690 — — | 184 10 — | Profits of Courts - | 194 15 — | 13 10 — |
| Earl of Northampton - | 20 — — | — | | 789 10 2 | 1,203 — 4 |
| | 868 — — | 325 10 — | | | |

*(continued.)*

Charter-house Revenue—*continued.*

| | Annual Rents. | Arrears due 5th January 1816. | | Annual Rents. | Arrears due 5th January 1816. |
|---|---|---|---|---|---|
| **Great Stainbridge:** | £. s. d. | £. s. d. | **Dunsby:** | £. s. d. | £. s. d. |
| John Kemp - - - | 430 — — | 215 — — | John Laurance - - - | 669 10 — | — |
| Rev. W. B. Ramsden - - | 5 5 — | 5 5 — | Thos Laurance - - - | 490 — — | — |
| Quit Rents - - - | 12 15 8 | 25 11 4 | Wm Richardson - - - | 387 — — | 387 — — |
| | 448 — 8 | 245 16 4 | Wm Carter - - - | 443 12 — | — |
| **Little Hallingbury:** | | | John Carter - - - | 292 — — | 146 — — |
| Henry Clark - - - | 200 — — | — | Rev. Wm Waters - - | 30 — — | 30 — — |
| John Houghton - - | 135 — — | 67 10 — | Richd Caswell - - | 670 — — | 335 — — |
| Nath. Dorrington - - | 376 — — | 376 — — | Cottages - - - | 184 2 6 | 184 2 6 |
| Quit Rents - - | 10 16 5 | 21 12 10 | Tithes - - - | 20 15 — | 20 15 — |
| Profits of Courts | 5 — — | | Timber and Underwood - | 164 6 — | 164 6 — |
| | 726 16 5 | 465 2 10 | | 3,351 5 6 | 1,267 3 6 |
| **Little Wigborow:** | | | **Elcombe:** | | |
| Edwd Wray - - - | 480 — — | — | John Bathe - - - | 426 6 3 | 213 3 1½ |
| Quit Rents - - | 6 15 9 | 13 11 6 | James Bathe - - - | 445 10 — | 222 15 — |
| Profits of Courts - - | — | | Timy Maskelyne - - | 400 — — | 200 — — |
| | 486 15 9 | 13 11 6 | B. P. Bennett - - - | — 10 — | 1 10 — |
| **Elmstead:** | | | J. King - - - | 400 11 — | 200 5 6 |
| Chas Josselyn - - | 358 5 — | | Wm Matthews - - | 413 9 8 | 206 14 10 |
| **Fryans and Jackletts:** | | | Richd King - - - | 262 — — | 131 — — |
| James Blakely - - | 308 — — | 462 — — | R. Don King - - | 619 5 6 | 309 12 9 |
| **Castle Camps:** | | | J. Matthews - - - | 292 — — | 146 — — |
| Willm Button - - - | 240 — — | 120 — — | John Edwards - - | 445 — — | 222 10 — |
| Richd Collier - - | 700 — — | 350 — — | Willm Brown - - | 293 16 4 | 146 18 2 |
| John French - - - | 210 — — | 105 — — | Willm Wallis - - | 2 8 — | 4 16 — |
| Jas Leonard - - - | 120 — — | — | Quit Rents and Interest - | 17 14 10¼ | 17 14 10¼ |
| Jas Paritt - - - | 130 — — | 325 — — | | 4,018 11 7¼ | 2,023 — 2¾ |
| Quit Rents - - - | 33 3 4½ | 137 4 7½ | **Thickwood:** | | |
| Profits of Courts - | 32 13 — | — | James Woodham - - | 170 — — } | 203 7 6 |
| Timber and Underwood - | 296 6 — | 296 6 — | now | | |
| | 1,762 2 4½ | 1,333 10 7½ | Robt Beckenbrow - - | 33 5 — } | |
| **Balsham:** | | | Joseph Penchin - - | 228 — — | 228 — — |
| John Kent - - - | 492 — — | 253 18 — | Quit Rents - - - | 1 3 2 | 5 2 — |
| Lewis Kent - - - | 457 17 — | 475 14 — | | 432 8 2 | 436 9 6 |
| Cottages - - - | 7 18 — | | **Higney:** | | |
| Quit Rents - - - | 45 17 4 | 49 7 6 | John Bromhead - - | 680 — — | 1,020 — — |
| Profits of Courts - | — | | Timber and Underwood - | — | |
| Timber and Underwood - | 195 5 8 | 195 5 8 | | 680 — — | 1,020 — — |
| | 1,198 18 — | 974 5 2 | **Hartland:** | | |
| **Buslingthorpe:** | | | Rev. Wm Chanter - - | 240 5 — | 240 5 — |
| Saml Turner - - - | 440 — — | — | Willm Ryder - - | 114 — — | 114 — — |
| John Lowther - - - | 230 — — | 115 — — | Willm Baglehole - - | 14 — — | 14 — — |
| C. Mason - - - | 294 1 — | 161 1 6 | | 368 5 — | 368 5 — |
| John Moody - - - | 30 — — | 45 — — | | | |
| Overseers of the Poor - | 1 1 — | 1 1 — | | | |
| Timber and Underwood - | 258 9 — | 258 9 — | | | |
| | 1,253 11 — | 580 11 6 | | | |

ABSTRACT of the TOTALS of the FARM RENTS, and of the Annual Amount of Interest and Dividends, with the Arrears thereof.

| | ANNUAL RENTS. | ARREARS due 5th January 1816. |
|---|---|---|
| | £. s. d. | £. s. d. |
| Farm Rents - - - - - | 20,578 17 11 | 11,012 18 6¼ |
| Quit Rents - - - - - | 184 2 — | 381 15 6¼ |
| Manerial Profits - - - - | 578 8 — | 13 10 — |
| Timber and Underwood - - - | 914 6 8 | 914 6 8 |
| Dividends and Interest - - - | 123 17 6 | 361 7 4 |
| Manciple - - - - - | 4 18 4 | — |
| Property Tax - - - - - | - - - | 229 1 2 |
| £ | 22,384 10 5 | 12,912 19 2¼ |

Balance of Cash in the Receiver's hands, 6th January 1816 - £. 2,809. 7. 1.

*Rt Barbor,* Receiver.

CHARTER-HOUSE.—State of the EXPENDITURE of the Hospital for One Year, from 5th January 1815 to 5th January 1816.

| Expenditure as to the Establishment: | £. | s. | d. |
|---|---|---|---|
| For Salaries to the Master and Officers, with their usual Allowances - - | 2,633 | 6 | 8 |
| Pensions to the Poor Brothers - - | 1,549 | 9 | 4 |
| Exhibitions to Scholars at the Universities - - - - - | 1,230 | — | — |
| The Manciples Fee and Allowances - | 83 | — | 8 |
| Wages and Gratuities to the Servants and Nurses - - - - | 496 | 5 | 8 |
| Provisions for fifty-two weeks, of Diet - - - £.3,596 8 6¾ Bread - - - 523 3 7¾ Beer - - - 577 13 1 | 4,697 | 5 | 3½ |
| Apparel and Linen - - - | 736 | — | 3 |
| The Apothecary's Bill £.129 5 5 Extra Nursing and Allowances for the Sick 194 10 11 | 323 | 16 | 4 |
| Candles - - - - | 180 | 15 | 3 |
| Lighting Lamps, and Tin Ware - | 80 | 14 | 6 |
| Water Rent - - - - | 26 | 8 | — |
| Fuel - - - - - | 543 | 5 | 9 |
| Taxes, Rates and Assessments on the Master's Lodge, and the Officers and Servants' Apartments, with Stamp Duties on Acquittances - | 320 | 18 | — |
| Stated Allowances to the Register - - - £.40 — — Receiver - - - 17 5 — Auditor - - - 7 17 — | 65 | 2 | — |
| Disbursements by the Housekeeper - £.119 2 — Matron - - - 58 19 8½ Laundress - - - 46 19 6 Gardener - - - 50 13 2 | 275 | 14 | 4½ |
| Annuities to Wall and Roberts, £.10. each - - - - - - | 20 | — | — |
| Repair and renewal of Furniture for the Pensioners and Scholars, and of Kitchen Utensils - - - - | 191 | 2 | 9 |
| Reparation of the Buildings within the site of the Hospital - - - | 1,443 | 17 | 9½ |
| Stationary and Printing - - - | 15 | 12 | 6 |
| Insurance of the Hospital and Officers' houses from Fire - - - | 58 | 19 | 6 |
| The Surveyor's Bill - - - | 76 | 6 | 10 |

Expenditure as to the Estates, Trust Monies, &c.

| For the Two Exhibitions on Lady Holford's foundation | £. | s. | d. |
|---|---|---|---|
| Lady Holford's foundation - - - - - | 55 | — | — |
| Stipend to the Rector of Dunsby - 180 — — Vicar of Southminster 20 — — Curate of Hartland - 60 — — | | | |
| Composition for the Tithes of Buslingthorpe - - | 140 | — | — |
| Expenses of the progress to hold Manerial Courts | 40 | 2 | — |
| Salaries and small Allowances to the Bailiffs - | 133 | 9 | — |
| Land Tax and other Outgoings on the Quit Rents - - - - - | 7 | 17 | 3 |

| | £. | s. | d. | | £. | s. | d. |
|---|---|---|---|---|---|---|---|
| For Quit and Chief Rents and fixed Payments on the Estates - - - - | 5 | 3 | 7 | | | | |
| Taxes, Rates and Expenses on the Woods in hand - - - - | 657 | 12 | 6½ | | | | |
| Reparations on the Farms at Elmstead, Higney, Dunsby and Elcombe, by order of Assembly, including two Surveyors' Bills of £.71. 18. and other incidental Expenses on the Estates - - - - - | 1,353 | 13 | 3½ | | | | |
| The Annuitants at Elcombe - - - - - | 90 | — | — | | 2,742 | 17 | 8 |
| Besides, Money invested in the purchase of Exchequer Bills - - - - | 3,041 | 2 | 5 | | | | |
| Money invested in the purchase of Consols 3-per-Cent. Annuities, in the name of the Governors, arising from the sale of five Exchequer Bills, and Interest and Dividends | 5,292 | 15 | 4 | | | | |
| Investment of the accumulated Dividends of Bishop Benson's Legacy | 35 | 6 | 6 | | 8,369 | 4 | 3 |
| TOTAL - - £. | | | | | 26,160 | 3 | 4½ |

The Charge on the Receiver, for the Year ending on the 6th January 1816, is made up as follows:

| | £. | s. | d. |
|---|---|---|---|
| Balance in the hands of the Receiver on the 6th of January 1815 - - - - | 4,715 | 13 | 8 |
| Arrears of Rent, &c. due at the same time | 10,487 | 5 | 5¼ |
| Produce of Exchequer Bills sold, and invested in Stock - - - - | 4,136 | 2 | 9 |
| Dividends of Stock bought therewith - | 158 | 17 | 5 |
| Amount of Rental for the year 1815 - | 22,384 | 10 | 5 |
| TOTAL Charge - - £. | 41,882 | 9 | 8¼ |

Discharge for the Year above-mentioned:

| | £. | s. | d. | | £. | s. | d. |
|---|---|---|---|---|---|---|---|
| Expenditure on the Establishment - - - | 15,048 | 1 | 5½ | | | | |
| Do on the Estates, &c. - | 2,742 | 17 | 8 | | | | |
| Investments in Exchequer Bills and Stock - - - | 8,369 | 4 | 3 | | | | |
| Arrears of Rent, &c. due on the 6th January 1816 - | 12,912 | 19 | 2¾ | | 39,073 | 2 | 7¼ |
| BALANCE in the hands of the Receiver, carried to the next current Year's Account - - - | | | | | 2,809 | 7 | 1 |

Have

Have you got a list of scholars on the foundation, and of exhibitioners ?—I have.

[They were delivered in, and read, as follows :]

## SCHOLARS on the Foundation of the CHARTER-HOUSE :—1816.

| GOVERNORS. | NAMES. | NAMES. | NAMES. |
|---|---|---|---|
| The King - - - - | Thomas Blair. | Wm King. | |
| — King - - - - | Wm Battiscombe. | | |
| — Queen - - - | Chas Dawkins. | John Awdry. | |
| Abp. of Canterbury - - - | Willm Legge. | | |
| Lord Chancellor - - - | John Hewlett. | Vincent Surtees. | |
| Abp. of York - - - - | Wm Hinchliffe. | | |
| Earl of Harrowby - - - | Chas Dickens. | Thomas Bonney. | |
| Duke of Marlborough - - | Geo. Humphrys. | George Spencer. | Edwd Holloway. |
| Marquis Camden - - - | Thos Powys. | Chas Chester. | |
| Earl Spencer - - - - | Benjn Hallowell. | John Hall. | |
| — of Chatham - - - | Henry Fuller. | Mountague Wynyard. | |
| —— Liverpool - - - | Henry Pye. | Charles Boyle. | John Barker. |
| —— Moira - - - - | | | |
| Earl Grey - - - - | Willm Jago. | | |
| Lord Viscount Sidmouth - - | Edwd Churton. | John Blackburne. | Willm Allen. |
| Lord Grenville - - - | Josiah Humphrys. | Arthur Frederick. | |
| — Ellenborough - - - | Henry Reade. | Henry Farnall. | Thos Docker. |
| — Erskine - - - - | Willm Perry. | John Smith. | |
| The Rev. Dr. Fisher, Master - | Chas Proby. | Philip Fisher. | |
| The late Bishop of London - | Luke Rutton. | | |
| The Rt. Hon. Wm Wyndham - | Wm Geo. Wright. | | |
| The late Master the Rev. Dr. Ramsden - | Wm Ramsden. | | |
| The Rt. Hon. Spencer Perceval - | Maurice Beauchamp. | | |

*M. A. Dixon*, Housekeeper.

---

## CHARTER-HOUSE EXHIBITIONERS, 5th January 1816.

George Pearson, B.A.
Henry George Phillips, B.A.
George Chetwode, B.A.
Philip Scott Fisher, B.A.
Richard Lynch Cotton.
Thos Francis Hale.
Henry Baker Tristram.
Mordaunt Barnard.

Edward Newton Young.
Nathl William Halward.
Edmund Henry Penny.
William Fisher.
Thos Cozens Percivale.
Chas Carr Clerke.
William Holland.
Francis Clerke.

Charles Ogle.
Charles Anthony Hunt.
Henry John Gunning.
Henry Hutton.
Henry Wm Buckley.
Peter Puget.

TOTAL - 22.

---

Have you got the form of the warrant of nomination ?—I have.
Is the same form used for a pensioner and scholar ?—It is.

[It was delivered in, and read, as follows :]

I Do hereby nominate and appoint
of                          in the county of                          to
be a                        of the foundation in Charter-house, on the
vacancy now in my disposal. Dated this          day of          17

To
    The Master and Register of   }
Sutton's Hospital in Charter-house. }

---

Mr. *William Allen*, again called in, and Examined.

FROM your observation upon the state of education among the lower orders, what should you say was the proportion of uneducated poor in the country generally ?—As far as our inquiries have gone, it has appeared that, taking the whole population, about one in twenty would require education upon the general plan ; that is, we calculate that one-twentieth part, including all ages, require to be assisted in education.

Do you mean, that supposing the population of England and Wales to be ten millions, about five hundred thousand require education ?—Certainly ; I think that they have not the means of obtaining it without assistance.

Mr.
*William Allen.*

469.

What

Mr.
William Allen.

What should you calculate would be the expense, upon the British and Foreign school plan, of giving education to that number?—The expense will vary according to local circumstances; where the number of children are sufficient to form a school of 500 or 600 in one place, the total expense per annum, in my opinion, need not exceed 200 *l.* or so much. We generally calculate that the expense per head, in the largest schools, should not exceed five or six shillings; but it is obvious that local circumstances, such as the price of provisions, the rent of premises, &c. will cause a difference in different places.

Should you think twelve shillings a head a fair average, taking schools of all sizes into account, one with another?—Yes.

Do you mean thereby to cover the expenses of school-rooms?—All expenses, except those requisite for the first erection of the building; but, as I stated before upon my last examination, the expense of every school upon the British and Foreign Society plan, consists in the salary of the master, the rent of the room, and about 20 *l.* more or less, according to the size of the school, for apparatus, together with the expenses of school-rooms, fuel, &c.

Then do you mean to calculate that from three to four hundred thousand pounds a year would suffice for the education of all the poor now uneducated?—Certainly; if the sum of 400,000 *l.* could be devoted to that purpose, every child requiring this sort of education might be provided with it throughout England and Wales, so as to leave not an uneducated person in the country; and in my opinion a much smaller sum would suffice.

Do you consider this as a moderate or large estimate?—Certainly as a large estimate.

Can you give the Committee any estimate, generally, of the expenses of a school-room?—The school-room at Kingsland, in the neighbourhood of London, was erected for a less sum than 400 *l.* and will contain 300 children; but in many parts of the country, an old barn or an old warehouse might be found, which would prevent the necessity of erecting a new building.

Should you say that, generally speaking, in the neighbourhood of London, a building for 500 *l.* would admit from 500 to 600 children into the school?—I should think from four to five hundred. It is to be recollected, in estimating the expense for a certain number of scholars, we calculate upon the number of children who shall be at any one time receiving the benefits of education in one school-room, but it never happens that the total number are always present. Thus in a school-room which is calculated to hold 1000 children, you will never get more than between 800 or 900 to attend at one time, and that is particularly the case in manufacturing districts; persons will keep their children at home a day or two for certain purposes of business, but still they are getting about three or four times as much instruction as they would procure in a Sunday school.

Suppose a grant were made merely of the money required to build the school, and the annual expenses were to be defrayed by subscriptions, would such meet with assistance, in your apprehension, in the progress of the system?—In my apprehension it would do every thing, because it would encourage benevolent persons in the neighbourhood to promote school associations throughout their districts, on the plan recommended by the British and Foreign School Society, in which the poor themselves would become interested in the education of their children, and receive it, not merely as an act of charity, but as a thing which they themselves had subscribed for.

Have you seen many instances of schools upon the new plan, in which the children paid a small sum?—At Northampton, in my journey to the North, I found an excellent school established upon the plan of the British and Foreign School Society, which had been supported by subscriptions, but those having fallen off, it occurred to the managers to endeavour to interest the parents of the poor children in the support of the school, and they accordingly received from them small subscriptions, which by the last accounts received appear to be sufficient to support the school entirely; and in many of the schools upon our plan, the parents pay one penny per week for the education of their children.

Is there no risk, if money were given for the commencement of the undertakings, by erecting or providing schools, new buildings would in every case be erected, instead of the more economical mode being resorted to of finding old barns or warehouses adapted to the purpose?—So general is the conviction now entertained among benevolent persons throughout the kingdom, of the great importance of

educating

educating the poor, that nothing more would be required, in my opinion, than to assist such benevolent individuals in providing suitable school-rooms in the most economical way.

In the estimate formerly made of the number of uneducated children, do you refer to those who at the commencement of the plan in contemplation would then be to be provided for?—My estimate was made upon the supposition that nothing had been done hitherto, and that the sole question was, how to provide for the want of education.

Would not this number of uneducated children be diminished in the course of the first two years?—If this plan were put into action, in the course of less than one year the whole might be provided for, and the number would be materially diminished; inasmuch as the want of education, notwithstanding all which has been done, is now so great, that we calculate, upon the total average of the kingdom, that about one half of the poor attend no school at all.

Would the annual expense be diminished in the same proportion?—It would be diminished, but not in the same proportion as the numbers decreased, because the expense of the schoolmaster would be nearly the same; the number of children requiring to be educated, after the arrear had been disposed of, would only consist of those who were arriving at the age of six years; but at the beginning of the plan it would be necessary to provide means for children from six to fourteen years of age.

Would it be necessary then, in contemplation of this diminution of the number to be provided for, to begin by erecting schools sufficient to accommodate the whole of the larger number; or might not some temporary accommodation be found for the larger number, and permanent schools only provided for that number requiring education, which would probably be permanent?—Under the circumstances of the case, it would appear advisable to provide substantially for the permanent education of the lower number, and to resort to some temporary expedients for educating the arrear at present unprovided for.

At what time did you make the calculation of 500,000?—About two years ago.

Have you not deducted from the 500,000 the number that have been since educated?—No; it is to be remarked, that since the period of this calculation, the progress of the British system and that of similar establishments for education has been exceedingly great; so that the total number requiring education, will be considerably smaller than the number stated.

Did you include in that number those children at that time receiving education in any establishment for the purpose?—The calculation, as I before remarked, was founded upon the want of education, which we discovered in attempting to form schools in several districts.

Suppose a place is large enough to maintain a school upon the National plan, and one upon the British and Foreign plan, so that Churchmen may send their children to both indiscriminately, and Dissenters to the British and Foreign school, would the two systems at all interfere with one another in such a place, whatever they might do in a smaller place?—If there were funds capable of supporting both, they need not interfere with each other; we had an example of a town large enough to support two schools, one upon each system, in which, if I mistake not, the same gentleman is president of both.

Have you more than one instance of that kind?—I do not recollect another instance of the kind.

Do you know an instance in which the same person might not be president of both schools, and the same benevolent people who could conduct the management of one, might on the other hand do so with the management of the other?—I certainly know instances of benevolent individuals who are disposed to be equally active on either system, from a firm conviction that education is one of the principal means of raising the moral character of the poor; and though they would certainly prefer that plan which would provide it indiscriminately for their denominations, yet they are so earnest that the poor should be educated, that they will render assistance to every attempt of the kind.

Suppose a place is too small to support a school upon both plans, do you see any means of teaching Dissenters there upon the new system?—The great probability is, from the experience we have had, that the want of co-operation between the parties will, under such circumstances, prevent the establishment of any school at all; there are several places in the kingdom now in which that is the case; it is not large enough to support two, and they cannot agree upon one.

469.

Suppose

Mr.
William Allen.

Suppose a National school were established, at which the children of Churchmen were taught the catechism and obliged to go to church, and the children of Dissenters not obliged to go to church, but only to attend some place of worship, and to be employed in some way, while the other children were learning the catechism; what would prevent the Dissenters from sending their children to such school?—My opinion is that they would very generally send them. But the difficulty in supporting such a school would arise from this circumstance, that some of the subscribers would conscientiously object to the appropriation of any of the funds to the teaching any peculiar creed, from a conviction that that ought to form a part of the duty of the minister of each religious profession.

Do children belonging to the Church attend schools upon the plan of the British and Foreign School Society?—In great numbers; within my knowledge there are several schools upon our plan, where from eight to nine tenths of the children belong to parents of the Establishment; and it is the constant endeavour of the promoters of this system, that those should all attend the Established Church regularly, while the others are required to attend such place of worship as their parents may prefer.

Are any attempts made to draw over those children to dissenting tenets?—I never heard of a solitary instance of it.

Do many of the children of Churchmen in those schools in point of fact conform to the discipline of the Dissenters?—No instance has come to my knowledge.

Do you mean no instance of any such child attending a meeting-house?—Certainly.

Have you heard of any objections being taken by parents to sending their children to schools on the British and Foreign plan, upon the grounds of their being converted?—Not the slightest, in any one instance.

Did that apprehension exist at first?—I am not aware of it.

THIRD

# THIRD REPORT.

(pp. 169——270.)

## MINUTES OF EVIDENCE

Taken before The SELECT COMMITTEE appointed to inquire into the EDUCATION of the Lower Orders of The Metropolis.

*Ordered,* by The House of Commons, *to be Printed,* 19 *June* 1816.

# WITNESSES.

# THIRD REPORT.

## MINUTES OF EVIDENCE

Taken before the SELECT COMMITTEE on the EDUCATION of the Lower Orders of The Metropolis.

*Jovis, 6° die Junii,* 1816.

HENRY BROUGHAM, Esquire, in The Chair.

*John Rickman*, Esquire, delivered in the following Paper :   *John Rickman, Esq.*

**AMOUNT of CHARITABLE DONATIONS, for the Maintenance of SCHOOLS in *England* and *Wales* :**

Extracted from the RETURNS, made by the Minister and Churchwardens, of CHARITABLE DONATIONS for the Benefit of Poor Persons, pursuant to the Act 26° GEO. III.

| ENGLAND: Counties of | ANNUAL PRODUCE: MONEY. £. s. d. | ANNUAL PRODUCE: LAND. £. s. d. | ANNUAL PRODUCE: RENT CHARGE. £. s. d. | TOTAL Annual PRODUCE. £. s. d. | Parishes and Places possessing Donations | Number of Donations. | Of which for mixed Purposes. |
|---|---|---|---|---|---|---|---|
| BEDFORD | 119 18 8½ | 333 5 8½ | 75 15 — | 528 19 5 | 29 | 50 | 11 |
| BERKS | 261 7 3 | 1,168 11 7 | 353 1 — | 1,782 19 10 | 44 | 91 | 11 |
| BUCKS | 377 4 6 | 934 6 10 | 171 17 2½ | 1,483 8 6½ | 47 | 61 | 12 |
| CAMBRIDGE | 139 4 4½ | 851 6 10 | 120 12 5 | 1,111 3 7½ | 38 | 60 | 5 |
| CHESTER | 213 12 — | 293 13 4 | 224 18 7 | 632 3 11 | 33 | 69 | 6 |
| CORNWALL | 179 8 2 | 197 13 10 | 42 5 6¼ | 419 7 6¼ | 35 | 48 | 3 |
| CUMBERLAND | 23 17 6 | 70 — — | 24 — — | 117 17 4 | 16 | 23 | 2 |
| DERBY | 94 18 — | 1,111 16 8 | 117 8 7 | 1,324 3 3 | 62 | 125 | 23 |
| DEVON | 315 10 6¼ | 1,140 13 10 | 260 1 8 | 1,716 6 10½ | 118 | 185 | 6 |
| DORSET | 146 13 6 | 1,529 5 1 | 140 5 — | 1,816 3 7 | 39 | 69 | 12 |
| DURHAM | 141 5 — | 72 10 — | 13 4 — | 226 19 — | 10 | 16 | 3 |
| ESSEX | 230 10 4½ | 1,380 12 8½ | 291 4 11½ | 1,902 8 —½ | 62 | 85 | 7 |
| GLOUCESTER | 428 13 4½ | 1,525 4 5¼ | 310 14 — | 2,264 11 9¼ | 84 | 123 | 16 |
| HEREFORD | 53 9 9¼ | 345 16 4 | 84 3 4 | 483 9 5¼ | 35 | 47 | 8 |
| HERTFORD | 203 9 — | 821 13 8 | 104 2 — | 1,129 4 8 | 34 | 56 | 9 |
| HUNTINGDON | 217 — 6 | 248 9 — | 22 7 9 | 487 17 3 | 26 | 42 | 4 |
| KENT | 622 5 2 | 1,203 — 6½ | 978 — 4 | 2,803 6 —½ | 81 | 138 | 8 |
| LANCASTER | 695 4 11 | 2,272 15 1 | 203 1 9½ | 3,171 1 9½ | 102 | 178 | 17 |
| LEICESTER | 275 10 2½ | 1,214 16 3¼ | 435 15 6 | 1,926 1 11¾ | 64 | 105 | 11 |
| LINCOLN | 101 8 4 | 1,817 14 11¼ | 279 — 5 | 2,198 3 8¼ | 108 | 159 | 9 |
| MIDDLESEX | 1,480 5 4 | 2,692 7 6 | 823 18 2 | 4,996 11 — | 64 | 151 | 19 |
| MONMOUTH | 549 — — | 121 2 — | 1 16 — | 671 18 — | 7 | 8 | 3 |
| NORFOLK | 123 17 10 | 729 13 3 | 278 — — | 1,131 11 1 | 51 | 60 | 16 |
| NORTHAMPTON | 183 4 6 | 1,757 8 11½ | 295 1 8 | 2,235 15 1½ | 72 | 121 | 10 |
| NORTHUMBERLAND | 71 10 — | 173 8 — | 45 — — | 289 18 — | 22 | 27 | 4 |
| NOTTINGHAM | 93 14 — | 374 13 — | 58 — — | 526 17 — | 43 | 65 | 6 |
| OXFORD | 127 11 —½ | 361 11 —½ | 175 15 2 | 664 14 1½ | 56 | 77 | 1 |
| RUTLAND | 4 18 6 | 45 — — | 5 — — | 54 18 6 | 10 | 11 | — |
| SALOP | 141 3 4 | 684 11 4 | 96 — — | 921 14 8 | 43 | 81 | 6 |
| SOMERSET | 420 17 11½ | 1,296 17 — | 310 14 4 | 2,028 9 3½ | 89 | 134 | 14 |
| SOUTHAMPTON | 931 2 8 | 717 12 10 | 459 18 — | 2,108 13 6 | 62 | 108 | 9 |
| STAFFORD | 149 — 6 | 1,323 19 5 | 148 12 4 | 1,621 12 3 | 60 | 108 | 6 |
| SUFFOLK | 89 6 4 | 1,614 — 11½ | 212 13 6 | 1,916 — 9½ | 71 | 124 | 6 |
| SURREY | 876 6 — | 1,413 13 2 | 154 15 1 | 2,444 14 3 | 43 | 92 | 16 |
| SUSSEX | 410 19 6 | 796 3 5 | 260 10 — | 1,467 12 11 | 57 | 78 | 7 |
| WARWICK | 328 15 10 | 1,411 13 11 | 663 19 10 | 2,404 9 7 | 57 | 79 | 6 |
| WESTMORLAND | 19 17 2 | 117 17 — | - - - | 137 14 2 | 8 | 22 | 1 |
| WILTS | 354 4 — | 534 9 — | 185 15 — | 1,074 8 — | 60 | 94 | 8 |
| WORCESTER | 222 12 6¼ | 2,798 14 1 | 39 10 8 | 3,060 17 3¾ | 53 | 92 | 7 |
| YORK, East Riding | 236 18 7¼ | 494 19 2 | 148 2 4 | 880 — 1¼ | 47 | 62 | 6 |
| — N. Riding | 164 18 1 | 1,358 7 5 | 364 15 2 | 1,888 — 8 | 73 | 95 | 7 |
| — W. Riding | 695 2 3¼ | 3,287 7 5 | 620 15 7½ | 4,603 5 3¾ | 133 | 292 | 9 |
| Total ENGLAND (carried forward) £. | 12,415 17 —½ | 42,638 13 5¼ | 9,601 1 11¼ | 64,655 12 5 | 2,248 | 3,716 | 359 |

495.

*(continued.)*

Amount of Charitable Donations, for the Maintenance of Schools in England and Wales—*continued*.

| WALES: | ANNUAL PRODUCE: | | | TOTAL Annual PRODUCE. | Parishes and Places possessing Donations. | Number of Donations. | Of which for mixed Purposes. |
|---|---|---|---|---|---|---|---|
| | MONEY. | LAND. | RENT CHARGE. | | | | |
| Counties of | £.   s.   d. | £.   s.   d. | £.   s.   d. | £.   s.   d. | | | |
| ANGLESEY - - - | 33 — — | 9   9 — | -   .   . | 42   9 — | 6 | 6 | — |
| BRECON - - - | 85   6   8 | 16 — — | 30 — — | 131   6   8 | 12 | 16 | — |
| CARDIGAN - - - | 9   14 — | 35 — — | -   -   - | 44   14 — | 5 | 8 | — |
| CARMARTHEN - - - | 43 — — | 13   5 — | 28   15 — | 85 — — | 12 | 19 | 1 |
| CARNARVON - - - | 22   5 — | -   -   - | 2   13   4 | 24   18   4 | 7 | 9 | — |
| DENBIGH - - - | 57   3 — | 78   7   9½ | -   -   - | 135   10   9½ | 10 | 20 | 1 |
| FLINT - - - | 67   6 — | 57   14 — | 41 — — | 166 — — | 13 | 28 | 1 |
| GLAMORGAN - - - | 7   10 — | 141   12   6 | 25 — — | 174   2   6 | 9 | 11 | 1 |
| MERIONETH - - - | 28   16 — | 27   6   8 | 15 — — | 71   2   8 | 6 | 9 | — |
| MONTGOMERY - - - | 22   7   2 | 43   8 — | 11 — — | 76   15   2 | 12 | 20 | — |
| PEMBROKE - - - | 87 —   4 | 57   2 — | 12 — — | 156   2   4 | 14 | 21 | 2 |
| RADNOR - - - | 5 — — | 154   2 — | 13 — — | 172   2 — | 13 | 15 | — |
| Total WALES - £. | 468   8   2 | 633   6   11½ | 178   8   4 | 1,280   3   5½ | 119 | 182 | 6 |
| ENGLAND (Brought forward) | 12,415   17 — ½ | 42,638   13   5¼ | 9,601   1   11¼ | 64,655   12   5 | 2,248 | 3,716 | 350 |
| TOTAL ENGLAND & WALES - £. | 12,884   5   2½ | 43,272 —   4¾ | 9,779   10   3¼ | 65,935   15   10½ | 2,367 | 3,898 | 356 |

BY whom and for what purpose was this abstract prepared?—It was prepared by me in the latter end of the year 1807, at the desire of The Speaker, in consequence of a Bill which had been brought into Parliament by Mr. Whitbread in the preceding Session.

Up to what date were those returns?—They were the returns for the year 1785. By an Act of the last Session, the 55th of the King, cap. 47, still further information was directed to be procured on the same subject.

The Rev. *John Sleath,* D.D. and Mr. *William Henry Lane,*
called in, and Examined.

*The Rev. John Sleath, D.D. and Mr. W. H. Lane.*

(*To Dr. Sleath.*) YOU are High Master of St. Paul's school?—Yes, I am.

How long have you been in that situation?—Nearly two years.

(*To Mr. Lane.*) What are you?—Accountant to the Mercers' Company.

Upon what foundation is the school?—The foundation of Dr. John Colet, dean of St. Paul's in the year 1512.

Was it founded by charter?—By the warrant of Henry the 8th, on the supplication of the dean.

Have you got the copies of that warrant and supplication?—I have.

[They were delivered in, and read, as follows :]

SUPPLICATIO ad Regiam Maiestatem

IN the moste humble wyse shewith and besechith youre mooste gracious highnesse youre contynuall oratour John Colet deane of the cathedrall churche of Seynt Paule wīn your citie of London, That where youre said oratour to the pleasur of God and for and in agmentation and encrease as well of connyng as of vertuouse lyvyng wīn this yoʳ realme hathe nowe of late edifyed within the cimitory of the saide cathedrall churche a Scole house (wherein he purposith that children as well borne and to be borne w'yn youre said citie as elsewhere) to the same repayring shall not oonely in contynuance be substancially taughte and lernyd in laten tung, but also instructe & informed in vertuouse condiciouns, which by Goddes grace shall largely extende and habunde to the comōn well of the people of this youre realme, and to the grete coumfort and comoditie of your grace and to youre heires, to have yoñg childern of youre realme bothe in conyng and vertue graciously brought up in avoydyng many folde vices which these dayes for lake of suche instruccion in youth been gretly rooted and contynued in yong people, to the greie displeasur of God And for the ppetuall cōtynuance of the charges of the same, for ever to be borne paied and susteyned according to such ordre and direccion as youre saide oratoʳ by the spẽall favour and licence of your highnesse purposith to make and ordeyne, he intendith to geve and mortyse landis and tenementis of the clere yerely valew of fifty and three poundis in the countie of Buk, to soñ body corporat at his denomynacion In consideracion whereof it may please yoʳ hignesse of yoʳ most habudat grace & goodnesse, by your gracious ires patent undʳ your grete seale in due forme to be made, to graunt & licence your said oratoʳ to geve & graunt mañs londs and tenements in the said countie of the clere yerely valour of fyfty and three poundis above all charges to som body corporate, and licence to the same body corporat the same landes and tenements to receyve and take to thentent biforesaid, eny statute of landes and tentˢ to mortmayne not to be putt notw'standing, and that w'oute fvn fee or other charges therfore to be paide or borne to youre grace And youre said oratour shall daiely pray to God for the prosperitie of your moste noble and royall estate long to endure.

WARRANT

*£. 53. p'ann. by Lands in the county of Bucks.*

WARRANT cum manu Regia assignat.

*The Rev.*
*John Sleath, D. D.*
*and*
*Mr. W. H. Lane.*

To the King our Sovaigne Lorde,

PLEASETH yoᵣ Hignesse of yoᵣ Mooste Noble and habundant Grace to graunt unto your feithfull Chapeleyn John Colet Deane of the Cathedrall Church of Seynt Paule w'in yoᵣ Citic of London, your gracious Lrēs Patentꝰ in due forme to be made according to the tenour ensuyng

Rex omnibus ad quos ̄ec̄e

Saⱡtm Sciatis q̃d nos considerãtes piū ꝓpositū dilecti nobis mag̃ri Joħis Colet sacre theologoie doctoris decam eccⱡie Catħ Sancti Pauli Londoñ in edificatiōe jam cujusdã Scole in Cimiterio dc̄e eccⱡie pro pueris in eadem scola erudiendis in bonis moribȝ & litteratura pro meliori sustentatiōe unius Mag̃ri & uniȝ ostiarij sive duoꝛ ostiarioꝛ ejusdē et aliaꝛ rerū necessariarū iƀm fiendarū de grã nr̃a spĩali ac ex certa sciēna & mero motu nr̃is cōcessimus et licentiã dedimus ac per presentes cōcedimus et licentiã damus pro nobis & heredibȝ nr̃is quantū in nobis est. Custodibȝ et cōmunitati misterij m̃cerie Civitatis Londoñ et successoribȝ suis q' ipī et successores sui dominia Maneria terras tenementa redditus revsiones servicia et hereditamēta quecūq, ac alias possessiones quascunq, ad annuū valorem Quinquaginta & trium libraꝛ ultra oōia onera et reprisȝ a quacūq, persona sive a quibuscūq, personis ea eis dare concedere ligare vel assignare volente seu volentibȝ. Licet de nobis in capite vel aliter aut de alij psonis vel psona mediate vel iōmediate teneañ acquirere et recipere possint. Habenđ et tenenđ sibi & successoribȝ suis imppetuū et eidem psone sive eijsdem psonis q̃ᵈ iꝑe dominia maneria terras tenemēta reddit⁹ revsiōes servicia et cetera ꝑmissa. Custodibȝ et cōmunitati mistere predce et successoribȝ suis ꝑdcis ad annuū valorem ꝑdictum in forma ꝑdca dare concedere ligare vel assignare possint et valeant Similiter licenciã dedimus & cōcessimus ac damus et concedimus spĩalem per ꝑsentes absq, impedimento impeticiōe seu grauamine nostri vel heredum aut successoꝛ nr̃oꝛ Justic̃ Escaeꝛ vicecomitum ballinoꝛ seu alioꝛ ministroꝛ nr̃orum quoꝛcūq, volumus insuper et concedimus per pntes ejisdem custodibȝ et comunitati mistere predce et successoribus suis q̃d ipī et successores sui habeant et obtineãt: et ħere et obtinere possint. tam psentes Lrãs nr̃as pateñ q̃m oōia et omīnoda brevia ac Lrãs regias executorias et confirmatorias in hac parte de tempore in tempus fienđ et prosequenđ absq, aliquo fine et feodo inde in Cancellaria nr̃a heredū vel successoꝛ ñroꝛ seu in hanapio ejusdē Cancellarie ac alibi quoquo modo taxanđ imponenđ fienđ soluenđ et capienđ. Et q̃d custos sive clericus Hanaperij predce aut ejus deputaꝛ iƀm pro tempore existeñ. inde quieti et in compoto suo ad Scc̃m nr̃m et heredū ñrorum reddenđ exonerati existant imppm̃. Statuta de terris et tenemētis ad manū mortuam non ponenđ aut aliquibȝ alijs statutis actibȝ ordinationibȝ restrictionibȝ sive mandatis in contrariū factis editis sive ordinatis aut fienđ seu ordinanđ aut aliqua alia causa re vel materia quacunq, aut eo q, expressa mentio de certitudine premissoꝛ seu de alijs donis sive concessionibȝ prefatis custod ibȝ et comunitati mistere predicte et successoribȝ suis antea factis in ꝑsentibȝ immine existit in aliquo non obstan. In Cujus Rei ēc̄.

Memorandū q̃d tenor psentiu prosequtus fuit secundum Rectum cursum legis et cōsuetudinis Regni Anglie videl' Warant superius scriptᵣ cum manu Regia assignaꝛ direcꝛ ad signetum Regium v't per eundem Warant penes clericos eiusdem signeti remaneñ plene liquet de Recordo; virtute cuius Warant exiuit aliud Warant sub signeto Regio verbatim custodi privata sigilli regij v't per eundem Warant penes eunde custodem privati sigilli remaneñ plemus apparet virtute cuiꝯ Warãt exiuit privatum sigillū pari forma Cancellario Anglie v't ꝑ eundem privatū sigillū penes eunde Cancellariū remaneñ apparet ad largū cuius ꝑtextu idem Cancellarius fieri fecit litteras Regias pateñ sub magno sigillo Regio signaꝛ in forma subscripta.

Have you a copy of the statutes?—I have.

[It was delivered in and read, as follows:]

## Num. 5.—The STATUTES of St. Paul's School.
### Prologus.

JOHN COLLETT, the sonne of Henrye Collett, Dean of Paules, desiring nothyng more thanne education and bringing uppe children in good maners and literature, in the yere of our Lord A.M. fyve hundredth and twelfe, bylded a schole

iu

The Rev.
John Sleath, D.D.
and
Mr. W. H. Lane.

in the Estende of Paulis church of CLIII to be taught fre in the same; and ordeyned there a maister and a surmaister and a chappelyn with sufficiente and perpetuale stipendes ever to endure, and sett patrones and defenders governours and rulers of that same schole the most honest and faithful fellowiship of the Mercers of London And for because nothing can continue long and endure in good ordre without lawes and statutes, I the said John have expressed and shewed my minde what I wolde shoulde be truly and diligentlye observed and kepte of the sayde maister and surmaister and chapelyn, and of the mercers governours of the scole, that in this boke may appere to what intent I founde this schole.

### Capitulum primum de

#### MAGISTRO PRIMARIO.

IN the grammar scole founded in the church yard of Paules at the Estende in the yeare of our Lorde 1518 by John Colet deane of the same churche, in the honour of Christe Jesu in pueritiâ, and of his blessed modir Marie, in that scole shall be firste an highe maister This hyghe maister, in doctrine learnyng and teachinge shall directe all the scole; this maister shall be chosen by the wardens and assistance of the mercery, a man hoole in body, honest and vertuous, and lerned in good and cleane Latin literature, and also in Greke, yf such may be gotten; a wedded man, a single man, or a preste that hath no benefice with cure nor service that may lett the due besinesse in the scole.

The Mercers shall assemble togither in the scole house with such advise and counsell of well literatur and learned men as they can gett; they shall chose this maister, and give unto him his charge, saying unto him on this wyse

" Sir, we have chosen you to be maister and teacher of this scole, to teache the children of the same not all only good literature but allso good maners, certificeing you that this is no rome of continuance and perpetuite but upon your dewtie in the scole And every yere at Candlemasse, when the mercers be assembled in the scole-house, ye shall submit you to our examination, and founde doinge your duetie according ye shall continue, otherwise reasonable warned ye shall contente you to departe, and you of your partie, not warned of us, but of your mynde in any season willing to departe, ye shall give us warnyng XII monthes before, without we can be shortlyer well provided of another.

" Also being maister, ye shall not absente you but upon license of the surveyors for the tyme being.

" Also yf any controversy and stryfe shall be betwixt you and surmaister or the chapelyne of the scole, ye shall stande at the direction of the surveyors being for that yere."

And yf the chosen maister will promise this, than admytt him toit, and name him and stall him in his seat in the scole, and shew him his lodginge, that is to say, all the sellers bynethe the halle the kytchin and butterye, and over that the hool storye and chambers, and in the house roofe the litell middel chamber and the galarye on the south side As touching all the storye of chambers nexte underneth the galary he shall nothing meddell withall And they shall geve him the ymplements of his house by indenture.

All these lodgings he shall have fre without any payment, and in this lodging he shall dwell and kepe housholde to his power.

His wagis shall be a mark a weke, and a lyvery gowne of iiii nobles delivered in cloth.

His absence shall be but onys in the yere, and not above XXX dayes, which he shall take conjunctim or divisim Yf the maister be syke of sykeness incurable, or fall into such age that he may not conveniently teache, and hath bene a man that longe and laudably hath taught in the scole, thanne let another be chosyn, and by the discrete charitie of the mercery let there be assigned to the olde maister a reasonable levinge of x¹. or otherwise as it shall seme convenyent, so that the olde maister after his longe labor, in no wise be lefte destitute Yf the maister be syke of sikenesse curable, yet neverthelesse I will he shall have his wagis, and in suche sekeness yf he may not teache, let hym reward the undermaister for his more labour somewhat according Yf the undermaister be in literature and in honest lyfe accordynge, then the hygh maisters rome vacante let him be chosen before another.

The hyghe maister shall have the tenement of Stebenhith, now in the hands of Crystofer Myddelton, to resorte unto, whiche tenement the mercers shall mayntein and repayre.

### The SURMAISTER.

There shall be also a surmaister, some manne vertuouse in livinge and well lettered, that shall teache under the maister, as the hygh maister shall appoynt hym, some single man or wedded, or a preste that hath no benefice with cure nor service that may let his due diligence in the scole.

This surmaister the hyghe maister shall chose as often as the rome shall be voyde, a man hoole in body, and when the high maister hath appointed him upon one, he shall call to the scole the surveyors of the scole, and before them he shall say to the surmaister on this wise:—" Sir, before these my maisters here, the surveyors of this scole, I shew unto you that I have chosen you to be under maister of this scole,

and

and to teache alway from tyme to tyme as I shall appoynte you, and supply my rome in my absence when it shall be granted me by my maisters the mercers wardens and surveyors And for such more labour in my absence I shall somewhat se to you as my maisters here shall thinke best." Thanne the surveyors shall exorte the surmaister diligently to do his dewtie, and shall say unto hym on this wise: " Your rome is no perpetuite but according to your labor and diligence ye shall continue, otherwise found not according and reasonable, warned of us ye shall departe Yf it shall be so that at any tyme ye will departe of your own mynde, ye shall give us a half years warninge.

" If any controversy be betwixt you and the highe maister, ye shall stande at our discretion in every thinge."

Yf he will promise this, thenne let the mercers approve the election of the surmaister, and assigne him his lodgeing in the old Chaunge.

His wagis shall be vi s. viii d. a weke, and a lyvery gowne of iiii nobles delivered in clothe; he shall go to comyns with the hyghe maister if he may conveniently.

He shall be absent in all the yere not above xxx dayes, and yet than for cause reasonable, and with licence had of the highe maister and also of the surveyors.

In sekenes curable, as aches or suche sekeness, for a tyme he shall be tolerated and have his full wagis.

Yf after his commynge he fall sick into sickenes incurable, as lepry or Frenche poxe, or after his longe labor in the scole fall into age ympotent, thenne I commit him to the charite of the mercers, they of the coler of the scole, to provide him a lyvinge as it may be possible, praying them to be charitable in that behalf.

### Of both MAISTERS at onys.

Yf both maisters be sicke at onys, thenne let the scole cease for that while.

Yf there be suche sicknesse in the citie contagious, that the scole cannot continue, yet neverthelesse both maisters shall have their wagis, being always readie for to teache.

Neyther of these maisters shall take office or lectorshype or proctorshype, or any such other besiness, which shall let their diligence and their necessary labor in the scole; yf they do, and warned lawfully, yf they will not cease from suche besiness, than lett them be warned to departe.

Lett the highe maister se the schole to be kept cleane by the poor childe, and be swepte every Satorday, and also the leades, and from tyme to tyme to call upon the mercers for necessary reparations.

### The CHAPELYN.

There shall be also in the scole a preste, that dayly as he can be disposed shall singe mass in the chapell of the scole, and pray for the children to prosper in good life and in good literature, to the honour of God and our Lord Christ Jesu At his masse, when the bell in the scole shall knyll to sacringe, then all the children in the scole, knelynge in their seats, shall with lift upp handes pray in the time of sacringe After the sacringe, when the bell knylleth agayne, they shall sitt downe agayne to theire books learninge This Preste, some good honest and vertuouse man, shall be chosen from tyme to tyme by the wardens and assistance of the mercery; he shall also learne, or yf he be lerned helpe to teache in the scole, if it shall seme convenient to the highe maister, or else not He shall have no benefice with cure nor service, nor no other office, nor occupation, but attende allonly upon the scole; he shall teache the children the Catechyzon and instruction of the Articles of the faythe and the x Commandments in Inglishe.

His wagis shall be viii l. by the yere, and a lyvery gowne of xxvi s. viii d. delivered in clothe.

His chamber and lodginge shall be in the newe house in the Old Chayn, or in the maisters lodging, as shall be thought beste.

He shall not have his rome by writinge or at seale, but at libertie according to his deserving.

His absence may be once in the yere, yf it nede be, as yt shall seme best to the surveyors of the scole for that yere, And than with license askyd and obteyned of the said surveyors.

In sekeness he shall be nothing abridged of his wages But let it be sene that he be hoole in body when he is chosen.

Yf he fall to unthriftiness and misbehaviour, after lefull warning let him be repellid, and another chosen within viii dayes, or assone after as can be.

### The CHILDREN.

There shall be taught in the scole children of all nations and contres indifferently, to the number of cliii, according to the number of the seates in the scole; the maister shall admit these children as they be offirid from tyme to tyme; but first se that they can saye the Catechyzon, and also that he can rede and write competently, else let him not be admitted in no wise.

A childe

The Rev.
*John Sleath, D.D.*
and
*Mr. W. H. Lane.*

A childe at the first admission once for ever shall paye iiii d. for wrytinge of his name, this money of the admissions shall the poor scoler have that swepeth the scole and kepeth the seats cleane.

In every forme one principall childe shal be placid in the chayre president of that forme.

The children shall come unto the scole in the mornynge at vii of the clocke both winter and somer, and tarye there untyll a xi, and returne again at one of the clocke, and departe at v And thrise in the day prostrate they shall say the prayers with due tract and pawsing as they be conteyned in a table in the scole, that is to say, in the mornynge and at noone and at eveninge.

In the scole in no time in the yere they shall use talough candell in no wise, but alonly waxe candell at the costes of theyr friends.

Also I will they bring no meate nor drinke nor bottel, nor use in the school no breakfasts nor drinkings in the tyme of learnynge in no wise, yf they nede drincke let them be provided in some other place.

I will they use no cockfightinge nor rydinge about of victorye, nor disputing at Saint Bartilimewe which is but foolish babling and losse of time I will also that they shall have no remedyes (play-dayes) Yf the maister grantith any remedyes, he shall forfeit xl s. totiens quotiens, excepte the kynge or an archbishopp or a bishop present in his own person in the scole desire it.

All these children shall every Childermas daye come to Paulis churche and hear the childe Bishop sermon, and after be at the hygh masse, and each of them offer a i d. to the childe Byshop, and with them the maisters and surveyors of the scole.

In general processions when they be warned, they shall go twayne and twayne together soberlye, and not singe out but say devoutlye tweyne and tweyne vii Psalmes with the letanye.

To theyr urine they shall go thereby to a place appointed, and a poore childe of the scole shall se it conveyed awaye fro tyme to tyme, and havs the avayle of the urine; for other causes, yf nede be, they shall go to the watersyde.

Yf any childe after he is receyved and admitted into the scole go to any other scole to learne there after the manner of that scole, than I will that such childe for no mans suite shall be here after received into our scole, but go where him lyste, where his frendes shall thincke shall be better learninge And this I will be shewed unto his friendes or rather that offer him at his first presenting into the scole.

## What shall be taught:

As touching in this scole what shall be taught of the maisters and learned of the scholers, it passeth my witte to devyse and determyne in particular, but in general to speake and sume what to saye my mynde, I would they were taught always in good literature bothe Laten and Greke and good autors such as have the verrye Romayne eloquence joyned with wisdom, specially Cristen autors that wrote theire wisdome with clean and chaste Laten other in verse or in prose, for my intent is by this scole specially to encrease knowledge and worshipping of God and our Lord Christ Jesu and good Christen life and maners in the children And for that entent I will the children learne first above all the Catechizon in Englishe, and after the Accidens that I made or some other, yf any be better, to the purpose to induce children more spedely to laten speeche And then Institutum Christiani Hominis, which that learned Erasmus made at my requeste, and the boke called Copia of the same Erasmus And then other authors Christian, as Lactantius Prudentius and Proba, and Sedulius and Juvencus and Baptista Mantuanus, and suche other as shall be thought convenient and most to purpose unto the true laten speeche All Barbary all corruption all Laten adulterate, which ignorant blind foles brought into this worlde, and with the same hath dystained and poysonyd the old laten speche, and the veraye Romayne tongue, which in the tyme of Tully and Salust and Virgell and Terence was used, which also Sainte Jerome and Sainte Ambrose and Sainte Austen and many holy Doctors lerned in theyre tymes, I saye that fylthines and all suche abusion whiche the later blynde worlde brought in, whiche more rather may be called blotterature than litterature, I utterly abannyshe and exclude out of this scole, and charge the maisters that they teache alwaye that is beste, and instruct the children in Greke and redynge Laten, in redynge unto them such autors that hathe with wisdome joyned the pure chaste eloquence.

## The Mercers.

The Honourable Company of Mercers of London, that is to saye, the maister and all the wardeins and all the assistence of the fellowshyppe, shall have all the care and charge, rule and governaunce of the scole, and they shall every yere chose of their compayne 11 honeste and substantiall men, called the surveyors of the schole, which in the name of the hoole felowship shall take all the charge and besiness about the schole for that one yere They shall oversee and receave all the landes of the scole, and see them repayred from tyme to tyme by their officers; and such officer as they appoint to be renter or to other besyness of the scole, for his more labor in the scole besyness, I wyll he have xx s. a yere, and a gowne price x111 s. 4 d.

The

*The Rev.*
*John Sleath. D.D.*
*and*
*Mr. W. H. Lane.*

The surveyors of the scole shall come into the scole vi days before Xtmasse, vi dayes before Ester, vi dayes before Saint John Baptiste daye, and vi dayes before Michaelmass, and paye the highe maister and the surmaister and the preste their quarter wages, and at the latir end of the yere they shall gyve accompte to the maisters wardens and assistence of the felowshype.

Their accompts shall be about Candlemasse, three dayes before or three dayes after Candlemasse  In that daye appoynted shall be an assembly and a litell dinner ordeyned by the surveyors not exceedinge the pryce of fower nobles.

In that daye they shall call to a rekening all the estate of the scole and see the accompte, and discharge the olde surveyors, and to the younger choose another; and in that daye after the accompte they shall geve to the maister warden a noble, if he be present, or else not; to eche of the other wardens v s. if they be present, or else not.

To the surveyors, eche of them xl s. for theyre labors for that yere; for theyr ryding and vysiting of theyre landes, to eche of them xl s. yf they ride.

The clerke of the mercery shall inacte all things that daye, and have for his labor iii s. iiii d.

See that the stuarde bring in his court rolles ear he have his fee.

See that the bayliffes renewe their rentalls every yere  Let not the landes of the schole but by the space of five yeres.

That is spared that daye in rewardes and charges, lett it be put in the treasure of the scole.

They shall dyvers tymes in the quarter come to the scole and see how they do.

Every year, at the foot of the accompte, all ordynary charges done, the overplus of the monye, which at this daye is extemed, this I hooly gyve to the fellowshippe of the Mercery, to the mainteyning and supporting and repayring of that longeth to the scole from tyme to tyme.

And albeit my mynde is that they shall have this surplusage for thentent above seyd, yet nevertheless I will the said surplusage, as much as shall be spared of it above reparations and casuelties, at every accompte be brought and put in a cofir of iron gyven of me to the Mercers, standynge in their hall, and there from yere to yere remayne aparte by itself, that it may appere how the scole by the owne selfe mainteneth itself, and at length, over and above the owne lyvelehode, if the saide scole shall grow to any further charge to the Mercery, that than also that may appere to the laude and prayse and meryte of the sayde fellowshippe.

### Libertye to declare the STATUTES.

And notwithstanding these statutes and ordinances before written, in which I have declared my mynde and will, yet because in tyme to come many thyngs may and shall survyve and grow by many occasions and causes, whiche at the making of this booke was not possible to come to mynde  In consideration of the assured truth and circumspect wisedom and faithfull goodnes of the most honest and substantial felowshype of the Mercery of London, to whome I have commytted all the care of the schole, and trustyng in theyre fidelitie and love that they have to God and man and to the scole, and also belevying verely that they shall allwaye drede the great wrath of God  Both all this that is sayde, and all that is not sayde whiche hereafter shall come unto my mynde while I live to be sayde, I leve it hoolely to theyre discretion and charitie, I mean of the wardens and assistances of the fellowshype, with suche other counsell as they shall call unto them, good lettered and learned men, they to adde and to diminishe of this boke, and to supply in it every defaulte  And also to declare in it every obscuritie and darknes as tyme and place and just occasion shall require, calling the dredefull God to loke uppon them in all suche besyness and exorting them to feare the terrible judgment of God, which seeth in derkness, and shall render to everye man accordinge to his worke  And finally prayinge the great Lorde of Mercye for theyre faythful dealing in this matters, now and alweye to send unto them in this worlde much wealthe and prosperyte, and after this lyfe muche joye and glorye.

### The LANDES of the Scole:

| | £. | s. | d. |
|---|---|---|---|
| Fyrste of the olde scole - - - - - - - | — | 20 | — |
| Item the 4 shopes in the holde of Berel - - - - | 4 | — | — |
| Item the tenements in Bridge-strete - - - - - | 8 | 6 | 8 |
| Item the tenements in Soperlane - - - - - | 6 | 13 | 4 |
| Item the tenements in Podinglane - - - - - | 6 | 13 | 4 |
| Item the holdes without Aldgate - - - - - | 6 | 18 | — |
| Item the maners and landes and tenements in the counte of Buck | 52 | 11 | 9 |
| Item the maner of Vach in Barton, with the members - - | 8 | 4 | 6 ob. |
| Item the maner of Berwicke - - - - - - | 8 | — | — |
| Item of landes in Colchester - - - - - - | 3 | 13 | 4 |
| Summa - - - - - - | 72 | 9 | 7 ob. |

Item

|  | £. | s. | d. |
|---|---|---|---|
| Item a tenement and certain closes late in the holde of William Role, by the yere | — | 1 |  |
| Item a tenement and a close late in the holde of Clyfton | — | 26 | 8 |
| Item a close late in the holde of Maister Wellis | — | 23 | 4 |
| Item another littell close in the holde of the same Maister Wellis | — | 5 | — |
| Item a barn late in the holde of the same man | — | 6 | 8 |
| Item of Edmonde Roll for 4 acres of lande of the backeside of White-hart-strete | — | 5 | — |
| Item of Chrystopher Hall for certain lande late John Atfeux, by the yere | 7 | — | — |
| Item of the same Hall for 8 acres of lande in London felde | — | 16 | — |
| Item of Mr. Crystofer Middleton for a certen tenement there | — | 20 | — |
| Item 4 little tenements there | — | 13 | 4 |
| Item 9 acres pasture next the place there | — | 30 | — |
| Item a place with gardens there | — | 40 | — |
| Summa | 18 | 16 | — |

|  | £. | s. | d. |
|---|---|---|---|
| Payde to the Bishopp of London yerely at 4 termes of londes and tenements before | — | 52 | 4 |
| Summa clar | 16 | 3 | 8 |
| Summa totalis | 122 | 4 | 7 ob. |

|  | £. | s. | d. |
|---|---|---|---|
| Whereof deducted for the shoppes in the holding of Berell for a certain tyme | 4 | — | — |
| Remayneth clere | £. 118 | 4 | 7 ob. |

Charges Ordinaire outpayde yerely:

|  | £. | s. | d. |
|---|---|---|---|
| To the High Maister | — | 52 | Marc. |
| The Under Maister | — | 26 | Marc. |
| The Preste | 8 | — | — |
| Theyre lyverye | 4 | — | — |
| The Supervisours | 4 | — | — |
| For the visitation of landes | 4 | — | — |
| The Clerke | — | 3 | 4 |
| The Maister Warden | — | 5 | — |
| To Stuardes | — | 40 | — |
| To Bailyffs | — | 40 | — |
| The costes of the dyner | — | 26 | 8 |
| The Officer of the Mercery, renter of the scole | — | 20 | — |
| For his gowne | — | 13 | 4 |
| Summa | 79 | 8 | 4 |

So resteth to the reparations suytes casuelties and all other charges extraordinarye - - - - - - - - 38. 16. 3. ob.

JOANNES COLETT
fundator nove Scole
manu mea propria.

(*To Dr. Sleath.*) From what class of children are the scholars of Saint Paul's school taken?—That is a question I am hardly prepared to answer; but the generality of boys that have been educated at Saint Paul's school, have consisted of boys in the neighbourhood, generally speaking, though it is open to the whole world.

Of what rank in society are they generally?—Being newly elected myself, I can hardly say; but I should think principally of the clergy, the professional gentlemen and medical men in the neighbourhood; and a great many gentlemen in Doctors' Commons have received their education in Saint Paul's school.

Is it a free school?—In respect to tuition, it is free; the only fee that is required and paid, is one shilling upon the entrance of each boy.

Is there any allowance provided for the board or lodging of the scholars?—None, it is merely tuition.

Is the admission in the Mercers' Company?—In the Mercers' Company, and the officer delegated by them is the acting trustee for the year.

Is the number of boys limited?—To one hundred and fifty-three.

Are the statutes above mentioned observed in all respects, as nearly as the change of circumstances and times would permit?—I believe so; there is a discretionary
power

The Rev.
John Sleath, D.D.
and
Mr. W. H. Lane.

power left to the governors, to act according to circumstances, and upon which they have acted.

What is the amount of the fund appropriated to the school?—I cannot say.

(*To Mr. Lane.*) Have you no idea of the revenue of the school?—There is a separate revenue for Saint Paul's school; but the answer to this question should come from the clerk of the company.

The Committee do not want to know within a pound or two?—I think, as near as I can say, between four and five thousand a year; but with respect to this statement of accounts, I should much rather that it came from the clerk of the company, who is the proper officer and representative of the company.

How is this money expended generally, without going into details?—By payments to the masters of the school, and the incidental expenses of the establishment.

As nearly as you recollect, what are the annual expenses of the school?—They are very uncertain.

Do they ever amount to four or five thousand a year?—They do.

(*To Dr. Sleath.*) What is the high master's salary?—600 *l.* a year, and a house.

Any other emoluments?—None, except that there is a house appropriated to the high master, at Stepney, besides the house in the church-yard, which is little or no emolument.

(*To Mr. Lane.*) What is the salary of the sur-master?—About 300 *l.* a year; rather more, perhaps 320 *l.* or 330 *l.*

A house?—Yes.

Are there any other salaries upon the establishment?—Yes; there are other masters, and an usher or chaplain.

Any others?—A fourth master, and assistant master to the high master.

What salaries have the chaplain and assistant master?—Between two and three hundred pounds a year each.

Have they houses?—The usher has, but not the assistant master.

Are there any other salaries?—There are payments from the school funds to the officers of the company, and various other expenses.

What sort of payments are made from the school funds to the officers of the company?—The payment to the clerk is 100 *l.* a year, the accountant 40 *l.* and two beadles are paid the sum of 5 *l.* each.

Are there any other payments made to the officers of the Mercers' Company?—There is a surveyor accountant, who admits the scholars, and who is in fact the acting trustee for the year as to admissions, and who maintains a communication between the master and the court of wardens; he has four pounds a year according to the statutes, and the surveyor assistant has the same.

Are there any other salaries or payments?—There is a porter boy, who has two pounds, likewise according to the statutes.

Are there any rents to pay?—No rents, that I recollect.

Any taxes?—Many taxes upon the school-houses.

About how much do they amount to, one year with another?—That is a question I am sure I cannot answer.

Are the repairs heavy?—They are occasionally heavy, because the school has been built many years. There is an annuity, to the late high master, of about 1000 *l.* a year.

Who is the late master?—Dr. Roberts; he had been high master forty-five years, and was a man of great merit.

(*To Dr. Sleath.*) Has the high master any advantage from taking boarders in his house?—That is entirely a private concern, which of course he is allowed to do.

(*To Mr. Lane.*) Are there any other annuities upon return?—No others, that I recollect.

Are there any pensions to boys going to college?—Very great; but part of those are paid out of a separate estate, being a benefaction founded by Lord Camden, which is quite separate from the estate of St. Paul's school itself.

How many of those exhibitioners are there?—There are seven who now receive it; but the number is not limited.

What are those exhibitions worth?—100 *l.* a year.

For how many years?—The time is not limited, but it is usually seven years; those seven are paid out of the Camden benefaction.

How many are paid by St. Paul's school?—I think there are about five or six holding exhibitions, but the number is uncertain; they are 50 *l.* a year.

For

For how many years?—They may hold them for seven years.

Are they usually given to the same boys that have the Camden exhibitions?—Never to the same.

How are the exhibitioners chosen?—By the court of wardens of the Mercers' Company, and the trustees of the school.

Are any premiums given upon apprenticeships?—The school is strictly classical; there are no apprenticeships, nor any further expense, upon the boys leaving the school, except such as go as exhibitioners.

## Mr. *William Edward Ward*, called in, and Examined.

YOU are clerk of the Mercers' Company?—I am.

Have you got an account of the income and expenditure of St. Paul's school?—No, I have not; but I believe I can answer to the general items.

What is the gross average income of the school?—About 5,200 *l.* to 5,300 *l.*

Whence does that arise?—It arises from landed estates, and the interest of money in the funds.

What are the expenses of the establishment?—The expenses of last year exceeded the income upwards of 1200 *l.*; that excess is in some measure to be accounted for by 1500 and odd pounds being expended upon the inclosure of Aston Clinton in Buckinghamshire, part of the Dean Colet estate belonging to the school.

Of what is the expenditure generally made up?—The bulk is in the masters' salaries; and there is a very large pension allowed to the old master, who has retired, after filling the situation about forty-five years, and who is a very old man, to whom an allowance of 1000 *l.* per annum is made.

What is the whole amount of the other salaries?—The high master, 618 *l.*; the sur-master, 307 *l.*; the usher, 227 *l.*; the assistant master, 257 *l.*; and an annuity allowed to the late sur-master's widow, of 60 *l.* per annum.

What are the other expenses?—The repairs last year were 284 *l.*; the taxes were 109 *l.*; insurances, 163 *l.*; surveyor, 167 *l.*; law charges, 36 *l.*; literary prizes, 47 *l.*; sundry other disbursements, 123 *l.*; purchase of books, and rebinding the greater part of the books in the library, 410 *l.*; poundage paid to the receiver, 142 *l.* and a fraction; exhibitions in the last year, 225 *l.*; property tax on masters and officers salary, and for the servants of the company, 180 *l.*; salaries to the officers of the company, clerk, accountant, and beadles, 171 *l.*

Are those salaries to the officers of the company by the order of the founder?—I do not know that there is any thing in the ordinance of the founder to that effect.

What are the other disbursements, generally?—There are the expenses of the apposition dinner, when the scholars are examined, and when they make their orations; and several other things; and that, I believe, will account for the difference. The repairs are sometimes greater than they were last year. The expenses generally are within about 200 *l.* of the receipts, they have been within the last five years, exclusive of the extra expense attending the inclosure last year.

Are there any other salaries or emoluments, besides those you have mentioned, that go to the Mercers Company?—No, I do not know of any others that go to the Mercers Company, besides those I have mentioned.

What becomes of the overplus of the money?—It is carried to account, and when there is a sum sufficient, it is funded for the benefit of the school.

Is there any considerable sum which has been funded in this way?—There is 11,000 *l.* I believe, in the South Sea Stock, and 15,000 odd hundred pounds in the Reduced. I think it is 11,000 *l.* in the South Sea Stock.

Is that 26,000 *l.* Stock the result of accumulations wholly?—In a great degree so.

Have you a power, under the warrant or statute, for applying it to any other purpose?—I apprehend not, for any other purpose whatever.

Have you a power to found new exhibitions?—The Dean, in his ordinance, gives a power (foreseeing that great alterations might take place in time and manners) to make new statutes and ordinances for the better regulation of the school: it is the same power that, I believe, is usually given in cases of that kind.

Is there any intention of enlarging the school on that power?—It is the wish of some to enlarge the school, and also to afford additional education. It is a thing that is not determined on. I mean as to enlarging the education, it has been thought that it might be of importance to afford them the advantage of writing, learning accounts, and the lower parts of the mathematics; but that is a thing which has not been put in practice, nor is such a scheme determined on.

Has

Has the stock you mentioned been accumulating since the first foundation of the school?—It has been accumulating, I should suppose; I cannot exactly say, to speak to it with any degree of correctness; it must have been, a considerable number of years.

Suppose it had been found expedient to appropriate the surplus to a more extensive plan of education, are you aware of any thing in the charter or constitution of the school to prevent it?—I know it is thought by many, that if we were not confined to the local situation which we conceive we are, that greater benefit might be derived.

But suppose you had funds for establishing a large free school annexed to the grammar school?—The founder has certainly never had any thing of that kind in contemplation, because he intended it expressly for a grammar school.

Do you think you are bound to educate no more than 153 boys; or do you not imagine the founder intended that 153 boys at least should be educated?—We conceive we are not bound to educate more than 153.

Have many of the statutes been altered since the foundation?—None, in my recollection.

How is the school lighted?—By wax tapers.

### The Reverend *Philip Fisher*, D. D. called in, and Examined.

YOU are the master of the Charter-house?—Yes.

Do you know any thing of the boys who are at present upon the foundation of the Charter-house?—Of some few of them.

Are the boys generally of the same class in society as the town boys?—I do not know how to answer that question; they are most of them the sons of gentlemen of very confined income and of large families; I do not say there are no exceptions to that, but that is the general description, and I conceive such to be the objects of the charity from its first institution in the year 1611. Four years after the foundation, I find an order made by the governors to this purpose; " We will and ordain that none shall be admitted as poor scholars of this hospital, but such whose parents or friends are not well able to maintain them and bring them up in learning." Each governor nominates according to his rotation; and the practice has been, as far as I know, to take those of the description I have mentioned.

Without entering into particulars from what you know of the circumstances of the individuals at present upon the foundation, do they come within the above description?—Yes, all of them, as far as I know. The person of my name, who appears there, is a nephew; I have myself had at different times three sons upon the foundation, presented by three other governors. And with reference to the evidence given by a former Witness, with respect to my preferment, I beg leave to add, that all those presentations were given to my family before the last and largest increase of my salary at the Charter-house, and before I became possessed of the bulk of my church preferment; so that I considered my own children at the time strictly within the above-mentioned description: my eldest son, indeed, was upon the foundation before I myself was appointed master.

### The Reverend *Thomas Cherry*, Head Master of Merchant Taylors' School; and

### The Reverend *Launcelot Sharpe*, Fourth Master of the said school;

### Called in, and Examined.

(*To Mr. Cherry.*) ON what foundation is Merchant Taylors' school?—The school is supported by the Merchant Taylors' Company.

When was it founded?—It was founded in the year 1561.

Was it founded by the Company?—It was.

There is no charter?—No; the school is entirely dependent upon the Company, and, for what I know, they might withhold their support.

Is there any statutes or rules for the regulation of the school?—None, except what were made by themselves when the school was founded; they called in several learned men to assist them in making regulations, and they have been adhered to.

What class of boys are taught there?—It is not confined to any particular class of boys; but the Company have always considered it as open to any persons who

meant

meant to bring up their sons decently: according to the statute, they should be recommended to the school by the master and wardens of the company, but in general they have been put in by myself promiscuously as they occurred.

How many boys are taught?—I think the last account (for there is an account every year, which is signed by the master of the school) amounted to 215.

Is it a free school?—I do not see how it can be called a free school, because no boy can come into the school but what is subject to the payment of 5 l. a year; every boy who comes into the school pays me a quarterage of 10 s., and 12 s. for breaking-up money each quarter, and they also pay for their own books.

Have the masters any salary from the company?—Yes, they pay their own masters; they pay me 120 l. a year; I believe 20 l. of that was for fuel money, which was left originally by Thomas White, the founder of St. John's College Oxford. The company have thirty-seven fellowships at Oxford, besides seven exhibitions to Cambridge of 40 l. a year each, for about seven years, till they are masters or in orders; but they (the latter) are not in the gift of the Merchant Taylors' Company, they are in the gift of the master of the school; they have likewise six civil law fellowships to St. John's College Oxford, of 50 l. each, for superannuated boys at nineteen years old.

Are there any lands or funds belonging to the establishment, besides those which you have mentioned?—I am not conscious that there are. Such of the exhibitions as are in the gift of the Merchant Taylors' Company do not amount to 5 l. each, arising from legacies to the company, all of which go to St. John's College Oxford, confining it to their own boys.

What are the boys taught?—Latin, Greek, and Hebrew, a complete classical education, and nothing else; we do not consider ourselves as a charity school; the boys are only day scholars, except they happen to board with the masters, which is a private concern.

## Mr. *John Pickton*, called in, and Examined.

ARE you schoolmaster at the Borough Road?—I am superintendent of the establishment for training masters, but am acting in the capacity of schoolmaster at present, in consequence of that situation being vacant.

How many boys are there at present upon the establishment?—Five hundred.

How many girls?—Two hundred and fifty.

How many are now upon the establishment, training as masters?—Twelve training as masters; including four Africans, the expense of two of whom is partly defrayed by the African Institution.

Are those persons now training for masters, boarded as well as taught?—Boarded and clothed.

From whence do those twelve come?—The eight Europeans are chosen from boys in schools in different parts of the country, lads of superior talent; the committees of such schools are encouraged to retain them till they are about the age of sixteen years, when the committee of the Parent Institution engage to receive them on the establishment, and to provide for them till schools are ready for them, and to supply them on application from country committees for the management of such schools.

What is the expense of their board and clothing?—The expense of their board, including servants' keep and wages, and all incidental expenses, is forty guineas a year each.

How long have they been upon the establishment?—From three to six or seven months; the Africans longer, as they were to be educated as well as trained in the practice of the system.

How long does it take to educate one of those masters completely?—The fact is, as far as their knowledge of the system goes, they are educated before they come to us, having been brought up in the schools, and of course acquired a knowledge of the system upon which they are conducted, and have merely to acquire the art of governing schools.

How long will that be?—About six months.

Suppose a boy, who has no knowledge of the new method, but has only learned to read and write in the ordinary way, is brought to your institution, how long will he take to train as a master?—He may go through all the departments of the school in the same length of time as under the other circumstance, but he will neither make an efficient or permanent master; in most instances where masters

have

Mr.
John Pickton.

have been so trained, the moment a better situation offered, they quitted the management of the school, and the committee were required to send down a lad who had been previously educated as well as trained in the Parent Establishment.

How long a time would it take to make an efficient master, under the circumstances last described?—I should think twelve months practice; by this I mean, that he should not only have a complete knowledge of the principles and the details, but also have acquired complete expertness in every branch of the school itself.

Have you known young boys undertake the management of large schools upon the new system?—Lads from sixteen to eighteen years of age have taken the management of schools from 100 to 400 boys.

What is the youngest boy you ever knew teach a school?—About fifteen.

How do the Africans you have mentioned, come on?—They have made great progress in their learning; their abilities are quite on a par with Europeans, and the lad who made the greatest progress in learning in a given time, was an African; he was totally ignorant of his letters, and at the expiration of sixteen months could read the Bible well, could write an excellent hand, and was acquainted with the rule of three; and furthermore, he laboured under ill health four months out of that sixteen, and was rendered incapable during that time of studying much.

How old was he?—About thirteen.

Do you know what part of Africa he came from?—Sierra Leone.

Was he a son of one of the settlers there, or was he brought from the interior?—I suspect the former.

What language did he speak, when he came?—English, pretty well.

What colour of Black was he?—Dark copper; but his complexion very much improved; after he had been in the country a few months, he grew lighter.

Was this owing to bad health?—I apprehend it was in a great measure; but I have observed generally the complexion grows lighter.

Where is he now?—In Sierra Leone.

How long has he been gone out?—About eighteen months.

What has he done since?—He has been engaged in the management of a school there, either altogether, or assisting another.

Do you know any particulars of the school he is teaching?—I do not.

How long have you been in the habit of teaching under the Lancasterian system?—Twelve years.

Have you perceived any difference in the manners and morals of the boys, in the course of their education?—Much improvement.

Have you made the same observation as to the children who have been educated in the school, and now grown up?—I have, particularly.

Do you observe many of the children acquire a thirst for reading?—Very much so; and as a proof of it, in most schools a circulating library is attached to the schools, and the desire for becoming members of that library is very great; it operates as a very powerful stimulus to good behaviour, and improvement in learning.

What sort of books do they generally read?—Natural history; general history of our own and other countries; and voyages and travels.

Have you known any considerable number of boys, educated at the new schools, becoming afterwards common day-labourers?—A very large number.

What kind of work do they do?—Tailors, shoemakers, and porters; seamen, some of them; one lad I know, went out as a soldier, and has arrived at the rank of a captain in the Army, and was with the Duke of Wellington in some of his late campaigns.

Have you had occasion to observe those who have become common day-labourers, after their education at a new school, and to see whether they continue to have a turn for reading?—As far as my observations have reached, that generally has been the case.

Are the lower people in general anxious to have their children taught?—Very much so; but I generally observe that those parents who have been educated themselves, are the most anxious for the education of their children.

Are the children at the Borough Road compelled to go to church on a Sunday?—They are obliged to attend some place of worship, such as their parents prefer; but in the majority of cases they attend Sunday schools, and follow the course, respecting attending places of worship, which is laid down at their respective Sunday schools. Perhaps two-thirds attend Sunday schools; of the remaining one-third, I should think, two-thirds attend the Established Church.

Are

Are the others Dissenters of different sects?—Yes; Jews and Catholics included.

Have you found any difficulty started by Catholic parents, or the priests, to sending the children to your school?—None at all.

Have you found any difficulty among the persons belonging to the Established Church, in sending their children to your school?—None whatever.

There is no catechism taught at your school?—None; and the reading lessons used are exclusively from the Scriptures, without note or comment.

Can you say how many Catholics you have at your schools?—The number is very considerable; I cannot say the proportion.

As to Jews?—There are about six, not more; and we never find the parents object to their reading the Testament.

Do you give any *viva voce* explanation of the Scriptures, when they read them?—No.

Do you take any means to learn whether the boys understand what they read?—The verses that they read are converted into questions, and the answers are given in the literal language.

Are the questions *viva voce* questions, or written questions?—*Viva voce* questions; when I said that explanations of the Scripture were not given, I meant that no person stood up and explained them to the whole school.

Are your selections of scriptures chiefly from the New or the Old Testament?—Both.

Are they numerous?—Very numerous; but we read the Testament and Bible likewise; the selections are not made for the sake merely of having selections, but to suit the different degrees of progress the children have made.

What governs your selection of parts to read?—They read regularly through.

Are the kind of questions you mentioned, applied to all the parts you read?—All the parts.

And always follow every lesson?—Not regularly, but generally.

If a boy answers wrong?—Then the next boy is required to correct him, who takes precedence on so doing.

Do you find this mode of answering questions serve much to keep up the attention of the boys?—It does very much.

And is to them a pleasant exercise?—I never found it contrary; in fact, children do what they are told to do.

What do you conceive to be the greatest operative means of keeping up a lively attention with boys?—The first boy in each company is furnished with a badge of distinction; if he retains that badge, he is entitled to a ticket at the close of the exercise, a number of which procure him a reward; but if he forfeits his place from inattention, or having committed an error, he forfeits his ticket to the one who takes precedence of him, and so toties quoties.

And whoever has the ticket at the end of the lesson, is entitled to the reward?—Yes.

One ticket is thus employed in each class?—One ticket or badge in each company.

How many does a company consist of?—Nine; the classes are divided into companies, consisting of nine each.

Of what do the rewards consist?—Principally articles of clothing.

Given to the boys, or sold at low prices?—Given to the boys, in exchange for tickets obtained for attention or good behaviour.

Do you give rewards on any other occasions?—No.

Is a boy entitled to any superior reward, when from his progress he is raised to a higher class?—Yes; his reward is then sixteen times greater than for being first boy in a company.

That is, it is equal to sixteen tickets?—Yes.

Does any other circumstance entitle a boy to a reward?—There are some other small occasions, but they are but trifling.

Do you on any occasion give books?—Very seldom.

What is your course with respect to punishments?—Forfeit of tickets, and confinement after school hours, are our punishments.

To what extent do you carry that confinement?—The repetition of offence brings with it the repetition of the punishment, and the confinement of half an hour is considered equivalent to one small offence, and the forfeiture of one ticket will liberate them from that half hour's confinement.

How

How do you proceed in the case of those punishments not producing the desired effect, or in the case of graver faults?—Graver offences have double, and in some cases treble portion of confinement or forfeiture; there is a certain scale of punishments, for such a crime, such a punishment.

Is there any expulsion?—Sometimes.

For what class of offences?—Truantism, or incorrigible misconduct during school time.

Do you meet with instances of lying, swearing, or thieving, amongst the boys?— Very seldom; and with regard to thieving, I do not recollect that I ever knew an instance.

With respect to lying?—Lying and swearing are vices to which the boys attending the school in the Borough Road are very little addicted, and when they are found guilty of them, particularly the former, it appears to arise from thoughtlessness more than a depraved mind.

What are the punishments annexed to those faults?—In some cases I find it unnecessary to punish at all; talking to a boy, and making him sensible of his error, has produced great effect; when that has failed, solitary confinement for two hours: we generally give them four times as long as common school offences.

In case you find a boy incorrigible, you resort to expulsion?—Yes.

Have you found any bad effects arise, as to self-conceit or pride on the part of the cleverest boys?—Not at all; there is a regular gradation among the monitors as among the boys, and the system of itself provides an effectual check to the risings of conceit.

What is that check?—It is by the master superintending the principal monitor, and by their situation being made so valuable to them that they shall report immediately, any thing that may be improper among the subordinate monitors.

What check have the principal monitors themselves?—The master.

How does the master proceed?—The monitors have certain duties to perform, the master acquaints them with those duties, he requires them to perform them in a certain way, which he points out; as long as they continue to do so to his satisfaction, they continue their offices, but no longer; and if a boy were to misbehave himself through conceit, he would be dismissed from his office. All other punishments have been discontinued.

With respect to the boys of colour training for schoolmasters, whom you mentioned, were they educated throughout at your school?—Three out of the four were; one could read a little when he came, the others could not.

How long have they been at the school altogether?—From twelve to fifteen months, from their first coming.

Have you any other boys of colour in the school now?—Two as scholars; one supported by the subscriptions of a shilling a week from some benevolent individuals; the other is a lad who has been to sea for some years, and has accumulated a considerable sum in wages and prize money, and is now living upon that money to get education; he is now about twenty-one years of age, and takes his lessons with the school-boys of the ages of eight or nine years.

And is suffered to do so without meeting with any insults from the other boys?—Yes.

In selecting the four you have mentioned to be educated as schoolmasters, were you guided by any motives but a wish to educate for that office those boys who appeared the most likely to fulfil it well?—Two of the four were brought from Sierra Leone, by private gentlemen, and placed on the establishment by the consent of the committee; one is supported by one of the gentlemen in question, the other partly at the expense of the African Institution, and the other two were liberated from slavery.

Are they as promising boys, for the office for which they are intended, as the generality of Europeans that you educate for the like use, are?—Certainly, three out of the four.

And with respect to the other, do you mean to proceed in educating him to be a master, or do you imagine it would not answer?—That will depend upon the pleasure of the committee; he may do probably for a small school, though he has not the same talent and ability as the others have.

The others, you think, have very good talents?—Very excellent, I would say.

Does the school decrease or increase?—At this season of the year it is increasing.

Is that greater or less than it was this time last year?—Greater.

Con-

Considerably?—I think by about 40 or 50 boys.

Could you educate many more boys than you have?—The room will seat about 540.

The girls and the boys are not educated in the same room?—No.

What share of the 500 boys attend upon the average, do you imagine?—From 350 to 400; it depends upon the season of the year.

At what season have you the fullest attendance?—About midsummer.

When the slackest?—The months of November, December, and January.

What do you consider the cause of this?—Want of hats and shoes principally; not so much of other clothing.

What may the difference be in round numbers, between the attendance at mid-summer and the attendance at January?—Perhaps from 50 to 80, not more.

Was the school ever larger?—It formerly contained upwards of 1000 boys, out of which number from 700 to 800 attended, but in consequence of the change of the neighbourhood, the leases of a number of small houses having expired, and they being pulled down, the great proportion of the poorer population are removed to other parts of the Metropolis, and the number is in consequence considerably reduced, probably one-half.

What may be the average attendance of the 220 girls?—The school-room will not accommodate more than 200, and it is generally nearly full.

Do they attend differently, at different periods of the year?—In the same proportion as the boys.

From the same cause?—From the same, I apprehend.

Does the committee often inspect the schools?—There is a regular inspecting committee, who visit the school weekly; but the committee as a body do not inspect the school regularly.

Would the funds of the school be adequate to educate 1000 boys?—The funds of the school are blended with the funds of the institution for training schoolmasters; but I apprehend that very little in addition to the present annual expenditure of the school would be sufficient for the education of double the number at present educated, which would be 1000.

When this school was full, did it educate a greater number of schoolmasters at a time?—The number has never been limited.

In practice, was it greater than it is now?—The number has varied from six to thirty or upwards.

Have the masters whom you have sent out after such education, in general given satisfaction?—Those particularly who have been brought up in the school as school-boys have uniformly given satisfaction; those who have been sent from different parts of the country, and who were not brought up in the school on the plan, have in many cases been removed; some on their own account, from having procured better situations, or from not having given satisfaction; in many of those cases, lads who have been chosen from the schools, and have been trained as masters, have been appointed to succeed them, and have given satisfaction.

Do you conceive that the three Africans now educating for schoolmasters, are promising, at least as likely to give satisfaction, as the Europeans which you commonly select from other schools, and educate for the same purpose?—If I may judge from their dispositions and manners, and from the progress they have made in their education, I would say equally so.

Do you find their dispositions and manners, as well as abilities, equal to the Europeans you educate?—Generally; they are constantly with the Europeans; they board at the same table, and sleep in the same apartments.

How does the climate agree with them?—Tolerably well; they require a great deal of care and nursing; we have buried one out of nine.

Do you think you have been able to make improvements on Mr. Lancaster's plan?—The mechanism of the system, I conceive, is improved.

Are the improvements of such importance as to produce visible effects in the education of the school now, compared with what it was before they were made?—Not materially.

Are there any other schools conducted on your principles, in Southwark?—There is one in the parish of Bermondsey.

Who conducts it?—A person of the name of Beavitt; the school is in White's Grounds Bermondsey.

Is it a school of considerable size?—About 300 boys, I believe.

Any girls?—No girls.

Do

Do you know of any other schools conducted upon the same system?—There are two, one in the City Road and one in Spitalfields, the masters of whom are both present.

Did you hear Mr. Allen's evidence yesterday?—Yes, I did.

Do you agree in all respects generally, with that part of it which relates to the general expense of the school, and the want of the means of education?—With regard to the education I entirely agree with him, and I rather think he has under-rated it.

Generally, or in any particular quarter?—Generally: an inquiry has been under-taken in Southwark, under the direction of the Southwark Auxiliary School Society, and I apprehend it will appear, when the results are laid before this Committee, that the number of uneducated children will amount to 6 or 7000 in about 12,000 children, within a district the population of which is about 100,000, notwithstanding the school in the Borough Road has been established so many years, and has been the means of educating at least 12,000 children.

Have you any idea of the number of uneducated children, within a moderate distance of the school in the Borough Road?—I have not.

Do the children who attend the school in the Borough Road make any payments?—None at all.

Are they the children of parents incapable of paying, chiefly?—The major part of them certainly are.

Suppose those who are capable of paying were required to contribute a small sum, as a penny a week, what would be the effects of that arrangement, in two points of view; first, in disinclining the parents to send their children; and secondly, in creating invidious distinctions between that class of children who pay, and that who do not?—With regard to the first point, I would observe, that the experiment has been tried in the girls' school, requiring every girl to bring a penny a week, not as a payment for education, but to be returned to her, at the expiration of six months, in articles of clothing, provided she has attended regularly; and in no case, to my knowledge, has a child been withdrawn or the penny refused to be paid by any one parent. With respect to the second point, I think if a plan of that kind were adopted, it would be desirable that the whole of the children in any one school should pay, as it perhaps might create invidious distinctions, and would occasion a great deal of trouble in selecting those who were found capable of paying, from those who were not.

Have you known any instances of parents who rather objected to sending children to a mere charity school?—I do not recollect any one instance.

Among parents filling superior stations of life?—In some schools in the country, in country villages, and small country towns, I have known little tradesmen and shopkeepers anxious to send their children to a school on the British system, considering that they made great progress in their education, and that their habits were very much improved, who were unwilling to send them to a free school; in such cases it has occurred to them to become subscribers, and in virtue of their subscription to recommend their own children.

Do you not consider it to be beneficial to the lower orders, that if they possibly can afford, they should not receive their education for nothing?—I think so. In the plan of forming school associations in the district embraced by the Southwark Auxiliary School Society, lately established, it is a part of their plan to require the parents to subscribe a penny or more a week, according to their circumstances, and to make them members of the association, giving them the same privileges, in virtue of their subscriptions, as a member of any other society. This plan has been found to succeed so well in Bible associations, that they entertain great hopes it will be equally applicable to school associations.

Do you know whether they can at present judge from experience, of the success they are likely to meet with in this way?—From the observations I have heard made by some gentlemen who have recently canvassed that district, to ascertain the want of education, it appears that there is a very general disposition among the poor to become subscribers, according to their circumstances; and as soon as the plan can be carried into effect, they have no doubt but a considerable proportion of the revenue of every school may be derived from such source.

From the effects which you have found produced by your own school in its neighbourhood, should you imagine that the defect of education that you have mentioned as likely to be found to exist in Southwark, would be remedied by establishing

a sufficient

Mr.
John Pickton.

a sufficient number of similar schools in convenient situations?—I have no doubt of it; when I say so, it is not the result of my own observation, but of those who are more in the habit of visiting families than myself in Southwark; and schools might be formed to suit the local conveniencies of the poor.

What do you conceive to be the annual expense of your school, not including the expense of those twelve intended for schoolmasters?—In the boys' school, from 140*l.* to 150*l.* a year, independent of rent; and in the girls', about 70*l.* or 80*l.*

Who pays your rent?—The school-room is free, having been built for the purpose.

What is allowed to the master?—I reckon the master's salary at 80*l.* a year; but that is much lower than would be given to the master of any other school, on account of a young man of eighteen or nineteen being sufficient to take management of the school under my own superintendence, which would not be the case in another school of the same number of children.

Do the society pay any thing for tuition, except to the master?—No.

What is paid to the mistress of the girls?—She receives 50*l.* a year.

A house to live in?—No.

Has the master a house?—He has.

Is the master found coal and candle?—No, he is found nothing; he resides at the establishment for training schoolmasters.

Do you imagine 50*l.* a year would procure a mistress, in ordinary cases, for a similar school?—It certainly would.

Can you form any estimate of the extent to which the British and Foreign school system exists?—I have nothing to say in addition to the evidence of Mr. Allen upon the subject: the number of schools for boys and girls, I apprehend, is above 300 in Great Britain.

How many are educated, upon the average, in each school?—I should think from 150 to 200; because we have many very large schools in some parts of the country, and some have only 50 or 60 boys.

Do you agree with Mr. Allen as to the expense of this system of education?—Yes, quite; the evidence received from Mr. Allen was arranged between us, on the subject of the annual expense of the schools.

Suppose a place is too small to maintain both a National school and one upon the British and Foreign school plan, then there would be a difficulty of educating the children of sectaries; but suppose that the place is large enough to maintain one upon both plans, what inconvenience do you apprehend can arise from there being one upon the National establishment?—I know of none, certainly.

In London, therefore, do you apprehend that the two societies at all interfere with one another?—I think not at all; I cannot see any reason why they should.

Do you find that Dissenters and Church people send their children with equal readiness to your school; or do one description of persons send them more readily than the other?—I have not observed the least difference in either party.

Do you find many Dissenters so desirous of having their own peculiar tenets taught to their children, as to be unwilling to send them to such a school as you have described yours to be?—I have never observed such an unwillingness in any one instance; they never say any thing about creeds; they merely wish to get their children educated.

Have you had any experience in Sunday schools?—I myself have been a teacher, and I have found that those children who had no means of receiving education during the week made very slow progress.

How long should you say a child, receiving no other education during the week, would take to learn to read tolerably, taking the average?—At least from two to three years, most certainly.

How does it happen, then, that in general children are found to learn quicker at Sunday schools?—Because a great proportion of them receive six days instruction during the week.

Do you mean, by taking instructions during the week, that they attend other schools?—Yes.

Suppose a child has only instruction at a Sunday school, with the little accidental helps he may meet with at home during the week, without going regularly to another school, how long do you think such a child would take to learn to read?—From the knowledge I have of the number of children who attend both day and Sunday schools, and from the connexion I have had with both, I certainly think that,

under

under those circumstances, a child could not be taught to read in less than a year and a half or two years.

When you say taught to read, what proficiency in reading do you allude to?—So as generally to understand what they read.

What progress do you make in your week-day schools?—I have known many children learn reading, writing, and the elements of arithmetic, in one year; but this is not the average.

What do you esteem the average to be?—From one year and a half to two years.

How long have you been connected with Sunday schools?—I am not now connected with a Sunday school, but I have been connected about two years; it was found difficult in the school with which I was connected to procure teachers, and as it was known that I was connected with the Institution in the Borough Road, it was deemed advisable to introduce the new mode of teaching to read into that school, whereby a number of teachers might be saved, and one person might be competent to manage the whole; the number was about 100 boys; that plan is at present practised, and with very great success. A great number of schools throughout the country have adopted the new mode of teaching. One young man, the master of a day school on the British system, in Lincolnshire, has, during the last year and a half or two years, succeeded in establishing nearly twenty Sunday schools, in all of which he has introduced the new mode of teaching practised by the British and Foreign School Society; those schools contain from 1000 to 1500 children. I mention this, to show the applicability of the plan to Sunday-school teaching. There are also many other Sunday schools on the plan, in different parts of the country.

### Mr. *John Tacey*, called in, and Examined.

WHAT school are you connected with?—A British and Foreign Society's school.

Have you the superintendence of a school?—Yes.

Where is it situate?—North-street, City Road.

How many children are taught there?—The total number at present is 605.

How long have you been in it?—Three years and three months.

Were you taught at the Borough-road school?—Yes, I was apprenticed to Mr. Lancaster.

You have heard the evidence of the last Witness?—Yes.

As far as your experience and observation goes, do you agree with him?—Yes, I agree with him in every thing he has mentioned.

How long have you been engaged in this system of education, altogether?—Six years, in three different schools.

What is the annual expense of your school?—The annual expense, not including the rent of premises or ground-rent, is about 160l.

What is the school rent?—The building is partly purchased for 1800l. which is to be paid by instalments of 300l.

How many children can it accommodate?—About 800.

What is the reason it is not full?—There is no want of schools in that district; the means of educating the poor is principally wanted; there are no more applications for admission.

Do you mean, that there are no poor children in your neighbourhood uneducated?—None without the means of being educated.

What other schools are there in that district, besides your own?—I do not know exactly.

Upon what is your opinion founded, that there are the means of education for all the poor in your neighbourhood?—The room being so commodious for the education of a greater number of children, and having no applications, at least not enough to fill the school, and there being many other charities in the same neighbourhood.

Is it a poor neighbourhood?—I do not know much of the neighbourhood.

Is it a very populous neighbourhood?—Yes.

Do you know any thing of Sunday schools?—I do not; but there are upwards of 500 of my children attend at Sunday shools.

Mr. *Thomas Harrod*, called in, and Examined.

*Mr.*
*Thomas Harrod.*

WHAT school are you connected with?—Spitalfields British and Foreign School.

How many children are educated there?—500.

How many is the school capable of educating?—About 700; it was built for 1000, and at the first two years of the establishment there were about from 700 to 800 daily attended, but there was not sufficient room to accommodate those conveniently; we were obliged to reduce the number of desks, which reduced the number of boys; it will now accommodate about 600.

To what do you ascribe your not being full?—For want of means, the parents have not the means of paying.

How much do the children pay at your school?—Thirteen pence per quarter; it was opened at first for a number of free scholars, but the funds were so low, that without the assistance of the boys it could not have gone on, and therefore they were obliged to stop admitting free scholars, and the children were obliged to pay.

Are the poor in that neighbourhood unprovided with the means of education?—Yes, from that reason.

Can you form an estimate of the number of poor children there may be uneducated?—Within the immediate neighbourhood of Spitalfields, I should suppose there are 400 or 500 boys uneducated, and without the means of education.

In how large a district do you consider there are that number?—Taking in only the parishes of Spitalfields and Bethnal Green.

What is the population of those two parishes?—I really do not know; I judge from an inquiry that I made last week in only a few streets, and I found the number in each family very considerable who were remaining in the house, and whose parents were very anxious to get them, now they were out of employment, into schools; those boys had been formerly for a short time in this school, but were taken out in consequence of their parents being in full employ, which is not the case now, and which makes them anxious to have them re-admitted, if they could, without any expense, not being able to pay themselves.

Do the parents seem desirous of the education of their children?—Very.

How long have you been engaged in education upon the new plan?—About fifteen years.

Have you heard the last two Witnesses examined?—I have.

Do you agree with them?—Yes; only that in Sunday schools they are not able to do any thing more, in the time stated, than read.

How long do you think they take to learn to read in Sunday schools, if they have no other means of instruction?—About two or three years, I should imagine.

*Veneris, 7° die Junii,* 1816.

HENRY BROUGHAM, Esquire, in The Chair.

---

Mr. *William Crawford,* called in, and Examined.

ARE you a member of the committee of the Spitalfields Lancasterian school in Spicer-street?—I am.

Have any measures been lately taken to ascertain the extent of the want of education among the poor in the neighbourhood of Spitalfields?—Inquiries have been made in the neighbourhood of Spitalfields, and it appears that in 2,091 families that have been visited, and containing 5,953 children, there were 2,565 children, from six to fourteen years of age, without any education.

Who made those inquiries?—Several gentlemen were called together for the purpose.

Did you make your inquiries in the poorest part of Spitalfields, or in a part where the poor did not so much abound?—Generally all over Spitalfields; we selected various districts.

Would those districts be a fair sample of the neighbourhood of Spitalfields in general?—I think they would.

What portion of that neighbourhood do they include; a third, fourth, fifth, or what?—They include the whole of Spitalfields, and some part of the immediate neighbourhood.

Do you mean the whole of Spitalfields parish?—Yes, and some part of the parishes immediately adjoining.

In what parish or parishes was that part of the neighbourhood?—A part in Bethnal Green, and, I think, part in Shoreditch.

Was the district examined, too extensive for the attendance of children on one school, or was it not?—I think it was too extensive for the children to attend one school.

What school is there now in that district or neighbourhood?—I have a list of the schools for the instruction of the poor in Spitalfields, the Old Artillery Ground, and Norton Falgate; which embraces nearly the whole of the district which has been examined.

[It was delivered in, and read, as follows :]

LIST of SCHOOLS for the Instruction of the CHILDREN of the POOR, in Spitalfields, the Old Artillery Ground, and Norton Falgate.

| PLACE. | Description. | Day School. Boys. | Day School. Girls. | Sunday School. Boys. | Sunday School. Girls. | Clothed. | Treasurer. | Master or Mistress. | Expenditure. | |
|---|---|---|---|---|---|---|---|---|---|---|
| Spitalfields - - - | Parochial - | - | 56 | 54 | - | - | Clothed | E. Merrick, Esq. | Master & Mistress | 450. | |
| D° - - - - - | D' - - | - | - | - | 70 | 100 | - - | Mr. Brown - - | - - - | 80. | In this School the Committee hire Teachers, and give as rewards to the children articles of Clothing. |
| Raven-row - - - | Methodists - | - | - | - | 254 | 227 | — | — | — | — | |
| Montague-street - | British System | - | - | 100 | - | - | - - | Mrs. Buxton - - | Mistress. | — | |
| D° - - - - - | Protestant Dissenters | - | - | - | 200 | 200 | — | — | — | — | |
| Wood-street - - - | D° - - | - | 50 | 50 | - | - | Clothed | - - - | Master & Mistress | 450. | |
| White's-row - - - | D° - - | - | - | - | - | 100 | - - | Miss Good - - | - - - | 30. | The Teachers in this School subscribe towards its support. |
| Hope-street Chapel | D° - - | - | - | - | 100 | 120 | - - | Mr. Stirtevant - | - - - | 10. | |
| Artillery-street - - | D° - - | - | - | - | - | 90 | — | — | — | — | |
| Crispin-street - - | D° - - | - | - | - | - | 70 | — | — | — | — | |
| Steward-street - - | D° - - | - | 21 | 21 | - | - | Clothed | J. Wilson, Esq. - | Master & Mistress | - | On Sundays a Dinner is provided at the School-house for the Children. |
| Elder-street - - - | Sir George Wheler's Chapel | - | - | 36 | - | - | D° - | Mr. Fouche - - | Mistress - - - | 100. | |
| Spicer-street Spital-fields - - - - | British System | - | 350 | - | - | - | - - | Mr. Gurney Barclay | - - - | 140. | This School can accommodate 700;—but owing to the embarrassed state of its finances, the Committee do not admit any children gratuitously; the pay is one penny per week. |
| Total - - | | 477 | 261 | 670 | 907 | | | | | |

Are

Are any of those schools out of that district?—Not any.

Did you find the want of education to be chiefly among the very poorest?—Yes.

In what proportion among the very poorest, should you apprehend?—About seven eighths.

What reason do the parents allege, in general, for not sending their children to school?—They allege principally poverty.

What other reasons do they also allege?—In some cases the necessity of employing the children during the day.

Were those cases numerous, in which they spoke of the necessity of employing the children during the day?—Not very numerous; the silk trade at present is very dull, and does not now afford much employment for children.

Do you imagine that in a good state of the trade there would be an objection to children going to school, in that neighbourhood, from the wish of the parents to employ them?—I believe a considerable number in that neighbourhood would be kept by their parents from attending the school on that account.

Do the parents in general seem very desirous of education for their children?—Very desirous.

Do they make any stipulations about it, and say they should not like such and such a sort of school?—Not in any case, among the families I visited.

But seem satisfied with good education, in whatever shape it might be presented?—Exactly so; they appeared anxious in their inquiries when schools would be opened.

Did they make any inquiries about the clothing of their children, as if they expected that would be a necessary condition in their appearance?—Not generally.

Did any considerable number?—Not any considerable number.

In what state did the children appear, in cases in which the want of education which you have mentioned was expressed; did they appear dirty and miserable?—In a very miserable condition.

Was there any great deficiency in their manners; were they uncivil?—There seemed considerable wildness in the manners of the uneducated children, and their persons were generally very dirty.

Their looks were not like those of children who were accustomed to go to school?—Certainly not.

There was a want of that civility and propriety of behaviour which is amongst those children who go to school?—Yes.

Most of those children are employed in the silk business, when at work?—The greater proportion of them.

In the Lancasterian school, mentioned in the paper just delivered in, as capable of accommodating 700, but as having but 350 children, do you conceive that the pay of a penny per week per child, demanded in that school, is the reason that it is not full?—I believe it is the reason with many parents for not sending their children to that school.

Have you reason to think it would be full if no pay were asked of the children?—I think it would. I beg leave to observe, that many of the parents are very ignorant and insensible of the advantages of early instruction, and are therefore apt to neglect sending their children; or, if they are sent, their attendance is very irregular; another cause of non-attendance is the distress which now prevails in Spitalfields, which is beyond description; many of the children are kept from school from the want of clothing and shoes.

Have any of the other schools, contained in the above paper, room for more children than at present belong to them?—I believe the Sunday schools have; the others are parish schools, or charity schools.

Can you state in what degree they have room for more, respectively?—No, I cannot.

Have you reason to think that, taken collectively, they would hold considerably more children than are now in them?—I think they would.

Do you imagine that their not being full is owing to the same cause you have mentioned, in speaking of the Lancasterian school?—In some cases the schools will not accommodate a greater number.

But

Mr.
*William Crawford.*

But in those schools which would admit a greater number, do you imagine that the present deficiency in numbers is owing to the causes that you stated as operating in preventing the Lancasterian school from being full?—I am not prepared to answer that question.

When you speak of 350 children as now belonging to the Lancasterian school, you mean to speak of the number on the books?—No, the number actually attending.

Do you know how many are upon the books of the school?—I am not exactly prepared to say what that number is.

Do you know of any measure in contemplation to remedy the non-attendance of the children belonging to it?—With respect to the indifference of parents, and the want of clothing, I apprehend that if district associations were established on the principle recommended by the British and Foreign School Society for their associations, those difficulties would in a great measure be removed. It has been proposed that local societies be formed in districts containing from four hundred to five hundred poor children, and that schools should be established for the accommodation of that number; the most reputable characters among the lower orders would be invited to co-operate with their more affluent neighbours, in visiting from house to house, and from apartment to apartment, in order to impress upon the poor the benefits which schools impart; such of the poor as could afford it, would be encouraged to subscribe one penny per week; weekly visits to the poor, to collect the pence, would serve to interest their feelings in the education of their children, and keep the subject constantly before their minds. Frequent communications with the poor, on subjects connected with the welfare of their children, have a beneficial tendency on the minds of the parents.

Has this plan been tried in any district you are acquainted with?—It has not been adopted in London; but an association has been formed upon this principle at Northampton, which has completely succeeded.

When was it formed?—About eighteen months ago.

Do you know whether a similar system has been adopted in any other quarter?—An auxiliary school society has been established in Southwark, for the purpose of forming associations of this description; but this society is not yet in action.

Have you had any experience of the comparative effects of day schools and Sunday schools in imparting learning to the poor?—I have been for some years a teacher in a Sunday school in Bishopsgate parish, and I have been in the habit of attending a day school on the British and Foreign system.

What have been your conclusions from what you have seen, as to the comparative progress?—I consider that a boy would learn to read, write, and cipher, at a day school on the British and Foreign system, in one fourth part of the time in which he would learn to read only at a Sunday school.

What did you find the average time requisite to teach children to read at Sunday schools, who have not had the advantage of attending day schools?—About four years.

In that time would they read fluently?—I think they would.

What are the comparative effects on the manners of the children who attend the Sunday schools and day schools?—In general the children who attend the day schools attend Sunday schools; but there certainly is a considerable difference in the habits of those who attend Sunday schools only, to the disadvantage of the latter.

If a child attended a day school and also a Sunday school for a year and a half, and another child attended only a day school for four or five years, which should you think would have the advantage, with reference to the effects produced on manners and habits?—I should think the child who attended the day school, from the restraint which the day school would impose on him.

Do you ground your opinion on instances now in your mind, or on your general impression of what would be likely to be the effect?—From personal observation, and from the impression which has been made on my mind, from being in the habit of attending both schools.

Do you find from your experience that almost all the children who attend day schools, also attend Sunday schools?—I think they do, generally. There is a numerous class of children whom it is very difficult to get to school; I allude to the children of the very lowest description of poor; these children may be seen wandering in the streets, without shoes or stockings, and generally exhibit a miserable appearance;

Mr.
William Crawford.

appearance; their habits may be traced to parental neglect; many of these children are turned into the streets in the morning by their parents, and dare not return in the evening unless they take with them a certain sum, the fruits either of mendicity or of crime.    There are other children, who are quite deserted by their parents. In Covent Garden market there are between thirty and forty boys, who are accustomed to sleep under the sheds and baskets every night, and when they rise in the morning have no other means of procuring subsistence but by the commission of crime.    I submit to the Committee, that these children can only be benefited by institutions which combine employment with instruction.    If schools of industry could be established in the most populous districts of the Metropolis, they would be the means of saving a number of destitute youth, who are training up in the most dangerous habits, and are often impelled as it were into the commission of crime.

Are those children, in general, in a state of complete ignorance?—It is very rarely indeed that any of those children can read.

Would their parents send them to a school if one was open, without pay, to receive them?—In some cases I do not think they would.

For what reason?—I have repeatedly called on the parents of children of this description, in the hope of inducing them to send their children to school, but I have often been unable to succeed in my endeavours.

For what reason?—They allege the want of clothing for the children, and the necessity of employing them during the day.

Are those parents in the lowest condition of life?—The very lowest.

Do they derive a profit from the mendicity of their children?—In many cases they do.

Do the parents avow this, when you mention it to them?—The parents do not avow it, but the children acknowledge it.

Can you guess how much a child may make by begging for its parents, in a day?— I should apprehend about two shillings a day by begging; the profits however which they have derived from begging have been much lessened since the publication of the Report on Mendicity.

Are there many children of the description you have now alluded to, in the Metropolis?—I should apprehend that there are between four and five thousand.

Do you consider that those children are withheld by their parents from schools, for the reason you have given?—I do; but I consider that if the children could earn a livelihood by attending schools of industry, their parents, in a number of cases, would cheerfully send them.

How much could a child earn at the schools of industry you refer to?—That entirely depends upon the manufacture they are engaged in; in some trades, the profits of children are very considerable.

Do they ever amount to 2 s. a day?—They frequently do.

Do you think children would earn more by those employments than they do by begging and thieving?—I think they would by begging, but not by thieving.

Then do you apprehend that those parents, whom you have described, would prefer having their children earn less by an honest calling, than more by a dishonest one?—In a number of cases I think that the parents would prefer placing their children at schools of industry, though with less profit, from a fear of the punishment attendant on the commission of crime.

Do you allude to those parents whom you have already described as having the 4 or 5000 children you have mentioned.—I do.

Do you conceive there is any considerable proportion of these parents who would prefer having their children earn more by begging and thieving, and would refuse to send them to the schools alluded to?—I believe that proportion would not be very considerable.

Do you conceive that nothing short of compulsion would induce such parents to send their children to school?—I think that nothing short of compulsion would effect that object, with such persons.

In estimating the number you have mentioned, do you include the Borough and Surrey side of the River generally?—I do.

Mr.

Mr. *Thomas Heaver*, called in, and Examined.

WHAT are you?—I am a member of the British and Foreign School Society, and a director of the Spicer-street school, Spitalfields; I have been a member of the committee of the Spicer-street school ever since its formation.

You have heard the latter part of the last Witness's examination?—I have.
Do you agree with him in his account of poor children?—I do.

Have you had occasion to examine any of the gangs of juvenile depredators who have been lately confined in Newgate?—Very frequently, for the last twelvemonth.

Are you a member of any committee for the purpose of that examination?—I am a member of an association for inquiring into the causes of juvenile delinquency.

How many of those persons may you have examined?—I have examined individually about one hundred in prison, and a considerable number out of prison.

What has been the result of that examination?—I found them very generally in a complete state of ignorance, having no idea either of religion or morality.

Of what class of society were they, generally speaking?—Principally children of the lowest description, frequently abandoned by their parents.

Can you form any estimate of the probability of such parents allowing their children to go to school, if the means of instruction for nothing were provided?—I think if schools were opened gratuitously, that the greatest portion of such parents might be induced to send their children to them; but yet there are some so insensible to the advantages resulting from instruction, that no persuasion would effect it.

State any further information upon this subject which you may have procured, relating to these young delinquents above referred to?—I have generally found that their prepossession for street gambling, and associating with lads of the same loose character as themselves, have deluded their minds so strongly as to make them insensible to any dispositions except those of the most depraved description; but yet, when opportunity has offered to select some from the group or gang, and to reason with them tenderly upon the excellence of religion, they have been made sensible of the error of their ways; when kept separate for a time, the most pleasing results have arisen; I know of upwards of twenty boys who have been snatched from these vile associations, and are now in a fair way of being restored to society; but I have always found it expedient to take them from their parents, where the parents had been the cause of the delinquency of the child. The free use of spirits by the parents appears to me to be one of the primary causes of that laxity of moral principle which is now so evidently prevalent among the lower orders of the community.

Did you perceive any indisposition to education in the children themselves?—At first I did; but after conversing with them seriously on the advantages to be derived from education, they admitted it, and said they should rejoice to go to school.

Mr. *Samuel Bevington*, and Mr. *Charles Beavitt*, called in, and Examined.

(*To Mr. Bevington.*)  HAVE you paid a great deal of attention to schools in your neighbourhood?—I have been treasurer to the one in our parish some time.

What school is that?—Bermondsey and St. John's.

(*To Mr. Beavitt.*) What are you?—Schoolmaster to the above-mentioned school.

(*To Mr. Bevington.*) What is the nature of that school?—It is on the British and Foreign system, and supported by voluntary contributions.

How many is it calculated to hold?—Four hundred.
Boys and girls?—Only boys.

How

Mr.
Samuel Bevington,
and
Mr. C. Beavitt.

How many are there who attend it at the present time?—The average attendance is 260, but we are increasing daily.

Is there any clothing found?—We have given shoes and stockings by way of rewards for their merit tickets.

How do you account for there being only 260, if your school would contain 400?—We have not taken sufficient pains, till the present time, to inform the poor that their children might come; we found that out by inquiries made within the last few days; yet within another week our school will be quite full.

How long has the school been established?—I think this is the fourth year.

Have you an account with you of the expenses attending that school?—No, I have not; but they have averaged about 200 l. a year.

Do you recollect the items of that expense?—Rent, 80 l. a year; master, 100 l.; rewards and incidental expenses, 20 l.; it has been rather more than 200 l. I would observe, that the attendance at the school is only 260, the number on the books is about 320; and from the short time that is necessary for each boy, we have on education as many as 400 in the year; 100 go out, and 100 come in.

Do you limit the admission to any particular age?—No; as soon as a boy is competent to take his form in the sand class we admit him.

How long, upon the average, do you find it necessary to continue them in this school, coming in in the sand class?—We have never been so full as to be obliged to discharge any, but I suppose we shall soon. There are seven or eight boys under seven years of age, who have not been in the school more than one year and a half, who can read the Testament sufficiently well for their parents to understand them, although they did not know their letters when they came in.

How long have you been engaged in superintending the new system of education?—About four years.

Have you any information respecting the free school in Grange Road?—I received this paper from Mr. Nottage, the treasurer.          [It was delivered in.]

Can you give the Committee any information respecting a free school in Cherry-garden-street?—Yes; there is a Sunday school for 200 girls, out of which 60 are selected for daily instruction, and six of those are clothed; and twenty boys put under the care of the schoolmaster for daily instruction: it is done by voluntary contributions, and is under the superintendence of Mrs. Townshend.

Is this a school in which the British and Foreign plan of instruction is introduced?—No, it is not.

Are the master and mistress persons who are paid for their attendance?—Yes.

Do the children who are educated in your school upon the British and Foreign plan, attend divine service regularly on a Sunday?—Yes; those whose parents state a wish for their going to church, are always taken there by the master; and care is taken that all the others attend some place of worship, which is generally under the superintendence of the Sunday school.

Do you recollect the proportion of boys and girls who attend church, and those who go to other places of worship?—About 70 to church, out of the 360; there is a National school, which has diminished our number of church boys.

The remainder all attend meeting?—Yes.

Is it any particular meeting they attend?—No, they go to some Sunday school or other; there are three principal ones that take them.

Have you found any repugnance on the part of Church of England people to send their children to the schools?—No.

Can you give the Committee any information as to the proportion of the Dissenters to the Church of England people in the district, generally?—No, I cannot; our population is 20,000, and the church will only hold 1200, galleries and all: there is a large Methodist meeting in the parish, but it is attended very much by those not belonging to the parish.

Do you find any reluctance on the part of the lower orders to send their children to school?—No, not at all.

Have you in your neighbourhood many very poor persons?—Not of the lowest order; lodging is too dear; it is a manufacturing neighbourhood, where a great deal is earned.

Have

Have the lower orders of your neighbourhood sufficient means of education?— They have not sufficient means generally; but I expect, for a populous parish, it is the nearest competent of any parish round London. The boys and girls together are 900, between five and fourteen years old, who do not receive any education. I should wish to observe generally, that the order and regularity necessary to be sustained by so large a number, is perhaps of more use to the habits of the children, than even the instruction we give them.

*Mr.*
*Samuel Bevington,*
*and*
*Mr. C. Beavitt.*

*Charles Barclay*, Esquire, a Member of the Committee, made the following Statement:

*Charles Barclay,*
*Esq.*

I HAVE made inquiry respecting the schools in the Borough of Southwark, and I find that in St. Saviour's parish there is a parish school, founded in 1707, containing 80 boys, which is the full number the school will contain; it has an annual income, arising from land and stock, of 153 *l.* 17 *s.* 6 *d.*; there is a subscription to the amount of 164 *l.* 18 *s.*; the annual expenses are 301 *l.* 15 *s.* 6 *d.*; the children are clothed, and 5 *l.* given as an apprentice-fee when they leave the school. In the same school there are fifty boys in addition, who are educated, clothed, and apprenticed under the will of Mrs. Newcomen, which is dated the 12th December 1664, and enjoins the wardens of St. Saviour's to clothe once a year twenty-one poor old decayed men or women, and to educate and put out apprentice four boys and girls. They have fifty boys and fifty girls. The charge of educating, clothing, and apprenticing the children, is about 500 *l.* annually, and the income arising from lands and stock is 560 *l.* There is likewise another girls' school, established in 1702, in which 50 girls are educated, which has an income arising from stock, of 59 *l.* 7 *s.* and annual subscriptions to the amount of 149 *l.* 2 *s.* The annual expense is about 220 *l.* and these girls are likewise clothed. There is likewise a free grammar school, founded in 1562, in which there are now thirty boys, but the school would contain 100. The annual certain income arising from land and stock is 380 *l.*; and the annual expense is about 300 *l.* independent of repairs. In all these schools there is no sum paid by the parents towards the education of their children. There is likewise a school connected with the National School Society, of which I have not yet got the return. In Saint Olave's parish there is a girls' school, founded in 1733; there are forty girls now in the school, but it would contain, if full, sixty. They have an income arising from stock, and gifts from the corporation of the free grammar school, of 90 *l.* per annum; and the remainder of the annual expense, which amounts to 345 *l.* 8 *s.* 2 *d.* is defrayed by private contributions. In this school three girls only pay for their education, at the rate of four-pence per week. There is likewise a boys' school in the said parish, of which I have not yet got the return.

*Sabbati, 8° Junii, 1816.*

HENRY BROUGHAM, Esq. in The Chair.

Mr. *William Crawford*, being again called in, made the following Statement.

Mr.
*William Crawford.*

IN my former examination, I referred to the benefits which would arise from the formation of local associations for the instruction of the poor, upon the plan recommended by the British and Foreign School Society; I particularly mentioned an association of this description, which had been established at Northampton; and as the Committee desired me to furnish them with further particulars respecting it, I now present a statement explanatory of the nature of that association. It appears that before its formation, but 50 children attended the school; there are now upwards of 1000 receiving instruction.

[The following Statement was delivered in, and read:]

THE formation of Education Associations is of vital importance to the support of schools. The plan which has been adopted at Northampton is so worthy of universal imitation, that it has been deemed expedient to insert an outline of the method which is there adopted in a Penny per Week Society in aid of the Lancasterian school. At the time when this society was instituted, the funds of the school were so low that the committee feared the necessity of shutting it up. No sooner was the plan set on foot, but the subscription was rapidly filled, a sufficient sum was procured to pay the salary of the master, and to leave all the larger subscriptions disposable for the expenses of the building. The importance of the establishment of this school for promoting the education of the poor is very striking. Previously, scarce more than fifty children received a gratuitous education; now there are upwards of 1000.

A few of the subscribers, amongst whom are some of the most respectable persons in the town, or their children (who join the society by way of sanction or example) pay quarterly, but the bulk is collected regularly every week; and a rigid adherence to this practice is strongly urged; it has many advantages; it keeps up the spirit of the institution, and the smallness of the sum is not felt, any defalcation is sooner discovered, and any probable new subscriber is more likely to be pointed out. So punctual to their time are two of the collectors in particular, that they generally, when they enter a house, find the penny on the table waiting for them; and they have never lost a single subscriber since the commencement of the plan. In relation to the more respectable subscribers it may not be amiss to remark, that to prevent any ostentation or jealousy, no individual is allowed to subscribe more than a penny, though many members of the same family contribute their mite.

## " PENNY PER WEEK SOCIETY

In aid of the LANCASTERIAN School at Northampton, instituted 22d February 1813.

Great good with little labour—Public benefit without party zeal.

" THE committee for managing the above society, feel great pleasure in stating that the number of subscribers very far exceeds their most sanguine expectations; upwards of 450 names are now on the list, and there is great reason to expect many more will be added; they at the same time feel it incumbent on them, for the information of those subscribers who are unacquainted with the regulations of the society, to lay before them an outline of the plan on which it is conducted.

" A general receiver has been appointed for the whole town, the town divided into five divisions, and a sub-receiver for each division; each division subdivided, and a collector for each sub-division: the collectors to call on the subscribers every Monday, except on those who wish to pay monthly or quarterly, and to pay the amount of their collections every Tuesday to their respective sub-receivers; the sub-receivers to pay their weekly receipts to the general receiver every Wednesday; and the general receiver to pay the amount of his receipts every fourth Thursday to the treasurer or secretary of the Lancasterian School.

" The committee, consisting of the general and sub-receivers, meet as often as is necessary; and a general meeting of the receivers and collectors will be held quarterly at the schools, for the examination of the books, &c. Every person having any part in the management of the society, acts gratis; and in case of illness, or any other impediment in any of the collectors, the general or sub-receiver will collect in their stead. The general or sub-receivers will go round with the collectors at least once in six months to the subscribers, and give them any information they may wish for respecting the society. By order of the Committee,

W. *Stanton*, Secretary."

Mr.
*William Crawford.*

COLLECTOR's ACCOUNT for 26 Weeks, or Half a Year:—North Ward.

| SILVER-STREET; (Mr. Rands, Collector.) | January, | | | | | February, | | | | March, | | | | April, | | | | | May, | | | | June, | | | |
|---|---|---|---|---|---|---|---|---|---|---|---|---|---|---|---|---|---|---|---|---|---|---|---|---|---|---|
| SUBSCRIBERS : | 1. | 8. | 15. | 22. | 29. | 5. | 12. | 19. | 26. | 5. | 12. | 19. | 26 | 2. | 9. | 16. | 23. | 30. | 7. | 14 | 21. | 28 | 4. | 11. | 18 | 25. |
| | d. | d. | d. | d. | d. | | | | | | | | | | | | | | | | | | | | | |
| Mr. Wilson   -   - | 1 | 1 | 1 | 1 | 1 | | | | | | | | | | | | | | | | | | | | | |
| Mr. Thomas   -   - | 1 | 1 | 1 | | | | | | | | | | | | | | | | | | | | | | | |
| | 1 | 1 | | | | | | | | | | | | | | | | | | | | | | | | |
| | 1 | 1 | &c. | | | | | | | | | | | | | | | | | | | | | | | |
| | 1 | | | | | | | | | | | | | | | | | | | | | | | | | |
| | 1 | | | | | | | | | | | | | | | | | | | | | | | | | |
| | 1 | | | | | | | | | | | | | | | | | | | | | | | | | |
| | 1 | | | | | | | | | | | | | | | | | | | | | | | | | |
| | 1 | | | | | | | | | | | | | | | | | | | | | | | | | |
| | 1 | | | | | | | | | | | | | | | | | | | | | | | | | |
| | 1 | | | | | | | | | | | | | | | | | | | | | | | | | |
| | 1 | | | | | | | | | | | | | | | | | | | | | | | | | |
| | 1 | | | | | | | | | | | | | | | | | | | | | | | | | |
| | 1 | | | | | | | | | | | | | | | | | | | | | | | | | |
| See Sub-receiver's Account   -   - } 1s. 2d. | | | | | | | | | | | | | | | | | | | | | | | | | |

SUB-RECEIVER's ACCOUNT.—AN ACCOUNT of the Subscription of ONE PENNY per Week, for the North Ward:—(See Collector's Account.)

| SUB-DIVISION. | COLLECTORS. | £. | s. | d. |
|---|---|---|---|---|
| 1. Silver-street   -   -   -   -   - | Mr. Rands -   -   -   - | — | 1 | 2 |
| 2. Sheep-street   -   -   -   - | Mr. Earl   -   -   -   - | — | 1 | 4 |
| 3. Bearward-street and Bullhead-lane -   - | Mr. Raynolds -   -   - | — | 1 | 6 |
| 4. Church-lane   -   -   -   - | Mr. Vaughan -   -   - | — | — | 6 |
| 5. North-end -   -   -   -   - | Mr. Ager -   -   -   - | — | 1 | 3 |
| 6. Kingshead-lane -   -   -   -   - | Mr. Rands -   -   -   - | — | 1 | 7 |
| | Received   -   £. | — | 7 | 4 |

RECEIVED                     1815, of Mr. *I. S.*                     Seven Shillings
and Fourpence, being the weekly collection for North Ward.

*T. S.* General Receiver.

GENERAL RECEIVER's ACCOUNT.—General ACCOUNT of the PENNY PER WEEK SOCIETY, in aid of the Lancasterian School at *Northampton*, for One Month ending June 5th, 1815.

| DIVISIONS *. | SUB-RECEIVERS. | May 15. | | | May 22. | | | May 29. | | | June 5. | | |
|---|---|---|---|---|---|---|---|---|---|---|---|---|---|
| | | £. | s. | d. | £. | s. | d. | £. | s. | d. | £. | s. | d. |
| North -   -   -   - | Mr. Sharp   -   - | — | 7 | 4 | | | | | | | | | |
| East   -   -   -   - | Mr. Todd   -   - | — | 5 | 6 | | | | | | | | | |
| South -   -   -   - | Mr. Hedge   -   - | — | 4 | 8 | | | | | | | | | |
| West   -   -   -   - | Mr. Hedge   -   - | — | 6 | 6 | | | | | | | | | |
| Chequer -   -   - | Mr. Stanton -   - | — | 3 | 10 | | | | | | | | | |
| Villages -   -   - | Mr. Sharp   -   - | — | 8 | 2 | | | | | | | | | |
| | £. | 1 | 16 | — | 2 | 4 | 6 | 1 | 18 | — | 1 | 15 | —. |

| May | 15 | -   -   -   -   - | £.1 | 16 | — |
|---|---|---|---|---|---|
| — | 22 | -   -   -   -   - | 2 | 4 | 6 |
| — | 29 | -   -   -   -   - | 1 | 18 | — |
| June | 5 | -   -   -   -   - | 1 | 15 | — |
| | Total Monthly Account   - | £.7 | 13 | 6 |

RECEIVED                     1815, of Mr. Sharp, Seven Pounds Thirteen
Shillings and Sixpence, on account of the Lancasterian School.

*J. B.* Secretary.

In the collection of Taxes, Northampton is divided into the above Five Wards instead of Parishes.

*George Giles Vincent,* Esquire, called in, and Examined.

YOU are Chapter Clerk of the Dean and Chapter of Westminster?—I am. I feel myself, from the office I hold, to be in a very awkward situation, for I feel bound to give no evidence without the consent of the Dean and Chapter.

[Mr. *Vincent* delivered in the following Paper, containing the Prescription of the office held by him :]

" Hic etiam Juramento teneatur de Secretis Capituli minime revelandis et quod nulli exceptis Decano et Canonicis Commentarios Collegii aut alia quæcunque Munimenta his evidentias Colli vel ostendat vel exemplaria illorum descripta tradat sine decani (custeo absenti) Prodecani et Capituli expresso consensu et mandato."

Have you taken the oath?—No, I have not been sworn; but I conceive it is equally a breach of my duty to give evidence without the consent of the Dean and Chapter.

[The Witness delivered in the following Paper :]

" Sint **duo** præceptores quorum alter Archidasculus alter Hypodidasculus vocetur. Ille Grammatices vel Artium Magister, hic Baccalaureus Artium ad minimum sit, si commode fieri potest—Horum gubernationi omnes discipuli subjecti subjecti sunto utrique religiosi docti honesti et laboriosi sint ut pios eruditos ingenuos et studiosos efficient discipulos.

Discipuli sint numero 40

|  | *s.* | *d.* |
|---|---|---|
| Schola Grammaticalis. | | |
| Discipuli quadraginta singuli, pro liberatura | xiij. | iiij. |
| - - - - - - - - - - pro commeatu annuo, | lxˢ | xᵈ |

Is this paper which you have given in the only part of the muniments in your custody which relates to the school at Westminster?—It is from the statutes; it does not contain the whole, but it contains all that immediately applies to the particular subjects there mentioned. There are a variety of other smaller matters, and particularly with regard to the qualifications of the discipuli sint numero 40.

Are there any other papers, relating to the expenses of the school?—None of the statutes; there is concerning clothes, but no particular sum; they are to be of a grave colour, and so on.

Nothing respecting the finance?—No; and the stipends of the schoolmasters, and so on.

Are the stipends specified?—Yes.

Are they the same as those deposed to by former Witnesses?—I cannot bear them in recollection; but they are but small, and that I should suppose includes board.

What are the parts of the statutes relating to the qualifications of the discipuli; produce the same?—I submit to the Committee, that to answer this question, it would be advisable the Dean should be summoned.

Do you consider that you ought to have the permission of the Dean to produce those statutes?—I do; I have not his permission.

In whose custody are those papers?—They are ordinarily in mine, as the proper officer; but merely for the use of the Dean and Chapter, nobody else.

[The Witness was directed to produce the statutes.]

[The Witness produced the book containing the statutes.]

What is the rule in those statutes, respecting the elections into the university?—It is described under the title Modus autem electiones esto.

[The Extract was read, as follows :]

" Primum legatur hoc statutum de electione discipulorum deinde septem he Electores jusjurandum dent se neminem in discipulum gratia odio, aliave animi perturbatione vel præmeo adductos sed eum solum quem testimonio conscientiæ permoti maxime idoneum judicaverint electuros.

" In omnibus Electionibus sit scrutinium semper apertum, Eligendos in Collegium Trinitatis Cantabrigiæ nominabit Magister ejusdem cui si tres e reliquis Electoribus consenserint aut dño decani is electus habeatur eodem modo eligendos in ecclesiam Christi Oxon' aut in Collegium Westmii nominabit decanus ejusdem cui si tres e reliquis aut dño Collegiorm præfecti consenserint is electus esto. Quod si post tria aperta scrutinia nec tres cum singulis præpositis nec ipsi tres præpositi
quod

*G. G. Vincent,*
*Esq.*

quod absit de uno cooptando consenserint tum hi pro Electis habeantur ne frustretur Electio quos dño præfecti aut eorum vicarii in discipulos dictorum collegiorum nominaverint tot autam eo tempore eligantur quot per annum sequentem discedentiu' loca in dictis collegiis suppleant. Deinde eo ordine quo indicta collegia electi fuerint discipuli eorum nomina parentele comitatus et oppida quibus nati fuerint in tribus Indenturis per Ludimagistrum scribentur. His Indenturis tres præfecti aut eorum vicarii nomina sua subscribant ut cum loca aliqua discipulorum in dictis collegiis eo anno vacua fuerint eo ipso ordine in sua Collegia sine ulla tergiversatione admittantur. Hic ordo electionis singulis annis observetur et novæ indenturæ fiant veteres indenturæ post inceptam novam electionem abrogentur. Et quamvis cupimus plurimos e nostris discipulis Westmonasterii ad Academias in dicta Collegia quotannis promoveri tamen ne incertus sit omnino numerus sex ad minimum videlicet tres in ecclesiam Christi Oxonii et tres in Collegium Trinitatis singulis Annis (si aut tot loca vacua in dictis Collegis Academicis aut tot idoneii e nostris discipulis Westmonasterii reperti fuerint) admitti volumus.

" Plures autem optamus se ita præfatis Electoribus commodum videbitur. Et hoc omnibus quorum interest vel interesse potent innocescere volumus per præsentes.

" Cautum sit semper quot uno scrutinio unus solum discipulus non plures simul eligantur.

" In Sumptus vero moderatos tam decani Eccliæ Christi et suorum quam Magistri Collegii Trinitatis et suorum tempore electionis impensos Collegium nostrum Westmonaster' suppeditabit utrique præfecto aut eorum vicariis."

What is the rule respecting the election on the foundation?—It is described under the title, Appendix pro discipulorum Electione in Collegium Westmoñ.

[The Extract was read, as follows:]

" Neminem in Collegium nostrum qui in dicta schola nostra annum integrum ante tempus electionis educatus non fuerit nec plures uno ex eodem Comitatu in una electione elegi aut admitti volumus. Praterea nullus hæres qui jam sit aut qui futurus sit patre mortuo hæres cujus hæreditas summam decem librarum excesserit in hunc numerum co-optetur. Electi autem quamprimum loca vacua fuerint suo ordine flexis genibus a Decano vel eo absente Prodecano publice in aula aut ante prandium aut ante cœnam admittantur his verbis.

" Ego N. Decanus vel pro Decanus hujus Collegiatæ Ecclesiæ admitto te N. in discipulum scholarem hujus Collegii juxta statuta ejusdem. In nomine Patris et Filii et Spiritus Sancti Amen."

Lieutenant Colonel *James Williamson,* called in, and Examined.

*Lieut. Colonel*
*James Williamson.*

YOU are commandant of the Royal Military Asylum at Chelsea?—I am. Is this establishment purely military?—Entirely so.

When was it founded?—It was founded in 1803; the first children were received in that year.

It was founded by His Royal Highness the Commander in Chief?—It was.

From what classes are the children taken?—They are the children of soldiers of the regular army.

Are they educated for the army merely?—No, they are not educated for the army merely, it is a voluntary choice; the boys are allowed a preference, whether they will volunteer for the army, or be apprentices to trades, or go to service; it is a voluntary act of the child.

How many children are there upon the establishment?—850 boys and 400 girls, at Chelsea; we have an infant establishment, for 100, at the Isle of Wight.

Connected with your establishment?—Yes; we do not take them into our establishment till they are five years old, and able to dress themselves; they are taken in at the Isle of Wight as soon as they are born.

How long do you keep them?—Till they are fourteen.

You board, lodge, and clothe them?—Yes, and educate them.

What are they taught?—Reading, writing, and arithmetic.

Is the new plan of education adopted?—It is.

Is it found to succeed?—It succeeds uncommonly well; there was a difficulty in instructing the children before, because they all depended upon one man, now they instruct one another on Dr. Bell's plan.

Are the children disciplined or trained after the military fashion?—Yes, in a certain degree; they are taught to march into the schools and into the dining-halls in a regular manner, but nothing further; there is no further military exercise, but the saluting the officer in a military way.

Has the establishment been long enough on foot to enable you to see its advantages in training recruits?—Certainly; there have been many instances of our boys

495.

who

*Lieut. Colonel*
*James Williamson.*

who have gone into the army, who have been made very useful non-commissione?
officers, and have been found very useful in the Regimental Office as clerks, and so on.

From their superior education?—Yes. Several of our boys have been killed in
action, and several wounded.

About what proportion of the boys may go into the army?—About one third
volunteer in the first instance; and sometimes, from the master's failing in business,
or from disagreement, they come to me, and beg I will recommend them to some
regiment, after they have been bound apprentice.

About what age do they volunteer into the army?—At fourteen; we do not
keep them after fourteen.

And you do not allow them to volunteer before?—No.

Do they volunteer generally on limited or unlimited service?—It is unlimited
service, they are not allowed to volunteer for limited service; but that is not a regulation of the Institution, but an order of the Commander-in-Chief; they leave our
Institution at fourteen; and as to those that volunteer into the army, I take great pains
to find out if they have any parents, and if they have any parents, I consult them
whether it is with their approbation that they go into the army. I think the children
who have no parents, of whom we have great numbers, always volunteer into the
army; where they have parents, they generally persuade them to the contrary.

At what age do they go out to trades or manufactures?—At fourteen; we do not
keep them after fourteen, for the boys and girls are not separated, and may have
communication, and it might be dangerous keeping them beyond that age; that is,
the boys are in the right wing of the building, and the girls in the left; we prevent
them getting together, but on dark winter nights they might do it. This is a statement of the petitions remaining unexamined on the 8th of June 1816, according to
the four classes by which we are bound by our rules to give preference.

[It was delivered in, and read, as follows:]

| DESCRIPTION. | BOYS. | GIRLS. | TOTAL. |
|---|---|---|---|
| 1st Class.—Complete Orphans - - - | — | — | — |
| 2d Ditto.—Fathers dead - - - - | 37 | 62 | 99 |
| 3d Ditto.—Mothers dead - - - - | 26 | 13 | 39 |
| 4th Ditto.—Fathers and Mothers living - | 168 | 101 | 269 |
| TOTAL - - | 231 | 176 | 407 |

*Lieut. Col. Williamson.* This is a statement of our number at this moment.

[It was delivered in, and read, as follows:]

State.

ROYAL MILITARY ASYLUM, Saturday, 8th June 1816.

| | MEN. | | | | | | | | | | | | | | WOMEN. | | | | | | | | | CHILDREN. | | Alterations since last Return, Viz. 15th May 1816. | | | | | | |
|---|---|---|---|---|---|---|---|---|---|---|---|---|---|---|---|---|---|---|---|---|---|---|---|---|---|---|---|---|---|---|---|---|---|
| | Commandant. | Adjutant & Secretary. | Quarter Master & Steward. | Chaplain. | Surgeon. | Serj.t Major. / Serjeants. | Quarter Master Serj.t | Hospital Ditto. | Master Tailor Ditto. | Master Shoemaker Ditto. | Porter Ditto. | Pioneer Corporals. | Drummer. | Matron. | Assistant Matron. | Schoolmistress. | Cook. | Assistant Cooks. | Laundress. | Assistant Laundresses. | Hospital Nurses. | Companies Nurses. | School-masters. | BOYS. | GIRLS. | — | Admitted. | Volunteered for the Army. | Apprenticed. | Delivered to Parents. | Detained by Parents. | Deserted. | Dead. |
| Present - - | 1 | 1 | 1 | 1 | 1 | 1 | 1 | 11 | 1 | 1 | 1 | 1 | 1 | 2 | 1 | 1 | 1 | 4 | 1 | 3 | 1 | 3 | 5 | 28 | 762 | 350 | Boys - | 1 | 5 | 7 | 1 | 1 | - | - |
| Sick - - | - | - | - | - | - | - | - | - | - | - | - | - | - | - | - | - | - | - | - | - | - | 1 | - | | Hospl - 37 | Hospl - 17 | Girls - | 2 | - | 5 | 3 | - | - | - |
| Total - | 1 | 1 | 1 | 1 | 1 | 1 | 1 | 11 | 1 | 1 | 1 | 1 | 1 | 2 | 1 | 1 | 1 | 4 | 1 | 3 | 1 | 3 | 6 | 28 | 799 | 367 | | 3 | 5 | 12 | 4 | 1 | - | - |

|  | B. | G. |
|---|---|---|
| Isle of Wight, for the benefit of Sea bathing - | 8 | 13 |
| Teaching at Gibraltar and Quebec - | 4 | — |
| At the Military College, Sandhurst - | 2 | — |
| Total - - | 14 | 13 |

RECAPITULATION:

| | Boys. | Girls. | Total. |
|---|---|---|---|
| Effective - - - | 799 | 367 | 1,166 |
| Wanting to complete - | 51 | 33 | 84 |
| Establishment - - | 850 | 400 | 1,250 |

*Lieut.*

*Lieut. Col. Williamson.*—This is a Return of the manner in which the children have been disposed of.

*Licut. Colonel James Williamson.*

[It was delivered in, and read, as follows :]

Return of CASUALTIES among the Children in the ROYAL MILITARY ASYLUM, *Chelsea*, from the commencement of the Institution, 29th August 1803 to the 8th June 1816, inclusive.

| YEAR. On the 24th Dec. | Number of Children in the Asylum. | | | Dead. | | | Deserted. | | | Apprenticed. | | | Delivered to their Parents by Order of the Commissioners. | | |
|---|---|---|---|---|---|---|---|---|---|---|---|---|---|---|---|
| | Boys. | Girls. | Total. | Boys. | Girls. | Total. | Boys. | Girls. | Total. | Boys. | Girls. | Total. | Boys. | Girls. | Total. |
| 1803 - - | 76 | 47 | 123 | — | — | — | — | — | — | — | — | — | — | — | — |
| 1804 - - | 381 | 199 | 580 | - | 2 | 2 | - | - | - | - | - | - | 4 | 2 | 6 |
| 1805 - - | 591 | 285 | 876 | 8 | 2 | 10 | 1 | - | 1 | - | 5 | 5 | 17 | 8 | 25 |
| 1806 - - | 650 | 287 | 937 | 4 | 7 | 11 | 2 | - | 2 | 3 | 14 | 17 | 5 | 4 | 9 |
| 1807 - - | 660 | 290 | 950 | 15 | 5 | 20 | 1 | - | 1 | 35 | 20 | 55 | 14 | 11 | 25 |
| 1808 - - | 713 | 321 | 1034 | 2 | 2 | 4 | - | - | - | 34 | 16 | 50 | 18 | 11 | 29 |
| 1809 - - | 784 | 341 | 1125 | 6 | 3 | 9 | - | - | - | 30 | 24 | 54 | 25 | 7 | 32 |
| 1810 - - | 724 | 346 | 1070 | 15 | 2 | 17 | - | - | - | 55 | 29 | 84 | 47 | 8 | 55 |
| 1811 - - | 793 | 399 | 1192 | 10 | - | 10 | - | - | - | 58 | 59 | 117 | 38 | 19 | 57 |
| 1812 - - | 792 | 391 | 1183 | 7 | 5 | 12 | 1 | - | 1 | 54 | 53 | 107 | 17 | 6 | 23 |
| 1813 - - | 789 | 396 | 1185 | 9 | 3 | 12 | - | - | - | 45 | 48 | 93 | 13 | 7 | 20 |
| 1814 - - | 834 | 392 | 1226 | 6 | 9 | 15 | 1 | - | 1 | 75 | 59 | 134 | 16 | 9 | 25 |
| 1815 - - | 819 | 382 | 1201 | 8 | 1 | 9 | 1 | - | 1 | 57 | 62 | 119 | 15 | 2 | 17 |
| 8th June 1816 | 799 | 367 | 1166 | 4 | 2 | 6 | - | - | - | 32 | 21 | 53 | 7 | 5 | 12 |
| Total - - | - | - | - | 94 | 43 | 137 | 7 | - | 7 | 478 | 410 | 888 | 236 | 99 | 335 |

*Continued below.*

*Repeated.*

| YEAR. On the 24th Dec. | Number of Children in the Asylum. | | | Detained by their Parents when on Pass. | | | Volunteered for the Army, and joined their Regiments. | | Alterations since last Return, viz. 15th May 1816. | Boys. | Girls. | Total. |
|---|---|---|---|---|---|---|---|---|---|---|---|---|
| | Boys. | Girls. | Total. | Boys. | Girls. | Total. | Boys. | Total. | | | | |
| 1803 - - | 76 | 47 | 123 | — | — | — | — | — | | | | |
| 1804 - - | 381 | 199 | 580 | 1 | 1 | 2 | — | — | Admitted - - - | 1 | 2 | 3 |
| 1805 - - | 591 | 285 | 876 | 4 | 2 | 6 | 1 | 1 | Dead - - - - | — | — | — |
| 1806 - - | 650 | 287 | 937 | 7 | 3 | 10 | 15 | 15 | Deserted - - - | — | — | — |
| 1807 - - | 660 | 290 | 950 | 6 | 1 | 7 | 19 | 19 | | | | |
| 1808 - - | 713 | 321 | 1034 | 6 | 1 | 7 | 24 | 24 | Apprenticed - - - | 7 | 5 | 12 |
| 1809 - - | 784 | 341 | 1125 | 6 | 5 | 11 | 27 | 27 | Delivered to their | | | |
| 1810 - - | 724 | 346 | 1070 | 12 | 5 | 17 | 51 | 51 | Parents - - - | 1 | 3 | 4 |
| 1811 - - | 793 | 399 | 1192 | 8 | - | 8 | 25 | 25 | Detained by their | | | |
| 1812 - - | 792 | 391 | 1183 | 9 | 5 | 14 | 47 | 47 | Parents - - - | 1 | - | 1 |
| 1813 - - | 789 | 396 | 1185 | 9 | 1 | 10 | 52 | 52 | Volunteered for the | | | |
| 1814 - - | 834 | 392 | 1226 | 11 | 3 | 14 | 40 | 40 | army - - - - | 5 | - | 5 |
| 1815 - - | 819 | 382 | 1201 | 8 | - | 8 | 27 | 27 | | | | |
| 8th June 1816 | 799 | 367 | 1166 | 3 | - | 3 | 15 | 15 | | | | |
| Total - - | - | - | - | 90 | 27 | 117 | 343 | 343 | | | | |

*Lieut. Col. Williamson.*—These are estimates of the expense of provisions and clothing.

Estimate of the Weekly and Annual Expense of Provisions for a Serjeant, Nurse, Boy and Girl, belonging to the ROYAL MILITARY ASYLUM, *Chelsea*, for the year 1816.

| RANK. | Weekly Allowance. lb. oz. | PROVISIONS. | Weekly Expense. £. s. d. | Annual Expense. £. s. d. |
|---|---|---|---|---|
| Serjeant or Nurse. | 7 — | Bread - - - - 2 d. lb. | — 1 2 | |
| | 4 — | Beef - - - - 5 - - | — 1 8 | |
| | 2 — | Mutton - - - - 5 - - | — — 10 | |
| | — 8 | Bacon - - - - 5 - - | — — 2 ½ | |
| | 1 — | Butter - - - 10 ½ - | — — 10 ½ | |
| | — 8 | Cheese - - - - 6 - - | — — 3 | |
| | 7 — | Potatoes - - - - ½ - | — — 3 ½ | |
| | | ½ pint of Peas - - - - | — — 1 | |
| | | 10 quarts and 1 pint of Beer, 12/ p' B¹ | — — 10 ½ | |
| | | Salt, Pepper, &c. - - - - | — — 1 | |
| | | £. | — 6 4 | |
| | | Per annum - - £. | | 16 11 2 |

*Lieut. Colonel*
*James Williamson.*

Estimate of the Weekly and Annual Expense of Provisions—*continued*.

| | Weekly Allowance. | PROVISIONS. | | Weekly Expense. | | | Annual Expense. | | |
|---|---|---|---|---|---|---|---|---|---|
| | | | | £. | s. | d. | £. | s. | d. |
| Boy or Girl. | $\frac{12}{20}$ | of a Quartern Loaf of Bread - - | | — | — | 7$\frac{3}{4}$ | | | |
| | 1 lb. 8 oz. | of Beef - - - 5 d. per lb. | | — | — | 7$\frac{1}{2}$ | | | |
| | — 8 oz. | Mutton - - 5 — | | — | — | 2$\frac{1}{2}$ | | | |
| | — 3 | Suet - - 8 — | | — | — | 1$\frac{1}{2}$ | | | |
| | — 6 | Cheese - - 6 — | | — | — | 2$\frac{1}{4}$ | | | |
| | 4 12 | Potatoes - - 0$\frac{1}{2}$ — | | — | — | 2$\frac{1}{4}$ | | | |
| | — 12 | Flour - - - 2 — | | — | — | 1$\frac{1}{2}$ | | | |
| | | 1 Gill of Peas | | — | — | 0$\frac{1}{2}$ | | | |
| | | 1 Quart $\frac{5}{6}$ & $\frac{1}{2}$ of Milk, 3 d. p' p$^t$ | | — | — | 5$\frac{1}{4}$ | | | |
| | | 2 Qu$^{ts}$ 1 Pint & $\frac{1}{2}$ of Beer, 12 s. p' B$^l$ | | — | — | 2$\frac{3}{4}$ | | | |
| | | $\frac{7}{16}$ of a lb. of Oatmeal, 1$\frac{3}{4}$ d. - - | | — | — | 0$\frac{3}{4}$ | | | |
| | | Salt, Pepper, &c. - - - - | | — | — | 1 | | | |
| | | | £. | — | 3 | — | | | |
| | | Per Annum - - - - - £. | | | | | 7 | 16 | 10$\frac{1}{2}$ |

ESTIMATE of the Expense for clothing a Serjeant, Pioneer, Boy, Nurse, and Girl, belonging to the ROYAL MILITARY ASYLUM, Chelsea ; for 1816.

| RANK. | CLOTHING. | | £. | s. | d. | £. | s. | d. |
|---|---|---|---|---|---|---|---|---|
| Serjeant - - | 1 Hat and Cockade - - - - - - | | — | 10 | 1 | | | |
| | 1 Coat - - - - - - | | 1 | 15 | 3 | | | |
| | 1 Waistcoat - - - - - | | — | 9 | 6$\frac{3}{4}$ | | | |
| | 1 Pair of Breeches - - - - - | | — | 10 | 6$\frac{1}{2}$ | | | |
| | 1 Pair of long Gaiters - - - - | | — | 5 | 5$\frac{3}{4}$ | | | |
| | 1 Stock and Clasps - - - - | | — | 1 | 3 | | | |
| | 1 Great Coat every five years, at £. 1. 5. - | | — | 5 | — | | | |
| | | | | | | 3 | 17 | 2 |
| Pioneer - - | 1 Hat and Cockade - - - - - - | | — | 3 | 6 | | | |
| | 1 Coat - - - - - - | | — | 15 | 8$\frac{1}{4}$ | | | |
| | 1 Waistcoat - - - - - | | — | 3 | 3$\frac{1}{4}$ | | | |
| | 1 Pair of Breeches - - - - - | | — | 5 | 8$\frac{1}{2}$ | | | |
| | 1 Pair of long Gaiters - - - - | | — | 5 | 5$\frac{3}{4}$ | | | |
| | 1 Pair of Chevrons 6 d. Stock and Clasps 1/3 - | | — | 1 | 9 | | | |
| | 1 Great Coat every five years, at 15/ - - | | — | 3 | — | | | |
| | | | | | | 1 | 18 | 5 |
| Boy - - - | 1 Leather Cap per annum - - - - | | — | 1 | 6 | | | |
| | 1 Winter Jacket - - - - - | | — | 6 | 6$\frac{1}{4}$ | | | |
| | 1 Summer Jacket - - - - | | — | 5 | 11$\frac{3}{4}$ | | | |
| | 2 Pair of Breeches (lined) at 6/ - - - | | — | 12 | — | | | |
| | 5 Shirts every two years, at 3/3 each - - | | — | 8 | 1$\frac{1}{2}$ | | | |
| | 3 Pair of Stockings per annum, at 1/3 - - | | — | 3 | 9 | | | |
| | Mending Stockings - - - - | | — | 1 | — | | | |
| | 5 Pair of Shoes every two years, at 4/ - - | | — | 10 | — | | | |
| | Mending Shoes, per annum - - - | | — | 4 | — | | | |
| | Mending Clothes, d$^o$ - - - | | — | 1 | — | | | |
| | Fatigue Dress, - d$^o$ - - - - | | — | — | 6 | | | |
| | | | | | | 2 | 14 | 4$\frac{1}{2}$ |
| Nurse - - | 1 Straw Bonnet and Ribbon every two years, at 4/ | | — | 2 | — | | | |
| | 1 Red Gown every two years, £. 1. 3. 9$\frac{1}{2}$. - - | | — | 11 | 10$\frac{3}{4}$ | | | |
| | 1 Shawl every two years, 4/6 - - - | | — | 2 | 3 | | | |
| | 1 Calimanco Petticoat per annum - - - | | — | 6 | 5$\frac{3}{4}$ | | | |
| | 1 Flannel - d$^o$ - - d$^o$ - - - | | — | 4 | 7$\frac{3}{4}$ | | | |
| | 1 Linsey-woolsey d$^o$ - - d$^o$ - - - | | — | 4 | — | | | |
| | 1 Linsey-woolsey Jacket d$^o$ - - - | | — | 5 | 6 | | | |
| | 1 White Apron - - - - - - | | — | 5 | 1$\frac{1}{2}$ | | | |
| | 1 Check d$^o$ - - - - - | | — | 2 | 11$\frac{1}{4}$ | | | |
| | 1 Hessian d$^o$ - - - - - | | — | 2 | 9$\frac{1}{2}$ | | | |
| | 1 Muslin Neck-kerchief - - - - | | — | 2 | — | | | |
| | 1 Pair of Gloves - - - - - - | | — | 1 | 3 | | | |
| | | | | | | 2 | 10 | 10$\frac{1}{2}$ |

(*continued.*)

Estimate of the Expense for Clothing a Serjeant, Pioneer, Boy, Nurse, and Girl—*continued.*

| | CLOTHING. | £. | s. | d. | £. | s. | d. |
|---|---|---|---|---|---|---|---|
| | 1 Straw Bonnet and Ribon every two years, at 3/6 | — | 1 | 9 | | | |
| | 1 Linsey-woolsey Bonnet per annum - - - | — | — | 10¼ | | | |
| | 1 Linsey-woolsey Gown - - dº - - - | — | 5 | 11¼ | | | |
| | 1 Red Gown - - - - - dº - - - | — | 10 | 8¼ | | | |
| | 2 Flannel Petticoats - - dº - a' 2/4¼ - | — | 4 | 9½ | | | |
| | 5 Shifts every two years, a' 2/8 - - | — | 6 | 8 | | | |
| | 5 pair of shoes dº - a' 4/ - - - | — | 10 | — | | | |
| | Mending shoes, per annum - - - | — | 4 | — | | | |
| Girl - - - | 3 pair of Stockings per dº a' 1/3 - - | — | 3 | 9 | | | |
| | Mending Stockings dº - - - | — | 1 | — | | | |
| | 1 White Apron - - dº - - - | — | 2 | 8¾ | | | |
| | 3 Pinafores - - dº 2/ - - - | — | 6 | — | | | |
| | 1 White Tippet - - dº - - - | — | — | 8½ | | | |
| | 1 pair of Gloves - - dº - - - | — | 1 | 1 | | | |
| | 2 Night Caps - - dº /4¾ - - - | — | — | 9½ | | | |
| | 1 pair of Stays - - dº - - - | — | 1 | — | | | |
| | Mending Clothes - dº - - - | — | 1 | — | | | |
| | Fatigue Dress - - dº - - - | — | — | 6 | | | |
| | | | | | 3 | 3 | 4½ |

Is there any library attached to the establishment?—Yes, there is, for the use of the children.

How does it happen that the number is not complete?—There are 84 vacancies just now; we are obliged to keep a number of vacancies for children that come from abroad; there is a barrack fitting up at Southampton, for an additional 400 boys.

Do you think that this number, when completed, will be sufficient to receive all the children who may require it, during peace?—I should think in time of peace it would.

How many have you at present on your sick list?—Twenty-nine boys and twelve girls.

Your establishment is in general healthy?—Very much so; I think we lose in general about one per cent. per annum.

Mr. *John Daughtrey*, called in, and Examined.

ARE you acquainted with the state of the children of the poor of the Metropolis?—I have for several years been in the constant habit of visiting the poor in Spitalfields, and I have also been a regular visitor of a large Sunday school, by which I have seen a good deal of the state of poor children.

To what school do you refer?—The school in George-yard Drury-lane.

How many children are in that school?—About 600 in that school; but in several schools connected with it, in Hinde-street Lambeth, Westminster, &c. there are in the whole about 3,000.

What observations have you made upon the effect of Sunday school instruction?—To speak generally, I have observed that it has had the most salutary effect upon the children who have been instructed, and also in numerous instances upon the families with which those children were connected; they not only preserve vast numbers of the youthful poor from ignorance and contamination, but have been the means of forming the character of multitudes. I myself know not a few, who but for Sunday-school instruction might have been among the worst members of society, but who are now young persons of exemplary character, and are steadily and actively engaged in communicating to others that instruction which has proved so useful to themselves.

Their moral character is improved by the instruction they receive?—Most decidedly. My visits to the habitations of the poor have enabled me to see the effect at home, which as a mere visitor of a Sunday school I should not have had the same means of seeing.

Have you observed much difference in the families where the children attend Sunday schools, from those where they do not?—A very marked difference in many cases, especially where the children have attended Sunday schools a sufficient length of time for such effects to appear.

What

Mr.
John Daughtrey.

What difference have you observed between Sunday school children and others whose education is neglected?—I have, I think I may almost say uniformly, observed that Sunday school children, such as have been in Sunday schools for any length of time, to be more respectful in their behaviour, and cleaner in their persons.

What class of the poor generally send their children to Sunday schools?—Chiefly mechanics and the labouring poor; we find it more difficult to get the children of the most degraded classes.

Do you conceive there are a great number uneducated, in the Metropolis?—Certainly still a great number.

Have you found that, in your visits to the poor of Spitalfields?—We have found it even there where Sunday-school education is carried to a greater extent than in some other parts of the town; we are seldom out a single evening without meeting with children who have not before attended any Sunday schools, or had any advantages of education; of course in such cases we endeavour to induce the parents to send such children.

Are the parents of those uneducated children desirous that their children should receive instruction?—In most cases, when the advantages are pointed out to them, they seem truly desirous of it; and we have succeeded in inducing the parents of many scores of poor ignorant children, to send them to various schools in that neighbourhood.

Do you conceive that a great number of poor children in the Metropolis would be entirely destitute of education, but for Sunday schools?—Certainly they would, especially when trade is at all in a flourishing state; we then find comparatively few of those who are able to work, that have not some regular employment which must totally prevent their attending a day school; and of those who may not be old enough to work, one at least in most large families is necessarily detained at home.

Some of the children are employed to nurse the younger?—Frequently so, and in other ways assisting their mother.

If the means of education were provided for all poor children on the week-days, do you still think there would be any occasion for Sunday-school instruction?—I certainly think there would, for the reasons just stated, and because Sunday schools afford peculiarly favourable opportunity for impressing the minds of the youthful poor with a sense of their moral and religious duties, upon which their conduct and character in future life so much depend.

What do you think is the cause of the ill conduct of so many of the children of the poor in the Metropolis?—In great numbers, to the want of education, undoubtedly, and especially of that kind of education which connects with it a due observance of the Sabbath, and a constant inculcation of the truths and duties of religion; there is the root of the evil; other causes might be mentioned, such as bad company, gambling, &c. but I consider these as rather effects of the grand cause just mentioned. It is no slight advantage of Sunday schools, that they are directly calculated to preserve from the infection of evil associates, as that is the chief day on which bad and neglected boys assemble and corrupt each other.

Do you think Sabbath-breaking is productive of many evils in the Metropolis?—My observation inclines me to attribute to it a great part of the immorality which is to be found among the lower classes.

Have any particular facts fallen under your own notice on that subject?—The opinion has, I may almost say, been forced upon me by the great body of facts and instances that have fallen under my notice in visiting the poor; with me it is no theory; I had not been many months engaged in this work before I was necessarily led to the opinion, and the correctness of it has been most fully confirmed in my mind by subsequent observation and experience. Neglecters and breakers of the Sabbath, among the poor, are almost always careless about the character and habits of their children; they are often idle and dirty themselves, and their families have consequently little domestic comfort; whilst those who pay a strict and proper regard to the duties of this day, are, in nine cases out of ten, found to be sober, honest, cleanly and industrious, and particularly anxious for the welfare of their offspring. I shall not be understood as attributing this great superiority of character to a mere formal attendance on public worship, unconnected with the sacred truths which are there inculcated, and to the influence of these truths and duties upon their minds; they clearly need such a weekly monitor, and we find little consistent morality among them which is not produced in this way.

Do the children in Sunday schools generally attend public worship?—In all the

Sunday

Sunday schools that I am acquainted with, they attend public worship; we consider it as of the greatest importance to habituate them to this.

Do you conceive special benefits arise from this early attendance on public worship?—Yes, certainly.

Do you conceive that the advantages which children derive from Sunday-school instruction are confined to the benefits of the Sabbath merely; or are there other benefits, which you have not stated?—By no means to the Sabbath; many of the children learn considerable portions of moral and sacred poetry and scripture, and other pieces, which the teachers think likely to be useful to them, during the week; they are also furnished with suitable books for weekly reading, from a circulating library attached to the school.

Have you had any opportunity of observing how Sunday-school children conduct themselves in their respective families?—I had lately an opportunity of inquiring into that circumstance, relating to a considerable number of the children who attend the Sunday school in George-yard Drury-lane.

Whence did that opportunity arise?—The sub-committee of that school thought it necessary, in consequence of some charges which they had heard against its moral tendency, or at least against the character of the children who attended there, to inquire into the insinuation, and also, at their own habitations, into the character of the children and the condition of their parents.

Do you mean a report from Newgate, brought against the National and various other schools?—I refer to that report.

What was done by the sub-committee in consequence of hearing of that report?—The sub-committee met to take it into consideration; and though they were most fully convinced that the charges were altogether unfounded, they thought it proper to make a general visitation to the habitations of the parents of the children, in order to make inquiries on the subject.

What was the result of their investigation?—The result of that investigation was highly satisfactory; they not only found that there was not the least shadow of ground for any of the charges brought against the school, but that the school had been productive of a much greater quantum of good than they had supposed.

Did they find any instances of great good having resulted to the children?—Yes, and not only to the children, but to the families in which they live.

Did you visit many of the families?—In connexion with a friend I visited about fifty of the families.

You were completely satisfied with the result of those visits?—Not only completely satisfied, but much encouraged by the good we saw and heard of, beyond any thing we had formerly supposed. In the course of this investigation, it was found that the homes of the children comprising the upper classes in the school, almost universally wore a decent and comfortable aspect, and the parents appeared tidy comfortable people; whilst those of the lower classes were observed to be generally of an inferior order. As the classes were visited by different persons, we were not aware of this general distinction, till the committee met to read their respective reports. Upon examination, it was ascertained that the time which the children of the sixth, which are the upper classes, have been in the school, averages about three years and a half; and that of the children in the lower classes does not exceed a few months: it is therefore a fair and natural inference, that much of the difference, even in the parents and families, is produced by the influence of the school.

Are the teachers in that and the other schools with which you are connected gratuitous?—All of them gratuitous.

Do you find gratuitous teachers most beneficial in Sunday schools?—Certainly they are. I would beg to state here, that gratuitous teachers have always appeared to me to be one main excellence of the Sunday school system; it appears to me calculated to secure Sunday schools from those abuses and that decay to which we know other establishments of that nature, where the teachers are paid, become liable. I would beg here just to state why I think so. It cannot be doubted that most persons who engage in the humble and laborious work of teaching in Sunday schools, do it from a pure and benevolent motive; and if at any time their zeal and interest in the school should decline, they have no inducement in the nature of pay or reward to continue their services, and of course withdraw from the school; and there is never any difficulty in supplying their place with persons who have the necessary zeal and other qualifications, both for teaching poor children to read, and

for

for instructing them in all the duties of religion. As I am not a teacher, these remarks from me will not be thought improper.

Have you observed a particular affection towards the children fostered in the minds of the teachers?—I have certainly seen that.

Do you find respect and affection from the children to their teachers?—Yes, generally, when they have known each other any length of time; and I have always found this extremely favourable to their improvement, and to useful impressions upon their minds; both the tone of feeling which pervades the mind of the teacher, which I have already accounted for from what must be his character and conduct, and the respect and affection induced by that on the mind of the children, are extremely favourable to a right impression on the mind.

Both with respect to their moral conduct and religious principles?—Yes.

Are the teachers in the habit of visiting the children and their parents?—In all the schools with which I am at all connected, there are small societies for the express purpose of visiting children when they are ill; indeed the children are always visited when they have been absent, to inquire the cause of that absence; and when ill, they are stately visited from a society, called "The Sick Children's Friend Society," and some trifling relief afforded to the parents, from a fund raised chiefly by the teachers, but not entirely.

What opinions have the parents expressed of the general conduct of their children, in the late visits you have paid?—The parents have, without any exception, appeared strongly impressed with a persuasion of the advantages of the school, and of the good it had been the means of effecting on the conduct and minds of their children. I would beg here to state, that the school to which I more particularly allude, being in the neighbourhood of the two principal theatres, the state of society in the courts and alleys all round that neighbourhood, where the children chiefly live, is certainly very profligate and corrupt, and this we found most of the parents were fully aware of; they considered, and stated indeed, great numbers of them, that they considered the Sunday school as the best preservative of their children from the surrounding infection; that keeping them as much as they could from the streets, and sending them to the Sunday school, appeared to be the two circumstances on which their chief hopes were founded.

Are there a great number of persons of bad character living in that neighbourhood?—Certainly; it is impossible to pass through the streets in that neighbourhood without discovering that; I allude to the courts about Drury-lane.

What do you conceive would be the best means of extending the benefits of education among the lower classes of society in London?—The formation and support of new schools where they are wanted.

Do you find that children in Sunday schools make greater proficiency than in day schools?—We have been repeatedly told, both by the parents and friends, that the children learn more on the one day, Sunday, and make a greater progress, than on all the other days in the week.

What time does it take to teach a child in a Sunday school to read; from its letters, to read the Bible; a child of six or seven years of age?—I am not prepared to speak precisely; I have not made an observation on the time.

Has it been the frequent remark of parents, that the children have made greater progress in Sunday than in day schools?—It has been, certainly.

Do you use the new system?—We have a monitor in every class, but they are closely dependent on the teacher; it is an essential part of our plan, to give moral and religious instruction to the children individually as well as collectively, and of course the monitors alone could not do this.

How many teachers usually attend?—About seventy is the whole number, and about thirty attend at the same time; they change alternately.

Do you conceive that if school-rooms could be provided, and sufficient funds raised to defray the expenses of Sunday schools, that gratuitous teachers could be found in sufficient numbers to carry on the instruction of children on a larger scale?—I feel certain there would, from the great zeal and interest every where felt, among young persons of well-regulated minds, for the good of the rising generation of poor children; and it would, in my opinion, be a great public benefit to bring into this employment a greater number of such persons; in general, they could not of course bestow their labour on any other day.

Does any other information occur to you upon this subject?—I can add, it is a fact of universal observation, that in the course of even a few weeks after the
admission

Mr.
*John Daughtrey.*

admission of children to a Sunday school, there is often a visible improvement in their appearance; their persons are cleaner, they are dressed in a more tidy decent manner. Trivial as this circumstance may appear, it has a salutary influence both on the individual children themselves, and upon the families to which they belong. This improvement in the dress and appearance of newly admitted children results chiefly, I have no doubt, from their observation upon others and the force of example; they see all their fellow scholars in their Sunday clothes at least clean and tidy, and they naturally become anxious to resemble them. A school in which the children meet only on week days, and where they are expected to appear in their working clothes, and are generally dirty, presents of course no such stimulus; nor indeed do those charity schools in which they have clothing provided for them; the uniform in which such children appear is supplied from the time of their admission, without the exertion of even a wish on the part of the children, and, not being a common dress, can be no object of imitation in other children of the families. I have also made an observation, accounting, I think, for the greater improvement which children sometimes make in Sunday schools, namely, that the anxiety which the teachers feel in the good of the children, leads them to devise plans and modes to awaken and keep up the attention of the children, which interests them, and attaches them to the school.

Would not the same advantages apply to a day school under the direction of an active committee?—Certainly I apprehend they would, or in some measure.

Have you visited many hundred families in Spitalfields?—Many hundred.

How long have you been in the habit of visiting the poor in Spitalfields?—I have been in the constant habit of visiting the poor in Spitalfields about five years.

Have you any further observations to make on the effect of the observance of the Sabbath on those families?—With regard to children, I have observed that a regular attendance on public worship, and a due observance of the Sabbath, when it once becomes habitual, forms perhaps the strongest restraint from evil with which a young person can be surrounded; it is the best outward defence of all virtuous conduct, and is broken through with the greatest difficulty. It is no doubt owing to this, that many of those who suffer for their crimes, speak of the open violation of the Lord's day as the first bold step in their iniquitous course; they felt, that when those restraints were completely thrown off, they were abandoned to their own evil propensities. From the closest and most unprejudiced attention I have been able to pay to the condition of the poor, I must also beg to state, that no means will in my opinion produce any radical improvement in the morals of the poor, upon a general scale, which do not prominently include the religious observance of the Sabbath. I may also be permitted to add, that being acquainted with a considerable number of intelligent persons who are in the constant habit of visiting the poor, and who have various modes of thinking on other subjects, they all agree in this, That ignorance and the profanation of the Sabbath lie at the root of the prevailing immorality of the lower classes.

Are you acquainted with any society where any considerable number of persons are employed in visiting the poor?—The Spitalfields Benevolent Society, of which I am a steward, has between thirty and forty regular visitors of the poor.

Is this their general opinion?—This is certainly the opinion of the whole of those persons.

Are you acquainted with visitors of the Stranger's Friend Society?—I know many of them.

How many are employed in that society, do you imagine?—Between three and four hundred.

Have you ever been present at any meeting of the visitors of that society?—I was present at a meeting of the visitors a few days ago; their annual meeting.

Do you understand that the opinion you have delivered, with respect to the observance of the Sabbath, is the same with that which is entertained by the generality of those visitors?—Having heard many of them express their sentiments upon that and other occasions, I think I can state that it is the uniform opinion of those laborious and exemplary persons. I am not a member of that excellent institution any further than as a subscriber, but I have had an opportunity of knowing the qualifications of its visitors, and the way in which they discharge the duties of their office; and I am sure that 350 such persons, continually in action among the lower orders, relieving the distressed, and giving instruction and advice to the ignorant and immoral, must be a real blessing to society.

How

How long have those persons been in the habit of visiting the poor?—Many of them for twelve or fourteen years.

Is it their regular and constant practice to visit the poor?—I believe they never pass a week without doing so, if in health.

How many families do they visit in the course of the week?—Sometimes eight or ten. But with regard to the Spitalfields Society, I may just observe, that on account of the great distress there, some of the visitors have had of late not fewer than forty or fifty cases each. Those of us who are engaged in business attend to them in an evening, or in the intervals of worship on Sundays.

What effect has been produced upon the minds of the poor, by being visited by those benevolent institutions?—I think a most salutary effect.

Have you any reason to believe that in the present distress which prevails in Spitalfields, the poor have submitted to their circumstances in quietness, in consequence of the benevolent aid of those societies?—That is I believe not only the opinion of the visitors of the poor there, but also of the very best informed persons, manufacturers and others, who have long resided in Spitalfields, and are well acquainted with the temper of that immense mass of poor. These gentlemen, I know, ascribe their present peaceable temper to the moral influence which has been diffused among them by means of Sunday and other schools, visiting societies, &c., and to the relief which the benevolent public have afforded them under their various distresses.

Do you belong to the Soup Society in Spitalfields?—Yes, I am a member of the committee.

What are the boundaries of the Stranger's Friend Society?—The Stranger's Friend Society has, I believe, no limit; it extends throughout the whole of the Metropolis.

How is it managed?—By a general committee and sub-committees, who meet weekly in their different districts.

You have stated, that the best effects have resulted from the efforts of the Spitalfields Benevolent Society; what is the general condition of the poor in Spitalfields, at present?—They are still in a most destitute condition.

Can you form any idea of the number of persons out of employment at this time?—I should think at least 5,000 weavers, besides the numerous dependents on their looms; as dyers, warpers, windsters, &c. Persons out of employ, of other trades, are numerous, but it is much more difficult to ascertain how many.

What should you conceive to be the whole number of labouring poor in that district?—I have heard the whole population exceeds 100,000, I mean the population of the district usually called Spitalfields, which comprehends the parish of Christ Church Spitalfields, St. Matthew Bethnal-green, Mile-End New Town, and part of Shoreditch.

In your estimate do you include women and children?—Yes.

Under the present distress in Spitalfields, there has been no disturbance?—Not the least tendency or movement towards it.

Have you heard that Spitalfields was formerly much disturbed in times of general distress?—I have understood that in some former times of distress there, it was not without considerable difficulty they were kept quiet; indeed, from the immense assemblage of poor in that quarter, so little intermixed as they are by persons of the superior classes of society, this would in all probability be the case at the present moment, did not the causes which have been mentioned happily correct and counteract such a tendency.

Have you reason to believe, from the increased benevolence of the respectable part of society towards the poor in Spitalfields, and the increased means of instruction afforded to the children of the poor, such disturbances have been prevented?—There can be no doubt that these causes have silently but powerfully operated to prevent them.

Do you think there are fewer poor, in consequence of the establishments for education?—The state of trade in that district at the present time necessarily reduces great numbers to extreme poverty, whatever their characters may be.

Otherwise the means of instruction would better their condition?—Unquestionably.

You consider that their actual condition is bettered by the education they receive?—Certainly.

That they are more industrious and frugal in consequence?—Certainly.

Are the five thousand weavers whom you state to be wholly out of employ in Spitalfields, relieved by the parish?—The parish of Christ Church relieves all

proper

proper applicants; we have not found that so generally to be the case in some of the other parishes. When the poor apply for relief, they too often insist upon their coming into the workhouse, to which the decent part of them feel a very material and just repugnance, and they consequently struggle on without relief. It must however be admitted, that the parishes are overburthened with applicants.

Do you conceive there has been an increase since the year 1811?—There has been a considerable return from the Army and Navy lately, but not in such numbers as to make a striking difference. As I have so strongly insisted upon the importance of the due observance of the Sabbath, as tending to improve the moral and temporal condition of the poor, I would beg to observe, in order to obviate an objection which may be made, that it is imagined by some persons, that the poor, being confined to labour during the week, absolutely require such recreation in the air as is compatible with the strict duties of the Sabbath, by walking in the country, and such like, on the Sundays. The time, however, which ought to be spent in attendance upon divine worship, is not devoted by the idle and profligate, as some may suppose, to an innocent walk out in the suburbs of the town, but more frequently in lounging in their filth, and drinking either at home or in the public houses; this we know, from repeated and frequent visits, is the real state of the case, with regard to a large proportion of the poor that neglect the Sabbath. If they do leave town, it is generally to join some disorderly assemblage called together about dogs or birds, a fight or a race; these things, as may be supposed, often end in quarrelling and drunkenness; and instead of being refreshed and rested by the proper use of the merciful institution of the Sabbath, their health and comfort suffer; they rise on the Monday morning languid in their bodies, and, if not too insensible, with remorse in their minds; they are often unable, and always indisposed for labour after a Sunday so spent; and this I apprehend to be the reason why, among persons of this description, Monday is also a day of idleness and dissipation. We find among those poor people who are in the regular habit of frequenting public worship, and properly observing the Sabbath day, they do not, as the others do, make Monday a day of idleness, and a lost day to their families.

These observations you mean to apply to the lower classes of the poor in Spitalfields?—I do.

Do you imagine that Sunday schools are inconsistent with such recreation as it is necessary for the poor to have on the Sunday?—By no means.

Do you think that recreation for the poor, by taking a walk on the Sunday after attendance on divine worship, is a good practice, or not?—I certainly think that poor persons may take such walks to recreate themselves, very innocently, provided they do not interfere with the proper duties of the day; but I hesitate to say that it is a good practice, because I know very few who do take them innocently, who are not led into temptation by such means, and into bad company; they too often call at public-houses, and end the day in a way which they probably did not design when they began it.

Do you think it practicable in the vicinity of Spitalfields, for poor people to take walks on the Sunday without being exposed to the danger of being led into scenes of dissipation?—I think it impracticable.

Have you not found that the condition of the orderly and well-regulated poor is much improved, by the rest and refreshment of the Sabbath, and the walks that they take to and from places of worship?—Undoubtedly it is the case.

Are not their health and spirits much recruited by the rest and comfort of the Sabbath?—They are; when properly used, the Sabbath is a day both of bodily and mental rest, it is an occasion for calling off their attention from the trials and perplexities of this life to the hopes and prospects of a better.

Mr. *Frederick Augustus Earle*, again called in, and Examined.

YOU are clerk to Mr. Parton, the vestry clerk of St. Giles's Bloomsbury?—I am. Is there a new school building there at this time?—There is.

When was it begun?—In the month of March; the old premises were pulling down at that time.

What is the nature of that school?—It is by the will of Mr. Shelton, in 1672. He left certain houses in Parker's-lane, to trustees, who out of the rents were to lay out, for buying on Michaelmas day twenty gowns for twenty poor men and women of St. Giles's, 15*l*. that was estimated at, and ten gowns for St. Martin's, 7*l*. 10*s*. and five for Covent Garden, 3*l*. 15*s*.; then to provide a schoolmaster to teach fifty

children

children of the poorest sort, thirty-five of St. Giles, ten of St. Martin, and five of Covent Garden, and to pay the said master 20 l. a year; they were likewise to provide the master with a gown once a year, which was estimated at 1 l. ; to provide a coat yearly for each of the scholars, 15 l.; to lay in two chaldron of coals annually (that sum is not estimated ;) to pay the devisor's heir-at-law 10 l. ; and to apply the surplus in placing out some of the boys apprentices, which amounted to 72 l. 5 s. The premises at that time appear to have been let partly in tenements to poor people, at rents amounting to between 50 l. and 60 l. a year, and were afterwards let on building leases at 25 l. 10 s. per annum. The school was conducted till the year 1763, when, it being greatly indebted to the parish, and the income reduced to 25 l. 10 s. it was discontinued; the rents from that time have been laid out in the Funds, to accumulate under the direction of the vestry, and the account has been annually audited. The old premises are now let from Lady-day last at 48 l. a year, and the consols now standing in the trustees names, with the accumulation, amount to 7,212 l. 8 s. 9 d. It is considered when this school is built, it will be able to be conducted agreeably to the testator's intentions.

What will be the expense of the erection of the school-house?—The expense of the new erection will be 814 l.

How many children will it accommodate?—Fifty.

How many rooms will there be?—I think only one large school-room, and a room for the master, which is to be his residence.

Is that building on leasehold or freehold ground?—On leasehold.

For what term?—Sixty-one years.

At what rent?—A rent of 40 l.; but the school-room is upon the first floor, and the lower part is merely a gateway, in which there is to be a large yard, in which it is in contemplation to have a stone-yard for the parish; one is now rented at 30 l. a year, so that there will be a ground-rent only of 10 l. a year.

Who are the trustees?—It is in the vestry; the trustees named under the will, were the minister and churchwardens, but the vestry have the management of this.

Of whom do the vestry consist?—They consist of seventy-eight gentlemen, with the churchwardens.

Who are the leading men among them, who take a part in the management of this business?—There are a great many of them; the Lord Chancellor is on the vestry, but he never attends; Mr. Becket of Gower-street attends, Mr. Richard Parkes of Broad-street, Mr. Charles Stable of High-street, Mr. Peter Ludgate of Holborn, Mr. John Waddell of High-street, and others.

Who is the builder of the new school?—Bedall & Hanse, of Holborn; it is under the direction of Mr. Edward Morley, of Thornhaugh-street, who is the surveyor.

Are either Mr. Morley, or Bedall & Hanse, members of the vestry?—No, quite unconnected with the vestry.

The building is done by contract?—It is, and the lowest price taken.

Do you conceive that you are limited in the number of boys you should receive into that school?—It is considered so; and it is a question whether the funds would provide for more, in the way that it is the testator's intention they should be provided for.

How are the expenses of this new building to be discharged?—From the funded property. It was thought that when the original lease of the old school-house was out, it would be about the proper time to re-commence the school.

### Mr. *Edmund Ludlow*, called in, and Examined.

HAVE you made a survey of the parish of Saint Saviour Southwark?—I have made a survey of part of it lately, with a view to the building of another school for such children as may want instruction.

What is the result of your observation upon that survey?—The district that I surveyed with Mr. Fell, is about a quarter of the parish; there were upwards of 400 children in that part of it, without the means of instruction.

Was there any indisposition in the parents to give them instruction?—They seemed all very desirous of doing it, but they were too poor to afford it.

How many do you estimate in the whole parish, to be without the means of instruction?—I have not seen the return yet.

Is it the poorer part of the parish which you visited?—It is. There are several schools in the parish, established schools.

Are there any foundations?—There is a grammar school founded by Queen Elizabeth.

Is

Is that by charter?—Yes.

How is it endowed?—By houses; I believe it is under five trustees.

How are the trustees chosen?—They are nominated by the survivors, and chosen by twelve inhabitants, who meet and generally choose the person that the four surviving trustees name.

What is the present revenue of that school?—I think it is about 380 l. a year, but I am not quite certain; it is not kept up at all.

How many children are educated there?—I believe at present not above 25.

What is the general number?—It is capable of holding about 100.

Why are there so few?—It is a grammar school, and the poorer classes do not see the advantage of learning Greek and Latin.

What is the master's salary?—I cannot exactly say.

Do you know the yearly expense of the school?—I believe the present expense is about 200 l. a year; they have been purchasing about 300 l. stock within the last three or four years.

What are the boys taught?—Greek and Latin under the charter of Queen Elizabeth, and since they have added writing and arithmetic.

Are there any other funds, besides those left by Queen Elizabeth?—30 l. a year, paid by the parish.

Who appoints the schoolmaster?—The five trustees appoint.

Is there any assistant schoolmaster?—A writing master.

Has the master a house?—Yes.

You do not know his salary?—I think the salary is about 60 l. now; but it is intended to increase his salary, and that of the writing master, and to try to make the school more beneficial.

What does the rest of the money go to?—It has been laid by to accumulate for the repair of the school; it is a large ancient school.

Were there ever any more scholars than 25?—Formerly, I believe, there used to be a great many, but of late years there have not been so many.

Are they boarded, or only taught?—Only taught.

Not lodged or clothed?—No.

Of what classes in society are the children?—All classes have a right to go there.

Does the charter oblige the master to teach Latin and Greek?—Yes.

What other schools are there in your parish?—There is a school for 80 boys, and another for 50 girls, where they are clothed and instructed.

Is that by foundation or subscription?—It is partly subscription and partly arising from the will of Mr. Newcomen, and other persons.

Do you know what the yearly income of that is?—It is estimated that the children cost about 3 l. each for clothing and instruction; so that it would be about 400 l. a year.

Does the school expend its whole income?—Nearly the greater part of the income arises from voluntary contribution.

Are they obliged by their charter to clothe the children?—There is no charter. There is also a school upon the new plan in Redcross-street, which has been established about two years.

For how many?—About 120.

Would it accommodate more?—No, it is about full. It is in consequence of this school being so small, that some gentlemen have lately been going round to see how many wanted instruction, with a view to the erection of a new school. The girls school is not on the new plan; a mistress and her niece attend it. There are no other schools in that parish, but a great many of the children in that parish go to the school in the Borough Road.

Have you any other observations to make, as to the result of your observation?—On going round, we found that whenever the children were instructed, the houses were always more clean, and the families more comfortable; as soon as we opened a door we could tell whether the children were instructed, by seeing whether they were decent, and from their ready and obliging manner in giving an answer. There was no instance where the parents did not seem very desirous of having their children instructed. From what we have already ascertained, there are more than 1500 children in the whole parish, who are not instructed; that bears a very large proportion to those who are instructed.

What proportion do you consider it as bearing?—There are not, in Sunday schools and all, above 500 instructed at present in that parish.

Does that include those who go to the Borough Road?—No.

*William Thomas Woodham*, Schoolmaster at the Foundling Hospital; and *Michael Barrett*, Treasurer's Clerk at the Foundling Hospital;

Called in, and Examined.

*(To Mr. Woodham.)* HOW many children are taught in the schools at the Foundling Hospital?—One hundred and ninety-five, boys and girls; there are not more at present.

Does that include all the foundlings belonging to the hospital, who are at years capable of being taught?—Yes.

When are they dismissed from the Foundling?—At the age of fourteen.

*(To Mr. Barrett.)* How many other children are there in the Foundling at this time?—All the children who are younger are in the country, under two inspectors; the one in the Surrey district, and the other in the Kent district.

Are they in houses belonging to the establishment?—No; the neighbouring people take them to nurse.

*(To Mr. Woodham.)* Is the new plan of education adopted in the school?—It is.

How long has it been adopted?—About six years, I believe.

*(To Mr. Barrett.)* How many children are there altogether in the country?—There are about 180 boys and girls.

How many in the house altogether?—About 195.

There are about 370 in all?—Yes.

Are there any other expenses belonging to the Foundling, except the maintenance and education of those children?—I believe not.

Are the accounts printed yearly, for the use of the proprietors?—They are.

Have you got the last balance sheet with you?

[It was delivered in, and read, as follows :]

State of the CASH ACCOUNT of the FOUNDLING HOSPITAL; from December 31st, 1814, to December 31st, 1815.

| RECEIPTS: | £. | s. | d. | £. | s. | d. |
|---|---|---|---|---|---|---|
| BALANCE in the hands of the Treasurer on the 31st December 1814 | - | - | - | 321 | 18 | 7 |
| Dividends; viz. | | | | | | |
| 3-per-Cent. Consols, £. 27,144  5 — Jan. Dividend, including Property Tax, £. 407  3  3 | | | | | | |
| — — — July - dº 407  3  3 | 814 | 6 | 6 | | | |
| New South Sea Ann. 34,000 — — Janʸ - dº 510 — — | | | | | | |
| — — — July - dº 510 — — | 1,020 | — | — | | | |
| 3-per-Cents. Reduced, 33,648  7  11 April - dº 504 14  6 | | | | | | |
| — — — October dº 504 14  6 | 1,009 | 9 | — | | | |
| Bank Stock - - - 1,000 — — April - dº 50 — — | | | | | | |
| — — — October dº 50 — — | 100 | — | — | | | |
| Since sold { 4-per-Cents. 337 10 — April - dº - - - | 6 | 15 | — | | | |
| Long Ann. - 2 10 — Mids. - dº - - - | 1 | 2 | 6 | | | |
| | 2,951 | 13 | — | | | |
| Produce of the Chapel, including Pew Rents, &c. - - - | 2,902 | 15 | — | | | |
| Rents - - - - - - - - - - | 4,672 | 1 | 6 | | | |
| Property Tax, on account of the Rental - - - | 253 | 2 | 5 | | | |
| Received by the Childrens Work - - - - | 77 | 8 | 9 | | | |
| Ditto - by Annual Subscriptions - - - | 17 | 17 | — | | | |
| Ditto - by Sale of miscellaneous Articles - - - | 14 | 18 | 5 | 10,889 | 16 | |
| GENERAL BENEFACTIONS: | | | | | | |
| Benefaction of James Baillie, Esq. - - - - | 52 | 10 | — | | | |
| Ditto - of the Committee of the Stock Exchange, as " being part of the Money detained from Lord Cochrane, the Hon. A. C. Johnstone, and Mr. R. G. Butt, on account of a Fraud committed on the 21st February 1814" - - - - | 100 | — | — | | | |
| Ditto - of John Ranicar Park, M. B. - - - | 50 | — | — | | | |
| Ditto - of Stephen Gaselee, Esq. - - - - | 50 | — | — | | | |
| Ditto - of Donald McLean, Esq. - - - - | 52 | 10 | — | | | |
| Ditto - of James Dunlop, Esq. - - - - | 52 | 10 | — | | | |
| Ditto - of a Gentleman unknown, by William Curtis, Esq. | 20 | — | — | | | |
| Ditto - of Henry Collingwood Selby, Esq. - - | 50 | — | — | | | |
| Ditto - of W. V. - - - - - - - | 5 | — | — | | | |
| Unknown - - - - - - - | 30 | — | — | | | |
| Cash found in the Boxes - - - - - | — | 16 | — | 463 | 6 | — |

(continued.)

State of the Cash Account of the Foundling Hospital—*continued.*

| | £ | s. | d. | £ | s. | d. |
|---|---|---|---|---|---|---|
| **LEGACIES:** | | | | | | |
| Legacy of Samuel Gist, Esq. - - - - - - | 90 | — | — | | | |
| Ditto - of Mrs. Letitia Pitts - - - - - - | 90 | — | — | | | |
| | | | | 180 | — | — |
| **Improvement of the Hospital Estate:** | | | | | | |
| Sold £. 337. 10. — - 4-per-Cents. - - - - | 274 | 7 | 3 | | | |
| 1,614. 12. 9. - 3-per-Cents. Consolidated Annuities - | 1,000 | — | — | | | |
| | | | | 1,274 | 7 | 3 |
| **MECKLENBURGH SQUARE:** | | | | | | |
| To Rent of Keys of Admission into the Square - - - | - | - | - | 87 | 3 | — |
| Balance due to the Treasurer on the 31st December 1815 - - | - | - | - | 30 | 11 | : |
| | | | £. | 13,247 | 2 | — |

| | £ | s. | d. | £ | s. | d. |
|---|---|---|---|---|---|---|
| **PAYMENTS:** | | | | | | |
| Butcher - - - - - - - - - - | 1,256 | 19 | 2 | | | |
| Baker - - - - - - - - - - | 666 | 10 | 9 | | | |
| Butter and Cheese - - - - - - - - | 442 | 12 | 3 | | | |
| Beer - - - - - - - - - - | 186 | 13 | 6 | | | |
| Coals - - - - - - - - - - | 295 | 8 | — | | | |
| Candles and Oil - - - - - - - - - | 109 | 11 | 4 | | | |
| Salaries - - - - - - - - - - | 652 | 17 | — | | | |
| Milk - - - - - - - - - - | 459 | 12 | 9 | | | |
| Miscellaneous - - - - - - - - - | 164 | 4 | 4 | | | |
| Stationary and Printing - - - - - - - | 92 | 5 | 4 | | | |
| Potatoes - - - - - - - - - - | 37 | 13 | 9 | | | |
| Garden Expenses - - - - - - - - - | 206 | 9 | 3 | | | |
| Grocery and Corn Chandlery - - - - - - | 227 | 8 | — | | | |
| Medicines and other Infirmary Expenses - - - | 133 | 8 | 4 | | | |
| Furniture - - - - - - - - - | 324 | 18 | 6 | | | |
| Education - - - - - - - - - | 149 | 15 | 2 | | | |
| Laundry - - - - - - - - - - | 137 | 12 | 2 | | | |
| | | | | 5,543 | 19 | 7 |
| Clothing, and House Linen - - - - - - | - | - | - | 1,375 | 19 | 1 |
| Repairs - - - - - - - - - - | - | - | - | 1,860 | 2 | 9 |
| Taxes - - - - - - - - - - | - | - | - | 223 | 4 | 11 |
| **Maintenance of ADULTS and CHILDREN out of the Hospital:** | | | | | | |
| For Children under Mr. Livings' Inspection - - - | 1,068 | — | — | | | |
| Ditto - - - Mr. Vine's - Ditto - - - - | 829 | 2 | 2 | | | |
| Adults with several Persons, and for Invalids at the General Sea-bathing Infirmary, Margate - - - - - - | 126 | 6 | 2 | | | |
| | | | | 2,023 | 8 | 4 |
| **CHAPEL EXPENSES, included under the following Heads:** | | | | | | |
| Salaries of the Rev. the Preachers and Readers - - - | 357 | — | — | | | |
| Ditto of the Organist, Attendants, and Singers - - - | 145 | 8 | — | | | |
| Sundry Expenses - - - - - - - - - | 189 | 6 | 3 | | | |
| | | | | 691 | 14 | 3 |
| **Improvement of the Hospital Estate:** | | | | | | |
| Paid for Boundary Wall to the Estate - - - - | 388 | 15 | 4 | | | |
| - - for Iron Gates to Porter's Lodge - - - - | 49 | 9 | 6 | | | |
| - - for Sewers - - - - - - - - | 25 | — | — | | | |
| - - for Paving - - - - - - - - - | 136 | 8 | — | | | |
| Purchase of £. 301. 17. 9. 3-per-Cent. Reduced Annuities - | 180 | — | — | | | |
| Sundries - - - - - - - - - - | 8 | 8 | — | | | |
| | | | | 788 | — | 10 |
| **GENERAL CHARGES:** | | | | | | |
| Poundage on the Collection of Rents - - - - | 126 | 10 | 10 | | | |
| Insurance of Hospital Building - - - - - | 15 | — | — | | | |
| Contribution for Watching and Lighting the Eastern side of Mecklenburgh-square - - - - - - - | 26 | — | — | | | |
| Sundries - - - - - - - - - - | 72 | 6 | 6 | | | |
| | | | | 239 | 17 | 4 |
| Interest of Money on a temporary Loan made by the Treasurer - | - | - | - | 22 | — | — |
| **MECKLENBURGH SQUARE.** | | | | | | |
| Paid for one year's Wages to Gardener - - - - | 40 | — | — | | | |
| - - for Tool House in centre, &c. - - - - - | 98 | 1 | 1 | | | |
| Sundries - - - - - - - - - | 38 | 10 | 7 | | | |
| | | | | 176 | 11 | 8 |
| PREMIUMS to those young Persons who served their Apprenticeship faithfully - - - - - - - - | - | - | - | 81 | 18 | — |
| Premiums with Apprentices, and a Subscription to Mr. Oldknow, for Marple Chapel - - - - - - - - | - | - | - | 90 | 4 | — |
| Gratuities to Servants - - - - - - - | - | - | - | 130 | 1 | 3 |
| | | | £. | 13,247 | 2 | — |

March 19th, 1816.

*John Heath.*
*D. M{c}Lean.*

FOUNDLING HOSPITAL.

Children remaining alive, the 31st December 1814  -  352
Received in the year, to the 31st December 1815 -  -  58
                                            410

Have been Apprenticed, and sent to Sea, within the said
    year  - - - - - - - - -  26
Died  - - - - - - - - -  13
Children in the hospital in London, 31 December 1815 - 192
Children at Nurse in the Country  - - -  179
                                            410

*Note.*—Exclusive of the above number of Children, Sixteen Adult Individuals are wholly provided for by the Hospital.

---

Plain Needlework is done by the Girls in this Hospital, at the following Prices; viz.

|  |  | s. d. | s. d. |
|---|---|---|---|
| A full-trimmed Shirt or Shift | from | 2. o. to | 3. 6. |
| A plain ditto | | 1. 6. — | 2. 6. |
| Sheets, per pair | | 2. o. — | 3. 6. |
| Table-cloths | | 0. 9. — | 1. o. |
| Children's Frocks | | 2. o. — | 3. 6. |
| Napkins, per dozen | | 1. 6. — | 2. o. |
| Gravats, per dozen | | 3. o. — | 4. o. |

All other articles proportionably reasonable.
Further information may be had of the Matron of the hospital.

---

The age of reception is within twelve months from the birth. In order to the reception of the child, the previous good character and the present necessity of the mother, and the desertion of the father, must be inquired into; and also whether the reception of the child, together with the secrecy observed as to the misfortune of the mother, will be attended with the consequence of her being replaced in a course of virtue, and in the way of obtaining an honest livelihood. Where these circumstances can be ascertained on the testimony of credible persons, the unfortunate mother is requested to apply herself with her own petition, and be assured that both recommendation and patronage will be unnecessary and useless.

The general committe sits, for examination of petitions for admission of children, every Wednesday morning, precisely at ten o'clock.

---

What is the annual revenue of the Foundling Hospital?—About 10,000 *l*.

Whence does it arise?—From ground-rents and stock.

Does any part of it arise from subscriptions?—Very little now.

About how much, do you think?—About 45 *l.*; between 45 *l.* and 50 *l.* the annual subscriptions: there are very few other subscriptions; there may be 50 *l.* or 100 *l.* a year; formerly there was a great deal more.

When was that established?—In 1739; that was the date of the charter.

Is there a power of making bye-laws?—Yes.

Have there many changes been made lately in the regulations of the hospital?—No, I believe not.

*(To Mr. Woodham.)*—Do you know whether any alteration has been recently made in the terms of admission?—No, I do not.

*(To Mr. Barrett.)*—Do the expenses nearly cover the income?—Yes, fully.

Do the hospital pay any ground-rent?—No.

Are the leases granted by the hospital near expiring?—No, they have yet sixty years or upwards to run.

What may be the estimated income, when they draw in?—That I am quite unable to say.

Were they 99 years leases?—Yes.

In what does the expense of 10,000 *l.* a year chiefly consist?—That will appear by the cash account.

What is the salary of the secretary?—One hundred guineas.

Any house or perquisites?—No, except that he has sixpence in the pound for collecting the ground-rents.

What salary has the treasurer?—Nothing at all; he has a house to live in.

Has

Has he the use of the balances?—He has the money in his hands.

What is the balance generally in hand?—Not more than 300 *l.* or 400 *l.*

*(To Mr. Woodham.)*—What is the salary of the schoolmaster?—Sixty pounds. And a house?—I reside in the house.

*(To Mr. Barrett.)*—What is the salary of the matron?—Sixty pounds to the matron, and 20 guineas to the sub-matron

They both live in the hospital, of course?—Yes.

Is there any assistant schoolmaster?—No.

What other servants are there?—Treasurer's clerk, steward, and messenger.

What is the steward's salary?—Sixty guineas; he resides in the house.

What is the chaplain's salary?—Sixty pounds.

He does not live in the house?—No, he does not.

What other salaries are there?—The preacher and reader.

How much are they?—The morning preacher has 120 guineas, and the evening reader has 40 *l.* and the alternate evening preachers 60 guineas each.

Have you a copy of the charter?—I have.

[It was delivered in, and read, as follows :]

The ROYAL CHARTER establishing an Hospital for the Maintenance and Education of Exposed and Deserted young Children.

GEORGE the Second, by the grace of God of Great Britain France and Ireland King, Defender of the Faith, &c. To all to whom these presents shall come, greeting :

WHEREAS Our trusty and well-beloved subject Thomas Coram gentleman, in behalf of great numbers of helpless infants daily exposed to destruction, has by his petition humbly represented unto Us, That many persons of quality and distinction, as well as others of both sexes (being sensible of the frequent murders committed on poor miserable infants by their parents, to hide their shame, and the inhuman custom of exposing new-born children to perish in the streets, or training them up in idleness beggary and theft) have by instruments in writing declared their intentions to contribute liberally towards erecting an hospital after the example of other Christian countries, and for supporting the same, for the reception maintenance and proper education of such helpless infants, as soon as We should be graciously pleased to grant our letters patent for that good purpose; That several legacies having been bequeathed for the same, to be paid by executors when any such hospital shall be properly established here ; The petition therefore hath humbly prayed us, that We would be graciously pleased to grant our royal charter for incorporating such persons as We shall think fit, for receiving and disposing of charities for erecting and supporting an hospital for the reception maintenance and proper education of such cast-off children or foundlings as may be brought to it, under such rules and regulations as to us may seem meet :

We taking the premises into our royal consideration, and being desirous to promote so good and laudable an establishment, are graciously pleased to gratify the petitioner in his request.

Know ye therefore, that We of our especial grace certain knowledge and mere motion, have willed ordained constituted and appointed, and by these presents for us our heirs and successors do will ordain constitute declare and grant, That our right trusty and right entirely beloved cousins Charles duke of Richmond, Charles duke of Grafton, Henry duke of Beaufort, John duke of Bedford, William duke of Devonshire, Charles duke of Marlborough, John duke of Rutland, John duke of Montagu, Henry duke of Kent, James duke of Hamilton and Brandon, Thomas Holles duke of Newcastle, William duke of Portland, John duke of Argyle and Greenwich, William duke of Manchester, James duke of Chandos, Lionel Cranfield duke of Dorset, and John duke of Roxburgh; our right trusty and right well beloved cousins Edward earl of Derby, Theophilus earl of Huntingdon, Henry earl of Pembroke, James earl of Salisbury, James earl of Northampton, Edward earl of Warwick and Holland, Daniel earl of Winchelsea and Nottingham, Philip earl of Chesterfield, William earl of Essex, George earl of Cardigan, Richard earl of Burlington, George Henry earl of Litchfield, Augustus earl of Berkeley, Richard earl of Scarborough, William Anne earl of Albemarle, William earl of Jersey, Henry earl of Grantham, Francis earl of Godolphin, George earl of Cholmondeley, James earl of Abercorn, James earl of Findlater, Charles earl of Portmore, Archibald earl of Hay, Edward earl of Oxford, and Mortimer Philip earl of Stanhope, James earl of Waldgrave, Benjamin earl of Fitzwalter, Spencer earl of Welmington, and Thomas earl of Malton ; our right trusty and our well beloved cousins Henry viscount Lonsdale, John viscount Lymington, Pattel viscount Torrington, Henry viscount Palmerston, John viscount Tyrconnel, and Charles viscount Dillon ; our right trusty and well beloved William lord Abergavenny, Algernon lord Percy, John lord Delaware, William Ferdinand lord Hunsdon, William lord Byron, William lord Craven, John lord Carteret, Charles lord Butler of Weston earl of Arran, John lord Gower, John lord Hervey, Charles lord Cathcart, Thomas lord Foley, Allen lord Bathurst, Robert lord Walpole, John lord Monson, Thomas lord Lovell, William lord Harrington,

Philip

Philip lord Hardwicke, William lord Talbot, and William lord Sundon; the lords and others of our privy council, now and for the time being; our right trusty and well-beloved councellors Henry Pelham esquire, sir William Lee knight, chief justice of our court of king's bench, John Verney esquire, master of our rolls, sir John Willes knight, chief justice of our court of common pleas, sir John Comyns knight, chief baron of our court of exchequer, Arthur Onslow esquire, speaker of our house of commons, and Stephen Poyntz esquire; our trusty and well beloved sir Thomas Hanmer, sir Erasmus Philips, sir Nathaniel Curzon, sir James Lowther, sir Michael Newton knight of the bath, sir Humphrey Monnoux, sir George Fettiplace, sir William Morrice, sir Philip Parker Long, sir William Wyndham, sir Miles Stapylton, sir James Dashwood, sir William Williams, sir John Stanley, sir William Courtenay, sir George Page, sir Hans Sloane, sir Abraham Elton, sir Rowland Hill, and sir Edward Hulse, baronets; our right trusty and well beloved councellors sir Paul Methuen knight of the order of the bath, and sir Charles Wager knight; our trusty and our well beloved sir John Barnard, sir Robert Baylis, sir George Champion, sir Francis Child, sir Joseph Eyles, sir Joseph Hankey, sir John Lequesne and sir William Rous, knights and aldermen of our city of London; sir Conrad Springhall, sir Roger Hudson, sir William Joliffe, sir William Perkins, sir Chaloner Ogle, and sir John Gonson, knights; our trusty and well beloved Benjamin Avery, doctor of law; our trusty and well beloved Richard Mead, Thomas Crow, Caleb Cotesworth, Benjamin Hoadley, Matthew Lee, Joseph Letherland, Edward Willmott, Robert Nesbitt, Abraham Hall, and John Bamber, doctors of physick; our trusty and well beloved Dudley Ryder, esquire, our attorney general; our trusty and well beloved John Strange esquire, our solicitor general; our trusty and well beloved Micajah Perry esquire, lord mayor of our city of London; our trusty and well beloved Vere Beauclerk esquire, commonly called lord Vere Beauclerk; our trusty and well beloved Thomas Pelham, Robert Trevor, George Doddington, Anthony Allen, Thomas Archer, Edward Ash, John Bance, Joseph Banks, Walter Baynes, Jonathan Belcher, George Berkeley, Stephen Bisse, Martin Bladen, Nathaniel Brassey, Stamp Brooksbank, James Brudenell, Peter Burrel, Alexander Hume Campbell, Delillers Carbenell, Thomas Cartwright of Northamptonshire, Walter Cary, Samuel Clerk, John Codrington, William Conolly, Thomas Cook, James Cook, James Cornwall, John Cotten, William Cooper, Charles Cutts, Peter Delme, Benjamin Devink, Edward Digby, John Dodd, Richard Edgecombe, James Fall, William Fawkner, Joseph Fawthorpe, Samuel Feak, Martin Folkes, William Gore, Henry Gough, John Hampden, Charles Hanbury Williams, Edward Harley, William Hart, Herring Hart, Peter Hartopp, Jacob Harvey, John Hetherington, John Hill, William Hogarth, Samuel Holden, Richard Hollings, John Hollister, Philip Honywood, Thomas Horner, Jacob Houblon, Richard Howard, Thomas Hucks, Archibald Hutcheson, Alexander Hume, Stephen Theodore Jansen, Edward Jasper, Thomas Inwen, Paul Jodderell, Peter King, Matthias King, James Lambe, Thomas Lane, Charles Leigh, John Legg, Samuel Lessingham, Thomas Lewis, William Lock, Henry Marshall alderman of our city of London, Sidney Meadows, Peter Meyer, Owen Meyrick, and John Milner, esquires; Colonel John Mordaunt, Benjamin Moyer, Henry Muilman, Henry Neal, Robert Nettleton, Henry Newman, Thomas Newnham, Robert Norman, Nathaniel Price, Thomas Pearse, Walter Plummer, Henry William Portman, George Proctor, George Purvis, Moses Raper, John Rawlenson, Jones Raymond, John Raymond, John Read, Thomas Revel, Richard Richards, and Henry Rolle, esquires; Captain William Mabbott, Henry Rowe, Joseph Russell, John Sawbridge, Thomas Scawen, Augustus Schutz, John Schutz, William Sharp, William Sloane, Edward Southwell, John Spencer, Stacey Spencer, Temple Stanyan, Edward Stephenson, Arthur Stert, Alexander Stewart, William Stewart, John Talbot, James Theobalds, Peter Theobalds, Joseph Thompson, Robert Thornton, William Tillard, Robert Tothill, and Edward Town, esquires; Captain Robert Hudson, Horatio Townsend, Gerrard Van Neck, James Vernon, Samuel Underhill, George Wade, Anthony Walburge, Edward Walpole, John Walton, Thomas Watts, Lewis Way, Thomas Weddall, Taylor White, Francis Wilks, Watkin Williams Winne, Adam Williamson, William Woolaston, Josias Wordsworth, John Woowen, Matthew Wymondesold, John Yeamans, William Young, and Joseph Wyndham Ash, esquires; our trusty and well-beloved Robert Atkins, George Arnold, David Barclay, Osmond Bevour, Thomas Beckford, Samuel Bosanquet, David Bosanquet, William Braund, John Barnaby, William Coleman, Samuel Craghead, Richard Dawson, Conrad Desmeth, Edward Dodd, James Douglas, Roger Drake, William Dunster, Christopher Emmott, John Furley, John Gascoyne, Peter Gamon, Richard Glover, Peter Stephen Godin, John Gore, William Gosselin, John Hambury, John Hayward, William Hunt, Edward Hunt, Theodore Jacobson, John Lister, James Lock, Joshua Lock, Baltzer Lyell, Benjamin Lythieullier, Gilbert Malcher, Henry March, Isaac Milner, John Mucklow, Abert Nesbitt, Nathaniel Newnham the younger, Richard Partridge, John Phillips, William Rawstone, John Rudge, Charles Savage, Peter Simond, Samuel Skinner, William Snelling, John South, Henry Sperling, Thomas Thomas, Samuel Travers, Samuel Trench, and Mark Wayland, merchants; John Waple and William Watts, gentlemen; Andrew Drummond, Benjamin Hoar, James Martin, and Thomas Snow, bankers; Richard Buckley brewer, Peter Collinson mercer; William Cheselden, Peter Saint Hill, William Petty, John Belchier, and John Winchester, surgeons; William Maunt stationer, Sylvanus Bevan druggist, John Knapton bookseller; and the said Thomas Coram the petitioner; and others, as shall from time to time be elected in the manner hereinafter directed, they and their successors, be and shall for ever hereafter be, by virtue of these presents, one body politick

politick and corporate in deed and in name, by the name of The Governors and Guardians of the Hospital for the Maintenance and Education of Exposed and Deserted young Children, and them and their successors by the same name we do by these presents, for us, our heirs and successors, constitute and declare to be one body politick and corporate in deed and in law, and by the same name they and their successors shall and may have perpetual succession; and that they and their successors by that name shall and may for ever hereafter be persons able and capable in the law, and may have power, notwithstanding the statute of mortmain, to purchase have take receive and enjoy to them and their successors, manors messuages lands rents tenements annuities and hereditaments, of whatsoever nature or kind, in fee and perpetuity, or for terms of life or years, not exceeding the yearly value of four thousand pounds beyond reprizes, so far as they are not restrained by law, and all manner of goods chattels and things whatsoever, of what nature or value soever, for the better support and maintenance of such poor deserted children as shall be received into the said hospital in manner hereinafter mentioned; and also to sell grant demise exchange and dispose of any of the same manors messuages lands and tenements whereof and wherein they shall have any estate of inheritance, or for life lives or years as aforesaid; and that by the name aforesaid they shall and may be able to sue and be sued, plead and be impleaded, answer and be answered unto, defend and be defended, in all courts and pleas whatsoever of us our heirs and successors, in all actions plaints matters and demands whatsoever, and to act and do in all matters and things relating to the said corporation in as ample manner and form as any other our liege subjects, being persons able and capable in the law, or any other body politick or corporate in this part of our kingdom of Great Britain called England, lawfully may or can act or do; and that the said corporation for ever hereafter shall and may have and use a common seal for the causes and businesses of them and their successors, and that it shall and may be lawful for them and their successors to change break alter and make new the said seal from time time as they shall think fit.

*Name of the Corporation.*

*Power to enjoy £.4,000 a year;*

*and Goods and Chattels.*

*To sue and be sued.*

*May have a common Seal.*

And for the better execution of the purposes aforesaid, We do declare and grant, That the said corporation and their successors for ever, shall have one president, six vice presidents, and one treasurer; and that John duke of Bedford be the first president; that the said Micajah Perry, the said lord Vere Beauclerk, the said Joseph Eyles, the said Martin Folkes, the said Peter Burrel, and the said James Cook, be the six first vice presidents; and that the said Lewis Way be the first treasurer of the said corporation; each of them respectively to continue in their several and respective offices of president vice-presidents and treasurer, until the second Wednesday in May one thousand seven hundred and forty, and until others shall be chosen in their respective rooms.

*One President, six Vice Presidents, and one Treasurer.*
*Names of the first in those offices;*
*to continue until the second Wednesday in May 1740.*

And our will and pleasure is, That the said president vice-presidents and treasurer, and the rest of the members of the said corporation, also above-named, or as many of them the said president vice-presidents and members as conveniently can, may, within forty days next after the date of this our grant, meet together at such time and place as the said president shall appoint by summons or other notice, which he is by these presents empowered and required timely to issue for that purpose to the said members, or such of them as live within the cities of London or Westminster or the borough of Southwark, or within two miles thereof, where they or the major part of them then present may chuse by ballot one or more secretaries, and such other inferior officers and servants as shall be thought convenient and useful for the purposes of the said corporation, and to serve in the said offices respectively until the second Wednesday in the month of May one thousand seven hundred and forty, and until others shall be elected in their respective rooms, unless they shall sooner die or be removed; and at such meetings one or more committee or committees shall be chosen out of the members of the said corporation, to consist of such number and persons as to the said general court shall seem proper, which committee or committees shall continue until the second Wednesday in the month of May in the said year one thousand seven hundred and forty, and shall have power to direct manage and transact all the business affairs estate and effects of the said corporation, and take in receive maintain and employ such poor deserted children, according to such rules and directions as shall be made and established from time to time by general courts; to which said general courts we do by these presents, for us our heirs and successors, give and grant full power and authority to make and establish such rules and directions, for the reception maintenance and employment of such poor deserted children, as they or the major part of them shall think meet fit and convenient from time to time; and for that purpose such committee or committees may erect or purchase such fitting place to be an hospital for the reception of such children.

*First Meeting within 40 days.*

*May chuse one or more Secretaries and other Officers and Servants, to serve until the second Wednesday in May 1740.*

*One or more Committee or Committees to be chosen, to continue until the second Wednesday in May 1740; have power to direct manage and transact and take in Children according to such Rules and Directions as shall be made by General Courts.*

*May erect or purchase a fitting place to be an Hospital.*

And our further will is, That on every second Wednesday in the month of May yearly there shall and may be a general meeting of the governors and guardians of the said corporation, in the said hospital, or some other convenient place until the said hospital be made ready to receive them, for the electing by ballot all succeeding presidents vice-presidents treasurers and committees, out of the members of the said corporation, by majority of votes of all the members then personally present, to continue in their respective offices until the second Wednesday in the said month of May following, and until others shall be chosen in their respective rooms; and that all succeeding secretaries and other inferior officers and servants be annually appointed, or oftener if needful, by the major part of the governors and guardians for the time being, then present at their general meeting, and in case of an equality of votes, the president, or in case of his death or absence, the vice-president first named in the list of vice-presidents then present, to have a double or casting vote, and at such salaries as they shall think reasonable.

*Every second Wednesday in May yearly, to be a General Meeting to elect by Ballot all succeeding Presidents, Vice-presidents, Treasurer and Committees, to continue until the second Wednesday in May following. All succeeding Secretaries, Officers and Servants, to be annually appointed, or oftener if needful, at General Meetings.*

495.                                                                                                    We

We will moreover, That there shall be every year four stated general meetings of the governors and guardians of the said corporation, to be held on the first Wednesday after Lady-day, Midsummer, Michaelmas, and Christmas-days respectively; at which meetings and no other, the said corporation, or the major part of the members thereof then present, shall and may execute leases for years, and make bye-laws for the well-government of the said corporation; which bye-laws, not being repugnant to the laws and statutes of this our realm, shall and may be effectually observed and kept: Provided nevertheless, and our will is, That no such bye-laws so to be made by this corporation shall be binding, until the same shall be confirmed by some succeeding general meeting, and that the same method be observed in the altering or repealing any bye-laws after they shall have been so confirmed; and the members to be present at such quarterly meetings, or the major part of them then present, are hereby impowered from time to time to remove and displace any officers or servants belonging to the said hospital, for misdemeanors, at their will and pleasure, and to put others into their rooms from time to time; and we do hereby also impower the committee for the time being, or any five or more of them, on any just cause, to suspend remove and displace any inferior officers or servants, and to put others in their rooms until the next general or quarterly court or meeting.

Provided, that no act, in any quarterly or other general meeting, be valid, unless thirteen or more members be present, and the major part of such as shall be present be consenting thereto.

We will moreover, That the said corporation and their successors, or the major part of such of them as shall be present at any yearly or quarterly court, or other general meeting, which the president has by these presents power to summon at any other times, as there shall be occasion, may from time to time by ballot elect and choose such fit and able persons to be governors and guardians as they shall think most likely to encourage and promote the charitable designs of the said corporation; which governors and guardians so elected shall, from and after such election, be adjudged and deemed members of the said corporation, and as such shall be summoned and admitted to vote and act by virtue of these presents, as fully and effectually to all intents and purposes as if their names respectively were particularly inserted to be members thereof in and by this our charter.

And we will moreover, That the said corporation and their successors shall have power to authorize and appoint such persons as they shall think fit to take subscriptions, and to ask of all or any of our good subjects and gather and collect such monies as shall by any person or persons, bodies politick or corporate, companies or other societies, be contributed or given for the purposes aforesaid, and may revoke and make void such authorities and appointment as often as they may see cause so to do.

And our further will and pleasure is, That the said corporation shall and may cause fair and just accounts in writing to be kept of all receipts payments and doings by them their officers and agents respectively, in relation to the premisses, which shall be liable to the view and inspection of any subscriber or subscribers, benefactor or benefactors, upon occasion; which said account shall on the twentieth day of December in every year, or within fourteen days after, be examined audited adjusted and subscribed by the members present at such meeting, or the major part of them.

We will moreover, That all persons who shall subscribe and pay to the said corporation to the amount of twenty pounds or more, or of forty shillings or more annually, shall have free liberty to inspect the said hospital, and inform themselves of the state thereof, and of the manner of nursing dieting managing instructing and employing the children therein.

And further we will, That in all general courts the president, or in case of his death or absence, the vice-president first named in the list of vice-presidents then present, be the chairman of the said court, and to have a voice in case of an equality of votes.

And lastly, our will and pleasure is, That these our letters patent or the inrolment or exemplification thereof, shall be good firm valid and effectual in the law, according to our royal intentions hereinbefore declared, and shall be taken construed and adjudged, in all our courts or elsewhere, in the most favourable and beneficial sense, and for the best advantage of the said corporation and their successors, any omission imperfection defect matter cause or thing whatsoever to the contrary thereof in any wise notwithstanding, without fine or fee, great or small, to be for the same in any manner rendered done or paid to us in our Hanaper or elsewhere to our use.

In witness whereof, We have caused these our letters to be made patent.

Witness Ourself at Westminster the seventeenth day of October in the thirteenth year of our reign.

(By writ of Privy Seal)                                    COCKS.

*Lunæ,* 10° *die Junii,* 1816.

HENRY BROUGHAM, Esq. in The Chair.

The Reverend *Basil Woodd,* called in, and Examined.

YOU are minister of Bentinck Chapel, Mary-le-bone?—I am.

How many years have you been officiating minister of that chapel?—I think thirty-one years.

Is it a chapel of the established church?—Yes.

Have you attended considerably to the instruction of the poor, since you have been minister there?—Within the last eighteen years I have; I began a school in the year 1798, which was supported at my own expense, and which interested me in the education of children, and then I brought it before the congregation, and placed it upon a larger scale.

You mean you applied to the congregation for pecuniary assistance?—Yes, I introduced it to the congregation by a sermon and collection, and collected about 80*l.*

What is the size of that school now?—It educates one hundred children, fifty boys and fifty girls.

Are they of the poorest description?—Yes, some of them are; they are the children of labouring poor.

Are they educated gratis?—Quite gratis, it is merely a day school; the children are educated, and clothed in part. The number that have passed through the school since its first establishment, is twelve hundred children.

How long do children now stay, upon the average, in that school?—About three years.

At what age do you take them in?—Between nine and ten; we call it ten.

Do you make any provision for them when they leave the school?—No, only supplying them with a Bible and Prayer Book, but nothing for their future maintenance.

Do you conduct the school according to the new plan of education?—Dr. Bell's method is in part adopted; it is adopted, excepting as to the particular point of monitors; we have not monitors in the way they have at the National school.

What has been your reason for departing from that part of Dr. Bell's plan?—I thought that the children who were monitors acquired a very disgusting degree of self-importance.

Have you found this, both in the boys and girls?—Yes.

How long have you departed from that part of Dr. Bell's plan?—I think nearly from the very first time that that method was at all adopted in the school; I thought the children were left too much to the management of children.

Did you find bad effects follow from that?—Yes.

Be so good as to specify them?—I thought there was a want of exactness, particularly in the pronunciation, that crept in by that means, and there was often a partiality which the monitors manifested towards their favourites.

How long did you try Dr. Bell's plan without alteration, before you introduced this change?—I hardly know, I do not think quite half a year, not above two or three months; the alteration that we made was to change the monitors more frequently, under the idea that it would preserve more the level of rank among the scholars, and prevent that self-importance.

How frequently do you now change them?—We leave it to the discretion of the superintendent of the school; but the plan which I first adopted upon the change, was to change the monitors every day.

Are they changed as often at present, in general?—It is left to the discretion of the superintendent.

How frequently do you conceive they are in fact now changed; every week, or every three or four days?—I should think about that.

Have you found this change correct the evils which you before experienced?—Yes, I think it does; it prevents an individual assuming that great self-importance.

Does it correct the evil sufficiently in practice?—I think it does.

Have you found the other parts of Dr. Bell's plan, which you have retained, beneficial?—I think the plan is admirable for fixing the attention of the children, and fully occupying their time.

Does

Does it produce the effect of great rapidity in their advancement in learning?— I think it certainly does, and I think it is impossible for a child otherwise than to learn when put into those kind of classes.

Do you experience any bad effects besides those you have particularized, and which you have corrected?—No.

In what time do you think that a child now, who comes to you without any knowledge of reading, attains to reading easily and satisfactorily, upon the average?— I should think a child in half a year would learn to read tolerably.

So well as to read the Bible with ease and satisfaction to itself?—That depends a great deal upon the child's natural genius and capability of instruction; we see such an amazing difference between different children.

Do you find children in general, who have come to you without any knowledge of their letters, read with fluency and ease in the Bible at the end of a twelve-month?—Yes, I think some of them do.

Do most of them in a year and a half?—I should think most of them do, or less than that.

Is three years about the average time they stay with you?—We generally give the girls two years for reading and working, and then one year for writing and ciphering and working; they keep up the reading at the same time.

When the children leave your school, are they generally well informed in those branches which you teach them?—I think they are; as to ciphering, they only learn the four first rules.

Do you use any methods to explain to the children what they read?—The general custom is, after every lesson that they read, to ask them what they recollect of it, and to put it in the form of questions.

Do you find that answer the purpose of opening their understandings and increasing their knowledge?—It does; they used to read without any idea at all of what they read.

Do you find they now take a greater interest in what they read, than they did before?—Yes; they read now with interest and attention.

Do you find a good effect on their dispositions and habits, in consequence of this course of explanation?—I should think in general that was the fact; as to religious education, I always examine them before they leave the school individually, and I have been very highly gratified with their general knowledge of the principles of the Christian religion; there is certainly a great deal of pains taken in the school as to their religious principles.

By yourself or by the master?—By both of us. I principally attribute it to this: they learn the church catechism first of all; then a card of prayer, extracted from the liturgy, with a number of short questions upon it; and a short system of the Christian doctrine expressed in the words of scripture, selected from Bishop Gastrell's Christian Institutes; and perhaps I should mention that they also learn the catechism of the duty of servants, which I drew up for their use.

Are there any other schools in your neighbourhood?—There are four that are connected with Bentinck Chapel; I have stated what we call Bentinck school, which consists of the very poor of the neighbourhood.

Is Bentinck school sufficient to accommodate the poor in that neighbourhood?— Nothing to be named.

What should you state the deficiency to be in that neighbourhood?—I should not think Bentinck school accommodated one-tenth. I was going to mention, there is another school connected with it, Bentinck Sunday school, which consists of about three hundred boys and girls; these are called Bentinck schools, because they are entirely supported by Bentinck Chapel.

Do you consider the means of education for the poor in that neighbourhood to be defective?—Yes, as to accommodation of numbers.

Can you form any estimate of the number of poor children who are destitute of the means of instruction in the parish of Mary-le-bone?—No, I cannot; Mary-le-bone is so very large a parish, that I do not know how to form an idea of that.

Is the district with which you are particularly acquainted, much inhabited by the poorer classes?—It is, much beyond any other part of the parish, arising from this circumstance, that there are a great number of houses built upon what we call sufferance, upon ground belonging to the Bishop of London, and liable to be removed at six months notice; they are permitted to live there upon paying a small annual rent for the ground, and, when notice comes for them to quit, are permitted

to

to remove the materials, which produces a very strange scenery; they pull the house down, and carry the materials to a distance, and build it up again.

In what part of Mary-le-bone parish is this?—The north-west, adjoining the Edgware-road. The adjacent part of Paddington parish, and the other side of the Edgware-road, I suppose, contains about six hundred small huts of this description. The district I particularly allude to, is called Lisson-place and the Gravel-pits.

What may be the population of that district?—I hardly know; I should think there must be four or five thousand within half a mile extent of Bentinck chapel, but I speak by guess.

Do you find a general disposition among the poor to have their children educated?—Very much so; there were no schools at all, till I set up these schools about eighteen years ago, in that part of the parish.

Of what classes do they consist chiefly?—Labourers.

Irish?—A good many; the circumstance of the Paddington canal has brought a vast number of poor people into the neighbourhood.

From the country?—Yes; and likewise the circumstance of their being permitted to run up these temporary kind of houses, for which they pay no rent, except a small ground-rent; these small houses have all been built within the last twenty years; then they have the advantages of little gardens attached to them, where they plant potatoes and vegetables, and they have the advantages of a clearer air than in the lanes and alleys of the parish.

Do they live in great misery, these poor people?—Many of them in extreme misery; many of the working poor at wages of twelve and sixteen shillings a week.

How do they employ their children?—I think the children in general seem to have no employment at all.

Do they send them out begging?—Many do.

Do you apprehend there would be any indisposition in the parents to send those children, whom they now employ in begging, to schools, if such were provided?—I should think there would not, in most instances.

Should you say, that within the last eighteen years, during which you have known the district particularly, that the lower poor were improved, or otherwise?—I think the general civilization is considerably improved.

Is their conduct improved generally?—I should think it is; there is a very great increase in their attendance at public worship, which is always attended with the increase of other comforts. When I first went to Bentinck chapel, I do not suppose twenty poor people attended, and I may say now not short of 300 attend every Sunday.

Are they more decent in their appearance?—A great deal more so.

Are many of the lower Irish in the district Catholics?—A great many; we admit them promiscuously into the school, and never ask any questions.

You find no indisposition among them to receive instruction?—No, they are very ready to receive it.

Do you perceive any disposition in the priests to prevent the parents from sending their children?—I do not know that they ever opposed it, or that the priests knew it; I have thought it most prudent not to say any thing to the Catholic parents on the subject of it, but to receive the children upon their applications, and to let them go through the same mode of religious instruction as the other children in the school.

On the part of the parents themselves have you perceived no objection at all, or difficulties?—None at all; I have never made it a point that the Catholic children shall attend at the chapel, but they have always come with the other children; if I had made a point of it, perhaps they would not have come. We have other schools connected with the chapel, besides those.

State what, and how many?—One is called the school of industry or spinning school; this consists of twenty children, little girls, clothed, boarded, and educated, by private subscription; of this, Mrs. Basil Woodd has the entire management.

Of course the education is the same as in the others?—Yes. We have another, called the Philological school; this school is an humble imitation of Christ's Hospital, except that it is a day school, but it gives exceeding good education; and in addition to the common education there is provision for French, Greek, Latin, drawing, and mathematics; it is a free-school designed for the sons of clergymen, of officers, and of respectable reduced tradesmen.

The terms might be such as to render it impossible that the poorer classes should enjoy the advantages of it?—Yes.

What

What are the numbers in it?—One hundred; and I believe about 1200 have passed through the school since its institution, which is about twenty-five years, and supported by private subscription; the Duke of York is patron, and Lord Teignmouth is president.

The children of parents of different religions are equally admitted to the Philological school, as to the others you have mentioned?—I do not recollect we ever had any in the Philological school excepting Protestants and members of the church of England; we have made no exceptions. As to the other schools, whoever applied was always admitted in regular order. The great evil that we experience, as to the schools in the neighbourhood, is, that we have no places of worship that can receive them.

You find that the want of places of worship in the neigbourhood is a serious obstacle to the establishment of schools?—Yes; we can only have the schools at one single service in the course of the Sunday.

Can you admit children at Bentinck chapel twice on the Sabbath?—No, only once; we have three services at the chapel, but we can only admit the children once.

Do you think it would be a great inducement to parents to send their children to these schools for education, if there were places of divine worship to which they might be sent?—It would to some of them, I have no doubt; but I am sorry to say that the poor do not much attend themselves; there has been a great improvement in their attendance, but I question very much if one person in seven houses ever goes to any place of public worship.

Do you find the comforts of the families materially increase, when they attend divine worship?—I think to many of them it gives habits of sobriety and cleanliness, independent of religion.

Does greater misery prevail among the lower classes of Irish, in your neighbourhood, than among the English and Scotch, if there are any Scotch?—I think many of them live in a very wretched way; in many instances every room has a distinct family; even the back kitchen as well as the front kitchen has a distinct family; little tenements of half-a-crown a week each.

Are you at all acquainted with the state of education in any other district of the Metropolis?—I am a governor and trustee of the Parochial school, and also the great National school, which is in the heart of London; and I attend them occasionally.

What is the whole number of children educated in the schools connected with Bentinck chapel?—Five hundred and twenty.

Can you tell, from your observation of Sunday schools, what is the comparative progress which a child makes there, and in a day school; for instance, how long will a child take to learn to read at a Sunday school?—I should think, if they were attentive, they would be able to learn to read in half a year, but not to read well.

Would they take a year and a half to read well?—I should thing they would; then there is a great difference in teachers, our teachers are all gratuitous teachers, and some are much more expert and attentive at it than others.

## Mr. *John Lush*, called in, and Examined.

YOU are secretary to the St. Giles and St. George Bloomsbury school?—I was, but have now resigned.

Do you consider the funds of that school to be perfectly well applied in the education of children?—Yes, I do.

Do you recollect a resolution having been moved at a meeting of the trustees, by Mr. Justice Bayley, prohibiting any person who acted as a trustee from having a contract, or in any way dealing for the supply of the school?—I do.

Was that resolution adopted?—No, it was not.

When was it proposed?—I think it was proposed in the Spring of 1814.

Was it proposed by Mr. Justice Bayley?—There was a proposal made in the first place by Mr. Thistleton, at the quarterly general meeting on the 14th of January 1814.

Was Mr. Justice Bayley present and in the chair?—Mr. Justice Bayley was present when it came forward for confirmation, he was not present at the time it was first brought forward.

When Mr. Thistleton proposed it, what reception did it meet with?—It passed the board of trustees unanimously.

Then what did you mean in your former answer, by saying the resolution was rejected?—When it was brought forward for confirmation at the quarterly general
meeting

meeting of the trustees and subscribers, in the month of April 1814, it was rejected; Mr. Justice Bayley was then in the chair.

Is a resolution not a rule, until it is adopted by a quarterly general meeting?—No.

Has a resolution of the trustees, previous to such confirmation, no force whatever?—It has no force, unless it receives a confirmation from a quarterly meeting.

Would a resolution passed by the trustees the day after one quarterly meeting, have no force until it received confirmation by the next quarterly meeting?—Any proposal that is made at the trustee meeting, must stand for confirmation at a subsequent meeting.

But is it of no force whatever until it is so confirmed, during the three months?—It is not. By the regulations of the school, the trustees cannot make any regulation until it is submitted to a general meeting; they may recommend a regulation to a general meeting, but they cannot enforce it.

So that the Committee are to understand, that a regulation proposed by the trustees, and adopted by them, has no force or effect whatsoever until it is confirmed by a general meeting?—Certainly not.

And binds nobody?—No.

Then in what do the powers of the trustees consist?—The mere management of the school, and to carry into execution the laws that are laid down.

Do the trustees not employ the contractors and persons that furnish the school?—They do.

Then would not a resolution of the trustees, that no contractor should be employed, who was a trustee, have perfect force previous to confirmation as to that point?—No, it would not, because it does not become one of the original resolutions; the trustees are restricted from making any regulations at any of their meetings, that shall clash with any of the original resolutions of the school.

But if the trustees are the persons who employ the contractors, if they make a resolution not to employ a certain class of persons as contractors, will that resolution not be effectual upon themselves?—It certainly will be effectual, if the trustees pass the resolution; it must be binding upon their own conduct.

When this regulation was proposed at the quarterly general meeting, what took place?—The matter, with various other things, was laid before the board for confirmation, and was objected to by many of the trustees.

Did they state the grounds of their objections?—No, they did not state any grounds; but I have no doubt in my own mind, that the ground was on account of their being interested themselves.

Was it put to the vote?—It was, and rejected.

Did Mr. Justice Bayley support it?—Mr. Justice Bayley did support it.

Did Mr. Justice Bayley immediately resign as a trustee?—No; Mr. Justice Bayley then submitted a resolution of his own, which was put, and negatived.

What was the purport of that resolution?—I forget the exact purport.

What was the substance of it; to what did it refer?—The substance of it was, that no person acting as a trustee should supply the house with any article in which he dealt, or that he should have any vote upon the payment of any such accounts.

Did Mr. Justice Bayley resign after that?—Mr. Justice Bayley never resigned, but he withdrew, and, I believe, has never attended the school since.

Then in point of fact, do the trustees supply the school with necessaries?—No doubt of it.

Do you consider this as politic in the management of the funds?—No; with respect to the parties supplying the house with articles, that they are very improper persons to sit at the board, either to make an order for goods, or discuss the payment.

Is this a copy of the resolutions to which you have referred in your evidence?—It is.

[It was delivered in, and read, as follows:]

" Resolved unanimously, That no trustee or subscriber shall be eligible to attend any of the trustee meetings, during the time he shall be appointed to serve the charity, whereby he is to receive a pecuniary compensation, unless specially summoned by order of a previous meeting.

" Resolved unanimously, That every trustee or annual subscriber qualified to attend the meetings of trustees, shall be eligible to attend all subsequent meetings, so soon as his successor is appointed to serve the charity; except the meetings at which his accounts shall be audited or ordered for payment.

" Resolved,

" Resolved unanimously, That the eight annual subscribers from the present list of trustees, elected to serve the office for the year ensuing, go out by rotation ; and that no person shall be eligible to be elected for a longer space than two successive years ; and that no such elective trustee shall be eligible to go to the ballot, until he shall have been out of office for the space of two years."

I beg to observe, that these resolutions were proposed on the 14th January 1814, and carried unanimously.

Was Mr. Justice Bayley present when those resolutions were carried?—No, he was not.

Was he present when they were rejected at a subsequent meeting?—He was; and it was upon those resolutions being rejected, that Mr. Justice Bayley moved a resolution to the following purport, That no trustee or subscriber attending any meeting, shall be allowed to vote on any question in which he may be personally interested. This motion of Mr. Justice Bayley having been made, was rejected instantly, and therefore was not recorded on the minutes.

Did Mr. Justice Bayley retire?—No, he staid the evening, but he has never attended any meeting since.

The Reverend *William Lonfield Fancourt,* and Mr. *Henry Brent,*
called in, and Examined.

*(To Mr. Fancourt.)* YOU are master of the grammar school St. Saviour's?—I am ; the school is purely classical.

*(To Mr. Brent.)* What are you?—Secretary of this school.

*(To Mr. Fancourt.)* Have you a copy of the charter relating to this school?—I have.

[It was delivered in, and read. as follows :]

ELIZABETH Dei gratia Anglie Francie et Hibernie Regina, fidei defensor, &c. Omnibus ad quos presentes ire pervenerint salutem. Cum dilecti subditi nostri Willus Emerson, Jofies Sayer, Ricardus Ryall, Thomas Cure, Johannes Oliff, Thomas Pultor, Thomas Bill, Thomas Osbourne, Ricardus Baptist, Willus Browker, Cristoferus Cambell, et Willus Gefferson, et alij discreti et magis probiores inhabitante parochie Sancti Salvatoris infra burgrum nostrum de Southwerk in comitatu nostro Surr ex eor pia affecio et boni dispositionis pro erudicone institucone et instruccone pueror et juvenu ejusdm parochie ad eor cust labores et onera non modico sumptuosa in laudabili forma et ordine infra predictum burgum et parochiam scholam grammaticalem nuper designaverunt et erexerunt in qua pueri et juvenes tam pauperum qui divitum inhabitancium infra predictam parochiam ingenue et prospere in grammatica iustruanter et educantur ad comuncm utilitatem omnium inhabitancio parochie predicte prout ex fide dignis informamur cumq, etiam ijdm subditi ñri inhabitantes parochie predce nobis humiliter supplicaverint ut scolam predictam sic per eos designatam et erectam continuam habeat successionem Et ut eis munificiaciam et gratiam nostra Regni in ea parte exhibere et extendere velimus nos nedum premissa verum eciam bonam piam et laudabilem intenconem predictor subditor nostri in premissis considerantes cupientesq, intime quantum in nobis est ea omnia et singula que ad bonam educationem et instrucconem pueror et juvenu quoquomodo concernere poterint augmentari de gratia nostra speciali ac ex certa scientia et mero motu nostris volumus concedimus et ordinamus pro nobis heredibʒ et successoribʒ nostri qᵈ scola predea sic per inhabitantes parochie Sancti Salvatoris ut prefertur designita et erecta infra dictam parochiam Sco Salvatoris in Southwerk de cetero sit et erit una scola grammaticalis pro educacone institucone et instruccone pueror et juvenu parochianoſ et inhabitanciu ibidem in grammatica perpetuis futuris temporibʒ duratur Et qᵈ scola illa vocabilᵐ libera schola grammaticali parochianoſ parochie Sancti Salvatoris in Southwerk in comitatu Surr ac scholam illum de uno magistro seu pedagogo et uno subpedagogo sur hippodidasculo pro perpetuo continuator erigimus creamus ordinamus declamarus fundamus et stablilimus per presentes Et ut intentio nostra predict meliorem sortiatur effectum Et ut terr tenementa reddit revencoes et alia proficua ad substentacoem et manutencoem scole predict concedend
assignand

*The Rev.*
*W. L. Fawcourt.*
*and*
*Mr. Henry Brent.*

assignand et appunctuand melius gubernenter pro continuacõe ejusdm volumus concedimus et ordinamus q^d de cetero imperpetuum sint et erunt infra parochiam Sancti Salvatoris predict̃ sex homines de discrecioribȝ et majis probioribȝ inhabitantibus ejusdem parochie pro tempore existen qui erunt et vocabuntur gubernatores possessionu' revencionu' et bonoȓ dicte scole grammaticalis vulgariter vocat̃ et vocand libere scole grammaticalis parochianoȓ parochie Sc̃i Salvatoris in Southwerke in comitatu Surȓ Et ideo sciatis q^d nos assignavimus eligimus nominavimus constituimus et declaravimus per presentes dilectos nobis prefatos Thomam Cure, Ricardum Ryall, Johannem Oliff, Thomam Pulter, Thomam Bill, et Willm Bowker, inhabitant' parochie predict̃ fore et esse primos et modernos gubernatores possessionu' revencionu' et bonoȓ dicte libere scole grammaticalis parochianoȓ parochie Sancti Salvatoris in Southwerk in comitatu Surȓ ad idem officui bene et fidelit̃ exercend̃ et occupand a dat̃ presentuȓ durante vita esc̃ Et q^d ijdem gubernatores in re facto et nomine de cetero sint et erunt unũ corpus corporatu' et politiqu' de se imperpetuum per nomen gubernator possessionu' reventionu' et bonoȓ libere scole grammaticalis parochianoȓ parochie Sancti Salvatoris in Southwerk in comitatu Surȓ incorporat̃ et erect̃ ac ipsos Thomam Cure, Richardum Ryall, Johannem Oliff, Thomam Pulter, Thoma Bill, et Willm Bowker, gubernatores possessionu' reventionu' et bonoȓ libere scole grammaticalis parochianoȓ parochie Sancti Salvatoris in Southwark in comitatu Surȓ per presentes incorporamus ac corpus corporatum et politiqu' per idem nomen imperpetuum duratu' realiter et ad plenu' creamus erigimus ordinamus facimus et constituimus per presentes Et ulterius volumus ac per presentes pro nobis heredibȝ et successoribȝ nostris concedimus q̃d ijdem gubernatores possessioñ revencioñ et bonoȓ dicte libere scole grammaticalis parochianoȓ parochie Sancti Salvatoris in Southwark in comitatu Surȓ habeant successionem perpetuam et per idem nomen sint et erunt persone habiles apte et in lege capaces ad habend̃ recipiend̃ et perquirend̃ maneria terȓ tenementa prat̃ pascuã pastuȓ rectorias decimas reddit reverc̃oes servicia possessionas revenc̃ones et hereditamenta quecunqȝ tam de nobis heredibȝ vel successoribȝ nostris qui de aliqua alia persona sive aliquibȝ alijs personis quibuscunqȝ Et ordinanimus et decernimus per presentes pro nobis heredibȝ et successoribȝ nostris q^d quandocunqȝ contigerit aliquem vel aliquos deoȓ sex gubernatoȓ pro tempore existeñ mori seu alibi extra parochiam Sancti Salvatoris in Southwerk predict̃ inhabitare aut cum familia sua decedere q^d tunc et tociens bene liceat et licebit alijs deoȓ gubernatoȓ superviventibȝ et ibidem cum familijs suis comorantibȝ et duodecem alijs discretis et magis probioribȝ inhabitantibȝ predc̃e parochie Sancti Salvatoris in Southwerk per eosdem gubernatores eligend̃ et nominand̃ vel majori parti eoȓdem aliam idoneam personam vel alias idoneas personas de inhabitantibȝ parochie Sc̃i Salvatoris predict̃ in locum vel locos sic morientis vel morientiu' aut cum familia sua sic ut prefertur decedentis vel decedenciu' in deo officio gubernatoȓ successoȓ eligere et nominare Et hoc totiens quotiens casus sic acciderit Et ulterius volumus ac pro nobis heredibus et successoribus nostris per presentes concedimus prefatis gubernatoribȝ et successoribus suis q^d de cetero habeant comme sigillum ad negotia sua premiss̃ et cetera in hijs literis nostris patentibȝ express̃ et specificat̃ seu aliquam inde parcellum tantumodo tangeñ vel concerneñ desernituȓ Et q^d ipsi gubernatores per nomen gubernatoȓ possessionu' revencionu' et bonoȓ libere scole grammaticalis parochianoȓ parochie Sancti Salvatoris in Southwerke in comitatu Surȓ placitare et implacitari defendere et defendi respondere et responderi possint et valeant in omnibus et singulis causis quarelis accionibus realibus personalibus et mixtis cujuscunqȝ generis fuerint sive nature in quibuscunqȝ placeis locis et curiss̃ nostris heredum vel successoȓ nostroȓ seu alioȓ quoȓcunqȝ coram quibuscunqȝ justiciaȓ et judicibus ecclesiasticis et secularibus infra regnu' ñrum Angl̃ seu alibi Et ad ea ac omnia et singula alia faciend̃ agend̃ at recipiend̃ prout et in eodem modo quo ceteri ligei nostri persone habiles et capaces in lege infra idem regnum ñrum Anglie faciunt et facere posterint in curijs placeis et łoas predict̃ et coram justiciarijs et judicibus supradc̃is Et ulterius de ampliori gracia nostra dedimus et concessimus ac per presentes pro nobis heredibus et successoribus nostris damus et concedimus prafatis moderius gubernatoribȝ scole

predict̃

*The Rev.*
*W. L. Fancourt.*
*and*
*Mr. Henry Brent.*

predict̃ et successoribus suis q̃ᵈ ipsi et successores sui cum advisamento
episcopi Wintoñ pro tempore existeñ   Et in absencia ejusdm episcopi pro
tempore existeñ cum advisamento alicujus alterius probi et erudit̃ hominis
plenam postetatum et authoritatem habeant nominandi et appunctuandi
pedagogum et subpedagogum sive hippodidasculum scole predce totiens
quotiens eadm scola de pedagogo et subpedagogo vacuet fuerit   Et q̃ᵈ ipĩ
gubernatores cum advisamento episcopi Wintoñ predict̃ pro tempore existeñ
de tempore in tempus faciant et facere valeant et possuit idonea et salubria
statua et ordinac̃ões in script̃ concerneñ et tangem ordinem gubernac̃oem
et dirrecc̃oem pedagogi et subpedagogi ac scholariu' scole predict̃ pro tempore existeñ ac stipendii et salarii eõdm pedagogi et subpedagogi ac alia
eandem scolam et ordinac̃oem gubernac̃oem preservac̃oem et disposic̃oem
reddit et revencionu' ad sustentac̃oem' ejusdm scole appunctuand̃ tangeñ
et concerneñ   Que quidem statua et ordinac̃ões sic fiend̃ volumus concedimus et per presentes precipuus inviolabiliter observaris de tempore in
tempus imperpetuum Ita q̃ᵈ statuta et ordinac̃ões sic fiend̃ non sunt contraria
ad statuta Regni nostri Anglie   Et insuper volumus ac per presentes pro
nobis heredibus et successoribus nostris concedimus q̃ᵈ nulla persona preter̃
pueros et juvenes parochianõ et inhabitantiu' parochie predict̃ et alias personas ejusdem parochia in predict̃ schola educatur̃ aut in grammatica instru-
eretur nisi eadem persona per gubernatores scole predict̃ pro tempore
existeñ prius admittatur   Et ulterius de uberiori gratia nostra dedimus et
concessimus ac per presentes pro nobis heredibus et successoribʒ ñris
damus et concessimus prefatis moderius gubernatoribʒ possessioñ revencionu' et bonõ dicte libere scole grammaticalis parochianõ parochie
Sancti Salvatoris in Southwark in comitatu Surr̃ et successoribʒ suis licen-
siam spĩalem liberamq̇ et licitam facultatem potestatem et authoritatem
habend̃ recipiend̃ et perquirend̃ eis et eõ successoribʒ imperpetum ad
sustentac̃oem et manutenc̃oem scole predict̃ tam de nobis heredibʒ et successoribʒ nostris q̃m de alijs quibuscunq̇ personis et alia persona quacunq̇
maneria messuagia terras tenementa rectorias decimas et alia hereditamenta
quecunq̇ infra regnu' ñrum Anglie seu alibi infra dominia nostra dumodo
non tenetur de nobis heredibʒ vel successoribʒ ñris immediate in capite et
non excedunt clarum annu valorem quadraginta librar̃ statuto de terris et
tenementis ad manu' mortuam non ponend̃s aut aliquo alio statuto actu
ordinac̃oe seu provisione aut aliqua alia re causa vel materia quacunq̇ in
contrariu' inde habit fact̃ edit ordinat̃ seu provĩ in aliquo non obstañ
Et volumus ac per presentes ordinamus q̃ᵈ omnia exitus redditus et reven-
c̃oes omnia predict̃ terr̃ tenementõ et possessionu' imposterum dand̃ et
assignand̃ ad sustentac̃oem scole predict̃ de tempore in tempus convertantur̃
ad sustentac̃oem pedagogi et subpedagogi scole predict̃ pro tempore existeñ
et ad sustentac̃onem et manutenc̃oem domus et edific scole ill̃ et terr̃ tenementõ et possessionu' predict̃ et non aliter nec ad aliques alios usus seu
intenc̃oes   Et volumus ac per presentes consedimus prefatis gubernatoribʒ
q̃ᵈ habeant et habebunt has l̃ras ñras patentes sub magno sigillo ñro Anglie
debito modo fact et sigillat absq̇ fine seu feodo magno vel parvo nobis in
hanaperio ñro seu alibi ad usum ñrum proinde nobis hered̃ vel success̃ ñris
quoquomodo reddend̃ solvend̃ vel faciend̃   Eo q̃ᵈ expressa mencode vero
valore annuo aut de certitudine premissõ sive eor alicujus aut de alijs Doĩus
sive concessionibʒ per nos vel per aliquem progenitor sive predecessor norum
prefatis gubernatoribʒ ante hæc tempora fact in presentibʒ minime fact existit
aut aliquo statuto actu ordinac̃oe promissione proclamac̃oe sive restricc̃oe
inde in contrariu ante hæc tempora fact edit ordinat̃ seu provĩs aut aliqua alia
re causa vel materia quacunq̇ in aliquo non obstant   In cujus rei testimonij
has l̃ras ñras fieri fecimus patentes teste me ipsa apud Westmonaster̃ quarto
die Junii anno regni nostri quarto per breve de privato sigillo et de data
predca authoritate Parliamenti.                        P. CORDELL.


It appears by this charter to have been confirmed by Act of Parliament?—
It has.

In what year should you suppose?—1562, I should suppose; that is the date of
the charter.

(*To Mr. Brent.*)   Is this an authentic copy of the charter?—It is.

Were

*The Rev.*
*W. L. Fancourt,*
*and*
*Mr. Henry Brent.*

Were there rules made in 1562 for the government of the school?—There were.

Are those rules thus laid down observed, and have they always been so?—They have.

Is it a free school?—Yes.

(*To Mr. Fancourt.*) What children are taught? The parish children, if their parents choose to send them, and from the five parishes, if there are not 100.

Are the children of persons of all classes, as well rich as poor, taken?—They are.

(*To Mr. Brent.*) What are the yearly revenues?—380 *l.* a year.

Arising from what?—Estates.

What are the expenses?—Abut 300 *l.*

What becomes of the overplus?—It is laid out in the repairs of the building, which is very large.

Are you confined to one hundred?—Yes, by the statutes.

In whose gift is the mastership?—The bishop, who appoints the governors chosen by the six trustees, and confirmed by the bishop of Winchester, who is visitor of the school; and we have an examination every year on the 17th of November. We have at present two boys on the foundation at college, one an exhibitioner.

To what college is the exhibition?—To any college in either university.

How is the exhibitioner chosen?—The best scholar.

What is the value of the exhibition?—20 *l.* from the school, and 12 *l.* from Christ church, which is left to the school in preference to any other school.

(*To Mr. Fancourt.*) What is the master's salary?—64 *l.*

And a house?—Yes.

(*To Mr. Brent.*) What do the other expenses of the school consist in?—The repairs and the salaries are the only expenses we have.

What is the sub-master's salary?—74 *l.*; but he has no house.

What other salaries are there?—No other salaries, except some to inferior servants. There is 20 *l.* a year belonging to the writing school, which has been left since.

Is there a writing school kept?—Yes, there is.

Who is the writing-master?—It has generally been connected with the sub-master, but it is now to be separated.

Is this 20 *l.* a year included in your 350 *l.*?—Yes.

How is the other 200 *l.* a year spent?—In the insurance of the building, and the repairs; the exhibition is not included in it.

Do the repairs and insurance amount to 270 *l.* a year?—Not annually; one year with another about 100 *l.*

Then there is about 170 *l.* accumulating yearly?—Yes; and when it has accumulated to a certain sum, we buy stock with it.

How much of the 350 *l.* arises from land, and how much from stock?—It is chiefly from estates; the stock is only about 60 *l.* a year, and all the rest from estates.

What are the premises upon which 100 *l.* is spent in insurances and repairs?—It is a very large building, and the school-house is spacious likewise; the assessed taxes upon the house are 18 *l.* a year.

(*To Mr. Fancourt.*) Is the master allowed to take boarders?—Yes, forty private pupils between the two masters.

Are those forty included in the hundred who attend the school?—Yes, I believe they are; but there is some doubt about that.

In point of fact, is it so?—It has never been put to the point, because we have never had 100.

What is the average number you have?—From 30 to 35, to 40 and 45.

How do your numbers happen never to be full?—The school itself is not altogether in bad repute, but certainly the finances of the school have been such as not to have the best instructors, which we could otherwise have had. Our average number is sometimes from 45 to 47; I cannot exactly answer the reasons why it is, neither have I right to answer; it is a matter of private concern between me and the governors. I have not the least doubt of the school being capable of instructing and receiving boys to the number of fifty; I do not suppose it would ever reach beyond fifty, because we are in the vicinity of two schools, Merchant Taylors' school and St. Paul's school; and we have a school of the same description, St. Olave's grammar school, whose finances enable them to have a much greater number, but who are always generally full; they have two classical masters, and, I believe, four or five writing masters; that will answer so far the reason why we are not full.

You are aware that Merchant Taylors' school is a pay school?—It is so; but it would take off a number from the middling ranks of St. Saviour's, because what

they

*The Rev.*
*W. L. Fancourt,*
*and*
*Mr. Henry Brent.*

they pay is trifling, and the advantages connected with the university are very great; and in point of fact, boys have left our school for that.

With respect to St. Olave's school, what is the revenue of that, do you know?—By report alone 1500 *l.* a year.

When was it founded?—Very near the same time as ours; I think they have the same charter.

Is it a free school?—I believe it is. I was asked a question which I believe I did not fully answer; that at the school, boys have been admitted of every rank and degree and trade, and among others, the lowest class have been admitted, and that is one objection why the better class have not sent their children in such numbers; it has been objected to. Now if the Committee refer to this document, they will find that the original foundation was not for the very lowest, but for the poorer mechanic and tradesman, who could not afford to give a liberal education to his boy. At our school, the admission fee at that time, and the other fees, amounted to 15*s.* a year, which in these days must have been equal to two pounds, and two pounds at the present time would exclude numbers who have hitherto received their education entirely from me. The chief boys who have been educated by me, have been, lately, of the lowest class, except a few of my private pupils, who have been admitted by right upon the foundation.

How long has this admission fee been disused?—Never; the admission fee is half-a-crown, and upon examinations, five shillings to the head master, and half-a-crown to the sub-master; there is likewise so much for brooms and other articles, per quarter, which has never been demanded; it was calculated it might amount upon the average to fifteen shillings a year at that time.

What is the actual pay now, a year?—At present just the same, only half-a-crown.

### Mr. *James Millar*, again called in, and Examined.

*Mr.*
*James Millar.*

WHAT are those papers you have in your hand?—They are the returns of the schools in Upper Rotherhithe, Christ-church, and Lambeth.

[They were delivered in and read, as follows:]

SOUTHWARK:—Returns of the SCHOOLS in Upper Rotherhithe, Christchurch, and Lambeth.

| Instituted. | Where situated. | Description. | Day School. Boys. | Girls. | Sunday School. Boys. | Girls. | If Clothed. | Treasurer or Secretary. | Master or Mistress. | Annual Expense. | REMARKS. |
|---|---|---|---|---|---|---|---|---|---|---|---|
| | | | | | | | | | | £. | |
| **Upper Rotherhithe:** | | | | | | | | | | | |
| 1796 | Church-street - - | Parochial Church | 43 | 25 | - | - | Clothed - | George Lee - - | Alex' Corson - | — | |
| — | - - D° - - - | Society - D° - | 12 | - | - | - | D°- - - | - - - - - - | - - D° - - | — | |
| 1798 | - - D° - - - | Church - - - | - | - | 50 | 50 | Partly - | Rector - - - | Mr. Williams - | — | |
| 1811 | Albion-street - - | Methodist - - | - | - | 120 | 50 | - - - | Enoch Fowler - | Sundry, gratuitous | 30 | |
| 1798 | Cherry-garden-st. - | Independent - - | 20 | - | 80 | - | - - - | J. Curling, Esq. - | W. E. Davies - | 40 | |
| — | - - D° - - - | - - D° - - - | - | 62 | - | 35 | Partly - | Mrs. Townsend - | Mrs. Allibon - - | 140 | |
| | | | | | | | | | | | |
| **Christchurch:** | | | | | | | | | | | |
| 1802 | Castle-yard, Gravel-lane - - - - | Sunday School Society - - | - | - | 160 | 177 | - - - | - - - - - - | Sundry, gratuitous | 35 | |
| 1799 | Surrey Chapel - - | - - D° - - | - | - | 192 | 196 | - - - | - - - - - - | - - D° - - - | — | |
| 1713 | Green Walk - - | Parochial - - | 100 | 40 | - | - | 60 clothed | Rev. Mr. Mapleton | - - - - - - | 400 | |
| | | | | | | | | | | | |
| **Lambeth:** | | | | | | | | | | | |
| 1700 | High-street { Blue coat } | Church - - - | - | 37 | - | - | 21 clothed | { Mr. Lett, Narrow Wall - } | } Mrs. Henderson | — | |
| 1751 | - D° - Grey-coat | - D° - - - - | - | 71 | - | - | 30 clothed | Mr. Evans - - | Mrs. Ayns - - | 366 | |
| 1804 | - D° - - - - | Methodist - - | - | - | 260 | 260 | - - - | J. Butterworth, Esq. | Sundry - - - | 600 | * Bell and Lancasterian. |
| 1816 | Paradise-row - - | Dissenters - - | - | - | 30 | 40 | - - - | Mr. Goss - - - | Mr. Carver - - | — | Expenses not yet made out. |
| 1806 | White-hart row - | - - D° - about | - | - | 80 | 70 | - - - | Mr. J. Farmer - | { M. Garham and others - - - } | } 45 | |

* This being only a Sunday school, it is probable the expenditure is overrated.

From a paper which has been put into my hand, containing an account of the want of education in the several parishes of Southwark, it appears that in about four thousand families visited, containing 11,470 children from five to fourteen years of age, there are 6020 without being provided with the means of education.

Have you paid any attention to the sufficiency of schools which at present exist, for affording the means of education to the uneducated children ?—I have for many years considered the provision for their education very deficient; and from such returns as I have seen in the present inquiry, I should apprehend the day schools do not provide for much beyond a ninth or tenth part of the want of education, the Sunday schools for one-third or perhaps a little more, and that there would still be a majority unprovided for, in some places nearly two-thirds.

Have you seen any experiments tried, of making the poor subscribe small sums to the education of their children ?—I have not seen it myself, but I have had information of the experiment being tried at Weymouth, for instance; and at Kingsland, I believe, it is tried.

What sums do they subscribe at those schools ?—One penny per week is what is given at those two schools.

Are you acquainted with the Scotch plan ?—Yes ; I have seen a great number of schools in Scotland.

What is the plan of those schools ?—The master is usually paid a very small salary provided by the parish ; his principal remuneration is by receiving in general about eighteen pence a quarter from each of the children, and the poorest person will rather want provisions than neglect that payment for his children.

What do they teach ?—English, writing, arithmetic, and in many instances, Latin.

Can you form any estimate of the amount of salary which a schoolmaster in Scotland obtains from those two sources you have described ?—That depends much upon the extent of the parish ; in some places it is very small, perhaps not exceeding thirty or thirty-five pounds a year, and from that it may extend, in larger parishes, to seventy or eighty, seldom much more. They have also what is called Sabbath schools; but reading is never necessary to be taught at those schools.

You are aware that by law in every parish in Scotland there must be a school ?—Yes.

Do the last answers refer to those parish schoolmasters ?—Yes.

In what way is a supply of proper schoolmasters procured in Scotland at such low salaries ?—It is not a very uncommon thing for young men who are educating for the church, to spend a year or two in that way, to help out their expenses; perhaps three or four years.

Is it not a very common thing to object to candidates for holy orders as parish schoolmasters ?—I am not aware of that, it may be.

Did you never see advertisements in the newspapers, for schoolmasters, in which it is said, None who are educating for the church are to apply?—I believe it is often tried in that way, by way of getting permanent masters, which would be of course preferable.

Do you not know that a principal part of the supply of schoolmasters are from young men who are educating themselves at the time they are teaching the school, intending to go out to the West Indies as book-keepers ?—I dare say there may.

What age are the parish schoolmasters generally ?—I cannot speak generally to that, but I have seen them as young as eighteen.

Are the lower orders in Scotland much better educated than they are in England ?—Vastly better, there is no comparison; they come to possess that information which I should conceive is impossible to be got by any Sunday school system.

Have you had an opportunity of comparing the education of the lower orders in Scotland, with that of the education of the lower orders in the Northern counties of England ?—I cannot say I have in the North of England; Manchester I have noticed a little.

How is it at Manchester ?—Far below the standard of the Scotch education, though a great deal has been done there in Sunday schools, perhaps as much as in any part of the kingdom. There are schools in Manchester for about 11,000 children, that I have seen.

But Cumberland and Northumberland you have not had an opportunity of examining ?—No, I have never stopped in them.

What is your opinion of the progress made by children in Sunday schools ?—I think there are instances of their reading pretty well ; but, without they stay a long while, the major part of them will read but indifferently.

What

What time do you refer to, when you say a long time?—I should think upon an average three years; and I have frequently noticed, that when children have read well, they have had parents who have exercised them at home, or had other means which have forwarded them greatly.

Did you ever make any observation, whether the girls learnt in a shorter time than boys?—I have thought the girls made more advances in reading than the boys, and I have imputed it to the probability of their playing truant less than the boys do. I should think the children in Sunday schools, upon the average, will take three years before they can read tolerably well.

Have you made any inquiries with a view to ascertain how far it is probable that the poor would subscribe to the maintenance of schools?—In some returns which I have seen, where they have been visited, in that paper which I have delivered in with regard to Southwark, for instance, there have been a considerable number marked, who have expressed their willingness to subscribe; and from the willingness of persons to subscribe for Bibles, there does not appear to be any doubt upon that subject, if they were visited by respectable people, who would point out the advantages; some of those persons who have visited them, have been received very favourably upon the subject.

Is there a general disposition to encourage and take advantage of education?—I am afraid I can hardly say in general; there are many who are insensible of those advantages, and at present there is a considerable number who plead a want of work and the difficulty of the times.

Is there any indisposition to send their children to schools when the means of education are provided cost free?—I think not, generally; there is no indisposition among those who have had instruction themselves, which seems to be a sort of consequence of the little instruction persons aim at for their children.

Do you apprehend there is a general indisposition to pay a small sum, as a penny per week?—I think not, without they were in circumstances where they could not subscribe through poverty.

Is the want of clothing, in the district you have visited, an objection to the sending of many children to school?—It is a very common objection in all schools; the parents say they cannot send them, for want of decent clothing and shoes.

Do you know of any children sent to the British and Foreign schools, who have been clothed by what is called the Juvenile Benevolent Society?—I have not heard of any: in inquiries of another kind, I have found the Juvenile Benevolent Society have very often clothed boys, as far as their funds would allow.

Are any girls clothed in the central school of the British and Foreign School Society?—Some of them are partly clothed by their own weekly subscriptions of one penny, which is laid out, by a committee of ladies, in articles at the first cost, and which does much more towards their clothing than they could have done. I suppose the ladies add to the stock.

What objection have the Dissenters to send their children to the schools upon the National plan, supposing they were not obliged to attend church on a Sunday, or to learn the Catechism?—I believe almost all the Dissenters that I know any thing of, provide for the education of their own children; they must be very poor indeed, if they do not.

Are you a Dissenter yourself?—I am. Our principal object is rather for others to be educated; we wish Catholics, and others, completely to get the benefit of instruction.

Do you mean that all Protestant Dissenters have the means of education for their children of all classes?—I know of none of them that do not get their children instructed, of the lowest order of all that I know.

Are you not alluding to some particular class?—No, I speak generally.

Do you mean that all over London the Dissenters of the lowest classes have the means of education?—I should think, unless they were very poor indeed, generally so.

Does it not follow, that if Dissenters have the means of education, every person has the means of education?—I mean the Dissenters in general; I speak of the persons who are careful in providing means of education for their children.

Do you allude to the poorer classes of Dissenters?—There are none so very poor that they could not do something if they chose.

Do you mean that Dissenters have better means of education for the poor, than members of the Church?—Not so much that, but I think they make greater exertions; I do not think they have better means.

Are

Are you not aware that a great proportion of the children who are educated at the British and Foreign schools are Dissenters, and not attending schools of their own sect?—I suppose they may; but I think they would pay a small contribution, if it was asked.

Do you mean that, supposing these British and Foreign schools were not in existence, the Dissenters have schools of their own capable of educating all the children belonging to them?—I do not think the schools that are provided on charitable foundations are sufficient in point of number.

Do you think, comparatively speaking, the generality of Dissenters are better educated?—I should not wish to confine that observation to Dissenters.

Why do not the Dissenters send their children to the National schools, if they are not obliged to go to church, and learn the Catechism?—I think they could have no other objection, certainly.

So that, in your opinion, they would send them, if those two objections could be got over?—I have no doubt of it.

Suppose that you required that each child should give security for attending his own place of worship, would there be any objection to Dissenters sending him to school?—Certainly not.

Have you had an opportunity of observing the progress made by children in the National schools and the British and Foreign Society's schools?—I have several times looked at them as well as I could, and I think the National schools provide for reading in some points of view superior, at least the children read materially better; but I suppose they are not quite so rapid in their movements; the writing department, I think, of the British system is decidedly superior.

Do you know any thing of the Catholic schools in London?—In consequence of an attack made by a Report, which the Committee may have heard of, by Mr. Godinge, of Newgate school, I paid a good deal of attention to one of the schools there attacked, at Lamb's Buildings near Moorfields, and I was fully satisfied that the school was extremely well conducted, that it had done a great deal of good among a considerable number of the very lowest class of Irish people, and their regulations as to going from the school so correct, and all the other parts of their management, that I felt considerable astonishment at any charge being applicable to such a school.

Can you speak distinctly with respect to the accuracy of the Report to which you allude, in other particulars?—From answers which I have seen, I am convinced it is greatly exaggerated, if there be any foundation at all for the assertions.

What has been the result of your inquiries with respect to juvenile depredations?—That the number of boys must be very considerable; I have always thought they did not much exceed 5000, and not much less, I dare say; some have estimated them at more.

Do you mean the boys who are occupied chiefly in begging and thieving?—Chiefly so, and who appear, from their connexions, to be initiating in it.

Whose parents profit by their crimes, and who would not allow them to attend schools, though cost-free?—I cannot say that; the parents profess that they would be glad to see their children instructed or employed.

Do you mean that the parents of those 5000 children, who profit by their depredations, would rather see them instructed?—A great many of them, whom I have conversed with, profess such a disposition; but some allowance must be made for their attention to truth, which is very material indeed.

Do you in point of fact believe that parents would allow their children to give up those circumstances which are profitable to them, and allow them to attend schools?—I have some difficulty in answering that question, because I think many of the children, if they were not removed altogether from their present association, could not be fixed to any thing like attendance at schools.

Of the five thousand you have mentioned, do you consider that there is a certain proportion whom no facility of obtaining instruction could draw to schools?—I should think there is.

Can you tell what proportion?—No, that must be wholly conjectural.


### The Reverend *Joshua King*, called in, and Examined.

YOU are rector of Bethnal-green?—I am.

How long have you been rector there?—About seven years.

Do poor abound in your parish?—Very much indeed.

Are

Are they a quiet and orderly set of people, or the contrary?—Excepting on particular occasions, they are tolerably well conducted; but there are dreadful scenes of riot and disturbance in the parish occasionally, arising from bullock-hunting principally, and the natural consequence which proceeds from disorderly public-houses.

Have they in general been educated, or not?—I am sorry to say that I deplore much the great want of education that prevails in the parish, which I apprehend is the pregnant source of crime; in our immense population, which consists of nearly 40,000, we have only two schools under the Establishment; in the one, there are 70 girls and boys educated, in the other school, there are 50 that are educated and clothed; those are the only schools we have under the Establishment in our parish.

Have you any large schools near the boundaries of your parish, to which your children go?—None under the Establishment.

What other schools, not under the Establishment?—I cannot speak to that positively; I believe the Methodists are educating a very considerable number, what number I cannot say; but theirs are principally Sunday schools.

You mean the Wesleyan Methodists?—Yes, I believe they are principally.

Are there no Catholic schools in your neighbourhood?—No.

Are there many Catholics in the parish?—I do not think there are.

Do you know how many schools the Methodists have?—I do not.

Does any other religious denomination exert itself in education there?—I do not think they do particularly.

Is there any British and Foreign school, or Lancasterian school?—There is a Lancasterian school in an adjoining parish, in Spitalfields.

Do many of your children go to it?—I believe many of them, but I do not know what number; it is a penny a week school.

Do you conceive that, after all, a very large proportion of children are un-educated?—Very large indeed.

Can you state what proportion?—It is impossible.

Much more than half are uneducated, you think?—Very considerably more, I should apprehend; including all the schools of every denomination, there are not, I conceive, more than 1200 at the extreme, out of a population which I conjecture to be 40,000.

Do you conceive there is a general desire for education?—I think education might be conducted to a very considerable extent in the parish, beyond what it at present is; but the children of the lower orders of people very early become useful in earning something towards their own maintenance, in my parish, in winding silk and other such employments; and therefore I apprehend it would not be an easy matter to prevail upon many of the parents to send their children to school.

That would be an objection to sending them to day schools, but not to sending them to Sunday schools; what do you think of the practicability of getting the greater part of them to attend Sunday schools?—I think many of them might be induced to attend Sunday schools; but some would not, except remuneration in the shape of clothing was held out, or in some other way to induce the parents to send them; I give that as an opinion, from this circumstance, that although the children whom we are educating under the Establishment are so very few, yet the applications for admission are not so numerous as we could expect.

Even though you give clothing as well as education?—Yes.

Is there a great proportion of Dissenters in the parish?—Very great indeed.

Do you not conceive that the objections which Dissenters may have to send their children to schools on the National establishment, is one cause of the deficiency you have mentioned?—I think I have assigned a reason before, that they find them useful at so early an age, in earning something towards their own maintenance; that I consider the principal cause.

May not the cause assigned in the preceding question be a secondary cause?—It certainly may.

Do you conceive the education is well conducted at the schools on the establishment which you have before mentioned?—Not so well as it might be.

Would not the parents be more ready to send their children to a better conducted school?—I do not think that would be a matter of consideration with them, the circumstance of their having clothing is, I apprehend, the principal inducement.

But if they saw a greater advancement in learning among the children who went to a better conducted school, would not that be an inducement to send them?—As far as our notions of things go, it certainly would, but I do not know how far it might operate upon the minds of people themselves destitute of education.

Do

Do you not uniformly find that those who have themselves received instruction, are anxious that their children should have the same advantage?—Yes, I think they are principally the better informed people who make applications for their children to be admitted into our schools.

If some small advantage could be held out, of clothing and pecuniary assistance to poor parents, your applications would probably be increased?—Not with respect to these particular schools, but to Sunday schools it would.

Have you any Sunday schools under the Establishment?—None.

Are you not of opinion it would be highly desirable to try a plan for Sunday schools in your parish?—Unquestionably it would, if we had adequate means.

Is there any building that could be applied to the purpose?—I do not know of any; I was very desirous a few years ago of establishing a Sunday school, and applied to the parish officers for the use of the committee-room for the purpose, but, being unsuccessful in my application, the plan was abandoned.

You meant the committee-room to answer the purpose of a school-room?—Yes; it is shut up on a Sunday, and I thought it would have been no great concession on the part of the parish officers, if they had lent it to us for such a purpose.

Have any individuals in the parish ever applied to you, expressing a wish to promote the institution of Sunday schools?—One gentleman alone, I think his name is Everett; and it was in consequence of that application from him, that an application was made to the parish officers for the use of the committee-room.

And upon the failure in that point, no further effort has been made?—No.

When was this application made to the parish officers?—I think about two years ago.

Are crimes very frequent in your parish?—The police magistrates could speak more to that point than myself; but I have observed a great deal of disorderly conduct, and I attribute much of it to the want of education.

Do you observe a considerable difference in the conduct of those who are educated and those who are not?—It is natural to conceive that those who have received education would be the more orderly, but it is impossible to distinguish individuals among so many thousands.

Is your workhouse crowded with juvenile objects?—Yes.

Do they receive any education in the workhouse?—They are taught to read, but their education is very badly attended to.

Is there a regular schoolmaster?—There is a pauper in the house who is called schoolmaster, a man who, I think, with proper encouragement, would cause the children to make greater proficiency than they do.

Has he a stipend given him by the parish, to instruct the children?—I believe not.

Is he one of the persons confined in the workhouse?—Yes, he is; and therefore I do not suppose he has any allowance from the parish.

Is particular attention paid to the morals of those juvenile objects in the workhouse, by the matron or other person, or whoever happens to be the governor?—I have not an opportunity of forming an opinion, for by the time they are capable of perpetrating crimes, they are sent down to the country to be employed in manufactures.

What is the general manners of children in the parish, that of civility or rudeness?—Rude and unmannerly in the extreme, being under no sort of control.

What is their appearance, with regard to cleanliness?—Filthy, and very ragged.

Can you conceive a greater blessing to them, than being induced to receive education?—None greater, and nothing more likely to correct their manners and produce a reform.

Do you conceive it possible, in the present state of the parish, for its minister to make the impression he would wish on its inhabitants?—Certainly not, it is utterly impracticable; for so populous a parish, there is only one parish church capable of containing about twelve hundred persons.

Do the poor frequent it much?—As far as our accommodation will allow, our aisles are overflowing.

Do those who attend, behave in an orderly manner?—They do.

Should you conceive, if there was more room, there would be a greater attendance?—No doubt about it.

495.

Are

*The Rev.*
*Joshua King.*

Are there any chapels of ease, or episcopal chapels of any kind, in the parish?—There is an episcopal chapel, which has been erected within the last two years, and which is as full as it can hold; but the greater part of the seats, I apprehend, are appropriated to the use of the rich.

But do you conceive that a population with such manners and habits as you have described to prevail among the poor, would be induced to attend Divine Service, until some change was wrought in them?—Not till you have laid the foundation by education; there are many more who would attend, but the principal number of course would not, having no ideas of religion.

Are there many Methodist or other dissenting places of worship in the parish?—A considerable number.

Do you consider them to be increasing?—Very rapidly.

Are they well attended in general?—That I cannot say.

Do you happen to know whether the children of Dissenters are more regular in their attendance at those places of worship, than those of the Established Church?—I apprehend not; their schools are principally Sunday schools, and they take the children to some place of worship; our children are also brought from the workhouse, and from the schools, to the church on the Sunday; but it is very evident to me that the establishment of a Sunday school or Sunday schools in the parish would be productive of a great deal of good, for many of the children now educated at Dissenters Sunday schools belong to parents of the National Establishment, who, it is natural to suppose, would prefer sending their children to Sunday schools belonging to the Establishment, if any such existed.

You attribute the fact, of children of parents of the National Church being sent to Dissenting schools, entirely to the want of affording them the means of instruction under the Establishment?—Certainly.

Had you any experience of a parish differently situated, before you went to the parish of Bethnal Green?—Excepting what I saw in the country, where there were generally free schools. One very great benefit resulting from Sunday schools would be, preventing the children from joining those riotous assemblages in Hare-street fields, or the field adjoining the church, every Sunday, which consist of many hundred persons, principally boys and men, who assemble, fight dogs, hunt ducks, gamble, and enter into subscriptions to fee a drover for a bullock to hunt on the Sunday evening, or for their diversion on Monday.

So that the effect of these assemblies is in fact to make Monday completely an idle and riotous day?—Yes, it is; for as soon as the bullock is driven into a populous part of the parish, hundreds and thousands join in the chace, and leave their looms: they consist principally of boys and men.

Do you imagine that suitable means of education would greatly tend to lessen the evil of drunkenness?—Unquestionably.

Do you consider that the good effects of education extend to the parents, as well as to the children, who may themselves have been without the means of instruction?—That education produces such an effect, to a certain extent, is, I believe, universally admitted.

*Martis*, 11° *die Junii*, 1816.

HENRY BROUGHAM, Esquire, in The Chair.

---

Mr.
F. A. Earle.

Mr. *Frederick Augustus Earle* delivered in Plans of Shelton's charity school, now building in St. Giles's : from which it appeared, that it is one story high, built over a gateway, and is 21 feet in front, widening to 23 feet behind, and is 20 feet in depth ; and that upon the same floor there is the master's room, 12 feet by 4, and a bed-room 10 feet 6 inches by 8 feet, with a passage and a small closet ; the whole expense of building which is to cost upwards of 800 *l.*

The Reverend *John Campbell*, called in, and Examined.

The Rev.
John Campbell.

ARE you connected with any charity schools at Kingsland ?—Yes ; I have been connected with them ever since their commencement.

In what year did they commence ?—About fifteen years ago the Sunday schools commenced on a very small scale ; in the year 1808, we commenced the day school.

How many children have you in the day school at Kingsland ?—Two hundred boys in the large school, and one hundred girls in the small school.

What are the dimensions of your large school-room for boys ?—Seventy feet in length, thirty in breadth ; seventeen feet in height at the one end, and fourteen at the other ; the floor ascends at the back part.

When you speak of the height, do you mean the height of the walls ?—Of the walls.

Is the ceiling plastered ?—No, it is open.

Have you an additional height in the roof, independent of the height of the walls ?—Considerably.

What is the height altogether, including the roof ?—I do not know as to that.

What was the expense of the erection of the large school-room ?—Including fittings-up within the walls, about 430 *l.*

Does that include desks and forms, and all other fittings-up belonging to the rooms ?—Yes.

How many children will that school-room contain ?—Three hundred, exclusive of the aisles all round, for carrying on the system so as not to be crowded.

And also room for the master's desk, and other conveniences ?—Yes.

On what plan are the schools conducted ?—On the British system.

How many girls have you in the school-room ?—One hundred.

What is the annual expense of supporting both schools ?—One hundred and fifty, exclusive of the clothing for eighty girls, which is by private subscriptions.

How is the money to pay the expenses raised ?—By annual subscriptions, and one collection in the chapel yearly.

How many children have passed through your schools since the commencement in 1808 ?—About two hundred have gone from us ; there were not so many at first as we now have ; it was a considerable time only for two hundred children in the first school ; and it was not taught upon the Lancasterian scheme at all till that new school-house was built last year.

How long does a scholar remain in the school, upon the general average ?—We receive them at five years of age, and they continue till fourteen, if their parents do not take them away.

Do the children in general continue so long ?—No, they mostly come in at the ages of eight, nine, and ten.

At what age do they leave the school ?—Generally about fourteen.

Have you observed any but good effects resulting from this school at Kingsland ?—Many have gone from the school to be servants in families, and apprentices ; and behaving well, many of their parents have adopted sober habits in consequence of the change that was effected in their children ; and there is a marked difference between children newly admitted, and those who have been some time there, they are more rude and rebellious at first admission than those who have been some time at school.

But

But the change in the neighbourhood is most visible since the commencement of the schools.

Was the neighbourhood of Kingsland notorious for persons of bad character before the institution of those schools?—Yes, in general, the lower orders in the village were extremely wicked and riotous; the place abounded in bull fights, men fights, intoxication, and thieving; that I know from good information: the old inhabitants frequently speak of the remarkable alteration in those respects.

Does your school extend to the village of Haggerstone?—We have one or two children from New Haggerstone, not Old. We have only a few children from Haggerstone. The children being taught to read, has produced a desire in their poor parents, who are mostly rude brickmakers, to be able to read. To gratify those desires we began an adult evening school last November, from 6 to 9 o'clock, four nights in the week; at the opening 40 attended, which soon increased to 110, who continued regular attendants all winter to Lady-day; many of them, being thus kept from the public-houses, were overheard to say, in the brickfields, by their master, that they had saved to their families from 4s. to 6s. per week by attending school; and on those, as on savages, reading has a civilizing influence.

Do you find that education renders children less industrious, or females less inclined to enter upon service?—No; though there are instances of females who must have been servants, but for the school; by their acquiring additional knowledge of needlework, they have been able to commence milliners and mantuamakers for themselves; there are various instances in which they would have been servants, had they not had this education at school.

You do not mean to say that the education at school prevents a great number from being servants?—No.; but their education has raised them higher in life.

Have you been in the habit of visiting the parents of children sent to your school?—Frequently we do; that is, the members of the committee do.

Has that intercourse between the members of the committee and the parents of the children, been followed with good effects to the families of the poor?—Yes, by the distribution of the Scriptures among them, and by relieving and conversing with them when sick, which we attend particularly to with respect to the school parents.

Do the visits which are paid by the school, for the relief of the sick poor, promote the education of children in charity schools, by giving an opportunity to the visitors to recommend to the parents to send their children to those charity schools?—Yes, both by their having an opportunity of recommending their sending their children to school, and likewise the parents feel an obligation to gentlemen or ladies, who thus visit, to take their advice.

Have any instances come to your knowledge of children turning out ill after they have received instruction in those schools?—I and several of the gentlemen in the management of the school had a meeting, within a few days, to inquire into that very circumstance, and we could only find six who had turned out bad since the year 1808.

Did you make this inquiry in consequence of a Report unfavourable to schools having been made from the prison of Newgate?—Yes.

Did you find that that Report rested upon any solid foundation?—We called a meeting, as I have stated, at which there were present the two masters of the largest brick-field in Kingsland, also the mother of one of the boys, Fox, who was confined in Newgate; and Pond, who also had been confined in Newgate, his father was there; and we did not find one charge respecting Kingsland substantiated.

Did you understand that any of the boys apprehended for public offences had formerly been in Kingsland school?—Yes, three.

Had they been expelled from the school for misconduct?—I should mention in the first place, we do not expel for bad conduct, we suspend them; they had been once or twice suspended, and afterwards dismissed for bad conduct, previous to their committing those deeds for which they were imprisoned.

Did the master of the brick-field give any particular evidence of the beneficial effects of the school?—He mentioned that he had never heard of the meetings of boys and girls in the brick-fields for the bad purposes that had been stated in the Report from Newgate.

Is it your practice to expel children of bad character from the schools when they are discovered?—Not at first; we generally suspend them for a time, on vicious conduct appearing; there is no fixed time, sometimes three weeks or a month; and on amendment receive them back, and sometimes receive them back a second time. If they appear irrecoverable, they are expelled.

. Are

*The Rev.*
*John Campbell.*

Are the girls and boys schools quite distinct and separate from each other?—Perfectly distinct.

Are there pains taken to prevent any improper communication between the sexes?—They always go out at different times, one before the other considerably, with that view.

Have you known of any evils resulting from the intercourse of boys and girls in that school?—None.

Are your schools open to all religious denominations?—Yes, to all.

Do you oblige the children to attend any particular place of worship?—No; when we find that the parents do attend a place of worship, we recommend the children to go with their parents, and also the parents to see that they do go.

But if you had reason to believe the parents did not attend with their children, then should you take them to Kingsland chapel?—Then in that case, having two parts of the gallery in the chapel fitted up for the reception of the children, we should oblige them to go there.

What do you conceive are the general advantages of those schools?—They appear to me to promote civilization among the lower orders, industry, greater attachment to their children, and cleanliness.

Are there any and what defects in the present system of charity schools, which you think might be remedied?—We know of none; the master says that he could teach three times the number with the same facility as the present number, that he could teach 600 as easily as 200.

Have you not room to accommodate them?—No.

And you think the children become exalted in the minds of their parents, and there is a stronger reciprocal attachment between the parents and their children?—That has very often been manifested; the children reading to their parents, raises them in the estimation of their parents, being unable to acquire any information from books, if their children are absent.

And the children possessing education, seem more valuable in the eyes of their parents?—Yes. One circumstance that led the Catholics in Ireland in a certain district, I think it was in the vicinity of Belfast, to wish to obtain reading for part of their family, was the issuing the one-shilling, two-shilling, and five-shilling notes; there were instances of men going with their cow to market, and bringing home a five-shilling note instead of a five-pound one; in consequence of this, they resolved that at least one of their children should be able to read, to accompany them to market, to distinguish notes; the priests could never successfully oppose that measure; and that was the commencement in Ireland of a desire among the lower orders of Catholics to read.

Have you travelled in the Southern parts of Africa?—I have.

Is it your travels in that part of the world of which an account is published?—Yes.

What effects have you observed resulting from education upon the savage nations in Southern Africa?—I should first state, there are part of three nations who are capable of reading, the Hottentots, the Griquas, and the Namacquas; a considerable number of those nations have been taught by the missionaries to read, and, from the statement of those missionaries when I was present with them, they considered their reading as particularly conducible to promote civilization. I am so convinced of the civilizing influence of such instruction, that among the Wankelnes where I was (where, a short time before, Dr. Cohen, Lieut. Donnovan, and twenty of the Cape regiment had been all murdered) that were reading among that people taught for one year, I could with the utmost facility visit that nation; I think the influence of instruction is so powerful.

What language have they learnt to read?—Those three nations that I have mentioned before, can speak the Dutch language as well as their own.

Were there any tracts distributed among them in the Dutch language?—Yes.

Of what description?—Published by the Religious Tract Society in London.

Were they able to understand, as well as read, the tracts which had been so distributed?—The same as the lower orders in England. I will here just state one fact: I got twelve of the Hottentots who accompanied me in the interior of Africa, on our return to Cape Town, fully instructed in the British system of education, on purpose that they might commence, upon that plan, a school at Bethelsdorp, which is about 550 miles from the Cape.

In what direction?—South-east, towards the Indian ocean. About four months ago, I received a letter respecting that school, stating that upwards of sixty Hot-

tentots,

tentots, who ten months before knew not their letters, could read the Dutch Testament as well as the missionaries.

You found the Hottentots as quick in receiving their education, as the people in England?—Nearly so; it brings them into a new world to be able to know what a book says, it is completely a new world. I may mention here, that I have found nothing so difficult as to convey to the conception of a savage how a book spake. I attempted with the King of Lattakoo, to make him understand it, but he and his principal men all shook their heads, and said it was impossible to understand it; I took a journal that lay before me, in which I had inserted, from the lips of his uncle, the names of his forefathers, who had been kings before him (the government is hereditary;) this I read to the king and his chief men, on which they perceived that I had formerly stated the truth, but had no idea how the book gave me that information; the king inquired if it would be possible for them and their children, by the instructions of a white man, to understand what books "said" (there is no other way of conveying reading, they can form no idea of what reading is, it is only speaking;) he and his people seemed highly gratified when I stated, that in the course of a few moons after the arrival of a teacher, they should be able to understand reading as well as myself. The missionaries have not yet arrived there, so that I can give no idea of the success.

Could you favour the Committee with any sentiments upon the best plan of extending the benefits of education to the lower classes of the Metropolis?—I have no particular plan to recommend; the plan of the schools on the British system appears to me best calculated for effecting that end.

### Robert Owen, Esq. called in, and Examined.

HAS your attention been directed to the education and circumstances of the lower orders?—Yes, it has been particularly directed to those objects, for the last twenty-five years.

How long have you been settled in Scotland?—Upwards of sixteen years, in the superintendence of the cotton mills at New Lanark.

You do not come from that part of the country originally?—No, from Wales but immediately from Manchester.

Have you attended practically to that subject?—I have been daily, during twenty-five years, occupied in practice, and my late proceedings have been entirely directed by the result of that practice.

How many persons have you generally had under your care?—From 500 to 2300 during the whole of that time.

Have you adopted the new mode of education among them, and upon what plan?—I have adopted a combination of the Madras and British and Foreign systems, with other parts that experience has pointed out.

What is your opinion of the advantages of the new plan?—That it gives great facility to children to acquire a knowledge of reading, writing, and arithmetic, and the girls sewing; these acquirements are learned in a much shorter time on the new than on the old plan.

What is the result of your observation, with respect to the comparative advantages and disadvantages of the two modes adopted by the National Society, and the British and Foreign School Society?—As they are now practised, the Madras system possesses an advantage over the British and Foreign; by the former, the children learn to read in a shorter time and in a more accurate manner; in other respects I do not think there is much difference.

Do you think that whatever difference there is, is on the side of the National or on the other, in those other objects?—It is difficult for me to decide which of them ought to be preferred, each possesses its peculiar advantages.

Do you consider, the other things being equal, there is no very material difference between the advantages of the two systems?—I think the difference is very immaterial; but I consider the Madras system as having disadvantages which is made up by its superiority in reading, and I think the British and Foreign has the advantage in other parts; which prevents me saying which, as a whole, is the best.

To what do you ascribe the superiority of the Madras system as to reading?—To the very distinct manner in which the boys are instructed in every part of reading, from the letters to the end of their instruction, particularly as I have seen it practised in the National school in Baldwin's-gardens.

Do you mean the distinct manner in which they pronounce the words; or did you

*Robert Owen.
Esq.*

mean to extend your answer to understanding what they read?—To the distinct manner in which they pronounce the words, and to the manner also in which the attention of the children is directed to the whole subject.

You conceive that their minds are more attentive to the subject and sense of what they read there?—They are necessarily obliged to attend more to every detail before them, than is required from the children under the British and Foreign system.

Did you remark any difference under the two systems, in the mode of explaining the sense?—It is generally much more fully explained under the National system than in the British and Foreign.

So as to lead the child to enter more into the subject, and to understand it better?—Yes, and to bring some of the mental faculties forward more rapidly.

Did you observe any difference in the manners and looks of the children attending those different schools, indicative of the superior knowledge or obedience in the one compared with the other?—I have been very much interested with the general appearance and manner of the children under the two opposite systems; I have often been pleased with the performances of the children in Baldwin's-gardens, and I have been particularly pleased with the appearance of the children in a large school in Newcastle-upon-Tyne, under the British and Foreign system.

What should you say were the most prominent circumstances in the appearance of the children in Baldwin's-gardens and at Newcastle, which pleased you?—In the school at Newcastle the appearance of the children was particularly gratifying, even more so than the children at the National school in Baldwin's-gardens, and I think the cause may be explained to arise from the longer time the children attend the school at Newcastle, than is customary for the children to attend in the school in Baldwin's-gardens; there are no manufactories in the neighbourhood of Newcastle to induce the parents to withhold the children from attending the school, and I found, upon inquiry, that the children remained in this school about four years upon an average, while in other situations in the manufacturing districts, at Manchester and Leeds, the children do not remain upon the average longer than three or four months.

How long do you imagine they remain upon the average at the National schools in London?—I have generally made the inquiry at most of the schools in which I have been, but I am not quite sure of the time mentioned by Mr. Johnson, the master of the National school in Baldwin's-gardens; less than four years, and the impression upon my mind is even less than two.

With respect to the appearance of the children in the National schools and the British and Foreign schools in London; where the children attend in a general view, under similar circumstances, do you think there was any distinction?—I have found a considerable difference to arise from the manner in which the school was conducted, either by the master or mistress, or the parties who interested themselves in the general superintendence of the school. It occurs to me at present, that I saw a number of girls in one of the British and Foreign schools, under apparently remarkably good habits; and I attribute it principally to two circumstances I have mentioned, namely, the mistress appeared to take a very lively interest in the instruction of the children; and I know there are many of the visiting females who also take considerable interest in the general superintendence of it.

You esteem it to be a very considerable object, where the thing is practicable, that children should continue at school for a greater length of time than is necessary merely to teach them to read and write?—I consider the facility with which children acquire the common rudiments of learning, an unfortunate result of the new system; for as they are now practised, the children too rapidly become possessed of learning, and they have not time to acquire those habits and dispositions which have always appeared to me to be of more importance than the acquirement of those rudiments of learning.

Has it fallen at all in your way to observe, whether knowledge very speedily acquired, is more readily lost and forgotten than that which is acquired somewhat more gradually?—Yes, I think it is much more speedily lost when it has been rapidly acquired. In confirmation of this opinion, from experience, I have been led in the establishment at Lanark, to receive children at the age of three years, principally for the purpose of preventing them acquiring bad habits, which they would have done, if they had been permitted to ramble in the streets among children who were ill instructed, and whose habits were bad; and also for the purpose of giving them good habits, and for settling the knowledge they acquire

more

Robert Owen,
Esq.

more firmly in their minds; they are continued in the school afterwards for seven years.

In giving explanations, it is very possible to make a child understand each sentence taken singly, and that yet at the end of his reading he shall have little or no notion of the general subject on which he has been reading?—Surely.

Have you seen the practice of that mode of explanation and its effects, as compared with the mode of explanation which not only explains each sentence to the child, but also gives it a general view of the subject?—I have not seen that put into practice, in any situation that occurs to me at present, in a manner satisfactory to myself.

Have you found the parents are too apt to take children out of the school as soon as they can perform the mechanical parts of reading and writing fluently, and, as the parents think, exceedingly well, without perhaps having their minds much opened?—I have found that practice very generally to prevail.

Do you not esteem it a great evil, and one which should if possible be counteracted?—I esteem it a very great evil.

Do you think that it would be an improper sacrifice with respect to mere reading and writing, if a child were not to advance so very rapidly in them as to induce its parent to take it away before its mind were in a measure opened and its good habits tolerably well formed?—In lieu of considering it to be any sacrifice made upon the part of the parent or child, I think it would be a benefit to both.

Has it ever happened to you to observe the bad effects produced on the dispositions of children, from the extremely rapid progress in mere reading and writing; that they become self-conceited in consequence?—I have found the children have derived very little benefit from being rapidly instructed in reading and writing, particularly when no attention has been given on the part of the superintendent to form their dispositions and their habits.

What is the plan adopted by you?—The children are received into a preparatory or training school at the age of three, in which they are perpetually superintended, to prevent them acquiring bad habits, to give them good ones, and to form their dispositions to mutual kindness and a sincere desire to contribute all in their power to benefit each other; these effects are chiefly accomplished by example and practice, precept being found of little use, and not comprehended by them at this early age; the children are taught also whatever may be supposed useful, that they can understand, and this instruction is combined with as much amusement as is found to be requisite for their health, and to render them active, cheerful and happy, fond of the school and of their instructors. The school, in bad weather, is held in apartments properly arranged for the purpose; but in fine weather the children are much out of doors, that they may have the benefit of sufficient exercise in the open air. In this training-school the children remain two or three years, according to their bodily strength and mental capacity; when they have attained as much strength and instruction as to enable them to unite, without creating confusion, with the youngest classes in the superior school, they are admitted into it; and in this school they are taught to read, write, account, and the girls, in addition, to sew; but the leading object in this more advanced stage of their instruction, is to form their habits and dispositions. The children generally attend this superior day school until they are ten years old; and they are instructed in healthy and useful amusements for an hour or two every day, during the whole of this latter period. Among these exercises and amusements, they are taught to dance; those who have good voices, to sing; and those among the boys who have a natural taste for music, are instructed to play on some instrument. At this age, both boys and girls are generally withdrawn from the day school, and are put into the mills or to some regular employment. Some of the children, however, whose parents can afford to spare the wages which the children could now earn, continue them one, two, or three years longer in the day school, by which they acquire an education which well prepares them for any of the ordinary active employments of life. Those children who are withdrawn from the day school at ten years of age, and put into the mills or to any other occupation in or near the establishment, are permitted to attend, whenever they like, the evening schools, exercises and amusements, which commence as from one to two hours, according to the season of the year, after the regular business of the day is finished, and continue about two hours; and it is found that out of choice about 400, on an average, attend every evening. During these two hours there is a regular change of instruction, and healthy exercise, all of which proceed with

such

such order and regularity as to gratify every spectator, and leave no doubt on any mind, of the superior advantages to be derived from this combined system of instruction, exercise, and amusement. The 400 now mentioned are exclusive of 300 who are taught during the day. On the Sunday, the day scholars attend the school an hour and half in the morning and about the same time in the afternoon ; and the evening scholars, as well as their parents and other adults belonging to the establishment, attend in the evening, when either some religious exercises commence, or a lecture is read, and afterwards the regular business of the evening Sunday school begins. These proceedings seem to gratify the population in a manner not easily to be described, and, if stated much below the truth, would not be credited by many ; inspection alone can give a distinct and comprehensive view of the advantages which such a system affords to all parties interested or connected with it.

How many masters have you in the day schools ?—Generally ten or eleven ; in the evening schools usually two or three more.

Is the expense of this institution considerable ?—It is, apparently ; but I do not know how any capital can be employed to make such abundant returns, as that which is judiciously expended in forming the character and directing the labour of the lower classes. I have made out a short statement of the expense of the instruction of the Institution at Lanark, and the expense of the instruction for 700 scholars, part taught in the day and part in the evening, supposing schools to be erected and furnished : One rector or superior master, at 250 *l.* per annum ; ten assistants, males and females, at 30 *l.* each on the average; light, heat, and materials of all kinds, 150 *l.* ; making together 700 *l.* or 20 *s.* per year for each child, which if taken under tuition at three years old, and retained to the age of ten, would be 7 *l.* each, for forming the habits, dispositions, and general character, and instruction in the elements of every branch of useful knowledge; which acquirements would be of more real value to the individual, and through him to the community, than any sum of money that at present it would be prudent to state. The expenses attending the exercise and amusements are all included.

Have you any means of estimating the expense of instruction under the common day-school plan ?—It varies according to circumstances; I have heard the examinations of the former Witnesses upon this point, and I consider their estimates to have been too low; it is very possible to give a cheap nominal instruction, but to me such instruction appeared to be the least beneficial to the individual and to the community.

What is the expense of building a school in the cheapest manner, capable of instructing 500 or 600 children ?—That will vary very much in different parts of the kingdom, depending materially upon the facility with which the materials for building can be procured.

Should you think 800 *l.* a large sum for this purpose, on the average?—No, not if the school is to be made complete in all respects for the purposes of a useful education.

Is it too small a sum for the purpose ?—I think 1000 *l.* would be a better average in many situations.

Exclusive of the expense of the school, what should you say was a fair expense for educating a child in a school of 500 or 600 children ?—To educate a child in the manner, which appears to me to be most useful to a child and to the community, the expense would not be much less than 20 *s.* per head.

Increasing upon a smaller number of children, and diminishing upon a larger number, of course ?—Not very materially, because I contemplate a material change from the present practice ; I would recommend the schools to have a much greater number of masters.

Do you consider a greater number of masters to be absolutely necessary, than is given upon the new plan?—Yes.

Does not this sacrifice the great advantage of the new plan, which consists in enabling one master to teach a great number of children ?—I consider that circumstance to be a defect in the present system; it is impossible, in my opinion, for one master to do justice to children, when they attempt to educate a great number without proper assistance.

What are the obstacles to children being taught at the National schools?—The principles on which the schools are founded, which oblige the children of Dissenters to learn the Catechism, the Litany, and to attend the Established Church on a Sunday.

Do you believe that that prevents many Dissenters from attending?—I can have

no

*Robert Owen,*
*Esq.*

no doubt of it; particularly because many Dissenters have had no godfathers or god-mothers at the children's baptism, and when their children are compelled to repeat the catechism of the Church of England, they are compelled solemnly to repeat falsehoods.

How does a Dissenter's child answer the question respecting godfathers or god-mothers in the catechism?—In the usual mode.

Suppose a Dissenter's child, in answer to that question put, says " I had no god-father or godmother," what objection would be made by the catechist?—That it was not the regular reply to the question that they put.

Would there be any objections to admitting such questions as that, and to confine the Catechism to such parts as both Dissenters and Churchmen can answer?—I know of none ; but I am not competent to speak upon such a subject.

From what you have seen of the managers of such schools, do you apprehend there would be any objection, on their part, to such a modification of the Cate-chism?—I should think not.

If those difficulties were got over, and the children allowed to attend their own place of worship, what objection could there be to Dissenters sending their children to the National schools?—None, that I know of.

In a small place, not capable of maintaining more schools than one, do you apprehend that the establishment of the National school prevents the lower orders from being educated at all?—I think it very probably would.

Suppose in any one town, where two schools may be established, one upon each principle ; do you apprehend that that exclusive plan can have any bad effects?—Yes.

What are they?—I consider the children would be necessarily trained, in some degree, in opposition to each other, and not in those principles of cordiality towards each other, which would be so beneficial in general society ; and therefore, that one general system of instruction would be far more beneficial.

What has been your own practice with reference to religious instruction?—That no child has been asked to learn any particular religious creed, contrary to the wishes of its parents.

Can you give the Committee the ages of the children in your establishment?—This paper contains them.

[It was delivered in, and read, as follows :]

| Males. | | | | Females. | | |
|---|---|---|---|---|---|---|
| 35 | - | - | - | 25 | of 3 years old. |
| 27 | - | - | - | 19 | - 4 | ———— |
| 29 | - | - | - | 30 | - 5 | ———— |
| 27 | - | - | - | 21 | - 6 | ———— |
| 34 | - | - | - | 22 | - 7 | ———— |
| 26 | - | - | - | 24 | - 8 | ———— |
| 30 | - | - | - | 23 | - 9 | ———— |
| 38 | - | - | - | 34 | - 10 | ———— |
| 246 | - | - | - | 198 | | |
| | | | | 246 | | |

444 from 3 to 10 inclusive.

| Males. | | | Females. |
|---|---|---|---|
| 155 | - | - - | 124 |
| | | | 155 |

279 from 6 to 10 inclusive.

The Reverend *James Blenkarne*, called in, and Examined.

*The Rev.*
*James Blenkarne.*

YOU are assistant minister of the Established Church at Saint Olave's?—Yes, I am ; I was curate.

What is the Saint Olave's school?—It is called Queen Elizabeth's Free Grammar School.

Have you got a copy of the charter?—I never saw the charter ; the governors are in possession of it.

How many children are educated at that school?—Two hundred and seventy we have now in the three schools.

Are

The Rev.
James Blenkarne.

Are you master?—I am.

Of what ages are those children?—They are of various ages : I have masters under me.

What are the children taught?—They begin with English, reading, and accounts, Latin and Greek : I am the master of the grammar school.

Is it a day school?—Yes.

None boarded?—No.

How many is the school founded for?—I believe the number is indefinite; but it will not contain many more than 270, which has been the greatest number. We have three distinct schools. There are sixty boys in the grammar school, of which I am the head master: the second master of that school is also a clergyman and a master of arts. Then there are three masters in the English school, which consists of 170 boys : there are two masters in the writing school, in which school there are 30 upon what we call writing; when they are more advanced they are allowed that privilege, after about thirteen.

At what age are the boys admitted?—About six or seven years; as soon as they can read we admit them into the English school.

How long do they remain in?—Generally till they are about fourteen; but with regard to the boys in the Latin school, it rests with the parents: we have two exhibitions, and they may go to the university, if their parents think proper.

Do the children pay any thing?—No, they have every thing free.

What are the funds of the school?—That I cannot exactly speak to; it consists of estates and freehold houses; but what the real income of the school is I cannot positively speak to.

What are the expenses of the school?—The head master has 115 l. a year, and a house to live in; the second master of the grammar school has 100 l. only, no house; the head master in the writing school has 100 l. a year, and a house to live in; the second master in the writing school has 75 l. a year; the first master in the reading school has 90 l. the second, 75 l. and the third, 65 l. The boys have their books and every thing found them, they are not put to the least expense possible; the governors find them books of all kinds, which, I should suppose, amounts to about 70 l. a year. The school was originally founded by some inhabitants of the parish; but the name, I believe, as far as I can learn from information, of the Free Grammar School Saint Olaves, it went by that name, I believe, ab origine.

Do you know the date it bears?—No, I cannot tell that; the charter was renewed in Queen Elizabeth's time, and she begged it might be called after her name, and it has been so ever since. Saint John's parish includes part of Saint Olave's, therefore we take that in.

They are equally entitled?—Yes.

Have you mentioned all the expenses that you know of?—I do not know of any other expenses; there are two charity schools, and I believe they give 30 l. a year to each.

Have you any knowledge at all of the funds?—Not the least.

Do they consist only of estates and houses?—Yes, I believe that is all.

Who are entitled to admission into the school?—Any who belong to the parish are entitled to admission through the governors.

Are any admitted into the school who do not belong to the parish?—No, it is confined to the two parishes.

Are there two exhibitions in general?—Yes. I have been master of the school twenty-seven years, and I have sent only two; one, my own son, who has been sent to the university with an exhibition of 70 l. a year, and another, Mr. Abdy, with an exhibition of 50 l. a year.

Are those the only two?—Those are the only two I have sent since I have been master.

Who has the general management of the funds of the school?—The sixteen governors. There is one warden for the year, and every thing is paid by him.

Who is warden?—Mr. Allen Shuter.

Are there any children of the lower orders in the school?—We do not object to any on that account.

Mr.

Mr. *Morris Lievesley*, called in, and Examined.

YOU are secretary to the Foundling hospital?—Yes.

How many children are provided for at present in the Foundling?—Four hundred.

How many boys and how many girls?—Two hundred of each.

What are they instructed in?—The boys are instructed in reading, writing, and accounts, upon Dr. Bell's system; and the younger boys are taught knitting, for the purposes of the children in general.

To what age do they remain in the school?—Between fourteen and fifteen.

What do you do with them generally?—Apprentice them out to trades, or as menial servants.

With a premium?—Without, invariably: if a boy was maimed, or imbecile in mind, we might give ten pounds, but that is with great caution.

What are the girls instructed in?—Needlework; and eighteen of them have two hours a-week to learn writing and accounts, and the master finds that quite sufficient; and as they go out, others are placed in their room.

All the girls learn to read and write, in succession?—Yes, and they are also in the same succession placed in the laundry and in the kitchen; that is our constant practice.

Has any change been lately made in the rules of receiving children into the Foundling?—At one time it was the practice, and it continued for many years, that children were received into the hospital upon the presentation of 100*l.*; that resolution which authorized the admission, was rescinded I believe in the year 1801, since which no children have been admitted into the Foundling with money.

How are they admitted?—By petition, the mother personally appearing.

How long is it since foundlings have ceased to be admitted?—I believe in the year 1759, when Parliament withdrew their annual grants, and then the hospital was forced to depend upon their own resources.

Do the women come as strangers in general?—They are all strangers, without recommendation.

What are the appointed days for receiving petitions?—Wednesdays, throughout the year, at ten o'clock in the morning.

Do the women bring their children with, or leave them?–Never.

What is the consequence of the petition?—The mother is personally examined, and that examination, with the petition, is put into the hands of the officer who makes the inquiry, and reports to the Committee on the following Wednesday.

Who is the officer?—Mr. Atcheson.

What is his designation?—Late schoolmaster; I believe he has been there forty years.

When are the children received?—The children are generally received once in six weeks upon the average; when we have admitted half a dozen children, we have a baptism, and the nurses are sent for from the country.

At what ages?—All ages under twelve months.

May any body bring the children, besides their mothers?—Any person having the ticket of admission.

At what age do the girls leave the school?—Between fourteen and fifteen, the same as the boys.

And put out to service in the same way?—Yes, to menial service.

Have you any further information to give to the Committee?—Whenever any of our girls from the hospital fail in their duties during their apprenticeships, we apprentice them to Mr. Oldknow, a cotton-spinner at Mellor near Stockport; and in upwards of fifty cases, Mr. Oldknow has succeeded in making them useful members of society, in fact he has never failed.

*Mercurii, 12° die Junii*, 1816.

HENRY BROUGHAM, Esquire, in The Chair.

———

Sir *Samuel Romilly*, a Member of the Committee, Examined.

WILL you be kind enough to inform the Committee whether the relator in an information upon a charity in the Court of Chancery is subject to any costs?—The relator is subject to all the costs of the suit ; he is subject to be ordered to pay the costs, if the court shall think there was no foundation for the complaint.

What is the relator in such suit?—Any private individual who thinks that a charity has been abused, may file an information in the name of the attorney general, subject of course to the attorney general's approbation, complaining of such abuse, and by so making himself the relator to the attorney general, he subjects himself to all such costs as the court may ultimately determine ought to be paid by the person who promoted that suit.

Have any measures been taken lately to diminish the costs on such applications?—There has been an Act passed, which is the 52d George III. cap. 101, which was brought in at my suggestion, and which enables any person to present a petition to the Lord Chancellor, or the Master of the Rolls, or the Barons of the Exchequer, complaining of any abuse of a charitable trust ; and that Act provides that the case may be heard in a summary way upon affidavits without the forms of pleadings in equity, and all the proceedings upon it are by the Act exempted from the stamp duties : that Act has greatly diminished the expense of bringing complaints of the abuses of charitable trusts before courts of justice. The costs of an information are in general extremely high, so high that it must be an act of great imprudence in any person to become relator in such a suit, unless it is quite clear that he shall be able to establish in evidence such a case of abuse of trust as will induce the court to make the defendants pay the costs of it, or at all events to order that the costs be paid out of the estate itself; and I have known many cases in which the costs, if paid out of the charity estate, would make it impossible that the purposes of the charity could be fulfilled for many years.

Are the costs upon a petition, under the regulations of the Act above referred to, considerable?—Comparatively they are very inconsiderable ; there may be cases in which there are many affidavits, where the costs may amount to a good deal.

Suppose a charity in a remote part of the country, would the costs of a proceeding by petition, in the case of abuses of such charity, be considerable?—I do not think the remoteness of the place where the charity was established would make any difference in the costs, the evidence must be by affidavit, which may be as well taken in the country as in town ; a town agent must be employed, but I believe that occasions no additional costs, the solicitor employed pays the fees of the town agent.

Must it not be necessary to send some person to town on purpose, in such a case?—I believe in such cases it is very frequently done ; but as the court decides only upon the written evidence, I do not imagine that in any case it is necessary.

Should you consider 50*l.* to be a large amount of costs in a proceeding of this nature?—In a proceeding under a petition, I should consider it a very large demand ; but at the same time I ought to say that I really know very little of the amount of costs.

If the allegation of petitions are contested by the defendants, might not that lead to an increase of expense?—It certainly might, very considerably.

May the court, upon a proceeding of this sort by petition, direct an issue or examination upon interrogatories in the common way?—I do not apprehend the court could direct an examination of witnesses upon interrogatories ; but undoubtedly if upon any important fact there was contradictory evidence upon the affidavits, I apprehend the court might and certainly would direct an issue to try those facts; and the trial of such issue would be attended with very considerable expense.

Have many informations been filed, notwithstanding that Act?—I am not able to answer that question ; I do not know what informations have been filed, I know

495. nothing

nothing of informations till their time of coming on to be heard; and it is not likely that many would come to a hearing in that period, since the Act was passed in the present state of business in the Court of Chancery.

Would a litigious defendant, availing himself of the forms of court, be enabled to protract the proceeding, and increase the petitioners expenses?—I think not; in an information, the defendant may protract the proceedings for a great length of time, and may increase the expense very considerably, but in a proceeding under the Act he has no means of doing it.

### Mr. *Henry Smith Speck*, called in, and Examined.

YOU are clerk to the Corporation of the Saint Olave's free grammar school?—Yes, I am.

Have you brought the accounts of the school?—It is impossible for me to get at the accounts, as they are in the strong room, under the care of three of the governors.

From what do the revenues of the school arise?—From lands and tenements, and from monies in the funds.

What is the whole amount of the revenue?—Now about 1400 *l.* a year.

How much of it arises from rents?—The whole, within 53 *l.* a year.

What are the expenses of the establishment?—The whole revenue is expended.

What are the salaries paid out of it?—We have a head master, who has 115 *l.* a year, and a house; the second master has 100 *l.* a year, and no house; the first writing master 100 *l.* a year, the principal reading master 90 *l.* a year, the assistant writing usher 75 *l.* a year, the second reading master 75 *l.* a year, the under writing master 65 *l.* a year, the clerk 50 *l.* a year, and the messenger 20 *l.* a year; we have also an engine keeper, at two guineas a year.

What are the other expenses of the school?—There are certain trifling expenses; there are payments made, for bread, which are distributed to the poor.

How is the other 700 *l.* expended?—We have the liberty of sending, by the charter, two boys to the university; we have lately had one only, for which 50 *l.* a year has been allowed; there are various donations to the poor of the parishes of St. Olave and St. John, given at different times of the year; all the books necessary for the use of the school, together with slates and stationary, and every thing that they use, is found at the expense of the charity, and the masters are not on any pretence suffered directly or indirectly to take any fee or reward from the scholars.

Are the donations to the poor under the charter?—They are; we have the power so to do.

Have you the copies of the two Charters?—I have.

[They were delivered in, and read, as follows:]

ELIZABETH by the Grace of God, of England France and Ireland Queen, Defender of the Faith, &c. To all men to whom these our present letters patent shall come, greeting: Whereas our well-beloved subjects the inhabitants of the parish of Saint Olave within our borough of Southwark in our county of Surrey, of their godly affection and good disposition for the bringing up, education, institution and instruction of children and younglings of the said parish, at their no little cost labour and charge, in laudable order and form have of late ordained and erected in the aforesaid borough and parish one grammar school, in the which children and younglings, as well of rich as the poor, being inhabitants within the aforesaid parish, are instructed and brought up liberally and prosperously in grammar in accidence and other lower books, to the common utility and profit of all the inhabitants of the parish aforesaid, as we are credibly informed: And whereas the same our subjects of the parish aforesaid, the inhabitants, have made humble supplication unto us, that the said school so by them ordained and erected may have continual succession, and that we would extend and shew our liberality and princely grace to them in that behalf; WE, considering not only the premises, but also the good godly and laudable intent of the same our subjects in the premises, and entirely desiring as much as in us lyeth to augment and increase all and singular those things which may any way concern the bringing up and instruction of children and younglings, of our grace especial certain knowledge and mere motion, We will grant and ordain, for us our heirs and successors, That the aforesaid school, so by the inhabitants of the parish of Saint Olave aforesaid ordained and erected within the said parish of Saint Olave in Southwark, from henceforth is and shall be one grammar school, for the bringing up institution and instruction of the children and younglings of the parishioners and inhabitants therein, as well in grammar as

in

Mr.
*H. S. Speck.*

in accidence and in other low books and in writing, at all times hereafter to endure; and that that school shall be called " The Free Grammar School of Queen Elizabeth of the parishioners of the parish of Saint Olave in the county of Surrey;" and that school of one master or schoolmaster, and one under schoolmaster or usher, for ever to endure, for to do erect treat ordain declare found and establish by these presents. AND that our intent aforesaid may take the better effect, and that the lands tenements rents revenues and other profits for the sustaining and maintaining of the said school to be granted assigned and appointed, may be better governed; for continuance of the same, we will grant and ordain, That from henceforth for ever there be and shall be, within the parish of Saint Olave aforesaid, sixteen men of discretion and most honest inhabitants in the said parish for the time being, which shall be and be called governors of the possessions revenues and goods of the said free school, commonly called and to be called " The Free Grammar School of Queen Elizabeth of the parishioners of the parish of Saint Olave in Southwark in the county of Surrey;" and therefore know ye, that we have assigned chosen named and appointed, and by these presents do assign, our well-beloved Anthony Bushe, clerk, parson of the parish church of Saint Olave in Southwark aforesaid, William Bond, clerk, minister of the parish church aforesaid, William Wilson, Charles Pratt, John Lambe, Olave Burr, Thomas Poore, Thomas Bullman, William Lands, Richard Harrison, Thomas Harper, John Charman, Robert Cowthe, Christopher Woodward, James Heath, and Thomas Pynden, inhabitants of the aforesaid parish of Saint Olave in Southwark, hereafter and now to be the first present governors of the possessions revenues and goods of the said Free Grammar School of Queen Elizabeth of the parishioners of the parish of Saint Olave in Southwark in the county of Surrey, and the same office well and faithfully to exercise and occupy from the day of the date of these presents, during the life of them and the longer liver of them; and that the same governors in matters deeds and name from henceforth be and shall be one body corporate and politic of themselves for ever, by the name of " The Governors of the possessions revenues and goods of the Free Grammar School of Queen Elizabeth of the parishioners of the parish of Saint Olave in the county of Surrey" incorporated and erected, and them the governors of the possessions revenues and goods of the Free Grammar School of Queen Elizabeth of the parishioners of the parish of Saint Olave Southwark in the county of Surrey, by these presents we do incorporate, and one body corporate and politic by the same name for ever to endure, we do really and as fully create erect ordain found and confirm. And furthermore, we will, and by these presents for us our heirs and successors do ordain and grant, That the same governors of the possessions revenues and goods of the said free grammar school of Queen Elizabeth of the parishioners of the parish of Saint Olave in Southwark in the county of Surrey, have perpetual succession, and by that name they be and shall be persons able apt and in law of capacity to have receive get and possess lordships manors lands tenements meadows feedings pastures parsonages tythes rents revenues services possessions reversions goods chattels and hereditaments whatsoever, or what kind nature or sort soever they be, to them and their successors, in fee and perpetuity, as well for us our heirs and successors as of any other person or persons whatsoever; and also to give grant demise and assign the same lands tenements and hereditaments, and to do and execute all and singular other deeds and matters by the name aforesaid; and that they the said governors be impleaded, answer and be answered unto, defend and be defended, in all and singular actions suits quarrels causes matters and demands, real personal and mixt, of what kind nature and sort soever they be, or whatsoever places or courts of us our heirs and successors, or of others whosoever, or before whatsoever justices and judges, ecclesiastical or temporal, within our realm of England or elsewhere, and all and singular the same to make do and receive in such sort and in the same manner as the other our liege persons able and in law capable within the same our realm of England may and be able to implead and be impleaded, answer and be answered unto, defend and be defended, and have get receive give grant and demise. And furthermore we will, and for us our heirs and successors by these presents do grant to the aforesaid governors and their successors for ever, from hencefore, one common seal to serve for their business in the premises and others in these our letters patent expressed and specified, or some part of the same only touching and concerning. And furthermore we grant ordain and decree by these presents, for us our heirs and successors, That whensoever it shall happen one or more of the said sixteen governors for the time being to die, or inhabit elsewhere without the parish of Saint Olave in Southwark, or from thence with his household to depart; that then and so often it shall be well and lawful for the other said governors over living, or the greater part of them, then dwelling and inhabiting within the parish of Saint Olave in Southwark, to elect and name another meet person or meet persons of the inhabitants of the parish of Saint Olave aforesaid to succeed in the office of governor, in the place or places of him or them so dying, or with his or their household so departing, and that so often as it shall chance or happen. And moreover of our abundant grace, certain knowledge and mere motion, we have given and granted, and by these presents for us and our successors do give and grant to the aforesaid new governors and their successors, and the greater part of them, That they and their successors, with the advice of the

Bishop

Bishop of Winchester for the time being, and in the absence of the same bishop for the time being, with the advice of some other honest and learned man, have full power and authority to name and appoint a master and under master or usher of the aforesaid school so often as the said school of the said master and under master shall be wanting; and that they the said governors for the time being from time to time may make and be of power and validity to make mete and wholesome statutes and ordinances in writing concerning and touching the order government and direction of the master under master and scholars of the school aforesaid for the time being, and the wages or hire of the same master and under master, and other things touching and concerning the same school, and the ordinance governance preservation and disposition of the rents and revenues aforesaid for the sustentation of the said school to be appointed; with which said statutes and ordinances for to be made, we will and grant, and by these presents command to be observed inviolably, from time to time for ever, for that the statutes and ordinances so to be made be not contrary to the statutes of our realm of England. And moreover we will, and by these presents for us our heirs and successors do grant, That no person having children and younglings of the parishioners or inhabitants of the parish aforesaid, and other persons of the same parish, be brought up or instructed, unless the same persons be first admitted by the governors of the school aforesaid for the time being. And furthermore know ye, That we, in consideration that the aforesaid governors of the said Free Grammar School of Queen Elizabeth within the said parish of St. Olave in Southwark in the county of Surrey, and their successors, may the better from time to time sustain and bear the charges of the same schoolmaster and under master thereof, of our grace especial, certain knowledge and mere motion, have given and granted, and by these presents for us our heirs and successors do give and grant to the aforesaid now governors of the possessions revenues and goods of the Free Grammar School of Queen Elizabeth of the parishioners of the parish of Saint Olave in Southwark in the county of Surrey, and their successors, special licence free and lawful liberty power and authority to have receive and get to them and their successors for ever, as well of us our heirs and successors as of others, whatsoever person or persons, manors messuages lands tenements parsonages tythes and other hereditaments whatsoever within our realm of England or elsewhere within our dominions, which are not holden of us our heirs and successors immediately in thrift or by knight service, for that they do not exceed the clear yearly value of fifty pounds; the statute of lands and tenements not to be put in mortmain, or any other statute act or provision or any other thing clause or matter whatsoever to the contrary thereof, had and set forth ordained and provided in any thing notwithstanding. And further we will and by these presents do ordain, That all the issues rents and revenues of all the aforesaid lands tenements and possessions hereafter to be given and assigned for the maintaining and sustaining of the school aforesaid, from time to time be converted to the maintenance of the master and under schoolmaster of the said school for the time being, and to the sustaining and maintaining of the house and buildings of that school, and the lands rents and possessions aforesaid, and not otherwise, or to any other purposes or intents. And we will and by these presents do grant to the aforesaid governors, That they have and shall have these our letters patents under our great seal of England in due manner made and sealed, without fine or fee great or small to us in our hanaper or elsewhere to our use for the same, to us our heirs and successors by any means to be rendered paid or done, because that expressed mention of the true yearly value or certainty of the premises or any of them, or of other deeds or grants by us or by any of our progenitors to the aforsaid governors before this time, in these presents is not made, any statute act or ordinance provision or restraint to the contrary made set forth ordained and provided, or any other thing cause or matter whatsover in any thing notwithstanding. In witness whereof we have caused these letters to be made patents. Witness Our seal at Coromby this twenty-seventh day of July in the thirteenth year of our reign.

---

CHARLES the SECOND, by the Grace of God King of England Scotland France and Ireland, Defender of the Faith, &c.   To all to whom these presents shall come, greeting: Know ye, whereas our noble predecessor Queen Elizabeth of ever blessed memory, by letters patent under her great seal of England bearing date the six and twentieth day of July in the thirteenth year of her reign, out of her grace and favour did grant unto the inhabitants of Saint Olaves in the borough of Southwark in the county of Surrey, free liberty to erect a Grammar School within the said parish, for the education and instruction of children and youths of the parishioners and inhabitants of the said parish in learning and good literature; and that the said school might be the better managed, did grant and ordain that from thenceforth there should be perpetually within the said parish of Saint Olaves sixteen men of the discreetest and most able and honest inhabitants of the said parish for the time being, who should be called governors of the possessions revenues and goods of the aforesaid school; and the said school to be called the Free Grammar School of Queen Elizabeth of the parishioners of the parish of Saint Olaves in Southwark, in the said county of Surrey, and that the said sixteen persons successively from time to time for ever should be governors of the possessions revenues and goods of the aforesaid school; and that the said governors should be one body politic and corporate for
ever,

ever, in deed and in name, by the name of the Governors of the possessions revenues and goods of the Free Grammar School of Queen Elizabeth of the parishioners of the parish of Saint Olaves aforesaid, and that the said governors by the name aforesaid should have perpetual succession; and the said Queen by her said letters patent did grant unto the said governors and their successors several other liberties privileges powers and jurisdictions as thereby, relation being thereunto had more at large, it doth and may appear : And whereas our loving subjects the present inhabitants of the parish of Saint Olaves aforesaid have humbly besought us that the school by them erected may have continual succession, and that we would be graciously pleased to extend our grace and favour to them ; NOW know ye, That we of our abundant grace certain knowledge and mere motion, for us our heirs and successors do ratify and confirm the said letters patent granted by our noble predecessor of ever blessed memory, and all the grants clauses jurisdictions liberties and privileges whatsoever therein contained mentioned or expressed; and we do hereby also declare and grant, that it shall and may be lawful for the governors hereinafter mentioned and inhabitants of the said parish of St. Olaves to have the benefit and enjoyment thereof in as large and ample manner as their predecessors the governors and inhabitants of the said parish of Saint Olaves did at any time heretofore enjoy the same. And we of our abundant grace certain knowledge and mere motion, being desirous by all proper ways and means to promote the good education and instruction of the children and youths of the said parish, and that the said school may be well regulated and governed, and the lands goods rents revenues and profits belonging to the said school may be managed and improved to the best advantage and profit to the uses hereinafter mentioned, we have assigned elected nominated and appointed, and by these presents do assign elect nominate and appoint, our well beloved subjects Richard Meggott doctor in divinity, one of our chaplains in ordinary, and rector of the parish church of Saint Olaves Southwark aforesaid; Thomas Barker esquire, one of our justices of the peace in quorum for the said county of Surrey; George Meggott the elder, William Fitzhugh, Jeremie Baines, Thomas Morgan, Charles Crayker, George Harvey, John Bateman, Tobias Selby, Symon Nicholls, Jacob May, Francis Miller, Anthony Rawlins, Anthony Allen, and John Brookes, inhabitants of the aforesaid parish of Saint Olaves in Southwark aforesaid, to be and who are and shall be present governors of the possessions revenues and goods of the said free grammar school, to exercise and enjoy the same office well and faithfully from the date of these presents, during their lives and the longest liver of them; and that whensoever it shall happen that one or more of the said governors shall die, or depart with his family out of the said parish, that then and so often it shall and may be lawful for the rest of the said governors and their successors, and the major part of them, one or more fit person or persons of the inhabitants of the parish of Saint Olaves aforesaid, who shall be conformable to the doctrine of the Church of England as now established, in the place or places of him her or them so dying, or with his or their families so departing, in the aforesaid office of governors successively from time to time to elect and nominate as often as occasion shall require, who shall be esteemed governors of the said school during the time and in manner aforesaid. And further we do by these presents, for us our heirs and successors, declare and grant, That the governors afore-mentioned and their successors shall be from henceforth one body politic and corporate in deed and in name by the name aforesaid, and that they and their successors from time to time for ever shall enjoy all the liberties jurisdictions powers and privileges whatsoever in the said letters patents of Queen Elizabeth granted; and it shall and may be lawful for the said governors and their successors from time to time to enjoy and exercise the authorities jurisdictions privileges and powers whatsoever in the said letters patents of Queen Elizabeth mentioned granted or expressed ; and them the said governors and their successors, or the major part of them, with the advice of the Bishop of Winchester, or any other honest and learned man, shall and may nominate and appoint one able schoolmaster, and such able usher or ushers, for the teaching of the Latin and English tongues, and also writing and casting accompts, as to the said governors and their successors, or to the major part of them, shall seem fit for the school aforesaid, as often as the said schoolmaster or usher shall be void, for the educating instructing and teaching of the children and youth of the inhabitants of the parish of Saint Olaves aforesaid, as well poor as rich ; and also that the said present governors and their successors, or the major part of them, from time to time, in case of insufficiency neglect or misdemeanors of the said schoolmaster or ushers, or either of them, shall have full power and authority at their wills and pleasure to displace amove and put out the said schoolmaster or ushers, or either of them, out of and from his or their places, for his or their said neglect insufficiency or misdemeanor, as to the said governors and their successors, or the major part of them, shall seem fit and expedient, and to nominate appoint and place some other fit person or persons in his or their rooms or places respectively ; and also that the said governors and their successors, or the major part of them, shall settle and allow such stipend and salaries to the said master and ushers from time to time as to the said governors and their successors, or the major part of them, shall seem fit ; and the said governors and their successors, or the major part of them, shall have full power and authority to make and establish fitting and wholesome statutes laws and ordinances in writing, for and concerning the order government and direction of

the

the said master ushers and scholars of the aforesaid school for the time being, and otherwise for the preservation and disposing of the rents and revenues aforesaid for the maintenance of the said school, which statutes laws and ordinances so to be made, we will and by these presents do command to be inviolably preserved and kept from time to time for ever, so as the same be not contrary, but agreeable to the laws and statutes of this our kingdom; and in case the said schoolmaster ushers or scholars, or any or either of them, shall refuse or neglect to perform and obey the said orders statutes laws and ordinances or any of them, so to be made by the said governors and their successors, or the major part of them, as aforesaid, that then it shall and may be lawful for the said governors and their successors, or the major part of them, to amove expel and put out such person and persons so neglecting or refusing to obey the said orders out and from the said school, and from any profit or benefit by and out of the same. And that the said governors and their successors may be the better enabled to support and sustain the burthen hereof from time to time, out of our special grace certain knowledge and mere motion, we have given and granted, and by these presents do give and grant, unto the aforesaid governors and their successors, special licence free and lawful power and authority to have retain and enjoy to them and their successors for ever, not only all those messuages lands tenements and hereditaments whatsoever which they now have and enjoy, or of right do in any wise appertain to the said school or to the maintenance and support thereof, but also receive purchase retain and enjoy any other manors messuages lands tenements and hereditaments goods or chattels whatsoever within our kingdom of England or elsewhere, so as they do not together in the whole exceed the clear yearly value of five hundred pounds, the statute of Mortmain, or any other statute ordinance provision, or any other thing cause or matter whatsoever to the contrary thereof notwithstanding. And we further will, and by these presents ordain, That all the issues rents and revenues of all the aforesaid lands tenements and possessions already given purchased or assigned, or hereafter to be given purchased or assigned, for the sustentation of the aforesaid school, shall be from time to time converted to and for the sustentation and maintenance of one schoolmaster, and such usher or ushers of the school aforesaid for the time being, as to the said governors and their successors, or the major part of them, shall seem fit; and for the erecting sustentation and maintenance of the house and edifices of that school, and of the lands tenements and possessions thereunto belonging; and for the support and defraying the necessary charges which the said governors and their successors shall expend in the managing performing and executing the trust hereby reposed in them; and for the maintenance and education of two scholars in the university, if any such shall be elected out of the said school, until they have severally taken their degree of batchelor of arts, being first brought up in the said school and inhabitants of the said parish, which scholars are to be elected by the said governors for the time being and their successors, or the major part of them, and to be allowed such maintenance, towards their education in the university, as to the said governors and their successors, or the major part of them, shall seem fit; and also for the setting out such poor scholars of the said school apprentices, and for the relief of such poor impotent persons of the said parish of Saint Olaves, as to the said governors and their successors, or the major part of them, shall seem fit; and for the erecting and maintaining a workhouse for the setting poor persons of the said parish of Saint Olaves at work; and not otherwise, nor to any other purpose use or intention whatsoever, although express mention of the true yearly value or certainty of the premises or of any of them, or of any other gifts or grants by us or by any other of our progenitors or predecessors, heretofore made to the said governors of the revenues and possessions of the Free Grammar School of Saint Olaves Southwark, in these presents is not made, or any statute act ordinance provision proclamation or restriction heretofore had made enacted ordained or provided, or any other matter cause or thing whatsoever to the contrary thereof in any wise notwithstanding. In witness whereof we have caused these our letters to be made patents. Witness Ourself at Westminster the second day of May in the six and twentieth year of our reign.

By writ of Privy Seal,<br>PIGOTT.

Are there any other expenses besides those you have mentioned?—We allow the charity school of Saint Olave's forty pounds a year, and the charity school of Saint John's thirty pounds a year, and occasionally afford assistance to the poor in the workhouses of both parishes; we are empowered to do it by the charter; and we allow five pounds a year to binding out as apprentices boys educated upon the school. Perhaps, when I say the whole of the revenues are expended, I am not altogether correct; because, in all their leases, the governors have reserved to themselves the power of granting licences, and a fine to be paid upon those licences: they have thought fit to apply those fines as a sinking fund against the rebuilding of the school, which is very ruinous. The licences are upon the underletting; there being a covenant in the leases, that they shall not be assigned without licence from the lessors.

What

Mr.
H. S. Speck.

What class of children attend this school?—The children of the rich as well as the poor; they are of all classes, but chiefly of the poorer classes.

How many attend the school now?—There are 260 now in the school.

Are they children of mechanics?—The children of mechanics and tradesmen: they must be inhabitants of the parish of Saint Olave or Saint John. The number now in the school is an excess of ten, for they calculate that the school cannot conveniently hold or educate more than 250. In addition to our masters, we have a public examination once a year by Dr. Sampson and Mr. Postan.

### The Reverend *William Page*, D. D. called in, and Examined.

The Rev.
William Page,
D. D.

YOU are head master of the Westminster school?—I am.

Is the number of boys upon the foundation always full?—Yes, always as full as in a certain sense it can be: if there is any deficiency, it is always between the times of admission: if the dean, or whoever is to admit, is out of town, they must wait for their return, or send a person for the purpose.

Have they supper as well as dinner?—They have; and a breakfast is provided for them, but at an hour at which it is very inconvenient to take it, according to the old regulations. Thirty-two of the boys are provided with gowns once a year, but not with caps.

When the boys go off to college, who are the electors?—If the master of Trinity and the dean of Christchurch agree upon the election, nothing further is said; but if they disagree upon the election of the boy, it is then put to the vote of the whole body of electors.

Is the dean of Christchurch limited in the number he takes?—No.

What are the Bishop's boys?—There was a Bishop Williams, I think, bishop of Lincoln, who left some small estate, I do not know what the proper description of it is, but something in lands, to found an establishment of four boys: their education is found them gratuitously, and they have a purple gown; and there is a small annual allowance, I think it is between six and seven pounds; but as it is such a trifle, we do not pay it them while they are at school, but let it accumulate till the time arrives when they may be admitted into St. John's College Cambridge; and we then pay them not only that accumulation, but something more, making it amount to about 20 *l.* a year for four years.

In whose nomination are the Bishop's boys?—In the dean and the head master.

### *William Blair*, Esq. called in, and Examined.

William Blair,
Esq.

WHAT is your profession, and where do you reside?—I am a surgeon, resident in Great Russel-street Bloomsbury.

From your residence in Bloomsbury, and your practice as a surgeon in that neighbourhood, will you inform the Committee of the observations you have made with respect to the state of the poor in St. Giles's?—I have resided about eighteen years in Great Russel-street, and have had very great opportunities of seeing the poor at their own habitations professionally, as connected with the Dispensary in that street.

Are they generally in a state of extreme ignorance?—They are the most uninformed body of persons I have ever come in contact with, they are extremely devoid of information; and speaking of the children generally, they are wholly without education.

Are they numerous in that neighbourhood?—So numerous, that every floor and every chamber of every floor is closely inhabited, several beds are frequently seen in one room, and several persons sleeping in one bed. I speak of that part of St. Giles which is comprised between High-street and Broad-street in the south, and Great Russel-street in the north, and from Tottenham Court Road in the west, to Charlotte-street Bloomsbury in the east.

Can you form an idea of the number of uneducated children in that part of St. Giles, in proportion to the whole parish?—I have reason to believe there are not fewer than 6000 Irish adults, and that probably their uneducated children must be at least three or four thousand.

*William Blair,*
*Esq.*

Do you know the amount of population of the parishes of St. Giles and St. George Bloomsbury?—I believe nearly 50,000. The poor Irish in that neighbourhood are a fluctuating population; and therefore the individuals who reside there at the present time, may not be half of the same individuals as were there three or four years ago.

Have you any knowledge of the schools established in St. Giles's?—I have a particular acquaintance with the school, called the Irish Catholic Free School, in George-street; with which I have been connected since its commencement in June 1813.

Is the system of education practised at those schools, the same as at other schools in the parish?—It differs in this: the elementary part of the education is conducted in a simple and mechanical way, like those of the British and Foreign schools; somewhat similar, but not so perfect, owing to the extremely wild and uncultivated state of the minds of the poor Irish. You cannot control and discipline them like those who submit to the discipline of the National Schools; and no books are there used for reading, but a spelling book and the Bible, to avoid controversy.

Do you exclude Protestant children?—The Schools are principally confined to the children of Irish poor, but we take in indiscriminately the children of both Catholics and Protestants.

At whose expense was the school established?—It is supported entirely by voluntary subscriptions. One of the treasurers, Mr. Clark, took the school-house; but the committee are responsible for the rent to him; I was the second person who joined in the institution, and I am quite aware who the individuals are that have the management of it.

Do you attend the committee meetings?—Frequently.

Can you state the effects of that school on the poor?—I have the fullest confidence that its moral effects have been very beneficial, not only upon the children but upon the parents; and many of the parents have themselves spoken to me in the most grateful manner, and expressed themselves contented that no interference had been attempted with their religious principles.

What number of children have you in the school?—Above 220 at present.

Are there any, and what difficulties in the way of extending the benefit of these schools to a greater number of children?—The difficulties are of two kinds; first, the want of funds; and secondly, the continued opposition of the Catholic priests, who supposed we were likely to interfere with the religious principles of the children.

Have their religious principles been in any manner interfered with in that school?—Not at all, to my knowledge.

Have the priests made opposition to the children of the Catholics coming to that school?—Always, from the beginning.

Have any steps been taken on the part of those who have the management of the school, with a view of removing those prejudices?—The schoolmaster has circulated printed papers, informing the parents of the children that no attempt ever was, or would be made to interfere with the religious views of the parents or their children, and that the children had been always conducted to St. Patrick's chapel every Sunday, without any obstacle being put by the committee; the committee have likewise in their Report, as well as by a letter written to one of the priests, stated that there never has been any endeavour made to proselyte the children, and that no such attempts would ever be permitted by any individuals whatever.

Has it been the sole object of the committee to communicate useful instruction to the poor children of Saint Giles's, and not to proselyte them to the Protestant faith?—This has been their sole object; and no instruction has ever been given besides what is conveyed by the spelling-book and Bible, by the simple reading of them: in fact, the spelling-book contains lessons from the Bible.

Has it been the intention and practice of the school to raise the moral character of the poor of St. Giles's, without any view of proselyting them to the Protestant faith?—This has always been the way of proceeding; and the parents of the Catholic children have repeatedly borne testimony to this point, as it regards their own children.

Do you know of any attempt to educate the Irish poor in other parts of the Metropolis?—Yes, a considerable attempt has been recently made in Mary-le-bone, principally for the benefit of the Irish poor about Calmel-buildings; which, I hear, was first taken up by Mr. Montagu Burgoyne.

Do

Do you know whether that establishment is continued, or not?—I have reason to believe that it is.

*William Blair,*
*Esq.*

Can you tell whether there be a disposition in the poor to allow their children to attend gratuitous schools?—I believe there is a very anxious disposition in general; and that parents in general are very anxious to embrace the opportunities that offer.

Do you think that they would be willing to pay a small sum, say a penny or two-pence a week, for the education of their children?—Many of the poor Irish in St. Giles's who are able, showed a willingness to make a payment when the school in question was first opened; but the committee did not think fit to continue that plan longer.

Was the plan discontinued because it was found that many of the poor Irish were literally unable to pay that small sum?—Partly on that account; but also because it created discontent among some of the parents, who discovered that the others did not pay, and therefore they thought there was a partiality: but I have the means of knowing that fourpence and sixpence a week is frequently given at another school in St. Giles's by the poor; this school is at the lower end of George-street.

Is the distressed state of the poor in St. Giles's a hinderance to their education?—Most undoubtedly; and we have this particular fact to illustrate it: when the distress of the poor has been extreme, as during the winter season, and an effort has been made by private subscriptions to relieve the immediate wants of the parents and the children, great numbers of the children who had been kept away, have again returned, and regularly attended the school.

Have you observed any, and what improvement in the minds of the children, from the instruction they have received in the Irish free schools?—I have found their minds greatly elevated; many of them could repeat whole chapters of the New Testament, which they had been accustomed to read to their parents in the evening.

Do they appear to understand the portions of Scripture committed to memory?—In a very intelligent manner.

Then is it your opinion that the moral and intellectual condition of the poor in St. Giles's might be much bettered by the extension of a plan of education among them?—I am perfectly convinced it would be greatly improved by the extension of some plan of education; and that the vicious state of the poor in St. Giles's particularly would not be so much a matter of complaint, if the children were better instructed.

Is it your opinion that the habits of the poor of St. Giles's, as well as their comfort and happiness, have been already improved by the existing institutions for edu-cation?—I have reason to believe that a great number of families have been considerably improved, and that the parents have become more orderly, sober and industrious; I have likewise been informed by a gentleman residing in Charlotte-street, that the state of the street during Sundays is materially different from what it was before our school was established, and that the number of loitering children about the streets and fields of a Sunday is materially diminished within the last three years.

And grown people also?—They are not so numerous; by far the greatest number of them are boys and girls.

Do you conceive that the condition of adults has been improved as well as that of the children?—I have been credibly informed of several striking instances of improvement in adults, and that some of them have left off their habits of gambling and rioting at the public-houses in Saint Giles's.

Do you suppose that institutions for education have produced general order and better conduct among the children?—I am quite persuaded of it.

Do you conceive that order in the children also produces order and better conduct in the grown-up people, their parents?—I have one proof of it in my own mind, viz. that of an evening, when the parents have it in their power, they will stay at home to hear their children read out of the New Testament, instead of frequenting the public-house.

Have the advantages of education become extended beyond the mere educating the children in reading and writing?—The moral consequences are also of great importance to the public.

Do you think that the poor have been diminished in the parish of Saint Giles, in consequence of the assistance of education?—I cannot say that. The number of casual poor is very considerable.

Do

*William Blair,*
*Esq.*

Do you find that the practice among the Irish poor, of sending their children, at a certain age, for education to Ireland, is very prevalent?—I have not heard of their sending them for education to Ireland.

Are the poor of Saint Giles's principally temporary residents, not staying for any length of time?—I believe principally; Saint Giles's parish is very well known in Ireland, and it is a common thing for the natives of Ireland to inquire when they come to England where Saint Giles's is, that they may lodge there.

When the poor leave the parish, they take their children with them?—Chiefly; but there are other parts of the Metropolis which are particularly frequented by the Irish; Saffron-hill, for instance.

Are you acquainted with the means of education in those parts?—No, not about Clerkenwell.

Are there other domiciled poor in the parish, who send their children to these schools?—Yes; but by far the majority are Irish Catholics. There is no exclusive admission of the Irish in this institution: the English, Scotch, or Welsh poor may send their children; but I imagine there are not more than thirty Protestants at present.

Are there any domiciled in the parish, who send their children to these schools?—I believe but few of them are at the schools in George-street.

What becomes of those children?—They continue with their parents. I believe not fewer than eighty or eighty-five out of every hundred are Irish.

From your professional knowledge, are you enabled to acquaint the Committee with the general state of the health of the poor in Saint Giles's?—They are very sickly where they are crowded close together, but in other respects they are as well in their health as the poor elsewhere.

Are the streets in the interior of Saint Giles's regularly cleansed?—They are exceedingly noisome, and neglected; so that it is the most offensive part of my professional duty to visit the poor in that vicinity.

Is it your opinion that the scavengers, or persons who should inspect the streets, do not sufficiently discharge their duty?—I am afraid the scavengers are seldom to be found in those streets: one thing I have sometimes remarked there was, that human beings, hogs, asses, and dogs, were associated in the same habitation; and great heaps of dirt, in different quarters, may be found piled up in the streets. Another reason of their ill health is this, that some of the lower habitations have neither windows nor chimneys nor floors, and are so dark that I can scarcely see there at mid-day without a candle. I have actually gone into a ground-floor bedroom, and could not find my patient without the light of a candle.

Are they lodging houses?—Yes, and let out by the night.

Do you know at how much per night each person?—From fourpence to sixpence per night for each individual; several persons lying in one bed, and several beds often in a small apartment. I have even known individuals to be without a single shred or piece of linen to clothe their bodies, perfectly naked.

Dr. Adams has observed in his book, that infectious complaints prevail throughout the year in the parish of St. Giles: has that fact come under your knowledge?—I have no doubt of the fact being so; and have often found that the great obstacle to my curing surgical diseases is the ill state of health arising mostly from filthiness, the people being sometimes covered with vermin.

Have you ever known professional men decline attending patients in St. Giles's?—I have known medical men who refused to go into the interior parts of St. Giles's, from personal fear, and because of the filthy state of the habitations. I believe that is common with medical men in the neighbourhood.

What do they apprehend?—Partly they are afraid of catching infectious diseases, and partly from apprehending they will be annoyed in their attendance by the ill behaviour of the lower orders.

Do you not then conceive that the health of those parts of the parish of St. Giles to which the benefits of education have been extended, has been materially improved by the extension of education?—I cannot say to what extent; but I have no doubt that, as far as the influence of education extends, it does improve their general condition, by promoting sobriety, cleanliness, and habits of industry.

Is

Is it your opinion that the prevalence of dram-drinking keeps them in poverty, and therefore prevents them from bettering the state and condition of their children?—I am perfectly convinced of the fact; and to show the extent of dram-drinking, I will name a circumstance to elucidate it: Having once had occasion to visit a patient near to a gin-shop in St. Giles's, during the few minutes I was absent, my coachman told me on my return that he had counted upwards of eighty people going into the gin-shop. I suppose my visit occupied not more than ten or twelve minutes.

*William Blair, Esq.*

At what hour of the day?—About one or two o'clock; and I have no doubt that the existence of so many gin-shops in that neighbourhood is one of the principal obstacles to bettering the morals of the lower orders.

Do they teach their children to drink drams?—Yes; and frequently the mother will give the young child in her arms a few drops of spirits.

Is it their practice to leave a small portion at the bottom of the glass for their children, when taking spirits?—I believe it is common.

Notwithstanding the wretched condition of the poor in St. Giles's, which you have described, do you not believe that by kindness and attention their general disposition might be much improved?—I have had many proofs of the gratitude of the lower orders in St. Giles's; and can scarcely ever go amongst them, but that some of the inhabitants come out to express their thanks, and say, " God bless you, sir; long life to you."

Has it come within your knowledge to find that they have expressed peculiar gratitude for the education afforded to their children?—I have frequently heard them express their gratitude; and in Saint Giles's, the poor Catholics, knowing that I was a Protestant, have themselves expressed their thanks for our attention to their poor children.

What is the capacity of the lower orders of the Irish poor, and of the children, for learning?—Fully equal to the capacity of the English or Scotch; and I have remarked, that the memory of the Irish children is remarkably good and retentive. I believe likewise, if they had the advantages of education which the English children have, they would, generally speaking, excel in intellectual exercises.

Mr. *William Waldegrave*, called in, and Examined.

WHERE do you reside?—South Sea Chambers, Threadneedle-street.

*Mr. W. Waldegrave.*

Have you had any opportunity of knowing the distress and ignorance of the lower orders of society in the Metropolis?—About a year and a half since, I connected myself with a society, whose object was immediately to associate with that class, to endeavour to raise a disposition to attend schools where that ignorance might be removed.

What parts of the town did you visit?—Principally Petticoat-lane, Essex-street, Wentworth-street, and the neighbourhood of Spitalfields and Whitechapel.

Did you find a great number of uneducated children?—A great number; but only a few of that number, or at least a small proportion of that number has come under my peculiar care; the Institution has not been established more than a year and a half.

What was the condition of the poor you visited?—Most miserable: I think I might instance it by one circumstance; the first essay I made was in Essex-street Whitechapel, it was about nine o'clock in the evening; I went into an apartment where there were nine people lying on the floor, and I believe without one comfort, not even a bed; there were three adults, the father and mother, and a man lodger, and six children of both sexes.

What was the size of the room?—A very small room.

What proportion, upon the scale of your visits, do you estimate are in this wretched-state?—I made my calculation some little time since upon a court in Essex-street, in which I think there are about thirty houses, and each house would average at least twelve persons; they are small houses. That would amount to three hundred and sixty persons in one court.

Do

Do you infer from the population of that court, that a great number of the poor in that district are in the same wretched condition?—I do most certainly, and have had an opportunity of witnessing it by going into several other courts.

Have you found, in the course of your visits, a disposition among the poor to sending their children to schools, to receive religious instruction?—Generally I may say that I have; but among some there has been an indisposition to it, or rather there has wanted a stimulus to send them.

What are the objections usually made?—They are generally two in nature; the first I think is inexcusable, they imagine that government employ us to collect their children for the Marine Society; the second is a pardonable pride almost, they say that their children have no clothing, and on that account they should not wish them to attend schools: and I may mention another objection which I have noticed, that a great proportion of them are Irish, and that the priests have such an effect upon their minds, that they are induced to withhold sending them to the Protestant schools.

Have you witnessed any beneficial results from the instruction of the children of the poor?—Upon the minds of some of the parents I think I have, and in the children particularly so.

What schools have you attended?—Attached to the society to which I belong, we have two evenings in the week for a conference with the children, which we find beneficial, it brings them together, and we have an opportunity of ascertaining what improvement they are making at the Sunday schools they attend.

What is the nature of your conference?—To examine the children what progress they make in the various schools to which they belong, and to distribute little rewards to those who have attended; by which means we discover their having attended the school regularly, and deliver a little reward for their attendance, which acts as a stimulus.

How many children come under your examination each day?—We are divided into districts, and in the North-east district there are under our care seventy-one children, the larger proportion are girls; I think I may say generally, we have about thirty girls and twenty-five boys, or about that proportion; the girls attend on the Tuesday and the boys on the Thursday evening.

How many are there in the other districts?—I am not prepared to tell that.

How many districts have you?—Eight.

What is the name of your society?—The Juvenile Benevolent Society.

Do you endeavour to procure clothing for those children who are the most destitute?—Our object is to clothe them; the society is designated " The Juvenile Benevolent Society for clothing and promoting the Education of the poor and destitute."

How many subscribers belong to your society?—I think about 200 in the whole.

Is that number increasing?—Daily, I think.

Have you any school belonging to your society?—None, no particular school; but we send the children to the school most contiguous to their situations, after being clothed.

Do you think, in the districts you have mentioned, there is a great deficiency in the means of education afforded to the poor?—No, I think that, generally speaking, there are means going forward very fast in those respective districts; there seems to be a want of re-action among the poor; amongst some of them, their habits of mendicity are such, that it leads them to give a preference to that, and they seem to find their children very useful servants.

Have you found that the profits made by employing their children in begging, have been an objection to their sending them to school?—I believe that is the real cause among them.

And the profits arising from their thefts also?—That is another very great one.

Is it your opinion that mendicity is a great hinderance to the instruction of poor children?—I do firmly believe it, from the experience I have had of the dispositions of the poor, that they find their children their best friends in that particular employment.

Do

Mr.
W. Waldegrave.

Do you not always find that the support the parents are daily receiving by the encouragement given to their children to commit depredations, is another principal reason why they do not wish to have their time employed in receiving education?—I have every reason to believe it. I can instance a circumstance of early depravity of one of those children : A child came to me to be clothed ; there was also a little girl from the same neighbourhood, whom I clothed ; and I requested the boy to take charge of the little girl, and see her safe home; when they had left the depôt of clothing, and had got near a pawnshop, he said to the little girl, " I wish you would return and get my treacle pot, which I have left ;" the little girl came, and a search was made, but no treacle pot could be found; during her absence, the boy went into the pawnbroker's, and pawned the clothes which he had just had given to him. This boy, I suppose, was about eleven years old ; and I had admonished him particularly, because I had some knowledge of his father.

Do you know the name of the pawnbroker, and the street in which he lived?—No, I do not, for the father would not give it me up, he would not mention the name of the pawnbroker.

How did you ascertain the fact of the boy pawning the clothes?—By special inquiry of the parents, who, after much investigation, confessed that it had taken place, that they had pawned them, but they would not give up the name or the duplicate.

Have you reason to believe that this boy or his parents supported themselves by improper means?—The man had no employ at the time ; and the woman complained of the same thing at that moment.

Had they any visible means of supporting their children, but by encouraging them to commit depredations?—It did appear that they had no means of maintaining themselves or their children, and this was a proof of that being the only means.

Do you know that pawnbrokers make any objection, on account of the youth of the child, to receiving the pledge?—There have been instances of many pawnbrokers refusing to receive these things of children of tender age ; but some have taken them, and we have got them out of pledge again.

At the time you clothe these children, do you give them to understand the clothes are a gift, or a loan?—We emphatically enforce upon them, that they are only lent to them for the purpose of enabling them to appear decent to attend Sunday and other schools.

In cases where you find a misuse of clothes so lent, by pawning or otherwise, do you take any measures, and if you do, what measures, to punish the pawnbrokers or receivers of them?—We should take no measures to punish the pawnbrokers, if we found them, but we punish the child by the suspension of any favour; as far as respects the children, after a frequent delinquency, and non-conformity to the regulations of the society, we either suspend or entirely reject them, or discharge them.

Where does your Society meet?—93, Bishopsgate-street.

*Jovis*, 13° *die Junii* 1816.

HENRY BROUGHAM, Esquire, in The Chair.

---

*Charles Butler*, Esquire, called in, and Examined.

Charles Butler,
Esq.

WHERE do you reside?—In Lincoln's-Inn.

From your knowledge of the Catholics in the Metropolis, are you of opinion that there is an indisposition among the parents of the lower orders to educate their children?—I never observed nor ever heard of it.

Have they in general the means of education?—No further than sending them to the Roman Catholic schools, and they are often prevented from doing that, by the want of shoes and other articles of dress.

Are there any obstacles to their sending them to the Protestant schools?—The great obstacle is, that a religion different from their own is taught at those schools.

Does this objection apply to sending them to schools upon the British and Foreign plan, where no catechism is taught?—It is an article of discipline of the Roman Catholic church, that the Bible in the vulgar tongue should not be put into the hands of the children or the absolutely unlearned; I state it as an article of discipline. which of course may be varied, but it is certainly at present a settled article of discipline.

Does the same objection apply to teaching them select portions of Scripture, without putting the whole Bible into their hand?—I apprehend that in strictness it does; but I should also apprehend that an arrangement might be made by the Roman Catholic prelates in England, that this should be adopted; I believe it is actually adopted in a school lately set up at Shadwell.

Were there Roman Catholic priests at the general meeting held this day se'nnight for the establishment of that school?—Several.

Were you present yourself?— No, I was not.

Did you understand that those priests expressed their approbation of the general object of that institution?—I understand that they did.

Do you apprehend that the Catholics could send their children to schools upon the National plan, were they obliged to go to church once a week, and to learn the English church Catechism?—No, certainly not

Suppose their going to church were omitted, and a certificate only required that the children had attended their own church; and suppose the Catechism were also omitted; would the Catholics object to sending their children to the schools upon those terms?—I should think that an arrangement might be made in which that would be conceded; but at present, standing singly, it is contrary to the Catholic discipline.

Do you apprehend there would be an objection to Catholic children attending general schools, if the Protestant version of the Bible were read in those schools?—Yes; the objection to the Bible being put into the hands of the unlearned is not an article of the faith, but an article of the discipline of the Roman Catholic church. There is a letter of Archbishop Fenelon expressly explaining this difference.

Do you believe that the parents of the lower orders, but for the interference of their priests, might be disposed to send their children (without making any nice inquiries into the matter) to such schools?—They are as much indisposed as the priests themselves.

Have you known this from your observation, or from report?—From my own observation.

Are there any penal disabilities in the statute-book affecting the education of Catholics?— There are some statutes, which I believe are completely obsolete in point of practice, but I believe they are still in the book.

Can you describe them?—No, I cannot, without looking into the statute-book. There are statutes in force, though not in use, which make it penal to teach a doctrine inconsistent with the established Catechism.

Are Catholic schoolmasters obliged to take out a licence for teaching?—They are obliged to take the oath prescribed by the 18th of His present Majesty, or that prescribed by the 31st of the same.

If

If they omit to take those oaths, to what penalties are they subject?—I cannot immediately recollect, but they are very serious.

*Charles Butler, Esq.*

Is it the practice of the Catholic schoolmasters to comply with those Acts?—I believe it is, generally.

What religious works are taught in the Catholic schools?—I believe none but the first and second Catechisms.

Do you know how many Catholic schools there are in London?—No, I do not; there is what they call the Associated Catholic Charities, which has three schools of about 700 children in all, and there is a school called St. Patrick's; at present I do not recollect any others in London.

Are there any Catholic schools at the East end of the town?—I believe there is one at Shadwell, at which I believe there are about eighty children.

How many children should you imagine are educated in the Catholic schools altogether in London?—I should suppose if you put it at 1200, you would put it high.

Do you imagine there are a great number uneducated?—An immense number.

Can you form an idea of the number?—No, I cannot.

Have you reason to believe there are thousands?—There are.

Is there a disposition among the Catholics to educate their children, if they had means?—Yes, but they are prevented for want of shoes and other things.

Have the Roman Catholic clergy a disposition to communicate instruction?—Very great; but they are worn down by fatigue.

Can Catholics devise property for the purpose of endowing schools?—No.

What prevents them?—The law of king William, and the statute of Edward the Sixth, of superstitious houses.

In case a Catholic devises property with a view of endowing a school, what becomes of the property so devised?—He devises it to a trustee, without expressing the trust.

If he expresses the trust, in what manner could the object of the devise be put aside?—By a bill in Chancery, as is frequently done in reported cases.

You have stated, that the practice is, in consequence of the statute, not to express the uses in the deed or will; suppose a trust made without expressing the uses, could no proceeding be had to compel the trustee to declare upon what uses he administered his trust?—He might be forced by a bill in Chancery; and in point of fact trustees sometimes, though men of honour, refuse to part with the trust fund; I know an instance at present, where a man of great honour withholds a sum of money, because he feels that he might be called upon by the Crown to refund it.

Then in point of fact, no Catholic can grant property legally or safely for the purpose of promoting the education of Catholics in this country?—Certainly not.

Suppose a Catholic were to leave money to endow a school for persons of all sects, in which no particular religious creed should be taught, and to which, of consequence, Catholic children would have access with others; would there be any illegality in such a bequest?—None, if the requisites of the statute of mortmain were complied with

Have you any idea of any plan which might be adopted, which would unite all sects, for giving instruction to the lower classes of society?—I apprehend that it cannot be effected better than by having an harmony of the Gospels in the English language, which might be approved by the Roman Catholic vicars-apostolic in England, and the Protestant bishops.

What part of the Bible is allowed to be taught in the Roman Catholic charity schools?—No part whatever of the Bible in the vulgar tongue; when a child is at school, he generally learns the New Testament in Greek, at about eight years old.

This cannot apply to the lower classes of society?—No.

What plan could be adopted, in which the Roman Catholics could agree with the Protestants in teaching the Scriptures?—I have already mentioned an harmony.

Do you know whether the Gospels in the Protestant version would be admitted by the Roman Catholic clergy?—Not in the vulgar tongue.

Would they in their own version?—I believe they would.

Would the Epistles be admitted by the Roman Catholic clergy in the vulgar tongue?—I believe to effect any general good, the arrangement of the whole New Testament would be admitted in the Catholic version.

Would the Old Testament be admitted?—There would be more objection to that than the New Testament.

Would

Would they admit the Douay version without the notes?—I believe they would, to effect a great purpose; it is an English version printed at Douay.

It is printed with notes?—Yes; there is no edition without notes.

Where is Douay?—In Flanders.

The objections that are made to this version, are rather to the notes than to the version itself?—Chiefly to the notes; but there has been an edition of the Douay version of the New Testament published within this twelvemonth, in which the greatest care has been taken to expunge every note that could offend the Protestants.

Is it a cheap edition?—No, it is about four shillings, and in one volume; there are in France numerous editions of the New and Old Testament without any note.

But in England and Ireland, have the Roman Catholic clergy ever allowed the New Testament to be circulated among their flock without notes?—No; I have stated it is an article of discipline of the Roman Catholic church, not to put the Old or New Testament, in the vulgar tongue, into the hands of the children or unlearned.

How has it happened in France that they have had the New Testament in the vulgar tongue?—In point of fact, there has not, for the last century, been in France (as I have informed myself from good authority) any objection to reading the Old or New Testament in the French tongue, or without notes, by any age or any description of people.

Has it been the practice in France to admit the authority of the church in the same manner which the Roman Catholics have admitted it in England and Ireland?—Certainly, it is one of the positions of the famous Bull Unigenitus.

What is the date of that Bull?—About 1710. I should wish to add, that I think an arrangement for the education of Catholic children at schools where the English version of the Bible is taught, might be managed by a proper spirit of conciliation on both sides, both among the Catholics and the Protestants.

### *Montagu Burgoyne,* Esquire, called in, and Examined.

HAVE you had occasion to pay attention to the state of the lower orders of Irish in any part of the parish of Mary-le-bone?—I have paid particular attention to it, and in so doing I have felt very greatly disappointed. What induced me to enter upon the inquiry, was seeing a great number of children, not only in a state of ignorance, but quite in an uncivilized state; I inquired of their parents, who were chiefly Irish, the cause of their children receiving no education, and they told me they were so entirely without clothing, that they were not fit to appear in any school. By the assistance of a charity called the Irish Calmel Society, I gave them clothing, the greatest part of which was soon sold; I then lent them clothes, but when they found it was not their own property, a great many discontinued attending the school. I found the greatest difficulty in procuring proper masters, and at last gave it up entirely to a school that was instituted by the recommendation of the Calmel Society, I may say instituted by the Associated Catholic Charities. I particularly recommended a Sunday school, in order to prevent the gambling and rioting of the children during the time of divine service; that Sunday school continues, and there is a tolerably good attendance in the morning, but none in the evening; and I observe the same gambling and rioting in Calmel Buildings that I first observed, a place that seems entirely put out of the law, the beadles and the parish officers pay no sort of attention to it; a murder was committed there some time ago, and I dare say others will be committed there in future. We found a great difficulty in procuring education for the Irish poor. It was absolutely necessary to have the consent of the priests, and they would not admit any but a Catholic master; and it was difficult to procure any Catholic master who was not an Irishman, most of whom in that line of life are not remarkable for their good character. I certainly have paid great attention to the subject, for on hearing of the great distress which the Irish poor children suffered on account of their parents not being employed, I visited all the Catholic schools in the Metropolis, and was told by the masters, that many of the children who came to those schools were very ill provided with the necessary sustenance for human life.

In your visits to those schools, did you find that the children were in a miserable state?—Very much so; the greater proportion of them diseased more than any children I ever saw; humours, lamenesses, ricketty, certainly the effects of negligence in infancy: and though they have increased so much in number, the number that dies is very great. It is a disgrace to this country, that they should be per-

mitted

mitted to live in that kind of way, so that absolutely their habitations become *Montagu Burgoyne,* *Esq.* a nuisance to every body, and prejudicial in the extreme to health; for medical men have stated to me, that they were afraid of the consequences to the neighbourhood; as any person may perceive who turns into Calmel Buildings out of Orchard-street. In that part of the town they are so closely packed, that in twenty-three houses I think there were very nearly seven hundred people : the whole place is such a scene of filth and wretchedness as cannot be conceived. Our committee have made various representations, but in vain, to the vestry of Mary-le-bone parish, to enter into measures to cleanse this nuisance. Besides those seven hundred people, there are upwards of a hundred pigs.

Have you any idea of the proportion of children that are left, to those that are born?—No, I have not; I can only tell the number of Irish children I have found in London. I made inquiry in every parish : it was a work of considerable labour, but paid for by the society; they are 7288 which I have collected, but I dare say I have not got half of them : here is the return of that inquiry.

[It was delivered in, and read, as follows :]

The POPULATION of the IRISH POOR resident in The Metropolis.

| | Children from 5 to 12. | | Children of all Ages. | Grown Persons. |
|---|---|---|---|---|
| | Boys. | Girls. | | |
| St. Mary-le-bone - - - - - | 168 | 130 | 515 | 645 |
| St. George's - - - - - - | 57 | 61 | 277 | 239 |
| St. James's - - - - - - | 37 | 43 | 95 | 155 |
| St. Martin's - - - - - - | 35 | 33 | 155 | 177 |
| St. Anne's - - - - - - | 16 | 38 | 120 | 128 |
| St. Giles's - - - - - - | 285 | 284 | 1,138 | 1,210 |
| St. Andrew's Holborn - - - - | 118 | 111 | 510 | 436 |
| St. George's Bloomsbury - - - - | 5 | 6 | 21 | 14 |
| St. Bride's, St. Dunstan's, and the Rolls Liberty | 14 | 10 | 48 | 47 |
| St. Paul's Covent-garden - - - - | 6 | 3 | 14 | 8 |
| St. Clement Danes - - - - - | 12 | 18 | 40 | 38 |
| St. Mary-le-Strand - - - - - | 4 | 2 | 10 | 11 |
| Aldgate - - - - - - - | 9 | 11 | 53 | 57 |
| St. Catharine's in the East - - - - | 10 | 9 | 37 | 34 |
| Whitechapel - - - - - - | 89 | 89 | 445 | 383 |
| Shadwell - - - - - - | 40 | 40 | 221 | 176 |
| Wapping - - - - - - | 3 | 3 | 12 | 10 |
| Limehouse - - - - - - | 10 | 9 | 47 | 48 |
| St. George's in the East - - - - | 129 | 87 | 278 | 274 |
| St. Dunstan's Ratcliffe - - - - | 26 | 26 | 67 | 61 |
| Poplar - - - - - - | 113 | 73 | 385 | 382 |
| St. Luke's - - - - - - | 43 | 33 | 123 | 149 |
| St. John's Clerkenwell - - - - | 18 | 14 | 46 | 44 |
| St. James's - D° - - - - - | 6 | 7 | 31 | 29 |
| St. Sepulchre's Within - - - - | 21 | 25 | 95 | 84 |
| St. Sepulchre's Without - - - - | 11 | 13 | 55 | 47 |
| Cripplegate - - - - - - | 31 | 35 | 134 | 134 |
| Aldersgate - - - - - - | 11 | 1 | 21 | 14 |
| Spitalfields - - - - - - | 33 | 32 | 119 | 87 |
| Bermondsey, and St. Olave, Borough - - | 73 | 70 | | |
| Christ Church - - - - - d° - - | 41 | 50 | | |
| St. Saviour's - - - - - d° - - | 58 | 50 | 791 | 760 |
| St. George's - - - - - d° - - | 13 | 9 | | |
| St. John's - - - - - d° - - | 16 | 10 | | |
| St. John's Westminster - - - - | 28 | 30 | 260 | 247 |
| St. Margaret's - d° - - - - | 26 | 25 | | |
| Bromley, West and East Ham - - - | 106 | 108 | 495 | 345 |
| St. George the Martyr - - - - - | 2 | 1 | 13 | 14 |
| Miscellaneous - - - - - - | 271 | 137 | 617 | 389 |
| | 1,994 | 1,736 | 7,288 | 6,876 |

Much pains have been used to make the above account, though it is by no means correct, as it is thought that a considerable number is omitted.

But to give the Committee an idea of the abhorrence to any person interfering with such kind of people and attempting to civilize them, a young man whom I appointed

Montagu Burgoyne, Esq.

pointed as assistant secretary, told me there was only one thing which he would not do to oblige me, and that was, having any connexion with the Irish poor, because he was very sure he should be massacred, that he could not pass by Calmel Buildings without being insulted, the men and women crying after him, " There goes one of Burgoyne's fellows."

Were those objections confined to the poor in Calmel Buildings?—Entirely.

Did you find among the other poor Irish in the Metropolis any objection to having their children educated?—Not absolutely an objection, but an indifference.

To what do you ascribe this peculiarly bad disposition of the Calmel Buildings' population?—Because they employ them in other things more beneficial to themselves.

What employments?—Begging and thieving. The great difficulties on account of religion are not to be wondered at, because they do not even agree among themselves. With submission, I think the two representations from Mr. Finigan and his opponents should be laid before this Committee.

Did you find any difficulty among these poor Irish, from their misapprehension of the views of the society?—There is always an indisposition in the lower ranks of people, when extraordinary pains are taken to serve them.

Were they suspicious of your having funds at your disposal, to which they were entitled?—They were.

Could you trace any effects from the labour of your society, with respect to the Irish in their own country?—A great number do come over; and now since Christmas I have been informed that many hundreds have come into the parish of Mary-le-bone; but what might be noticed is, that I have been found great fault with by some of the Catholics, in expressing a wish that some steps should be taken by Government to prevent any further increase of those Irish poor, who are not able to maintain themselves.

Is the object of your society the amelioration of the condition of the Irish poor?—It is so; but the objects of our society have been so much changed, from the scenes of distress that we have witnessed; the original object of our society was to that particular part, the population of Calmel Buildings, to try to civilize them; we found it was impossible to effect that, any further than by encouraging the education of the children.

You found the encouragement of education to be the best means of civilization?—Yes; and any thing we gave away was more confined to those whose children attended best; in times of distress we gave a small quantity of bread, and gave it to those people whose children were most orderly.

Do you consider that if the Catholic priests consented to the adoption of your plans, that the object of your labour would be principally accomplished?—Very much assisted, and for this reason, I have been with them all, and have been with the Bishop, who is a very enlightened good man as can be.

Then that at present appears to be the chief obstacle?—I think it is one great obstacle. I was extremely pleased with one proposition that was successful; for finding a great difficulty in satisfying the priests in the parish of Shadwell, I called a meeting of the Church of England, with some of the Catholics, some Methodists, and Presbyterians and other Dissenters, and a plan of education was agreed upon that was not entirely Lancasterian, inasmuch as the particular chapters of the New Testament pointed out by that system were omitted.

Are the priests sensible of and witnesses to this melancholy state of the condition of their poor?—Yes, certainly; but such is their apprehension of their being lost to their flock, and to what they think eternal happiness, that I have often had my doubts whether they wish them to be removed from the state of ignorance in which they are placed.

The great impediments, then, are points of religion?—Yes; the system upon which the schools of the associated charities was founded was the Lancasterian, but the principle is that of Dr. Bell's, inasmuch as they will not permit any education to be given without introducing religious instruction with it.

Have you observed any improvement in the state of the lower orders in the district you have mentioned, arising from the means of education that have been already offered?—I have heard of instances of parents being improved by the education of the children, which enables them to read to them.

Are many of those children reclaimed from those bad habits of begging and thieving?—Undoubtedly; but I have found the designs of our charity are very much

much curtailed, because the only true way of benefiting the children is by removing them from their parents, and putting them out as apprentices and servants.

Montagu Burgoyne, Esq.

What steps do the Catholic priests take to relieve the condition of the Catholic poor?—The number of priests is so small that they have it in their power to pay very little attention to it; but in justice to them, I must say they work extremely hard in attending the sick and dying.

Is it their practice to encourage education?—Some of them do not. The proportion of poor, both of people and children of Irish, now is astonishing, and most of the beggars in the streets, I would bet two to one, are Irish; I believe the older thieves make use of the boys to plunder, which is one of the advantages of not sending them to school.

Have you ever heard of a practice among the Irish poor, of sending their children to Ireland for education?—No; but I have known a great many who wished to be sent to Ireland, because they could not get employment here; I do not mean the children, but the family.

The Irish to whom you allude, are not domiciled in the parish, but go like itinerants?—No, they are domiciled; which brings to my recollection the complaint which we have frequently made, of not providing for any of the children, except they have been resident here for seven years.

Have you visited their lodgings?—Yes, a great many of them.

What have you seen?—Nothing but dirt and wretchedness.

Great numbers in one room?—Four or five in one room; that must be the case when there were 700 in 23 houses.

What was the state of their clothing?—Very bad indeed, hardly shoes and stockings, and often not breeches; you may see them tossing up halfpence on Sundays, but at the same time not have clothes to cover them scarcely.

Have they beds?—Yes, sometimes, but very miserable ones.

How many children to one family, upon the average, do you suppose?—I cannot tell.

What is the largest number of children to one family you have seen?—Eight or nine children.

All existing with one family in the same room?—Yes. I was very much disappointed the other day; we had put out from ten to twenty children with a Catholic woman, a Mrs. Haddingstead in Chapel-street, by whose means a great improvement had taken place in them; rewards were frequently given, but upon the discontinuance of those rewards, she could not show me more than four or five girls who staid with her, the rest having gone back to their wretched parents, attending wheelbarrows in the street, or begging, or some other low way of obtaining something for their parents: they were going on perfectly well as long as the rewards were continued, and the moment they were taken away, they went back to their parents.

Do you not attribute this circumstance to the neglected condition of that population, rather than to any aversion to education themselves?—I do not attribute it to any aversion, but certainly there was no inclination, as soon as the smallest advantage could be obtained by the employment of the children in ever so low a way.

What objection have the priests to their going to a Lancasterian school?—Because in the first place they read the Bible without note or comment, which is directly againt them; that is the grand attack against Mr. Finigan.

Do you think the public attendance of children on mass has been increased?—Certainly, because there is a regular school in the morning, where I suppose one hundred and forty children go regularly, and from thence go to their own place of worship; I tell them they need not be ashamed.

What, in your opinion, would be the best mode of establishing a system for their benefit?—The priests themselves will never consent, I am free to say; let religion stand upon its own ground, and educate in such a manner as not to preclude persons professing any religion being benefited by it; but then I must say that it becomes those who patronize education, to be particularly careful that the parents of children sent to such a school should not imagine that religion is not of any consequence, on the contrary, I think peculiar pains should be taken to instil proper notions of religion in the minds of the children, but it should not be done in the school. I have sometimes seen bad effects of children being educated in that kind of way, not going to any place of worship; there is one that I subscribe to, where we take particular care to have them go to some place of worship.

Is

*Montagu Burgoyne,*
*Esq.*

Is it not a point in the Lancasterian system to induce the children to go to their respective places of worship on a Sunday?—I believe it is.

The Catholic priests would not assent to a system of education but upon the exclusive system?—I believe they would not.

Upon their own?—Yes; that is the reason I say it is similar to Dr. Bell's.

Upon such an exclusive system the Catholic priests would co-operate with benevolent persons to relieve the condition of their poor?—I believe they would; I have no doubt that they would.

Is it your opinion the number of Irish poor is increasing or decreasing?—Increasing very rapidly, and how can it be otherwise; can any one be surprised that men will leave a part of the country where there is no provision for the poor, and prefer one where the principle of the law is, that no man can perish through want.

Is the capacity of the poor Irish children equal to the other poor, in their acquirement of learning?— Superior, I really believe; their quickness is prodigious.

Would not, then, a proper education lessen the number of poor?— Undoubtedly.

Had you any personal inspection of the mode of instructing children in your schools?—The British and Foreign system is generally adopted.

Is it under your own management, or is it left to the Catholic priests?—I do not interfere at all, nor do the committee to which I belong.

The mode of instruction is left to the priests?—It is left entirely to the committee of the school, who are permitted to visit it and report.

Do any means occur to you, of dealing with the parents among the low Irish, who will not send their children to be educated, from unwillingness to forego the profits of their begging?—There is only one mode, and that must be confined to those who receive assistance from the parish, because I have always contended, that the parish who maintains the family, has a right to have the children educated in such a way as not to be likely to continue burdensome to them. I am sorry to say that I hardly ever met with a parish who acted upon these principles. There is a sort of unwillingness in parish officers to interfere with the domestic affairs of a private family, be they ever so much distressed, or ever so much dependent upon the parish. There is nothing so much mistaken as the present management of the poor.

### The Reverend *William Gurney* M.A. again called in, and Examined.

*The Rev.*
*William Gurney.*

WHAT is the result of your observation, with respect to the advantages of children paying part of the expense of their own education?—I think that the advantages are very great: In the first place, from the parents it removes the unpleasant feeling of receiving charity, and, as they have not been in the habit of receiving pecuniary aid, it is desirable that that disposition should be kept up, for otherwise if they were in the habit of receiving even gratuitous education for their children, they might by degrees become very willing to receive pecuniary aid for the support of their families; that is one particular reason which, I think, renders the system of payment advantageous: besides, the poor generally value, and in fact every body values that which costs them something, more than that which costs them nothing. We find by experience in the West-street school, where the parents pay for their children, that they are more particular in sending their children regularly since they have paid, than formerly they were accustomed to do when they received education gratuitously, which can be proved by the books, showing the regular and daily attendance. It appears also that the children maintain a sort of superiority in their own minds, as to their view of the school in which they are, when compared even with those schools where clothing as well as education are given freely; the children are more careful about their dress and their cleanliness, because they go to a pay school, and they feel, and they express it frequently, that they belong to a superior class to those who are called parish children. It has been considered by the managers of the West-street school, that this sort of pride, if pride it may be called, is rather desirable than otherwise, because it makes the lower classes of people aim to keep themselves in a considerable degree independent of the higher orders; it gives them, of course, a propensity to industry and the exertion of their talents, and this in a great degree has an influence upon their morals, keeping them sober and steady in their outset of life, promising good fruits in old age. We have many instances of children brought up in this school, who have arrived to manhood, and who, by their orderly and constant attendance in their places on Sunday, show that their former education was not thrown away. And

it

it should be observed, especially as to the tendency of their education here, as in respect to the promotion of the interests of the Church of England, that several hundreds have in the course of a few years been actually made members of the Church of England by confirmation; more than 150 at one time, who had been educated principally in the school, were confirmed at St. Martin's church; thus showing that the system of education adopted in the school, which is to this effect, is beneficial; that nothing is taught in the school, relative to religion, which is not strictly agreeable to the church doctrine and discipline; but no child is required to learn or do any thing which may be contrary to the conscience and requisition of its parents.

*The Rev. William Gurney.*

Can you give the Committee any conjecture of the probable proportion of children whose parents are capable of paying in the way you have described?—If I may judge, from the experience of West-street school, I should calculate that about one third of those who may properly be called poor children, would be able to pay three halfpence a week for each child, because in the circuit perhaps of half a mile, with some few exceptions, we have found 400 children among the lower orders, whose parents could pay more than twopence a week; and I am satisfied that the payments of twopence a week by 600 children would pay the expenses of the education of 1200.

Are any children excluded from that school, on points of religion?—No.

What are the expenses of your school?—Two hundred and ten pounds per annum for 400 children.

Would the expenses be proportionately diminished as the number of children increased?—Yes.

How much?—I have calculated, that if 400 children can be taught for 210*l.*, 1200 may be taught for 380*l.*

Have you any other information to give, in addition to your former evidence upon the subject of St. Clement Danes' school?—I find, upon examining some official documents belonging to the parish, that the supplies by which the charity schools are kept up, are not merely, as I supposed, annual subscriptions, donations, and collections, but that there is considerable landed property; a number of houses, which appear, as far as I can collect at the present moment, to bring in a rental at least of 200*l.*; and that the leases of many of those houses will expire in four years from last Lady-day, which of course will make a very great addition to the funds of the school.

Who has the care and custody of it?—There are a number of trustees, and a treasurer.

Who is the treasurer?—His name is Johnson, a sword-cutler in Newcastle-street; and I am satisfied, as I observed before, that from this foundation, and the usual subscriptions, more money would be supplied than would educate all the children of St. Clement's parish, if the parents paid nothing; and of course, I should conceive, that if one-half of the income were expended in clothing the poorest so as to fit them to come decent to school, without giving offence to the other children, those who were willing to pay would make up the deficiency. I really think that might be the case in most districts, since I find St. Clement's, a great part of it, is as full of poor as any part of St. Giles's, in some of the houses of which, I know there are several in Clement's-lane, there must be near forty children, for every room has a family in it.

What difficulties do you apprehend from different descriptions of children attending the same school?—I think the difficulty would be to get them together, for the labouring mechanic who keeps his child tolerably decent in clothing, would be fearful of his child mixing with the very raggedest, he might get disease and vermin, and various other very unpleasant things, besides having his morals corrupted if they had been better taken care of before; because I have always found poverty and filth are accompanied with vice, generally on the permission of such practice, and I think that the removal of the former would tend very much to improve the latter, that is to say, that the removal of filth and so on, would remove the vice.

What would be the best plan, in your opinion, of educating the children of your parish?—If I might chuse, I would first of all have a large room prepared, capable of containing a number equal to the poor population of children; I should then, having got the room, devise means for acquainting myself with the inclinations of the parents, as to their ability and readiness to pay something towards the education of their children, and I conceive that I should find a considerable number who would be willing to pay from twopence to a halfpenny per week for such education; I have found also many who would make an excuse, that they could not send their

children

children to school for want of clothing, and that they could not of course pay any thing; I should therefore receive those at first who were willing to pay; and I should then like to have a power, if I were the manager, to go to the churchwardens and overseers with the names of certain children whose parents were willing that they should be educated, requesting them, and in fact insisting upon it, that they should immediately furnish a suitable decent dress which would conceal all defects of filth, with respect to those children, and fit them to appear in the school; and if I found, upon a calculation, that I did not want any pecuniary aid from the parish to carry on the school, thus including all the population, I would demand no money, but if there was a deficit on account of those very poor children, I should certainly think it right that the parish should supply that deficiency.

Do you think such a plan would tend to lessen the poor rates of the parish?— I do; on account of the habits of industry that would be excited, and on account of the various interests that would be combined together to find employment and occupation for the children thus trained up in habits of industry, and bearing a good character, which now they do not.

What do you suppose would be the expense of a room adequate to the purposes you have mentioned?—That question connects with it another observation: The expense of such a room as would do for a school might not be very great, if it was done upon the frugal plan of Mr. Lancaster; I cannot tell as to the amount, but I suppose it is a sum of money that might very easily be repaid by the school itself in a few years, fixing the rent to be merely the interest of the money laid out, but to pay a part of the principal every year, and leaving it also open to the occasional charity sermons or subscriptions or donations of serious people, whom I should chuse to assist in it; but, connecting it with another idea which I have already suggested, that of making every one of those schools a chapel of the Established Church, for the accommodation of the poor parents of these children, and which will be the ruin of the Established Church, comparatively speaking, if this system of education is carried on, unless you provide these children, after they have quitted the school, with a place of worship; they will go somewhere, either to the Catholic or Dissenting chapels, or to any place where they can be accommodated, and the Church is not that place.

Notwithstanding the expense of the school-room being borne by the parish, still you think the poor rates would be lessened by such establishment?—Considerably.

Have they room in the Methodist and dissenting chapels for the poor?—Yes, much more in proportion than they have in the churches.

Has it come to your knowledge that the parents of children who are of the church of England, go to dissenting chapels, for want of room in the church?— There is no doubt of it, and the children too.

When you speak of children, do you allude to boys as well as girls?--Both.

Considering that the girls should be as universally educated in the parish as the boys?—Yes.

Do you think that the increase of accommodation for the poor in places of worship connected with the Establishment, would facilitate the means of education, and the welfare of the Church itself?—Most certainly it would; I speak from experience.

Have you made any observation upon juvenile depredators, in addition to those you formerly stated to the Committee?—I think those children that come under that denomination, with all beggars, should be sifted, so as to fall each on his own parish, and as soon as that is done, if there remain any still who are of that description, and for whom you cannot find a parish, they must be educated where they are; but I should suggest their being educated (and I think their number would be but few) at the parish expense, either in another school-room appropriated to their use, or in the workhouse; in the workhouse, there is a room where they dine, and where service is performed, in that room, at least on the Sabbath day, not in times of divine service, they might be educated altogether as at a Sunday school, until they were in such a state of improvement, as to conduct, as to be recommended to the other school, as a sort of reward for good behaviour; my Sunday school originally was a sort of preparatory one to the day school.

Would it be practicable to register all parishioners?—O yes; I think there can be no doubt about it.

Do you think it would be useful?—I think it would; frequently, beggars in the street will not acknowledge that they belong to any neighbouring parish, but say that they live no where, and sleep in a brick field.

Mr.

Mr. *Francis Place*, called in, and Examined.

WHERE do you reside?—Charing-cross.

Have you attended to the state of the education of the poor in this Metropolis?—Yes.

Were you a member of the West London Association?—Yes, I was.

What is the result of your observation, with respect to the means of education?—I agree entirely with the account already given on this subject by Mr. Wakefield, and Mr. Biggs.

Have you seen the accounts already given in evidence, of the National, and British and Foreign School Societies' plans?—Some of them.

Have you seen the accounts given in, of the expense of education upon those plans?—Yes.

Do you hold that those estimates are accurate?—I cannot say as to the National school; I know that the accounts that have been given of the Lancasterian schools are all incorrect.

In what manner do you think the estimates are incorrect?—I was in fact appointed with three others, to inquire as to the actual expense of educating the children of the Lancasterian schools in London, and we found that the school in North-street, which was said to be a school for 1000 boys, would hold but 594, and could not admit more than 560 at one time; the master stated that the average number which attended for the last twelvemonth was 350, that was his estimate, and not the number actually ascertained by counting them out at any one time; we found the number under 300, at three several countings on different days; and from the items of expense we obtained from the secretary, the actual charge was 16 s. per head for those who did attend the school; the number on the books was more than twice the number in attendance, but that must necessarily be so in all schools where there is no inspection of the parents, to see that the children attend.

Although a school may not be capable of holding above 560 at any one time, may not 700 or 800 children receive the benefits of education at that school, from alternate attendance there?—No doubt more children get educated at every school than the number attending upon any given day.

Have you examined any other school with the same view?—The school in Spicer-street Spitalfields, calculated to hold 650; there were 308 boys in that school on one counting, 320 on another, and about the same number the third time; it would hold, if full, 660; and the actual expenses, as far as we could get them, were about 16 s. a head. For the lower number, we were obliged to go to the matter of fact, to ascertain what we could do with given funds, before setting about a school.

What was the result?—The result was, that the lowest estimate would be at the rate of 12 s. per head per annum.

Upon what number?—Upon about 500.

What should you take the expense to be for a school of 200 or 300 only?—It would be prodigiously increased.

Would not this sum of 12 s. per head be proportionately diminished as the number of children were increased above 500?—The largest number of children which one master would be able to manage would not exceed 600; we calculated on having schools for 600 in them; that was the result of all the Lancasterian schools in London.

Suppose a school capable of educating at one moment 600 boys; may not this be said to be a school for 800?—No, I think not; I think it would be calculated to mislead those who interested themselves about schools, they would be deceived as the calculations deceived us.

Suppose at any time 600 could be educated in a room, and 200 of those 600 were a floating number, should you think that this estimate of 200 is too great?—Yes, I think it is; I think it would not be found on actual examination that the fluctuation was from 600 to 800. There is no school in London which can contain, with any convenience at all, so much as the Spicer-street school, which is the largest. The school in the Borough-road would accommodate 480 boys; a space has since been added, and it will now admit 592 boys to be in the school; the number of boys in that school, at three several countings, averaged 307; and the expense per head for that number, independent of any rent, was about 12 s. a year.

Do

Do you suppose that is the minimum of the expense?—It is, because I think that has advantages which no other school has.

Of that 12s. per head, what proportion do you consider as rent?—None, at that school.

But the Committee mean generally?—We estimated the rent for a school capable of containing 600, which of course would include such taxes as the school would be compelled to pay, would be 70l. a year. There is a school in the Horseferry-road, which was built for 500, and, while under the care of the British and Foreign School Society, averaged an attendance of about 220 boys, and the cost, taking all charges together, was about one pound a head.

When you say that 600 could be taught at one moment, might not an arrangement be made for 200 of those 600 attending in such a manner, that 800 should be taught altogether in the course of one week?—It is possible; but it is an arrangement not at all likely to be made. The great difficulty in getting children to attend the school, is the want of inspection of their parents. It was intended by the West London Lancasterian Association to form the neighbourhood into sections, in each of which a number of inhabitants should undertake to see a certain number of children in regular attendance, so that the school list might not have a great number on it, when in fact a small number only attended. I have no doubt the schools could be all filled, if the parents were properly attended to.

Is there any indisposition on the part of parents to send their children to school?—It is evident there is, from the large numbers on the lists of the schools, and the small numbers that attend.

Do you apprehend that this is any thing more than inattention on the part of the parents?—Nothing more, and a persuasion, in the minds of many of them, that they play, and learn nothing.

If the parents themselves were better instructed, would not they put a greater value upon education?—They would.

Have you had an opportunity of comparing the merits of the two modes of teaching?—I think I understand the Lancasterian mode of teaching completely; and as far as I have observed, I think it greatly superior to the National mode.

Upon what points?—The children are more intensely employed, without suffering the same quantity of fatigue; at the National schools they stand for a long time, and are not permitted to sit, which fatigues the body and indisposes the child.

Do you not attribute a great advantage to the slates?—Yes.

Do they teach writing generally at the National schools?—I believe not; the arrangement in the school is for a small number only; but in the Lancasterian schools a boy learns to write the letter as soon as he can pronounce it.

Is that his mode of learning to write?—Yes. He is taught to read in the same manner, seated at his desk, and afterwards to repeat, against the wall. In the Lancasterian mode, the boys are occupied every minute in the exercise to which they are put; but in the other, they appear to wait for their turn; hence the Lancasterian must be the quickest way of teaching.

In point of experience, have you found it be the quickest mode?—I have not experience enough to know what is the quickest mode, but from what I have seen.

Is any creed enjoined in the Lancasterian schools?—None, nor any particular form of prayer.

Is there in the National schools?—Yes, the Creed of the church and the Catechism of the church of England. I found in the North-street school, from the books in that school, out of 1150 boys who were upon the books for a certain period, there were 595 of the Established Church, 516 Dissenters of various denominations, 35 who are stated to be indifferents, and 4 Jews, which makes 1150: they had not a Catholic in that school.

What do you consider to be the effect of those regulations, in excluding Catholics from attending those schools?—The result will appear in one school, from the statement I have just made.

Suppose a place is too small to maintain a school both upon the National plan and upon the British and Foreign Society plan; do you apprehend that in such place the poor of dissenting parents must go without education?—Most likely the influence of the parish officers will secure a number of subscribers to their own school, which will prevent the funds being large enough to educate any others, or if it has been established will prevent the continuance of it.

But suppose a place large enough to support schools upon both plans; do you apprehend that the exclusions adopted by the National system can in such place produce any bad effect?—No; unless meaning by " bad effect " the diminution of the number of children uneducated.

Do

Do you apprehend any other bad effects, of a different description?—No, I am not aware of any; I believe that in general the schools managed by the Dissenters will have more children than the others, from their prodigious activity which I observe they use in all the schools with which I have had any connexion.

*Mr. Francis Place.*

Do you believe that there are great numbers of poor in London, who would not allow their children to attend schools, because they derive profit from their begging and thieving?—I have no knowledge of it.

Do you consider that the morals of the lower orders of people are worse now, or better, than they were forty or fifty years back?—I am quite sure that the morals of the lower orders are infinitely improved; I think a distinction might be made between the working people and those who are completely dissolute, for in fact they do not belong to them; it will be found on inquiry that very few of the dissolute ever want work.

To what do you attribute that improvement?—The increased information.

In the analysis of the number of children in the North-street school, you have mentioned there were no Catholics?—No, there were not.

Do you know the reason of that?—No, I do not.

Mr. *Joseph Henry George*, called in, and examined.

ARE you one of the masters of archbishop Tenison's school, in King-street?— I am.

*Mr. J. H. George.*

When was it founded?—In 1700.

Was it founded by will, or deed of gift?—Deed of gift.

For what?—For the education of forty boys; the children of housekeepers to be taken first, then lodgers, and then the poor inhabitants, of the parish of St. James Westminster.

What are the funds?—I really cannot give an answer to that question.

What are the annual expenses?—The reader and schoolmaster, 120*l.* a year; writing-master, 50*l.*; clerk and agent, 25*l.*; organist and singing-master, 25*l.* 4*s.*

From whence do the funds arise?—From the letting of the pews of King-street chapel; we have the chapel, which is let out, and the emoluments of it pay for the education of the boys, and their books, and 6*l.* to put them out apprentice. There are also the rents of five houses.

What are the expenses of the chapel, besides those you have mentioned?— Morning preacher, 143*l.* 10*s.*; afternoon preacher, 84*l.*; besides beadle, pew-opener, &c. and other small salaries.

What becomes of the overplus of the funds?—It is laid out in buying stock.

[Mr. *James Millar*, being again called in, delivered in the following paper; which was read.]

*Mr. Millar.*

### SAINT GEORGE'S SOUTHWARK.

| Instituted. | Where situated. | Description. | Day School. Boys. | Day School. Girls. | Sunday School. Boys. | Sunday School. Girls. | If Clothed. | Treasurer or Secretary. | Master or Mistress. | Annual Expense. | Remarks. |
|---|---|---|---|---|---|---|---|---|---|---|---|
| 1796 | Stone's End - | Insolvent Debtors | 100 | 50 | - | - | - | Cha⁵ Barclay, Esq. | Ashley - - | £. 170. | Church Catechism. |
| | New Alley - | Parochial - - - | 60 | 40 | - | - | Clothed - | F. Young & A. Sterry | Wiggins - - | 560. | |
| | Borough Road | British System - | 500 | - | - | - | - - | Wᵐ Allen - - | Jnᵒ Pickton - | 140. | Exclusive of Rent. |
| | Do - - - | Do - - - | - | 250 | - | - | - - | Do - - - - | Eliz. Brewer - | 70. | - - Do. |
| | East Lane - - | Day and Sunday | 57 | - | - | - | 40 Clothed | - - - - | - - - | 180. | |
| | Prospect Place | Dissenters - - | - | - | 165 | 135 | - - | Southwark Union | Sundry, gratuitous | - | |
| | Kent Street - | Do - - - | - | - | 260 | 205 | - - | Do - - - - | Do - - - - | - | In these Schools some of the Children are taught Writing and Arithmetic two evenings per week, and the average Expense will be from 2/6. to 3/. each Child. |
| | Mint School - | Do - - - | - | - | 126 | 137 | - - | Do - - - - | Do - - - - | - | |
| | | | 717 | 340 | 551 | 477 | | | | | |
| | | | | 2,085 Total. | | | | | | | |

495.

(*Mr. Millar.*)   I also deliver in Accounts of the expense of the Peckham charity schools.

[They were delivered in, and read, as follows :]

Dr - - - The Treasurer in Account with the Peckham Female Charity School - - - Cr

| 1815. | | £. | s. | d. | 1815. May 4. | | £. | s. | d. | £. | s. | d. |
|---|---|---|---|---|---|---|---|---|---|---|---|---|
| | To Amount of Subscriptions and Donations  -  - | 129 | 14 | 8 | | Balance due to the Treasurer | 52 | 15 | 2 | — | | |
| | Received for use of School-room, from the Sunday | | | | | Mistress's Salary  -  - | 42 | — | — | 42 | — | — |
| 1816. April 11. | School  -  -  - | 3 | 5 | — | | Rent and Fixtures  -  - | 17 | 5 | — | 12 | — | — |
| | Collection at Camden Chapel  -  -  - | 20 | — | — | | Clothing, for Prizes -  - | 10 | 5 | 2 | 10 | 5 | 2 |
| | Received for Work  -  .  - | *10 | 4 | 9 | | Haberdashery  -  - | 2 | 11 | 5½ | 2 | 11 | 5 |
| | Due to Treasurer  -  - | 8 | 4 | 7 | | Printing, Slates, and Pencils | 7 | 11 | 6 | 7 | 11 | 6 |
| | | | | | | Coals  -  -  - | 3 | 4 | — | 3 | 4 | — |
| | | | | | | Paid to 1 d. per week Fund | 4 | 15 | 8 | — | | |
| | | | | | | Bricklayer's Bill  -  - | 11 | 4 | 8 | — | | |
| | | | | | | Painter's  -  do  -  - | 7 | 2 | 6 | — | | |
| | | | | | | Smith's  -  do  -  - | 2 | 12 | 8 | — | | |
| | | | | | | Carpenter's  do  -  - | 2 | 16 | 4 | — | | |
| | | | | | | Various incidental Expenses | 7 | 4 | 10½ | 7 | 4 | 10 |
| | £. | 171 | 9 | — | | £. | 171 | 9 | — | 84 | 16 | 11 |
| | | | | | | Work per Contra  -  - | - | - | - | 10 | 4 | 9 |
| | | | | | | Amount Expenditure  - | - | - | - | 74 | 12 | 2 |
| | | | | | | BALANCE due to the Treasurer  -  - | 8 | 4 | 7 | | | |

* The Clothing for Prizes made up in the School, has supplied the younger children with Work, and if paid for, would amount to £.2. 11. 3½. during the last year, in addition to the above sum.

### Lancasterian School at Peckham.

THIS School was opened the 10th of February 1813 ; since which time 240 boys have been admitted ; and there now remain 140 in the school, of which number 90 can read well in the Bible and Testament, and the others are making good progress in lessons of one, two, and three syllables ; 80 of the boys can write well on slates, and 68 write in copy-books ; 40 are perfect in the four first rules of arithmetic, and 70 are making good progress in those rules. Of 81 boys who did not know the alphabet when they were admitted into this school, 60 can read in the Testament.

The children attend the various places of worship in the village on Sundays, according to the religion of their parents ; and it is cause of much satisfaction to the Supporters of this school, that the good effects of its establishment are visible in the more quiet and orderly observance of the Sabbath, it having been remarked by many of the inhabitants, that the village is not disturbed on Sundays, as it was formerly, by the children playing about in a noisy and disorderly manner.

Previous to the opening of this school, there was no school for the boys of this hamlet, except a Sunday school, which had been established about 12 years, and in which from 20 to 50 boys were generally taught. There was also a school for 20 girls, which has lately been enlarged on the new system, and contains 75 girls, who are in good order, and are taught reading, writing, arithmetic, and needlework.

13th June 1816.                          *Henry Newman*, Secretary.

| | £. | s. | d. |
|---|---|---|---|
| Master's Salary -  -  -  -  -  -  - | 63 | — | — |
| Rent  -  -  -  -  -  -  -  - | 12 | 12 | — |
| Books, Slates, and Pencils -  -  -  - | 15 | — | — |
| Rewards  -  -  -  -  -  -  - | 5 | — | — |
| £. | 95 | 12 | — |

FOURTH

# FOURTH REPORT.

(pp. 275——324.)

## MINUTES OF EVIDENCE

Taken before The SELECT COMMITTEE appointed to inquire into the EDUCATION of the Lower Orders of The Metropolis.

TOGETHER WITH

AN

A P P E N D I X.

Ordered, by The House of Commons, to be Printed,
20 June 1816.

# WITNESSES.

# APPENDIX.

# FOURTH REPORT.

## MINUTES OF EVIDENCE

Taken before the SELECT COMMITTEE on the EDUCATION of the
Lower Orders of The Metropolis.

*Veneris,* 14° *die Junii,* 1816.

HENRY BROUGHAM, Esquire, in The Chair.

Mr. *Joshua Johnston,* Treasurer of Saint Clement Danes School, and
Mr. *Peter Jackson,* Schoolmaster of the said School ;
called in, and Examined.

*(To Mr. Johnston.)* WHAT are the funds of that Establishment?—The total receipts for last year were 852*l.* 6*s.* 2¼*d.* the disbursements 860*l.* 3*s.* 1*d.*

Whence do those funds arise?—They arise from charity sermons, from subscriptions, from rents, and from the interest of money in the funds.

What proportion arises from rents?—287 *l.* last year.

Rents of houses?—Yes.

From money in the funds ; how much?—101 *l.* 5*s.*

*(To Mr. Jackson.)* When was it established?—1702.

Was it established by charter?—I believe not.

Was it by will?—No, I believe not ; it was the voluntary subscriptions of the inhabitants.

*(To Mr. Johnston.)* How many children are educated at the school?—60 boys clothed and educated ; 20 girls are educated, clothed, and boarded.

What are the salaries?—The master's salary is 80 *l.* the mistress's 30 *l.*

*(To Mr. Jackson.)* Have they houses?—I have apartments found me.

Has the mistress?—She is resident in the house with the girls.

Are the boys lodged?—No, only clothed.

*(To Mr. Johnston.)* Who appoints the boys and girls upon this foundation?—They are all admitted by the committee ; there are 41 trustees, including a treasurer ; and the girls are admitted in the same way.

Are they the poorest children in the parish?—They are those that we consider to be so ; they are the people who petition to be admitted ; and we select those whom we think to be the greatest objects.

Does each trustee appoint?—It is done by vote of the board ; a notice is sent to every member of the committee, and they are elected by a majority. There have been two girls and four boys admitted last week.

In what state of life were the parents of the girls?—Poor people.

What are the parents particularly of those two girls whom you have mentioned?—I cannot speak to that ; I have no recollection of the particular circumstances of those two girls.

Were you present when they were admitted?—I was.

Were there any certificates of their parents being poor?—No.

How did you know their circumstances?—From the petition.

Was the petition attested by any person?—The petition must be signed by one subscriber, and then they are put upon the books, and brought before the board of trustees, and admitted as vacancies occur.

Is there any thing in the constitution of this school that obliges you to board the girls as well as to educate them?—I do not know that there is.

Have you always boarded as many as twenty?—No ; they have been increased from time to time.

What used they to be formerly?—They have been as low as eight.

If it were proposed to the trustees, instead of boarding twenty girls, to teach a larger

Mr.
*Joshua Johnston,*
and
Mr. *Peter Jackson.*

number of children without boarding, what reception would be given to such a proposal?—That must be for their consideration; it would be laid before the board of trustees, and they must decide upon it.

What do you think would be their objection to making such a change in the management?—I think they would be for its continuing as it is; I am of that opinion myself.

(To Mr. Jackson.) How long has it been in its present state, as to number?—About five years.

How many were upon the establishment then?—Eighteen.

(To Mr. Johnston.) Do you not think that a much greater good would be done to the poor in your neighbourhood, by educating without boarding a very great number of children?—I do not; there are Sunday and other schools of that kind, which educate as well.

Do you mean to represent that there are schools enough in your neighbourhood for all the poor children who want education?—I am not at all acquainted with that.

Suppose it were proved to you that there are a vast number of poor in that neighbourhood wholly destitute of the means of education, should you be of opinion it was more beneficial to the poor to board 20 girls than to educate 2000 poor children without boarding?—There are the 60 boys, as well as the girls.

The question supposes you are to continue to educate 60 boys, and that you are to educate 2000 children instead of 20 girls; do you think that is a most beneficial management of your funds to the interests of the poor?—We are obliged to act according as our committee direct.

The question is, whether you yourself are of opinion that this is the most beneficial mode of managing the funds?—It is the mode that I have decided upon in my own opinion.

Then do you mean to represent your own opinion to be, that it is more beneficial to the poor in your parish, who are destitute of instruction, to board 20 girls, than to educate, without boarding, 2000 children?—Yes, it is.

Do you consider that more good is done by boarding 20 children than by educating 2000?—Not if they were as fully educated.

Suppose the 2000 were as fully educated as the 20 are, but only not boarded; do you consider that more good is done by boarding 20 than by fully educating 2000?—No, I should think not.

But you are still of opinion that it is better to board 20 than to educate 2000?—There are the 60 boys as well.

Suppose the 60 out of the way, because this does not affect that; the Committee are talking of the 20 girls only?—Certainly a much larger number would be benefited; but then I should think that benefit would not be to the same extent, there could not be the same pains taken then as there are now.

Can a child not be educated fully without being boarded at the same time?—No doubt of it.

Do you mean to represent it as better to board one child than to educate 100?—No, I think not.

Do you mean to represent it as better to board 20 children than to educate 2000?—No, I do not think it is.

The expenses of the school being 860 l. what proportion of it goes to the support of the 20 girls?—The house expenses are 251 l. 9 s. 7 d.

Does that include the mistress's salary?—No.

How much is that?—30 l.

Has the mistress any perquisite?—No.

What is the rent of the house in which the girls live?—25 l.

Does that include the school-house?—Yes.

What proportion belongs to the school-house?—It is all in one rent.

Then is 306 l. the whole expenses of the house?—No.

What are the other expenses?—There were apprentice fees last year, of 12 l.; there was the tailor's bill, and linings for the boys breeches.

What are the expenses of the girls?—It is not separated.

What is the tailor's bill?—17 l. 7 s. 6 d.; linings for the breeches, 6 l. 5 s.; woollen-draper's bill, 68 l. 14 s.; linen-draper's bill, 58 l. 19 s. 10 d.; the vestry keeper, 3 l. 6 s.; 29 l. 9 s. 9 d return for property tax to tenants, in the last year's disbursements; 7 l. doctor's bill; 9 l. for books; 15 l. 8 s. 4 d. for taxes; 1 l. 4 s. insurance; 3 l. 15 s. for potatoes; 8 l. 16 s. haberdasher's bill; 9 l. for apprenticing; 16 l. 19 s. collector's poundage; 57 l. 10 s. 6 d. for 100 l. stock; 11 l. 7 s. 9 d. for stockings; 38 l. 5 s. for shoes; and 32 l. 12 s 6 d. for coals.

Are there any salaries, besides those two you have mentioned?—None.

Then it appears that the whole expense of educating these 80 children consists

of

of 110 *l.* to the master and mistress, 9 *l.* for books, 25 *l.* for rent, making in all, between 140 *l.* and 150 *l.* and that all the rest is for clothing and maintenance?—Yes; I have given in all the items.

Who furnish the school with the different articles?—The tradesmen of the parish.

Are any of those tradesmen trustees?—Yes, I believe they are.

Are they all trustees?—No.

Which of them is not?—I think there are only three trustees among them all.

Who are those?—There is Mr. Marchant.

What trade is he?—A woollen draper.

Who else?—Mr. Burnthwaite, linen-draper; Mr. Soulsby, coal-merchant.

Is there any butcher?—Yes; the butchers are changed every four weeks.

When one butcher is changed for another, is he not gone back to?—Yes, in his turn.

How many butchers do you employ altogether?—I think there are four or five, somewhere thereabouts.

Was no butcher ever a trustee?—Not that I know of: they are all subscribers; we always employ the subscribers.

Are the trustees chosen by the subscribers?—No.

How are they chosen?—The vacancy is filled by the committee themselves.

How many does the committee consist of?—Forty-one.

What is the number that generally attend?—It varies very much, sometimes twelve.

(To Mr. *Jackson.*) Who are those that most frequently attend?—Mr. Marchant, Mr. Burnthwaite, and Mr. Howell.

Who is he?—A baker and churchwarden.

Does he supply the school with bread?—In his turn.

Who else supplies it with bread?—There are five or six of them altogether.

Are they trustees?—No, they are subscribers.

[Mr. *Collier,* attorney and vestry clerk, and one of the trustees of the school, was here examined with the other Witnesses.]

(To Mr. *Collier.*) What other trustees frequently attend?—Mr. Ommaney, navy-agent, Mr. Alexander of New Inn, Mr. Nourse the builder, Mr. Harrison, and Mr. Anderson

Have you any expense of law proceedings in your bills?—Not a shilling.

Expense of leases?—None.

How are your houses let?—The house at Hampstead was let to Mr. Bridgman, I should not think much short of twenty years ago, who afterwards made improvements in it and sold it; then we have some houses in Belton-street, Long Acre, in which we are jointly interested with Saint Martin's and Saint Dunstan's; the estate was a joint lease granted by the three parishes, and expired about two years ago; it was re-let beneficially, but there was no expense to the school.

How are these given or devised to the school?—It was a legacy a century ago, or at least thereabouts.

You do not recollect whether it was upon any condition?—No, I do not; I believe merely in aid of the foundation.

Do you know what the foundation of the school is?—It was one of those that were established by the Society for promoting Christian Knowledge, somewhere about 1706 or 1707.

How are the trustees chosen?—They are in fact chosen by the subscribers; notice of the election is given in the church previous to the election; but it seldom happens that more than one or two who are not trustees attend. As to the mode of election, the name of every subscriber is put on the table, and those gentlemen who attend to vote, put their marks against such as they wish to be elected trustees; and it has often happened, when there is no cause of complaint, he has been re-elected.

During his residence in the parish?—There are two or three gentlemen, very respectable, who do not reside in the parish, who are trustees; Mr. Dickinson, of Great Queen-street; Mr. Townsend, of Bow-street, who was educated in the school, has been a constant subscriber, and last Sunday sent three guineas to the charity sermon, he is a trustee; there is likewise Mr. Johnston, in Saint James's-street, sword-cutler. When a vacancy happens by death or removal of a trustee, another is elected, by such as attend the election, once a year, and the vacancies are then filled up.

### The Reverend *Daniel Wilson,* M. A. called in, and Examined.

ARE you Minister of Saint John's Chapel Bedford Row?—I am.

Is it a chapel-of-ease to the parish church of Saint Andrew's Holborn?—It is.

Have

Have you any charity schools attached to that chapel?—There are two schools, one not immediately attached to the chapel, the other closely connected with it; the former is the Welsh School, in Gray's-Inn Lane, which has attended the chapel more than forty years, in which there are 105 children, entirely boarded, educated and clothed, the children of Welsh parents.

How is that school supported?—It is supported by voluntary subscriptions, and the interest of their funded property, but I am not acquainted with the particulars; the other school which attends the chapel, and is closely connected with it, is a school for religious instruction, which is held on the Sunday only, and consists now of 84 boys, and 84 girls.

What is the expense of that school?—The expense is about 120 *l.* a year, a little varying.

What are the articles of expense incurred in that school?—The salary of the master and mistress is the only direct article; the rest are in books and rewards.

Is any sum paid for rent?—There is no rent paid; the school attends in the chapel.

What is the plan of instruction in your Sunday school?—Our plan is not to teach the children to read, because we find a sufficient number of children apply who can already read; our plan therefore is to admit first of all the children of parents attending the chapel, and then generally of others residing in the neighbourhood. We admit them when they can already read, and instruct them generally in religion. We teach them the Catechism of the Church of England; we teach them the collects; we teach those that are old enough, the Epistles and Gospels; we require them to learn the texts of the sermons which they have heard on the preceding Sunday; and, where they have time, we occasionally set them to learn the Articles of the Church of England. These several lessons are not taught them at the time on the Sunday; they learn them during the week, and repeat them only on the Sunday at the time of their attendance at the chapel, when the great aim of the superintendents is to endeavour to enable the children to understand what they are doing, and not only to learn the things by rote.

Have you any teachers who are paid, besides the master and mistress?—No; but we have fourteen ladies and thirteen gentlemen, belonging to the chapel, who attend regularly without pay, besides supernumeraries, who fill up the vacancies of any persons who may occasionally be absent, so that about six or seven children only are under the care of one superintendent.

Do many of the children attend any day school in the course of the week?—I should apprehend not; but I have never made the inquiry; but I should rather conceive not; because they come to us after they have learnt to read, and of course are not a class of children that would so much require week-day instruction.

Have you observed any particular good resulting from your plan of instruction?—We think we have observed an almost incalculable measure of good; for the children frequently enter the school ignorant, rude, untaught; many of them absolutely not knowing the very first principles of religion in any way, negligent of their duty to their parents, and, in many cases, apparently open to all the vice or misery that such want of principles would lead to. As they go on in the school, we find that their knowledge of the general principles of religion, their observation of the Sabbath, their regard to conscience, and to their duty to God and man, and the affection they generally acquire for what is good, produce at the time the most important results, and, in their future life, those happy effects which you would naturally expect to follow.

Have you observed the good effects of instruction in the future life of some of them that have been children in your school?—Many such cases have occurred. One obvious good effect is, that, after the children have left the school, many of them voluntarily continue to attend divine worship on the Sunday. Indeed we see many who in their future life bear respectable characters; and in some cases we observe in them all that piety which we could wish to see in Christians. In short, they retain in general an affection for the school and the chapel, and for their instructors, during the remainder of their lives.

Have you known many children in your schools rise to creditable situations in life?—At present I have one who was a scholar in the school, who is now clerk of my chapel, and collector of various public charities; an exceedingly respectable, well-ordered man, in his station in life.

Do you conceive that those good effects have been produced by the religious instruction given in your schools?—I conceive so, under God's blessing, unquestionably; because all our instruction is founded upon the specific principles of
Christianity,

Christianity, the fear of God, and the revelation of his will in his Word. The children, as soon as they enter the school, have a Prayer-book given to them, the Church Catechism, Doctor Watts's Hymns for Children, a book of Collects, and, as soon as they can use it aright, a Bible; and the main point that we wish to aim at, is the planting the love and fear of God in the minds of the children; for which purpose the number of our superintendents is so considerable, that it enables them to take the utmost pains with their children.

How long does a child remain in your school?—It varies from three or four to seven or eight years, or even more. We admit them as soon as they can read. The common time is about seven years of age, and they remain till fifteen; some even as long as eighteen or twenty. The boys commonly remain after they are apprentices, their masters still allowing them to attend.

Have you observed any good effects arise to the parents and families of those children, from the instruction which the children have received in those schools?—We have observed many pleasing effects. The books which the children are furnished with in passing through the school, they take home and read to their parents. The parents generally consider the attention paid to their children, and the voluntary attendance of the gentlemen and ladies of the chapel upon the school, as a favour conferred on them, and they are led, in very many instances, to attend upon divine worship themselves. We do not make their attendance absolutely a condition, but we understand the school is for the children of families who come to the chapel; and though we are not very strict upon that point, it certainly encourages the attendance of the parents upon the Sunday. This end is promoted in another way. When I go up into the gallery myself, if any children are not in time, I ask the reason why they were not earlier in their attendance; perhaps they reply, that they were employed by their parents in a way which I think not right; I then make a remark or two to the children in an affectionate way, which I think they will probably carry home to their parents; and in this way a great improvement in the morals of the parents has been sometimes produced. In some cases, I should conceive that the reformation of the parents from habits of vice and irreligion has been in a great measure effected by these methods. One effect which we endeavour to produce in the girls, and which we think tends to benefit the parents, is, a strict regard to modesty, and a suitable dress.

In what way does religious instruction tend to make children good members of society?—I conceive that instructing the children in their duty, as immortal and accountable creatures, instructing them in the important doctrine of a future judgment; pointing out to them the great evil of lying, which we find at the foundation of almost all early sins and bad habits in children; teaching them a reverence for conscience, a sense of God's presence as every where with them; explaining to them the love to God in sending Jesus Christ into the world to save sinners, his readiness to pardon those who repent, and the eternal glory and happiness which he has promised to good children; all these principles, varying in the measure of course, with God's blessing, and other attendant circumstances, tend directly to lay in the children's minds the foundation of obedience to their governors in church and state, to make them contented with the station which Providence has appointed to them in the world, to teach them the subjugation of their passions, and the avoiding the company of dissolute and profligate and vicious characters; and in this way, to make them worthy, respectable and virtuous persons in their stations, and real blessings to society.

Of what description of character, and what class of society, are the teachers who volunteer their services?—They are persons who regularly occupy seats in the chapel, and live in the neighbourhood; the wives and sons and daughters of persons engaged in trade, or in the profession of the law; most of them very respectable people.

Do those voluntary teachers endeavour to give religious instruction to the children, as well as yourself?—They chiefly do this, my own attendance being of course very limited; their object is, in hearing them the lessons they have set them on the preceding Sunday, to explain them, and give them religious instruction.

You apprehend they are capable of bringing down religious truths to the understanding of the children?—Quite so; their object is particularly to interest the minds and affections of the children, and to make religion and their duty, as far as it can be, pleasing to them; and to bring down to their understandings all the main principles and duties of the Christian religion, according to the principles of the Church of England. Of course the degree in which this instruction is understood, depends upon the child.

What

*The Rev.*
*Daniel Wilson.*

What influence is produced upon the minds of the children, with respect to the observance of the Sabbath?—I conceive it to be one of the most prominent advantages of the school, because the regular attendance upon the Sunday is one point which we chiefly insist upon, and according to which, the rewards are given. The children are thus impressed with the evil of violating that sacred day, which being early implanted, commonly grows up to an habitual reverence for the Lord's day; a disposition of mind which in a great measure, so far as my observation goes, lies at the foundation of all moral and religious habits. I never knew any poor family become very vicious or miserable who observed the Lord's day; and I never knew a poor family happy, contented or virtuous, that did not observe it. The Sunday is in fact to the poor, if it is not conscientiously employed, a source of a thousand temptations; they are thrown off from the ordinary habits of industry; all the scenes of vice are open before them; and, being left without those principles of religion and morality, which the Sunday is the time of inculcating, they grow up nearly as heathens.

Do you conceive it of great importance to train up children in the habit of attending public worship on the Sunday?—Of great importance, unquestionably; because it is one of those duties which, if a person habitually violates, he soon loses all taste for; the conscience becomes hardened; the duty of making every thing yield to an attendance on public worship is forgotten. The person forgets also the benefits he derives from religious duties, and gives way to those multiplied calls and engagements, which no one can want, if he wishes to employ them as an excuse. By a contrary line of conduct, the best habits of a moral and religious nature are produced and strengthened in the mind.

Is there any accommodation in your chapel for the children of the poor to attend public worship?—When the school was established, the congregation subscribed and built a gallery, which will contain about 300 persons, on the two longer sides of the chapel, over the other gallery, not projecting into the chapel above one third the way of the larger gallery. The chapel is 90 feet long, and of course the two galleries are very extensive.

Do you conceive it would be a public benefit in the building of new churches, if a small gallery, of the form you have described, were built over the ordinary gallery, for the use of poor children?—I should think so; I believe it is so in the new church of Mary-le-bone; there are two galleries there, the one over the other. In my chapel, on a Sunday evening, when the children do not all of them attend, we open those galleries for free sittings, which we find a very great accommodation. They are quite crowded every Sunday evening with persons who perhaps otherwise would not attend public worship.

Do you recollect any particular instances of the good which you have spoken of, as resulting from the instruction given in your schools?—I have seen it lately. A little boy, perhaps ten or eleven years old, is gradually dying, I may say, with an abscess, but who really seems so resigned to God's will in the pain he suffers, is so sensible of the love of Christ his Saviour to him, and of the mercy of God in pardoning his sins, that he is dying happy and thankful for the instruction he has received. Several other such cases have occurred. Many cases have likewise occurred where the children have been untractable during the time of their being in the school, and yet afterwards in future life we have traced the good effects of what they were taught at this school, and the religious instruction which was there given.

What do you conceive is the advantage of the kind of respectable teachers you have mentioned as employed in your school?—The advantage is, that they are, generally speaking, better qualified for the particular duty of giving them moral and religious instruction than ordinary schoolmasters; or, if they were not, the difficulty and expense of getting that number of schoolmasters would be sufficient to recommend our method. Besides, as this is a voluntary thing, the manner in which they engage the affection of the children is a great advantage; and their own better education enables them both to understand religion themselves perhaps beyond what ordinary schoolmasters would, and to explain it more correctly and intelligibly to the children.

Is there a disposition in the poor to send their children to be taught?—A very great disposition; the number of applications we have for admission is much greater than the vacancies which occur in the schools. It is a most pleasing circumstance, that in all the inquiries we have made among the poor, there does appear a readiness to be taught, and to avail themselves of all the opportunities of obtaining for themselves and their children moral and religious advantages. Mrs. Wilson has found

this

The Rev.
Daniel Wilson.

this also in visiting the female poor on the occasion of a Bible Association established in the neighbourhood. There is the same disposition in the poor women to receive with gratitude every offer that is made for ameliorating their condition and instructing and helping them or their children.

Do you think this desire to have their children educated, has increased of late years?—I am not exactly able to say, because I have been in London only about six years, and have not had the opportunity of making a comparison; but from the accounts I have received from others, I should apprehend there was a considerable increase.

Have you any control over the children during the week?—In cases where notorious bad conduct occurs, the parents bring the refractory child before the committee; and I, if I am present (or some one else, if I am not) speak affectionately and yet firmly to the child, and inform it, that if its conduct in the week is not what it should be, we must exclude it from the school. We do not go to that extent, except in very bad cases.

Has the custom of bringing the children before you and the committee, a good effect upon their minds, in restraining them from bad habits?—The best of effects. We find a by far better effect produced by the fear of punishment, and by a love of their superintendents and schoolmaster, and a desire to please them, than by any direct punishment actually inflicted.

Have you found the children take a pleasure in attending school?—A great pleasure; united, as I should explain, with the system of rewards which we adopt in the conduct of the school. Our rewards are these: every Sunday the best child in the class receives a small tract, perhaps of the value of a halfpenny or not so much, which he takes home with him; he also receives a ticket, testifying his good behaviour and regular attendance: once a quarter, in addition to this, the best child in the class receives a prize of greater value, perhaps a book of two shillings value: and at the end of the year there is an annual distribution of prizes still more considerable, to those who have gone best through the year. The children become so desirous of accumulating these little books, as well as of obtaining the approbation of their teachers, that many children have a library, which they acquire in the six or seven years they are in the school, which they preserve with care through all their future life. It is pleasing to see the anxiety which parents manifest that the children should behave well, and get books, and have the rewards which are given in the school. We give no money.

What do the rewards consist of, beside books?—We have no rewards but books and tracts.

Have you any annual examination of the children?—We have only that kind of examination which I have referred to, in classing the children according to their behaviour during the year. But we have also all the children assembled once a year, generally on the first day of May, when a sermon is preached entirely to children, upon some little history from the Scriptures, that may interest them, or some other simple topic. After the sermon, we deliver before the committee and friends, the various books to the children. In addition to this, as the children leave the school from time to time, we bring them before the committtee; and I, if I am there, and if not some member of the committee, make them a present of a new Bible, large or small according to the merit which we consider the children to have, and we endeavour to impress upon them the importance of showing, in their future life and conduct, the good effects of what they have been learning in the school which they are then quitting.

Do you think any danger is to be apprehended by giving children knowledge, without communicating religious instruction?—Certainly there is a danger; because you give them information and a greater power, without at the same time a principle to direct that power. But when you teach them to read, and at the same time implant the main principles of Christianity, and an attachment to the Church of England, and to the worship of God on a Sunday, you not only give them knowledge, but the principles to use it aright; you keep them from pride and self-elevation, and from that abuse of knowledge, in reading improper books, to which they might possibly be tempted. Besides, in our schools we give the children books on which to employ their knowledge; and, above all, we endeavour from the beginning to make them understand that we give them knowledge on purpose to enable them to know their duty better, and serve God better in this world, and be prepared for heaven, and His favour in another world.

In speaking of attachment to the Church of England, you speak as a clergyman of that community?—Yes.

Do

Do you mean that you would confine religious instruction to children of the Church Establishment only?—I should be very far from wishing to exclude any children of any description from the advantage of religious instruction; and I should be equally far from wishing to impose on such children the principles of the Establishment to which they do not belong. All I meant to say was, that in a case where the great mass of our population are members of the Church of England, it is an essential branch of religious education, in my opinion, to unite an attachment, a moderate and an enlightened attachment to the Church, with the general principles of religion, morality, and virtue.

Do you receive the children of all denominations, who apply for admission into your school?—We make no very strict inquiry; though it is specifically for the children of those who attend at the chapel.

Do you teach the children the Church Catechism?—Yes.

You are willing to communicate instruction to all who apply, if you have vacancies?—Exactly so.

Do you conceive that the two things united, namely, reading and religious instruction, ever make the poor discontented in their stations, or less obedient to their superiors?—Unquestionably not. The direct tendency of the two, when united, is to produce those principles that lead to submission, contentment, humility, and in fact to all those dispositions and duties to which they are chiefly about to be called in the stations where Providence has placed them. We let nothing form any part of the knowledge we communicate, which tends to foster pride or self-elevation. We confine ourselves to those essential principles of Christianity and those duties resulting from them, which may best fit them for their stations in society, and may most directly lead to practical results. The very first thing we teach the female children especially is to correct the love of dress, and to lead them to aim at that respect every person acquires who behave well in their station; and to avoid on the other hand the contempt to which they will expose themselves, by aspiring to that which they can never attain, and which only draws upon them the displeasure of others and the anger of God.

Have you found the children of your school attached to the forms of the Church of England, from affection and habit?—Very much so; because when the children come to us they are necessarily ignorant, from their tender age, of what the Church of England is. But when they go on in the school, they become accustomed to our forms of instruction and devotion, and to all the various branches of that education in which they are trained; and this generally produces in the susceptible minds of children an attachment and preference to the Church which they have found connected with the blessings of a moral and religious education.

Have you any society for visiting the poor, attached to your chapel?—We have a considerable society for visiting the poor; the year before last, we gave away as much as 800*l.*

How are those funds raised?—Simply by subscriptions and donations. Last year also we had a collection sermon in the chapel for them.

How many visitors have you in the society to which you allude?—Stating upon recollection, I should think about twenty or twenty-four.

Do the visitors recommend the children of the poor to schools?—Constantly. The twofold object of the visitors is, to relieve their necessities, when they find them to be of good character, and to give them such advice as will benefit their children and families. Sometimes we have had the opportunity of benefiting a whole family of children, by directing their attention to schools, and pointing out the facilities for obtaining admission.

Do you conceive it of importance for bettering the condition of the poor, that visits should frequently be paid among the lower classes of society by respectable persons?—I think so; because it unites the different orders of society together; it leads the poor to consider the commendation and support of their superiors as dependent upon their good conduct; it enables their superiors both to know their actual character and wants, and to administer that particular kind of relief which their circumstances render most desirable.

Have any circumstances come to your knowledge of the effects of the want of education in the children of the poor?—Yes. The most deplorable effects follow from the want of education: One instance is now before me, of a very respectable woman apparently, with a family, who has one boy who has been inveigled by bad company. He is now engaged in committing little thefts. He is utterly incorrigible by any thing the parent can say; and the only hope of his not coming to the gallows,

is

*The Rev.*
*Daniel Wilson.*

is sending him to the Philanthropic Society. Such instances occur frequently where there has been no early education in the principles of the Christian religion.

Do you conceive there are many uneducated children in your part of the town?—I conceive there are a great number.

Do you think the proportion of educated children is very small, in comparison with that of uneducated children?—I should think it is.

Are there any National schools, or those upon the British and Foreign system, in your neighbourhood, except that in Baldwin's Gardens?—I am not aware that there are any.

Of what class in society are the persons employed in your society for visiting the sick poor?—The same respectable class of persons as the superintendents of the schools, young merchants or tradesmen, after they have done their duties in the City, and some lawyers; we have one or two barristers who attend.

As a clergyman, you see no impropriety in respectable laymen visiting the poor upon that plan?—I rejoice to have their aid; it requires of course judgment in the selection of your visitors, as it does in every other thing of the same nature; but it is a clergyman in fact multiplying himself into twenty or thirty persons, who go about to do for him what he cannot do himself.

Do you not consider that the attendance at divine worship is the principal act in the observance of the Sabbath?—The principal act certainly; but not the only one.

Do you consider that the system of your Sunday schools is productive of valuable benefits to individuals, and also to the nation, in proportion to the number?—I consider them to be so in the highest degree; it is communicating the greatest possible blessings to them in every relation in which they may stand, as individuals, as members of families, and as subjects of the realm.

Do you consider that the parents of the children are considerably improving, by associating with their children who attend your school?—There can be no doubt of it, in the several respects which I mentioned in an answer to a former question; for instance, bringing them to attend divine worship themselves is an extremely important benefit; another instance, is the correcting in them the habit of profane swearing, and of a variety of other vices, which those children are taught on a Sabbath morning to abhor, as violating the commands of God.

Do you not think that the educating of the poor, and their acquirement of knowledge, will tend much to lessen the poor rates of parishes?—I should think very much; because it tends directly to lessen those vices which throw the poor upon our parishes, and creates that proper spirit of independence and desire to do for themselves which directly leads to exertion. It gives them also the feeling that they are men, and reasonable beings; it raises them above the mere animal, and gives them a desire to appear creditable in their neighbourhood and connexions; it qualifies children for filling up stations which they otherwise could not fill; and it particularly forms that habit of industry and of regular employment which bars out many of those vices which interrupt the happiness of the poor, and reduce them to abject dependence.

Does it not raise them especially in the rank of society?—I think it does. There is nothing which raises a poor person so much, in a proper sense of the word, as a moral and religious character.

Have you observed that the present state of the Poor Laws has had any effect upon the education of the children of the poor, in a direct or indirect way?—As far as a very limited opportunity of observation allows me to answer, I should consider the Poor Laws as a most defective system; degrading to the poor, lavish at sometimes and parsimonious at others, and incapable of just and adequate discrimination. In a small parish in Oxfordshire which belongs to my father, he has himself superintended the conduct of the poor during the last few years, and he has reduced the amount of poor-rates very considerably, by endeavouring to excite the poor to rely on their own efforts, by promoting a spirit of industry, and breaking through the habit which had been established, of their expecting relief from the parish according to the number of their families, independently of their actual circumstances and wants; and also by not giving relief in money, but giving it in (what is sure to be for the good of the family) the immediate necessaries of life. The consequence is, the poor are better off, more contented and happy and respectable. I am almost certain, upon recollection, that the poor-rates have been lessened more than half.

Do you conceive that any general plan for extending education to the children of the poor, would be a public benefit?—A most incalculable benefit.

497. Does

Does it fall within your knowledge that there is a great want of accommodation for the poor in places of worship in the Establishment?—Most deplorable. In the parish where I reside there are about 30,000 inhabitants, and there are only, so far as I remember, four places of worship in the Established Church, viz. the mother-church of St. Andrew's Holborn, the church of St. George the Martyr, and two chapels. I do not suppose these four places would hold above 6,000 or 7,000 persons altogether, leaving 24,000 without the possibility of attending divine worship in the Church of England in our parish.

Is it your opinion that this want of accommodation is not only injurious to the morals and religious habits of the poorer classes, but that, by diminishing accommodation for Sunday-schools, is an obstacle to education?—It must be an obstacle in every view. There must be a building prepared for our schools, if it were not for my chapel, where they meet; it is in the chapel, and in the chapel alone, that the instruction is given.

Do you not think a plan for obliging every parish to educate their poor, would tend to save the parish in point of poor-rates, and be nationally very beneficial in a religious and moral point of view?—It certainly would, if it could be so arranged as not to stand upon the ordinary plan of parish business and parish officers, but to engage the well-educated and liberal part of the parish to interest themselves actively in behalf of the education of the poor.

Then the welfare of a parish depends considerably upon the industry of many, besides the parish officers, to promote those benefits?—Certainly; I should think so.

Have you formed any opinion of the comparative merits of the Lancasterian and the National system of education?—I should say, that certainly I conceive the benefits of knowledge to the lower orders to be so incalculably valuable, that I would risk any thing as to the mode of communicating it, in order that they might receive that benefit. At the same time I think it of high importance to inspire the great mass of your population already members of the Church of England, with a fixed and enlightened regard to their own religious establishment; and I consider further, the particular principles of religion upon which our church is founded, to be so essential to that religion, that I regard the National system, when it can be obtained, as having incomparably the advantage over the British and Foreign system. I am of opinion also, that the present system of Sunday schools, and especially schools for religious instruction on Sundays, is necessary where they can be had, because there you have your children addressed individually and specifically, by persons who have a particular regard for them, in small numbers. There also the observance of the Sabbath, and the progress of the children in religion, are more watched over, than in any great general schools can be the case. So that if National schools should spread over the whole Metropolis, I still think they would not supersede Sunday school instruction. As to a plan of mere mechanical instruction, without the great principles of Christianity being also inculcated, I cannot but view it as pregnant with very dangerous consequences to the public.

Do you consider that the Lancasterian system gave rise to the National establishment?—I think so; what the National Society might have done without the Lancasterian I really cannot say. I have always thought that Mr. Lancaster was the person who first excited a general anxiety about the education of the poor, and called up the exertions of Churchmen, and awoke them from their sleep, if I may use the expression.

Do you consider that there is now a great competition between the two establishments?—I should think there was.

Each active in doing good?—Yes; each in their way, and in different degrees.

Do you not think that the continuance of the Lancasterian plan preserves that competition?—I should think so. And yet it is an awkward thing to say so, when I approve of the one so much more than of the other; and yet I must think, considering what human nature is, and how things generally go on, it must be the case that the continuance of the Lancasterian schools is necessary to preserve the National ones in their full vigour.

And you think that competition is beneficial to both systems, in promoting activity and industry?—Yes, I should think it is.

### Mr. *Joseph Christian*, called in, and Examined.

WHERE do you reside?—In Wigmore-street.

Do you belong to any charity school in Mary-le-bone?—I am a trustee for the Mary-le-bone Institution for Instruction and Industry.

How

Mr.
Joseph Christian.

How many children have you in that school?—About 540.

What is the annual expense?—From 800*l.* to 1,000 *l.* a year.

How is it supported?—By voluntary contributions and annual subscriptions; there is also some funded property, which has been saved out of the annual subscriptions.

What is your plan of instruction?—It is precisely the same as the National Society; the school is actually united to the National Society.

Have you observed any improvement in the morals and behaviour of the children since they came to the school?—Yes; I think the improvement is very apparent.

To any considerable extent?—I can merely answer to their general conduct in the school, I cannot answer in any other respect; I am not in the habit of visiting their families, but their conduct certainly is very much improved in the school.

Are any of the children clothed?—One hundred and fifty are clothed, but partly from their own earnings.

What portion of the 800*l.* pays for the clothing?—About 100*l.*: Last year the expense of the clothing was 196*l.* and the earnings of the children contributed 96*l.* leaving 100 *l.* to be paid by the Society.

How are the boys employed?—In the straw business for hats, which are principally exported to the West Indies.

How are the girls employed?—In needlework; in plain work.

What hours are appropriated for instruction, and what for work?—Four hours are appropriated to instruction, and two hours to work.

Can you receive all the children into your schools, who apply for admission?—Yes.

Is there still a great number of uneducated children in your parish?—I believe there are.

Besides the Irish?—Yes; I found my opinion upon the great extent of the parish, and the small number of the schools, and not from my own observation.

Can you ascertain the reason why a greater number do not apply for admission into your school?—I really can scarcely answer that question: At every board-day, we have upon the average thirty applications; but still our numbers do not very considerably increase; we continue at about 500; and I attribute it to the circumstance of the poor allowing their children to remain so short a time in the schools, from the necessity of being obliged to have their children employed for their own support.

How many children would your schools contain, if they were full?—We could receive more than 540; but I am not prepared to say to what extent; I should suppose the school would contain about 100 more.

Where is it situated?—No. 82, High-street Mary-le-bone.

Are you connected with any Sunday school in that parish?—A Sunday school has lately been established, or rather added to this.

How many children are there in that school?—The numbers generally speaking, on the average, are about 300 that attend; they do not all attend.

What are they taught?—Entirely religious instruction; the Church Catechism, the Collects, and Watts's Hymns; they are made to read the Bible, and are examined as to the understanding of what they read.

Do the children all attend on the Sunday at the school?—No; about 300 on the average.

What is the reason that a large proportion of the day scholars do not attend the Sunday school?—Many of the children are the children of Dissenters, and they are not compelled to send their children on the Sunday; they are allowed full liberty to take their children where they please: the only question we put to the parents is, whether they do take them to a place of worship.

Are there any visible effects of the advantage of the Sunday school establishment?—I think the effects are visible, particularly in that part of the parish where the school is situate, not only arising from this Sunday school, but from another Sunday school in the neighbourhood.

What school is that?—It is connected with the chapel in Hinde-street.

How many children are there in that school?—I have understood between five and six hundred.

Have you any connexion with it?—No.

The school in High-street and that in Hinde-street, have you observed any material difference in the neighbourhood result from them?—I have; the visible effects are apparent, only judging from outward circumstances; the neighbourhood is comparatively quiet now, to what it was before these schools were established; very few children are comparatively seen loitering and idling about the street.

Was

Mr.
Joseph Christian.

Was that the case formerly?—It was; there is a greater degree of decorum apparent in the children, than there used to be.

Have you any society for visiting and relieving the sick poor in that neighbourhood?—Yes.

How is it supported?—By voluntary subscriptions.

Does this society contribute to increase the number sent to the school?—I apprehend it does.

Do the visitors recommend the poor to send their children to those schools?—Yes, the visitors make it a point, when they observe any children at the houses, to recommend their parents to send them to the school.

Who are the visitors?—They chiefly consist of ladies and gentlemen, members of the district society.

And members of the Church of England, generally?—Generally, not all.

Do the clergy take an active part in the society?—There are two clergymen who are the treasurers of the society; but they do not visit the poor, conceiving that it might interfere with the duties of the Minister of the parish.

Does the Minister of the parish approve of the principles of the society?—Yes, he so far approves of them, that he has said he will subscribe to our society, and as many others as may be established of the same description, provided no part of his parish is left without a society of that description; his objection to the society at first arose from its being partial.

Do you conceive that the societies for visiting the sick poor, and the schools for the instruction of poor children, have greatly improved the state of society in your neighbourhood?—I conceive they tend very materially to improve the lower orders of people, and more particularly the Sunday and other schools.

### Mr. *John Collins*, called in, and Examined.

Mr. John Collins.

ARE you schoolmaster of Hatton Garden school?—Yes.

Is the report which you have sent to the Committee drawn up from your own knowledge?—Yes; but I have made a little mistake, the correction of which I have got in my pocket.

What is the mistake?—I will give in the correction of it. [*It was delivered in, and read.*]

Are you qualified as a schoolmaster?—Yes.

In what particular parts of education?—Reading, writing, arithmetic, and mathematics.

Dr. Hutton recommended you, did he not?—Yes.

---

### *Sabbati*, 15° *die Junii* 1816.

### HENRY BROUGHAM, Esquire, in The Chair.

### The Reverend *James Yorke Bramston*, called in, and Examined.

The Rev.
J. Y. Bramston.

YOU are a priest in holy orders?—I am.

Suppose schools were established upon the National, or British and Foreign Society's plan, but without any Catechism being taught, or any obligation to attend Church, are you of opinion that there would be any impediment in the way of Catholic parents sending their children to such schools?—That might depend upon the kind of religious instruction. To the general question I should say, as a Catholic priest, I should be sorry for it. If I understand the question it is this, whether I conceive it would be advisable that Catholic parents should send their children to schools where there are persons of various religions; to go to that school where they are taught no religion at all; I conceive it is not advisable.

Do you mean because there is no religion taught at all?—No; what I mean is, that if you send a child to a school where no religion is taught at all, and where there is no Catechism taught, you h row a burden upon the priests, which they are not capable of bearing, and I have had experience of the effects of that; a number of Catholic children who used to attend for religious instruction twice a week at Saint George's Fields Chapel, went to the Borough Road school, and as there was nobody to look after them, they discontinued their attendance at the chapel, and there was no security for their continuing to learn the Catechism.

Could

*The Rev.*
*J. Y. Bramston.*

Could the difficulties be got over by teaching them at the school the Bible or certain select portions of it, which might be authorized by the Catholic clergy?—I should think they would not only not get over it, but it would increase the difficulty. I wish it to be distinctly understood, for it is my positive opinion from much experience, that the Bible, generally speaking, is unintelligible to children without explanation.

Do you admit the common people of the Roman Catholic persuasion to have the Bible, without notes to explain the text?—I never saw one without notes, and I do not know of any without notes, in England.

Might not a number of the most plain and intelligible parts of the New Testament be taught to children without note or comment?—It might, I suppose, from an approved edition. In our Catechisms, or books of devotion, which we give, there are extracts from the Bible and Testament.

Are there any cheap editions of the New Testament, of the Roman Catholic version, in English?—There are; I know of two.

From your knowledge of the Roman Catholics in London, do you imagine there is any indisposition on the part of the parents to allow their children to be instructed?—Quite the contrary.

Are there any difficulties that present themselves to prevent the instruction of the lower classes of children of the Roman Catholic persuasion?—I know of none; the only difficulty is in finding ways and means to instruct them.

How many children do you suppose are educated in the Roman Catholic persuasion in London?—I do not know.

Do you know whether there are many uneducated?—I do not know that.

Are there many children in the congregation under your charge, who are without the means of education?—We fear the greater part are without the means of education, except by charity.

Are the charities at present established in your neighbourhood sufficient for the purpose?—I should say there was a deficiency, but not a very material one; but I have not had an opportunity of fully examining the matter.

Do you think that sufficient religious instruction could be given to Catholic children, by simply teaching them certain selected parts of the Bible?—Certainly not; decidedly not.

Suppose they were taught those select passages at the school, could not sufficient religious instruction, in addition to this, be communicated upon Sundays?—No, it is not possible, considering the paucity of the clergy.

About how many are in your own congregation?—I have no means of judging exactly, it is a congregation that extends over a space of sixteen miles in circumference; but I have no means of estimating the number, except by the baptisms, which are about from 250 to 300; many of the parents carry their children over to Ireland, where they can leave them to be brought up more cheaply.

Do you happen to recollect whether the Catholic prelates have approved of certain select passages of Scripture being taught in the schools where Catholic children attend?—No, I do not know that they have; I have not heard of it, and should not think it probable.

Where there is no adequate school in the neighbourhood, is it your opinion that the parents of Catholic children could conscientiously send them to school, the master of which should be a Protestant, and where the spelling-book and the Protestant version of the New Testament were the only books used?—If the question means whether as a Catholic clergyman I could approve of it, I should say no; and as a Catholic clergyman I never could approve of it.

Do you think the affluent Roman Catholics in London are sufficient in point of number, to afford education to the great mass of the lower class of Irish?—No, I do not.

What religious works are taught in your Catholic schools?—I have already delivered them in.

Are the Scriptures used at all?—No further than I have mentioned. We do not approve of the use of the Holy Scriptures as a common school-book; we think such a practice calculated to lessen that respect which children should entertain for them.

Do you imagine it would be practicable for Protestants and Roman Catholics to unite in any system of general education for the poor?—I think it scarcely practicable.

Do you conceive that any plan could be adopted in which the Roman Catholics could agree with the Protestants in teaching the Scriptures?—Any portion of

Scripture

The Rev.
J. Y. Bramston.

Scripture taught to the Catholics, to be approved of by the Catholic priests, must be taught from the approved Catholic edition of the Scriptures.

Would you allow the Douay version to be taught to the lower classes of society, unaccompanied with notes?—I should answer to that, that I believe it is not at all the practice to give the Scriptures to the common people, without notes.

Are you acquainted with the Bull Unigenitus published by Pope Clement the XIth?—I am.

Is it allowed to be in force in the Roman Catholic church?—No doubt it is.

What was the object of that Bull?—That Bull embraced many objects; but none, I apprehend, at all relevant to the education of the poor.

It is your opinion that it is better for so many of the lower classes of the Roman Catholic persuasion to remain uneducated, than to be educated by Protestants?—I have not made up my mind upon that at all; but I should think it were better they were uneducated, than educated on a false principle.

Should you have any doubt about its being more beneficial to children being taught reading and writing without any religion, than remaining at home, where they must be taught neither reading, writing, nor religion?—I take that to be a question of great delicacy and importance; and after much reflection, and considerable experience, I have rather come to the conclusion, that, speaking *of this town*, it would be better for children not to be taught reading and writing at all, than to be so taught, without any moral or religious instruction. The dangers I apprehend from their being taught in this way, arise from the facilities and temptations afforded in a town like this, to employing their knowledge of reading and writing improperly. I confine this answer to a place like London.

Should you imagine, if a spirit of conciliation were manifested both by Roman Catholics and Protestants, that they might unite in a plan of education, where the Holy Scriptures are taught?—I do not feel myself competent to answer that question decisively; but I conceive not.

### The Reverend *James Archer*, called in, and Examined.

The Rev.
James Archer.

YOU are a priest in holy orders, and chaplain to the Bavarian Embassy?—I am.

Do you apprehend there would be any difficulty in teaching the lower orders of Catholics at Protestant schools, where select portions of the Scripture were read, and no catechism taught?—I think the difficulty would be insuperable.

In what does it consist?—Inasmuch as we cannot give a sanction to any of our persons being taught a version of the Bible which is not approved of by our Church.

Suppose the version approved of by your Church were taught?—If the version approved of by our Church were taught, we could have no difficulty as Catholics, but it would be for the Protestants to say whether they liked that or not.

Is there any Catholic version without notes?—None, that I know of; at least there is none in England that I know of, there may be some in foreign countries.

Do those notes always contain the peculiar tenets of your Church?—Wherever there is a peculiar controversy between the Churches, we generally affix a note to determine the sense of the controverted point to our tenets.

But might not children be taught such parts of Scripture without note, as both Churches agree upon; for example, certain parts of the Gospels?—They might be taught them, but at the same time, except they have a comment to explain them, we think it unsafe.

Do you consider that there is no part of the history of our Saviour in the Gospels that might be taught safely without comment?—Undoubtedly there is, that they might be taught safely; but I do not add to that, that we should approve of the use of that version.

Do you consider it to be dangerous to children to be taught reading and writing without religious instruction?—Dangerous as to their morals; it is beneficial perhaps as to the purposes of this life.

Is not a child, generally speaking, better off as to the means of obtaining moral instruction, for knowing how to read?—No; because every thing must then depend upon what books are put into his hands; he may become a great deal worse for knowing how to read.

But suppose a child to have parents of good sense and character?—I conceive that if the parent, or those persons who have the care of him, take care to put proper books into his hands, it is better for him to know how to read.

Might

*The Rev.*
*James Archer.*

Might not there be the same danger of improper books getting into the hands of a child, however much moral or religious instruction he might receive at the school?—Certainly there is danger of it, but we do not co-operate in it.

Do you not co-operate by giving him the means of reading?—If I give him the means of reading, and take no further care, I certainly do.

Then you consider that you stand acquitted of all blame by adding to the means of reading such instruction as may tend to make it safe?—Yes.

From what you know of the Catholic poor in this town, do you consider there are many of them without the means of education?—I do; but my situation does not enable me to know that particularly.

Do you allow children and unlearned to receive the Scriptures in the vulgar tongue?—With proper discretion, not promiscuously.

The Scriptures are not allowed without notes?—We never publish any without notes; and even with notes we do not sanction the promiscuous reading of them, but to such persons as we think will make a good use of them.

Are the Scriptures taught in the St. Patrick's school?—That I am sure I cannot tell.

Where there is no adequate Catholic school in the neighbourhood, can parents of Catholic children conscientiously send them to a school, the master of which is a Protestant, and where the spelling-book and the Protestant version of the New Testament are the only school books used?—If you will confine it to the spelling-book, and such things as a spelling-book contains, we will agree to it, not otherwise.

If an assurance were given that a child should hear nothing against his own religion, would there still be an objection to the Scriptures being taught?—Yes, except he were to hear a great deal for his own religion at the same time.

## The Reverend *Richard Horrabin*, called in, and Examined.

*The Rev.*
*Richard Horrabin.*

YOU are a priest in holy orders?—I am.

Have you heard the examination of the two last Witnesses?—I only heard Mr. Archer's examination.

Do you coincide with him in the answers he has given?—As near as possible.

Do you know whether there are many of the poor Catholics in this Metropolis, destitute of the means of education?—In the district where I am situated, which is the Eastern district of London, there are a great number.

Is there not a school now established at Shadwell?—Yes, the British Union School.

Is that school open to children of the Catholic persuasion?—Yes; children of all denominations.

Did any of the Catholic clergy attend the meeting for the foundation of that school?—There were many at the opening of it, but then it was not looked upon as an absolute sanction, till it was seen what arrangements might take place.

What arrangements have been made with respect to teaching the Catholic children?—The arrangement at present is, that the children shall go from the school at every written request of their pastor, to the places which he shall appoint for religious instruction; but it has never been settled exactly what lessons shall be read.

Has any sanction been given by the Roman Catholic clergy to the reading the lessons from the Scriptures, in that school?—I have said, no positive sanction has been given.

Has any approbation been expressed?—It is deemed practicable, that is to say, that certain portions of Scripture might be selected, which might be read.

Without comment?—The selection has not been made; a committee has been appointed for that purpose.

When did these proceedings take place?—Last Thursday week.

Could the Protestant Scriptures be allowed in that school, without the authority of the Vicar Apostolic?—I should say, no.

What number of uneducated children do you suppose there are at the East end of the town?—I calculate between six hundred and one thousand.

In what district?—The district we are in is Saint George's in the East, Saint Catherine's, part of Whitechapel, Shadwell, the hamlet of Ratcliffe, Limehouse, Poplar, Blackwall, and Wapping.

## Mr. *Frederick Matthew Waggoner*, called in, and Examined.

*Mr.*
*F. M. Waggoner.*

DO you know any thing of the proceedings that have been had with respect to Mr. Troutback's will?—I do; he bequeathed 2,000 *l.* for erecting an Orphan

hospital,

hospital, and the whole of his money, amounting with the accumulations to upwards of 100,000 l. to trustees, for erecting an additional wing or separate building to the charity school of Saint John of Wapping, and for maintaining and educating poor children of that parish.

Are there as many poor children as it would require such funds to educate?—Yes, more, within the parish.

Do you think that 5,000 l. a year would not educate the poor of the parish of Wapping?—The will is for the education, clothing, and maintenance.

What has been done with respect to it?—We understand that it has been set aside by the Court of Chancery, and that, the testator having no next of kin, the money has gone to the Crown.

Mr. *Joseph Henry George*, being again called in, delivered the following Papers; which were read.

"An Extract of the DEED OF SETTLEMENT made by his Grace Thomas Lord Archbishop of Canterbury, to his Nine Trustees, &c. for the use of the Parish of Saint James Westminster, September the 10th, 1700.

"THIS Indenture, made the Tenth day of September in the twelfth year of the reign of our Sovereign Lord William the Third, by the Grace of God of England Scotland France and Ireland King, Defender of the Faith, &c. Anno. Dom. 1700, Between the most Reverend Father in God Thomas by Divine Providence Lord Archbishop of Canterbury, Primate of all England, and Metropolitan, of the one part; and the Reverend Father in God John Lord Bishop of Norwich, William Wake doctor of divinity rector of the parochial church of Saint James within the liberty of Westminster and county of Middlesex, John Poulteney esquire, Samuel Trotman esquire, Orlando Bridgman esquire, John Tulley esquire, Isaac Newton esquire, John Outing gent. and Isaac Teret gent. of the other part.

"Whereas, &c. [here follows a recital of the said Lord Archbishop's title to certain pieces or parcels of Land in the Deed particularly described, and also his Grace's grant thereof, together with all erections and buildings erected and built thereon, unto the several other parties to the same Deed, upon certain trusts thereinafter mentioned.]

"And the said Thomas Lord Archbishop of Canterbury, out of his charitable disposition and for the further better support of the charitable work and uses hereinafter mentioned, hath on the day of the date of these presents paid and deposited into the hands of the said John Lord Bishop of Norwich, &c. the sum of 500 l. of good and lawful money of England, the receipt whereof they do hereby acknowledge and confess.

"And it is hereby declared by and between all the parties to these presents, That the respective grants hereinbefore made to the said John Lord Bishop of Norwich, &c. and the said sum of five hundred pounds as aforesaid by the said Thomas Lord Archbishop of Canterbury to them paid, are so made and paid to them upon special trust and confidence that they the said John Lord Bishop of Norwich, &c. and the survivors and survivor of them, and the heirs executors administrators and assigns of the survivor of them, shall and will permit and suffer the said Chapel or tabernacle, and the soil and ground whereon the same standeth, to be for ever hereafter used enjoyed and employed as a public chapel or oratory for divine service according to the liturgy and orthodox practice of the church of England, for the ease and conveniency of the inhabitants of the said parish of Saint James; and upon this further trust, that they the said John Lord Bishop of Norwich, &c. and the survivors of them, and the heirs executors and administrators of the survivors or survivor of them, so

soon as the same may or can conveniently be done, lay out the said sum of five hundred pounds to them paid as aforesaid, on the purchase of houses, lands or ground rents, the said purchase to be made to them the said John Lord Bishop of Norwich, &c. or such of them as shall be living at the time of such purchase, their heirs and assigns for ever.

"And the said Thomas Lord Archbishop of Canterbury doth by these presents direct order and appoint, That the produce or interest of the said 500 l. until the same be invested in lands as aforesaid, and the rents issues and profits of the said lands and tenements to be so purchased, from and after such purchase made, and also the rents issues and profits of all and singular the messuages lands and premises in and by these presents granted, over and above the ground rent and other rents payable out of and for the same, and all monies arising by the pews erected or to be erected in the said chapel there, shall be for ever hereafter taken and received by the said trustees and the survivors of them, and the trustees for the time being their heirs and assigns, or their order and appointment, and shall be applied laid out and expended in and about the charitable uses hereinafter mentioned (that is to say)

"In the first place, to find and provide from time to time, for ever hereafter, two able and orthodox ministers of God's word, to be Preachers in the said Chapel, the said preachers to be licensed by the Bishop of London for the time being; and in the second place, to find and provide for ever hereafter a sufficient Reader, to say divine service in the said Chapel every day throughout the year, morning and afternoon; and in the third place,

to

to find a clerk to officiate in the said Chapel; and in the fourth place, to find and provide, for ever likewise hereafter, one or more able and sufficient schoolmasters or schoolmaster, to teach and instruct poor Boys, natives and inhabitants of the said parish of St. James, in such manner as hereinafter is directed. And the said several preachers, reader, clerk, schoolmasters or schoolmaster, out of the rents issues and profits of the said premises, shall have and receive for their respective salary such sum and sums of money yearly as the trustees and directors of the said Charity for the time being shall think fit and appoint. And in the fifth place, for ever hereafter to keep the said Chapel houses and premises in good repair; and also to find and provide a ringer, pew-keeper, fire, candles, and other necessaries, to be used in and about the said Chapel. And in the sixth and last place, that in case the rents and profits arising in or by the said premises shall amount to more than what shall be appointed by the said trustees and directors of the said Charity for the time being, for the said two preachers, reader, clerk, and schoolmasters or schoolmaster, and for defraying the other charges for necessaries in and about the said Chapel, then and in such case the said Thomas Lord Archbishop of Canterbury doth hereby order and appoint the surplus of the said rents and profits, over and above what shall be so appointed by the said trustees and directors of the said Charity for the time being, for the said two preachers, reader, clerk, schoolmasters or schoolmaster, and for other charges in and about the said Chapel, shall be deposited and laid up by the said trustees for the time being, for the repairing the said tabernacle and houses, and for the discharging other contingent charges that shall or may happen or fall out in or about the same, or the execution of the said trust, or any way relating thereunto. And in case the rents and profits of the said premises, over and besides the necessary charges of or relating to the said trust, which shall be thereout first allowed, shall happen or fall out not to be sufficient to pay off and discharge the salaries that shall hereafter be appointed by the said trustees and governors of the said Charity for the time being as aforesaid, to and for the said two preachers, reader, and schoolmasters or schoolmaster, then and in such case the said two preachers, reader, and schoolmasters or schoolmaster, shall be abated out of the salaries to be appointed to and for them respectively, as the said trustees and directors shall think convenient.

"And as to the said schoolmasters or schoolmaster hereinbefore appointed to be provided, the said Thomas Lord Archbishop of Canterbury doth hereby direct and order, That such schoolmasters or schoolmaster from time to time to be appointed, shall for ever hereafter, gratis and without any fee gratuity or reward other than the salary that shall be appointed to and for him by the said trustees and directors as aforesaid, diligently instruct and teach in the tabernacle aforesaid, or in some convenient schoolhouse or place upon the said granted premises, such of the sons of the poor inhabitants of the said parish of St. James as by the trustees, governors, or directors of the said Charity for the time being, or any five or more of them, whereof the rector of the said parish of St. James for the time being to be one, shall be nominated and appointed, not exceeding the number of Sixteen Boys at one time. The said boys to be taught to read, write, cast accounts, and such other parts of mathematics as may the better qualify the said boys to be put out apprentices to such honest trades and employments as shall be thought meet for them.

"And it is hereby further ordered, That no boy shall be admitted into the said school until he hath passed the age of nine years; nor shall any such boy so admitted, continue in the said school longer than five years, to be accounted from such his admittance.

"And for the perpetuating the said charitable uses, and to the end the same may the better be carried on and duly from time to time performed, the said Thomas Lord Archbishop of Canterbury doth by these presents ordain and appoint, That when any four or more of the said trustees shall be dead, then the surviving trustees shall, by such ways and means as shall be thought convenient, convey and transfer the estate in law of and in the said premises, so as the same may be forthwith vested in such surviving trustees, and in so many other persons, inhabitants of the said parish (to be nominated by the surviving trustees) as shall together make up and complete the number of nine upon the trusts aforesaid; and that the same order and rule shall from time to time be always observed and continued.

"And it is hereby further ordained and appointed, That the trustees hereby appointed, and the trustees for the time being, together with the rector and head churchwarden of the said parish of St. James for the time being, shall be and are hereby appointed directors and governors of the said Charity.

"And the said Thomas Lord Archbishop of Canterbury doth hereby further ordain and appoint, That the said now rector, and every other rector of the parish church of St. James for the time being, by and with the consent and approbation of the other directors and governors, or of any five or more of them, for ever hereafter shall nominate and appoint the said preachers, reader, clerk and other officers in the said Chapel, and every of them, and the said schoolmasters or schoolmaster, and the said boys, and the boys to be taught and instructed by him or them; which said preachers, reader, clerk, and schoolmasters or schoolmaster shall continue in his and their said office and places during his and their natural lives.

"Provided always, That if any or either of the said preachers, reader, clerk, schoolmasters or schoolmaster, or boys or other officers so to be nominated by the said rector, or rector for the time being as aforesaid, shall at the time of such his nomination have any thing alleged

497.

*Mr. J. H. George.*

alleged or objected against him, for which the said trustees, or trustees for the time being, or the major part of them, shall judge him to be unqualified for or otherwise unworthy of the place to which he shall be nominated; that then and in such case the said rector, or rector for the time being, shall nominate some other person, and so continue to nominate one after another till such person be nominated by him as against whom the said trustees, or trustees for the time being, or the major part of them, shall not have any thing to allege or object as aforesaid.

Rules for the removal of Officers or Boys after their nomination.

" Provided also nevertheless, and upon this express condition, That if the said preachers, reader, clerk, or other officer belonging to the said Chapel, schoolmasters or schoolmaster, and boys, to be appointed as aforesaid, or any of them, shall wilfully neglect the duty belonging to their respective offices or places, or shall become of evil life and conversation, or for other reasonable causes shall be adjudged unfit for their said places or unworthy of the said Charity by the said directors and governors, or the greater number of them, that then and in such case it shall and may be lawful unto and for the said directors and governors, or the greater number of them, whereof the rector of the said parish of St. James for the time being to be one, to remove deprive and displace the said preachers, reader, schoolmasters or schoolmaster, clerk and other officers before mentioned, and the said boys, or any of them, from their respective places and employments, and to appoint others in their place and stead in such manner as is hereinbefore appointed; any thing hereinbefore contained to the contrary thereof in anywise notwithstanding.

The said Lord Archbishop of Canterbury to add, alter, or change any of the Trusts hereby created, for the advantage and better management of the Charity.

" Provided also further, That it shall and may be lawful unto and for the said Thomas Lord Archbishop of Canterbury, at any time hereafter during his natural life, by any deed or writing under his hand and seal, testified by two or more credible witnesses, for the advantage and better management and improvement of the said Charity, to add unto, alter or change any of the trusts limitations rules orders or directions hereinbefore limited and appointed; any thing hereinbefore contained to the contrary notwithstanding.

New Rules or Alterations to be made by the said Trustees or any five or more of them (the Rector being always one) with the consent of the Archbishop of Canterbury for the time being.

" Provided also further, That it shall and may be lawful unto and for the said trustees, directors or governors, or any five or more of them, whereof the rector of the said parish of Saint James for the time being to be one, by and with the advice consent and approbation of the Archbishop of Canterbury for the time being, and not otherwise, for the better advancement and promotion of the said Charity to make any new or other orders rules directions and appointments of and concerning the said Charity than what are hereinbefore appointed, so as such new orders rules directions and appointments be for the advancement and not any way prejudicial to the said Charity, and all other things do concerning the premises, for the advancing of the said charitable uses, for the glory of Almighty God, and the ease benefit and comfort of the inhabitants of the said parish of Saint James.

The Archbishop of Canterbury to be Supreme Visitor of the Charity;

whose determination in all matters relative thereto, shall be final and conclusive.

" And lastly, the said Thomas Lord Archbishop of Canterbury doth by these presents direct ordain and appoint, That the Archbishop of Canterbury for the time being shall be Supreme Visitor of the said Charity, and of all persons concerned therein, and of all matters relating thereto; and that the sentence and determination of the said Archbishop of Canterbury for the time being, in any matter relating to the said charitable uses, shall be final and conclusive to all persons concerned therein, without any benefit of appeal whatsoever.

" In witness whereof the parties first above named to these present Indentures have interchangeably set their hands and seals the day and year first above written.

(Signed)     Tho. Cantuar. (L. S.)

---

## KING-STREET CHAPEL FREE SCHOOL,

### Founded by Deed of Gift in 1700, by Archbishop Tenison.

| | |
|---|---:|
| Funds | £. 3,700. |
| Cash in hand | 650. |
| Officers, per annum | 750. |
| Annual Income | 800. |

*Joseph Henry George,*

No. 3, Chapel-court, King-street, Golden-square.

*Lunæ*, 17° *die Junii*, 1816.

HENRY BROUGHAM, Esquire, in The Chair.

---

Mr. *Thomas Bray*, called in ; and Examined.

ARE you treasurer of Mr. Emery Hill's alms-houses in the parish of Saint John Westminster?—Yes.

What is the nature of that charity?—There are six men and their wives, and there are six widows, that are supported and maintained under the will of Emery Hill.

Of what date is that will?—That I cannot say ; about a hundred years ago, I believe.

What was the money and property left for?—It was left for the support and maintenance of those widows ; and to have a clergyman to attend them, and so forth ; and as far as we have been able, we do it, as well as the funds and the property will afford it. There are ten governors.

What are the funds?—They are in the three-per-cents.

What is the annual amount?—I suppose about 400*l.* a year ; we have an estate too in Buckingham-street.

What does that produce a year?—I think the whole income, including the estate, is 400*l.* a year.

Is there any school connected with your charity?—There was to have been a school for some town boys, but there was not money enough to go on with it.

Was it in the deed of trust?—It was, and it is complied with as far as we are able to go.

How does the supporting these old people take 400*l.* a year?—There are the repairs of the church ; it is but lately we have come into such a sum of money as that.

What repairs do you allude to?—Repairs to the alms-houses, and the building of them ; and the repairs of the church, as I said before ; it was a long while before the charity came into possession.

When were the houses built?—More than twenty years ago.

How is the 400*l.* a year spent?—It is all accounted for in the management of the charity.

What salaries are there?—There is a salary to the clerk, that is only 10*l.* a year ; and the salary to the parson, that is 10*l.* a year ; the rest goes to the support of the old people, who have some 18*s.* a month, and some 14*s.* and coals and cloathing, but they have no provisions.

Have you any overplus of your funds?—We always keep, in case of any accident, about 100*l.* in hand.

Do you buy stock every year?—Not every year, but we buy it when we can ; there has been some bought very lately.

How much?—About 700*l.* stock.

Why did not you rather educate the children according to Emery Hill's recommendation, who did not recommend you to buy stock?—What we want is to establish this school, when we have money to do it ; that has been the plan.

How long have you been in the receipt of 400*l.* a year?—Not above a twelve-month, I believe.

What was it before that?—Barely enough to carry on our business.

When did you buy the 700*l.* stock?—I cannot tell.

Was it three years ago?—No, about three months.

Then it seems to have been more than sufficient?—We have renewed some leases, and we have had some fines paid us ; we were never to increase the rents, but to let them at the same rent, and to take fines, and so when those leases were out, a few years ago, we took the fines.

> [ *The Witness was directed to send a balance sheet of the accounts for the last year.*]

*Joseph*

*Joseph Butterworth*, Esquire, a Member of the Committee, Examined.

HAVE you had any, and what opportunities of knowing the state of the poor in the Metropolis?—I have for many years belonged to a Society for visiting and relieving the Poor at their own habitations; I have also for some years been Treasurer and Visitor to a Sunday-school Society which has nearly 3,000 children under instruction. Those institutions have given me considerable opportunities of knowing the state of the poor.

What is your opinion of the state of education of the lower classes?—From what I have personally observed, and heard from others of undoubted authority, I believe that a very large proportion of poor children is entirely uneducated, and in the most deplorable and wretched state, especially of the children of the Irish poor.

What observations have you made upon this want of education?—I have observed that ignorance in general produces vice in its most hideous forms, and that idleness, disobedience to the laws, and all kinds of profligacy, are its necessary consequences. The convicts at Newgate are generally uneducated. Some worthy persons with whom I am acquainted, were a few years ago in the habit of visiting the convicts at Woolwich, on a Sunday, with a view of communicating to them moral and religious instruction. At that time there were nearly 1,000 convicts, the greater part of whom could not read. I visited Newgate last year, in order to examine the state of a number of boys that were prisoners; I examined thirteen, nine of whom could not read. It is now notorious that a great number of children live by thieving in the metropolis. From inquiry it is found that many of them are without education and moral instruction. They acquire habits of vagrancy and depredation, which end in atrocious crimes. With this ignorance of moral obligation, is connected the evil of mendicity, which leads many children to acts of thieving. They are in the habit of gaming with the money which they beg, and when they lose their money they recruit their stock by criminal courses. I some time ago endeavoured to persuade some beggar children, near my place of residence, to attend school, and leave off their way of life, which I was not able to effect. Upon my last visit to Newgate I there found one of the boys whom I had spoken to in the street.

What, in your opinion, would be the best plan of promoting the education of the poor?—The further encouragement of the various societies for visiting and relieving the sick and distressed poor, which afford the best means of inspecting their real state, and of persuading them to send their children to schools; and secondly, to have a sufficient number of schools upon the National and British and Foreign school plans, and also Sunday schools.

Do you think it necessary to encourage both day and Sunday schools, and for what reason?—I am decidedly of opinion that both are necessary. Each has its peculiar use and excellencies; the day-school to instruct in reading, writing, and accounts; to preserve from idleness; to induce habits of industry, subordination, and order. The Sunday school is more particularly adapted to instruct in moral and religious duties, and therefore to raise the moral character of the poor upon its proper basis of true religion. Sunday schools are also useful and necessary, to teach reading to that numerous class of children who have not an opportunity of attending day-schools. There are a great number of poor children who are employed by their parents during the week, either in nursing younger children, attending to household work, or engaged in labour, who have no other opportunity than that afforded on Sunday of receiving instruction. Sunday schools have also the advantage of inducing the habit of attending public worship, and creating a reverence for the Sabbath day; points much insisted upon in all well-regulated Sunday schools.

Have you practically, in your observations on Sunday schools, seen particular good effects from them?—I have had many opportunities of seeing their good effects in a series of years; but more particularly of late my attention has been drawn to the subject, in consequence of some scandalous reports from Newgate, made to the disadvantage of schools in general, and among others of one of the Sunday schools of which I am treasurer. It was determined to visit the children and their parents at their own habitations, and thoroughly to investigate their several characters. Five hundred were so visited; I called upon upwards of eighty children myself, and I was highly satisfied with the general report made by their parents, friends, or employers, of the benefits they had received at the school, and of their general good behaviour. Much good also I found had been done to the parents themselves.

Many

J. Butterworth,
Esq.

Many had been induced to read the Bible, which they before had neglected, and also to attend public worship, which formerly they were not in the habit of doing. Many of the elder children in the same families who were once in the school were now grown up, married, and settled, of whom I heard from their parents very excellent accounts. I have the names, address, and particulars of many interesting cases which were visited. The political benefit of Sunday schools to society is incalculable; for not only the principles of loyalty and obedience to the laws are instilled into the minds of the children, but they are fitted to serve the State in various ways, by being taught to serve themselves in an industrious and honest course of life. The attachment of children to Sunday schools, and their improvement in them, is very considerable. A small school has lately been instituted in St. Giles's where some few of the teachers from a larger school were induced to attend, from the wretched state of that neighbourhood. The school has only been opened about four or five months, and its good effects are already very visible in the neighbourhood, and the progress of the children in learning is surprising. One boy, aged fourteen years, was admitted into the school on the 18th of February last, when he could not tell any letter in the alphabet, nor has he, since that time, had any instruction but what he has received in this school. He now spells well in the second spelling-book, and his desire for learning at present is so great, that his teacher expects he will be able to read his Testament well in six months more. His employment is that of selling fruit in the streets. He is much exposed to the bad effects of low company; but his parents have acknowledged with thankfulness the improvement in his behaviour, and the benefit he has received in the school. His sister was admitted into the school at the same time; she only knew her alphabet, and has made similar progress, to the great satisfaction of her parents, who state, that her conduct is also much improved; she is only six years of age. Another girl aged six years was admitted into this school on the 11th of February last, and did not know a letter at that time; she has now began to spell words of two syllables, and manifests an earnest desire to learn to read; she is constant and punctual in her attendance. Another girl was admitted on the same day; she only knew her alphabet at that time, but now reads so well that her next removal will be to the Testament class; she is fifteen years of age; she has no father nor mother; she shows so strong an attachment to the school, that she has brought eight or ten children since she first came, most of whom attend regularly. It is very common for children to bring their playfellows and neighbours to the school as scholars, and not unfrequently in the first instance even without the knowledge of their parents, having such a strong attachment to the schools themselves, which is produced principally by the attention, affection, and general mild conduct of the teachers towards them, and the general interest they take in their welfare. They have often shown great reluctance to leave the school, when of sufficient age to go to service. As visitor I have been in the habit of reading many respectful and grateful letters of thanks from the children for the benefits which they have received, and of which they appear to be deeply sensible.

What other plan do you think would improve the state of poor children in the metropolis? I think chiefly to enforce a due observance of the Sabbath, as I consider this, or the neglect of it, the root of infinite good or evil in society; and secondly, I consider it of great importance that trustworthy street-keepers should be appointed in every parish, with sufficient pay to make it worth their while to attend to their duty, in order to prevent gambling and other bad practices in the streets among children. In Spital-fields I know it is the practice to pay their watchmen or street-keepers sufficiently, and even to allow them a small pension for life, in case of their being disabled from attending to their duty, provided they have discharged it with fidelity. This has had the desired effect, and has preserved the streets from beggars, women of ill-fame, and other bad characters, who corrupt the young. Thirdly, I consider fairs in and about the metropolis, such as Bartholomew fair, Peckham fair, and others of that description, which produce large assemblies of the lower classes, to be exceedingly destructive of the morals of youth. That they produce the ruin of many young people, and that it would be a benefit to society if they could be suppressed. Fourthly, I have long lamented the increased evil of gaming in the public streets; this has become a dreadful snare to children: I lately examined twenty-two boys in Newgate, and found that tossing up for halfpence in the street had led most of them to thieving, and had proved their utter ruin. One boy, who had received a tolerable education, and whose father had been an honest worthy servant in a respectable

family

J. Butterworth,
Esq.

family for more than twenty years, with whom I am acquainted, was led to a capital crime entirely by gaming with halfpence in the street: such was the excessive excitement produced in his mind to obtain money for the purpose, that he was led to rob the till from time to time in a shop where he was employed, purely to obtain money for gaming; he proceeded from taking smaller to larger sums, till at length he was detected and capitally convicted. I may be permitted to add, that the activity of the police by no means keeps pace with the increase of juvenile crime, and that it appears to me that the most active exertions are necessary to disperse groups of boys, who assemble for gaming and unlawful purposes: innocent amusements for children are, I conceive, highly necessary and proper; but some restraint should be laid upon those amusements which have a direct tendency to produce vicious habits. I also think that as bad children contaminate the comparatively good, that some prison regulations should take place to prevent bad associations when they are committed to prison, from which they are generally discharged worse than when they were first sent; and thereby rendered more pernicious to their youthful companions than before. There is a remarkable case of juvenile depravity now in Newgate, which appears to me strongly to illustrate the sad effects of a want of education. A boy, not yet ten years of age, has been for three years living by depredation. He has been apprehended at least eighteen times, and as often discharged, on account of his youth. This little creature, who is only 3 feet $10\frac{1}{2}$ inches high, has been in the habit of creeping into shops and houses, and stealing every thing he could carry away. He has frequently taken journies into the country for the purpose of depredation. He has been detected at Hertford, Brentford and other places. At one time he went, with a thieving party of boys, within two miles of Portsmouth. He has been for many months together away from his mother, sleeping in barns and outhouses, when in the country, and in the sheds and baskets at Covent Garden when in town. He once took a till from a shop with nearly 50 l. in money: his share of the booty was about 12 l., which he spent in the course of a week, chiefly in gaming. He would toss up for four or five shillings at a time. He was in the habit of going regularly to the play when he had money. Associating with other bad boys, and tossing up for halfpence in the streets, first led him to thieving. After many escapes, he was at length detected in shop-lifting, capitally convicted, and was under sentence of death. He was respited, and is now under sentence of transportation for life. He could not read when he was first committed to Newgate, but his long habits of cunning, have induced a vicious sharpness of intellect. This extraordinary instance of youthful depravity may be traced up to a total want of education, and an utter ignorance of all moral principle; and perhaps should lead to the grave consideration of some plan for the instruction, employment and reformation of juvenile convicts, who, if let loose upon the public in their present state and habits, are likely to corrupt others. I understand there are now nearly forty boys in Newgate, many of whom have been often apprehended, and are old offenders.

Do you conceive that an increased attention to schools would increase the desire of instruction among the poor?—Most certainly: I have observed in Sunday schools that the more they are attended to, the more the scholars increase, the children bring others to school, and if sufficient schools could be provided and the public opinion could be so raised, as that it should be a reproach to children not to attend a school, which I believe is the case in Scotland, we should see a general eagerness among the poor for the instruction of their children.

Would ill-disposed children attend schools?—Certainly not, at first; but if public opinion could be properly raised on this subject, I should think in a short time many children, at present of indifferent character, would be desirous of instruction. In St. Giles's, I have reason to believe, that many boys, formerly of bad character, now attend a free-school opened for Irish children, and are more orderly in their behaviour. I would also mention to the Committee, a place called Cock Road, in the vicinity of Bristol, notorious for the residence of thieves of every description, and persons of the very worst character: About a year ago, some benevolent persons of Bristol, feeling for the children of those wretched creatures, offered to build a school, provided they would allow their children to attend; the parents were delighted with the offer, and uniting in the promotion of the design, did actually work a considerable time in digging the foundation of the school, and contributed much to the building of it, and now send their children regularly: Several teachers go over from Bristol on the Sunday, and a great improvement has already taken place in the characters of the people in consequence.

What,

What, in your opinion, should be done with vagrant children who would not attend school?—I consider this a very delicate subject, and one which involves many difficulties; but if, without interfering with the general liberty of the subject, they could be taken into any general or parochial asylum, such a plan might rescue multitudes from ruin. I have this very day been inquiring into a case which has excited my particular attention. A woman who had lived reputably was sometime ago left a widow; she is now in reduced circumstances; she applied to me for charitable help; I visited her apartment, and found six children, all girls, in the most deplorable situation, destitute of the common necessaries of life. Upon a minute investigation of the case, I had reason to believe that the woman has recourse to prostitution for support, and her children, if left to her care, will in all probability be led into the same course of life. I am not aware that parish officers could demand the care of the children, she not receiving parochial aid; but I lament that there are no means of rescuing some fine-looking girls from falling a prey to the vices of their mother. If parochial relief could in any measure be withheld from parents, who would not send their children to some school of their own choice, that might have a happy effect upon the lower classes of society.

*J. Butterworth, Esq.*

In your opinion, is there any general plan of instruction that could be formed for the education of the children of Irish poor indiscriminately?—I conceive the difficulty at present to be nearly insurmountable, as far as regards the Roman Catholics, unless the priests would consent to their being taught by Protestant masters, and to allow at least a portion of the Scriptures to be used in the schools; Protestants have always considered this to be of prime importance in the instruction of children; at the same time I conceive, that no interference should take place with regard to their religious principles. I have observed in some charity schools, that when Catholic children have accidentally come to the school, and were making improvement in reading, that they have been withdrawn. It has been generally understood to be by order of the priests, although I am certain that the pains taken with them were not to proselyte them to the Protestant religion. From the vicinity of my residence to the parish of Saint Giles's, where a large proportion of the Irish usually live, I have had many opportunities of observing their character, and I believe that many of their children are among the most abandoned and profligate throughout the metropolis, which I impute entirely to the want of education.

Might not some arrangement be made, by which the objections of the priests to allow children to attend schools under Protestant schoolmasters, might be removed?—This will depend upon the Roman Catholics themselves; but from what I heard stated by a clergyman of that persuasion on Saturday last, I fear that such an arrangement is impracticable.

Do you apprehend the difficulties of the Roman Catholic priests, to bottom themselves in fears that their children would be proselyted to the Protestant faith?—I apprehend they do; but, as I have already stated and believe, the sole object of many benevolent Protestants, is simply to convey instruction and raise the moral character of the children by means of schools.

Is it in your opinion practicable or desirable to unite all denominations of protestants in some general plan of giving instruction to the poor?—Considering the prejudices or partialities that exist, I scarcely think such a plan practicable where catechisms are insisted upon; but Mr. Green of Blackwall, has given in his evidence, some account of an approach towards union; if, however, it be not practicable to unite different denominations, I would much rather see rival schools than none at all. I am not sure, indeed, whether two systems are not, on many accounts, extremely desirable to stimulate each other, and if carried on without hostility, may be mutually useful to each other and to society. In a country like this, where the views of individuals are so various on religious subjects, I am not aware that an union of all parties in one specific and uniform plan, is necessary for the great end of general instruction: I apprehend, that if the national establishment were to pursue the excellent plan which it has adopted, to the full extent to which it is capable of being carried, and if at the same time the various other denominations of christians who cannot conscientiously join in those plans, were zealously to pursue their several systems of education (supposing the Bible to be always taught) I am of opinion that in a short period provision might be made for the education of the whole juvenile population of the country; and I apprehend that while every encouragement is given to the national shools, due encouragement might also be given to the British and Foreign school system, and to other schools not exclusively connected with the national establishment.

What

J. Butterworth,
Esq.

What could be done to promote the utility of parochial schools?—I think that the subscribers should more vigilantly attend to them, and in the selection of masters, attention should be paid to elect those who are best qualified for the office, and not to make the situation, as it too frequently is, a place of charity to the master, merely to serve an individual. That quarterly examinations of the children, and regular visitation of the parents to inquire after the characters of the children, would be attended with the happiest effects; and by those and similar means, the spirit of these institutions might be soon raised.

Is it an advantage to board small numbers of children in parochial schools?—I think not by any means. The expense of boarding a few, would give instruction to many, who at present have no education. Great National Establishments, such as Christ's Hospital, the Military Asylum, and the Asylum for the Deaf and Dumb, and others of similar magnitude, are in general well managed, and are great public blessings; but when several children live together, and are ill managed, it rather appears to me to be a waste of public money.

Is it desirable to clothe a certain number?—I think clothing, under certain limitations, has its advantages in various ways; it excites a disposition for neatness, cleanliness and decency among the poor, and I think has a good effect in inducing many persons to promote the interest of schools. The Annual Meeting at Saint Paul's is, I think, attended with many good effects, but I would rather reduce than extend the number to be clothed, in order to give instruction to all. It is a delightful sight to see so many children at St. Paul's at the Annual Meeting; but the deplorable state of thousands of poor children in the metropolis is, I think, more distressing than the other is gratifying.

Is it necessary, practically, to make greater exertions to promote schools, than those which are now made?—I think it absolutely necessary, otherwise the lower classes of society, from the increase of population and profligacy, will soon be reduced to the most deplorable state. If school-rooms could be built, or the rent be paid by Parliament, more schools might easily be supported by voluntary contributions. The riotous behaviour of loose young men and uneducated children on a Sunday in St. Giles's, and in the fields adjoining, and more particularly their conduct at the east-end of the town, near Bethnal-green, where great numbers usually assemble and spend the Sunday in dog-fights and other low amusements, convince me that some effectual plan should be adopted to promote the general education of the poor, and to restrain the habits of vice and profligacy.

What exertions would in your opinion best conduce towards promoting a more general plan of the instruction of the poor?—I know of no plan so effectual as for Parliament to afford aid to the building or towards the rent of schools, and thus excite public opinion in favour of education, and call forth local charity to a greater extent.

Would it, in your opinion, be desirable for Parliament to grant money to any besides National schools?—I know of no good reason against it. Perhaps it may be said that it would increase sectaries; but those who are best acquainted with the benevolent persons who take the most active part in charity schools, well know that their activities proceed simply from a desire to do good, and to lessen the sum of misery of the lower classes of society, and that it is not the view of making proselytes which stimulates their exertions. They would gladly give their time, labour and money to support schools, but the building or renting of them is found to be too burthensome. I believe many persons of the respectable Society of Friends, (the Quakers) much to their honour, have been particularly active in promoting schools upon the British and Foreign system, but I have never heard that they have made, or have attempted to make, proselytes to their society. I certainly think that the National schools should be liberally supported in the first place; but I know of no solid reason why Parliament should not grant assistance to those who may be desirous of sending their children to other schools. The country is equally interested in the welfare and happiness of those, who either from principle or accident, dissent from the Establishment, and it should be its policy to afford facilities that every part of the population may be rightly instructed in its duty to God and man; I apprehend that for such a useful object as the education of the poor, the national bounty would be well applied.

Is the profanation of the Sabbath a great evil in the metropolis?—I consider this as the root of incalculable evil amongst the lower classes of society; I consider the observance of the Sabbath as strongly indicating the state of public morals. Much has been said of the good morals of the people of Scotland, in consequence of their respect

respect for the Bible; but I believe they are as much owing to the strict observance *J. Butterworth,* of the Sabbath, which is quite proverbial in that country. I believe the profanation *Esq.* of the Sabbath is the ruin of thousands in London: the trade carried on in shops and by fruit-stalls, Sunday newspapers, public-houses, tea-gardens, &c. is most destructive of the morals of the lower classes of society.

What plan could be adopted to secure the attendance of children on public worship on the Sabbath?—I consider it to be the duty of all the managers of schools to see to this, which is of prime importance in all respects. The habit of attending public worship, if firmly fixed in the mind of the child, is seldom destroyed in riper years: but accommodation for the poor in places of public worship is greatly wanted in all our churches and chapels. I think it would be of great advantage to the public, if in all new churches and chapels accommodation could be made for the children of charity schools; and a gallery might easily be built over the ordinary gallery, for adults, which should not project so far as to deface the building, and would be a great accommodation to schools.

Do any other observations occur to you on the subject?—I would offer an opinion, that I think the poor might be induced to pay a penny or three halfpence a week to those schools for the instruction of their children. All benefits which are rendered too cheap are unduly estimated.

### Dr. *William Poynter*, Roman Catholic Bishop, and Vicar Apostolic of the London District, called in; and Examined.

HOW long have you been in your present situation?—In my present situation *Dr. Poynter.* as Vicar Apostolic I have been since the month of May 1812, when my predecessor, Dr. Douglas, died: I was Bishop before that, but had not the functions of Vicar Apostolic.

Do you conceive that the lower orders of catholics in London are destitute of the means of education, generally speaking?—I believe that many of the catholics of the lower orders in London are destitute of the means of education.

What are the difficulties, in your opinion, which prevent Catholic children from attending schools which are open to all sects?—That question is so general, that unless I know the particulars of what books are read in the schools, and other particulars, I cannot answer.

Suppose a school taught without catechism of any kind, without any obligation to go to church, and without any religious instruction of any kind, what objection would there be to Catholics sending their children there, they being free to give them religious instruction according to their own principles out of school?—To this question, supposing public schools where no catechism is taught, and where no religious instruction is given of any kind, whether Catholics can send their children to such a school; I say, that it is not advisable that Catholics should send their children to such a school.

Why?—Because Catholic education comprises religious instruction, or at least the means of their learning their catechism, and of preparing for the general instructions which they receive from their clergymen.

Could not those be taught out of school, while they were taught reading alone in school?—I do not conceive it could be by our Catholic clergy, considering the very small number we have, compared with the extent of our congregations.

Could not laymen give this religious instruction?—Laymen might teach the children to learn the letter and text of their catechism, but we could not permit laymen to explain the doctrine to the children.

You consider it contrary to the discipline of the Roman Catholic Church?—I do.

Then, at present, the number being so small of the Roman Catholic Clergy, is there not as great a deficiency of the means of religious instructions, as there would be if with the same small number of clergymen, the children should attend such schools?—No.

Might they not learn to read at those schools, and be taught religion out of school as much as they are at present taught?—Yes, I believe they might.

In short, do you apprehend that their merely learning to read, and nothing else at school, could interfere with their religious instruction out of school?—No, I do not conceive that it would.

What

*Dr. Poynter.*

What objection then would there be to sending those Catholic children to schools of the above description?—I answer, in the first place, that if it were possible to procure for them such an education as would afford them at the same time religious instruction, and the means of learning to read and write, and qualify them for some state in life, I should think it the duty of the Catholics to prefer such a system; but secondly, considering the plan proposed, I do not see that it is unlawful for Catholics to send their children to such a school.

Suppose that in those schools the children are taught lessons from the Scripture, but without any comment, should you consider this as removing the difficulty in any degree?—No, I should not.

How?—Because I do not consider the mere reading of the Scriptures, is a proper mean of communicating the necessary religious instruction to children.

Do you consider that it is any objection to sending children to those schools, that portions of the Scripture are taught without comment?—May I beg to ask, whether the Committee speak of the Catholic version, or any other?

No, the Protestant version; but supposing the selection to be made of passages which are the same in both versions?—I answer, that I could not in any manner approve of any Catholic children reading the Protestant version of the Scriptures.

Suppose the version is taken of those passages in which the two do not differ?—Even in that case I should think it contrary to my duty, and the constant discipline of the Catholic Church, to permit it.

For what reason?—The reason is, that the Catholic Church considers the sacred Scriptures as a precious deposit, which was originally committed by the Apostles to their immediate successors, and that the Catholic Church has always carefully preserved it, as it were in its archives, and has never permitted the faithful to read any other edition or version which is not duly sanctioned and authenticated by the authority of the Catholic Church; consequently I should act contrary to the constant discipline of the Catholic Church, if I were to approve of the Catholic children reading a version of the sacred Scriptures, which emanates from a body of Christians not in communion with the Catholic Church. Those are the principles of my answer.

Suppose passages were taken, which are exactly the same in the two versions, would the objection still occur?—If the passages be taken from a version made by any body of Christians not in communion with the Catholic Church, the objection would be the same.

Although the words are the very same?—Yes; because by approving it I should give a sanction to a version made by an authority which the Catholic Church in spirituals does not acknowledge.

Suppose the passages were taken from the Protestant version, and approved by the Catholic prelates, would there then be any objection to Catholic children being taught to read them by Protestants?—There would not be any objection to the children being made to read them by Protestants, provided it were confined merely to the reading of the text; but I might say that this would excite a certain alarm in general amongst the Catholics, if it were observed and practised.

According to the discipline of your church, are children and the unlearned allowed to read the Scriptures in the vulgar tongue?—They are, under certain regulations.

Of what nature are those regulations?—That they should not read them in the vulgar tongue, without the permission of their pastors.

Are they allowed to read them without notes?—They are only allowed to read the approved Catholic translations of the Scriptures, and we have no approved Catholic translations without notes.

Might not certain passages be selected which do not require notes?—Certainly; but I must beg to observe in general, out of the great respect which I feel for the sacred Scriptures, as containing the revealed word of God, I do not think it becoming that the sacred Scriptures should be made a school-book, for the purpose of teaching children to read.

Do you mean that there is something inconsistent with the nature of that volume, that copies of it should be suffered to lay about, and be ill treated in schools?—Most certainly I do.

Is it a part of the Catholic discipline, that each copy of the Catholic version of the Scriptures partakes in some way of the sacred character?—Certainly.

Suppose a selection were agreed to by the Catholic prelates, and that the books in which that selection was printed were different from the Scriptures, and were mere common school books, do you consider that the difficulty would be removed?—If

it

Dr. Poynter.

it contained merely the texts of the sacred Scriptures, it appears to me the difficulty would be the same.

Suppose it contained texts of Scripture along with other matter, would it retain the same character?—I should not conceive it would, in that case the general character of the book would no longer be considered sacred; I beg to add, there was never any prohibition at all in the Catholic Church against reading the Scriptures in Latin, but all the regulations referred to the translations in the vulgar tongue, and the church had two views, one that the translation should be such as was authorized by the Catholic Church; and secondly, that they should not be read by those from whose ignorance or dispositions the pastors of the Church had reason to fear that the reading of the Scriptures would be rather prejudicial than beneficial to them.

Are not the Scriptures at present allowed to be read in France, in the vulgar tongue, without notes?—I think I have seen one edition of the translation of the Scriptures in France, without notes, but I am not sure of it.

Are those translations with notes in the vulgar tongue, allowed to be read by people in France?—I cannot well answer to the practice in France.

Do you consider their reading of them as contrary to the discipline of the Church?—Their reading of them without the approbation and permission of their pastors, is not agreeable to the regulations made by the Council of Trent.

Suppose the Catholic pastors were to find a copy of the authorized version of the Scriptures in the possession of one of their flock, to whom they had not given such permission, what course would they take?—I think, that unless they judged that the reading of it would be prejudicial to the individual, that they would permit him to read it.

Would he insinuate to them, that his permission ought to have been asked?—I must say, that that entirely depends upon the ecclesiastical customs of the country, for some of those regulations of discipline are adopted in practice in some places, but are not followed in practice in others.

How would this matter be in England?—In England we generally permit the faithful to read the authorized Catholic version in the vulgar tongue, which are always accompanied with notes.

Do you apprehend any danger is likely to result from educating the lower orders without communicating at the same time religious instruction?—I do consider that the educating the lower orders without giving them any religious instruction, may be rather dangerous than beneficial to them; I beg to observe that I consider the preservation or correction of the morals of the lower orders is the principal object we should have in view in their education; and I am persuaded that this end could never be obtained without religious instruction; and on this subject, I express my firm conviction, that in order to preserve or correct the morals of the lower orders, they must not only be taught their duty to God and to society, but the great motives of performing their duty must be strongly enforced, which can only be done, in my opinion, by the instructions and exhortations which they receive from their pastors; and on this ground, I consider that it is in vain to expect that the morals of the lower classes will be improved, unless education comprises religious instruction.

Do you apprehend that the teaching of children to read, if unaccompanied with religious instruction, does harm?—I do consider that it might do a great deal of harm; it would enable them to read every thing that would tend to inflame their passions.

Does your observation apply generally to Catholics as well as Protestants?—Certainly; and most particularly to Catholics.

Why more particularly to Catholics?—I apply it more particularly to Catholics, because my duty obliges me to attend more to their instruction.

Does your observation apply to children in a large town as London more particularly, than to children in the country?—Much more so.

Does it apply at all, or in any considerable degree to children in the country?—It applies to children in large towns in the country, where I conceive the same occasions of evil will present themselves.

Does it apply to children in villages in country places?—According to the occasions of evil it must vary.

Then in point of fact, in large towns such as London, do you conceive that the children had better remain without any education at all, than with some education unaccompanied with religious instruction?—Certainly; education unaccompanied with religious instruction might be of service to them in the stations they would occupy in the world,

*Dr. Poynter.* world, but would not promote their happiness, I conceive, either in this life or in the next.

Are there not habits promoted by a course of education which would, in fact, promote their happiness in this life as well as that to come?—Certainly it might serve them in the world.

The Committee have understood that a very large proportion of the poor children of the Roman Catholic persuasion in London is uneducated; and they are desirous of knowing from you the best plan of giving them instruction; and for this purpose they would wish to know whether the Roman Catholic body themselves have sufficient funds for the instruction of the children of the poor of their own persuasion?—In the first place, I do not think that the Catholics have at present means adequate to the education of all the Catholic poor children in the metropolis.

Do you understand that there are many thousands of those poor children uneducated?—I cannot ascertain that; but I conceive the number to be very considerable.

Then if the Roman Catholics have not the means of giving instruction to their own poor, could the parents of those children conscientiously allow them to attend a school, the master of which is a Protestant, where the Spelling Book and Protestant version of the New Testament are the only school books used, and where a clear assurance is given that a child would hear nothing against his own religion?—Without answering directly to the conscientious part, which is a point of extreme delicacy, considering the situation I hold, and as every decision relating to conscience requires that the whole case, with all its circumstances and variations, should be considered; I beg to say, that the reading of the Protestant version of the Bible is a point to which I could never give my approbation.

Then as Vicar Apostolic you could not by any means consent for Roman Catholics to be taught the Protestant version of the Scriptures?—No, certainly not.

Could you allow any portions of that version to be selected for the use of the Catholic children?—No.

Not even those which convey moral instruction, not involving any doctrinal or controversial points?—I answer, in general, according to the principle which I laid down before, that I could not receive a portion of the Protestant Scriptures.

Could you devise any plan by which the poor children of the Roman Catholic persuasion could be educated by Protestants, consistently with the Catholic discipline?—Considering that Catholic education comprises religious instruction, I do not conceive that any plan of the nature proposed could be adopted, which would meet the desires of the Catholics, and in particular the pastors of the Catholic Church.

Are you aware that a great number of the children of the poor Roman Catholics in London are entirely destitute of education, and that they have fallen into vicious and bad habits, arising from their ignorance?—I conceive there are a great number. It is a fact we cannot deny.

Nevertheless, as a Roman Catholic bishop, could you consent to any attempt to better their moral condition by the instruction of Protestants, or must you not, consistently with your duty as Vicar Apostolic, refuse your assent to any attempts of the kind made by Protestants?—As a Catholic bishop, I do not judge that their morals could be improved but by religious instruction, and I could not consent for them to receive it from Protestants.

Then you conceive that the religious instruction which might be conveyed by teaching them to read the Protestant Scriptures would not better their moral condition, in your view?—Certainly not.

You mentioned that you conceived that children should be taught their duty to God and to society; the Protestants conceive that those great duties are taught children by reading the Scriptures; but is it your opinion that further instruction is necessary to accomplish this great object?—It is, decidedly.

You also stated that the great motives for the performing their duty must be strongly enforced, do you not believe that those motives are strongly enforced by the arguments and commands in the Holy Scriptures, according to the Protestant version?—Without saying more of the Protestant version than what I have said in my former answers, which we could not admit as Catholics, I beg to observe, that I do not conceive that children simply by reading the Scriptures would sufficiently learn their duty, or be able to apply to themselves, in a practical manner, those motives which would influence their moral conduct.

Do

Do you not imagine that children being taught to read moral lessons taken from the Scriptures, and to commit them occasionally to memory, might by this means receive moral and good principles in their minds without any further instruction?—I think not sufficient in general for a practical effect.

Then you conceive if a selection of moral precepts were made from the Scriptures and taught to the children, that such instruction would not be sufficient to produce right principles in their minds?— I do not think it would be sufficient.

If children were allowed to attend their own ecclesiastical instructors, in addition to such education in schools, you still think it would be objectionable if given by Protestants?—I object to the religious or moral instruction of the children given by Protestants, and beg to add that such are the occupations of the Catholic Clergy on Sundays, in the public chapels, that on those days they would not have leisure to attend to the instruction of those children, according to their wants.

And you could not allow children to be instructed by the laymen in the Catholic church in the articles of their faith?—Certainly we could not, consistently with the practice and discipline of our Church.

Do you know of any school lately established at Shadwell for the instruction of both Catholic and Protestant children?—I have heard of such a school.

Was any question proposed to you whether Roman Catholic parents could conscientiously send their children to that school?—Yes, such was proposed by Mr. Charles Butler.

What was your reply to the inquiry?—Considering that the reading lessons were to be taken from the Protestant version of the Scriptures, I answered Mr. Butler, that he knew that I should act in direct repugnance to the constant and universal practice of the Catholic Church, were I to approve of the reading by Catholic children, in a public school, of a version of the sacred Scriptures emanating from a body not in communion with the Catholic Church.

What was the result of that answer?—Mr. Butler sent my answer to Mr. Fletcher, a Protestant gentleman, who had taken an active part in the establishment of that school, which excited painful feelings in the mind of Mr. Fletcher.

Is it your opinion that Mr. Butler improperly committed himself in this business, without due authority from his ecclesiastical superiors, by giving an intimation to the Protestant gentlemen at Shadwell, that the Protestant version of the New Testament would be allowed by the Roman Catholic clergy in that school?—I do think so, indeed.

Have you any doubt of it?—None.

Did he afterwards apply to you to assent to the propositions which he had made?—Mr. Butler applied to me to know whether he could conscientiously take a part in the opening of the school.

What was your determination on that subject?—Mr. Butler had sent my note to Mr. Fletcher, and I declined sending any further written answer to Mr. Butler, but I sent the Rev. Mr. Hodson, one of my vicars-general, to explain my reasons to Mr. Butler for not answering.

What were those reasons?—Because I saw that Mr. Butler by his own conduct was drawing me into difficulties, which in the circumstances I wished to avoid.

Was Mr. Butler sufficiently acquainted with the principles of the Catholic Church to know, previous to any arrangement being made with the Protestant gentlemen at Shadwell, that his proposition in regard to the introduction of the Protestant version of the New Testament into that school could not be assented to by his ecclesiastical superiors?—I was persuaded that he was sufficiently acquainted with the principles of the Catholic Church in that regard, and therefore in my answer to him I referred to his own conviction, by saying, " You know that I should act in direct repugnance to the constant and universal practice of the Catholic Church," &c. I may add, that I conceived that the question proposed me by Mr. Butler, whether Catholics could conscientiously send their children to the school, was a question which should rather have been proposed to me by the clergy who direct the consciences of the people within their district, and therefore I did not think it my duty nor prudent to give a direct answer to Mr. Butler on that question.

Did you consider Mr. Butler's interference in that business to be irregular?—Yes; inasmuch as he proposed a question to me, whether the parents could conscientiously send their children to that school.

Did you understand that Mr. Butler had engaged to deliver an oration upon the occasion of opening that school?—I had heard it reported.

497.                                                                              Did

*Dr. Poynter.*

Did Mr. Butler attend the opening of that school?—I have been informed that he did not.

Was that in consequence of what passed between you and himself?—I think it was.

Had you expressed to Mr. Butler any wish to be examined before this Committee? —Certainly not; and I beg the Committee to understand that it was not my wish to appear before the Committee to give evidence on this occasion; and it having been signified to me that I was called at the suggestion of Mr. Butler, I beg to say, that Mr. Butler never consulted me to know whether it would be agreeable to me or not to appear before the Committee; and I apprehend that he wished to force me to give a public answer to those questions before the Committee, which from prudential reasons I had declined answering in private to him, and I am confirmed in this persuasion from the circumstance that the same questions have been proposed to myself and the other Catholic clergy who have been examined before the Committee, which Mr. Butler privately proposed to me, and to which I declined giving Mr. Butler a direct answer.

---

## *Martis*, 18° *die Junii*, 1816.

### HENRY BROUGHAM, Esquire, in The Chair.

#### Dr. *Poynter*, again called in, and Examined.

*Dr. Poynter.*

DID you understand that Mr. Finigan, the master of St. Giles's Catholic school, was a member of the Roman Catholic society at the time he commenced that school?—I know nothing of his character at the time he commenced that school; but before that, he had the character of being a Catholic.

#### *Joseph Fletcher*, Esquire, again called in, and Examined.

*Joseph Fletcher, Esq.*

IN your former evidence before the Committee, you stated, that 18,000 poor children were educated in your district; was that correct?—That must have been a mistake in copying; I stated 1,800, a part of which not being in the six parishes, made the actual number 1,540.

You also stated, that there were 1,400 poor Irish in those parishes; was that number correct?—That also must have been a mistake in copying; the number as represented by the Roman Catholic clergy is 14,000.

Are the parishes correctly stated in your former evidence?—Only five are mentioned, the parish of St. Catharine's, being one of the six, is left out.

How many of the uneducated children of the Irish poor do you believe are in that district?—I cannot say with any accuracy; I should suppose three or four thousand, there are that number at least.

Without any means of instruction whatever?—I believe without any.

You stated, that a society was about to be formed, and to be designated The British Union School; has that society been formed since your last examination?— The school was opened on the 6th of June.

Was it intended to admit the poor children of parents of the Roman Catholic persuasion as well as of Protestants?—It was intended to admit the children of the poor of every denomination.

What arrangements were made for this purpose?—The earliest meetings of the persons with whom the design originated, were attended by both Catholics and Protestants.

By laymen or clergymen?—Laymen exclusively.

What plan of instruction was proposed to be adopted?—The plan of instruction was detailed, and an address printed and circulated, with the plan annexed, a copy of which I will deliver in.

[It was read, as follows :]

" AN ADDRESS to the respectable Inhabitants, of every Religious denomination, residing in the Parishes of Saint Catharine's, Saint George Middlesex, Limehouse, Wapping, Shadwell, and the Hamlet of Radcliff: With the Prospectus of a

PLAN for the general Education of the Children of their Poor.

" THE exertions which have been made to prepare and give efficacy to a System of general Education for the Children of the Poor, and the powerful assistance that system has received by the union of all classes of professing Christians, have rendered argument
**unnecessary**

*Joseph Fletcher,*
*Esq.*

unnecessary to prove its expediency and advantage; the principle is firmly established upon a practical experience of its worth; it has been adopted by men of every denomination; and their association is attributable to that amiable and enlightened liberality of sentiment which is the peculiar characteristic of the present age. The happy effects of this friendly and cordial co-operation are valuable and extensive; the mist of ignorance is gradually dispersing, and there is abundant reason to believe that the time is fast approaching when every child shall be able to read the Bible. This animating and encouraging persuasion will induce its possessors to enlarge their sphere of action, that they may endeavour to convey to all who are in uninstructed poverty, the benefits of a system so admirably calculated to teach them the knowledge of their duty, and so fraught with future blessings to the world.

" There is not perhaps any part of the Metropolis in which the evil consequences arising from a want of Education are more painfully conspicuous than in the Eastern District, adjoining the River, inhabited by those very useful, industrious and laborious persons, who are employed amongst the shipping. Most of these men, so valuable to the community, have numerous families, and the produce of all their industry is barely sufficient to provide the necessaries of life; their children are supported with difficulty, but they cannot be taught; and the dreadful result of their misfortune is felt by every class of society. The neglected and awful situation of these Little Ones having a peculiar claim upon the Inhabitants of the district in which they reside, it has been proposed to provide a School for their reception, founded on a broad and liberal basis, where Christians of every denomination may cordially unite in the laudable endeavour to enlighten the minds of the rising generation. For this highly desirable purpose, several meetings have been held, and much pains taken to prepare the outline of a Plan adapted to receive all the Children of the neighbourhood, many of whom are the offspring of the Natives of Ireland, and whose parents are Catholics. These preparatory meetings have been attended by a number of respectable persons, Protestants and Catholics; and it has been resolved to submit the subject to the consideration of the Public, in the hope that something effectual may be done to increase the happiness of the Children of the Poor, and to render them useful and orderly members of society.

" It is further intended to solicit the attendance of the Inhabitants of the district at a General Meeting (of which due notice will be given) that the proposed Institution may receive their sanction and support.

" In pursuance of a Resolution of the preparatory Meeting—That a School should be instituted on a broad and liberal basis, in order to provide the means of Instruction of the Children of the Poor;—the attention of the Public is respectfully requested to the following

## PLAN.

" IT is proposed, That a Committee shall be formed, to consist of thirty-six persons of every religious denomination, who shall conduct the business of the institution; and that every minister residing in the district, or officiating at any place of public worship therein, shall be considered as part of the said committee, and have, if they require it, due notice of the meetings.

" That those lessons provided by the British and Foreign School Society in the Borough Road, consisting of *whole chapters of the Bible,* shall be used in the school; that they be selected and approved by the committee; and that no Catechism, tract, or any comment upon or explanation of the lessons, shall be introduced into the school, or be made by the teachers or visitors, but that their business shall be strictly and entirely confined to the written letter, and their duty consist in instructing the children in reading, writing, and arithmetic.

" That while due care is taken to prevent the introduction of any thing that could by the remotest construction be considered as likely to impress the minds of the children with the particular tenets of any religious society or persuasion, the committee, impressed with the deepest conviction of the importance of religion, and fully sensible of the danger that must ever attend a state of ignorance and infidelity, will strongly recommend, that every child committed to their care shall constantly attend Divine Service on the Sunday, both in the morning and afternoon; but in pursuance of this object, they will as carefully abstain from offering any bias or having any direction as to the place of their attendance; they will therefore require, that the parents or guardians of every child applying for admission shall attend the committee, and state at what place of worship they desire their children to attend on the Sunday, which shall be regularly entered on the books, and be open to the inspection of the respective ministers, who may, if they see fit, be furnished with any extract therefrom; and upon every written request of the said ministers, the children of their own denomination shall attend them at any place they may appoint.

" In preparing this arrangement, and in endeavouring thus carefully to guard against the imputation of desiring to possess any religious influence, the preparatory committee are actuated by an earnest desire to avoid the possibility of objection, by the hope to unite every Christian in the liberal endeavour to enlighten the understanding of the rising generation, and (thereby hereafter) to improve the condition of their fellow-creatures; thus rendering an important benefit to society, by enabling every individual to appreciate the blessing of Revelation, and to learn, by Divine instruction, their duty to God and man."

" *August* 10 1815."

" BRITISH

## " BRITISH UNION SCHOOL.

" T H E Public are respectfully informed, that immediately upon the former circulation of the annexed Address, a subscription was commenced; and the very liberal encouragement of the inhabitants of the district induced the Committee to pursue the benevolent resolution of the preparatory meeting. A School has been built, in a central situation, capable of accommodating six hundred boys, which will in a short time be opened for their reception, and where they will be educated in strict conformity to the original plan; and upon this broad and liberal principle, which will unalterably continue to be the basis of the insitution, the Committee most earnestly solicit the assistance and co-operation of every friend to the general instruction of the poor, to carry this highly desirable purpose into full effect.

" It is intended to adopt a system of reward for merit, to encourage diligence and orderly conduct in the children; that such reward shall consist of different articles of clothing, and that, according as the funds will admit, a certain number of the most deserving shall be annually clothed.

" A subscription of one guinea will entitle the subscriber to have three children constantly in the school; a donation of ten guineas will admit two, and a donation of five guineas one child, in addition to the number allowed for every annual guinea.

" The school is situated in Farmer-street, Shadwell; the present entrance for visitors is from Shakespeare's Walk, where it is proposed hereafter to erect a School for Girls, upon the same principle, under the direction of a female committee.—January 25, 1816."

What gentlemen of the Roman Catholic persuasion attended your meeting?—The person who attended the first meeting was a Mr. Sidney; but when the plan was finally arranged, it was attended by Lord Clifford's brother, the Honourable Robert Clifford; he suggested the alteration which is printed in italics, that the reading-lessons should consist of " whole chapters of the Bible."

Was this plan approved of by any other gentlemen of the Roman Catholic persuasion?—It was sent by Mr. Clifford's desire to the Thatched House tavern, where a meeting was to be held the next day of the Calmel Buildings Society: the secretary of that society was directed to write a letter to me; which letter stated, that at the meeting of the Calmel Buildings Society, the Earl of Leitrim in the chair, the plan had been read, was approved, and that, so far as related to the Irish poor, it should have all the assistance in their power. Mr. Mountagu Burgoyne, by the desire of the same society, requested that we would put down his name as a donation of ten guineas to the subscription.

Did you understand what gentlemen of the Roman Catholic persuasion had seen the plan and approved of it?—There were in the letter the names of three or four others, who I presume were Roman Catholics, but I do not know it.

Has Mr. Butler seen the plan?—I wrote to Mr. Butler, inclosing the printed plan, and he answered me, that it met his approbation.

Did he express a desire to give any further sanction to the Society?—He said he would subscribe, and that he should have great pleasure in attending the meeting when the school was to be opened, and in furthering its views.

Was a public meeting held on the opening of the school?—It was upon the 6th of June.

Who was in the chair?—His Royal Highness the Duke of Kent.

Did Mr. Butler attend that meeting?—He did not.

Do you know the reason why he did not attend?—I cannot say exactly what was the reason that he did not attend; the meeting was attended by several of the Roman Catholic clergymen.

Did they approve the plan?—I have no doubt of it, because the resident Roman Catholic clergyman the next day sent his subscription, with the assurance of his most cordial co-operation.

Did any clergymen attend the meetings of your committee, previous to the opening of the school?—Yes.

Did any Roman Catholic clergymen attend?—Yes.

Who?—The Rev. Mr. Horrabin.

Did he approve the proposed plan of instruction?—He did.

You have no doubt of his approbation?—Not any.

Did any other Roman Catholic clergyman attend any of your meetings?—No other Roman Catholic clergyman attended any of our meetings.

Was every clergyman entitled to attend the meetings of your committee?—Every minister residing in the district, or officiating at any place of worship therein, was considered as a part of the committee; and it was actually so stated in the printed plan; we carefully avoided distinguishing any, because we wished to give an equal admission to all.

And

And from all that transpired before the committee, the plan met with general approbation of both Catholics and Protestants?—It certainly did.

Have any of the Catholic children attended the school, in consequence of the arrangements previously made?—No children at present are admitted; we meet to-morrow for the first time to receive children, but great numbers of Catholic children are ready to come in; I have given letters of recommendation to the committee for several children of Irish parents to-day.

Have several Roman Catholic clergymen attended at any meetings of your committee?—One has attended frequently.

Have any others expressed their approbation of the plan?—One of them has attended frequently, and another, since the public meeting, has sent his subscription, and an assurance of his co-operation.

Who are those clergymen?—The Rev. Thomas Dobson is the first, and Mr. Horrabin.

Has Mr. Horrabin attended your meetings?—He has.

And has he expressed full approbation of the plan?—He has.

Has Mr. Horrabin subscribed to its funds?—He has.

And has expressed his full approbation of the proposed plan of instruction?—Fully.

You have stated, that there are a great number of poor Irish children in your neighbourhood; are they in general of a vicious character?—More ignorant than vicious.

Have you entertained any apprehensions that their vicious habits would corrupt others in the neighbourhood?—Not theirs particularly, but the vicious habits of uninstructed children neutralize the instruction received by the few who are educated.

And you conceive it of great importance to society, that some plan of instruction should be adopted for the benefit of the lower classes?—The want of such a plan was felt, and was the reason why this was instituted.

You still entertain sanguine hopes that the plan proposed will be carried into effect?—I hope and believe it will.

Has a committee been appointed to select chapters of the Bible for lessons?—There has.

Of whom is it composed?—Among others, Mr. Horrabin, the Roman Catholic clergyman, and Mr. Rudge, the clergyman of the Church of England, and myself, who am a Protestant Dissenter.

You have not yet agreed upon the chapters?—We have not yet set down to it.

Has it been agreed that you shall select chapters from the Protestant version?—Yes.

Are you quite certain of that?—Yes.

Did the Roman Catholic clergy approve of selections being made from the Protestant version?—They made no objections.

Have the Roman Catholics known and approved of this plan?—Certainly.

Has Mr. Horrabin approved of it?—Yes.

What Roman Catholics have approved of it, of the Roman Catholic laymen?—There has not been an objection made to it by any one.

And several have known of it?—All have known of it, who are upon the committee.

And you do not apprehend any objection from people of the Roman Catholic persuasion?—Not to the selection from the Protestant version, certainly not.

*Joseph Fletcher, Esq.*

### Mr. *George Ellis*, called in, and Examined.

YOU are solicitor to, and one of the trustees of, Emery Hill's charity?—Yes.

Have you got the foundation?—I have a copy of it.

Read that part of it relative to the education of the children?—" That 20 poore male children, children of poore men, and born in the said parish, shall be admitted to be taught free in the said schoole, without any charge to their parents; and to bee taught both English, Lattin, and to write and keep accounts, but especially to be well catechised and instructed in the principles of religion."

What is the amount of the expenses of the foundation?—Between 300*l.* and 400*l.* No children ever were admitted on the foundation, as far as I understand.

[Mr. *Simon Stephenson*, clerk to the trustees of Emery Hill's charity, was called, and delivered in the following Account.]

*Mr. George Ellis.*

*Mr. Simon Stephenson.*

The

The ACCOUNT of Mr. *Thomas Bray*, Treasurer of Mr. *Emery Hill*'s Charity, from 30th July 1814, to 30th July 1815.

Dr

| 1814. July 30th. | | £. | s. | d. |
|---|---|---|---|---|
| TO Cash received, Balance of last Account - - - - | | 140 | 15 | 5¼ |
| To one Year's Dividend on £. 2,097 4s. 3d. Reduced 3-per-cent. Annuities, due 5th April 1815 - - - £. 62 18 2<br>Property Tax deducted - - 6 5 8 | | 56 | 12 | 6 |
| To one Year's Dividend on £. 1,400. Reduced 3-per-cent. Annuities, due 5th April last - - - £. 42 — —<br>Property Tax deducted - - 4 4 — | | 37 | 16 | — |
| To one Year's Dividend on £. 950. Consolidated 3-per-cent. Annuities, due 5th July 1815 - - £. 28 10 —<br>Property Tax deducted - - 2 17 — | | 25 | 13 | — |
| Received of Mr. John Cierlaus, one year and a half Rent to Christmas 1814 - - - - - - £. 45 — —<br>Property Tax deducted - - 4 10 — | | 40 | 10 | — |
| Received of Messrs. Arnaud and Green, one year's Rent to Christmas 1814 - - - - - - £. 24 — —<br>Property Tax deducted - - 2 8 — | | 21 | 12 | — |
| Received of Mr. Telford, Executor of Mr. Hodgson, one year's Rent to Lady Day 1815 - - - - £. 55 — —<br>Property Tax deducted - - 5 10 4 | | 49 | 9 | 8 |
| Received of Mr. Wood, one year's Rent of Public House, due Michaelmas 1814 - - - - - £. 12 12 —<br>- - - - for House adjoining - - - 14 — —<br>26 12 —<br>Property Tax deducted - - 2 13 — | | 23 | 19 | — |
| Received of Mr. Mortimer, one year's Rent due at Christmas 1814 - - - - - - - £. 15 — —<br>Property Tax deducted - - 1 10 — | | 13 | 10 | — |
| To Cash received of Mr. Cowdry, one year's Rent due at Christmas last - - - - - - - - £. 20 — —<br>Property Tax deducted - - 2 — — | | 18 | — | — |
| BALANCE - - - - - £. | | 427 | 17 | 7¼ |

Cr

| 1814. | | £. | s. | d. |
|---|---|---|---|---|
| August 1 - | TO the poor People, one month's pay; viz. { 6 Married, at 18s. - - £. 5 8 —<br>6 Single - 14s. - - 4 4 — } | 9 | 12 | — |
| | To Mary Taylor, Wardour - - - - - | — | 3 | — |
| September 1 - | To the poor People and Wardour, as usual - - - - | 9 | 15 | — |
| October 1 - | To the poor People and Wardour, as usual - - - - | 9 | 15 | — |
| November 1 | To the poor People and Wardour, as usual - - - - | 9 | 15 | — |
| December 1 - | To the poor People and Wardour, as usual - - - - | 9 | 15 | — |
| 1815. | | | | |
| January 1 - | To the poor People and Wardour, as usual - - - - | 9 | 15 | — |
| February 1 | To the poor People and Wardour, as usual - - - - | 9 | 15 | — |
| March 1 - - | To the poor People and Wardour, as usual - - - - | 9 | 15 | — |
| April 1 - - | To the poor People and Wardour, as usual - - - - | 9 | 15 | — |
| May 1 - - | To the poor People and Wardour, as usual - - - - | 9 | 15 | — |
| June 1 - - | To the poor People and Wardour, as usual - - - - | 9 | 15 | — |
| July 1 - - | To the poor People and Wardour, as usual - - - - | 9 | 15 | — |
| | To the poor People a Gratuity of 5s. each, on 9th August 1814, agreeable to the Minutes of that day - - - - | 3 | — | — |
| | To Mrs. Taylor, for washing Surplices, for one year - - - | — | 5 | — |

*(continued.)*

The Account of Mr. *Thomas Bray*, Treasurer, &c.—*continued*.

C*

| 1815. | | £. | s. | d. |
|---|---|---|---|---|
| | To Expenses incurred at two Entertainments for the Governors and their Wives, pursuant to the Will - - - - - | 10 | — | — |
| | To George Ellis, Esq. Solicitor, his bill - - - - - | 18 | 2 | — |
| | To Matthew Burt, Smith, his bill - - - - - - | 4 | 4 | 6 |
| | To the Dean and Chapter of Westminster, one year's Ground Rent for Almshouses in Tothill Fields, due Michaelmas 1814 | 1 | 1 | 4 |
| | To one year's Water Rent to Dᵒ - - - - - - | 1 | 4 | — |
| | To one year's Insurance of Premises, Villiers-street, Buckingham and Rochester-row, to 26th February 1816 - - - - | 18 | 7 | — |
| | By Cash paid Messrs. Mitchell and Co. for 13 Chaldron of Coals at 72 s. shooting, &c. - - - - - - - - | 48 | 11 | 9 |
| | To Mr. John Jones, Plumber, his bill - - - - - | — | 8 | 6 |
| | To Mr. Simon Stephenson, Clerk to the Trustees, one year's Salary, due Midsummer day 1815 - - - - - | 10 | 10 | — |
| | To Mr. Dorset, for Turnery, his bill - - - - - | — | 4 | 6 |
| | To Mr. Glanvile, Carpenter, his bill - - - - - | 1 | — | 3 |
| | To Mr. Sutton, Bricklayer, his bill - - - - - | 2 | 17 | 4½ |
| | To the Vestry Keeper, attendance at two Meetings - - - | — | 2 | — |
| | To Thoˢ Williams, whose Wife was ill from an accident, and to Atkins, blind; at sundry times - - - - - - | 1 | 12 | 6 |
| | To Mary Taylor, for attendance upon the Sick - - - | — | 7 | 6 |
| | To sundry Stamps on receipt of Rents; Coach-hire, &c. - | — | 12 | 8 |
| | £.239. 10. 10½. | | | |
| | By Cash in hand, to balance - - - - | 188 | 6 | 8¼ *Sic Orig.* |
| | **BALANCE** - - - - £. | 427 | 17 | 7¼ |

Saint Margaret's Vestry Room, 31st July 1815.

The foregoing Account was examined and approved by Us,

> John Abington,
> Lytton Geo. Kier,
> J. F. Sheppard.

The foregoing was extracted from the Accounts relating to Mr. Emery Hill's Charity, and is a true copy.

> SIMON STEPHENSON,
> Clerk to the Trustees.

---

*Anthony Richard Blake*, Esquire, called in, and Examined.

WAS not the school now under the direction of Mr. Finigan, originally called " The Catholic school?"—To the best of my recollection it was called " St. Giles's Catholic school:" the word Catholic was certainly introduced into the title.

At what time was this?—About two years and a half ago.

Is it not now called " The Irish Free School?"—I never heard it called the Irish Free School, until I saw the printed evidence of Mr. Finigan before this Committee.

Are the scholars Catholics at the school?—I cannot state from my own knowledge; I know they are Irish, but I do not know whether they are Catholics or Protestants.

Are you a Roman Catholic?—I am.

Do not the Roman Catholics generally consider that the several gentlemen who have been active in establishing this school, are hostile in their principles to Roman Catholics?—I certainly did hear that some of the gentlemen who were upon the committee were rather marked for hostility to the Catholics, upon what is generally called the Catholic question. I particularly understood they had been concerned in a publication, called " A Correspondence on the formation of the Roman Catholic Bible Society," which was considered and felt by Roman Catholics as extremely injurious to them. There were annexed to that correspondence a collection of notes taken from Roman Catholic versions of the Testament, which had been published in the bitterest days of polemical acrimony, and were written in terms that Protestants might consider extremely offensive. I must also observe, that by the preface to this work, an idea was conveyed that it was the intention of the Roman Catholics, who were engaged in republishing a new edition of the Testament, to republish those obnoxious

*A. R. Blake, Esq.*

obnoxious notes, although the Roman Catholics had previously resolved the contrary, and inserted their resolution in several newspapers. There was also other matter in the publication which it was impossible for Roman Catholics to see without conceiving that the persons who sent it forth were pointedly inimical to them. The feeling of the Catholics, with respect to the publication of the notes, was, that they were produced with a view to excite a hostile feeling towards them in the minds of their Protestant brethren, and the publication took place about the time when the Catholic Relief Bill was before Parliament.

Did any suspicion appear amongst the Roman Catholics that the object of this school was Protestantism?—Upon hearing that Mr. Finigan had met with a great deal of opposition in his school, and not knowing any of the particular circumstances of the institution, I was a good deal surprized at it, and being rather in the habit of interesting myself in the promotion of order amongst the lower classes of Irish, I made some inquiries upon the subject, and I found that many of them were impressed with an idea that the real object of the school was to make proselytes of their children.

Did that idea prevail amongst the higher orders of the Roman Catholics?—It certainly did.

Of whom did you make those inquiries?—Several.

Can you name any individual?—Indeed I cannot; I have frequent applications made to me by the lower orders of Irish for assistance, and I do not know that I could give the committee the name of any one of them.

Have any attempts been made in those schools to proselyte the children to the Protestant faith?—Upon my word I do not know; except that I understand Mr. Finigan the master has become a proselyte.

Have the committee of that school taken any part against the Roman Catholics, as a committee?—Not as a committee; but I believe some of the members individually have.

Do you know that the Reverend Mr. Gandolphy went to that school in April 1814, and in an impassioned manner addressed the children, and ordered them to go home to their parents, declaring that the schools were a hypocritical and heretical institution?—I heard that Mr. Gandolphy did go to the school, and had interfered very warmly to induce the children to leave it, on the ground that the object of it was to make proselytes.

Did you understand that on the following Sunday he preached a sermon against it in the Spanish chapel?—I heard he did.

Did you understand that in consequence of that sermon, Mr. and Mrs. Finigan were much abused, and that acts of violence were committed upon the children of the school, and that the windows of the school-house were broken?—I did hear that acts of violence had been committed against Mr. Finigan, but I did not hear that they were occasioned by Mr. Gandolphy's sermon; I understood that there was a hostile feeling towards Mr. Finigan amongst the lower orders of the Irish, in consequence of their conceiving, as I have already stated, that whilst he called himself a Catholic, and the school, of which he was the head, Catholic, the real object was to induce the Catholic children to abandon their religion.

Do you think that these acts of violence would have been committed had no such sermon been preached, or if Mr. Gandolphy had not expressed himself strongly against the institution?—From the irritable nature of my countrymen generally, and particularly of the lower orders, I am myself persuaded that the idea that Mr. Finigan was not acting *bonâ fide* towards them, was alone sufficient to induce them to act very violently against him; I attribute, myself, the violent opposition he has received, to that idea, and not to any interference of Mr. Gandolphy; on the contrary, I am persuaded that Mr. Gandolphy and the other Catholic clergymen of London would be the first to discountenance any act of violence, whatever might be the cause.

Has any thing occurred since that period, within your knowledge, to contradict or confirm that idea in the mind of the Irish Catholics?—No, on neither side. I however beg not to be understood as expressing an opinion, myself, that Mr. Finigan practised or meant to practise any wilful delusion upon the Catholics.

As you have had frequent opportunities of knowing their sentiments, do you think there is a general disposition in favour of educating their children?—Most certainly; and I have myself endeavoured occasionally to get their children into the Lancasterian schools as well as the Catholic schools.

Have you observed in the habits of such of the Irish poor, whether Catholic or Protestant, as have been educated, any beneficial effects resulting from that education?—Upon my word I cannot say that I perceive much distinction in point of

morals

morals between those who are and those who are not educated ; my own opinion is, (if I am to give one) that education must enlighten, and of course improve their minds.

A. R. Blake, Esq.

Does it fall within your knowledge that, in Ireland, the Catholics and Protestants are educated indiscriminately at the same school ?—Certainly they are ; most of the classical Catholic schools are under the direction of the Protestants.

Mr. *Charles Francis Jameson*, again called in, and further Examined.

Mr. C. F. Jameson.

HAVE you any further information to give the Committee ?—Having observed out of 170 boys that have left the Horseferry Road school, 82 of which go to no school at all, and many of those boys do not know their letters, I have made it my business to examine into the conduct of several children who resort together for no other purpose than mischief and theft. Wishing to satisfy myself of this matter, I have watched their conduct since I was before this honourable Committee, and therefore I speak of my own certain knowledge of what I relate. There are three gangs of boys infesting at present Great Peter-street, Stratton-ground, St. Ann's-street and Orchard-street, and indeed all the avenues leading thereto, led by what is called the Pye-street Gang. Some of these boys I know, having been admitted into the Horseferry Road school two or three times each ; at the National schools several of them have also been admitted once and twice ; but they do not now attend any school ; they are six, eight, nine, ten, eleven and twelve years old, and many others. Their custom is, one boy goes in first for a small article, two others generally follow before the article is bought, and in the mean time the other part of the gang steal something. I have seen this process, because I have examined into it since I was here before. At other times bad silver and French money have been tendered, and before that has been refused to be taken, something has been stole by the other party. A party of these boys went a few days ago to a laundress's in Rochester-row, and, while the woman was taking in clothes from the drying ground, stole three shirts. Some of those boys I have dismissed in consequence : and some of the parents of the children that are in the school, knowing the character of those other boys, would not allow their children to mix with them : others I have dismissed for truantry. I have written several letters to their parents, to induce a reformation ; and I have frequently remonstrated with them on the conduct of their children, which has been treated with the greatest contempt : if at any time they have played truant, they have been constantly begged off ; and when sent for, the answer returned has been, that they had been wanted. A boy of the age of twelve years, who I had re-admitted into the school three times ; the first time I discharged him for telling stories, but at the request of the Rev. Isaac Saunders he was admitted a second time ; the second time I discharged him for stealing the flowers of a lady in the Horseferry Road ; he was re-admitted a second time at the request of the Rev. Isaac Saunders and some person belonging to his chapel : I at last discharged him in consequence of his stealing from the very school. Having missed a Bible and some other articles out of the school, I made it my business to watch : This was on the Saturday morning ; and having watched from four till six o'clock, I saw this boy get over the wall from the street, and so on the leads of the school, and opened a back door which goes down to the girls Sunday school ; and of course having then detected him, I discharged him for good. But the Rev. Mr. Saunders, wishing to try him again, took this boy into his own school, in hopes of producing a reformation, where he was a fortnight ; at the expiration of a fortnight, he was discovered in the Park by Mr. Bone, who is a subscriber to the West London Institution, with a Sunday-school tract in his pocket ; and having given an account that he had been admitted into the Horseferry Road school, of which Mr. Bone was a subscriber, and giving a very incorrect account as to the means and reason of his being turned out, induced Mr. Bone to call on the West London committee, in order to ascertain the reason ; at that committee it so happened I was in attendance ; the boy was then not there, but he understanding from some other persons that Mr. Bone had received information of his being turned out of the school in the true way, before he saw Mr. Bone he ran away from him, and he has not seen him since. But I am clearly given to understand that the boy at the present moment is the head of one as notorious a gang of pickpockets in St. Giles's as there exists in London ; and indeed I should have no difficulty in proving it, if I were called upon so to do. When I opened the Horseferry Road school on the 16th January 1815, I then had only thirty-seven boys ; and finding in the evening that the practice of the children was to knock at the doors of the inhabitants, I opened an evening school from six to eight, which I did merely for the

purpose

*Mr.*
*C. F. Jameson.*

purpose of keeping them out of the streets, for I never had a farthing for it, nor expected it. That evening school has a very short time been given up, in consequence of some information which I received from Mr. Lucas, one of the Society of Friends, in Millbank-street, stating, that in going round in order to collect the monthly subscriptions of the Bible Association, he discovered some (I cannot say how many) who refused any longer to pay. stating that if they had a Bible delivered to them, they did not know the letters of it. Mr. Lucas then stated to me the propriety of opening an adult school, instead of continuing the school for boys, which I expect will be carried into effect.

---

*Mercurii,* 19° *die Junii,* 1816.

### THOMAS BABINGTON, Esq. in The Chair.

Mr. *Thomas Augustine Finigan,* again called in, and Examined.

*Mr.*
*T. A. Finigan.*

IN your former evidence before this Committee, you stated that the Catholic priests had threatened the parents to deprive them of their religious privileges, if they suffered their children to read the Scriptures; do you wish to correct that part of your evidence?—I meant to say, if they suffered them to attend the schools.

You stated in your former evidence, that you were master of the St. Giles's Irish Free School; is that the correct title of it?—The correct title at present is, The Catholic School.

What is the proper title of it?—The proper title of the school at present is, The St. Giles's Irish Catholic Free Schools.

In your former evidence you omitted the word " Catholic," had you any reason for so doing?—Understanding that it was the intention of the committee to propose it at the next general meeting, as it gave such offence to the priests that they called at the school-house and asked how we dare to call it Catholic, as it was supported by Protestants, I therefore omitted the word in my description of the school.

Is it proposed to omit the word Catholic, merely to avoid giving offence?—So I understand, and for no other reason.

Were you a Roman Catholic at the commencement of this school?—I was, to June 1813.

Did you in June 1813 embrace the Protestant faith?—Not till the latter end of July.

Were you educated in the Roman Catholic religion?—I was, and as a candidate for priesthood.

You are now a Protestant?—I am.

Has considerable opposition been made to you in the conduct of that school?—In a considerable degree.

Did you understand that the parents of the children were impressed with an idea that the real object of the school was to make them proselytes to the Protestant faith?—No.

Have you any reason to believe that the opposition you met with proceeded from any idea of that sort entertained by the parents of the children?—The parents of the children have at all times treated me with the utmost respect, and even such parents as were prevailed on by the priests to withdraw their children, have frequently declared that it was wholly in consequence of the priests refusing them absolution in confession, that they kept them away. Many of them, when they got this absolution, brought their children back again to the schools, where they now continue. I also hold in my hand a number of documents, signed by the parents of the children, to prove the truth of what I now advance.

Have any attempts been made to proselyte the children to the Protestant faith in your school?—On the contrary, the committee at all times have given directions that they should attend such place of worship as their parents preferred, and some of the committee have proposed to rent a room for the admission of any of the Roman Catholic clergy who would meet the children, to instruct them in the principles of their religion. But no child has at any time been solicited to attend any place of worship, except such as their parents preferred, as I have already stated.

---

APPENDIX.

# APPENDIX.

Appendix (A.)

Copy of a CIRCULAR LETTER, dated 4th June 1816, addressed to the Masters, &c. of various Charity Schools in the Metropolis.

Committee on the Education of the Lower Orders,
June 4th, 1816.

SIR,

I HAVE to require that you will furnish me with Answers to the following Queries, with as little delay as possible :

1st. WHAT is the nature of the School with which you are connected?

2d. HOW many Children are educated there?

3d. WHAT are they taught?

4th. IS the new method of teaching adopted?

5th. ARE they clothed and boarded?

6th. WHAT is the Expense? distinguishing the Master's, Mistress's, and other Salaries.

7th. WHAT are the Funds, and how do they arise? Specify the particulars of the last year's Income.

8th. WHAT old Foundation Schools are there in your Parish; how are they endowed; how many do they teach; and what are their Expenses, distinguishing Salaries?

9th. CAN you estimate the Number of poor Children in your Parish who are without the means of Education?

10th. DO the Parents of such Children show any reluctance to have them educated?

I have to require that you will address your Answer to me, at the Select Committee on the Education of the Lower Orders, House of Commons.

I am your obedient Servant,

H. BROUGHAM,
Chairman.

EXTRACTS

EXTRACTS OF THE ANSWERS RETURNED

| NAMES OF SCHOOLS. | DESCRIPTION OF SCHOOLS. | Number of Children Educated. | What Taught. | Method. |
|---|---|---|---|---|
| Shoreditch Boys Charity School - | Parochial Male Charity School - | 100 Boys. | Reading, Writing, and Accounts. | New method. |
| St. George's, Southwark, Charity School - - - - | D° Male and Female D° - - | 60 Boys. 40 Girls. | D° D° D° D° and Needle-work. | New method not adopted. |
| Finsbury Charity Schools - - | (Not Parochial) Male and Female Charity Schools - - - | 31 Boys. 21 Girls. | D° D° D° and principles of the Estab. Church. | D° |
| St. Anne, Westminster, Charity School | Parochial Male and Female Charity School - - - - - | 130 Boys. 60 Girls. | D° D° D° D° with Needle-work, Knitting, &c. | New mothed partly adopted. |
| St. Paul, Shadwell, Charity School - | D° - - - - - | 45 Boys. 35 Girls. | D° D° D° and House-hold work and Sewing. | New method not adopted. |
| Protestant Dissenters Charity School | Dissenters Male Charity School - | 70 Boys. | D° D° | D° |
| Aldgate Ward Charity School - - | Auxiliary National School - - | 60 Boys. 40 Girls. | D° D° | New method. |
| St. John, Wapping, Charity School - | Parochial Male and Female Charity Schools - - - - | 50 Boys. 40 Girls. | D° D° D° and Needle-work. | D° |
| St. Paul, Covent Garden - - - | D° - - - D° - - - | 70 Children, (sexes not men-tioned). | Reading, Writing, and Arithmetic, &c. | New method. |
| St. Ethelburga Society School - | Male and Female Charity School - | 36 Boys. 20 Girls. | D° D° D° and Needle-work. | New method (in a great degree). |
| St. Pancras Female Charity School - | Parochial Female Charity School - | 54 Girls. | D° D° | New method not adopted. |
| St. Marylebone Institution for In-struction and Industry - - | Parochial Auxiliary National School | 319 Boys. 200 Girls. —— 519 | D° & in a branch of the Willow Hat-Manufacy. D° and Needle-work. | New method. |
| St. Alphage Charity - - - | Auxiliary National School - - | 18 Boys. 7 Girls. | D° D° | D° |
| St. Bride's Charity School - - | Parochial Male and Female Charity School - - - - | 40 Boys. 30 Girls. | D° D° D° D° & Sewing. | New method partially adopted. |
| Islington Charity School - - - | Parochial Male and Female Charity School - - - - | 250 Boys & Girls. | D° D° | New method. |
| Billingsgate Ward Charity School - | Male and Female Charity School, comprising five Parishes - - | 30 Boys. 15 Girls. | Reading, Writing, and Arithmetic. D° & Needlework. | New method not adopted. |
| Aldersgate Ward School - - | Parochial Male and Female Charity School - - - - | 40 Boys. 40 Girls. | D° D° D° D° | New method. |

TO THE FOREGOING LETTER.

| Number Clothed or Boarded. | Total Income. | Total Expense. | Sources of Income. | Amount of Salaries Paid. | REMARKS. |
|---|---|---|---|---|---|
| | £.  s.  d. | £.  s.  d. | | | |
| All Clothed. | 426  3  5 | 264 — — | Subscriptions and Sermons. From Stock, £. 59. 17. | Master, £. 120. | Not very many uneducated Children.—Parents anxious for the Education of their Children. |
| All Clothed, and 1 Girl Boarded. | 511  18  10 | 560 — — | Dº Dº From Stock, £.73. | Master, £.65. Mistress, £.45. | Cannot estimate the number of uneducated Children.—Parents anxious for their Children's instruction. |
| All Clothed. | 276  12  11 | 311  2  2 | Dº Dº From Stock, £.35. | Master and Mistress's joint Salary, £.64.  4. | Dº  -  -  - Dº |
| 60 Boys and 30 Girls Clothed. | 713  2  4¼ | 669  3  8 | Dº Dº Stock, £.183. 12. | Master, Mistress, &c. £. 286. 8. 1. | Number of Children without the means of Education unknown.—Parents reluctant to comply with rules of the School. |
| All Clothed. | Not stated equal to Expenses. | 280 — — | Dº Dº Stock, £. 48. | Master, £.40. Mistress, £. 30. | Parish populous; means of instruction inadequate.—Parents not averse to the Education of their Children. |
| All Clothed. | 512  7  3 | 257  8  3 | Dº Dº | Master, £.63. | Dº |
| All Clothed. | 687  13  7 | 581  4  9 | Dº Dº Stock, £.49. 10. | Master and Mistress, £. 81. Gratuity £. 30. | Cannot estimate the number of Children uninstructed.—Parents not reluctant. |
| All Clothed. | 473 — — | From 450 — — to 480 — — | Dº Dº Stock, £.60. | Master, £. 50. Mistress, £.30. | Dº  -  -  - Dº |
| All Clothed and Boarded. | Not stated. | -  -  - | Dº Dº | -  -  - | Number of Children uneducated unknown.—Parents appear reluctant to avail themselves of Education on the National Plan, because unaccompanied with Board and Clothing. |
| All Clothed. | 240  12  6 | 247  15  9½ | Dº Dº Stock, £.35. | Master and Mistress, £.63. | Not aware of any uneducated Children.—Parents anxious for the instruction of their Children. |
| All Boarded and Clothed. | -  -  - | -  -  - | Dº Dº | Mistress, £.35. Assistant Writing Master, £. 13. 13. Singing Master, £.5. 5. | Number of uneducated Children not stated. |
| 150 Clothed. | 1,167  17 — | 1,083  7  6 | Dº Dº Stock, £.15. 1. 6. | Master, £.83. 4. Mistress, £.38. 17. 6. Poundage on the Work, £.16. 7. 2. | Number of Children uneducated supposed to be 1,400 or 1,500 in this Parish.—Parents indifferent to their Children's instruction. |
| All Clothed. | 92  12  10 | 81  11  3 | Dº Dº Stock, £. 27. 10. | Master, £.19. 12. 2. Mistress, £. 2. 7. | Number uneducated unknown.—Parents strongly desirous of their Children's instruction. |
| All Clothed. | -  -  - | 260 — — | Dº Dº Stock about £.39. | Master, £. 42. Mistress, £. 30. | Opportunity of instruction afforded to all.—Parents not reluctant. |
| 46 Boys. 34 Girls. 80 Clothed | -  -  - | 525  14 — | Dº Dº | Master, £. 60. Mistress, £. 30. | Number uneducated supposed to be few. Parents not generally averse to their Children's instruction. |
| All Clothed. | 300  1  2 | 274  13  3 | Dº Dº From Stock, £. 34. 4. | Master, £. 50. Mistress, £. 20. | Not many uneducated Children.—Parents not reluctant to have their Children educated. |
| All Clothed, 2 Girls Boarded. | 421  2  6 | Not stated. | Dº Dº | Master, Fifty Guineas. Mistress, £. 40. | Number uneducated small.—Parents not averse. |

EXTRACTS OF THE ANSWERS RETURNED

| NAMES OF SCHOOLS. | DESCRIPTION OF SCHOOLS. | Number of Children Educated. | What Taught. | | Method. |
|---|---|---|---|---|---|
| St. Mary-le-bone Charity School - | Parochial Male and Female Charity School - - - - - | 54 Boys. 54 Girls. | Reading, Writing, and Arithmetic. D° and Needle-work, &c. | | New method not adopted. |
| Mile End Old Town Charity School | D° - - D° - - - | 120 Boys. 95 Girls. | D° | D° | New method. |
| Cordwainers and Bread-street Ward School - - - - - | Male and Female Charity School for 13 Parishes - - - | 50 Boys. 30 Girls. | D° | D° | New method not adopted. |
| Broad-street Ward Charity School - | Male and Female Ward Charity School - - - - - | 50 Boys. 30 Girls. | D° | D° | D° |
| Queenhithe Charity School - - (Vide Mr. Hatch's Evidence.) | Part of London Auxiliary National School - - - - - | | | | |
| St. George's, Westminster, School of Industry - - - - | Male and Female Charity School - | 175 Boys. 125 Girls. | D° | D° | New method. |
| Cripplegate Within Ward Charity School - - - - - | Ward Male and Female Charity School (comprising part of nine Parishes) - - - - | 50 Boys. 25 Girls. | D° | D° | New method not adopted. |
| St. Katharine's Charity School - | Male and Female Parochial Charity School - - - - - | 50 Boys and Girls. | D° | D° | D° |
| St. Dunstan's in the West Charity School - - - - - | D° - - D° - - - | 45 Boys. 35 Girls. | D° | D° | New method in great part adopted. |
| St. Leonard, Shoreditch, Charity School - - - - - | Parochial Male Charity School - | 100 Boys. | D° | | New method. |
| St. Giles in the Fields and St. George, Bloomsbury, Charity School - - - - - | Parochial Male and Female Charity School - - - - - | 101 Boys. 60 Girls. | D° | D° | New method not adopted. |
| Paddington Charity School - - | D° - - - - - - | 50 Boys. 50 Girls. | D° | D° | D° |
| Vintry Ward Charity School - | Ward Male and Female Charity School - - - - - | 30 Boys. 20 Girls. | D° | D° | D° |
| School House, Spitalfields - - | Male and Female Charity School - | 56 Boys. 54 Girls. | D° D° and Sewing. | D° | New method not adopted. |
| Bridge, Candlewick, and Dowgate Wards Charity Schools - - | Male and Female Charity School for six Parishes - - - | 60 Boys. 40 Girls. | D° D° and Sewing. | D° | New method partly adopted. |
| St. George the Martyr, Queen-square, Charity School - - | Parochial Male and Female Charity School - - - - - | 40 Boys. 30 Girls. | D° D° | D° D° | D° |
| Stockwell Charity School - - | Auxiliary National School - - | 70 Boys. 30 Girls. ——— 100 | D° | D° | New method. |
| Charity School, Bermondsey - - | Parochial Male and Female Charity School - - - - - | 50 Boys. 30 Girls. | D° | | D° |
| St. Thomas's Charity School, South-wark - - - - - | Parochial Male Charity School - | 30 Boys. | D° | | New method adopted. |
| Langbourn Ward Charity School - | Male and Female Ward Charity School - - - - - | 30 Boys. 20 Girls. | D° | | New method in part adopted. |
| Zoar-street School, St. Saviour, Southwark - - - - | Male and Female Free School - | 60 Boys. 40 Girls. | D° | | - - - - |
| St. Mary, Whitechapel, Charity School - - - - - | Parochial Male and Female Charity School - - - - - | 100 Boys. 100 Girls. | D° | | New method. |

TO THE FOREGOING LETTER.

| Number Clothed or Boarded. | Total Income. | Total Expense. | Sources of Income. | Amount of Salaries paid. | REMARKS. |
|---|---|---|---|---|---|
| | £. s. d. | £. s. d. | | | |
| All Boarded and Clothed. | 2,217 — 11 | 2,261 11 2 | Subscriptions, Sermons, &c. From Stock, £.105. | Master, £.52. 10. Assistant, £.24. Mistress, £.36. 15. Assistant, £.21. | Number uneducated supposed to be very great. |
| 30 Boys and 30 Girls Clothed. | 433 — — | 430 — — | D° D° Stock, £.139. | Master, £.100. Mistress, £.60. | Number uneducated unknown.— Many Parents have shewn reluctance to their Children being instructed. |
| All Clothed. | Not stated. | Not stated. | D° D° | - - - | Number uneducated, not great. Parents, not reluctant. |
| D° | 465 — — | About 420 — — | D° D° Stock and House, £.155. | Master, £.65. Mistress, £.35. | Number uneducated unknown. |
| All Clothed. | 2,260 17 7 | 1,855 12 2 | D° D° Stock, &c. £.195. | Master, £.135. Mistress, £.80. 5. Total, £.412. 7. | D° - - - D° |
| D° | 435 13 6 | 430 — — | D° D° Stock, £.30. | Master and Mistress, £.120. | About 100 uninstructed in this Ward. Parents happy to have their Children educated. |
| D° | 255 13 10 | 210 7 6 | Not stated. | Not stated. | Number uneducated unknown. |
| All Clothed. | 492 16 2½ | Between 400 — — and 500 — — | D° D° | Master, £.75. Mistress, £.40. | Number uneducated, supposed to be small. Parents not reluctant. |
| D° | 426 3 5 | 384 — — | D° D° Stock, £.59. 17. | Master, £.120. | D° - - - D° |
| Boys Clothed, Girls Clothed and Boarded. | 2,286 7 — | 2,155 12 9 | D° D° | Master, £.80. Assistant, £.40. Mistress, £.30. 5. | Number uneducated unknown. |
| 20 Boys and 20 Girls Clothed. | 250 — — | About 250 — — | D° D° | Master and Mistress, £.84. | - - D° - - |
| All Clothed. | 240 8 — | 213 — — | D° D° Stock, £.92. | Master, £.70. Mistress, £.40. | About 60 uneducated. Parents not reluctant. |
| Not stated. | Not stated. | Not stated. | Voluntary Contributions, &c. | Master, £.60. Mistress, £.38. | No Children without the means of education. Parents attentive to their Children's education. |
| All Clothed. | 642 4 3 | 667 7 2 | D° D° Stock, £.70. | Masters, £.40. Mistress, £.26. | D° |
| D° | 454 7 10 | About 400 — — | Voluntary Contributions, Stock and House, £.218. 5. | Master, £.100. Mistress, £.50. | D° |
| Neither Clothed nor Boarded. | Not stated. | About 175 — — | D° D° | Master, £.80. Mistress, £.40. | No means of estimating the number of uneducated Children. |
| All Clothed. | Not stated. | Not stated. | D° D° | Master, £.70. 2 Mistresses, £.80. | About 1,000 Children uneducated. —Parents anxious. |
| D° | 140 — — | 140 — — | D° Stock, £.40. | Master, between £.50. and £.60. | Number uneducated unknown. |
| D° | 417 8 11 | 403 8 8 | D° | Master, £.50. Mistress, £.30. | Not any uneducated. |
| — | Uncertain. | 90 — — | D° | Master, £.35. Mistress £.30. | — |
| D° | 864 12 6 | About 820 - — | D° | Master, £.100. Mistress, £.38. | Cannot estimate the number uneducated. |

EXTRACTS OF THE ANSWERS RETURNED

| NAMES OF SCHOOLS. | DESCRIPTION OF SCHOOLS. | Number of Children Educated. | What Taught. | Method. |
|---|---|---|---|---|
| St. Luke, Middlesex, Charity School | Parochial Male and Female Charity School - - - - - } | 185 Boys & Girls. | Reading, Writing, and Accounts. D° and Sewing. | New method not adopted. |
| Bethnal Green Charity School - | D° - - - - - - | 35 Boys. 35 Girls. | D° | D° |
| Tower Ward Charity School - | Male and Female Charity School, containing two Parishes, and part of three others - - - | 60 Boys. 60 Girls. | D° | New method in part adopted. |
| Castle Baynard Ward School - | D° - - - - - - | 34 Boys. 24 Girls. | D° | New method not adopted. |
| St. Andrew's, Holborn, Charity School - - - - - } | Parochial Male and Female Charity School - - - - - | 85 Boys. 85 Girls. | D° | New method. |
| St. Sepulchre's Boys Charity School | Parochial Male Charity School - | 51 Boys | Reading, Writing, and Arithmetic. | New method. |
| St. Sepulchre's Girls Charity School | Parochial Female Charity School - | 26 Girls. | Reading, Writing, Sewing, Knitt & Householdwork. | New method not adopted. |
| St. Mary, Newington, Sunday Schools | Sunday School for Boys and Girls - | 100 Boys & Girls. | Reading. | New method. |
| Lambeth, Boys Parochial School - | Parochial Male Charity School - | 300 Boys. | Reading, Writing, and Arithmetic. | D° |
| Lambeth Charity School, founded by Archbishop Tenison - - - | Female Charity School - - - | 36 Girls (but soon to be increased to 200.) | D° and Needlework. | D° |
| Charity School, White Hart Row - | Male and Female Sunday School - | 226 Boys & Girls. | Reading. | New method not adopted. |
| Free School, Grange Road, Bermondsey | Free School for Boys - - - | 60 Boys 20 Supernumeraries. | Reading, Writing, and Arithmetic. | — |
| Pentonville Charity School - - | Male and Female District Parochial School - - - - } | 55 Boys. 55 Girls. | D° | New method. |
| St. Ann, Aldersgate, Charity School | Male and Female Parochial Charity School - - - - | 90 Boys & Girls. | D° | New method not adopted. |
| Raine's Hospital and Schools - - | Male and Female Charity School - | 50 Boys. 50 Girls. | D° | D° |
| Poplar and Blackwall Charity School | Parochial Male Charity School - | 100 Boys. | D° | New method. |
| St. Mary, Rotherhithe, Charity School | Parochial Male and Female Charity School - - - - | 40 Boys. 25 Girls. | D° | New method not adopted. |
| Clerkenwell Charity School - - | Ditto. | 160 Boys. 80 Girls. | D° D° and Sewing. | New method. |
| Western School - - - - | } Associated Catholic Charities : (Vide Mr. Booker's Evidence.) | { 70 Girls. { 85 Boys. } | D° D° | D° D° |
| Eastern School - - - - | | { 90 Girls. { 180 Boys. } | D° D° | D° D° |
| Centre Division - - - - | | 200 Boys. | D° | D° |
| Sunday School, Church Street, Lambeth - - - - - - } | Sunday School for Boys and Girls - | 10 Boys. 16 Girls. | Reading, Writing, and Arithmetic. | D° |
| St. Mary-le-Strand, Charity School - | Parochial Male and Female Charity School - - - - } | 30 Boys. 12 Girls. | D° | New method partly adopted. |
| St. Giles, Cripplegate, Charity Schools | D° - - - - - - | 102 Boys. 100 Girls. | D° D° and Needlework. | New method adopted in the Gir's School, not in the Boys. |

TO THE FOREGOING LETTER.

| Number Clothed or Boarded. | Total Income. | Total Expense. | Sources of Income. | Amount of Salaries paid. | REMARKS. |
|---|---|---|---|---|---|
| All Clothed. | £.  s.  d.  808  19  7½ | £.  s.  d.  536  12  1 | Voluntary Contributions, &c. Stock £.195. | Masters, £.115.10. Mistress, £.89. 5. | Number uneducated apprehended to be very great. Parents by no means disinclined to their children being instructed. |
| D° | About 350 — — | About 350 — — | D° | Master, and Mistress's Salary,£.80. | Number uneducated unknown. |
| D° | 504 — — | 458 10 — | D° | Master, £.70. Mistress, £.50. | D° |
| D° | 373  5 10 | 377  5 — | D° | Master, £.40. Mistress, £.32. | D° |
| D° | 1,204 15 — | 1,077 11  5 | D° Stock £.228. | Master, £.100. Mistress, £.30. | D° |
| All Clothed. | Not Stated. | 237 — — | Vol^y Contributions & Funded Prop^y | Master, £.58. | Cannot estimate the number uneducated. |
| All Clothed, 4 Boarded. | 193 — — | 202 — — | D° Stock, £.30. | Mistress, £. 30. | D° |
| 15 Boys } Clothed. 15 Girls } | 65 — — | 58 — — | D° | Master 6s. per Week, Mistress 4s. D° | Uneducated poor children numerous. Parents rather indifferent. |
| 70 Clothed. | 411 17 11 | 412  8  4 | D° Stock £.49. 10. | Master, £.100. | Number uneducated unknown. |
| 20 Clothed. | Not stated. | 150 — — | Houses and Land. | Mistress, £.30. | Number uneducated considerable. Parents thankful for their children's instruction. |
| Neither Clothed nor Boarded. | 50 — — | Not stated. | Voluntary Subscriptions. | -  -  - | Number uneducated unknown. |
| D° | 150 — — | 150 — — | Houses, Land, &c. | Master, £.80. Ushers, £.50. | D° |
| 52 Clothed. | Not stated. | About 300 — — | Voluntary Contributions, Sermons. | Master and Mistress, £.80. | D° |
| All Clothed, from 25 to 30 Boarded. | D° | 1,141 12  6 | D° Stock £.452. 5. 4. | 2 Masters and 1 Mistress, £.150. | D° |
| All Clothed, 22 Girls Boarded. | 1,100 — — | 1,100 — — | Charitable Donations, Estates, Subscriptions. | Master, £.50. Mistress, £.30. | D° |
| 50 Clothed. | 14,808  6  2 | 14,649 11  7 | D° Stock £.24. | Master, £.100. | D° |
| All Clothed, 1 Girl Boarded. | 347  3  2¼ | 320  5 11½ | D° - Stock £.60. Freeh^d Estate, £.32. | Not stated. | Many poor Children uneducated in this parish. Parents not reluctant. |
| 60 Boys. 40 Girls. | 498 12  1 | 354 11 10 | D° Stock £.24. | Master, £.80. Mistress, £.50. | A great number of Children uneducated. |
| All Clothed. D° | Not stated. D° | Voluntary Subscr^s D° | D° D° | Mistress, £.40. Master, £.80. |  |
| D° 80 Clothed, 20 Clothed & Boarded. | D° D° | D° D° | D° D° | Mistress, £.40. Master, £.80. |  |
| D° | -  -  - | -  -  - | -  -  - | Master, £.80. |  |
| Neither Clothed nor Boarded. | 23 — — | 23 16  9 | Voluntary Subscriptions. | Master and Mistress, 5s. a week. |  |
| All Clothed. | 280 — — | 200 — — | D° | Master and Mistress, £.110. | Number uneducated unknown. |
| D° | Boys School. 472  5  2 Girls D° 649 19 — | 476  4  3 641  3  3 | Freehold Estates, Stock, &c. -  -  - | Master, £.84. Assistant £.60. Mistress, £.52. 10. 2 Assistants, £.42. | D° |

Appendix (B.)

Copy of a LETTER from GEORGE P. BRIETZCKE, Esq. dated 17th June 1816, inclosing Accounts of the Annual Amount of Charitable Donations for Schools in the Counties of *Middlesex, Surrey, Bedford, Berks,* and *Kent.*

SIR,

Poor Return Office, Whitehall,
17th June 1816.

I HAVE the honour to inclose the several Accounts hereafter specified, made out pursuant to the directions of the Select Committee on the Education of the Lower Orders in the Metropolis, as conveyed to me by Mr. Tomlins; viz.

1.—An Account of the Annual Amount of Charitable Donations for Schools in the County of Middlesex.

2.—An Account of the Annual Amount of Charitable Donations for Schools in the County of Surrey.

3.—An Account of the Annual Amount of Charitable Donations for Schools in the Counties of Bedford, Berkshire, and Kent.

I beg leave to observe, that I had originally intended to supply the Committee with separate Returns for each County in England and Wales respectively; but as it was found that the formation of these Returns would consume a considerable deal of time, it was thought proper to apply to you for fresh instructions; the result of which, herewith submitted, it is hoped will prove satisfactory.

I am, Sir,

Your most obedient humble Servant,

GEO. P. BRIETZCKE.

HENRY BROUGHAM, Esq.
　Chairman of the Committee,
　　&c. &c. &c.

## —No. 1.—

An ACCOUNT of the Annual Amount of CHARITABLE DONATIONS for Schools in the County of *Middlesex*, in the Year ending 25th day of March 1815, as specified in the Returns made in pursuance of an Act passed in the 55th Year of His present Majesty's Reign, intituled, " An Act for procuring Returns relative to the Expense and Maintenance of the Poor in *England*, and also relative to the Highways ;" so far as the same can be made up.

| COUNTY. | PLACE. | DESCRIPTION OF CHARITY. | ANNUAL AMOUNT. |
|---|---|---|---|
| | | | £.  s.  d. |
| MIDDLESEX | Hornsey - - | A Grammar School, at Highgate, for 40 Boys. | |
| D° - - | St. James and St. John, Clerkenwell | A Parish School  -  -  -  -  - | 92 — — |
| D° - - | D° - - - | Three Charity Schools, for clothing and educating. The Brewers School (free) for Education only. Also Five Sunday Schools. | |
| D° - - | St. Luke - - | Orphan School, Yellow-hammer School, Finsbury School, Lancasterian School, and Tabernacle Walbrook School. | |
| D° - - | St. Mary, Islington | A Parish School  -  -  -  -  - | 493 12  1 |
| D° - - | St. Mary, Stoke Newington - - | A Parish School  -  -  -  -  - | 45 15 — |
| D° - - | St. Anne, Limehouse | A Parish School  -  -  -  -  - | 93 16  4 |
| D° - - | St. Botolph - - | A Parish School  -  -  -  -  - | 3 — — |
| D° - - | St. Catherine - | A Parish School | |
| D° - - | Christ Church - | A Parish School  -  -  -  -  - | 178 — — |
| D° - - | St. George in the East | Middlesex Society, for clothing and educating 100 Boys and 50 Girls ; Tower Hamlet, for clothing and educating 40 Boys and 20 Girls ; Pell-street School, for clothing and educating 40 Children ; Roman Catholic School, for educating 65 Boys and 36 Girls (the Girls, and also 45 Boys, are clothed.) | |
| D° - - | D° - - - | Raine's Charities  -  -  -  -  - | 1,027 15  6 |
| D° - - | St. Leonard's, Bromley - | A Parish School  -  -  -  -  - | 167  4  4 |
| D° - - | St. Mary, Whitechapel - | A Parish School  -  -  -  -  - | 472 11  5 |
| D° - - | St. Mary, Stratford | A School under the Management of the Drapers' Company ; and a Dissenting School. | |
| D° - - | St. Matthew, Bethnal Green - | A Parish School. | |
| D° - - | St. Dunstan, Stepney | A Lancasterian School. | |
| D° - - | Mile End Old Town | Red Coat School. | |
| D° - - | Poplar & Blackwall | A School -  -  -  -  -  - | 6 14 10 |
| D° - - | D° - - - | A School for Boys and Girls, under the Direction of the East-India Company. | |
| D° - - | Ratcliffe, St. Dunstan's Parish - | Cooper's School, Ratcliffe School, Stepney Meeting School, Rose-lane Meeting School, Queen-street Meeting School. | |
| D° - - | Chiswick - - | A Parish School  -  -  -  -  - | 39 — — |
| D° - - | Ealing - - | A Parish School  -  -  -  -  - | 430 — — |
| D° - - | Fulham - - | A Parish School  -  -  -  -  - | 52 — — |
| D° - - | Hammersmith - | Latimer Charity School. | |
| D° - - | St. Mary Abbotts - | A Charity School, and House for the Master. | |
| D° - - | St. Luke's, Chelsea | A Parish School  -  -  -  -  - | 49 — — |
| D° - - | New Brentford - | Dividends of £.900 and £.500 3-per-cent. and £.36 per annum  -  -  -  - | 78 — — |
| D° - - | Great Greenford - | A Parish School  -  -  -  -  - | 169 — — |
| D° - - | Hanwell - - | A Parish School  -  -  -  -  - | 35 — — |
| D° - - | Norwood, in Hayes Parish - | A Parish School  -  -  -  -  - | 35 — — |
| D° - - | Uxbridge - - | A Parish School  -  -  -  -  - | 189  3  2½ |
| D° - - | Monkin, in Hadley Parish - | 1 Boy School -  -  -  -  - 1 Girl School -  -  -  -  - | 12 — — 16 10 — |
| D° - - | Allhallows - - | A Free Grammar School. | |
| D° - - | Harrow on the Hill | A Free Grammar School. | |
| D° - - | Hendon - - | A Charity School  -  -  -  - | 10  5  2 |
| D° - - | Pinner - - | A Parish School  -  -  -  -  - | 3 — — |
| D° - - | Little Stanmore - | A Free School. | |
| D° - - | Hampton - - | A Parish School  -  -  -  -  - | 299 — — |
| D° - - | Hanworth - - | A Parish School  -  -  -  -  - | 15 — — |

(continued.)

Donations for Schools in Middlesex—*continued*.

| COUNTY. | PLACE. | DESCRIPTION OF CHARITY. | ANNUAL AMOUNT. | | |
|---|---|---|---|---|---|
| | | | £. | s. | d. |
| MIDDLESEX | Littleton - - | A Parish School - - - - - - - | 9 | 11 | 10 |
| Dº - - | Staines - - | A Parish School - - - - - | 4 | — | — |
| Dº - - | Stanwell - - | A Parish School - - - - - - | 40 | — | — |
| Dº - - | Sunbury - - | A Parish School - - - - - - | 31 | 2 | 8 |
| Dº - - | Teddington - - | A Parish School - - - - - - | 27 | — | — |
| Dº - - | St. Andrew, Holborn | Auxiliary National School. | | | |
| Dº - - | St. Bartholomew the Great - } | A Parish School - - - - - | 29 | 12 | — |
| Dº - - | St. Botolph within | A Parish School - - - - - - | 645 | 1 | 9 |
| Dº - - | - Dº - - | { Bishopsgate Charity Schools, Bishopsgate Sunday School, St. Ethelburg Charity Schools, and Turner's Free School. | | | |
| Dº - - | St. Giles without - | { Two Charity Schools, one for Boys, and one for Girls; Protestant Society Schools for Boys and Girls. | | | |
| Dº - - | St. Sepulchre - | A Charity School - - - - - | 209 | — | — |
| Dº - - | St. Andrew, Holborn | { A Charity School for clothing and educating 40 Boys and 30 Girls. | | | |
| Dº - - | St. Mary-le-bone | { A Charity School for wholly maintaining and educating 108 Children; and School of Industry. | | | |
| Dº - - | Paddington - - | A permanent Charity School | | | |
| Dº - - | Twickenham - | A Parish School - - - - - - | 109 | 8 | — |
| Dº - - | Isleworth - - | A Parish School - - - - - - | 268 | 4 | 6 |

---

CHARITIES in the City of LONDON applicable to SCHOOLS.

| PARISH OR PLACE. | DESCRIPTION OF CHARITY. | ANNUAL AMOUNT. | | |
|---|---|---|---|---|
| | | £. | s. | d. |
| Allhallows, Mark-lane - - | A Parish School - - - - - | 5 | — | — |
| St. Anne and Agnes - - - | { St. Anne's Society School (St. Anne's-lane) founded in 1709 for 30 Boys and 30 Girls, who are clothed and educated (the six senior Girls are boarded;) they have also an Establishment at Peckham, in which 30 Boys are altogether provided for. | | | |
| St. Ann, Blackfriars, united to the Parish of St. Andrew by the Wardrobe - - - - | { A permanent Charity School, founded by Peter Jay, Esq. | | | |
| St. Augustine - - - | { Cordwainers and Bread-street Ward Charity School. | | | |
| Christ Church - - - | { Christ Church Hospital, containing 604 Children; and a School in Bull-and-Mouth-street, belonging to the Ward of Farringdon Within, containing 110, now about to be augmented upon Dr. Bell's system. | | | |
| St. Dunstan in the East - - | A Parish School - - - - - | 10 | — | — |
| St. Lawrence, Poulteney - - | A Free Grammar School. | | | |
| St. Leonard, East-cheap - - | A Parish School - - - - - | 5 | 18 | — |
| St. Mary on the Hill - - - | A Charity School. | | | |
| St. Mary Magdalen - - - | A Charity School. | | | |
| St. Michael, Pater Noster Royal - | A Grammar School. | | | |
| St. Stephen's, Coleman-street - | A Charity School. | | | |

City of WESTMINSTER.

| | | | | |
|---|---|---|---|---|
| St. Anne - - - - - | Two Schools. | | | |
| St. James - - - - - | For Parish Schools - - - - - | 90 | — | — |
| St. Mary-le-Strand - - - | For Parish Schools - - - - - | 22 | 4 | — |

GEO. P. BRIETZCKE.

## —No. 2.—

An ACCOUNT of the Annual Amount of CHARITABLE DONATIONS for Schools in the County of *Surrey*, in the Year ending 25th day of March 1815, as specified in the Returns made in pursuance of an Act passed in the 55th Year of His present Majesty's Reign, intituled, " An Act for procuring Returns relative to the Expense and Maintenance of the Poor in *England*, and also relative to the Highways;" so far as the same can be made up.

| COUNTY. | PLACE. | DESCRIPTION OF CHARITY. | ANNUAL AMOUNT. |
| --- | --- | --- | --- |
| | | | £.   s.   d. |
| SURREY - | Croydon - - | A Charity School for educating 28 Boys, and and a Charity for binding poor Boys Apprentices. | |
| Dº - - | Chipstead - - | A Parish School - - - - - | 38 — — |
| Dº - - | Mordon - - | A Parish School - - - - - | 27  17  2 |
| Dº - - | Sutton - - | A Parish School - - - - - | 6 — — |
| Dº - - | Ockley - - | A Parish School - - - - - | 8   8 — |
| Dº - - | St. Nicholas, Guildford - - | A Parish School | 30 — — |
| Dº - - | Esher - - - | A Parish School - - - - - | 30  14  6 |
| Dº - - | Farnham - - | One Bell's School, one Lancasterian School. | |
| Dº - - | Puttenham - - | A Parish School. | |
| Dº - - | East Moulsey - | A Parish School - - - - - | 6 — — |
| Dº - - | Weybridge - - | A Parish School - - - - - | 5 — — |
| Dº - - | Charlwood - - | A Parish School - - - - - | 8 — — |
| Dº - - | Foreign of Reigate | A Parish School. | |
| Dº - - | Ashtead - - | A Parish School - - - - - | 10 — — |
| Dº - - | Leatherhead - | A Parish School - - - - - | 26 — — |
| Dº - - | Richmond - - | A Parish School. | |
| Dº - - | Kew - - - | A Parish School - - - - - | 37  10 — |
| Dº - - | Epsom - - | A Parish School - - - - - | 50  18 — |
| Dº - - | Ewell - - - | A Parish School - - - - - | 20 — — |
| Dº - - | Albury - - | A Parish School - - - - - | 5 — — |
| Dº - - | Shiere - - | A Parish School - - - - - | 14  14  2 |
| Dº - - | Worplesdon - | A Parish School - - - - - | 6   8 — |
| Dº - - | Windlesham - | A Parish School - - - - - | 5 — — |
| Dº - - | Wonersh - - | A Parish School - - - - - | 8 — — |
| Dº - - | St. Mary Magdalen, Bermondsey | A Parish School - - - - - | 195 — — |
| Dº - - | St. Giles, Camberwell - - | Parish Schools - - - - - | 276 — — |
| Dº - - | Dº - - - | Camberwell Green Coat, and United National Schools; Dulwich College; Doctor Allen's School at Dulwich; Peckham National School; St. Ann's School, Peckham. | |
| Dº - - | Clapham - - | A Parish School - - - - - | 8 — — |
| Dº - - | St. Mary, Newington | A Parish School - - - - - | 62   1  2 |
| Dº - - | St. Mary, Rotherhithe - - | A Parish School - - - - - | 8   8 — |
| Dº - - | Streatham - - | A Parish School - - - - - | 20 — — |
| Dº - - | Barnes - - | A Parish School - - - - - | 117   7 — |
| Dº - - | St. Mary, Battersea | A Parish School - - - - - | 220 — — |
| Dº - - | Mortlake - - | A Parish School - - - - - | 37  10 — |
| Dº - - | St. Mary, Putney - | A School for educating and clothing 20 Boys. | |
| Dº - - | Tooting - - | A School for 30 Boys and 25 Girls - - | 30 — — |
| Dº - - | Wandsworth - | A Parish School - - - - - | 67  10 — |
| Dº - - | Wimbledon - - | A Parish School - - - - - | 20 — — |
| Dº - - | Blechingly - - | A Parish School - - - - - A Free School. | 32 — — |
| Dº - - | Godstone - - | A School to educate poor Children - - | 4 — — |
| Dº - - | Lingfield - - | A Parish School - - - - - | 7  10 — |
| Dº - - | Tandridge - - | A Parish School - - - - - | 4 — — |
| Dº - - | Chertsey - - | A Charity School for educating 25 Boys and 25 Girls, founded by the late Sir William Perkins. | |

*( continued.)*

Donations for Schools in Surrey—*continued*.

Borough of SOUTHWARK.

| PLACE. | DESCRIPTION OF CHARITY. | ANNUAL AMOUNT. |
|---|---|---|
| | | £. s. d. |
| St. John's - - - - | [Return not in.] | |
| St. George the Martyr - - | A great number of Charitable Institutions, supported partly by Gifts and Legacies left to them, but chiefly by annual Donations. | |
| St. Olave - - - - - | A Free Grammar School, founded by Queen Elizabeth; also a Girls' School, supported by voluntary Contributions. | |
| St. Saviour - - - - | Parish Schools - - - - - - | 793 17 5 |
| Ditto - - - - | St. Saviour's Grammar School, and St. Saviour's Institution for educating the Poor. | |
| St. Thomas - - - - | For Parish Schools £.600. 3-per-cent. Reduced - - - - - - The Protestant dissenting School, and St. Thomas's Charity for Boys. | 18 — — |

GEO. P. BRIETZCKE.

—No. 3.—

An ACCOUNT of the Annual Amount of CHARITABLE DONATIONS for Schools in the Counties of *Bedford*, *Berks*, and *Kent*, in the Year ending the 25th day of March 1815, as specified in the Returns made in pursuance of an Act passed in the 55th year of His present Majesty's Reign, intituled, " An Act for procuring Returns relative to the Expense and Maintenance of the Poor in *England*, and also relative to the Highways;" so far as the same can be made up.

|  | Total Annual Amount. |
|---|---|
| In the County of *Bedford* - - - - - - | £.510. 14. 5½. |
| —— of *Berks* - - - - - - | 1,725. 0. 6. |
| —— of *Kent* - - - - - - | 3,811. 16. 6¾. |

GEO. P. BRIETZCKE.